MW01618447

Atlas of
Physiology of the Muscular Fascia

By the same Publisher:

BERTELLI – Anatomy of the Eye

BOTTI – Aesthetic Surgery of the Aging Face, 6 DVD

CANEPA – Dysmorphic Syndromes & Constitutional Diseases of the Skeleton

CAVALLARO – Atlas of Arterial Surgery, 2 volumes

GIANNETTI – Textbook of Dermatology and Sexually Transmitted Diseases, 3 volumes

LIESSI – Atlas of Musculoskeletal MRA & MRI: Small Joints Pathology

MASSIRONE – Aesthetic Medicine

Intradermal Therapy (Mesotherapy), DVD 1
Fillers, DVD 2
Chemical Peeling, DVD 3
Botulin Toxin in Aesthetic Medicine, DVD 4
Lasers in Aesthetic Medicine, DVD 5

NAVA – Breast Reconstructive Surgery, 6 DVD

NAVA – Aesthetic Breast Surgery, 8 DVD

PEGORARO – Hospital Based Bioethics

PRETI – Advances in Clinical Prosthodontics

PULCINI – First Aid

RANERI – Pilates Fisios: The Silvia Raneri Method®

RUSCIANI – Textbook of Dermatologic Surgery, 2 volumes

SCANU – The PRALD Therapeutic Method

STECCO – Fascial Manipulation® for Internal Dysfunctions: Practical Part

STECCO – Fascial Manipulation® for Internal Dysfunctions

STECCO – Fascial Manipulation® for Musculoskeletal Pain

STECCO – Fascial Manipulation®: Practical Part

STECCO – Fascial Manipulation® Posters

Locomotor Apparatus
Internal Part

ZAOLI – Aesthetic Rhinoplasty, 2 volumes

Luigi Stecco

Atlas of Physiology of the Muscular Fascia

Presentation by
LEON CHAITOW
Honorary Fellow, University of Westminster, London
Editor-in-Chief, Journal of Bodywork & Movement Therapies

English translation by
AURÉLIE MARIE MARCHAND

PICCIN

ISBN 978-88-299-2745-6

Printed in Italy

To my wife Lena

FOREWORD

In order to understand the complexity fascial function and dysfunction, it is necessary to have an accurate appreciation of the constituents that make up these ubiquitous and versatile tissues, as well as of their coordinated physiological interactions and behaviors.

To achieve this it is suggested that a validated working model is necessary that simplifies reality.

Fortunately a number of excellent atlases and textbooks now exist that offer images of the architecture of fascia, from the microscopic to the macroscopic. What has been missing, however is a comprehensive English language description of the normal physiology of fascia: how it behaves in normal circumstances, as well as how to accurately and systematically identify both the nature and location of fascial dysfunction.

In this extensive and detailed text, Luigi Stecco, offers specific practical insights that merge appreciation of the anatomy and physiology of the multiple elements that make up myofascial biomechanical structures and how these operate in the body to produce integrated stability and movement, when operating normally.

Most importantly, from a clinical perspective, he then describes a wide range of reasoned functional assessment protocols that are able to identify and localize dysfunctional fascial features, whether these involve unidirectional, bidirectional or multidirectional myofascial actions and activities.

Symptoms associated with altered motor control, reduced ranges of motion and/or pain, may result from dysfunctional fascial features, including increased local densification (tissue stiffness) and/or altered sliding functions. Importantly, such changes need to be appreciated as being largely reversible – involving as they do altered function, but not necessarily pathology.

It is the well-thought-out descriptions of accurate, reproducible and practical evaluation methods, capable of leading to the identification of the locations of such changes, that makes Luigi Stecco's work so important. Critically, numerous studies have emerged that validate the reliability of the protocols associated with Fascial Manipulation®, the therapeutic method that has evolved from Stecco's years of dedicated research.

While a variety of methods of treatment and rehabilitation of painful and dysfunctional fascial structures have been proposed and studied, there are relatively few approaches that offer accurate identification as to which tissues and structures may be involved, or precisely where these are located.

The methods described by Stecco, in the objective examination process that leads to the identification of areas of fascial dysfunction, involve both palpatory assessments as well as functional movement tests that systematically evaluate and record the results of controlled movements in the sagittal, frontal and horizontal planes, involving all areas of the body.

These objective assessment methods are coupled with a subjective evaluation, incorporating factors such as age, trauma history, patterns of use in work and leisure activities, as well as previous medical history.

Using a combination of the results that emerge from both the objective and subjective examinations, a working hypothesis emerges on which subsequent treatment is based. The tests used are then repeated, following treatment, in order to evaluate functional and symptomatic changes. In this beautifully illustrated work Luigi Stecco has distilled his years of research into a carefully-crafted textbook that offers insights and practical guidelines, that are of immense potential value to practitioners and therapists of all schools - and for this he deserves our praise and profound thanks.

Leon Chaitow
Honorary Fellow, University of Westminster, London
Editor-in-Chief,
Journal of Bodywork & Movement Therapies

INTRODUCTION

Since 1543 (Vesalius, *De humani corporis fabrica*) until now numerous studies have been conducted on the anatomy and physiology of the musculoskeletal apparatus but overall the muscular fascia has been overlooked.

An image of Vesalius is reported on the cover of this atlas. The drawing represents the four new proposals on the anatomy and physiology of the fascia reported below:

- *Unitas* or myofascial (MF) unit, the chosen example is formed by the biceps brachii and brachialis muscles (anatomy), the vectors highlighted are those formed by both muscles on the fascia (physiology);
- *Sequentia* or myofascial sequence, the sequence formed by the flexor muscles of the upper limb was emphasized (anatomy) on the drawing, the tractions produced by the muscle insertions on the aponeurotic fascia (physiology) are indicated by the arrows;
- *Diagonalis* or myofascial diagonal, it is formed by points of fusion between different fasciae (anatomy), they coordinate the intermediate movements between two spatial planes (physiology);
- *Spira* or myofascial spiral, it is formed by the spiral arrangement of several muscles and by intrafascial collagen fibres (anatomy) which together with the retinacula coordinate global motor activities or gestures (physiology).

Therefore, this atlas aims at combining, through their fascial interactions, the anatomy of muscles with the physiology of muscle spindles and Golgi tendon organs. In particular, it seeks to:

- incorporate all the motor units implementing a specific movement in the myofascial unit;
- describe the myofascial sequences moving and maintaining body posture in all three spatial planes;
- underline the interaction between the spindles and the fascia (stretch reflex) for the management of motor schemes;
- explain the role of fascia in the physiology of global motor gesture.

These premises are supported by the following findings:

1. the peripheral myofascial architecture corresponds to the motor organisation of the central nervous system;
2. in all body segments, the intrafusal muscles create vectors in the perimysial fascia that have a specular disposition to the vectors formed by the extrafusal muscles;
3. the architecture of the muscular fascia corresponds to the management of segmentary movements, posture, motor schemes and global gestures;
4. the images of anatomical dissections examined according to these new proposals demonstrate that the fascia is at the service of body movement.

The first chapter offers explanations that facilitate the understanding of the next chapters, furthermore it reports on several studies supporting this new view.

The second, third and fourth chapters respectively present the MF units and MF sequences of the upper limbs, trunk and lower limbs.

On the first page of each of the above chapters, the regional anatomical image (anterior, posterior, lateral, medial and deep) of each limb or trunk is reported. These pictures illustrate the entire limb or entire trunk with the aim of highlighting the synergy of the entire limb and not the action of a single muscle.

Besides each image is a list of the primary or monoarticular muscles, the secondary or biarticular muscles and the synergic muscles. The last two intervene in motor scheme movements and not in unidirectional movements.

On the opposite page the photographs feature the four segments of the limb or trunk. These pictures show the movements performed by the MF unit in a specific spatial plane rather than by a single muscle.

The initial anatomical drawing is repeated again on the third page. It highlights the fascial compartments encompassing the primary and secondary muscles, both are implicated in limb movement in one spatial direction. The page opposite presents a photograph of the movement executed by the sequence of muscles along the entire limb.

The next page will present the same anatomical drawing elaborated to show the vectors forming the myofascial unit.

In the opposite page the dysfunctions highlighted represent what occurs in this harmonious movement if the fascia loses its elasticity. Indeed densification of the fascia does not allow for the correct functioning of the neuromuscular spindles and consequent excitation of the muscular fibres belonging to that MF unit.

On the next page the muscle insertions on the fascia are highlighted. Through these muscle insertions on the fascia each MF unit is able to adapt its strength to that of the proximal and distal MF units when the entire limb or entire trunk is implicated in a directional effort.

The opposite page features the role played by biarticular muscles in the peripheral motor organization. These muscles move the proximal and distal joints whilst maintaining a constant angle of variation between both articulations. The Golgi tendon organs placed between the tendon fibres intervene in regulating these variables.

The last four pages of each chapter show several photographs of anatomical dissections of the fascia. These pictures provide added visual explanation.

The fifth chapter presents the peripheral motor organization through the centres of fusion (CFs) and the lines of fusion of the fasciae (myofascial diagonals). The centres of fusion manage the intervention of two or three myofascial units throughout the passage from one direction to another (segmentary motor scheme). The MF diagonals perform the same function as the MF sequences: they synchronise the action of the centres of fusion that participate in movement of the entire limb or trunk along an intermediate trajectory between two spatial planes (global motor schemes).

The sixth chapter takes into consideration the helicoidal fibres (spiral) included in the aponeurotic fasciae. The retinacula of the ankle and wrist are the starting point of these spirals. The small muscles of the hands and feet take origin on these retinacula. The movements of these extremities create tractions on the helicoidal collagen fibres that spread in a distal-proximal direction along the aponeurotic fascia.

The spiral collagen fibres coordinate the recruitment of muscles having an opposite direction between two contiguous segments, as is the case in complex motor gestures.

ACKNOWLEDGEMENTS

I wish to thank my daughter Carla and my son Antonio for their advice and for the anatomical dissections they performed at the University of Paris and Padoua.

I wish to thank Dr. Piccin for the permission to use images from the textbook of Anatomy by Chiarurgi and initially elaborated by E. Giandotti.

I wish to thank the anatomical draftsman Marco Marzola who masterfully re-elaborated several images in order to yield a clearer depiction of the physiology of the fascia.

I wish to thank Paweł Poncyljusz for helping me in the correction of the drafts.

With special thanks to Lawrence Steinbeck and Edward Traum for their English language assistance throughout.

GENERAL INDEX

ABBREVIATIONS

Ia II	primary, secondary spindle afferent
an	ante i.e. forward movements
an-ca	ante-carpus or flexion of the wrist
an-th	ante-thorax or forward flexion
an-la-cl	motor scheme of ante-latero collum
an-la-di	motor scheme of the hand
an-me-	motor scheme of ante-medio…
bi	bilateral, both right and left
ca	carpus, wrist
CC	centre of coordination of the myofascial unit
cl	collum, cervical region
CF	centre of fusion
CP	centre of perception and site of pain
cp	caput, head, face and cranium
cu	cubitus, elbow
cx	coxa, thigh-hip
di	digiti, fingers, I-II-III-IV-V
er	extra, extrarotation, eversion
er-ta	extra-talus, extrarotation of talus, pronation
ge	genu, knee
hu	humerus, distal shoulder
ir	intra, intrarotation, inversion
ir-ta	intra-talus, intrarotation of talus, ankle supination
la	latero, lateropulsion
la-ca	latero-carpus, lateral deviation of the wrist
la-cl	latero-collum, lateral flexion of the neck
LL	lower limb
lt	left, limb or trunk
lu	lumbi, lumbar
m.	muscle, muscles
me	medio, mediopulsion, medial
me-cl	medio-collum, bring back to the centre
MF	myofascial, unit, sequence, spiral
n.	neuron
pe	pes, foot, tarsus, metatarsals, toes
pv	pelvis, pelvic girdle
re	retro, retropulsion, backwards
re-ca	retro-carpus, extension wrist
re-la-	motor scheme of retro-latero-
rt	right, limb or one side of the body
sc	scapula, proximal shoulder
ta	talus
th	thorax
TP	trigger point
TR	trunk
UL	upper limb

CHAPTER 1

BASIC PRINCIPLES OF THE MYOFASCIAL SYSTEM

PHYSIOLOGY OF MOVEMENT OF THE HUMAN BODY

In the physiology textbook of Baldissera (1996), human movement is described as: "Human behaviour is expressed through the movements imparted by skeletal muscles on the different body segments whilst under the control of the central nervous system. The organisational hierarchy of motor control may be portrayed as follows:

- the first level is made up of reflex movements consisting in a brief and stereotypical response to external stimuli (postural control);
- the second level is made up of automated movements which include movements with a cyclical pattern such as respiration and mastication, and other movement actions requiring the coordinated activation of muscular chains such as deglutition and scratching; automatic movements may be controlled by will;
- the third level is made up of voluntary movement which is associated with postural adjustments and automated voluntary movements like writing, riding a bicycle, etc.

The reflex and automatic activities are principally mediated by the neural axis whereas voluntary movements are elaborated in the telecenphalon".

In this atlas the previous hierarchical organisations of human movement are only partially left under the control of the central nervous system (CNS) since these are often connected to fascia:

- reflex movements are not exclusively mediated by the spinal cord (neural axis), and the coordinating element is found in the configuration of the fascia (myofascial unit, myofascial sequence and posture);
- automatic movements are initiated by will but are thereafter continued under the tensional control of the fascial architecture (i.e. deglutition with the stretching of internal fasciae, peripheral motor schemes);
- voluntary movements also include automated movements (ie. writing) that take advantage of the motor schemes memorised in the collagen tissue of the fasciae.

There are several schools of thoughts that study human movement:

- behaviourist, that reduce movement to a passive relationship such as cause and effect;
- cognitivist, that believe that motor sequences always stem from active decisions;
- ecologist, that sustain that the brain is not able to think in a detailed manner of the relative aspects of movement.

"The major speakers of the ecologist school (J. Gibson, M. Turvey, P. Kugler, J. Kelso and L. Grimaldi) hypothesise that:

1. the CNS utilises reflex to achieve movements; the threshold of muscle stretching is independent from the central commands reaching the alpha and gamma motor neurones;
2. a point of equilibrium exists in the various muscle groups; it depends upon the joint range of motion accomplished during movement and upon the degree of tension present at the level of the various muscles;
3. there are various thresholds of activation in a muscle that functions like a spring: an initial elongation may deform the muscle without it reacting, a second elongation may provoke the typical spindle reflex, a further elongation may provoke the tonic stretch reflex;
4. since muscular behaviour is only partially influenced by the superior central commands it must be assumed that, especially at the spinal level, the CNS possesses all the details of knowledge necessary to render all kinematic muscular variables possible" (Pirola V. 1998).

The above hypotheses from the Ecologists' school of thoughts find the following answers in the architecture of the fascia:

- the stretch reflex through its interaction with the neuromuscular spindles is regulated by the endomysium, perimysium and epimysial fascia;
- the various points of equilibrium created by intermuscular tensions may only be implemented by the muscular fascia placed along the myofascial sequences, along the diagonal and myofascial spirals;
- intrafusal muscles implement an initial stretch of the fascia (spring) and a second stretch passively intervening on the spindles;
- the details of peripheral knowledge of the CNS are not localised in the spinal cord, rather they have to be sought after in the conformation of the collagen fibres of the fascia.

Another author who substantially contributed to the understanding of movement is H. Kabat: "Every voluntary movement initiates and finishes in a posture that is based upon the activity of many reflexes[1].

During exercise against resistance, the enforcement of specific schemes of irradiation provides an effective tool to stimulate recovery in paralysed muscle groups. Experience has demonstrated that the irradiation schemes of diagonals and spirals are often more effective."

Kabat utilises the terms "motor schemes, diagonals and spirals" with a similar meaning between them.

[1] Reflexes may either inhibit or facilitate voluntary movement, and voluntary movement may either inhibit or facilitate reflexes. Moreover, a voluntary movement may facilitate another one: the synergists through the irradiation, and the antagonists through the subsequent induction. (Kabat H. 1954)

In the literature, the term "motor scheme" adopts different meanings based on which adjective it is combined with.

Generally, different terms are used to indicate the movements of the human body (Fig. 1.1, A):

- unidirectional movements are namely performed in a one spatial direction. These are themselves divided into segmentary movements managed by the MF units of flexion, extension, adduction, abduction, internal and external rotation, and into global postural movements managed by the myofascial sequences (see chapters 2, 3, 4);
- bidirectional movements are also divided into segmentary schemes, which are managed by centres of fusion for the intermediate transition of a joint between two motor directions, and global motor schemes managed by the myofascial diagonals arranged along an entire limb and along the trunk (see chapter 5);
- multidirectional movements may be coordinated by the retinacula of digiti-carpus, pes-talus and collum-caput or may be managed by the myofascial spirals in order to coordinate the global gestures of the human body (running, jumping, throwing) (see chapter 6).

These motor activities are organised at the level of the CNS in different cerebral areas[2] (Fig. 1.1, B):

a) an area responsible for unidirectional movements or movements implemented along the three spatial planes (Brodmann area 4 or precentral gyrus, M1);
b) an area handling complex or scheme movements (secondary motor cortex or premotor area located on the external surface of the frontal lobe, M2);
c) an area responsible for the unique motor gestures of mankind: handling, throwing, etc. (supplementary motor area, M2b).

The fascia organises these fundamental movements in muscles:

a) simple movements, implemented along the three spatial planes, are organized by the myofascial units, whilst the management of posture is managed by the myofascial sequences;
b) motor schemes, corresponding to the movement of a limb from one plane to another, are managed by the myofascial diagonals;
c) motor gestures, using the centres of fusion of two adjacent segments in an antagonist manner, are organised by the myofascial spirals.

In a mirror image to the central and peripheral motor organisations, the fascial architecture transmits the afferents of movements to the brain:

a) fasciae responsible for the perception of directional movements in each single segment (centre of perception of the myofascial unit) and for the perception of posture in three directions (receptors of the MF sequences);
b) fasciae reunited along the lines of fusion dedicated to the perception of body movement from one plane to the other (receptors inserted along the MF diagonals);
c) intrafascial collagen fibres arranged in spirals (Fig. 1.72, 1.73) suitable for the perception of motor gestures execution (throwing, pulling, etc.).

[2] The motor cortex may be divided into different functional areas: the *primary motor cortex* (M1) directly controls the execution of movements. The M1 area corresponds to Brodmann area 4, precentral gyrus in the ascending frontal circumvolution. The *secondary motor cortex* (M2) including: the *premotor cortex*, located in front of the M1 area and laterally to the external surface of the frontal lobe. It controls the organisation of movements in the proximal muscles and in trunk muscles, it contributes to the creation of motor schemes whilst taking direction and external stimuli into account. The *supplementary motor area*, located on the medial aspect of the frontal lobe, it presides over the coordination and the planning of complex movements. Namely those that implicate a sequence of movement or the coordination of movements in the distal limbs. (Hauk O. 2004)

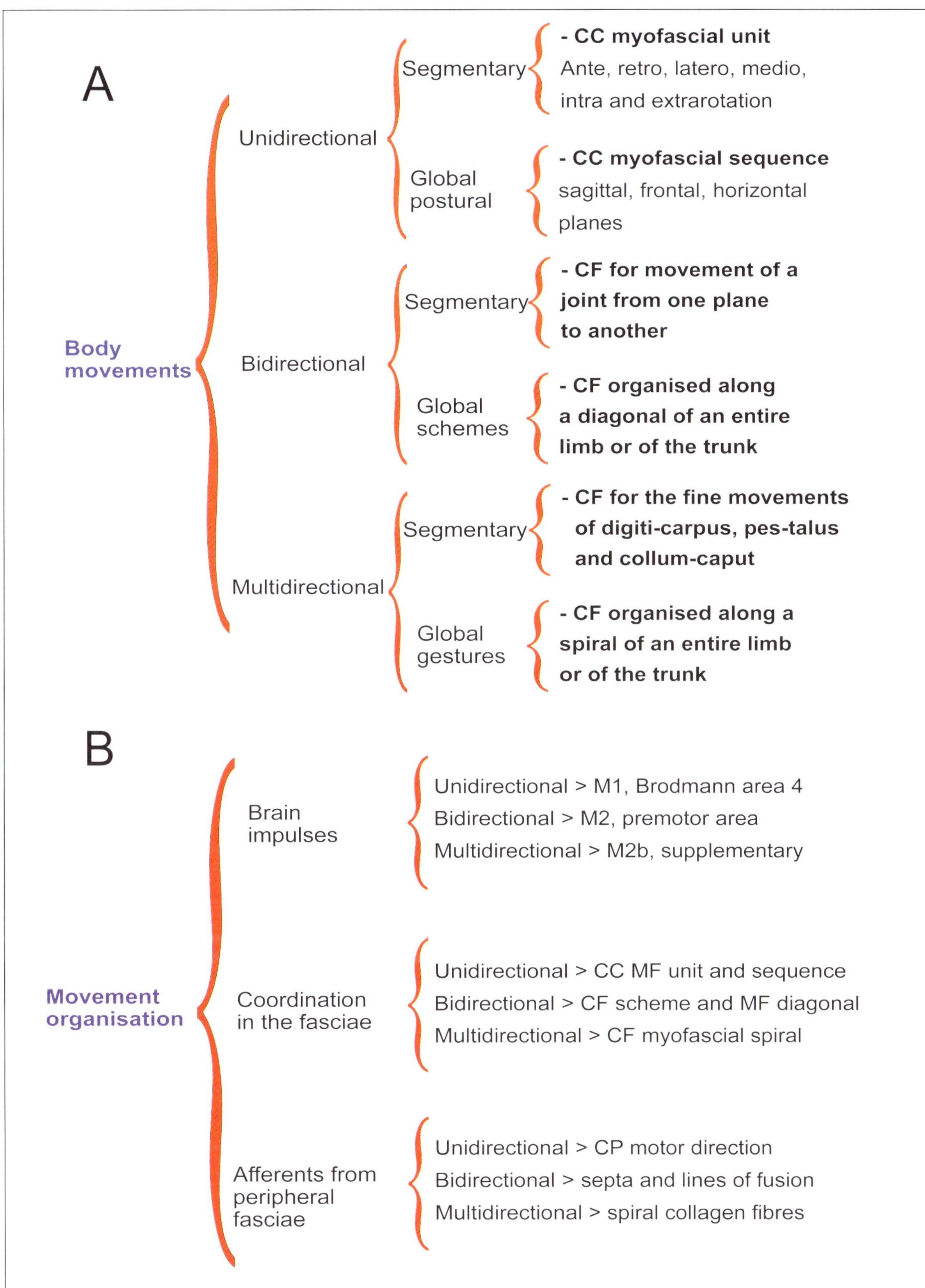

Fig. 1.1. Macroscopic division of the musculoskeletal apparatus based on fascial structures.

DIRECTIONS OF MOVEMENT IN THE THREE SPATIAL PLANES

Below is a phrase from Gray's Anatomy to demonstrate how the classic terminology on the movement directions of the human body presents some contradictions (Fig. 1.2): "Conventionally the anatomical position is considered: the standing body with palms facing forward. The terms freely used as synonyms are: anterior, ventral, flexion and palmar. The terms posterior, dorsal and extensor are opposite for the trunk and lower limb, but are not always correct synonyms. Indeed the surface of extension of the leg is anterior to the knee joint, the ankle and the foot. Readers may initially find these conventional terms slightly irritating, but it is essential for an unequivocal communication."

In anatomy the term "flexion" is used to be indicative of angle reduction between two bones forming a joint, yet this does not correspond to the motor directions programmed by the brain. Indeed bringing the thigh forward is defined flexion whilst bringing the knee forward is defined extension. Bringing the thigh backwards is defined extension whilst bringing the knee backwards is defined flexion.

Light, Georgopoulos[3], Kandel et al. have demonstrated that the stimulation of a motor neuron pool at the level of the motor cortex rarely produces the contraction of a single muscle. Often it is expressed in the activation of multiple striated fibres that are distributed along many muscle bellies which cooperate in movement management along a specific axis in one or more anatomical regions. This arrangement leads to the hypothesis of the brain organizing many movements in directional terms, namely according to the three spatial planes: sagittal, frontal and horizontal.

In accordance with the cerebral organization, the following terms are proposed for peripheral movements:

- antepulsion or antemotion for the forward movements of all segments of the body (Fig. 1.3);
- retropulsion or retromotion for the backward movements of body segments along the sagittal plane;
- lateropulsion or lateromotion for the movements away from the medial axis of the limbs and the trunk;
- mediopulsion or mediomotion for the movements towards the medial axis of all segments of the body;
- intrarotation for the forward or inward rotation of the limbs and the trunk;
- extrarotation for the backwards or outward rotation of the limbs and the trunk (Table 1.1).

Based on this vision, muscles are analysed according to directional myofascial sequences. For instance, the antepulsion or antemotion sequence of the upper limb, lower limb and trunk is formed by muscular fibres which contraction moves the various segments of the limbs and trunk forward.

Body movement has evolved at different times.

- The most primitive movements are those implemented along the spatial planes. Indeed lateropulsion or lateromotion is already found in the agnatha (lampreys). In gnathostomata fish mandibular movements have formed, namely opening and closing of the mouth which occurs on the sagittal plane. The muscles of the jaw then extended into the trunk allowing for retropulsion or retromotion and antepulsion.
- Rotational movements are required for terrestrial life. Along with the appearance of rotation, intermediate movements between one plane and the other are developed. These allowed for the possibility of carrying out motor schemes.
- In mammals, movement enriches itself with motor variables such as the cruciate movement of the limbs (or reciprocal limb movement) and running. These motor gestures require the connection between the anterior limb on one side and the posterior limb on the opposite side. The spiral fibres of the trunk are hence formed.
- Human beings also developed the fine gestures of the hand and the standing position. Therefore the hand and foot require that the proximal part of the limbs adapt to the needs of the extremities. The retinacula of the wrist and ankle are the starting point of spiral collagen fibres that are connected to the muscles of the entire limb through the septa.

[3] The neurons belonging to a precise cortex area in the primate may implement a precise movement in one of the three spatial directions. It was observed that the direction of movement may be anticipated when the specific action of a population of neurons is known. (Georgopoulos A.P. 1986)

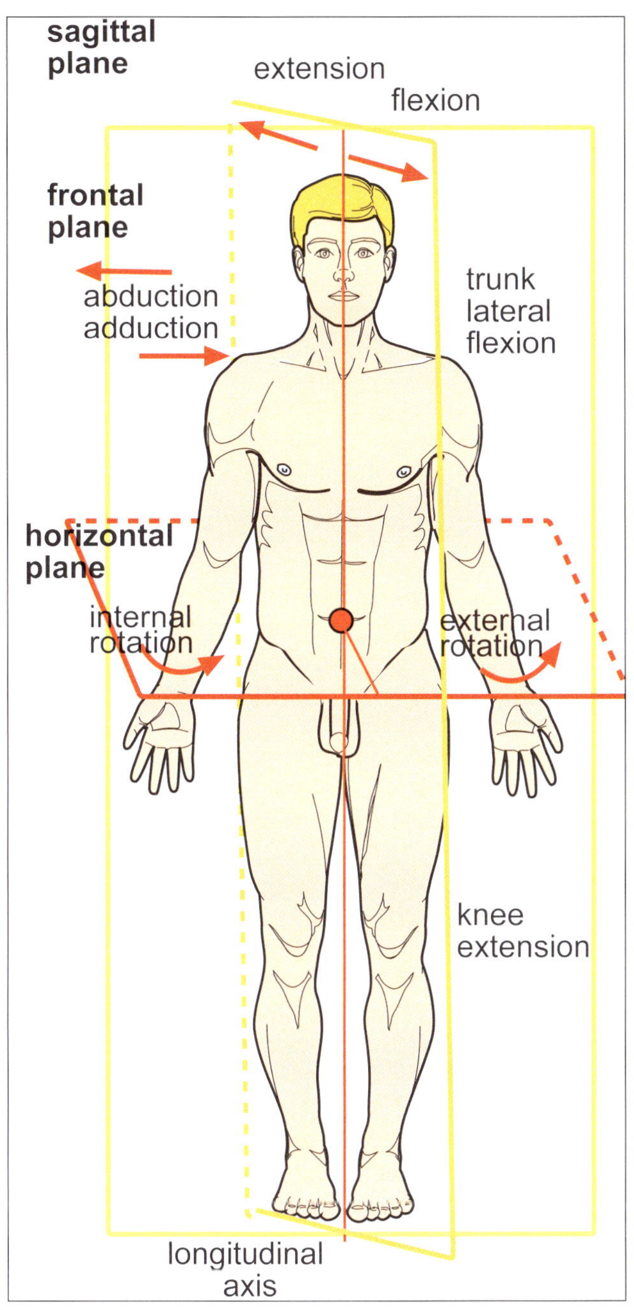

Fig. 1.2. Classic nomenclature of the movement guidelines in the human body.

sagittal plane
retropulsion
antepulsion
frontal plane
lateropulsion
mediopulsion
horizontal plane
intrarotation
extrarotation
longitudinal axis

Fig. 1.3. New nomenclature of movements based on the spatial directions.

Table 1.1. Names according to joint angle closure and names according to motor directions

Planes of space	Previous denomination	Motor directions	Abbrev.
Sagittal plane	▪ Dorsiflexion of the foot	Antepulsion	an
	▪ Extension, straightening of the spine	Retropulsion	re
Frontal plane	▪ Adduction, bringing towards to medial axis	Mediopulsion	me
	▪ Abduction, lateral flexion	Lateropulsion	la
Horizontal plane	▪ Internal rotation, pronation, …	Intrarotation	ir
	▪ External rotation, supination, torsion, …	Extrarotation	er

DIVISION OF THE HUMAN BODY IN SEGMENTS

In anatomical textbooks the human body is divided into segments and into joints (Fig. 1.4). In the upper limb the arm is located between the shoulder and the elbow, the forearm is located between the elbow and the wrist, and finally there is the hand. In the lower limb the thigh is located between the hip and the knee, the leg is located between the knee and the ankle, and then there is the foot. In the trunk there is the thorax, the abdomen and the pelvis. The head and neck together with the entire trunk form the torso.

The classical division considers the body segments as elements comprised between two joints. Instead, in this textbook the primary or monoarticular muscles are connected to a specific articulation and fascial compartment. The anterior and posterior parts of the trunk are not separable as could be inferred from these terms: thorax and back, abdomen and lumbar. In fact, the thorax works as a functional unit, as do the lumbar region and the pelvic girdle.

The bones of the wrist and ankle form a single segment. Indeed, there is no perception of the individual movement of the carpal or tarsal bones, rather the functional unit of the ankle and wrist is perceived.

In the upper limb, the scapula (sc) is an element of pivot. Its muscles may sometimes work together with the humerus (glenohumeral joint) and sometimes with the neck[4]. For this reason, the presentation of the MF unit scapula as an independent segment is not dwelled on.

In order to distinguish the new division of the body segments from the classical denomination, it was decided to refer to them with names derived from Latin (Fig. 1.5):

- caput (cp) or head, where three articulations are recognised: the six muscles of the eyeball (cp 1), the movements of the three ossicles of the middle ear (cp 2), the temporomandibular joint (cp 3);
- collum (cl) or neck, where the seven cervical vertebrae are perceived as a single unit;
- scapula (sc) or scapula, humerus (hu) or glenohumeral joint, cubitus (cu) or elbow, carpus (ca) or wrist, digiti (di) or fingers of the hand;
- thorax (th) or chest, where the twelve thoracic vertebrae, the ribs and the sternum act as a single segment;
- lumbi (lu) or lumbar region, formed by the five lumbar vertebrae and by the abdominal wall above the umbilicus;
- pelvis (pv) or pelvic girdle, where the pubis, the sacrum and the coccyx are perceived as a single entity;
- coxa (cx) or hip joint, genu (ge) or knee, talus (ta) or talocrural joint and pes (pe) or tarsal bones including the forefoot and toes.

Table 1.2 shows the Latin terms and their respective abbreviations indicating each segment.

In the body, there are therefore 14 functional segments[5], each of which is formed as follows:

- by a joint that may move in one or all three spatial planes;
- by motor units that implement movement of the joint in one spatial plane;
- by fascia that connects the ipsidirectional motor units together and also extends over the periarticular structures.

For instance, cubitus (cu) includes not only the elbow but also the muscles and fasciae moving the elbow in antepulsion and retropulsion. The elbow does not have a true movement of laterality or abduction but it has muscular fibres (brachioradialis, extensor carpi radialis longus and brevis) that contribute to the lateral stability of cubitus during the lifting of a weight. The muscles carrying out flexion and extension of the elbow are mainly located in the arm. The muscles implementing lateral stabilisation have their muscle belly in the forearm. Hence, the borders of cubitus extend from half the arm down to the proximal third of the forearm.

The borders of the anterior regions of the body are equal to the borders of the posterior regions.

[4] The infraspinatus fascia of the scapula forms a type of retinaculum from which six myofascial expansions detach: medially, superiorly, inferiorly, for the deltoid, for the teres minor and for the teres major. (Moccia D. 2015)

[5] Each anatomical component may be considered to be intimately connected while at the same time functionally isolated from the others. This seeming paradox is at the base of the neuromotor organisation. Coordination becomes the noble and essential pursuit to survival. Each region may generate a directional movement by giving origin to synergies that are reflected from one anatomical segment to the other, by coordinating or by isolating the motor components in multiple and complex configurations. (Forsythe M. 2014)

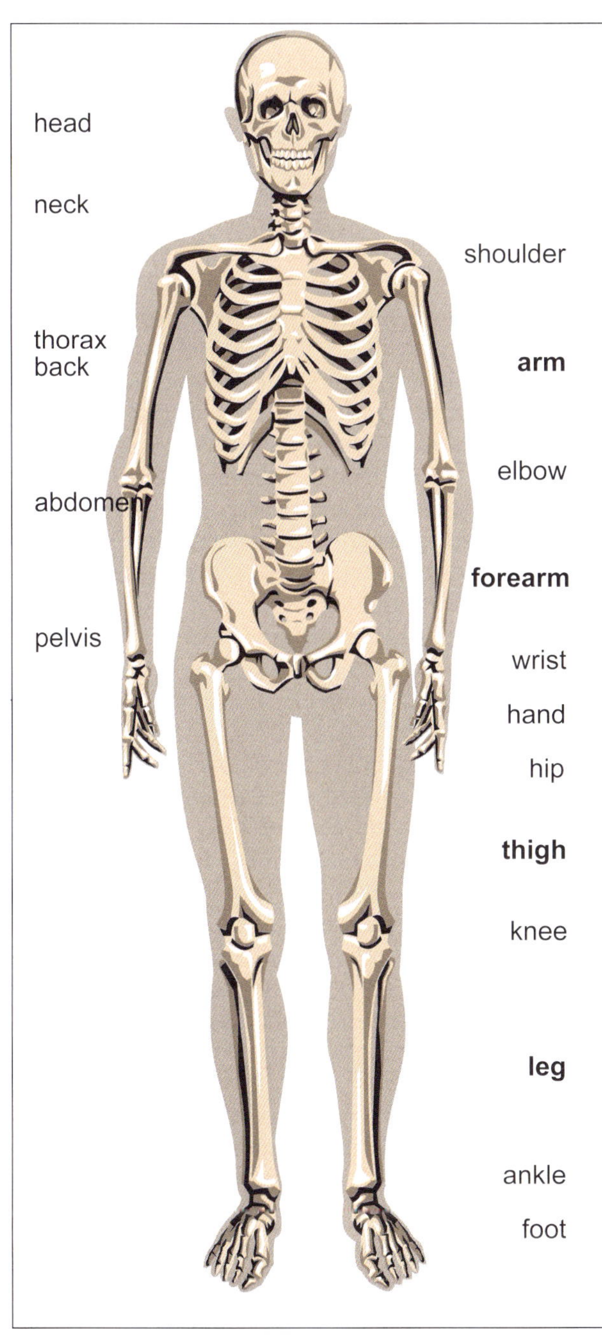

Fig. 1.4. Classic division of body segments.

Fig. 1.5. New proposal of division of segments.

Table 1.2. Abbreviations of the terms defining the new segments

Abbr.	Latin terminology	English words	Abbr.	Latin terminology	English words
cp	Caput	Head	ta	Talus	Ankle
cl	Collum	Neck	pe	Pes	Foot
th	Thorax	Thorax	sc	Scapula	Scapula
lu	Lumbi	Lumbar	hu	Humerus	Humerus
pv	Pelvis	Pelvis	cu	Cubitus	Elbow
cx	Coxa	Thigh	ca	Carpus	Wrist
ge	Genu	Knee	di	Digiti	Fingers

DIVISION OF MUSCLES IN MONOARTICULAR, BIARTICULAR AND SYNERGIST

Platzer writes the following on the functional division of the musculature with regards to the elbow joint: "The movements at the elbow joint are flexion and extension. All muscles that pass in front of the axis act as flexors and all those passing behind it act as extensors at the elbow joint. Since many muscles act on multiple joints, their names are not always appropriate for their function in relation to the elbow joint. In addition, their action at the elbow joint depends on the position of the neighbouring joints."

Platzer recognises that the name of the muscle does not always correspond to their function. It is noted that the extensor carpi radialis longus and brevis muscles also participate in elbow flexion. Not all the above muscles are activated simultaneously, rather they intervene during determined degrees of movement of the elbow joint. If the elbow is flexed with simultaneous internal rotation then the pronator teres muscle intervenes. If there is flexion with simultaneous abduction then the brachioradialis muscle intervenes for lateral stability. These muscular associations create the various motor schemes that are organised in the myofascial diagonals.

According to Gray a primary muscle and a synergic muscle exist for every joint: "One or more muscles constantly act to initiate and continue a given movement. They are called prime movers, an example is the brachialis in elbow flexion. In some cases the contraction of a prime mover, especially when the muscle extends over more than one joint, may produce additional movements. The latter are eliminated by the contraction of the synergic muscles."

Carroll A.M. and Bewener A.A. have ascertained that monoarticular muscles work in a specific manner for a determined direction, whilst biarticular muscles intervene in postural control[6].

Based on these observations each joint is therefore composed of (Fig. 1.6):

- a primary or principal or specific or monoarticular muscle. The largest number of motor units located there are connected to one specific direction;
- a secondary, biarticular or polyarticular muscle. The motor units operating on two joints are located there. For instance the biceps brachii muscle operates on both shoulder and elbow flexion;
- more synergic or motor scheme muscles. The motor units for two or three directions are located there. For example, the pronator teres muscle operates on flexion and pronation of the elbow.

The monoarticular muscle is the muscle containing the highest number of ipsidirectional motor units. Therefore, it is the first muscle upon which the central nervous impulse converges. Many muscles such as the triceps brachii have their monoarticular fibres fused with the biarticular ones (long head). Through these fascial connections, the activation of the primary muscle also involves the secondary and synergic muscles. Huijing et al. found that around 40% of muscular fibres have their origin on the perimysium[7], which in turn is connected to the epimysial fascia. During exertion and depending on the joint range of motion, the stretch also involves synergic muscles. The biarticular muscles adapt their intervention based upon the range of motion of the proximal joint compared to the distal joint. Both ipsidirectional mono and biarticular muscles are innervated by the same spinal cord level. This facilitates and speeds up the completion of the alpha and gamma reflex arc.

Platzer reports that this functional motor organisation corresponds to what is currently reported in the literature: "The most modern method to evaluate muscular function is electromyography. This method has shown that, with an increase in effort, more and more motor units become activated. Electromyography has demonstrated that all fibres are never all active at the same time. While some fibres are at rest, other contract, resulting in a uniform increase or decrease in tension. The accuracy of electromyography is limited by the difficulty of determining the relative contributions of different muscles to any given movement" (Platzer 2009).

[6] The muscles that operate on a single joint (monoarticular) have a different role compared to those operating on two joints (biarticular). The biarticular muscle seems to act mainly on postural control while the monoarticular muscle is specific for the movement of one joint. (Carroll AM. 2009)

[7] Huijing et al. (2005) demonstrated how 30-40% of the force generated by muscles is transmitted not along the tendon, but rather to the connective tissue surrounding the muscle. The presence of a constant basal tone of the muscular fibres maintains the spindles and the perimysial fascia in a state of permanent tension. Many muscular fibres do not necessarily extend from the origin to the insertion of the muscle but have tapered ends to the surrounding fascial structures. (Stecco C. 2015)

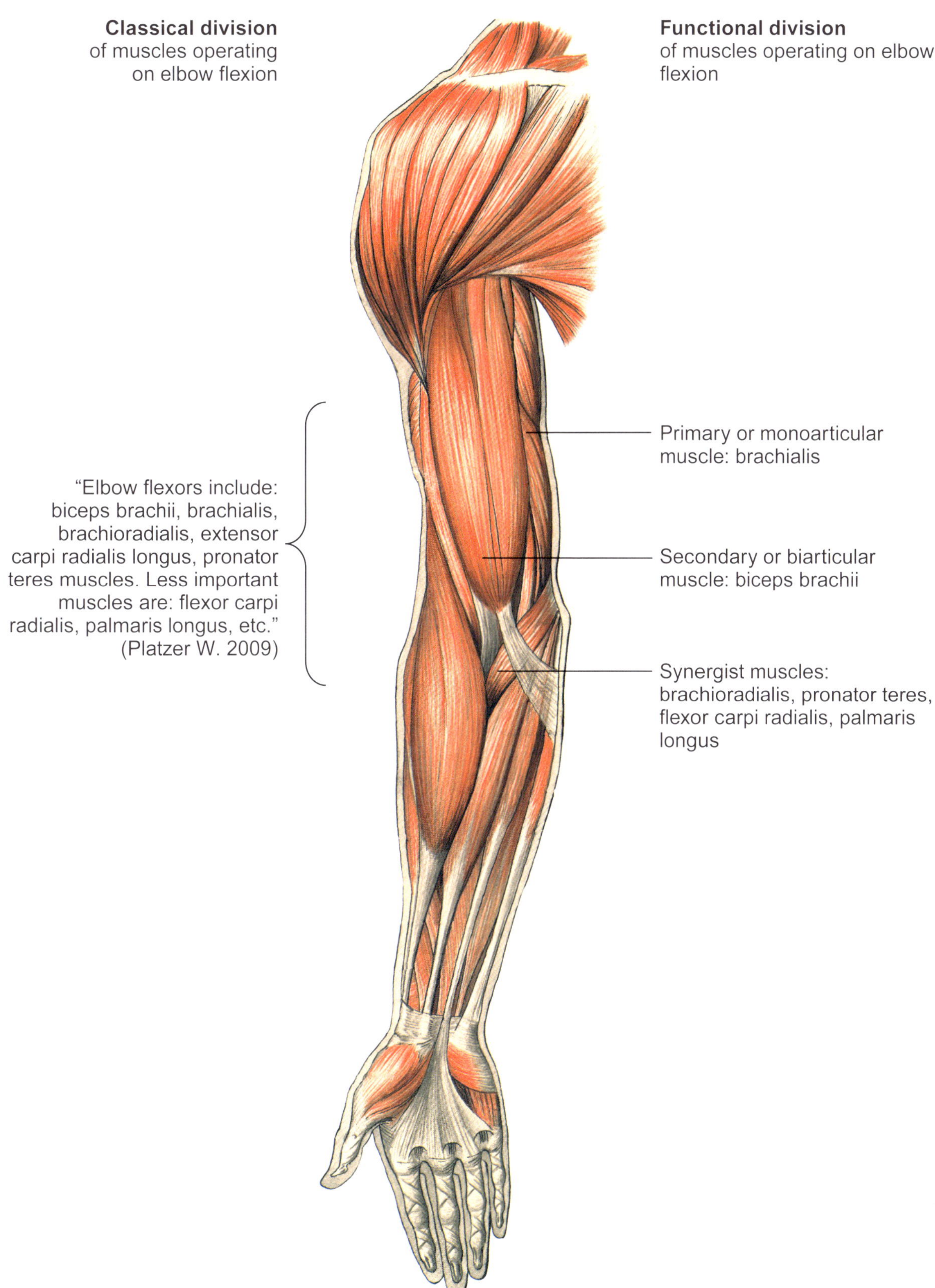

Fig. 1.6. Muscles of the upper limb, anterior view. Classical division on the left, new proposal on the right.
(From G. Chiarugi and L. Bucciante, Istituzioni di anatomia dell'uomo. Piccin Nuova Libraria, Padova 1983, modified)

MUSCULAR FASCIA

STRUCTURE OF THE FASCIA

The muscular fascia is a membrane formed of fibrous connective tissue. Proper connective tissue comprises both loose and dense connective tissue. Dense connective tissue is characterised by a large number of collagen fibres providing a definite resistance to traction and by elastic fibres allowing for a certain adaptability of the tissue. Muscular fascia may be classified within the dense regular connective tissue (Stecco C. 2015).

With a naked eye the examination of a strip of fascia lata (Fig. 1.70, 1.71, 1.72, 1.73) reveals that it is very resistant when stretched in the direction in which its collagen fibres are arranged, whereas it easily tears if stretched in the opposite direction. The examination of the same strip of fascia under a microscope reveals that it is formed by undulated collagen fibres mixed with elastic fibres (Fig. 1.7). Fibroblasts or cells dedicated to the formation of these fibres are present along these fibres. The fibres and cells are embedded in the ground matrix. The undulation and quantity of collagen fibres vary greatly in the various types of fasciae and connective tissues. All fasciae, muscular and visceral, must adapt to stretching therefore, there is a continuous transition between the resting position and that of stretching (Fig. 1.8). Following each stretch the elastic fibres must bring the fascia back to its resting position. The fascia is an anisotropic body inasmuch as the collagen fibres forming its exhibit different physical properties (elasticity, absorption, quantity) in different directions. The element that allows collagen fibres to elongate or shorten is the ground matrix in which they are embedded. If this substance goes from its fluid form (sol) to its dense form (gel) then the interfibrillar gliding is compromised. The densification of the ground matrix, and in particular that of the hyaluronan, is determined by various causes and primarily by overuse and trauma (Stecco A. 2014).

The four principal forms of muscular fasciae and their structures are examined below.

- The aponeurotic fascia (Fig. 1.9) is formed by two or three layers of collagen fibres as for instance the fascia lata. Each layer is formed by unidirectional collagen fibres and is separated from the underlying one by a layer of loose connective tissue. The content of the fibrous layers is approximately 80% of collagen fibres and only 1% of elastic fibres (Stecco C. 2009).
- The epimysial fascia (Fig. 1.10) is formed of type I and III collagen fibres and of approximately 15% elastic fibres (Sakamoto 1996). An example is the fascia surrounding the vastus medialis of the quadriceps muscle. The collagen fibres have an angle of incidence of 55° with respect to the arrangement of muscular fibres. The collagen layer of the epimysium is free to glide since it is separated from the aponeurotic fascia by an external layer of loose connective tissue. It is also separated from the perimysial fascia by the internal layer of loose connective tissue. The collagen layer of the epimysial fascia is not completely independent since multiple septa detach themselves from the epimysium and insert in both the overlying aponeurotic fascia and the underlying perimysial fascia.
- The perimysial fascia (Fig. 1.11) is formed by few type I fibres and many type III and IV collagen fibres. An example is the membrane surrounding the secondary bundles of vastus medialis. Type I fibres have a diameter up to ten times greater than those of the endomysium (Purslow P.P. 1989), allowing for a notable resistance to traction. The perimysium has an external layer of gliding and an intermediate layer of collagen fibres. These fibres are arranged at an angle of 55° at rest with respect to muscular fibres, but this angle reduces to 20° when the fibres are stretched (Rowe R.W. 1981). This layer of collagen fibres is separated from the endomysium by a thin layer of loose connective tissue whilst also offering insertions to the ends of the neuromuscular spindles.
- The endomysial fascia (Fig. 1.12) is mainly formed by type III, IV, V collagen fibres. An example is the membrane surrounding the primary bundles of the vastus medialis muscle. These are associated with the basal lamina overlying each muscle fibre (Standring et al. 2008). The abundance of ground substance present in the endomysium makes it the fundamental element for the gliding of the various muscular fibres. The alpha axon terminates on the endomysium through the motor endplate.

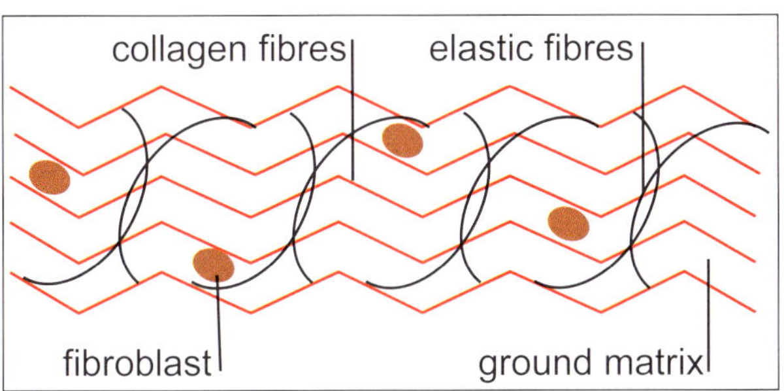

Fig. 1.7. Arrangement of collagen and elastic fibres at rest or in a relaxed state.

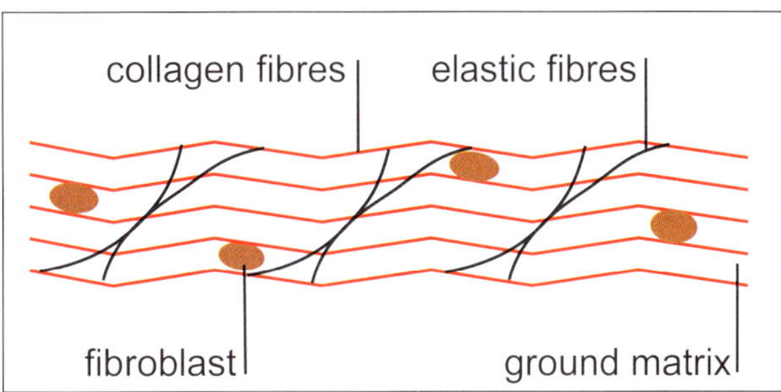

Fig. 1.8. Arrangement of collagen and elastic fibres under tension.

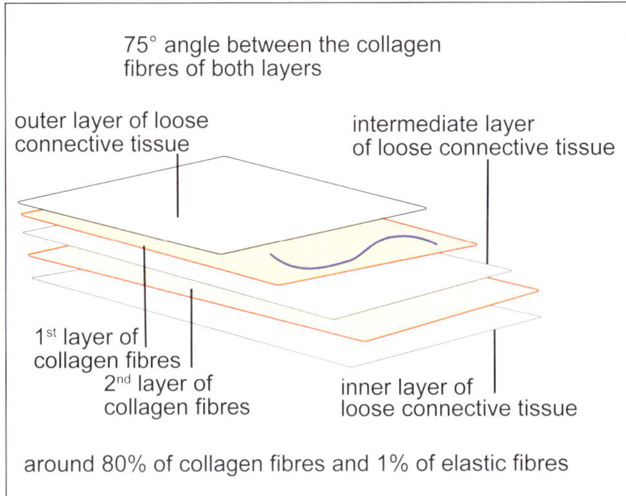

Fig. 1.9. Aponeurotic fascia. It is composed of two or three independent layers of collagen fibres arranged longitudinally, transversely and obliquely.

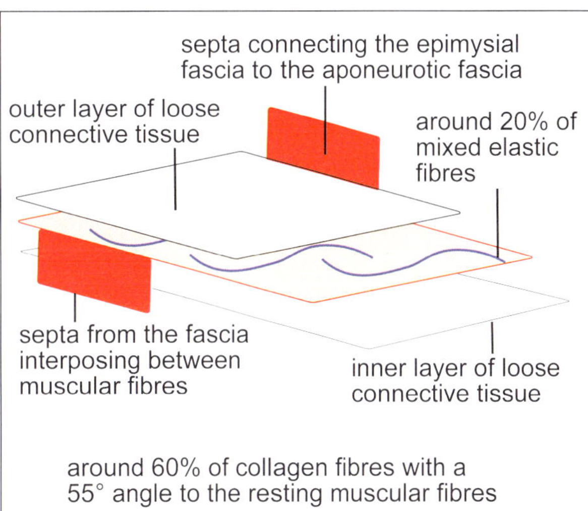

Fig. 1.10. Epimysial fascia. It extends between the underlying muscles through the septa and it connects to the overlying aponeurotic fascia.

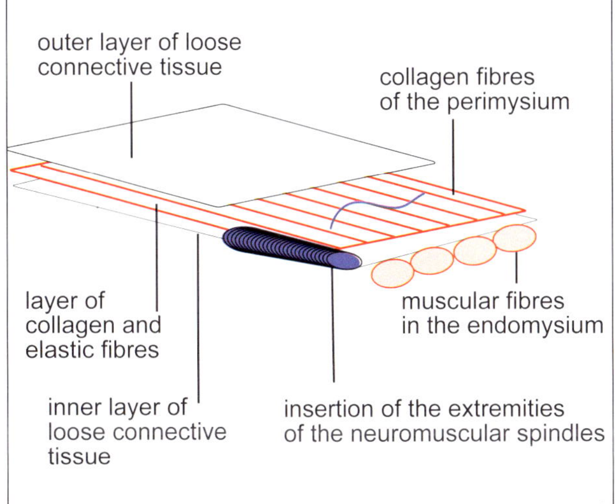

Fig. 1.11. Perimysial fascia. Part of the collagen layer is free to glide over the endomysium and part is in direct contact with the neuromuscular spindles.

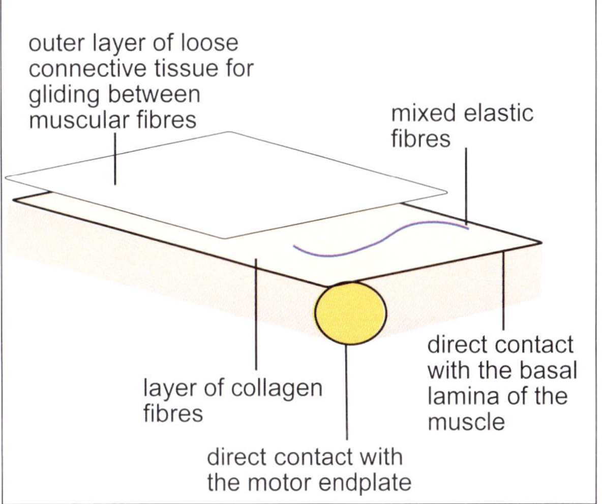

Fig. 1.12. Endomysial fascia. The layer of collagen fibres is in direct contact with the basal lamina overlying each muscular fibre. The motor endplate terminates on it.

DIVISION OF MUSCULAR FASCIA IN LAMINAE

In anatomy textbooks the fasciae of the trunk are divided in laminae. Below is a quote from Chiarugi followed by some important discrepancies that are highlighted. "The fasciae of the large muscles of the trunk (Fig. 1.13): a first connective lamina, the fascia of the external oblique muscle, extends on the superficial aspect of this muscle on both fleshy parts and its aponeurosis. A second connective lamina is interposed between the external and internal oblique muscles. A third lamina is located between the internal oblique and the transverse muscle. The transverse fascia is a connective lamina differentiated from the deep fascia of the transverse muscle and on which the peritoneum is stratified. The preperitoneal connective tissue is found between the transverse fascia and the peritoneum." (Chiarugi G. 1975)

The first connective lamina, laid over the large muscles of the abdomen is a true fascia whilst the second and third laminae that are interposed between muscles are gliding loose connective tissue. Only the laminae containing the internal oblique and transverse muscle in their bilamination are true fasciae with a function of coordination and perception. These laminae then continue onto the aponeurosis formed by the rectus sheath.

During anatomical dissections layers of loose connective tissue are found between all the muscular fasciae, but these only have a function of facilitating the gliding between various muscles. The fascial laminae must contain the muscle, send septa inside it and form a continuity with other muscles.

For instance, the superficial lamina of the deep fascia of the trunk wraps around the gluteus maximus muscle and then proceeds in a spiral with the opposite latissimus dorsi muscle. On the anterior trunk the right and left serratus anterior and pectoralis major muscles continue in a spiral with the contralateral external oblique muscle.

The intermediate lamina of the trunk is a cushion fascia since it allows gliding between the musculature belonging to the deep lamina and to the superficial lamina. The serratus posterior inferior and superior, the gluteus medius and the internal oblique muscles are enclosed in the intermediate lamina.

At the level of the neck (Fig. 1.15) the muscular fascia is also divided into three laminae. The superficial lamina wraps the neck forming two sheaths holding the sternocleidomastoid and the trapezius muscles. The intermediate lamina mainly refers to the hyoid muscles with the levator scapula and the splenius muscles. The deep lamina is divided between the prevertebral and paravertebral muscles.

In anatomical textbooks[8], the fasciae of the limbs are described without distinguishing between the aponeurotic fascia spread superficially, the intermediate lamina connecting with the rotator muscles, and the epimysial fasciae wrapping the muscles (Fig. 1.14). In the limbs, the fasciae are not arranged in three concentric laminae as in the trunk, rather the aponeurotic fascia wraps the entire limb and sends intermuscular septa between muscles.

The aponeurotic fascia of the limbs is formed by the tendinous expansions of the large muscles of the trunk. These muscles are called appendicular since from the trunk they insert onto the appendices (limbs). Their distal tendons do not insert on bones but send large tendinous expansions that form the aponeurotic fascia; for instance, 80% of the gluteus maximus tendon forms a part of the fascia lata (Stecco A. 2013). Along the limbs the muscles insert onto the aponeurotic fascia directly or through tendinous expansions, the lacertus fibrosus being an example. The aponeurotic fascia of the limbs is not uniform and it contains the retinacula of the ankle and wrist that are sometimes improperly called ligaments. The retinacula continue into the collagen fibres arranged in spirals along the limbs.

The epimysial fascia is located underneath the aponeurotic fascia. This fascia does not glide above the muscles like the aponeurotic fascia, but it fuses with the perimysium surrounding the underlying muscular fibres.

The deep lamina of the fascia of the limbs mainly forms the interosseous laminae on which the deep postural muscles of the lower limbs insert (bipedal posture of humans).

[8] The leg fascia continues from the fascia lata. On its anterior aspect it is more robust proximally and there it adheres and gives insertions to the underlying muscles. Distally above the malleoli, transversal fibrous bundles appear and become very robust, these form the transverse ligament of the leg. The posterior aspect of the leg fascia overlays the triceps surae muscle. It sends a sheath to the anterior aspect of triceps surae which is attached to the surface of the muscles of the deep layer. (Chiarugi G. 1975)

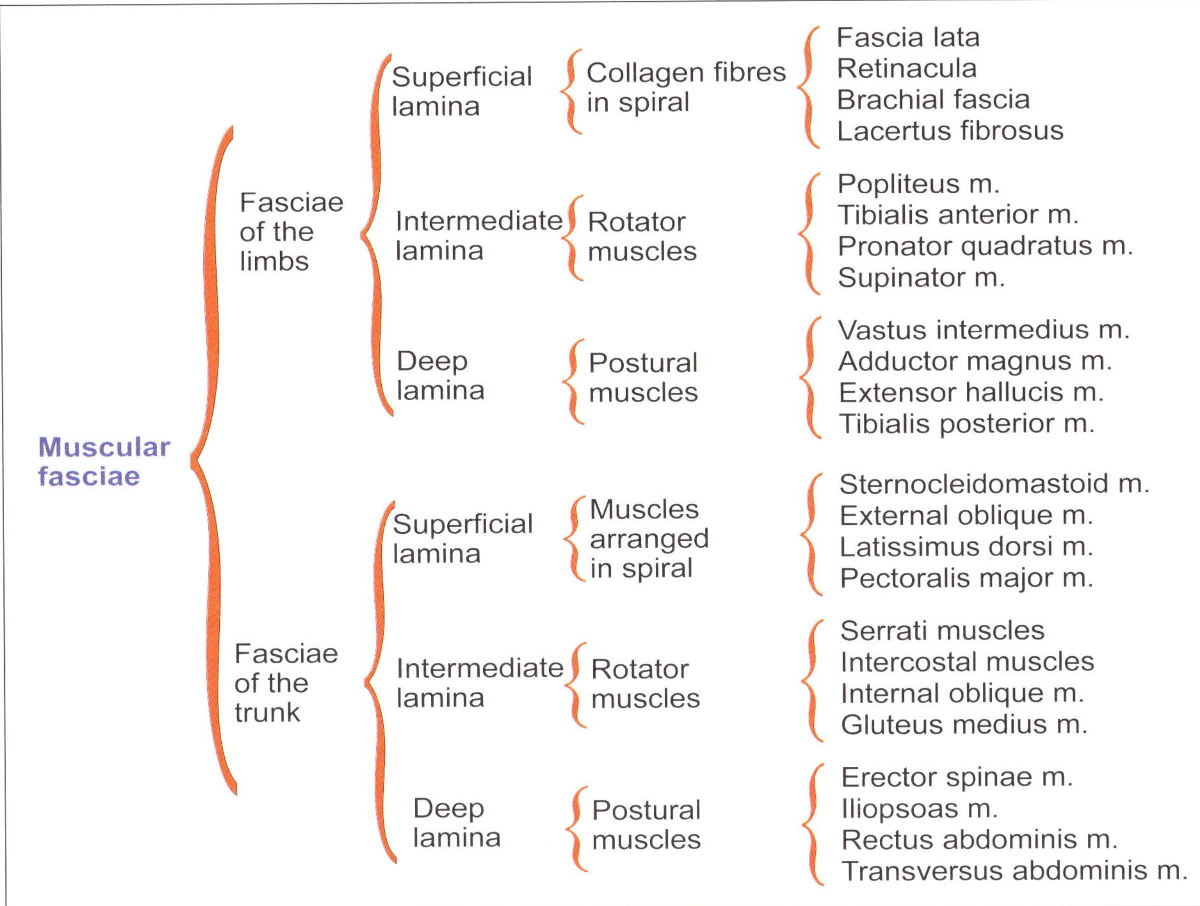

Fig. 1.13. Division of the fasciae of the limbs and trunk in layers.

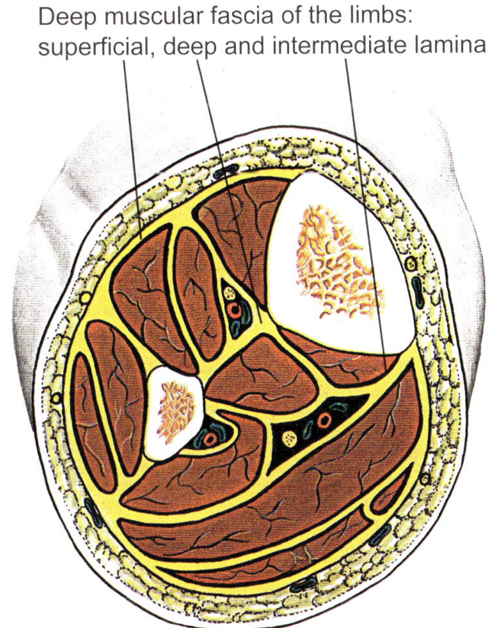

Fig. 1.14. Transverse section of the leg, medial third. *(From G. Chiarugi and L. Bucciante, Istituzioni di anatomia dell'uomo. Piccin Nuova Libraria, Padova 1983, modified)*

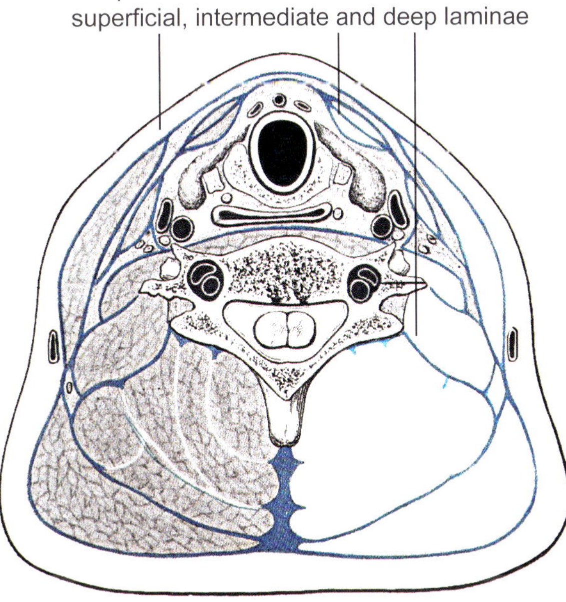

Fig. 1.15. Transverse section of the neck at the level of C6.
(From G. Chiarugi and L. Bucciante, Istituzioni di anatomia dell'uomo. Piccin Nuova Libraria, Padova 1983, modified)

DIVISION OF THE ARTICULAR COLLAGEN STRUCTURES ACCORDING TO MOTOR DIRECTIONS

During dissections Anatomists have removed all fascial connections to point out the single parts composing the joints. Instead it would be opportune to connect the periarticular structures together whilst following a precise motor organisation. In the elbow for instance (Fig. 1.16), ligaments are not a separate entity but rather they are in continuity with the tendons and fasciae. The ligaments are often divided in several bundles: the ulnar ligament has an anterior, a transverse and a posterior bundle. Each is able to perceive a determined directional stretch and to stabilise the joint during a precise movement. The continuity of ligaments with tendons explains why Golgi tendon organs are also found inside ligaments whereas these nerve endings have usually been related exclusively to tendons. On this topic Gray states that: "The type III joint nerve endings are identical to the Golgi tendon organs by structure and function: they are found in the articular ligaments but not in the articular capsules. They are receptors with the function of preventing excessive articular effort through the inhibition of adjacent muscles" (Gray H. 1993). The interaction between the Golgi tendon organs and the ligaments in coordinating joint range of motion between two adjacent joints will be explained later on.

The intermuscular septa are often in continuity with ligaments. For instance, the lateral intermuscular septum of the arm is continuous with the collateral radial ligament which in turn provides insertion to the supinator muscle. During elbow movement, this arrangement allows the proximal stretch of the lateral septum and distally that of the supinator muscle.[9]

Muscle insertions are also present on the joint capsule (Fig. 1.16, 1.17). For instance: "the terminal part of the common tendon of the triceps muscle casts some muscular bundles on the synovial membrane of the elbow (tensor of the synovium muscle). Given its attachment on the joint capsule of the elbow, when the brachialis muscle contracts it pulls the synovia and avoids its entrapment between the bony heads. The muscular bundles of the supinator muscle have been described, these may be interpreted as tensors of the annular ligament of the radioulnar joint" (Chiarugi G. 1975). The insertions of the brachialis and triceps muscles on the joint capsule not only help to prevent its impingement but they also provide feedback in order to adjust the contraction of these muscles at various joint angles.

The joint capsule is formed of two layers: the synovial membrane secreting the synovial fluid, and the external fibrous membrane in continuity with all the other fascial collagenous structures.

Chiarugi writes that the ligaments often give insertions to tendons, give origin to muscles (supinator) or are the continuation of intermuscular septa. This statement increases in significance if looking at it from the point of view of fascial continuity and directional perception (captions of Figures 1.16 and 1.17).

The directional nature of the fascial architecture found in the elbow is also evident in the shoulder and hip joints but the analysis below will be focussed on the knee joint.

The collateral ligaments of the knee are the continuation of tendons. The lateral collateral ligament is enclosed within a bundle of the biceps femoris tendon and this ligament corresponds to the insertion of the peroneus longus tendon.

The medial collateral ligament is in continuity with the adductor magnus tendon: "the distal tendon of adductor magnus, at the insertions on the medial condyle, is one with the medial intermuscular septum" (Chiarugi G. 1975). The medial meniscus of the knee is adherent to the joint capsule and to the medial collateral ligament (Fig. 1.17).

Retinacula are also an extension of the tendinous insertions. For instance, the patellar retinaculum is formed by the tendinous expansions of the vastus lateralis and vastus medialis of the quadriceps muscle.

Many tendons come to an end in a manner similar to pes anserinus, namely as three tendinous expansions with as many fasciae:

- "the first part of the tendon of semimembranosus goes to the medial condyle of the tibia, the second part goes to the fascia of the popliteus muscle and the third part spreads out to the joint capsule forming the oblique popliteal ligament; these expansions form the deep pes anserine" (Platzer W. 2009);
- the tendon of the tensor fascia lata muscle (iliotibial tract) connects at the level of the knee with the interosseous membrane of the leg, with the fibular head and with the lateral condyle of the tibia.

[9] When the relationship between muscle spindles and the intramuscular connective tissue is considered, the role of the muscle spindles in peripheral motor coordination becomes evident. The muscle spindles are localised in the perimysium, and their capsule is connected to the epimysium and fascial septae. Strasmann et al. analysed the septum of the supinator muscle and found that many muscle spindles are inserted directly into the connective tissue of the septum. Studies have demonstrated that the extrafusal and intrafusal muscle fibres possess complex biophysical properties that contribute to muscle stiffness and/or laxity. (Stecco A. 2014)

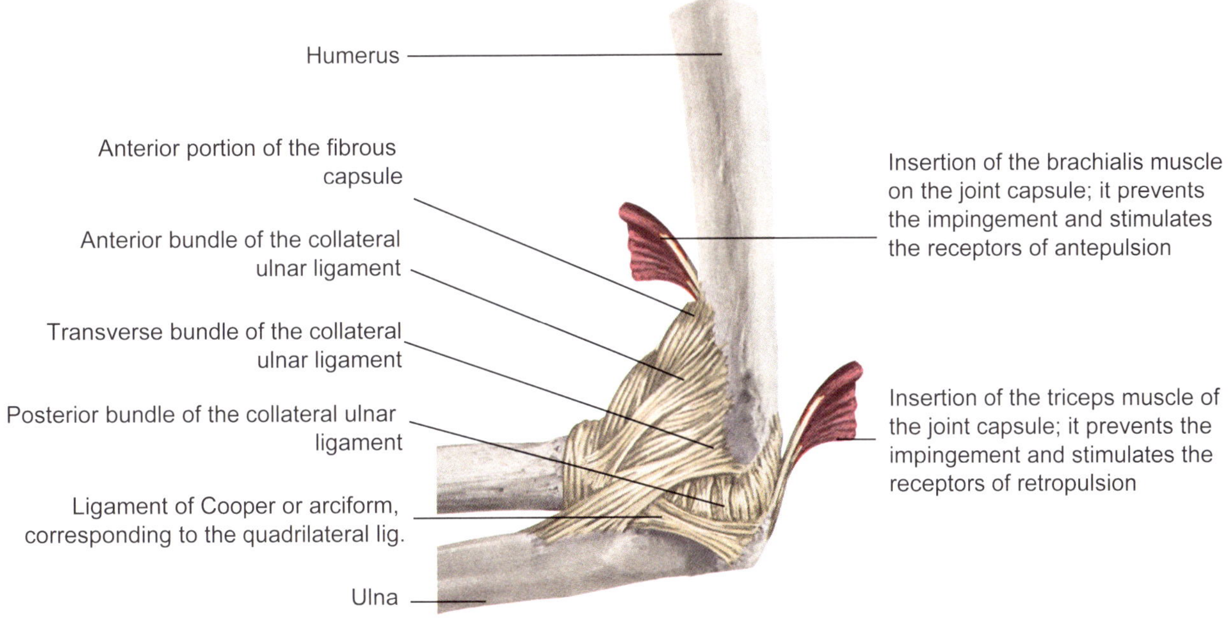

Fig. 1.16. Medial elbow joint. Each bundle of the collateral ulnar ligament is specific for the perception and stabilisation in one direction. The anterior bundle for antepulsion, the transverse bundle for intrarotation and the posterior bundle for mediopulsion. Each bundle of the collateral radial ligament is specific for a direction: the anterior for extrarotation, the lateral for lateropulsion and the posterior for retropulsion.

(From G. Chiarugi and L. Bucciante, Istituzioni di anatomia dell'uomo. Piccin Nuova Libraria, Padova 1983, modified)

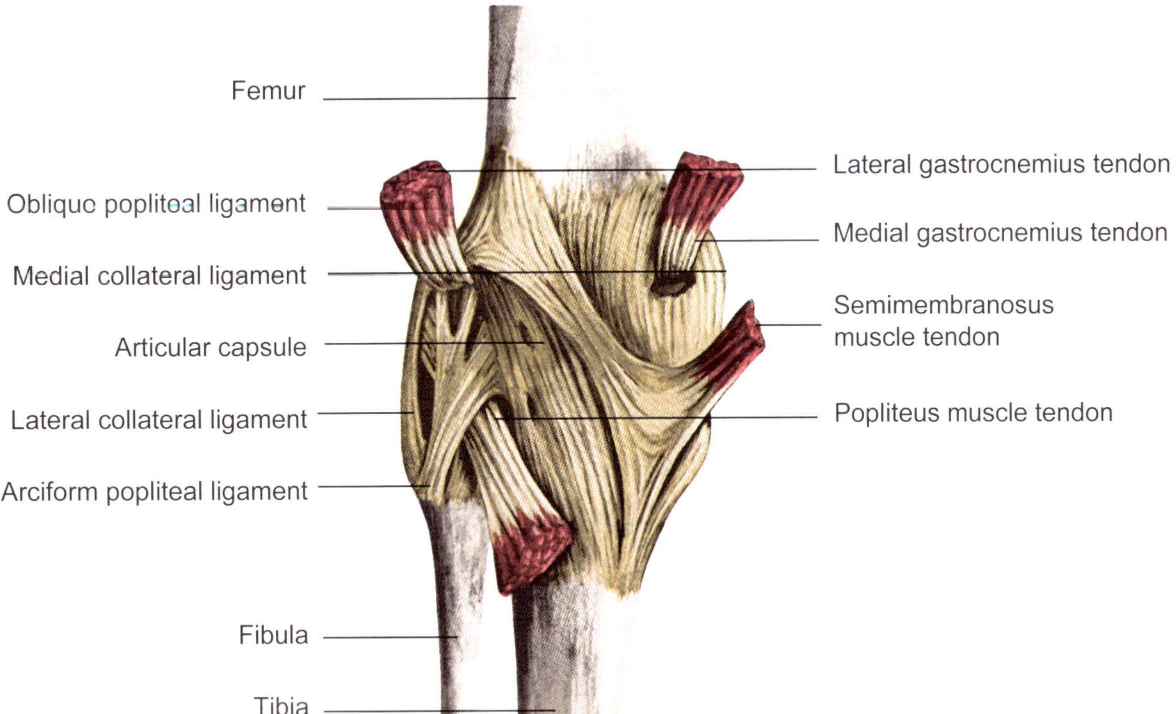

Fig. 1.17. Posterior knee joint. Each bundle of the popliteal ligament is specific for one direction: the arcuate bundle for extrarotation, the oblique bundle for intrarotation, the posterior bundle for retropulsion. Each ligament of the knee is specific for the perception and for the stabilisation in one direction: the lateral collateral lig. for lateropulsion, the medial collateral lig. for mediopulsion and the patellar lig. for antepulsion.

(From G. Chiarugi and L. Bucciante, Istituzioni di anatomia dell'uomo. Piccin Nuova Libraria, Padova 1983, modified)

DIVISION OF THE WRIST AND ANKLE FASCIAL SHEATHS ACCORDING TO MOTOR DIRECTIONS

The arrangement of the tendon sheaths of the wrist and ankle show how the fascia conforms itself to movement. In the palmar region of the wrist (Fig. 1.18, 1.19) the sheaths of the following muscles are present:

- flexor carpi ulnaris muscle that moves the wrist in mediopulsion (ME) or ulnar adduction;
- flexor carpi radialis muscle that moves the wrist in antepulsion (AN) or radial flexion;
- pronator quadratus muscle that moves the wrist in intrarotation (IR).

In the dorsal region of the wrist the sheaths of the following muscles are present:

- extensor carpi radialis muscle that moves the wrist in lateropulsion (LA) or radial abduction;
- extensor carpi ulnaris muscle that moves the wrist in retropulsion (RE) or ulnar extension or dorsiflexion;
- supinator, extensor digitorum and extensor pollicis longus muscles that implement extrarotation (ER).

The aforementioned muscles are associated with muscles that are derived from them; their tendons run in the tendinous sheaths of the wrist and connect to a specific finger giving each one a motor perception (Fig. 1.19):

- flexor carpi radialis muscle is associated with flexor pollicis longus muscle (AN);
- pronator teres and quadratus muscles are associated with flexor digitorum longus and brevis muscles (III and IV) (IR);
- flexor carpi ulnaris muscle is associated with flexor digiti minimi muscle (ME);
- extensor carpi ulnaris muscle is associated with extensor digiti minimi muscle[10] (RE);
- supinator muscle is associated with the extensor digitorum and pollicis longus muscles (III and IV) (ER);
- extensor carpi radialis longus and brevis muscles are associated with abductor pollicis muscle (LA).

The palmaris longus, extensor indicis and flexor indicis tendons are located in an intermediate position.

The extensor and flexor digitorum muscles are associated with intrarotation and extrarotation since as Chiarugi writes: "coinciding with each flexion and extension movement of the fingers, slight movements of rotation are encountered however, these cannot be performed voluntarily".

The fact that each finger of the hand is involved by a specific motor direction provides the hand the capability of stereognosis, or the ability to recognise an object through palpation with the eyes closed.

The muscle tendons responsible for wrist movements are connected to the superficial lamina of the antebrachial fascia whilst the tendons of the fingers are connected to the deep lamina.

The tendinous sheaths of the antero-medial ankle are connected to the following muscles (Fig. 1.20, 1.21):

- tibialis anterior muscle moves the ankle in antepulsion (AN) or dorsiflexion;
- flexor halluces longus muscle moves the ankle in mediopulsion (ME) or adduction;
- tibialis posterior muscle determines the intrarotation of the ankle (IR) or supination.

The tendons sheaths of the postero-lateral ankle are connected to the following muscles:

- triceps surae and plantaris muscles move the ankle in retropulsion (RE) or plantarflexion;
- peroneus longus muscle rotates the ankle in extrarotation (ER) or pronation;
- peroneus tertius muscle implements lateropulsion of the ankle (LA) or eversion.

The muscles dedicated to ankle movement are associated with muscles going to the forefoot:

- tibialis anterior muscle extends with the extensor hallucis longus muscle to the big toe of the foot (AN);
- flexor hallucis longus muscle[11] extends through strips towards the tendons of flexor digitorum longus (ME);
- tibialis posterior muscle extends with the flexor digitorum longus muscle towards the central toes (IR);
- the fascia of the triceps muscle extends with the lateral compartment of the foot containing the extensor digiti minimi muscle (RE);
- peroneus longus muscle extends with the peroneus brevis muscle at the base of the fourth and fifth metatarsal bones (ER);
- peroneus tertius muscle unites with the extensor digitorum longus muscle for the three central toes (LA).

In the foot, there is lack of perfect independence of the last four toes. The motor independence of the forefoot is implemented by the muscles comprised in the medial, intermediate, lateral and dorsal compartments.

[10] The muscle belly of the extensor digiti minimi, rather than being independent, may originate from the extensor carpi ulnaris muscle. (Chiarugi G. 1975)

[11] The tendon of the extensor hallucis longus muscle whilst running through the calcaneal sulcus is held in place by the deep layer of the laciniate ligament. In the foot it gives tendinous expansions to the flexor digitorum longus muscle for the second and third toe. Thence the usual appellation of the muscle is improper since its action also implicates movements of other toes besides those of the hallux. It adducts and supinates the foot and its deficit causes a flat foot. (Chiarugi G. 1975)

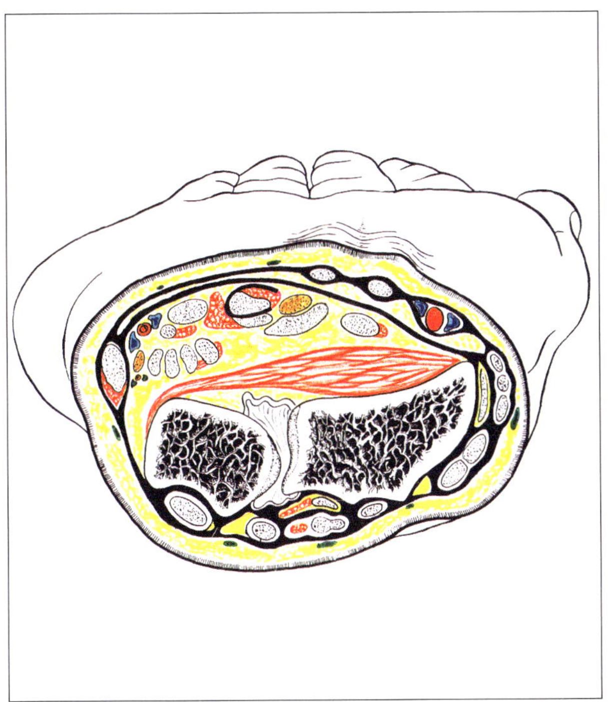

Fig. 1.18. Transverse section of the right forearm, at the inferior bony border.

(From G. Chiarugi and L. Bucciante, Istituzioni di anatomia dell'uomo. Piccin Nuova Libraria, Padova 1983, modified)

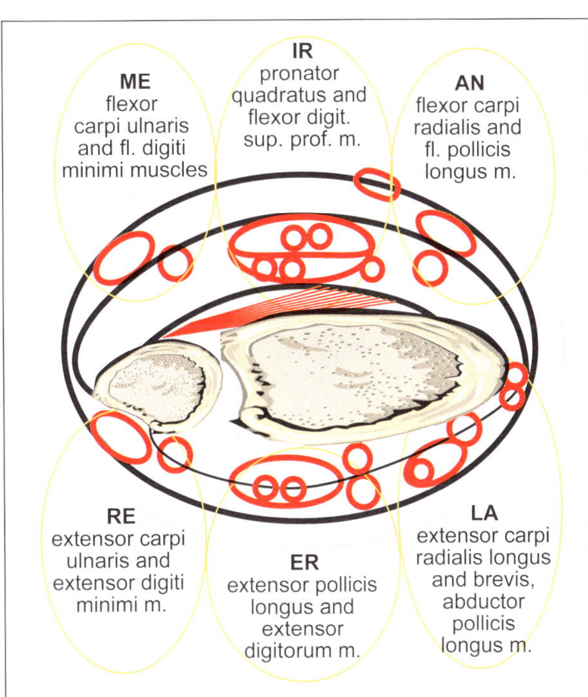

Fig. 1.19. Tendinous sheaths of the proximal wrist. The motor directions are indicated for each tendon.

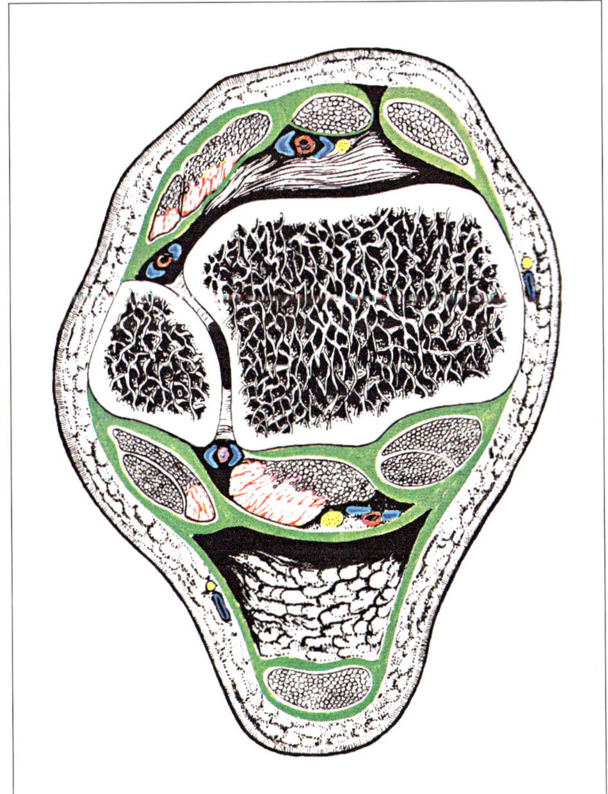

Fig. 1.20. Tendinous sheaths. Transverse-oblique section of the lower border of the left leg at the level of the malleoli.

(From G. Chiarugi and L. Bucciante, Istituzioni di anatomia dell'uomo. Piccin Nuova Libraria, Padova 1983, modified)

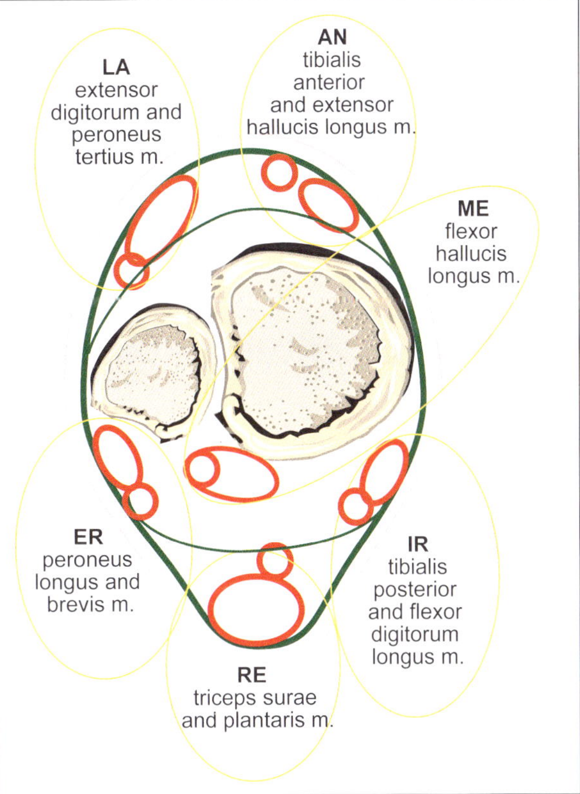

Fig. 1.21. Tendinous sheaths of the ankle and forefoot associated with specific motor directions.

DIVISION OF FASCIAL COMPARTMENTS ACCORDING TO MOTOR DIRECTIONS

Anatomists[12] have ascertained that the fascia forms septa and compartments[13] around muscles but have not shown them in relationship to motor directions. Testut highlighted the continuity of the leg compartments with those of the foot. "Fibrous septa divide the space included between the fascia and the bony plane in three compartments: a posterior compartment that stops distally at the calcaneus, a lateral and a medial compartment. The medial compartment continues proximally with the deep compartment of the posterior region of the leg and distally through the calcaneal canal, with the medial and intermediate plantar compartment."

Fascial compartments of the upper limb

Each compartment has a specific relationship (Fig. 1.22, 1.23, 1.24) with a motor direction. The anterior compartment (AN) of the shoulder (hu) and the arm (cu) continues into the forearm (ca) with the compartment of the flexor carpi radialis, the palmaris longus and the flexor pollicis longus muscles. At the level of the wrist and fingers (di) the flexor muscles of antepulsion converge towards the anterior tendinous sheath and towards the thenar eminence.

The lateral portion of the deltoid muscle (LA) continues into the arm through the lateral intermuscular septum and into the forearm with the compartment of the extensor carpi radialis longus and brevis muscles. Mediopulsion (ME) of the humerus, performed by the pectoralis major and latissimus dorsi muscles, continues into the arm through the medial septum and into the forearm through the compartment of the flexor carpi ulnaris muscle. Retropulsion (RE) of the humerus (hu) is performed by the spinal portion of the deltoid, latissimus dorsi and teres major muscles. Their fascia continues into both the triceps brachii (cu) and the extensor carpi ulnaris (ca) muscle compartments. The intrarotation muscles (IR) are connected to the medial septa and to the anterior aspect of the interosseous membrane. Conversely the extrarotation muscles (ER) are connected to the lateral septum of the arm and forearm.

Fascial compartments of the lower limb

The posterior superficial compartment of the leg contains the gastrocnemius muscles formed mainly of motor units responsible for the retropulsion of the ankle (RE). The lateral compartment contains the peroneus tertius muscle that participates in the lateropulsion of the ankle (LA). The posterior intermediate compartment contains the soleus muscle that mainly implements mediopulsion (ME) of the ankle. The deeper fasciae relate to the muscles (tibialis posterior and peroneals) responsible for intra and extrarotation (IR, ER).

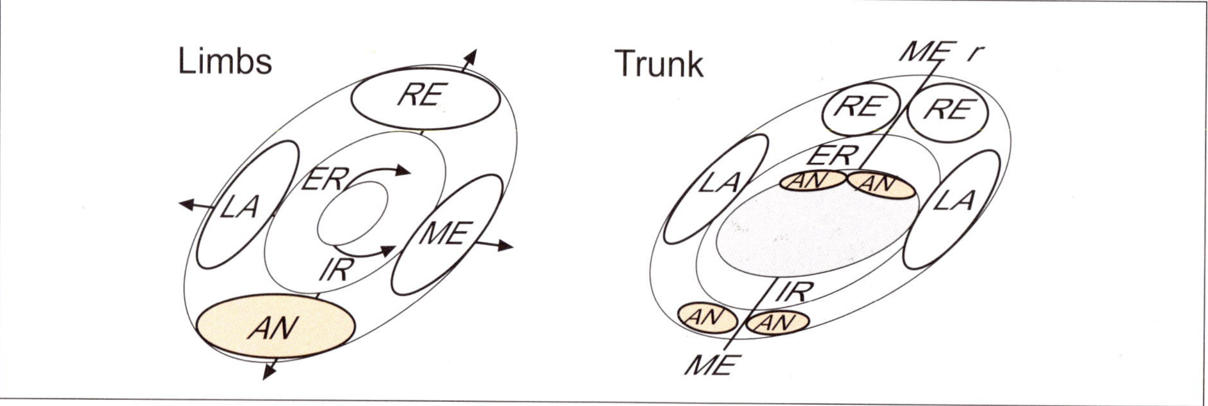

Fig. 1.22. Fascial compartments of the limbs compared to the arrangement of the trunk fascial compartments.

Fascial compartments of the trunk

The muscle compartments operating on the sagittal plane (Fig. 1.22, AN, RE) are distributed deep, and are the four anterior compartments (rectus abdominis and iliopsoas sheaths) and the two posterior compartments (erector spinae muscle).

The muscle compartments for lateral flexion (LA) are formed by the iliocostalis and the quadratus lumborum muscles.

The muscle compartments for trunk rotation (ER, IR) are formed by the muscles connected to the intermediate lamina.

[12] The connective tissue plays important roles in the functional organization of muscles. It provides mechanical consistency, whilst allowing independent movements of single fibres and transmitting contractile forces to adjacent structures. The deep fascia forms intermuscular septa isolating muscles into compartments. (Gray H. 1993)

[13] Muscles participating in the same action have a tendency to cluster. In the limbs the fascial compartments perform this function for instance the flexor compartment of the arm. The muscles participating to the same action have a tendency to be innervated by the same segment of the spinal cord. (Gosling J.A. 2003)

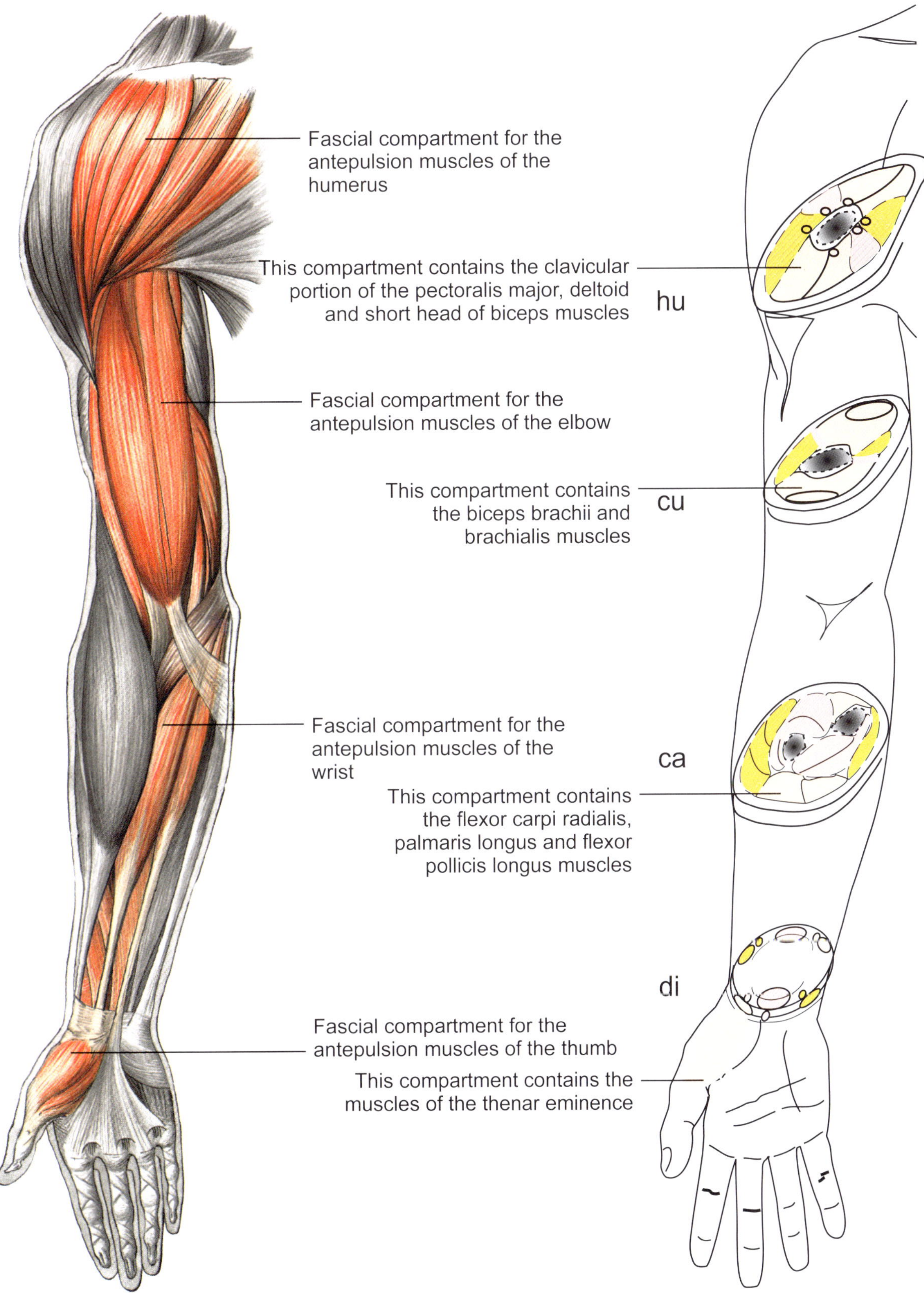

Fig. 1.23. Fascial compartments of the anterior region of the upper limb.

(From G. Chiarugi and L. Bucciante, Istituzioni di anatomia dell'uomo. Piccin Nuova Libraria, Padova 1983, modified)

Fig. 1.24. Transverse section of the upper limb segments with the various fascial compartments.

FROM THE MOTOR UNIT TO THE MYOFASCIAL UNIT

The motor unit[14] is formed by a single motor neuron going to the neuromuscular spindle connected to various muscular fibres. The muscular fibres of one motor unit contract in an all or nothing manner.

In each muscle, there are several motor units: for instance 500 neuromuscular spindles are present[15] in the soleus muscle and therefore 500 motor units. In each motor unit there are about 10 myonemae. Each myonema or primary fascicle is formed by around 10 muscular fibres wrapped by the endomysium[16] (Fig. 1.25). Each muscle fibre (myofibril) is reached by an alpha axon finishing with the motor endplate or neuromuscular junction.

If each motor unit was controlled by the brain individually, the management of motor gesture by the central nervous system would be extremely complicated[17]. The intervention of the neuromuscular spindles and their interaction on the fascia through the endomysium, perimysium and epimysium facilitate the task of the brain.

The ipsidirectional motor units are distributed in several muscles; for instance, the motor units for retropulsion of the talus are located in the soleus, and the medial and lateral gastrocnemius muscles (Fig. 1.26, A, B). If movement only occurs in retropulsion then all these units will intervene simultaneously. If, on the other hand, the retropulsion movement of the ankle goes from pronation to supination during gait, then the fascial stretch first activates the motor units of the lateral gastrocnemius and then those of the medial gastrocnemius muscle[18]. In this case the motor units intervene proportionally based upon the stretch on the fascia and upon the consequent activation of the spindles or inhibition of the alpha fibres from the Golgi tendon organs (Fig. 1.26 B).

Each myofascial unit is formed of four components:

- motor nerve component (Fig. 1.27): the alpha and gamma fibres of the neuromuscular spindles with the intrafusal muscle fibres, primary and secondary afferent fibres from the annulospiral and flower spray receptors;
- coordinating fascial component: the fascia connected to the ipsidirectional motor units regulates the intervention of the neuromuscular spindles and the tendon organs based on joint angle;
- mechanical muscular component: the extrafusal muscle fibres implement the movement of a specific segment towards one direction;
- joint perception component: the receptors embedded in the fascia are connected to the ligaments and to the joint capsule, which are stretched during movement in a specific direction.

Each body segment is served by six myofascial units (Table 1.3) which ensure for movement and stability in the three spatial planes (sagittal, frontal and horizontal).

- The names of the myofascial units are formed by the initials of the motor direction (i.e. an for antepulsion, re for retropulsion, etc.) and by the initials of the segment moved (i.e. cp for caput, cx for coxa, ca for carpus, etc.).

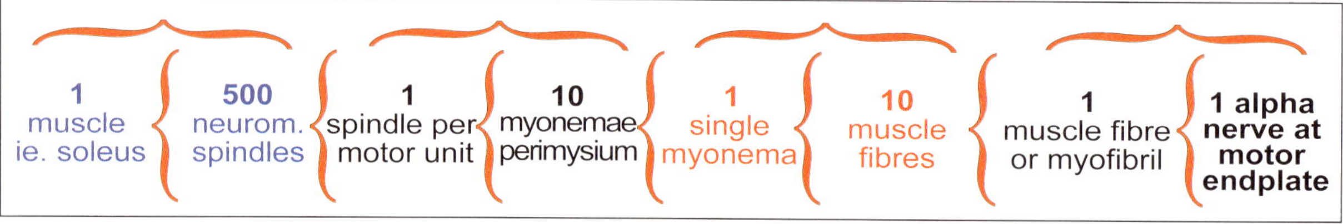

Fig. 1.25. Components of each voluntary muscle

[14] According to Sherrington, the neuromuscular unit is composed of the single spinal somatomotor neuron and of a group of around one hundred myofibrils innervated by it. (Chiarugi G. 1975)

[15] There are around 500 neuromuscular spindles in the soleus whilst they are only 156 in the gastrocnemius muscle; this demonstrates that the gastrocnemius has a different role to the soleus muscle. (Loram I. 2009)

[16] The length of the muscle fibres may vary from a few millimetres in the shorter muscles to many centimetres as in the sartorius muscle (15-30 cm). The manner of clustering of the fibres into primary fascicles organised by the perimysial septa varies based on the muscles. The biomechanical significance, the morphogenesis and the manner of innervation have been scantly studied. These must also be kept distinct from the motor units. (Gray H. 2009)

[17] The mechanism underlying the basis of motor neuron recruitment is not yet completely clear and it appears as an excessive simplification of the complex and real neuromotor organisation. (Kandell E.R. 1994)

[18] Recent researches, derived from morphological and anatomical studies on human muscles, confirm the existence of neuromuscular compartments. These data suggest that the muscular divisions may have a directional function, in fact different portions of a muscle may be recruited according to the task and the motor state. (English A.W. 1993)

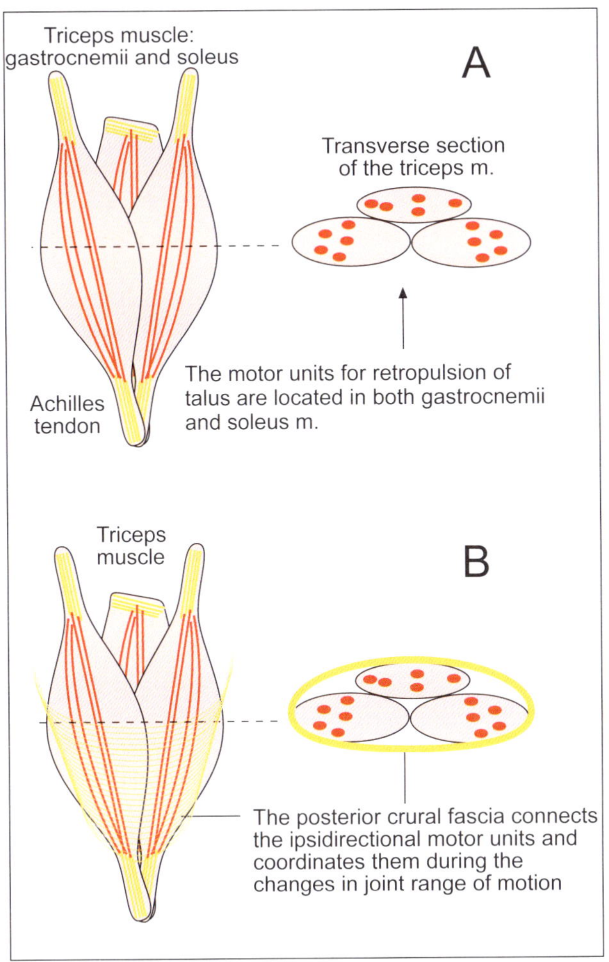

Fig. 1.26. Motor units of the triceps surae muscle.

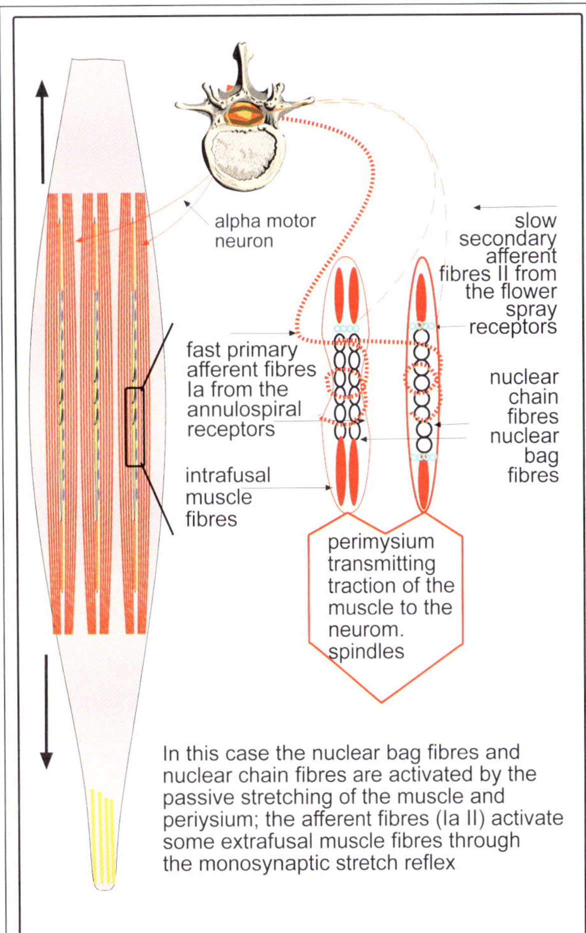

Fig. 1.27. Alpha-gamma circuit of a single motor unit.

Tabella 1.3. Summary table of the myofascial units (top row for motor direction, first column for segments)

	ante an	retro re	medio me	latero la	intra ir	extra er
caput cp	an-cp	re-cp	me-cp	la-cp	ir-cp	er-cp
collum cl	an cl	re-cl	me-cl	la-cl	ir-cl	er-cl
thorax th	an-th	re-th	me-th	la-th	ir-th	er-th
lumbi lu	an-lu	re-lu	me-lu	la-lu	ir-lu	er-lu
pelvis pv	an-pv	re-pv	me-pv	la-pv	ir-pv	er-pv
coxa cx	an-cx	re-cx	me-cx	la-cx	ir-cx	er-cx
genu ge	an-ge	re-ge	me-ge	la-ge	ir-ge	er-ge
talus ta	an-ta	re-ta	me-ta	la-ta	ir-ta	er-ta
pes pe	an-pe	re-pe	me-pe	la-pe	ir-pe	er-pe
scapula sc	an-sc	re-sc	me-sc	la-sc	ir-sc	er-sc
humerus hu	an-hu	re-hu	me-hu	la-hu	ir-hu	er-hu
cubitus cu	an-cu	re-cu	me-cu	la-cu	ir-cu	er-cu
carpus ca	an-ca	re-ca	me-ca	la-ca	ir-ca	er-ca
digiti di	an-di	re-di	me-di	la-di	ir-di	er-di

FROM THE MYOFASCIAL UNIT TO THE CENTRE OF COORDINATION

Studying the neuromuscular spindles without considering their insertion on the perimysium does not allow for the complete comprehension of physiology. "The neuromuscular spindles are inserted on the connective tissue surrounding the muscle fibres. Their contraction is completely inefficient in exerting force on the tendons, but it is used to regulate the sensibility of the receptors" (Chiarugi G. 1975). The regulation of the receptors' sensitivity should not be connected to proprioception but to their ability to shorten and to perceive the adaptability of the surrounding connective tissue. Characterising the spindles and Golgi tendon organs as muscular receptors is incorrect since these nervous organs are active[19] even in the presence of spinal cord lesion[20].

The studies of Gregory J.E. (2002) found that the facilitatory role of stretching through PNF (Proprioceptive Neuromuscular Facilitation) is not correlated to the proprioceptive information but to the viscoelasticity of the fascia and to its interaction with the neuromuscular spindles.

More recent research (Cronin N.J. 2011) confirms the role of neuromuscular spindles in control and in peripheral motor organisation. This regulation is determined by the interaction between the intrafusal fibres and the perimysium. Each voluntary movement is anticipated by the contraction of intrafusal fibres[21] determining an initial variation in muscle tone. In a resting state the annulospiral receptors are not active (Fig. 1.30, A). When the gamma impulse leaves the brain there is a contraction of the intrafusal fibres which will stretch both the perimysium upon which they are inserted and the equatorial plate of the spindle. Only if the perimysium is able to adapt to the traction operated by the intrafusal fibres will there be the activation of the annulospiral receptors (Fig. 1.30, B) that, through the afferent fibres (I, II), will activate the alpha impulse in the cord. The alpha motor neurone[22] is responsible for the contraction of the extrafusal muscle fibres carrying out joint movement (Fig. 1.30, C).

The centre of coordination (CC) of the myofascial unit

From their deep aspect, the epimysial fasciae send septa that are connected to the perimysium. This allows the perception of tractions stemming from the contraction of the muscle fibres belonging to the neuromuscular spindles[23]. The traction exerted by these intrafusal muscle fibres form vectors in the fascia (Fig. 1.29). These vectors converge towards a point of the epimysial fascia called Centre of Coordination (CC). The CC behaves like a coachman holding the reins of the motor units that act on a joint for a specific direction. Each motor unit is formed by both intrafusal muscle fibres preparing movement and by extrafusal muscle fibres implementing movement. Movement preparation is managed by the perimysial fascia that allows the activation of the annulospiral fibres and the closure of the afferential loop (Ia, II) by adapting to the stretch of the spindles. The afferent impulse triggers the alpha stimulus[24] determining the contraction of extrafusal muscle fibres implementing joint movement.

For instance, the centre of coordination (CC) ante-cubitus is formed on the anterior brachial fascia (Fig. 1.28), secondary to the traction of the muscle spindles included in the biceps and brachialis muscles. Some motor units of the ante-cubitus myofascial unit are distributed in the lateral part of the arm, their traction on the fascia forms the external parallelogram. Other motor units are distributed in the medial part of the arm where a second parallelogram is formed. The resultants of both these parallelograms form a third parallelogram which final resultant is arranged along the final direction of movement created by all these motor units. The centre of coordination is situated on the starting point of all these resultants.

Not all motor units are activated simultaneously during elbow flexion, rather they contract based upon the different tensions of the brachial fascia and upon the closure of the alpha-gamma circuit. When the elbow is flexed at 45°, the tension of the brachial fascia is different from when the elbow is flexed at 90°. This difference in tension is reflected on the perimysium and therefore on the neuromuscular spindles inserted into it.

The motor units would activate "all or nothing" if the stimulus were to be regulated by the central nervous system. Instead, they are progressively activated since their participation is determined by the interaction of the spindles with the perimysial fascia.

[19] The neuromuscular spindles facilitate peripheral motor reorganisation even after spinal lesions. (Takeoda A. 2014)

[20] The Golgi tendon organs remain active even in the presence of spinal cord lesion. (Downes L. 2015)

[21] The gamma circuit might seem essential in voluntary motor contraction of muscles since it would induce optimal muscle tone for an effective phasic contraction of muscles. Indeed, it seems demonstrated that each voluntary movement is preceded by a slight increase in tone of the interested muscular groups. (Mazzocchi G. 1996)

[22] It has been demonstrated that each alpha motor neuron innervates the muscular fibres of a single histochemical type. This means that the territory of innervation of a single alpha motor neuron is not distributed uniformly within a muscle. (English A.W. 1993)

[23] The fusimotor fibres provoke the contraction of the polar regions of the intrafusal muscle fibres. They regulate the response of the sensitive terminations and thus allow the "comparison" of programmed movements. (Gray H. 1993)

[24] The Ia afferent fibres are connected to the alpha motor neurons going to the same muscular compartment from which the afferent fibres originated. Therefore, during locomotion, the contraction is not of the entire triceps muscle, but only of some of its parts. (English A.W. 1993)

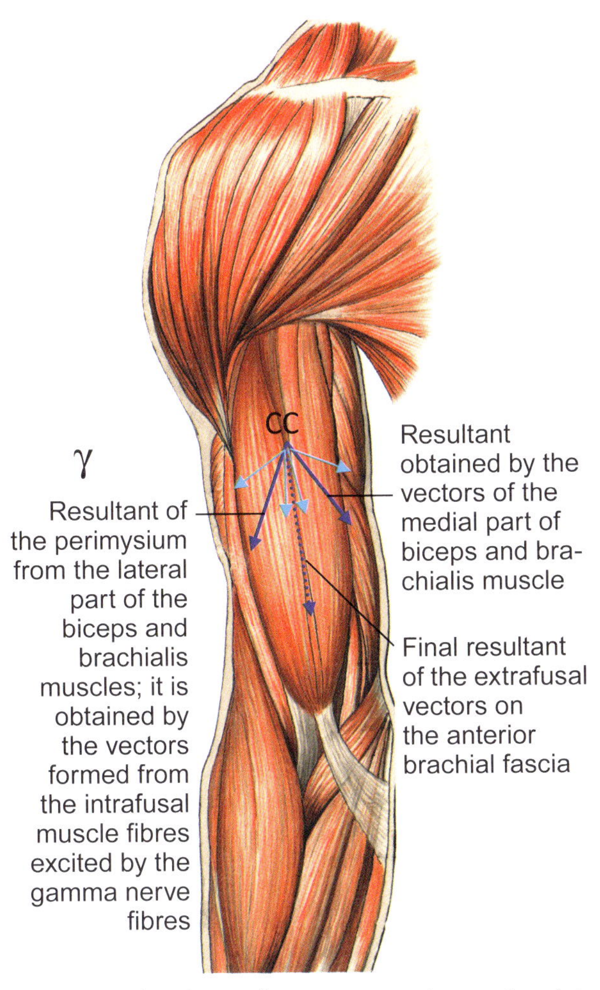

Fig. 1.28. Resultant of many converging vectors into the centre of coordination (CC).
(From G. Chiarugi and L. Bucciante, Istituzioni di anatomia dell'uomo. Piccin Nuova Libraria, Padova 1983, modified)

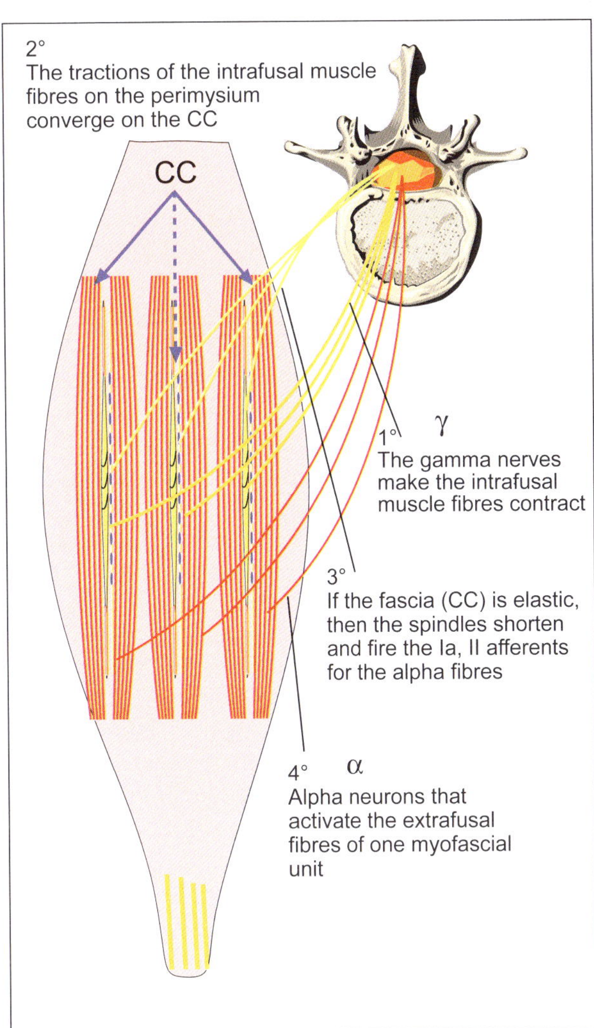

Fig. 1.29. Location of the CC or centre of coordination.

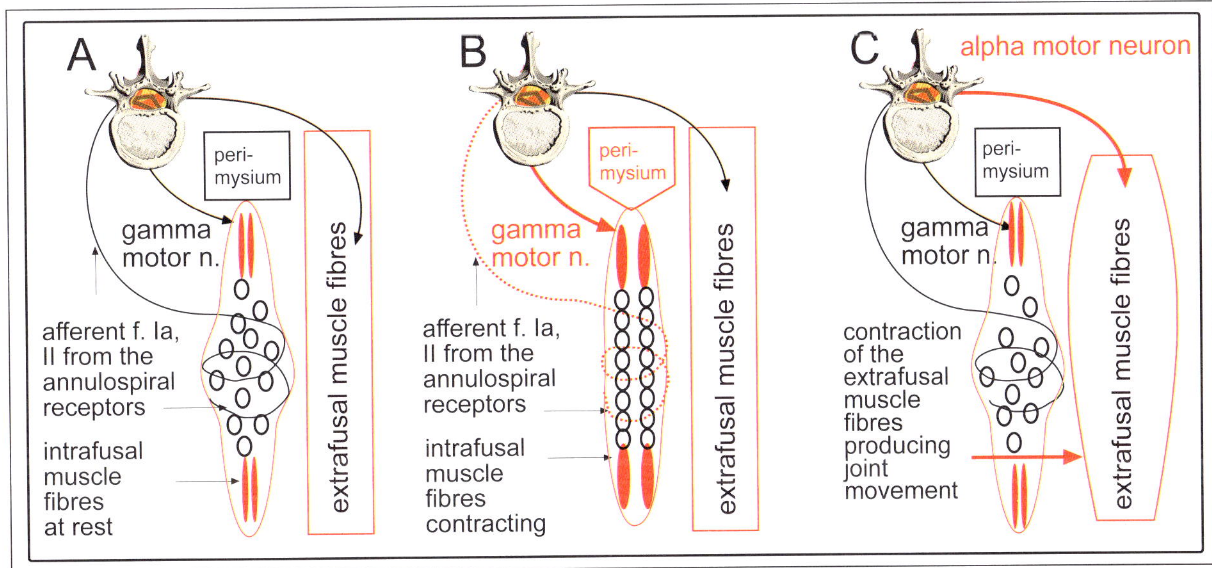

Fig. 1.30. Alpha-gamma circuit. A, circuit at rest. B, intrafusal fibres contraction preparing the movement. C, annulospiral afferent initiating the alpha motor neuron impulse and the extrafusal muscle fibre contraction.

FROM THE CENTRE OF COORDINATION TO THE CENTRE OF PERCEPTION

The centre of perception (CP) corresponds to the resultant of the muscular fibre traction on the fascia which is connected to the tendons and joint capsule of a specific myofascial unit (Fig. 1.31). "The afferents participating in the detection of body segment position and in the establishment of body scheme take their origin from joint receptors located in the capsules and ligaments surrounding the joints. The sensory nerve endings of joints have a different structure: some are similar to Pacini corpuscles, others to Ruffini corpuscles, others are simply free nerve endings. Many of them operate as stretch receptors; others belong to the category of nociceptors.

The receptors function as a goniometer measuring both joint range of motion and velocity with which it is modified. However, each receptor only covers a portion of joint excursion. A map of all joint receptors must be held to know the absolute value of range of motion, as is the case for higher centre neurons for somatic perception" (Baldissera F. 1996).

Joint receptors have two principal functions:

- sending afferents to the brain acknowledging that movement is executed according to the intended direction. This afferent is verified if the receptors are stretched according to the physiological vectors;
- safeguard the integrity of joint structures[25]; this task exploits pain, namely if the joint is stretched outside its physiological axis, then the receptors become nociceptors.

The Pacini and Ruffini organs are identical in the entire body and in all joint capsules, hence these would be able to convey information which would be lacking in providing the brain with a directional significance.

Only if these receptors are mapped along portions of fascia and in ligaments connected to a specific motor direction then do the afferents reach a specific higher centre creating perception related to that part of the body only.

The centre of perception (CP) of the myofascial unit

The centre of coordination (CC) is silent, in that one does not perceive the starter contraction of the intrafusal fibres. Indeed, during elbow flexion (Fig. 1.33) whilst the initial muscle contraction is not perceived, one perceives the sensation of elbow movement and possibly the sensation of muscle enlargement. The movement sensation of elbow flexion is determined by the stretch of the anterior elbow fascia[26] connected to the ligaments and joint capsule (CP) of the an-cu myofascial unit; whereas the sensation of muscular effort is determined by the stretch of the anterior fascial compartment of the arm caused by the increase in volume of the biceps and brachialis muscles. The brain receives the specific afferents for the programmed direction.

The proprioceptive afferent is therefore not provided by neuromuscular spindles or Golgi tendon organs but by the receptors embedded in specific sectors of the muscular and articular fasciae. The organs of Ruffini and Pacini are able to send back to the brain a precise motor direction, since they are inserted in ligaments and fascial compartments according to the three spatial planes (anterior, posterior, lateral, medial, internal, external compartments).

In summary: first, the brain sends the directional gamma motor impulse for a determined group of motor units. Second, the fascia laid out in the CC adapts to the traction of the intrafusal fibres. Third, the annulospiral endings send Ia, II afferents, and close the circuit (Fig. 1.32). Finally, the alpha impulses for the muscle fibres moving the joint are fired. This circuit, called the "gamma circuit", prevents muscular force from pulling the joint outside of its axis. If this feedback was not present many joint lesions would occur. From a clinical point of view, it can be observed that densification of the fascia in the CC creates both a motor deficit and a painful sensation in the CP as a result of anomalous tractions in periarticular structures and in joint receptors.

For all myofascial units, the vectorial resultant connected to neuromuscular spindles is matched by the vectorial resultant formed by the tendons responsible for the final movement (Fig. 1.31). Both resultants could be combined into a single parallelogram, since the tendinous forces are aligned with those of the spindles. However, a single parallelogram would lose the vision of both vectorial actions: one for the motor organisation of the muscle spindles and one for the perception of movement in the joint.

[25] The multifidus muscle is a key muscle that determines the stability of the lumbar spine. It was demonstrated that in the presence of acute low-back pain there is an alteration of the neuromuscular recruitment. Our studies demonstrate that the different regions of multifidus implement different functions: some produce movement, others control lumbar stability. (Rosatelli L.A. 2008)

[26] The thoracolumbar fascia is more sensitive to chemical stimulation compared to the muscles and the subcutis with regards to intensity, duration and irradiation of pain. (Schilder A. 2014)

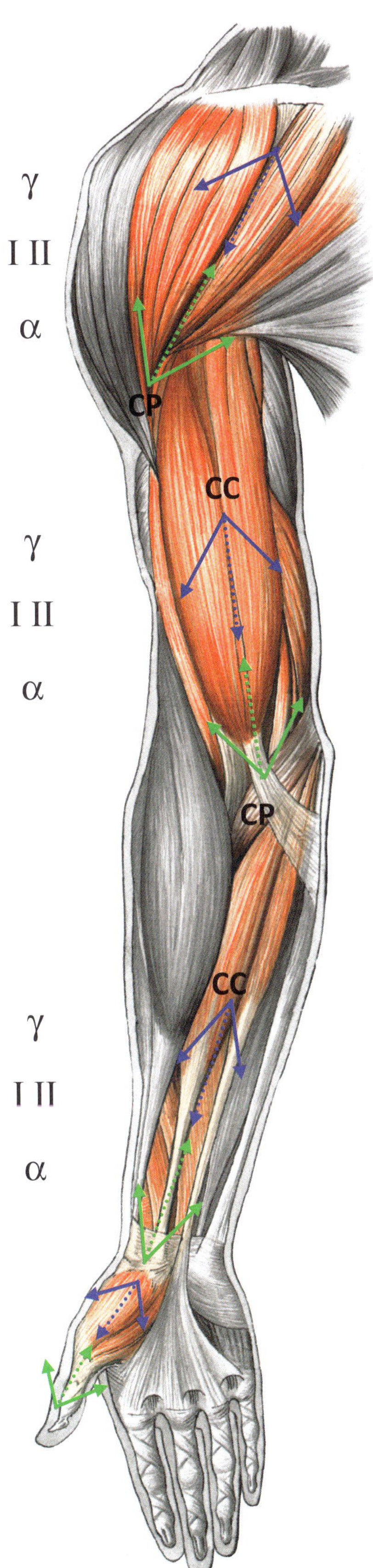

Fig. 1.31. Resultants composed of the CCs and CPs or centres of perception.

(From G. Chiarugi and L. Bucciante, Istituzioni di anatomia dell'uomo. Piccin Nuova Libraria, Padova 1983, modified)

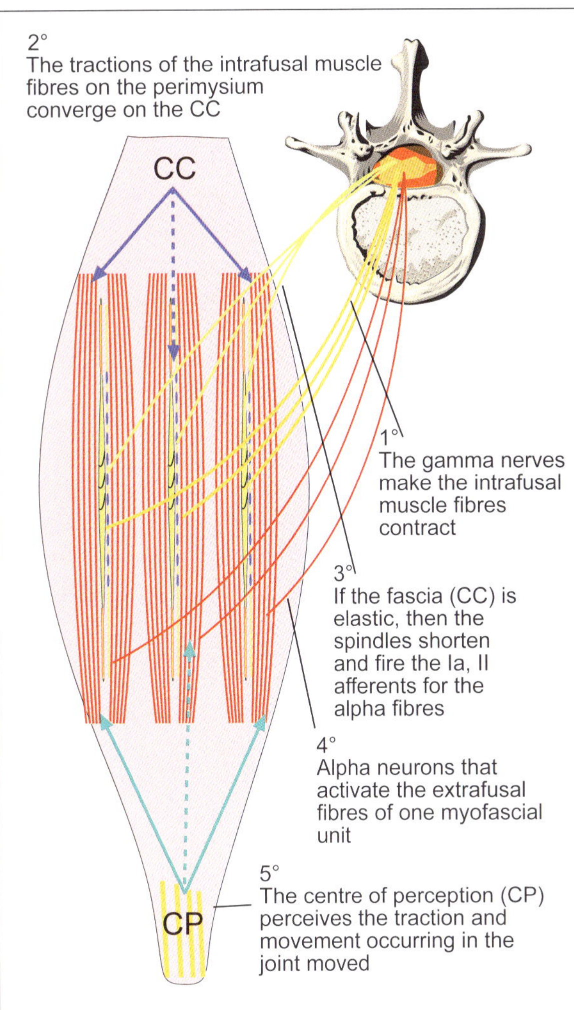

Fig. 1.32. The tractions of the spindles are on the perimysium (CC), whilst the tractions of the muscles are on the tendons (CP).

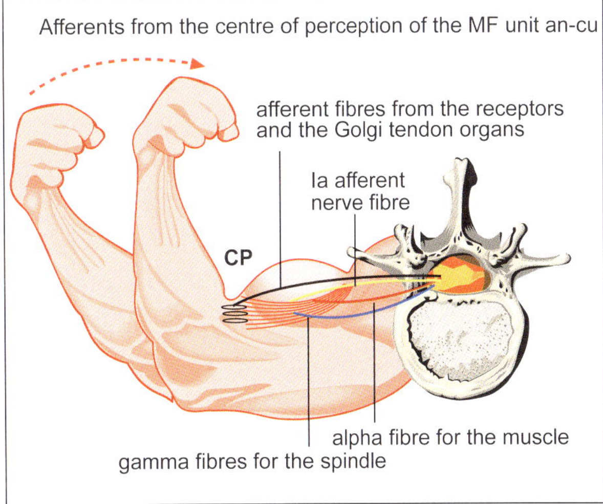

Fig. 1.33. During elbow flexion the action of the CC must be aligned with the resultant of the tendinous forces.

FROM THE CENTRE OF PERCEPTION TO THE LOCATION OF PAIN

If the fascia containing the vectorial centre is densified, then it will no longer adapt to the stretch of the spindles which in turn would not allow the enlargement of annulospiral fibres and would thus mute afferent impulses going to close the alpha-gamma circuit. In this case only some alpha fibres and hence only some muscular fibres would be activated resulting in an articular imbalance (Fig. 1.34). The vectorial resultant would no longer be aligned with the physiological movement and consequently an articular conflict would be created resulting in tractions on the receptors embedded in the capsule and ligaments (Fig. 1.35). All the periarticular structures normally working as a centre of perception for movement would become an area of friction, inflammation and pain.

For millennia, in the clinical practice of acupuncture, it has been understood that the needle is not to be inserted where pain is located but must placed in a point that causes pain. These points have the same location in all human beings. Many acupuncture experts claim that needle insertion reaches the muscular fascia.

More recently, Travell J. and Simons D. (1981) found that there are trigger points (TPs) at the muscular level which trigger referred pain if active. These active points are determined by the densification of the ground substance of the fascial connective tissue. Indeed, fascial alteration in the centre of coordination (CC or TP) determines a motor incoordination that is projected to the joint or along the myofascial sequence (referred pain). For instance (Fig. 1.36), if the antebrachial fascia is densified in its proximal third, then wrist pain is created during antepulsion (an-ca). In the presence of a flexor carpi ulnaris tendinosis, the search for the point should be performed not on the tendon but over the muscle belly (me-ca).

In the forearm the points of treatment are located on top of the muscle bellies and not on the joint or tendons. There are six points that correspond to the centres of coordination (CCs) for each of the six MF units, six acupuncture points and six trigger points (Table 1.4).

Nowadays the interest in fascia and its treatment has greatly increased (Schleip R. 2012). The placement of acupuncture points on the fascia has been hypothesized for several years by Heine H. (1988). The arrangement of the fasciae according to myokinetic chains is described by Myers T. (2006) and by other researchers (Chaitow L. 2014). The importance of the fascia in the treatment of the locomotor apparatus dysfunctions is reinforced in the textbook of Hammer W. (2007). All these authors argue that it is not useful to treat where the body senses pain but one must go back to its causes which almost always reside in the fascia over the muscle belly.

In the presence of a tendinosis, many therapists apply lotions or therapies to the inflamed tendon (CP) which may provide a momentary benefit. To resolve the problem in a definitive manner, the fascia at the level of the muscle belly (CC) must be manipulated. The transition from gel to sol of the ground substance allows the endomysium and perimysium to better coordinate the various motor units and to move the tendon along its physiological trajectory (CP). Only when the tendon glides in its sheath along a normal trajectory then friction is no longer created. It is the friction, created by on the tendon traction along inappropriate resultant vectors, that causes inflammation and tendinous cysts in an attempt to neutralise these non-physiological tractions.

Tabella 1.4. Comparison between acupuncture points, trigger points and centres of coordination

Acupuncture points	Trigger points	Centres of coordination
LU 6, at 5 cun from elbow crease	TP of flexor carpi radialis muscle	Centre of coordination ante-carpus
PC 4, between palmar tendons	TP of flexor digitorum superficialis muscle	Centre of coordination intra-carpus
HT 4, on tendon flexor ulnaris	TP of flexor carpi ulnaris muscle	Centre of coordination medio-carpus
LI 9, 3 cun under Quchi	TP of extensor radialis brevis muscle	Centre of coordination latero-carpus
TE 9, 5 cun below olecranon	TP of extensor digitorum muscle	Centre of coordination extra-carpus
SI 7, 5 cun proximal to wrist	TP of extensor carpi ulnaris muscle	Centro coordinazione retro-carpo

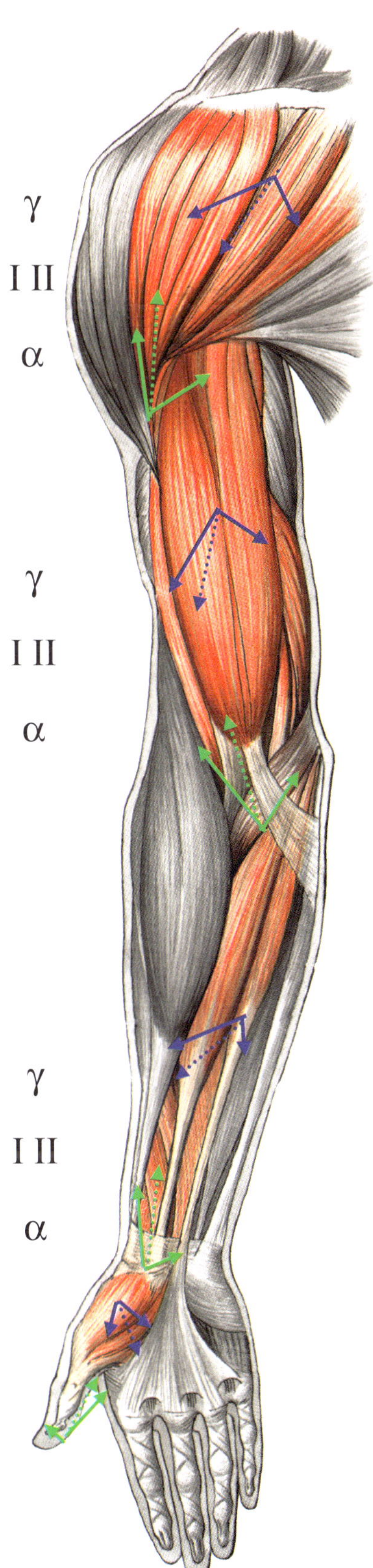

Fig. 1.34. Alteration in the CCs of the antepulsion MF units of the upper limb determine an incoordination in the CP.

(From G. Chiarugi and L. Bucciante, Istituzioni di anatomia dell'uomo. Piccin Nuova Libraria, Padova 1983, modified)

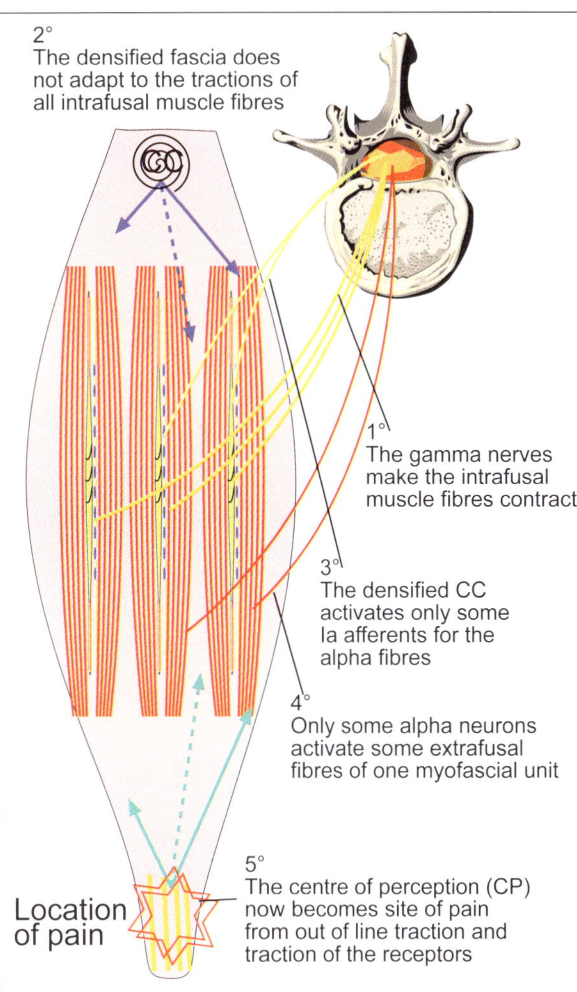

Fig. 1.35. If only some motor units are activated within a myofascial unit, then there is an abnormal traction of the tendon.

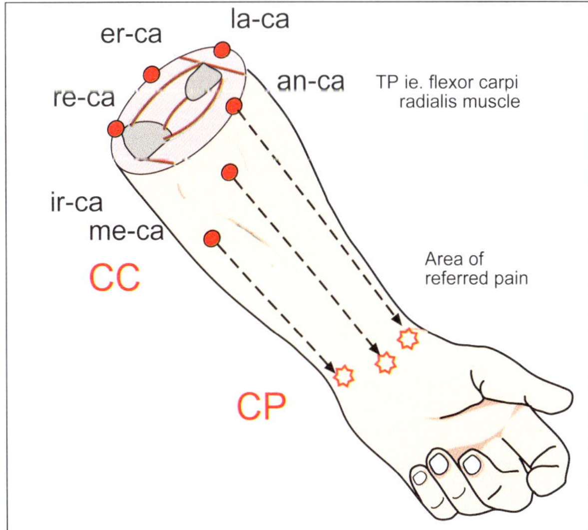

Fig. 1.36. Densification of the fascia in the CC results in pain in various tendons and in the wrist (CP).

FROM THE MYOFASCIAL UNIT TO THE MYOFASCIAL SEQUENCE

"Muscular fibres take origin on some fasciae and others insert on it" (Chiarugi G. 1975).

The origin and insertion of muscles on the aponeurotic fascia is reported in anatomy textbooks without relating it to motor physiology. For instance, in the anterior region of the upper limb (Fig. 1.37), the clavicular portion of pectoralis major muscle sends a tendinous expansion on the brachial fascia; during the contraction of this muscle the fascia is stretched in a proximal direction. The brachial fascia is continuous with the medial and lateral intermuscular septa from which the brachialis muscle originates, when contracting it determines a stretch in a distal direction of the same fascia (yellow arrows).

The biceps muscle inserts with a tendinous expansion (lacertus fibrosus) onto the antebrachial fascia (Fig. 1.75), where the flexor carpi radialis and palmaris longus muscles also originate. The biceps muscle (MF unit ante-cubitus) determines a traction in a proximal direction of the antebrachial fascia; the palmaris longus muscle (MF unit of ante-carpus) determines a traction in a distal direction.

The palmaris longus muscle through its distal tendon offers insertion to many muscles of the thenar eminence (Fig. 1.74). The contraction of palmaris longus muscle then pulls the thenar fascia in a proximal direction while the contraction of the thumb muscles (an-di) determines a stretch of the same fascia in a distal direction.

The tendinous insertions on the anterior aponeurotic fascia of the upper limb interconnect the MF units of antepulsion. The aponeurotic fascia is partially free to glide above the epimysial fascia and the longitudinal collagen fibres coursing within it therefore connect the proximal and distal muscular forces.

This connection helps in activating the neuromuscular spindles: "The primary endings of the spindles are very sensitive to muscular stretching and evoke excitatory post-synaptic action potentials in alpha motor neurons as soon as stretching is initiated (monosynaptic stretch reflex). The rapid increase in excitation causes the motor neurons to discharge at a frequency that is proportional to the velocity. This induces a rapid summation of the muscular discharge and a ready increase in force" (Baldissera F. 1996).

The monosynaptic reflex is so called because it is transmitted via only one synapse. The active or passive stretch of a muscle involves the flower spray and annulospiral nerve endings of the neuromuscular spindles. Their afferent impulses reach the cord and close the circuit which activates the alpha motor fibres (Fig. 1.38).

The stretch reflex recruits ipsidirectional MF units during two motor activities:

- during active effort (Fig. 1.39). For instance, when a person wants to pull on a rope, then the impulse leaves from the brain and activates several motor units through the alpha-gamma circuit. When effort increases, all the ipsidirectional MF units are activated through the stretch reflex. This automatism occurs as a result of the continuity of the anterior fascial compartments of the arm as well as their connections to the underlying muscles. When stretches vary in intensity, they result in a different muscular recruitment pattern;
- during passive stretching (monosynaptic reflex) (Fig. 1.40). For instance, when the flexed arm is suddenly stretched by an external force, the stretch of the entire anterior aponeurotic fascia of the upper limb determines the initiation, through the stretch reflex[27], of the myofascial units of ante-carpus, ante-cubitus and ante-humerus. This automatism is maintained even in the presence of a spinal cord lesion[28] since movement is governed via the neuromuscular spindles only by the activation of the alpha circuit.

The active or passive stretching along a fascial sequence determines not only the activation of motor units but also that of the receptors embedded in it. This activation facilitates proprioception from a specific direction. Thus, the stretching of the aponeurotic fascia not only synchronises the forces of ipsidirectional MF units, but also results in the proprioceptive afferent impulses reaching the brain being already codified for one direction.

The stretch of the neuromuscular spindles allows synchrony between the MF units arranged along a sequence, along a diagonal and along a spiral. The different types of recruitment arising from muscular forces are determined by the different course of the intrafascial collagen fibres through either longitudinal, transverse or spiral fibres.

[27] When the muscle lengthens and the muscle spindle is stretched, mechanically gated ion channels in the sensory dendrites are opened. This leads to a receptor potential that triggers action potentials in the muscle spindle afferents; the firing of the spindle Ia afferents stimulates the alpha motor neurons in the spinal cord causing reflex contraction of the extrafusal muscle fibres. At the same time Ia spindle afferents synapse in the posterior horn of the cord and stimulate inhibitory interneurons, which then depress alpha motor activity to the antagonistic muscles. Thus, the simple myotatic/stretch reflex acts as a servo-mechanism to maintain correct muscle tone. (Stecco A. 2014)

[28] The sensitivity of neuromuscular spindles to stretch persists even in the presence of spinal cord lesion. This demonstrates the function of the spindles in static and dynamic situations. (Macefield V.G. 2015)

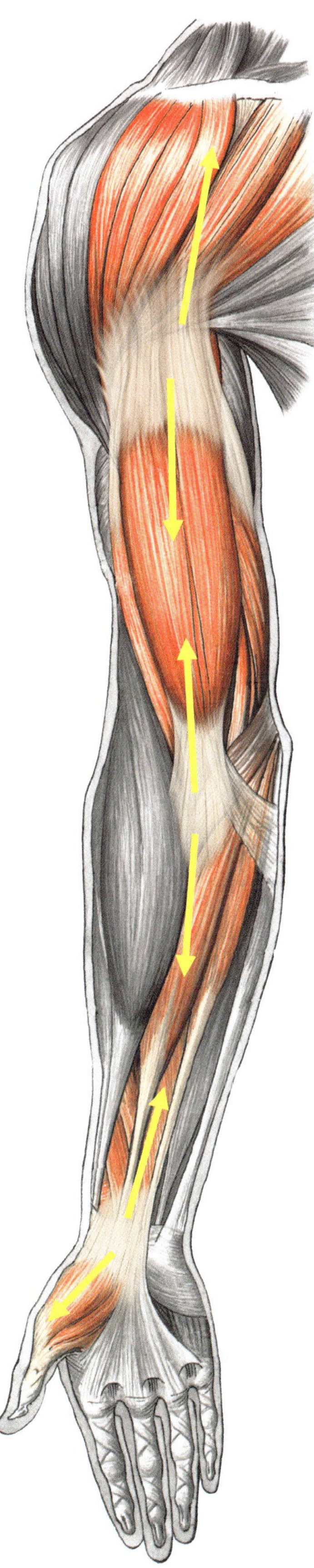

Fig. 1.37. Reciprocal stretch along the fascial sequence of antepulsion.

(From G. Chiarugi and L. Bucciante, Istituzioni di anatomia dell'uomo. Piccin Nuova Libraria, Padova 1983, modified)

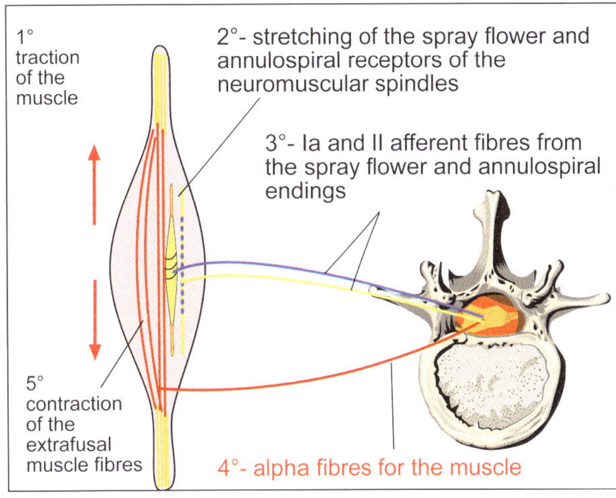

Fig. 1.38. Neural circuit of monosynaptic stretch.

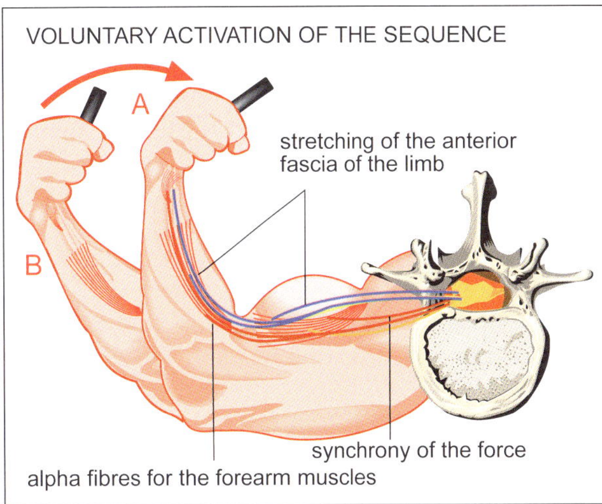

Fig. 1.39. Propagation of the active stretch in the sequence.

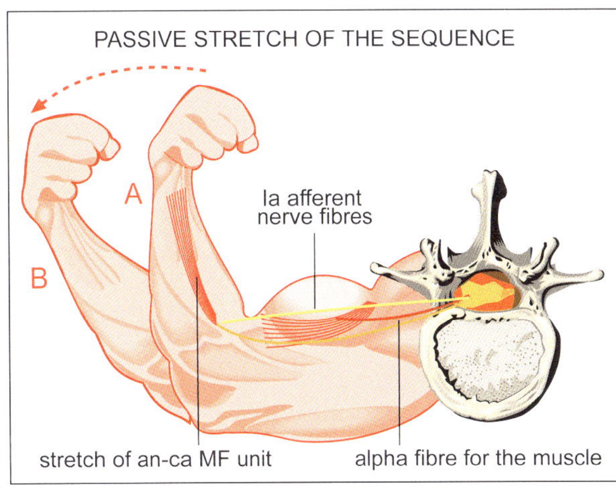

Fig. 1.40. Propagation of the passive stretch in the sequence.

FROM THE MYOFASCIAL SEQUENCE TO BIARTICULAR MUSCLES

In all MF units, there are biarticular (Fig. 1.41) and monoarticular muscles: the function of monoarticular muscles is to regulate the position of proximal body segments with respect to the position of distal segments; the function of biarticular muscles is to develop force within the MF unit to which they belong. For instance, in the ante-cubitus MF unit, the biarticular biceps brachii muscle acts upon the shoulder and elbow joints, whilst the monoarticular brachialis muscle only acts upon elbow flexion.

Parallel to the biceps muscle there is the humerus, which in turn articulates with the shoulder and the elbow.

Similarly, in the forearm, the flexor carpi radialis muscle participates in elbow and wrist flexion; it is positioned in parallel to the radius and ulna which articulate in the elbow and wrist. This architecture is repeated in all the joints and in all the MF units, therefore it must have a purpose.

The contraction of biarticular muscles is mainly regulated by the Golgi tendon organs[29] (GTO) in the following manner. The biceps brachii muscle has a proximal and distal tendon formed by collagen fibres arranged in series with specific motor units. These tendons are not inserted into small points but have a rather wide insertion in order to pull on different tendinous zones depending on joint position.

The contraction of monoarticular muscles is influenced by the GTO in the following way. The muscle fibres of brachialis directly originating from the bone (humerus) do not have angular variations and hence are not influenced by GTO, whilst the fibres originating from the intermuscular septa and the fibres connected to the tendon inserting on the ulna are regulated by GTO based upon angular variations of the elbow joint.

"The afferent impulses deriving from the Golgi tendon organs interact with the neuromuscular spindles in the postural and motor feedbacks. Both interact with the internal dynamics and the reactions to external disturbances.

The tendon organs provide joint position sense, they are able to control the joint angle position that the spindles are not able to perceive on their own. Often the tendon organs are aligned with the neuromuscular spindles. The exact nature of these impulses still remains unknown" (Kistemaker D.A. 2013).

The structure tendon organ of the helps in understanding its interactions with muscles.[30] "The Golgi musculotendineous organs are formed by the intertwinement of connective filaments intersecting the axon (Fig. 1.42, A). Depending on how the tendon is stretched there is a reduction in the space between the filaments with consequent squeezing of the nerve ending. This initiates the stimulus causing it to fire the receptor. Unlike the spindles, the Golgi receptors are activated when the force is generated by muscle contraction. Under isometric conditions, the activation of a single motor unit is sufficient to activate the Golgi receptors connected to it" (Baldissera F. 1996). The axon of the Golgi tendon organ cannot fire for each muscle contraction otherwise the body would work inefficiently. The axon only fires when tendon angulation pulls the collagen fibres obliquely rather than longitudinally. A longitudinal traction pulls the collagen fibres away from the axon whilst an oblique traction brings them closer. For instance, the biceps brachii tendon organs (Fig. 1.42, B, 1, 2, 3) are activated during both elbow and shoulder flexion and when returning to the initial position since there is an oblique trochlear angulation. The activation of the Golgi organs helps to adjust and stabilise the shoulder based on the variations of angulation during elbow joint range of motion. In the shoulder, the tendon of the short head of biceps muscle is arranged longitudinally to the muscle fibres whilst the tendon of the long head forms an angle of 90°. This tendinous arrangement of the biceps brachii muscle determines different stretches of the collagen fibres during the various degrees of elbow flexion and shoulder abduction. When the Golgi tendon organ fires its impulse, it inhibits the alpha fibres with which it is connected at the level of the spinal cord. This inhibition occurs when a smaller muscular contraction force is required during the variations in range of motion. The same process takes place in the tendons of flexor carpi radialis muscle (Fig. 1.42, 3) acting on both elbow and wrist flexion.

[29] The state of tonicity or tonus is reflexive in nature, it is determined by the impulses arising from proprioceptors (neuromuscular spindles and musculotendinous organs) of the muscle itself. The factor provoking these impulses is the degree of tension of the contractile mass and its proprioceptors. (Chiarugi G. 1975)

[30] It is unclear which tensions are signalled by the tendinous organs. What is known is that they are activated only with muscle contraction and that they are stretched in specific directions. (Proske U. 2002)

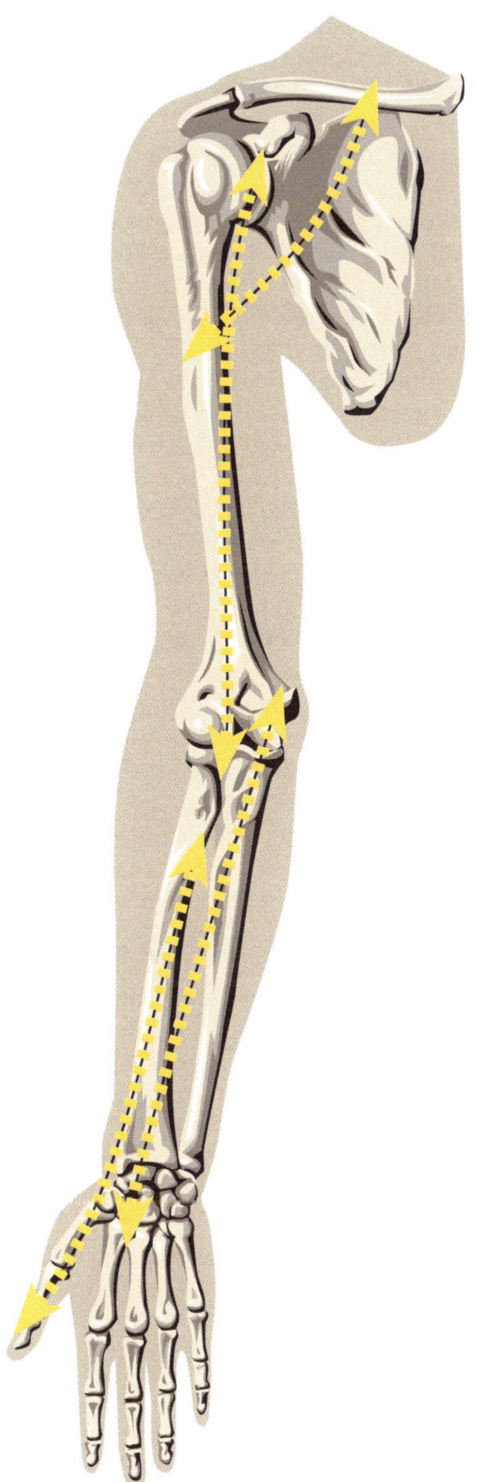

Fig. 1.41. Biarticular muscles of the ante sequence.

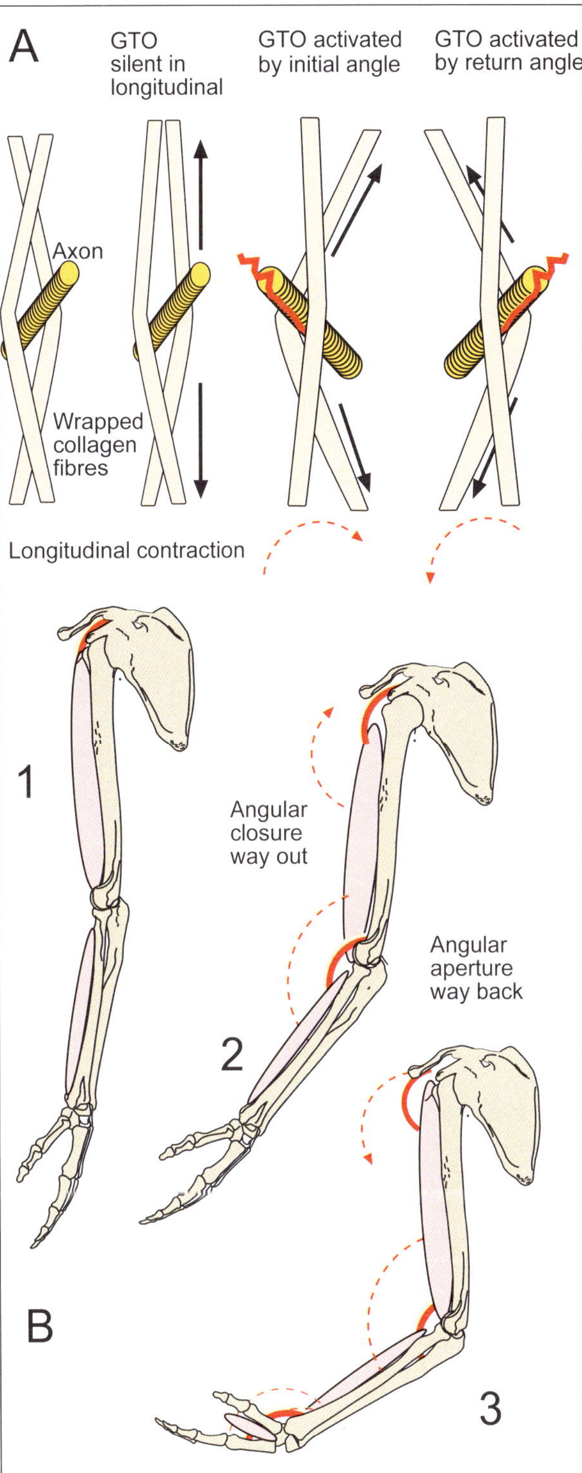

Fig. 1.42. Range of motion and activation of the Golgi tendon organs.

MYOFASCIAL SEQUENCE AND CONTROL OF POSTURE

The tonic contraction of the antigravitational muscles, maintaining the upright posture, is partly managed by the myofascial sequences in tune with spinal reflexes[31]. The continuous oscillations on the frontal and sagittal planes produce a stretch of the myofascial sequences with the consequent activation of their specific muscles through the stretch reflex.

"In the upright position, postural control must distribute the muscular forces in order to counterbalance the forces of gravity and impede falling either when the body is motionless or when moving. Posture requires the continuous tonic contraction of anti-gravitational muscles. In the upright posture, the body is subject to continuous oscillations both in antero-posterior and in latero-lateral directions" (Baldissera F. 1996).

The oscillations on the sagittal plane (Fig. 1.43) are managed by the two antepulsion sequences (one on the right, one on the left Fig. 1.44) and by the two retropulsion sequences (Fig.1.45). Each MF unit of the sequences for antepulsion and retropulsion, indicated by red dots on the figures, has tendinous expansions connected to the overlying fascia. When the body oscillates in antero-posterior, the fascial stretch also determines the stretching of the spindles[32] and thus the tone activation of the anti-gravitational muscle[33].

The oscillations on the frontal plane (Fig. 1.46) are coordinated by the lateropulsion and mediopulsion sequences. In the trunk, the mediopulsion sequence courses along the linea alba and supraspinous ligaments; both these fibrous structures continue into the limbs with the sheaths of the adductor muscles (Fig. 1.47). In the trunk, the sequence of mediopulsion is not formed by muscles since it only has the function of perceiving deviations from centration of the trunk. Both right and left lateropulsion sequences maintain centration along the line of gravity within the base of support (Fig. 1.48).

Each shift of the centre of gravity outside of the polygon-shaped base of support determines a stretch of the fasciae that, if prolonged in a unidirectional manner, will generate densifications in the fasciae leading to subsequent pain.

The centre of gravity is the point on which the resultant of the gravitational vectors acting on different points of the human body is applied. It oscillates between the upper third of the sacrum and the umbilicus depending on the posture of the subject being more or less lordotic.

The sequences of the horizontal plane are mainly activated during dynamic movement schemes.

The sequences of the horizontal and frontal planes connect the trunk with the lower limbs since the upright posture requires the continuous interaction of the trunk with both lower limbs.

In humans, unlike in other quadruped animals, the sequences of the upper limb operate with a certain independence, this has allowed the development of fine movements and gestures.

All sequences of the limbs and trunk reach the head that also contains the receptors for the tridimensional perception in space. The afferents located in caput namely sight (stereognosis[34]) and the three semicircular canals (vestibular control) must integrate with the afferents of the MF sequences.

"The three components of automatic postural control are: spinal control, vestibular control and visual control. Spinal control is formed by different reflexes: stretch reflex, tonic neck reflex, positive support reflex, placing reflex and crossed extensor reflex" (Baldissera F. 1996).

Stretch or spinal reflexes are the equivalent of the stretch reflex of the myofascial sequences, while the crossed extensor reflex is managed by the spirals.

---

[31] "Spinal reflexes: the internal organisation of the cord subserves a number of important reflex functions. The monosynaptic stretch reflex mediates muscle contraction in response to stretch of muscle spindles. The sensitivity of the stretch reflex is regulated by gamma motor neurons, which provide motor innervation to the spindle fibres. The stretch reflex is responsible for maintenance of muscle tone and is clinically tested as the deep tendon reflex." (Crossman A.R. 2000)

[32] The participation of the stretch reflex to the dynamic regulation of posture is demonstrated by postural disturbances secondary to blockage of the Ia afferent from the neuromuscular spindles. With decreased spindle afferents and therefore decrease of the stretch reflex, the body encounters large oscillations. These are only corrected when reaching such an amplitude to be reported by the vestibular apparatus. (Baldissera F. 1996)

[33] The afferent impulses from the Golgi tendon organs interact with the neuromuscular spindles in the postural and motor feedback. In humans the tendon organs control the posture better whilst the spindles act on running and walking. (Kistemaker D.A. 2013)

[34] The hypothesis is that there are two types of postural perception: one concerned with the interrelations between body and limbs, the other concerned with the perception of extra personal space. (Poske U. 2015)

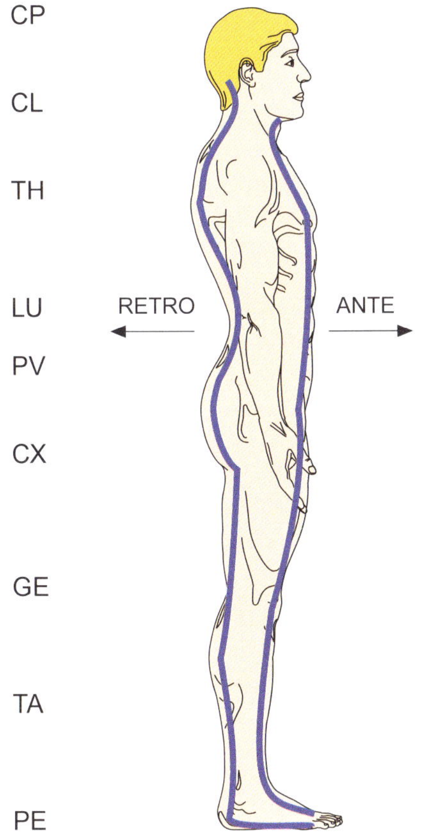

CP
CL
TH
LU
PV
CX
GE
TA
PE
RETRO
ANTE

Fig. 1.43. Sequences of the sagittal plane.

ANTE

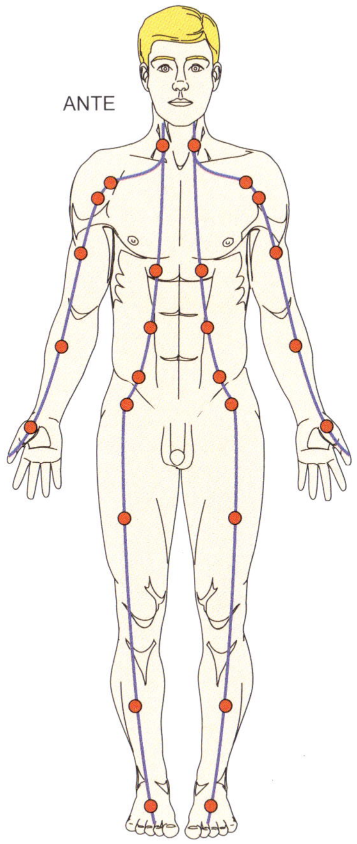

Fig. 1.44. Sequences of antepulsion.

RETRO

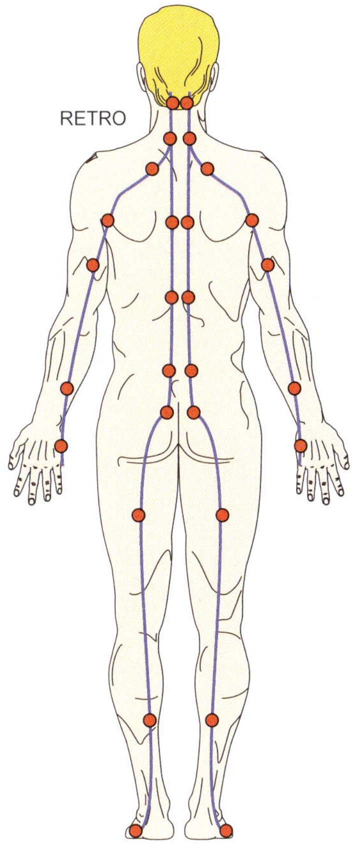

Fig. 1.45. Sequences of retropulsion.

CP
CL
TH
LU
PV
CX
GE
TA
PE
MEDIO
LATERO
LATERO

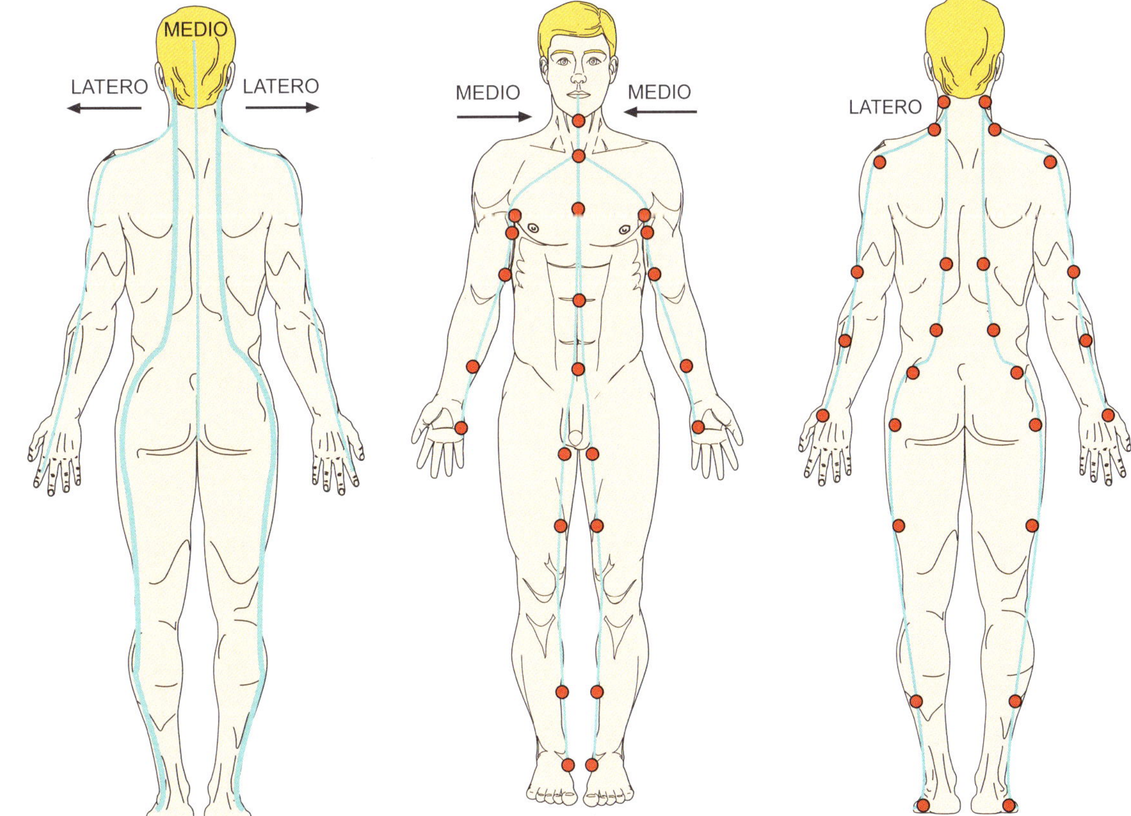

Fig. 1.46. Sequences of the frontal plane.

MEDIO
MEDIO

Fig. 1.47. Sequences of mediopulsion.

LATERO

Fig. 1.48. Sequences of lateropulsion.

FROM THE CENTRE OF COORDINATION (CC) TO THE CENTRE OF FUSION (CF)

The centres of fusion (CFs) are not located over the muscle belly like the CCs but they are found on the fascia connecting the muscle tendons involved in movements on more than one plane. The centres of fusions are so called since they are located in points where the fascial laminae fuse together to manage the interaction of multiple myofascial units. The centre of coordination manages the motor units within a muscle and the centre of fusion manages the myofascial units through the tendons. The centre of coordination intervenes in simple ipsidirectional movements, the centre of fusion acts upon global and complex movements. In the periphery the CFs, like the CCs, manage the "all or nothing" impulses coming from the central nervous system.

Motor schemes are generated in the brain (central pattern generators) and are implanted on the peripheral fascial structures. By itself the brain would not be able to produce all motor variables. Moreover, the motor patterns (ie. walking) and the internal patterns (ie. deglutition, respiration) must be distinguished; the first are under a predominant voluntary control, the second are under a predominant control from the autonomic nervous system. In this textbook, only the motor patterns or motor schemes connected to the musculoskeletal system are taken into consideration, namely those that must adapt the central nervous impulse to the changing demands of the external environment. For instance in a decerebrate cat (Gottschol J. 2009) the neuronal network for gait is located at the thoraco-lumbar level, the cat's gait may be modified by bending its head up or down; this demonstrates how the central nervous impulse may be partially influenced by the peripheral fascial tension.

Location of the CFs for carpus and talus

At the level of the wrist two retinacula are present: a superficial retinaculum is present between the superficial lamina of the deep fascia and a deep retinaculum (transverse ligament) is included in the deep lamina. Both these laminae fuse together in the medial and lateral aspects of the wrist where the following CFs are located:

- the CF of an-me-ca is in front of the flexor carpi ulnaris tendon. It manages the motor scheme obtained by the simultaneous intervention of the MF units medio-carpus and ante-carpus. The CCs of both these MF units are located on the muscle bellies in the forearm;
- the CF of ante-latero-carpus is midway between the tendons from the MF units of antepulsion and of lateropulsion. It coordinates the MF units of ante-carpus and latero-carpus;
- the CF of re-la-ca is close to the tendons of extensor radialis longus and brevis muscles. It manages the motor scheme obtained by the simultaneous intervention of the MF units latero-carpus and retro-carpus;
- the CF re-me-ca is close to the tendon of extensor carpi ulnaris muscle. It manages the motor scheme obtained by the simultaneous intervention of the MF units medio-carpus and retro-carpus.

At the level of the ankle (Fig. 1.50) the disposition of the CFs is mirroring to that of the wrist. The CFs in talus are also located where the deep lamina joins with the superficial lamina of the muscular fascia.

Location of the CFs for the trunk

In the trunk, the CFs are also localised where the laminae of the fasciae holding the muscles fuse together, these points of fusion coordinate the aponeurotic tendons (flat) of various muscles:

- in the lowback (Fig. 1.51) lateral to the erector spinae compartment there is fusion of the three laminae holding the external oblique, internal oblique and transversus abdominis muscles. This point corresponds to the CF re-la-lu located between the MF units of retro-lumbi and latero-lumbi;
- lateral to the spinous processes there is fusion of the aponeurosis of the latissimus dorsi and serratus posterior inferior muscles. This point corresponds to the CF retro-medio-lumbi;
- in the abdominal wall (Fig. 1.52) there is a mirror situation. Lateral to the rectus abdominis sheath there is fusion of three laminae holding the external oblique, internal oblique and transversus muscles. This point corresponds to the CF ante-latero-lumbi located between the CC of ante-lumbi and the CC of latero-lumbi;
- close to the linea alba (medio-lumbi anterior) there is also a junction of the three fascial laminae. The CF ante-medio-lumbi is located in this point.

The difference between the CFs of the limbs and the CFs of the trunk lies only in the structure of the tendons. In the limbs, the tendons are fusiform whilst in the trunk the aponeurosis are flat, therefore the CFs look like they are placed along lines of fusion.

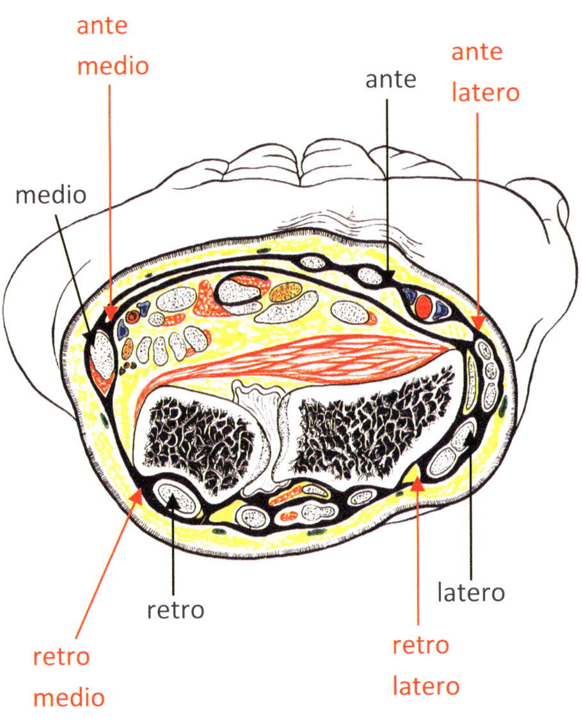

Fig. 1.49. Tendon sheaths of the wrist related to the motor directions (black) and points of fusion of the retinacula (red).

(From G. Chiarugi and L. Bucciante, Istituzioni di anatomia dell'uomo. Piccin Nuova Libraria, Padova 1983, modified)

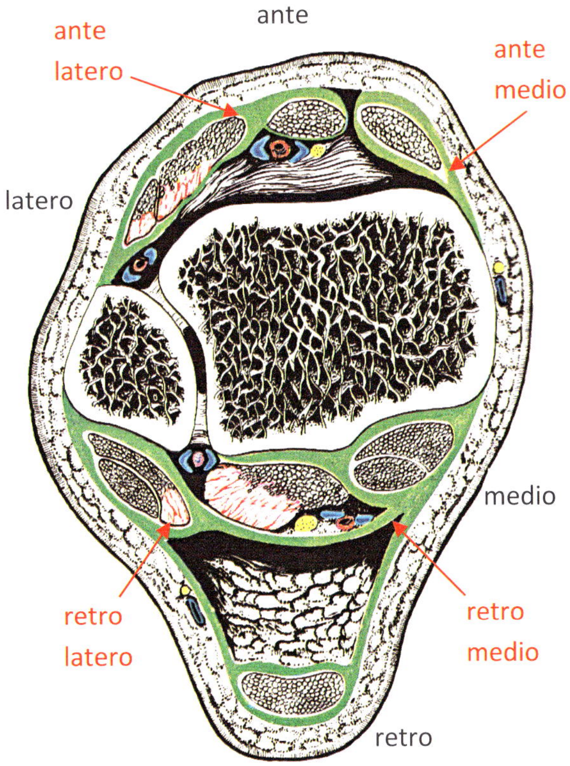

Fig. 1.50. Tendon sheaths of the lower aspect of the left leg at the level of the malleoli. Transverse-oblique view.

(From G. Chiarugi and L. Bucciante, Istituzioni di anatomia dell'uomo. Piccin Nuova Libraria, Padova 1983, modified)

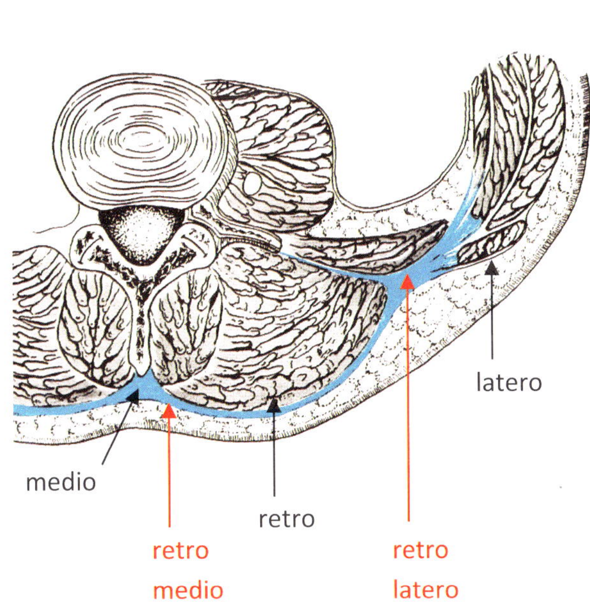

Fig. 1.51. Lines of fusion of the posterior fasciae of the trunk.

(From G. Chiarugi and L. Bucciante, Istituzioni di anatomia dell'uomo. Piccin Nuova Libraria, Padova 1983, modified)

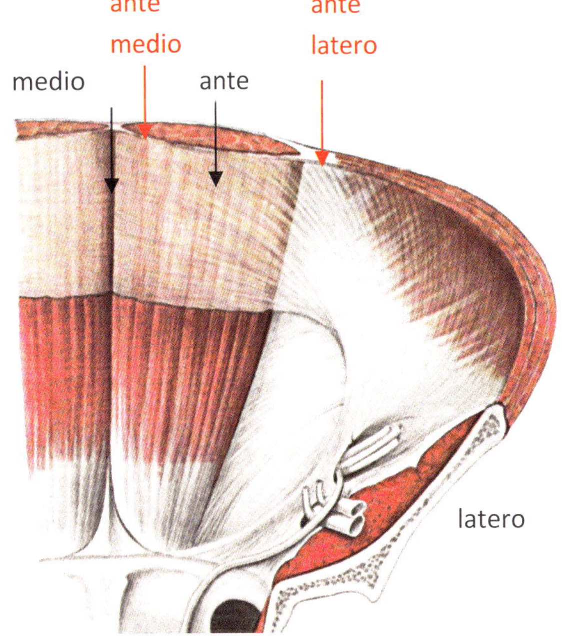

Fig. 1.52. Lines of fusion of the anterior fasciae of the trunk.

(From G. Chiarugi and L. Bucciante, Istituzioni di anatomia dell'uomo. Piccin Nuova Libraria, Padova 1983, modified)

CENTRES OF FUSION AND SEGMENTARY MOTOR SCHEMES

The centre of fusion (CF) coordinates the movement of one segment from one plane to another. To perform this task the CF uses the intervention of two or three myofascial units. The fascia located between two MF units implements the task through the control of the spindles and tendon organs. The CF is like the needle on a balance moving towards the direction where the cerebral programme requires the major force.

In the MF units, the CCs are located at the convergence of all the parallelograms. These are formed by the tensions produced by the intrafusal muscles having ipsidirectional motor units. In motor schemes, the CFs are located at the convergence of the two parallelograms formed by the two MF units (Fig. 1.53). For instance, the CF an-la-hu is in located the point of convergence of the vectors for the ante-humerus MF units and of the vectors for the latero-humerus MF unit[35]. The resultant for these two vectors is the needle of the balance (CF) that shifts between ante and latero according to the motor intention of the individual. The densification of the fascia corresponding to the CF results in aberrant coordination between both MF units.

Figure 1.54 helps explaining how a centre of fusion coordinates two centres of coordination.

- The centre of coordination of antepulsion of the humerus (CC an-hu) is located on the muscle bellies implementing shoulder flexion. When the limb is relaxed (Fig. 1.54, A) this point is silent; whilst when the limb is in movement, it is stretched by the intrafusal muscle fibres. The interaction between the perimysium and the spindles manages the distinct muscular recruitment encountered during the various degrees of shoulder flexion.
- The centre of coordination of lateropulsion for the humerus (CC la-hu) is located on the lateral belly of the deltoid muscle (Fig. 1.54, B), where the tractions of the intrafusal muscle fibres converge. The centre of coordination acts on the motor units activated for the frontal plane. During the variations in range of motion, the recruitment of the spindles[36] and motor units of lateropulsion will also vary.
- The centre of fusion of ante-latero-humerus (CF an-la-hu) is located on the anterior aspect of the tendinous insertion of the deltoid muscle (Fig. 1.54, C), the muscle fibres implementing antepulsion and lateropulsion of the humerus converge there. This CF manages the decline of intervention of one myofascial unit (an-hu) and the progressive participation of the other MF unit (la-hu). At the start of the movement the MF unit an-hu prevails, midway the forces of both ante and latero are involved equally; at the end of the motor scheme the forces of latero-humerus prevail. During these steps the rotational component is always involved.

The fascial structure itself coordinates all these variables. It is no longer spread over the muscle belly (CC) but is located in proximity to the tendons or on the point where the forces of two MF units (CF) converge. From this point the fascia can better manage both the neuromuscular spindles and the Golgi tendon organs.

This arrangement of CFs over the point of convergence of the tendons belonging to two main MF units is present in all body segments. Below are some other examples:

- the CF of an-me-hu is located over the humeral tendon of pectoralis major where the forces of adduction, intrarotation and antepulsion implemented by pectoralis major on the humerus converge;
- the CF of an-me-cu is located on the epitrochlea where the tendons of flexor carpi ulnaris (adduction), pronator teres (intrarotation) and flexor carpi radialis (antepulsion) muscles converge;
- in the CF of retro-latero-humerus, the deltoid muscle fibres for retropulsion, lateropulsion and extrarotation of the shoulder converge;
- in the CF re-la-cu, located underneath the epicondyle, the tendons of the supinator, extensor carpi radialis and extensor carpi ulnaris muscles converge. They implement the motor scheme of extra, latero and retro-cubitus with the proximal tendons, and the latero, retro, extra-carpus motor scheme with the distal tendons.

The fifth chapter addresses the analysis of the motor schemes, and the location of all the CFs of the human body will be analysed there.

[35] Synergy may happen between parts of muscles with different functions. For instance, the biceps brachialis muscle may act together with the brachioradialis muscle for elbow flexion, but their compartmentalization facilitates other tasks. (English A.W. 1993)

[36] The variations of tension-length in primary motors, antagonists and synergists is perceived by the receptors located in the various connective tissues and is integrated into the central nervous system. (Gray H. 1993)

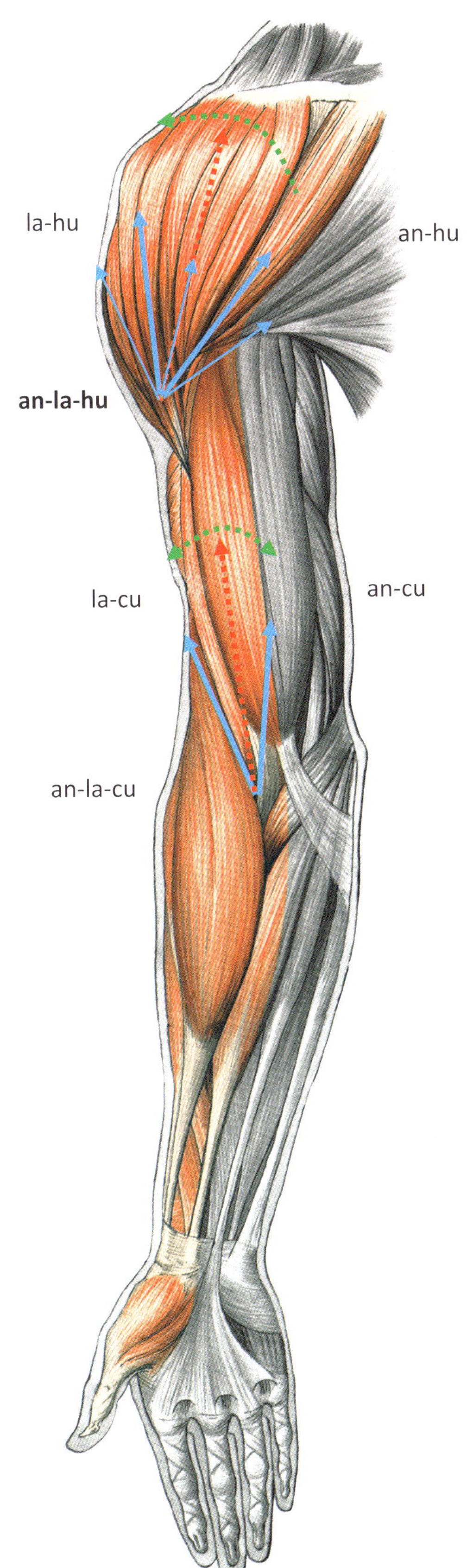

Fig. 1.53. Centres of fusion of ante-latero (upper limb).

(From G. Chiarugi and L. Bucciante, Istituzioni di anatomia dell'uomo. Piccin Nuova Libraria, Padova 1983, modified)

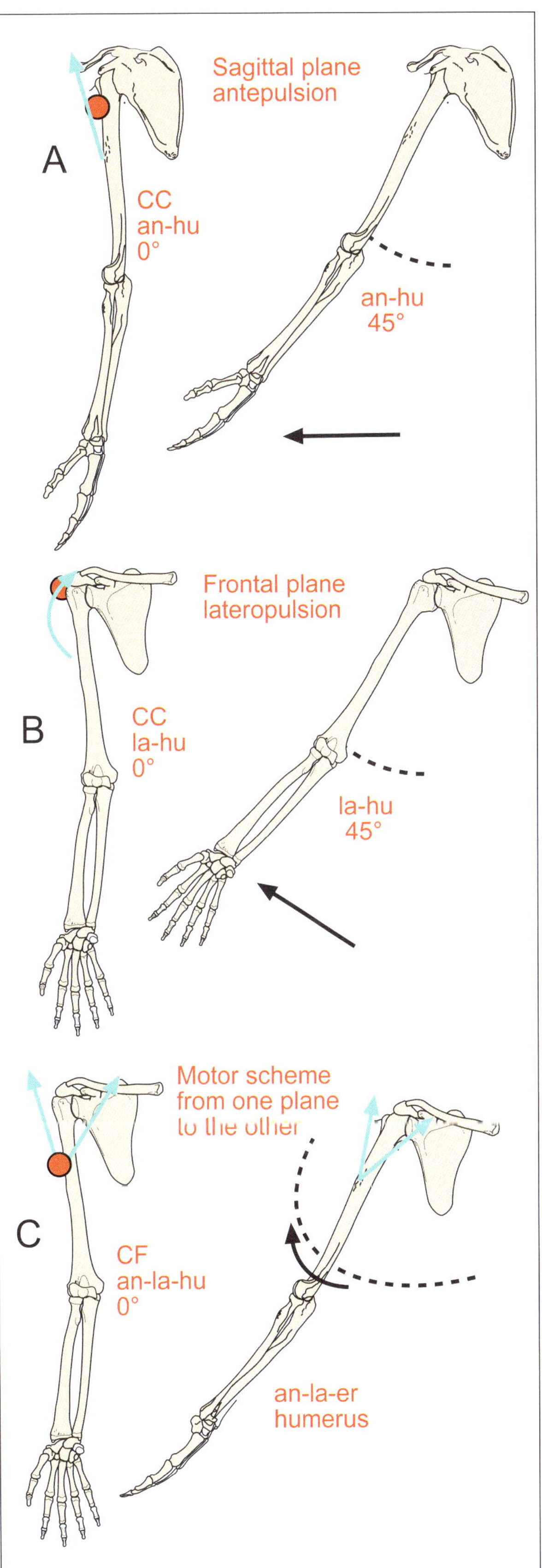

Fig. 1.54. Differences between CCs and centres of fusion (CFs).

CENTRES OF FUSION AND GLOBAL DIAGONALS

A diagonal is a line joining two non-consecutive angles of a geometrical figure.

In the anterior part of the upper limb (Fig. 1.55), the antepulsion sequence (blue line) forms one side of the polygon, the lateropulsion sequence forms another side; the clavicle and the wrist form the remaining two sides, the diagonal of ante-latero is located within this polygon. The course of the myofascial sequences corresponds to the fascial compartments; the course of the myofascial diagonals corresponds to the intermediate fascia. The ante-latero fascial sector of the upper limb connects together the an-la-hu CF to the an-la-ca and digiti CFs, passing through the CF of an-la-cu (Fig. 1.56).

The wrist retinacula connect finger movements to wrist movements; the ankle retinacula connect foot movements to ankle movements. Through this arrangement the distal part of the diagonals in the limbs informs the entire diagonal of the movements in the extremities. The proximal part of these diagonals also ranges over nearly 360° at the levels of the hip and shoulder; thus, the diagonal allows for the adjustment of the proximal part of the limb to the distal part.

The primary postural demands arise from the centres of perception in the head, the myofascial sequences must adjust the force of the MF units of the trunk and limbs to conform to those demands.

The myofascial diagonals and spirals start from the extremities since motor schemes and gestures are programmed by the brain for the movements of the hands and feet; the proximal part of the limb must adapt to the motor requirements of the extremities. In diagonals and spirals the contraction of the distal muscles determines the activation of the proximal CFs through the stretch reflex.

The stretch reflex is a monosynaptic reflex, in other words regulated at the level of the spinal cord, providing the following various automatic motor regulations:

1. fast, passive and sudden stretching: this stretch occurs when one stumbles, the stretch prevents falling or joint lesion;
2. active stretching along the spatial planes: this stretch develops along a myofascial sequence following muscular recruitment;
3. weak and continuous stretching: this stretch is necessary for maintaining the upright posture by counteracting the oscillations of the centre of gravity;
4. variable stretching with interaction of the Golgi tendon organs in the motor schemes managed by the diagonals of a limb;
5. weak stretching associated with the activation of both muscle spindles and Golgi tendon organs of two antagonist CFs; this is what is implemented by the intrafascial collagen fibres arranged in spiral.

Observing the fascial architecture and how it is connected to spindles and tendon organs, helps in understanding how the fascia manages these forms of stretches and the various types of automatic movements.

1. The muscular fascia (epimysium) continues inside the muscle (perimysium), the perimysium and endomysium offering insertions to the neuromuscular spindles. Besides the polysynaptic circuit, the monosynaptic reflex is also present: the passive stretching of the muscles propagates to the fascia and spindles causing the closure of the gamma circuit.
2. The fascia extending along a myofascial sequence is the element that perceives stretching during efforts and that transmits it to the synergic MF units.
3. Muscle tone is a constant reflex motor activity necessary in maintaining postural alignment; a movement outside of the centre of gravity creates stretching of the MF sequences and spindles.
4. The inverse stretch reflex is an inhibitory impulse activated by the contraction of the muscle itself and involving the Golgi tendon organs. It is an involuntary circuit since the motor impulse is derived from the spinal cord; the afferent impulses from the tendinous organ inhibit the alpha motor neuron causing relaxation of several specific muscle fibres.
5. The fascia of the perimysium is continuous with that of the tendon and forms the collagen structures for the Golgi tendon organs. The tendons are related to the retinacula and are in continuity with both the intermuscular septa (diagonals) and with the helicoidal collagen fibres (spirals).

Only when combining the fascial architecture with the neural architecture does it becomes possible to clarify the commonly nebulous interactions between neuromuscular spindles and the Golgi tendon organs.

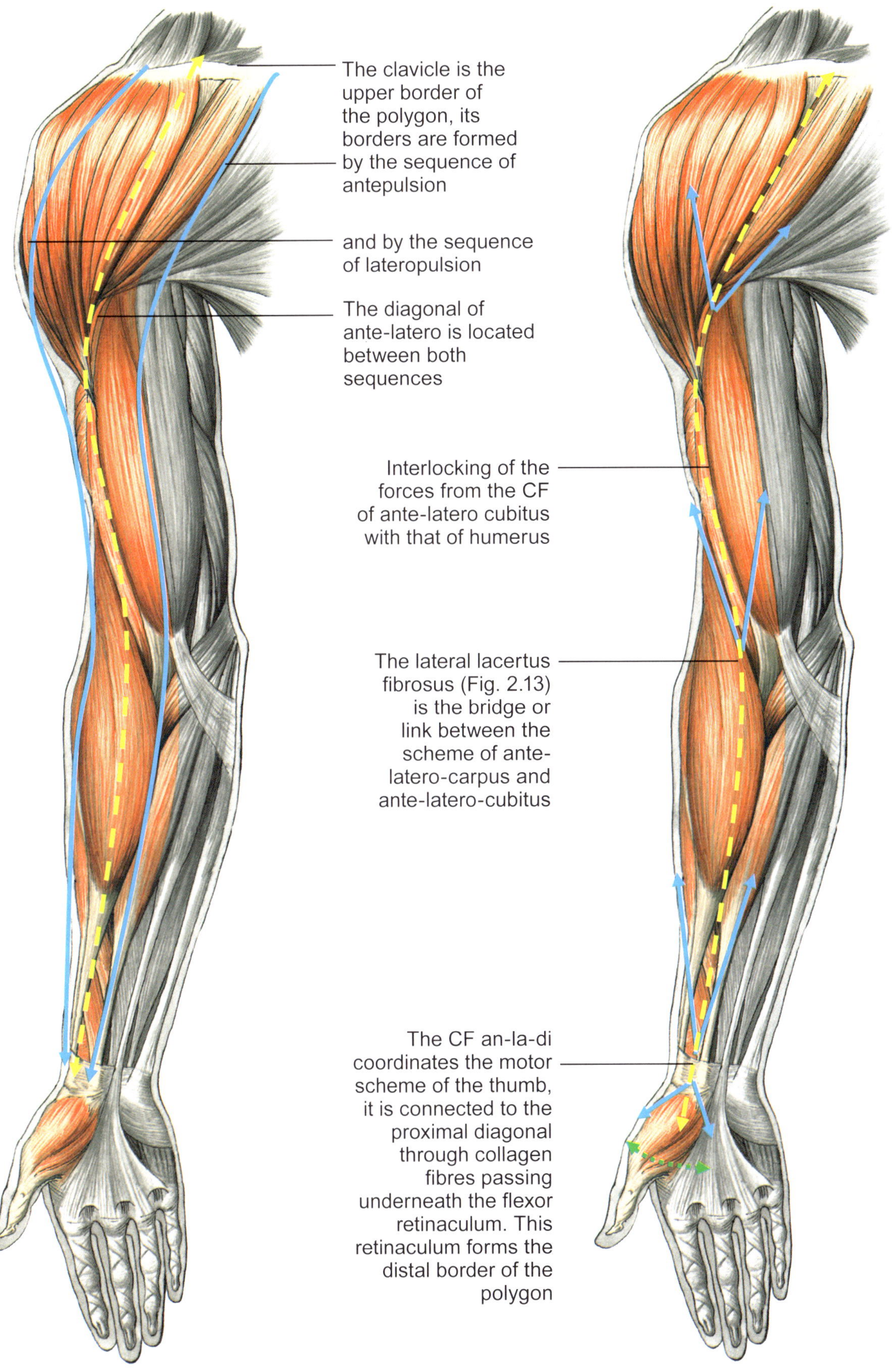

Fig. 1.55. Diagonal of ante-latero (yellow line) and sequences of ante and latero (blue lines).

(From G. Chiarugi and L. Bucciante, Istituzioni di anatomia dell'uomo. Piccin Nuova Libraria, Padova 1983, modified)

Fig. 1.56. Motor scheme for ante-latero in the four segments of the upper limb.

(From G. Chiarugi and L. Bucciante, Istituzioni di anatomia dell'uomo. Piccin Nuova Libraria, Padova 1983, modified)

CENTRES OF FUSION ASSOCIATED IN SPIRALS

The upright posture of the body is managed by the sequences having a rectilinear and parallel course to the spatial planes. The motor schemes involve the intermediate diagonals (Fig. 1.58, A). The motor gestures activate the centres of fusion that have an opposite action between them (Fig. 1.58, B). For instance, the gesture of playing the piano involves moving fingers in ante-latero and ante-medio, the wrist moving into retro-medio, the elbow moving into ante-latero and the shoulder moving into retro-medio. This description only demonstrates a single spiral, but certainly other spirals are also involved in this gesture. All these variables cannot be managed by the brain, the motor coordination of such gestures is under the responsibility of the spirals formed by spiral collagen fibres embedded in the deep fascia. The brain thinks about how to move the fingers of the piano player and the proximal segments of the limb will adapt their position based upon finger movements. In the cerebral motor cortex the sites corresponding to the hands and feet take up much more space compared to the remainder of all the limbs. Therefore, the motor organisation is not based upon muscle mass but rather upon the intentional movements of the extremities.

These spiral fibres of the deep fascia are also present in the lower limbs where they coordinate both complex reflexes such as the triple extension reflex and voluntary gestures such as walking[37] and running.

Both the reflexes (the crossed reflex, positive support reflex, placing reflex) and voluntary gestures must be aware of foot position to implement the disto-proximal motor organisation.

In the limbs, the muscle fibres of the hand and foot initiate tractions on the wrist and ankle retinacula. The retinacula determine the activation or stretching of one spiral or another. In the upper limbs, where grasping is predominant, the two prevailing spirals initiate on the palmar aspect of the hand, namely ante-latero-digiti (muscles of the thenar eminence) and ante-medio-digiti (muscles of the hypothenar eminence). In the lower limbs, where support is the predominant gesture, the two prevailing spirals are connected to the muscles of the sole of the foot inserting into the retinaculum of the peroneals (retro-latero-pes) or into the flexor retinaculum (retro-medio-pes).

From the extremities, the information sent back includes disto-proximal tensional information, micro and macrodynamic information:

- microdynamic tensions arise from the retinacula, these are determined by the small muscles of the hand and foot (Fig. 1.57, 1.74);
- macrodynamic tensions arise from the long muscles of the fingers and the toes, these connect the ipsidirectional muscles of the forearm and leg with the small muscles of the extremities. For instance, the tibialis anterior muscle continues into the extensor hallucis longus muscle on the first toe; in turn the extensor hallucis muscle is reached by the extensor digitorum brevis muscle, hence there are anatomical and tensional (physiological) connections during ankle and foot movements.

The collagen fibres of the retinacula are continuous with the collagen fibres contained in the aponeurotic fasciae of the forearm and leg. In the knee, the microdynamic and macrodynamic tensions are gathered in the patellar retinaculum, and in the superficial and deep pes anserinus. In the elbow, the microdynamic and macrodynamic tensions are gathered in the retinaculum formed by the lacertus fibrosus of biceps brachii (Fig. 1.75) and triceps brachii, and in particular the tensions gather in the lateral epicondyle (re-la-er) and in the epitrochlea (an-me-ir). In the shoulder and the hip, the aponeurotic fascia finishes respectively amongst the muscle fibres of deltoid (Fig. 1.76, 1.77) and gluteus maximus. Indeed these large muscles located in the shoulder and pelvic girdles give origin to the aponeurotic fascia of the limb through their tendinous expansions. These myofascial insertions transmit and receive the proximal tractions to and from the trunk and distal tractions to and from the limbs.

The spiral activates consecutive segments of antagonist MF units and interacts with both neuromuscular spindles and Golgi tendon organs of these MF units. Spirals have an oblique course determining a different traction on the intermuscular septa and epimysium compared to the longitudinal course of sequences and diagonals. This different arrangement allows excitation of both spindles and tendon organs that is different in its timing and modality. Therefore, the retinacula should not be relegated to the role of restraining the tendons[38], but should be considered for their role as transmission belts for the forces arising from the distal joint to the proximal joint. The tendons mainly remain in place because the flexor and extensor muscles of the fingers and foot are fixed to bone from underneath the retinacula (Fig. 6.15).

[37] Studies demonstrate that the crural fascia may be used by the body to transmit propulsive force, to maintain kinematic invariance and to modify the tensions from one joint to the next during level walking. (Stahl V.A. 2014)

[38] In some sites, close to the wrist and ankle, transversal thickenings in the deep fascia are fixed on bony prominences. These are retinacula; they are so called because they maintain the tendons passing underneath it in position. Otherwise, the tendons would bend during the respective activity of their muscles. (Gray H. 1993)

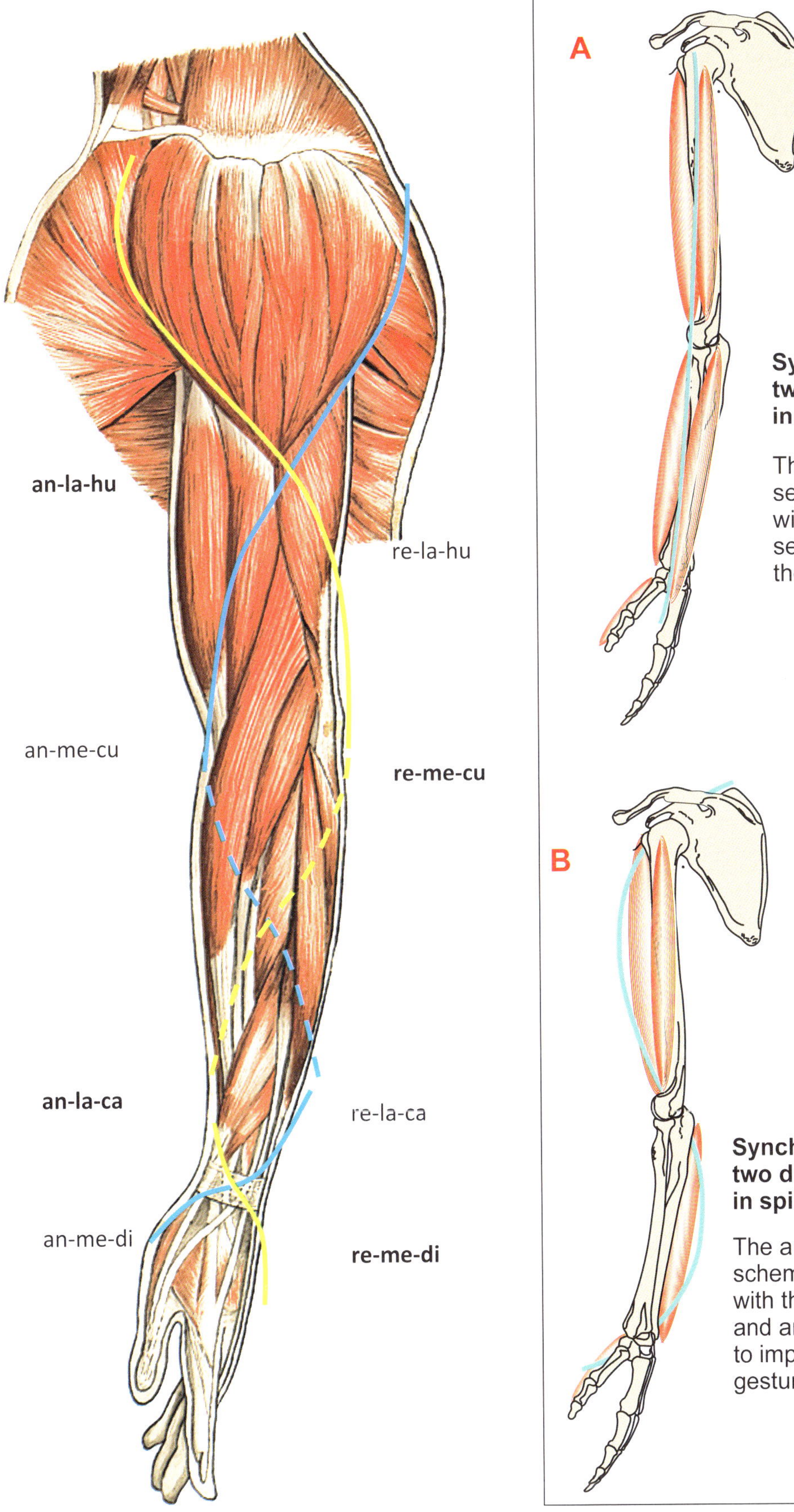

Fig. 1.57. Arrangement of the re-me-di spiral (yellow line, text in bold) and the an-me-di spiral (blue line).

(From G. Chiarugi e L. Bucciante, Istituzioni di anatomia dell'uomo. Piccin Nuova Libraria, Padova 1983, modified)

A

Synergy between two sequences in diagonal

The antepulsion sequence is associated with the lateropulsion sequence to establish the diagonal of ante-latero

B

Synchrony between two diagonals in spiral

The ante-latero-digiti scheme is associated with the retro-medio-carpus and an-la-cu schemes to implement a motor gesture

Fig. 1.58. Differences between the connections of MF units in diagonal and in spiral.

SPIRALS STARTING FROM THE HAND RETINACULA

The description of the sequences highlights the tendinous expansions of the proximal muscles on the distal fascia; this organisation responds to the needs of adapting the posture of the trunk and limbs to the perceptions registered by the cephalic receptors.

In contrast, the spirals highlight the expansions of the small muscles of the extremities onto the retinacula and tendons of the wrist and ankle muscles; this organisation meets the needs of adapting the position of the proximal limb segments to the movements requirements of the hand and foot.

In the palm of the hand there are three layers of small muscles (Fig. 1.60, 1.61) originating from the fasciae and retinacula. Their contraction extends into the forearm (Fig. 1.59) and determines the following microdynamic tensions:

- from the palmaris longus aponeurosis both palmaris brevis and abductor pollicis brevis muscles (Fig. 1.60, 1.74) have their origin; these proceed into the myofascial sequences of ante and mediopulsion;
- from the superficial flexor retinaculum several muscles from both the thenar (abductor pollicis brevis and flexor pollicis brevis muscles) and hypothenar eminences (flexor digiti minimi brevis muscle) (Fig. 1.61) have their origin; this retinaculum is called the palmar ligament by many anatomists;
- from the deep flexor retinaculum some muscles of both the thenar (opponens digiti minimi muscle) and hypothenar eminences (opponens pollicis muscle) have their origin; this retinaculum is called the transverse ligament of the wrist by many anatomists. The insertions of these muscles onto the retinacula give origin to the spirals of ante-medio and ante-latero.

Other muscles of the hand insert on the distal tendons of the muscles of the forearm. These determine the macrodynamic tensions:

- from the abductor pollicis longus tendon the abductor pollicis brevis muscle originates, the latter is connected to the extensor pollicis brevis muscle;
- from the flexor carpi ulnaris tendon a part of the abductor digiti minimi and the palmaris brevis muscles originate (Chiarugi G. 1975);
- the tendon of extensor pollicis longus unites with flexor pollicis brevis muscle;
- the abductor digiti minimi muscle connects the tendon of flexor carpi ulnaris to the extensor digiti minimi muscle;
- the four lumbrical muscles originate from the radial aspect of flexor digitorum profundus muscle and insert on the extensor digitorum muscle. Through their connection with the flexor and extensor tendons, the lumbricals promote the peripheral motor coordination between antagonist muscles.

On top of the above insertions of the small muscles of the hand on both retinacula and proximal muscles tendons, in the forearm the additional associations of the extensor and flexor pollicis longus muscles, extensor and flexor indicis muscles, extensor and flexor digitorum muscles with the extensor and flexor carpi muscles (macrodynamic tensions) must also be considered.

During the fine movements of the hand the voluntary activation of the small muscles, inserted onto the retinacula and tendons of the forearm muscles determines a disto-proximal stretching activating the neuromuscular spindles[39] (stretch reflex). This is confirmed by the fact that "when the hand firmly grasps an object, the hand allows for slight extension permitting the simultaneous contraction of the wrist extensors, in this position the finger flexors are able to exert maximal force" (Chiarugi G. 1975).

The motor organisation of the an-me-di spiral (Fig. 1.59) explains the observation of Chiarugi. A handshake determines the contraction of the hypothenar eminence muscles (ante-medio-digiti). The CF an-me-di coordinates flexion-adduction-internal rotation of the fingers with subsequent traction on the flexor retinaculum. The flexor retinaculum partly attaches to the styloid processes of the ulna and radius and partly continues into the retinaculum and the fascia of the extensors. This spiral tension allows the activation of the CF re-la-ca. This CF is located in the proximal segment and coordinates wrist extension-abduction-external rotation. The spiral climbs into the elbow and joins the lacertus fibrosus and the CF ante-medio-cubitus. Dissections (Fig. 1.75, 2.13) demonstrate that the lacertus fibrosus is not simply formed by a medial expansion. Proximally it is also continuous with the brachial fascia and distally with the antepulsion sequence and ante-latero diagonal.

[39] Studies demonstrate that dynamic disturbances activate the neuromuscular spindles and Golgi tendon organs. These provide for a feedback contributing to motor control. (Mugge W. 2009)

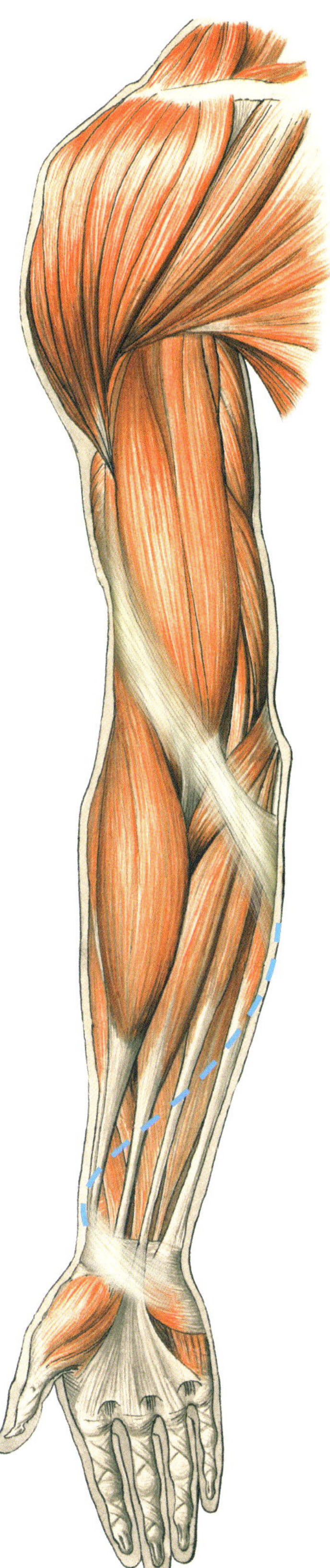

Fig. 1.59. Spiral starting from the muscles of the hypothenar eminence (an-me-di).
(From G. Chiarugi and L. Bucciante, Istituzioni di anatomia dell'uomo. Piccin Nuova Libraria, Padova 1983, modified)

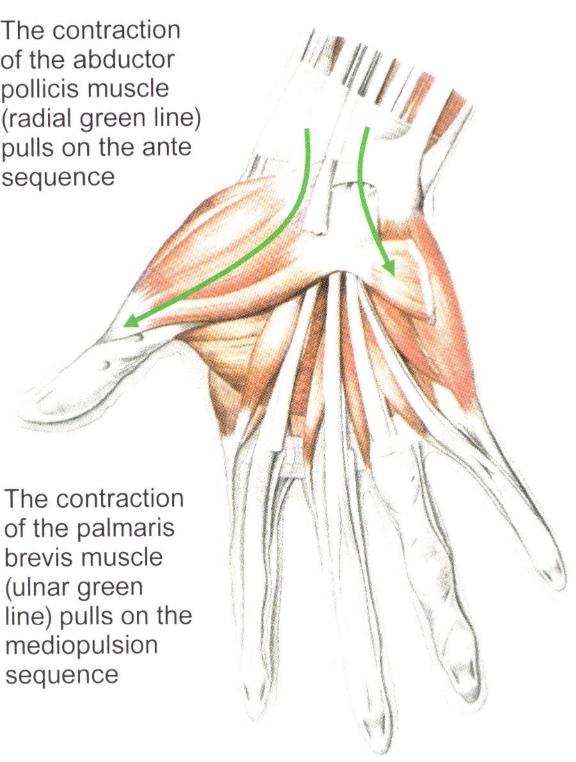

Fig. 1.60. Origin of the palmaris brevis and abductor pollicis muscles on the palmaris longus aponeurosis.
(From G. Chiarugi and L. Bucciante, Istituzioni di anatomia dell'uomo. Piccin Nuova Libraria, Padova 1983, modified)

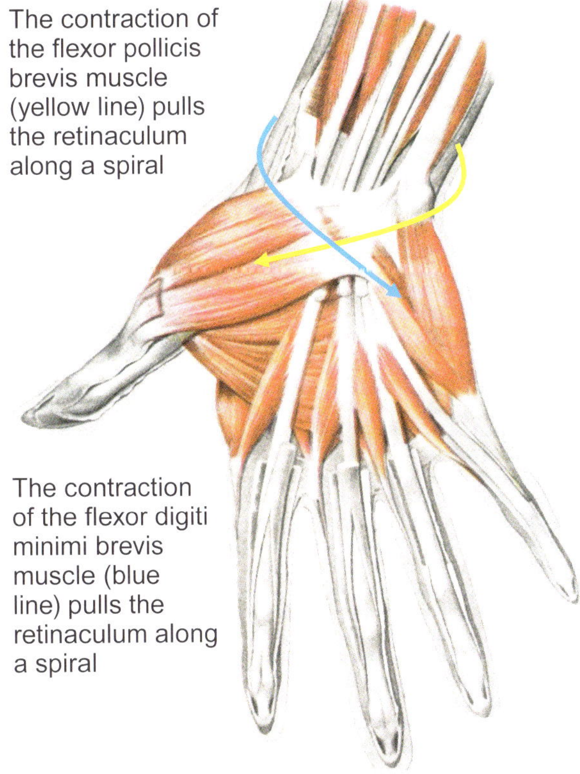

Fig. 1.61. Origin of the flexor digiti minimi brevis and flexor pollicis brevis muscles on the flexor retinaculum (superficial).
(From G. Chiarugi and L. Bucciante, Istituzioni di anatomia dell'uomo. Piccin Nuova Libraria, Padova 1983, modified)

SPIRALS STARTING FROM THE FOOT RETINACULA

The architecture of the foot fasciae is connected to that of the leg:

- the fascial compartments of the foot that are arranged longitudinally (Fig. 1.62) are connected to the myofascial sequences of the leg;
- the fascial compartments and foot retinacula that are arranged obliquely (Fig. 1.63, 1.64) are the start of the spirals ascending over the entire lower limb.

This interconnectedness manages the automation of the upright standing posture through the passive stretch of MF sequences, and manages the motor gestures through the stretching of spirals. Both postural and gesture activities often occur simultaneously; this is made possible by the different arrangement of the collagen fibres: sequences pull both the neuromuscular spindles and the Golgi tendon organs mapped longitudinally, whilst spirals activate the CFs related to the oblique fibres[40].

Below is an examination of how the spirals are activated during human gait. Their initial involvement starts with active foot movements; the stretching from the foot spreads proximally following the retinacula and spirals of the leg. Walking determines helicoidal foot movements and simultaneous opposing movements of the ankle[41]; knee retropulsion is associated with hip antepulsion; movements of the ipsilateral inferior limb are synchronised with the contralateral upper limb movements. All this is coordinated by the spirals embedded in the aponeurotic fascia of the limbs and by the spirals formed by the superficial muscles of the trunk.

The brain could not handle all the variables involved during gait; for instance, when the foot hits an obstacle, there is an immediate need to establish new motor and postural arrangements. This is possible since the foot, home to many autonomous mechanisms, presents numerous muscles that originate from the retinacula:

- extensor digitorum brevis muscle (Fig. 1.64) originates from the calcaneus close to the entry of sinus tarsi and from the inferior retinacula of the extensor muscles (Platzer W. 2009);
- abductor digiti minimi muscle originates from the calcaneal tuberosity, from the tuberosity of the fifth metatarsal bone and from the plantar aponeurosis; abductor digiti minimi is located in the lateral compartment of the foot (Fig. 1.62);
- adductor hallucis and adductor digiti minimi muscles take origin from the long plantar ligament; this ligament is deeper than the plantar aponeurosis but has the same course;
- quadratus plantae muscle (accessory flexor) inserts onto the tendon of flexor digitorum longus, it corrects its direction of traction (Benninghoff G. 1986);
- abductor hallucis muscle originates from the calcaneal tuberosity, from the superficial layer of the laciniate ligament and from the deep aspect of the plantar aponeurosis (medial compartment);
- flexor hallucis brevis muscle originates from the plantar aspect of the cuneiforms, from the plantar calcaneocuboid ligament and from the tendon of the tibialis posterior (Chiarugi G. 1975);
- flexor digiti minimi brevis muscle originates from the fifth metatarsal and from the long plantar ligament together with the opponens digiti minimi muscle;
- flexor digitorum brevis muscle originates from the inferior aspect of the calcaneus and from the proximal third of the plantar aponeurosis;
- lumbrical muscles originate from the tendons of the flexor digitorum longus muscle.

The above insertions of muscles on the retinacula are not aimed at developing force like bony insertions, rather they inform the leg muscles of the position of the foot during walking[42], jumping, etc. In this way the large muscles are able to adapt their force during the positional variations of the foot.

[40] During gait the gastrocnemius (myotendinous unit) lengthens and shortens by about 4.5 centimetres. This variation of length determines the different orientation of the muscular bundles, aponeuroses and tendons. These mechanisms are interdependent and are different during either active or passive stretch. (Herbert R.D. 2015)

[41] During the descent from a step, a peak of activation is observed in the medial gastrocnemius shortly before touching the ground, it is accompanied by the coactivation of tibialis anterior whilst during the first phase of stance the ankle is observed to be in a dorsiflexed position. (Pozzi F. 2013)

[42] Our studies allow us to say that the crural fascia is used for force transmission and to reduce the kinematic variables involved with limbs during locomotion. (Stahl V.A. 2014)

Lateral compartment of the foot in continuity with the sequence of retro
Intermediate compartment of the foot in continuity with the sequence of medio
Medial compartment of the foot in continuity with the sequence of intra

Fig. 1.62. Longitudinal traction of the sequences of retropulsion, mediopulsion and intrarotation (superficial layer of the fascia).

(From G. Chiarugi and L. Bucciante, Istituzioni di anatomia dell'uomo. Piccin Nuova Libraria, Padova 1983, modified)

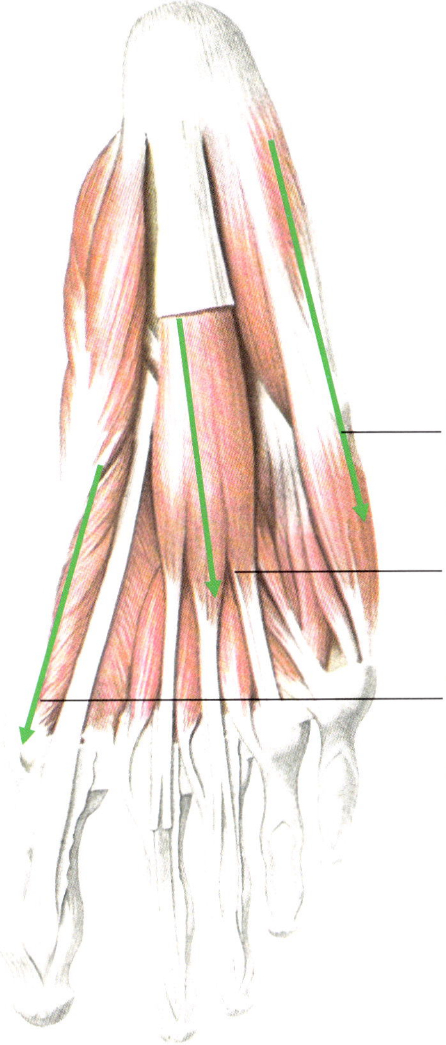

Spiral re-me-pe following the tendon of the flexor digitorum longus muscle
Spiral re-la-pe following the tendon of the peroneus longus muscle

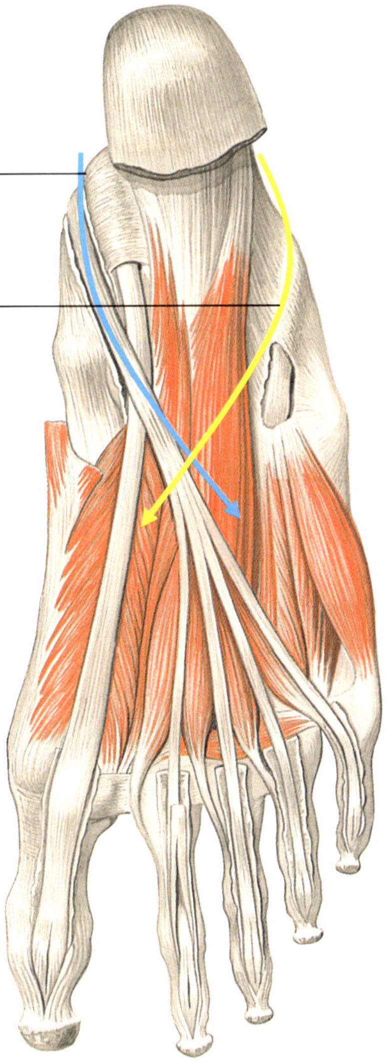

Fig. 1.63. Oblique traction of the spirals of retro-latero-pes and retro-medio-pes (intermediate myofascial layer of the sole of the foot).

(From G. Chiarugi and L. Bucciante, Istituzioni di anatomia dell'uomo. Piccin Nuova Libraria, Padova 1983, modified)

Superior retinaculum of the extensor muscles
Cruciform retinaculum of the extensor muscles
Extensor digitorum brevis muscle

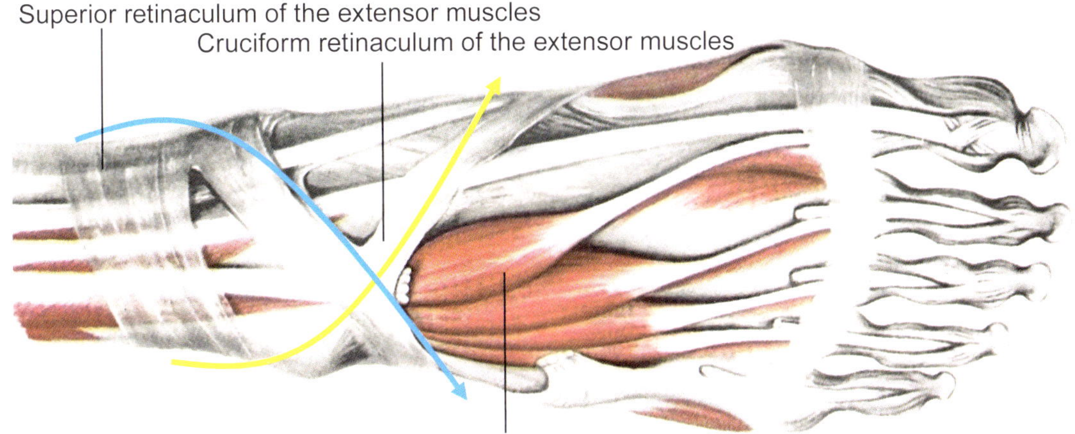

Fig. 1.64. Traction of the spirals of ante-latero-pes and ante-medio-pes (retinacula of the deep layer of the dorsum of the foot).

(From G. Chiarugi and L. Bucciante, Istituzioni di anatomia dell'uomo. Piccin Nuova Libraria, Padova 1983, modified)

MECHANOTRANSDUCTION IN SPIRALS

Mechanotransduction is part of the process through which sensory receptors or mechanoreceptors (MR) convert a mechanical signal into a nervous impulse or changes in membrane potential. This form of transduction relies on mechanically controlled ionic channels. The retinacula contain mechanoreceptors (Ruffini and Pacini corpuscules), their mechanical stretching is converted into changes in membrane potential through the ionic channels (Burkholder T. 2007). This electrical impulse then travels with afferent nerves to the CNS and provides proprioceptive afferents. There are also unconscious afferent impulses, like those of the annulospiral fibres, that do not reach the brain but stop in the spinal cord (monosynaptic reflex arc). Several researchers[43] have demonstrated that some reflexes are organised in the periphery without the intervention of the intraspinal neural reflex arc.

The hypothesis put forward is that in the motor organisation of the spirals, two other types of transmission may occur:

- the impulses are created via mechanotransduction by the receptors arranged in the retinacula of the ankle and wrist. These then travel through the oblique collagen fibres of the limbs and trunk and excite the CFs arranged along their path;
- the small muscles of the hand and foot cause a stretch of the retinacula, through the piezoelectric effect these stretches are converted into electrical potentials. These spread along the collagen fibres of each spiral, therefore exciting the CFs having an antagonist function between them.

"Piezoelectricity is a phenomenon through which some bodies are electrically polarised following a mechanical deformation. Vice versa they deform elastically if submitted to an electric field. The sign of polarisation is inverted whether the deformation is caused by compression or by traction" (Treccani 2015).

Collagen fibres respond to the piezoelectric effect (Langevin H. 2005) and the transmission of the electric potential follows the spiral collagen fibres[44]. The retinacula of the ankle and wrist are especially suitable structures for piezoelectricity, as are those of the elbow and knee; indeed these are inserted on bones holding them secure to allow stretching, whilst they offer insertion to the muscles pulling on them during movement.

These concepts may be explained through the examination of a single spiral of the upper limb (Fig. 1.65). When the thumb opposes, its muscles stretch the flexor retinaculum and determine a slight electric charge spreading along the spiral collagen fibres; these fibres are connected to the extensor retinaculum of the wrist (CF re-me-ca) and the anterior retinaculum of the elbow (CF an-la-cu).

The electrical conduction of spiral collagen fibres is supported by several scientific studies[45] and by clinical experience[46]; indeed patients sometimes may refer, when being manipulated on the wrist and ankle retinacula, the presence of small disto-proximal electrical discharges that do not follow the path of nerves but rather that of the spirals.

The electrical stimulation along the spiral is combined to the mechanical transmission in determining opposing movements between two adjacent segments. The spiral arrangement of the collagen fibres allows these "electrical conductors" to reach the centres of fusion localised in diametrically opposed positions. However, electric transmission does not exclude mechanical transmission. At the level of the knee, mechanical transmission from the sartorius muscle prevails, its spiral sheath connects the CF of retro-medio-genu to the CF ante-latero-coxa. In this case, the continuous repetition of the walking scheme and the higher force requirements of this gesture have joined the muscular fibres (mechanical transmission) to the collagen fibres (electric transmission).

The myofascial sequences operate through mechanical transmission where the contraction of one myofascial unit determines the direct stretch of the overlying fascia. The longitudinal continuity of fascial compartments determines the activation of the spindles in the next MF unit through the stretch reflex.

The myofascial diagonals and spirals are located in an intermediate position hence they take advantage partly of the myofascial stretch and partly of the bioelectric potential variation. Diagonals synchronise the action of the CFs arranged longitudinally whilst spirals excite the CFs with antagonist function located in two adjacent segments.

---

[43] The results demonstrate that the giraffe has little ability in responding precisely to sudden stimuli using only the nervous feedback, therefore there must be a peripheral organisation. (More H.L. 2013)

[44] The structure and piezoelectricity of the opaque membrane were not modified by the process of neutralisation. In transparent membranes the results show that the presence of an additional electrical transfer according to the alignment of the fibres. The piezoelectric response was ample in the collagen fibres of the tendon of a rat. (Denning D. 2014)

[45] Tendon has been shown to exhibit piezoelectric effects as well as streaming potentials when subjected to a mechanical stress. (West C.R. 2012)

[46] The third TP of the soleus muscle irradiates deep pain into the ipsilateral sacroiliac joint. In two cases it was observed that the area of pain irradiation reached the jaw. (Travell J. 1996)

MECHANOTRANSDUCTION ALONG SPIRALS

(Please start reading from the bottom of the page)

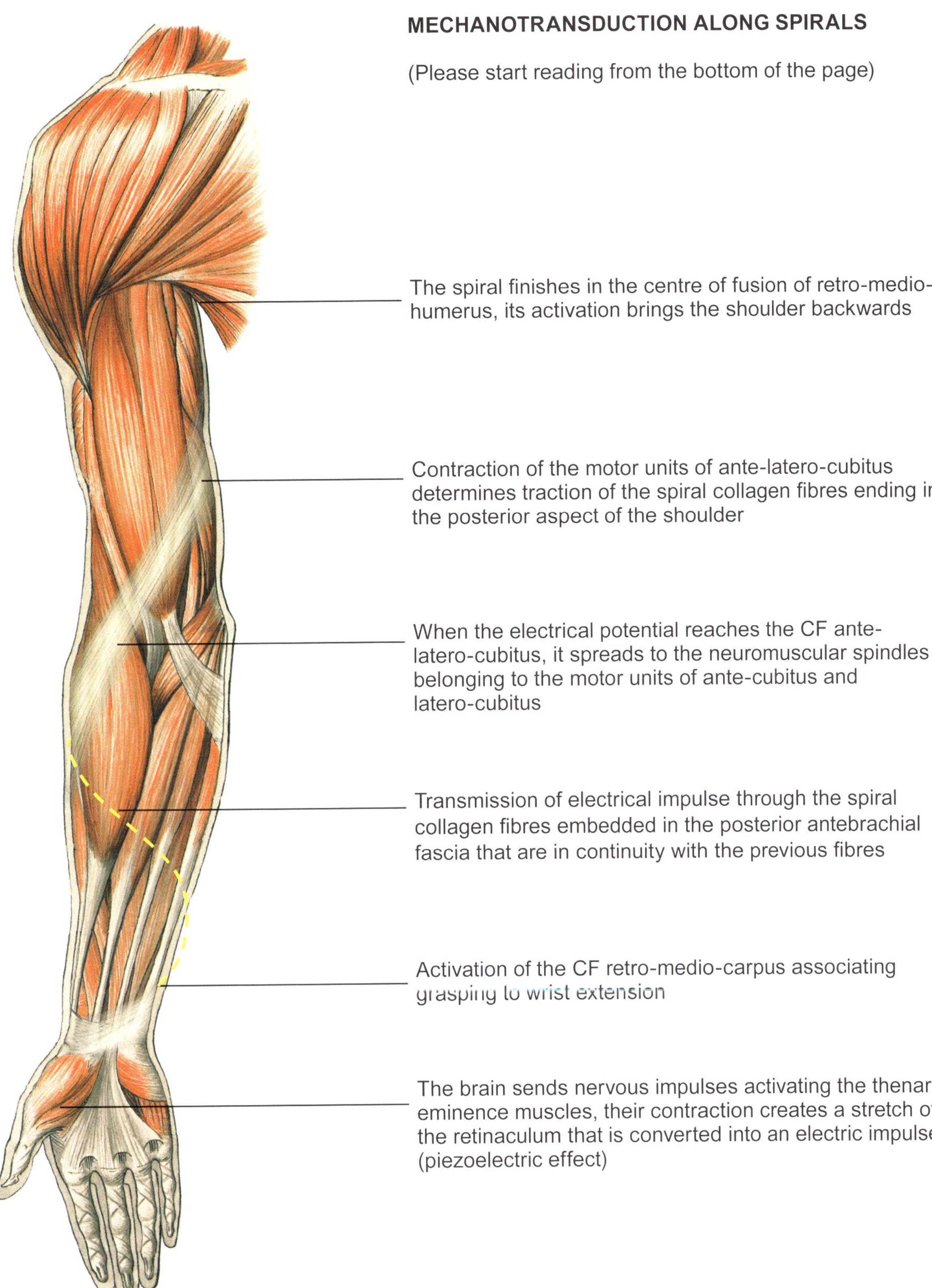

Fig. 1.65. Arrangement of the ante-latero-digiti spiral.

(From G. Chiarugi and L. Bucciante, Istituzioni di anatomia dell'uomo. Piccin Nuova Libraria, Padova 1983, modified)

TERMINOLOGY OF THE MUSCULAR FASCIA

In anatomy the term fascia describes a variety of connective tissues. Based on their appearance and their relationships they are called: superficial fascia (present in the entire subcutis of the body), fasciae of the nervous system (meninges: pia matter, arachnoid, dura matter), fasciae of the peripheral nerves (epineurium, perineurium, endoneurium), fasciae of the internal organs (visceral, vascular, glandular), and fasciae of the muscles and tendons.

In this atlas, the fasciae of the muscles and tendons are presented based upon their physiology (Table 1.5).

- *origin and insertion of tendons on the aponeurotic fascia through the paratenon.*

The paratenon has a function of facilitating the passage of vessels and nerves, as well as transmitting tension from the tendon to the fascia and from the retinacula to the tendinous tissue. Therefore, it can facilitate the interaction with the tendon organs and neuromuscular spindles (Centres of Fusion CFs).

Benninghoff[47] describes the continuity of the fascial structures of the muscle with those of the tendon, however, the terms used have since been revised and defined unequivocally during the 4th World Fascial Congress (Stecco A. 2013, Stecco C. 2015). The continuity of the perimysium with the paratenon connects the neuromuscular spindles to the Golgi tendon organs which then interact at the spinal cord level.

Tabella 1.5. Denomination of the muscular fasciae according to their function and localisation

Fasciae	Epi or external	Peri or intermediate	Endo or internal
In parallel to the muscle	Epimysium or deep muscular fascia	Perimysium or fascia connected to the **neuromuscular spindles**	Endomysium or fascia in continuity with the endotenon
In series to the muscle	Elastic fascia rich in proprioceptors	Aponeurotic fascia with longitudinal and oblique fibres	Insertions of the epimisial fascia on the aponeurotic one
In parallel to the tendon	*Epitenon or fascia in continuity with the epimysium*	*Paratenon or fascia connected to the **Golgi tendon organs***	*Endotenon or gliding fascia between tendon fibres*
In series to the tendon	*Elastic fascia united to the retinacula and to the receptors*	*Paratenon or fascia in continuity with the aponeurotic fascia*	*Insertion of the epitenon with the paratenon or mesotenon*

Fasciae arranged in parallel to the muscular tissue (Fig. 1.66, 1.67):

- epimysium: connective tissue that manages the function of the myofascial units;
- perimysium: connective tissue connected to the function of the neuromuscular spindles – Centres of Coordination;
- endomysium: connective tissue with gliding role between single fibres.

Fasciae arranged in parallel to the tendinous tissue either fusiform or flat (Fig. 1.68, 1.69):

- *epitenon: connective tissue in continuity with the epimysium and with the synovial tendon sheaths;*
- *paratenon: connective tissue connected to the function of the Golgi tendon organs;*
- *endotenon: connective tissue in continuity with the endomysium and muscle fibres.*

Fasciae arranged in series to the tendinous tissue:

- *receptor fascia: elastic connective tissue suitable to the activation of proprioceptors;*
- *aponeurotic fasciae connected to the retinacula-ligaments through longitudinal and oblique fibres;*

[47] Macroscopically it can be recognised that the single muscle is wrapped by a layer of connective tissue, the epimysium (external perimysium or external fascia) that continues around the tendon as epitendon. Bundles of muscle fibres of the muscle are circumscribed by connective septa (internal perimysium) from which the thinner connective fibres of the endomysium arise. The tendon is not merely the rigid whitish cord that is visible at the extremity of a muscle. It also continues inside the muscle itself, where it directly connects with the interstitial connective tissue. In tendons there is a division of the tendon fibres into bundles similar to that of the muscle fibres. They are wrapped by the epitendon (or external peritenon) and by the peritendon (or internal peritenon). (Benninghoff A. 1978)

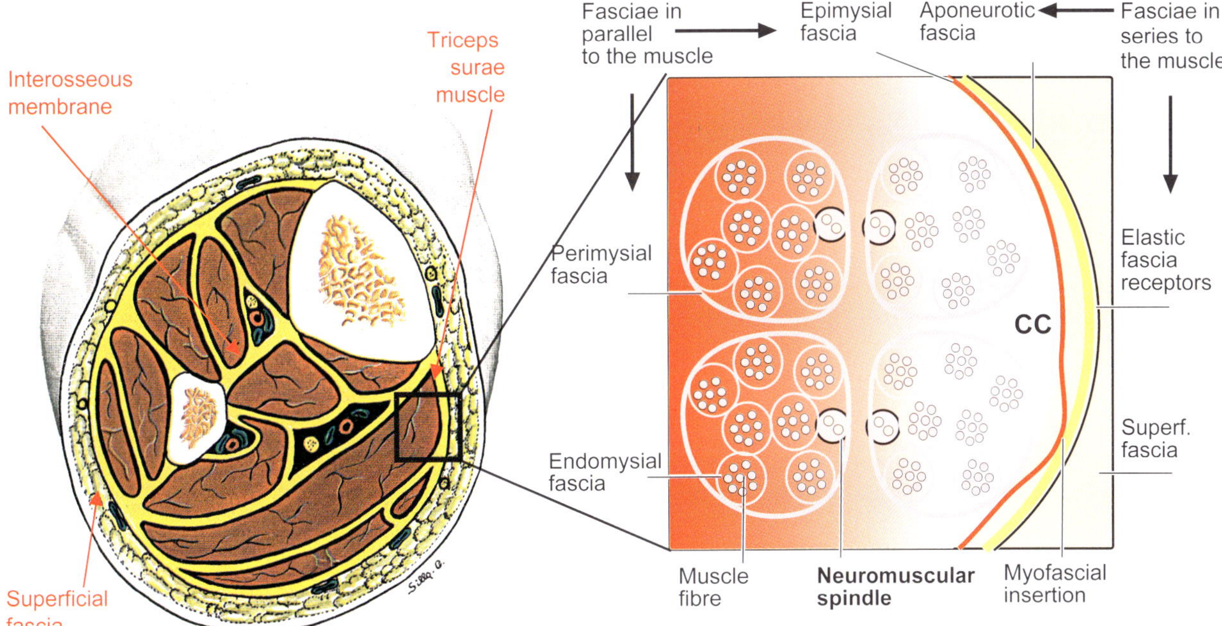

Fig. 1.66. Transverse section of the leg, medial third. *(From G. Chiarugi and L. Bucciante, Istituzioni di anatomia dell'uomo. Piccin Nuova Libraria, 1983, modified)*

Fig. 1.67. Detailed view of the transverse section of the medial triceps surae muscle with the fasciae in parallel and in series.

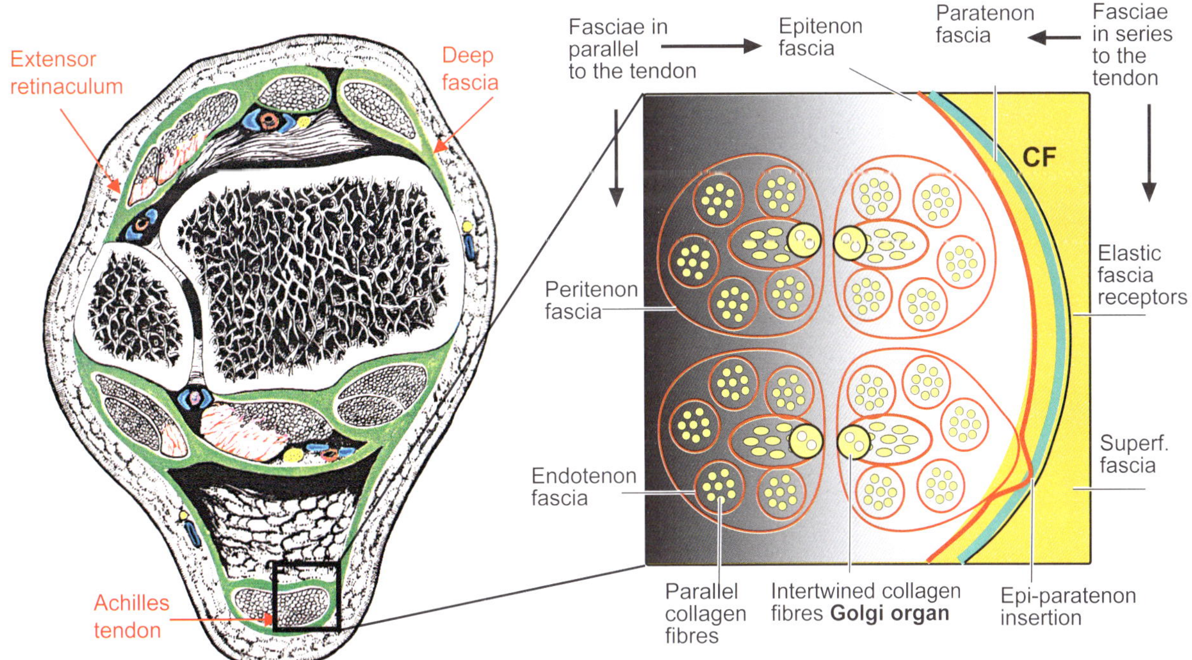

Fig. 1.68. Tendon sheaths, transverse oblique section of the lower left leg at the level of the malleoli. *(From G. Chiarugi and L. Bucciante, Istituzioni di anatomia dell'uomo. Piccin Nuova Libraria, Padova 1983, modified)*

Fig. 1.69. Detailed view of the transverse section of the tendon of the medial triceps surae muscle with the fasciae in parallel and in series.

ANATOMICAL DISSECTION OF THE FASCIA LATA

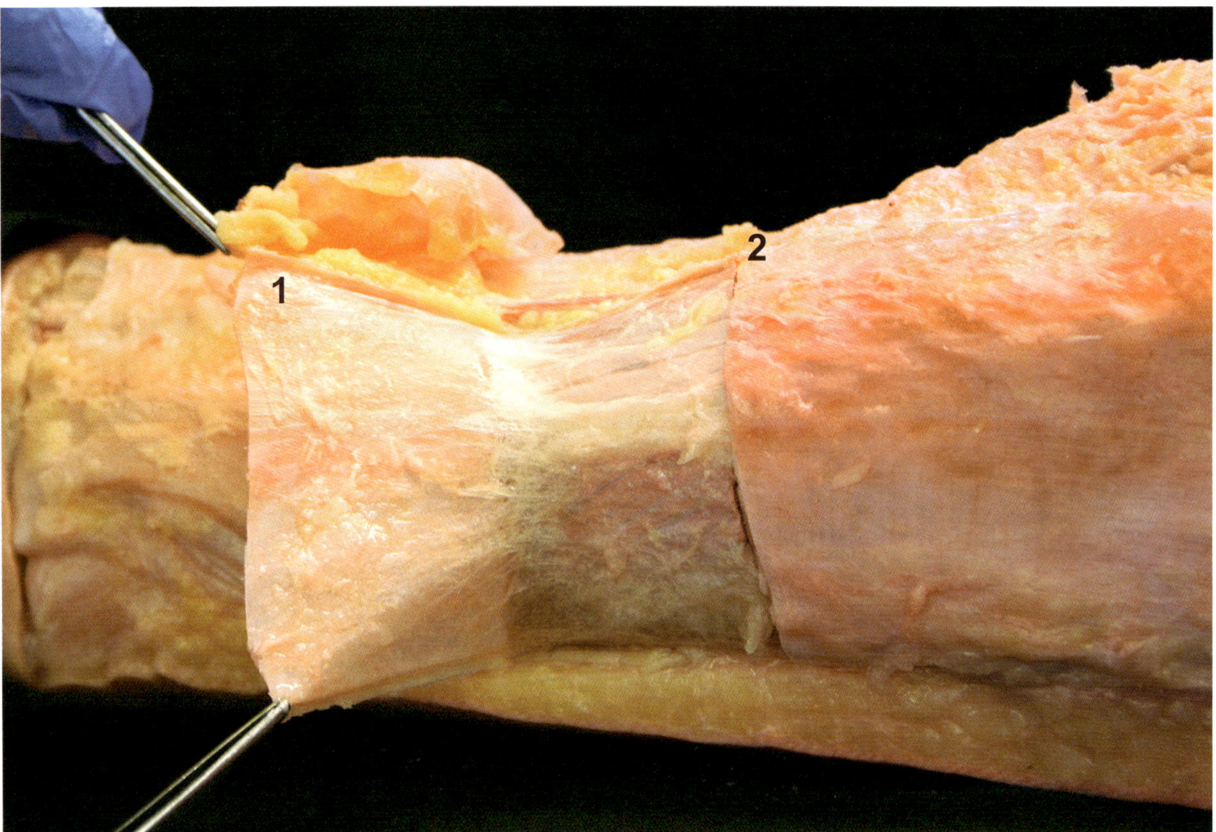

Fig. 1.70. Anterior fascia lata. The aponeurotic fascia is cut mid-thigh (2) and lifted inferiorly (1) to collect a strip of tissue.

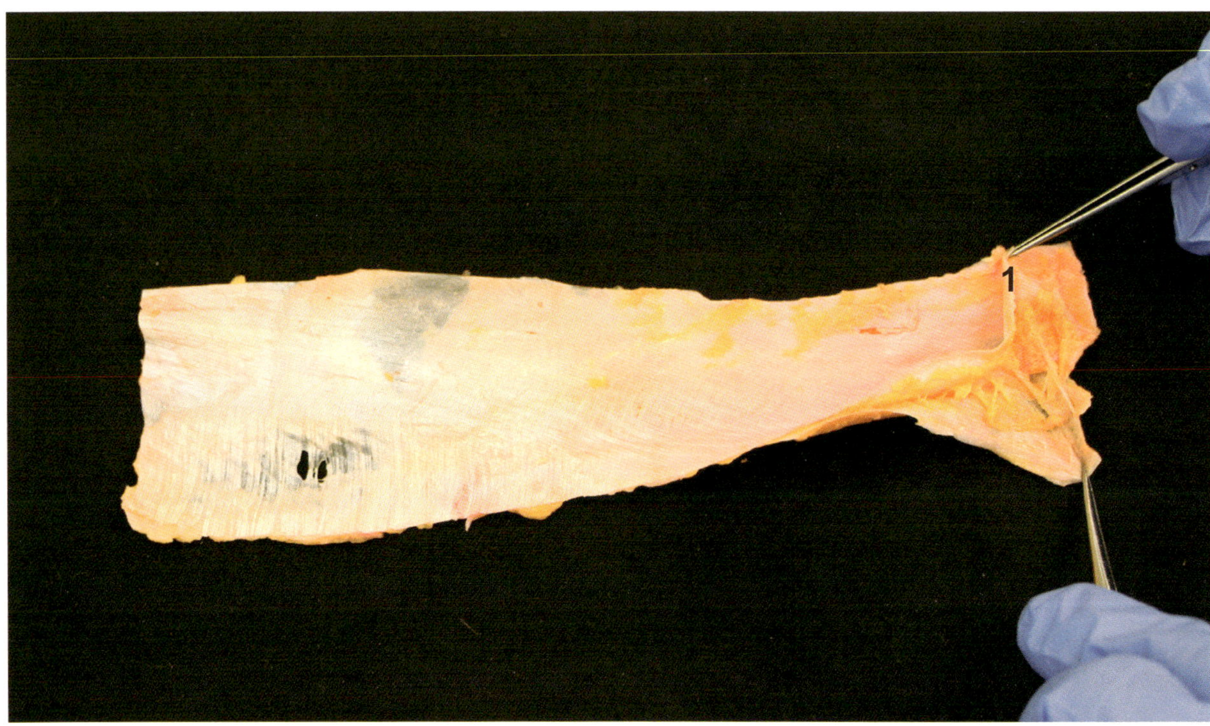

Fig. 1.71. Strip of fascia lata tissue. The aponeurotic fascia is formed by two or more layers of collagen fibres separated by loose connective tissue. Forceps are used to separate the two layers in order to examine a single layer (1).

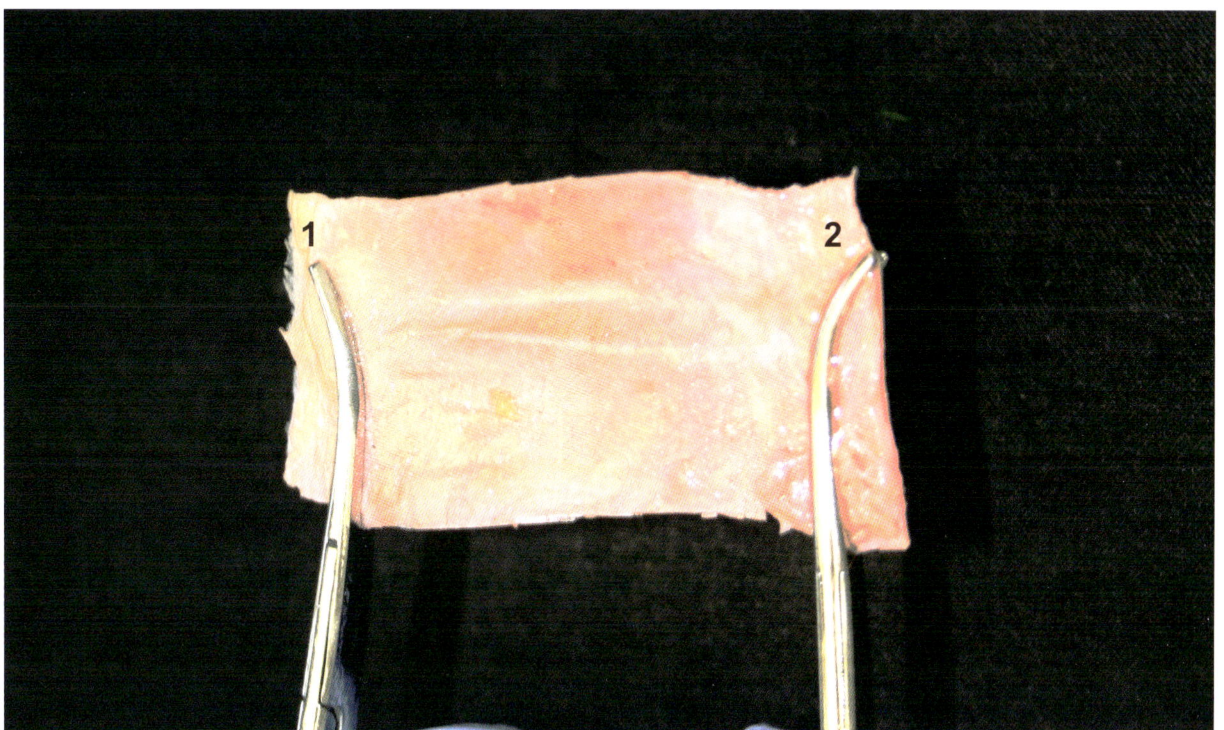

Fig. 1.72. Layer of fascia lata. Resistance to traction is tested by applying a strong pull towards the left (1) and towards the right (2) in accordance to the arrangement of the collagen fibres.

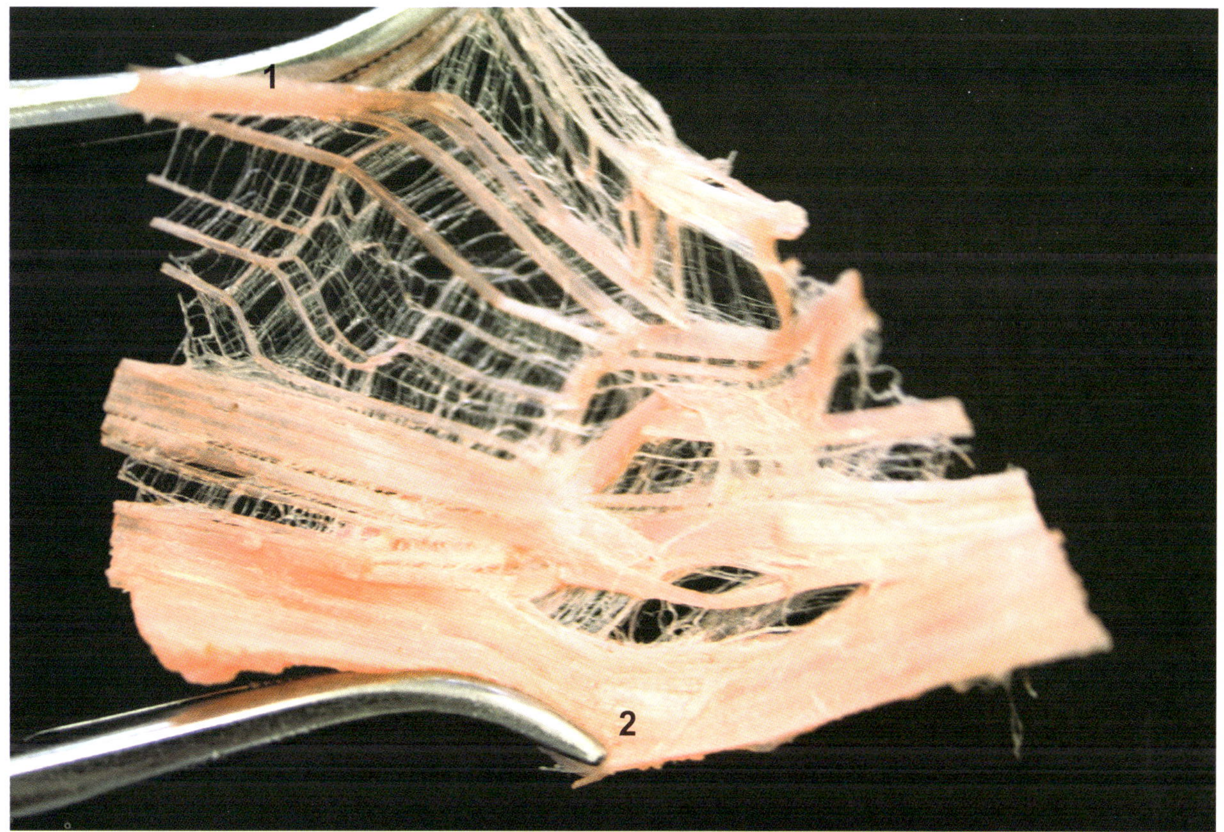

Fig. 1.73. Layer of fascia lata. The fascia tears when subjected to transverse traction (1,2), the force is applied transversally to the arrangement of the collagen fibres. Note the arrangement of the collagen fibres and the elastic fibres (thinner).

SPIRAL COLLAGEN FIBRES OF THE UPPER LIMB

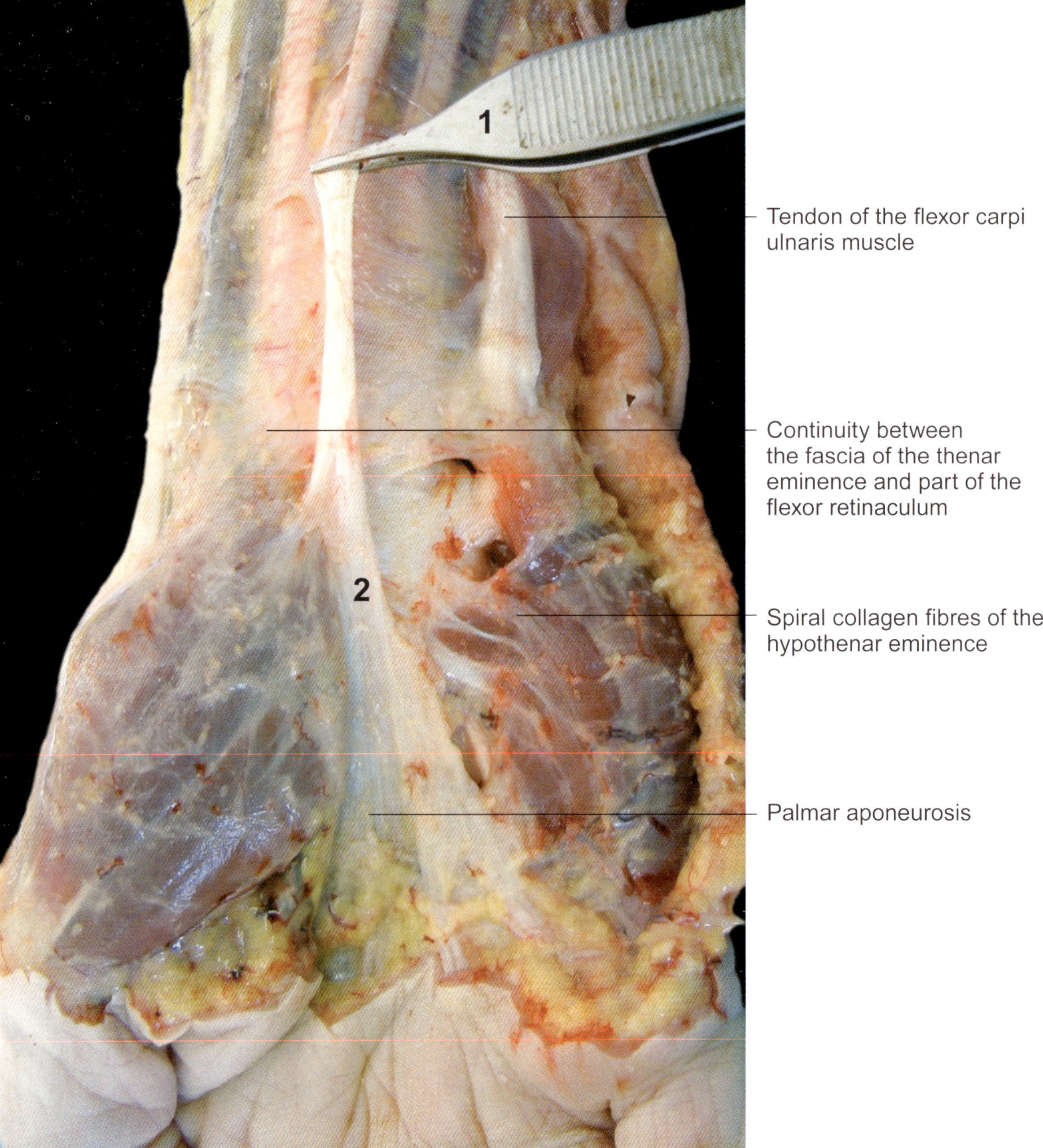

Fig. 1.74. Tendon of palmaris longus. The forceps (1) holds the tendon of palmaris longus and passively stretches it upward. This shows how the tendon tractions (2) the palmar aponeurosis and the fascia of the thenar eminence. Note how the fibres of the hypothenar eminence course underneath the tendon of palmaris longus.

In the figures horizontal lines indicate anatomical parts whilst numbers (1,2) indicate the physiology of the fascia. Namely number 1 indicates a determined action and number 2 indicates its effect.

SPIRAL COLLAGEN FIBRES OF THE UPPER LIMB

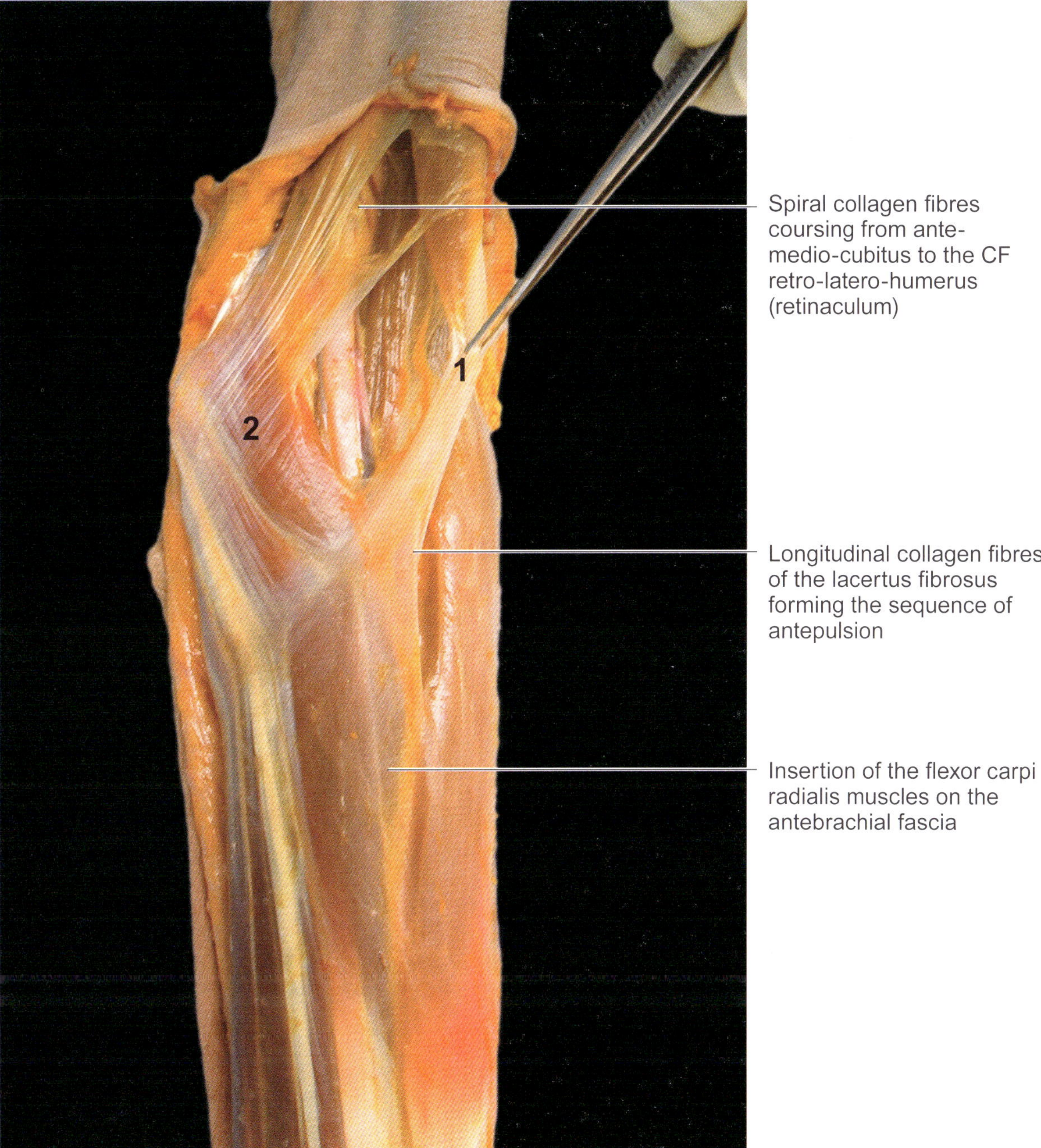

Fig. 1.75. Anterior view of the antebrachial and brachial fascia. The forceps (1) hooks onto the tendon of lacertus fibrosus demonstrating how it forms part of a spiral. The spiral ascends from ante-medio-cubitus towards the CF retro-latero-humerus; most spiral collagen fibres are in continuity (2) with the brachial fascia.

SPIRAL COLLAGEN FIBRES OF THE UPPER LIMB

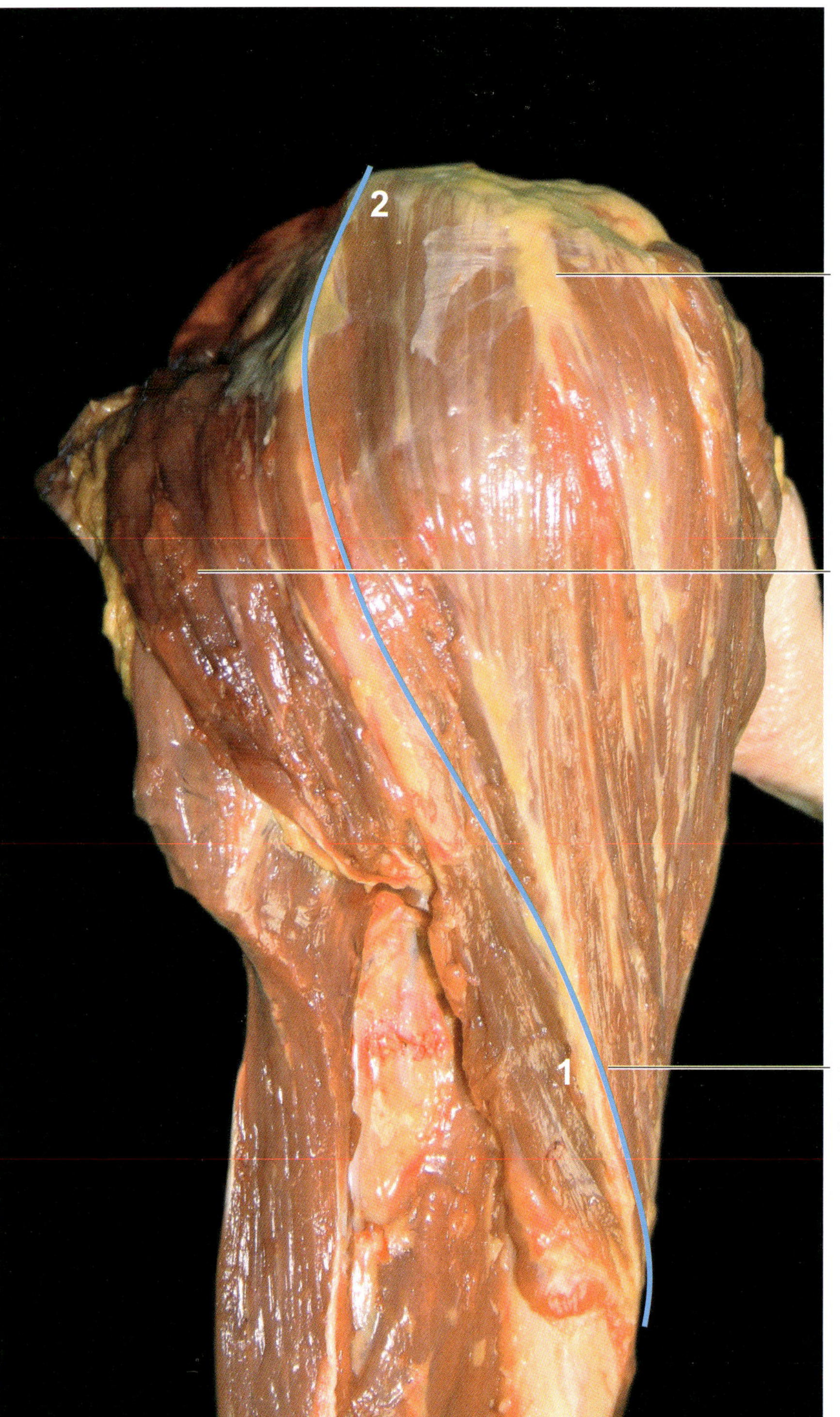

Fig. 1.76. Epimysial fascia of the deltoid muscle, CF retro-latero. In the shoulder and hip, the aponeurotic fascia of the limbs continues with the oblique intramuscular fibres of the deltoid and gluteus maximus muscles. The blue line indicates the arrangement of the muscular fibres connecting the CF of retro-latero-humerus (1) to the CF retro-latero-scapula (2).

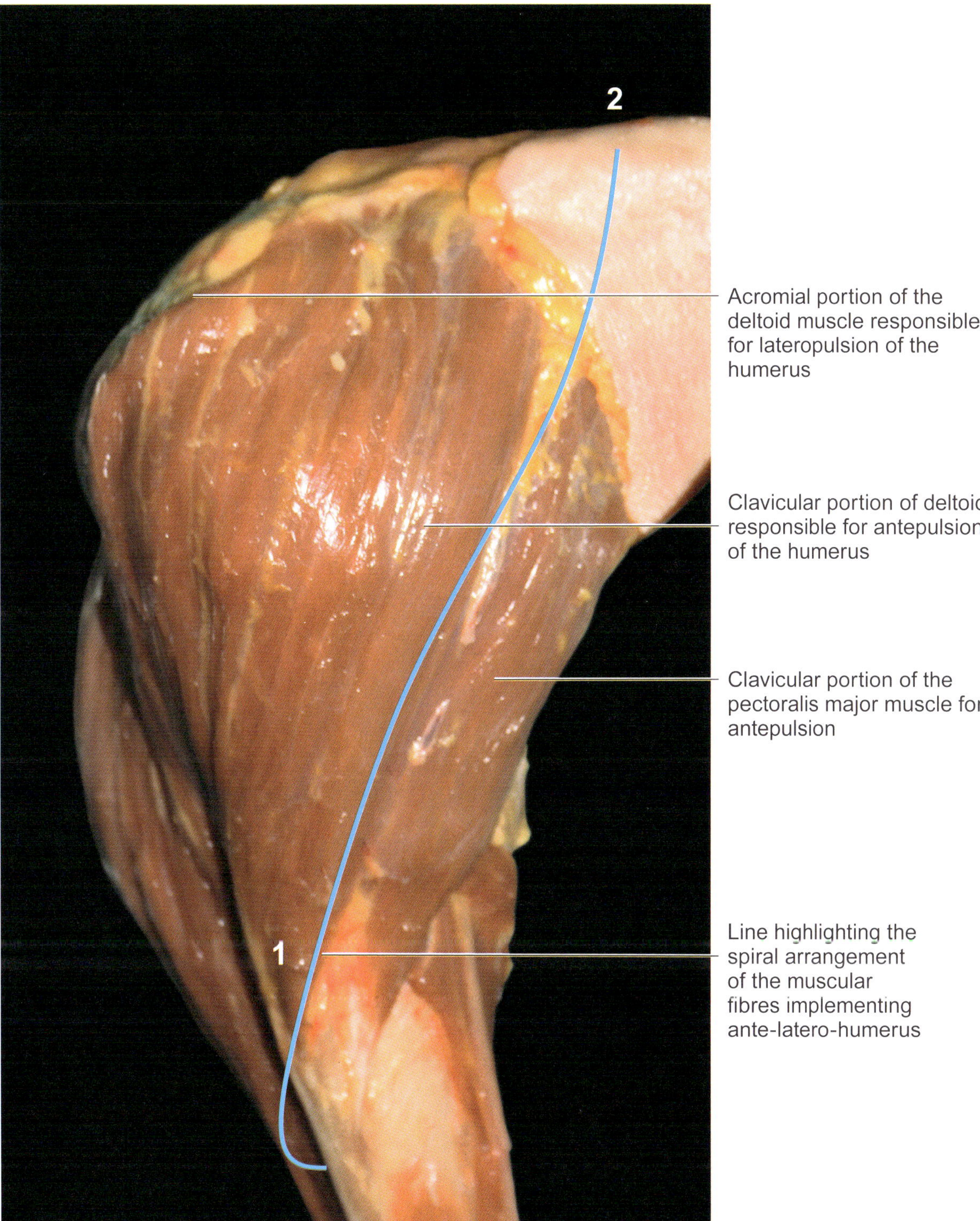

Fig. 1.77. Epimysial fascia of the deltoid, CF antero-latero. The brachial fascia and biceps brachii muscle are removed to show the ample insertion of the deltoid tendon. The spiral arriving from retro-medio-cubitus connects to the CF ante-latero-humerus. The latter (1) is located between the insertions of the deltoid and pectoralis major tendons and continues into the CF an-la-sc (2). In the spirals scapula works in synergy with humerus and not in opposition as is noted in other segments.

CHAPTER 2

CENTRES OF COORDINATION AND SEQUENCES OF THE UPPER LIMB

MYOFASCIAL UNITS AND UNIDIRECTIONAL MOVEMENTS OF THE UPPER LIMB (UL)

In the human body there are no individual muscles participating for individual movements, nor are there individual movements performed by individual muscles.

In the following chapters, the first anatomical drawing (Fig. 2.1) represents the classical view of muscles with a description of the movements implemented by the four main segments in the limbs or in the trunk. The photographs in the opposite page (Fig. 2.2-2.5) show the movements implemented in a specific spatial plane.

Segments are not able to move without involving both the stability and the synergy of the proximal and distal segments. Therefore, from a physiological point of view, it has more sense to examine the sequence of muscles involved when carrying out a specific motor direction instead of examining muscles individually (Fig. 2.6, 2.7).

The anatomical drawings, taken from Chiarugi's anatomical textbook, feature the region of the limbs and trunk in connection to the three spatial directions and hence to the MF sequences:

- the antepulsion sequence is visualised on the anterior view. It is formed by the fascial compartments of the upper limb containing the biceps brachii, flexor carpi radialis, flexor pollicis longus muscles, etc.;
- the retropulsion sequence is visualised on the posterior view. It is formed by the fascial compartments of the triceps brachii, extensor carpi ulnaris, extensor digiti minimi longus muscles, etc.;
- the mediopulsion sequence is visualised on the medial view. It is formed by the fascial compartments of the coracobrachialis, flexor carpi ulnaris, flexor digiti minimi longus muscles, etc.;
- the lateropulsion sequence is visualised on the lateral view. It is formed by the fascial compartments of the lateral deltoid, extensor carpi radialis, extensor indicis muscles, etc.;
- the intrarotation sequence is visualised on the deep anterior muscle view. It is formed by the fascial compartments of the subscapularis, pronator teres, flexor digitorum longus and brevis muscles;
- the extrarotation sequence is visualised on the deep posterior muscle view. It is formed by the fascial compartments of the infraspinatus, supinator and extensor digitorum longus muscles.

Each myofascial unit moving a segment of the upper limb in one spatial plane is composed of:

- a primary muscle corresponding to a monoarticular muscle. It is called primary since it acts mainly in the direction and on the segment of that MF unit;
- a secondary muscle corresponding to a biarticular muscle. It is called secondary since it intervenes in more than one movement and on more than one segment;
- one or more synergic muscles. These intervene when implementing the motor schemes in one segment.

Nearly all the motor units of a primary muscle participate to the specific movement of that MF unit. For instance, nearly all motor units of the brachialis muscle intervene in elbow flexion or antepulsion of cubitus.

The motor units of secondary muscles participate in more than one movement. For instance, the biceps brachii muscle contains motor units for elbow flexion, elbow supination, shoulder flexion and humerus abduction.

The motor units of synergic muscles are activated during motor schemes or spiral movements. For instance, the brachioradialis muscle contributes in elbow flexion but it also stabilises the elbow during the motor scheme of ante-latero-cubitus.

The neuromuscular spindles of the mono and biarticular muscles of each myofascial unit (Fig. 2.8) create small tensions on the perimysium. These vectors converge towards a unique vectorial centre called centre of coordination (CC). For each myofascial sequence the four MF units are reported along with the vectors formed during their physiological activities.

The opposite page illustrates the vectors in the presence of dysfunction (Fig. 2.9) namely in the presence of a fascial densification.

On the following page, the tendinous expansions on the aponeurotic fascia are illustrated, these create longitudinal vectors that are able to activate the synergy between the MF units belonging to the same sequence through the stretch reflex (Fig. 2.10).

The biarticular muscles (Fig. 2.11) manage the ranges of motion between two adjacent joints through the Golgi tendon organs arranged in their tendons.

The photographs of anatomical dissections aim at supporting the above myofascial organisations.

ANTERIOR REGION OF THE UPPER LIMB, ANTEPULSION SEQUENCE

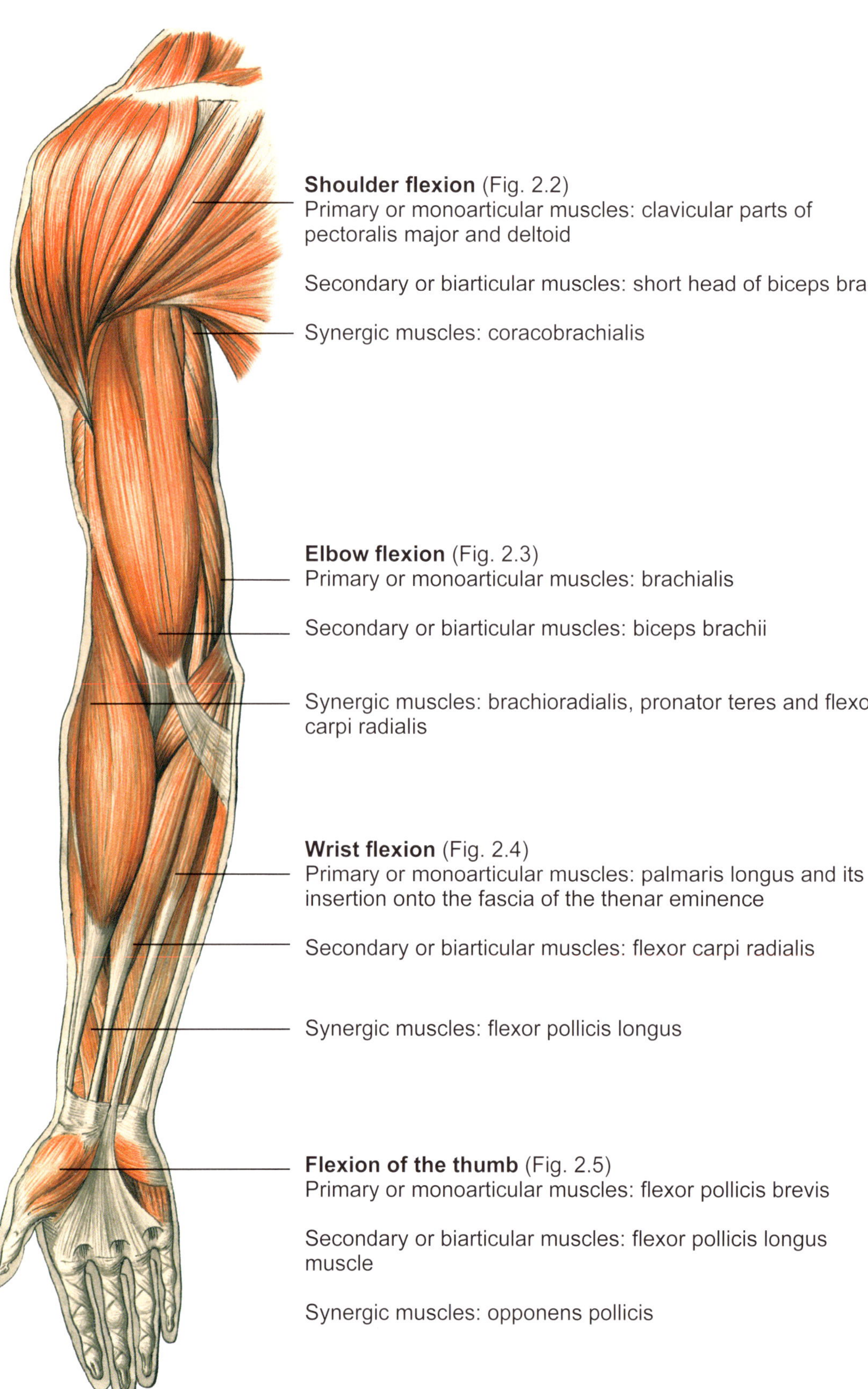

Fig. 2.1. Anterior region of the upper limb.
(From G. Chiarugi and L. Bucciante, Istituzioni di anatomia dell'uomo. Piccin Nuova Libraria, Padova 1983, modified)

SEGMENTARY MOVEMENTS IMPLEMENTED BY THE MF UNITS OF ANTEPULSION

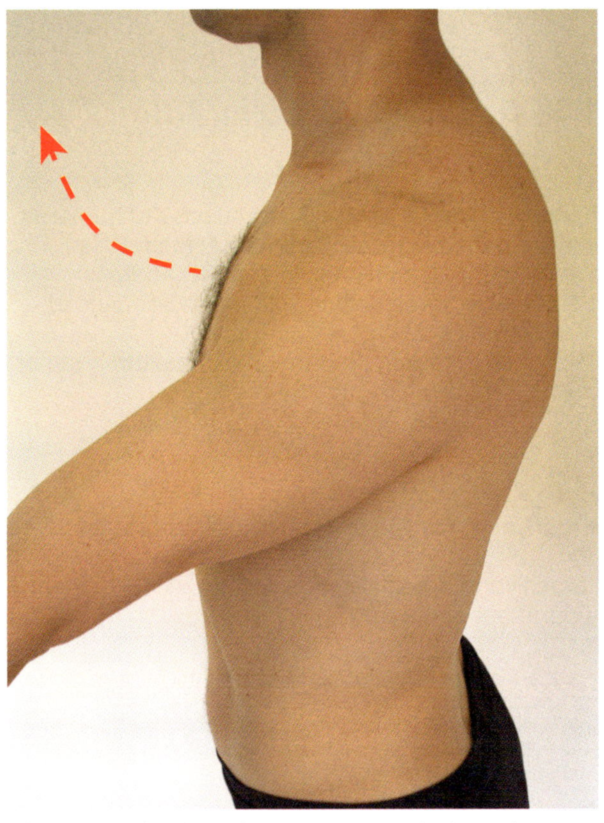

Fig. 2.2. Shoulder flexion, managed throughout its range by the myofascial unit of ante-humerus.

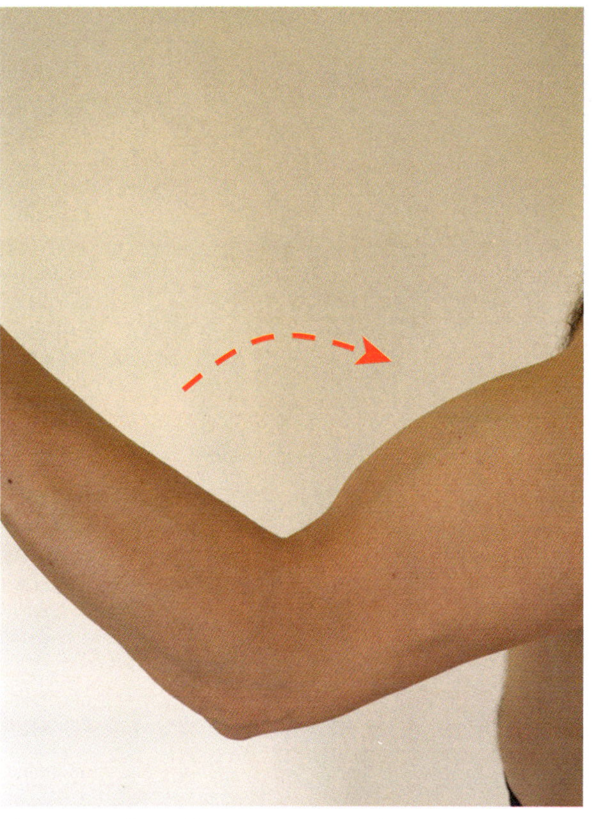

Fig. 2.3. Elbow flexion, managed throughout its range by the MF unit of ante-cubitus.

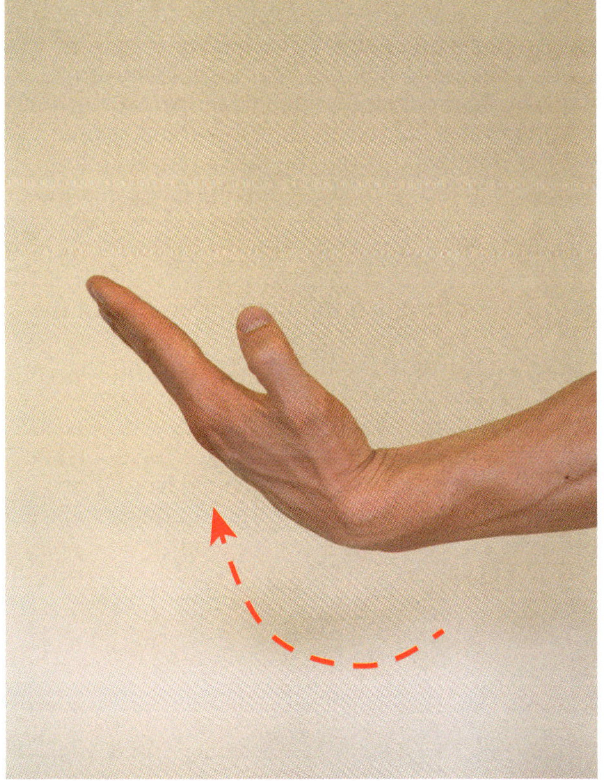

Fig. 2.4. Wrist flexion, managed throughout its range by the MF unit of ante-carpus.

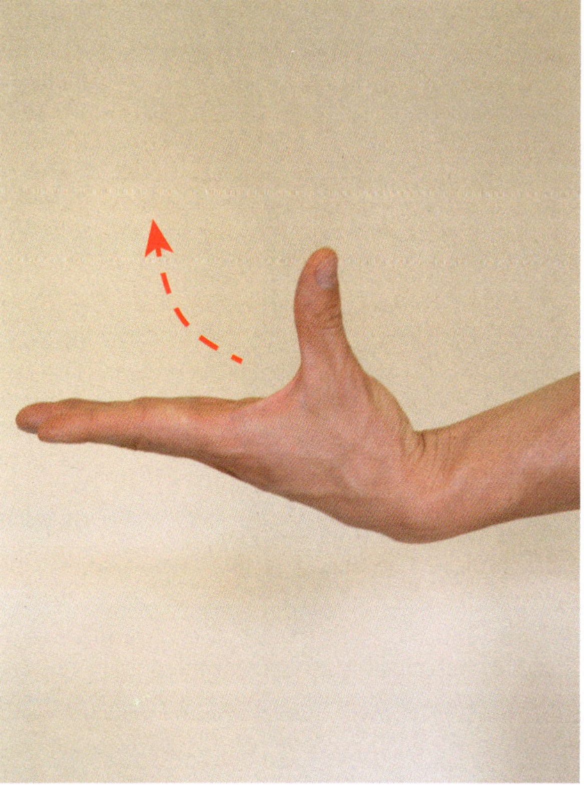

Fig. 2.5. Thumb flexion, managed throughout its range by the MF unit of ante-digiti (pollicis).

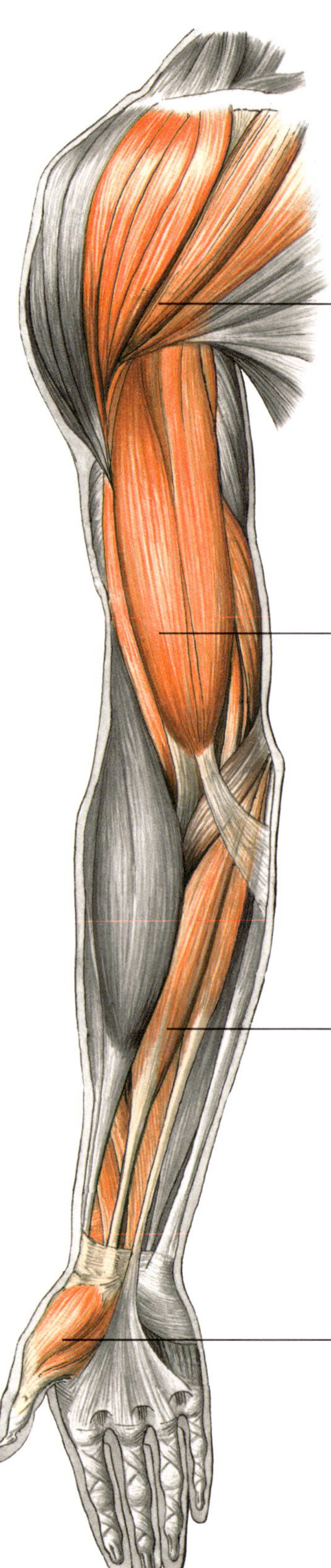

COMPARTMENTS FOR THE MUSCLES OF ANTEPULSION, UPPER LIMB (Fig. 2.7)

Fascial compartment for the antepulsion muscles of humerus
The fascia covering the pectoralis major muscle and the clavicular portion of the deltoid muscle sends numerous septa between muscle fibres uniting with the motor units of antepulsion for both muscles.
This fascia also connects with the tendon of the short head of biceps brachii.

Fascial compartment for the antepulsion muscles of cubitus
The biceps brachii and brachialis muscles are included in the anterior compartment of the arm.

"The anterior brachial fascia close to the muscle bellies consists essentially of circular fibres. Towards the shoulder and elbow areas, these are associated with robust longitudinal and oblique fibres. Proximally these fibres are formed by the pulling action of the tendinous anchorages of pectoralis major and deltoid" (Lang J. 1991).

Fascial compartment for the antepulsion muscles of carpus
The flexor carpi radialis and palmaris longus muscles are included between the septa that are interposed between the brachioradialis, flexor digitorum and flexor carpi ulnaris muscles. The neuromuscular spindles of the antepulsion motor units of the wrist are inserted on the perimysium that in turn is connected to the epimysium and the latter with the septa.

Fascial compartment for the antepulsion muscles of the thumb
The fascia overlying the muscles of the thenar eminence is connected to the tendon of the palmaris longus muscle and the flexor retinaculum. The flexor hallucis brevis muscle takes origin from the tendon of palmaris longus (antepulsion sequence). Besides their fascial origin (coordination) these muscles also have a deep insertion onto bones (lever force).

Fig. 2.6. Fascial compartments for antepulsion muscles.
(From G. Chiarugi and L. Bucciante, Istituzioni di anatomia dell'uomo. Piccin Nuova Libraria, Padova 1983, modified).

GLOBAL MOVEMENT IMPLEMENTED BY THE ANTEPULSION SEQUENCE

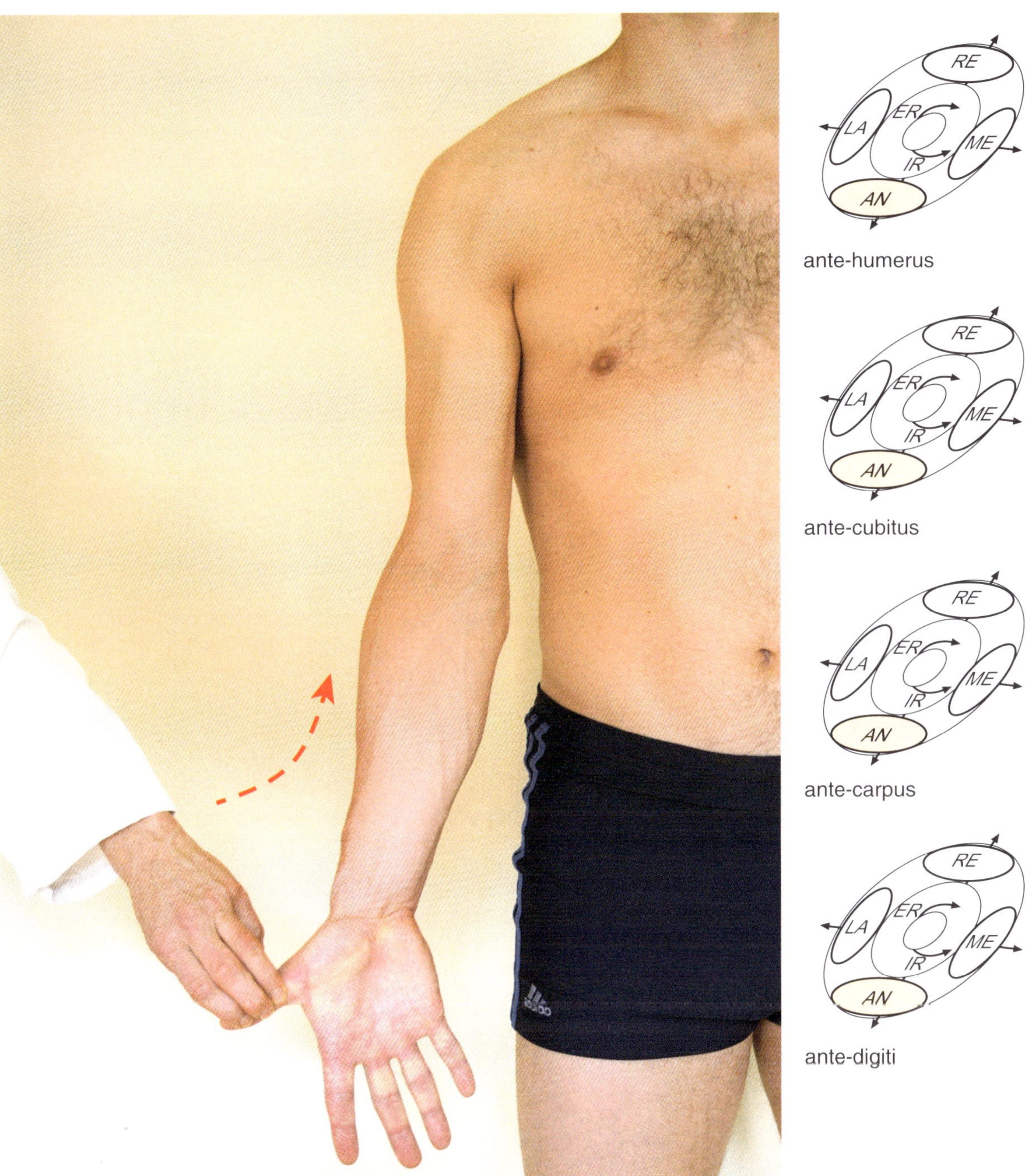

Fig. 2.7. Contraction of the antepulsion sequence bringing the entire upper limb anteriorly.

When the brain programmes for forward upper limb movement, the ipsidirectional motor units included in the fascial compartments of the anterior region of the upper limb are then activated.
The contraction of the antepulsion motor units included in the anterior fascial compartments determines the stretch of the overlying fascia and the activation of proprioceptors. The afferents from the antepulsion sequence return to the brain confirming the occurrence of the movement according to the programmed direction.

PHYSIOLOGY OF THE ANTEPULSION MF UNITS IN THE UPPER LIMB

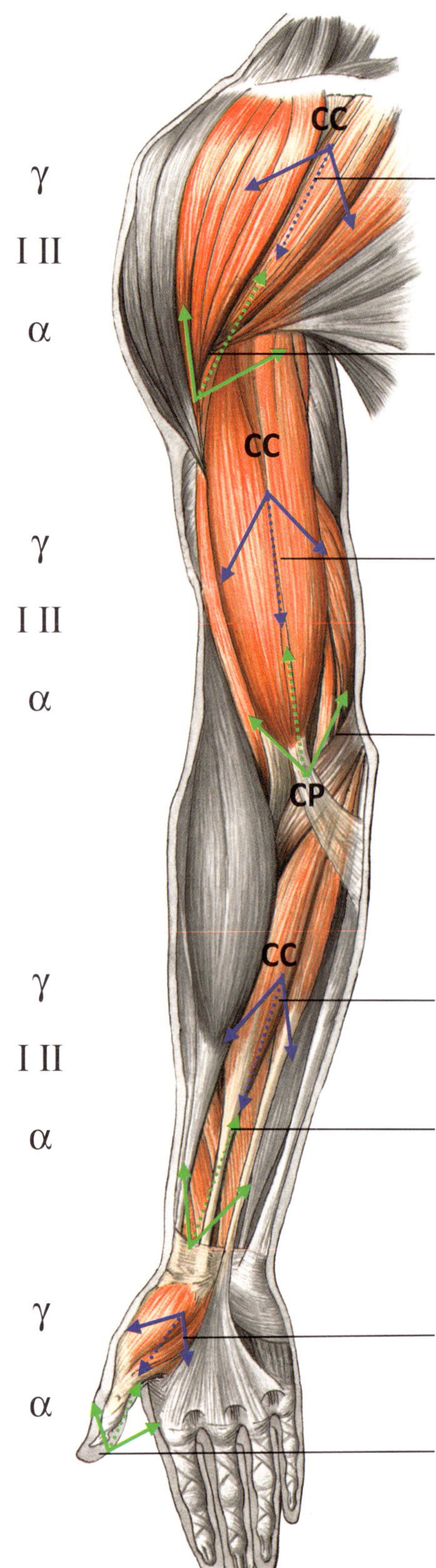

Myofascial unit of ante-humerus (an-hu)
The gamma motor neurone stimulates the intrafusal muscle fibres creating tractions on the perimysium of the deltoid, short head of biceps brachii and pectoralis major muscles (CC).
The adaptability of the perimysium allows the afferents I, II to close the circuit, to trigger the alpha impulse and to contract the extrafusal fibres of the MF unit ante-humerus.

Myofascial unit of ante-cubitus (an-cu)
The gamma motor neurone stimulates the intrafusal muscle fibres of the biceps brachii and brachialis muscles. Their tractions on the perimysium converge on the belly of the biceps brachii muscle (CC).
The adaptability of the perimysium allows the afferents I, II to close the circuit triggering the alpha impulse. This stimulus causes the contraction of the extrafusal fibres of the MF unit ante-cubitus carrying out elbow flexion (CP).

Myofascial unit of ante-carpus (an-ca)
The gamma motor neurone stimulates the intrafusal muscle fibres creating tractions on the perimysium of the flexor carpi radialis and palmaris longus muscles (CC).
The adaptability of the perimysium allows the afferents I, II to close the circuit, to trigger the alpha impulse and to contract the extrafusal fibres of the MF unit ante-carpus.

Myofascial unit of ante-digiti (an-di)
The gamma motor neurone stimulates the intrafusal muscle fibres creating tractions on the perimysium of the flexor pollicis brevis and abductor pollicis brevis muscles (CC).
The adaptability of the perimysium allows the afferents I, II to close the circuit, to trigger the alpha impulse and to contract the extrafusal fibres of the MF unit ante-digiti (thumb).

NB. In these figures, the abbreviations CC and CP are not reported for each MF unit due to space limitations.

Fig. 2.8. Normal functioning of the gamma circuit.
(From G. Chiarugi and L. Bucciante, Istituzioni di anatomia dell'uomo. Piccin Nuova Libraria, Padova 1983, modified).

ARTICULAR CONFLICTS IN THE ANTEPULSION UNITS IN THE UPPER LIMB

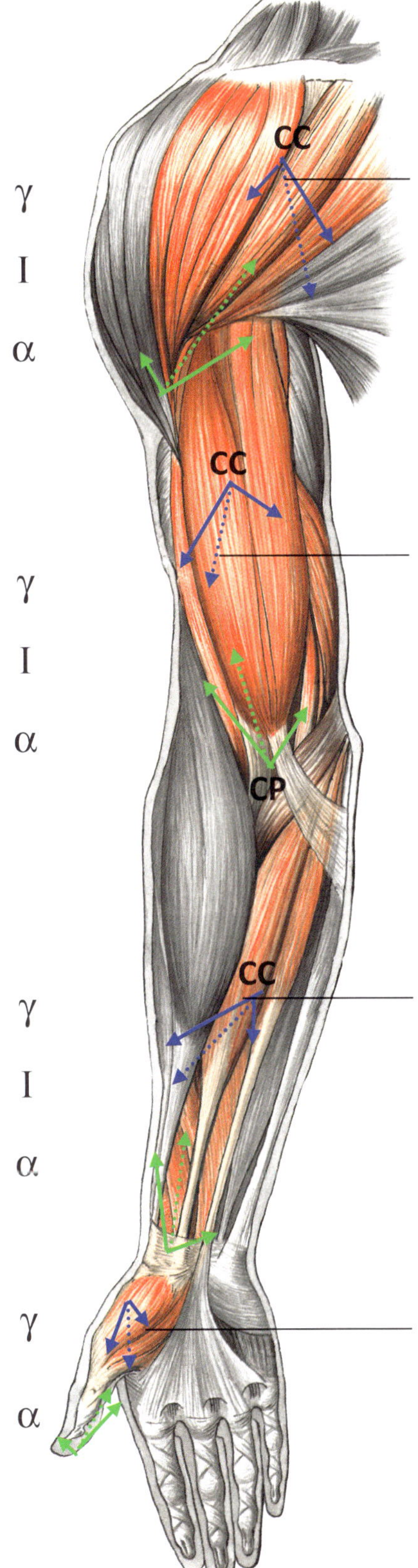

Pain during antepulsion of humerus
If the fascia located midway in the sulcus between the deltoid and the clavicular portion of the pectoralis major muscle (CC) is densified, then the afferents from a few neuromuscular spindles are not fired and their alpha circuits are not activated.
The contraction from the extrafusal muscle fibres that are activated shifts the tendinous resultant outside of its physiological axis. Consequently, a conflict occurs at the glenohumeral joint and the deltoid tendon.

Pain during antepulsion of cubitus
If the fascia located midway of the arm over the biceps brachii muscle belly (CC) is densified, then the afferents from a few neuromuscular spindles are not fired and their alpha circuits are not activated.
The contraction from the extrafusal muscle fibres that are activated shifts the tendinous resultant outside of its physiological axis. Consequently, a conflict occurs at the elbow joint (CP).

Pain during antepulsion of carpus
If the fascia located over the muscle belly of flexor carpi radialis (CC) is densified, the afferents from a few neuromuscular spindles are not fired and their alpha circuits are then not activated.
The contraction from the extrafusal muscle fibres that are activated shifts the tendinous resultant outside of its physiological axis. Consequently, a conflict occurs at the carpal joints and sometimes a compensatory cyst may be formed in the flexor carpi radialis tendon.

Pain during antepulsion of the thumb
If the fascia located over the centre of the thenar eminence (CC) is densified, then the afferents from a few neuromuscular spindles are not fired and hence their alpha circuits are not activated.
The contraction from the extrafusal muscle fibres that are activated shifts the tendinous resultant outside of its physiological axis. Consequently, a conflict occurs at the metacarpophalangeal and interphalangeal joints.

Fig. 2.9. Dysfunctions of the gamma circuit.
(From G. Chiarugi and L. Bucciante, Istituzioni di anatomia dell'uomo. Piccin Nuova Libraria, Padova 1983, modified).

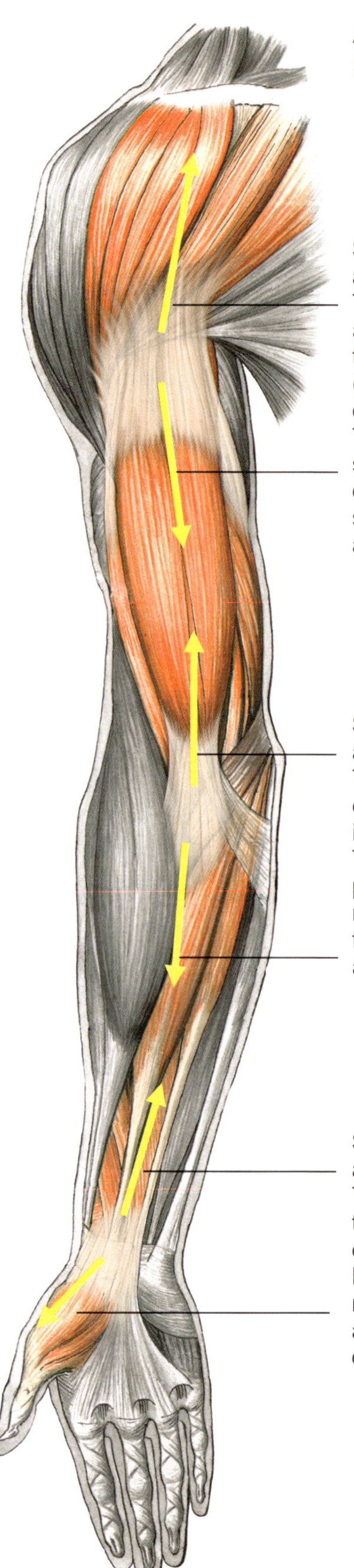

ANTEPULSION SEQUENCE AND STRETCH REFLEX

Synergy between the MF units of ante-humerus and ante-cubitus
The more superficial muscle fibres of pectoralis major and deltoid give origin to a tendinous expansion forming the aponeurotic fascia of the anterior region of the arm (Fig. 2.12). The contraction of the ante-humerus MF unit determines a proximal traction of the anterior brachial fascia. The brachialis muscle originates from the intermuscular septa of the brachial fascia, hence during its contraction it determines a distal traction. These myofascial insertions synchronise the involvement of the an-hu MF unit with that of an-cu.

Synergy between the MF units of ante-cubitus and ante-carpus
The more superficial muscle fibres of biceps brachii give origin to a tendinous expansion (lacertus fibrosus) that inserts into the aponeurotic fascia of the forearm (Fig. 2.13). The contraction of the ante-cubitus MF unit determines a proximal traction of the anterior antebrachial fascia. Many muscle fibres of the flexor carpi radialis originate from this fascia, its contraction determines a distal traction of the anterior antebrachial fascia.

Synergy between the MF units of ante-carpus and ante-digiti
The muscle fibres of palmaris longus give origin to a tendinous expansion forming the fascia of the thenar eminence (Fig. 2.15). The contraction of the ante-carpus MF unit determines a proximal traction of this fascia. The muscles of the thenar eminence originate from this fascia and the flexor retinaculum, their contraction determines a distal traction of the retinaculum.

Fig. 2.10. Synergy of the antepulsion sequence in the upper limb.
(From G. Chiarugi and L. Bucciante, Istituzioni di anatomia dell'uomo. Piccin Nuova Libraria, Padova 1983, modified).

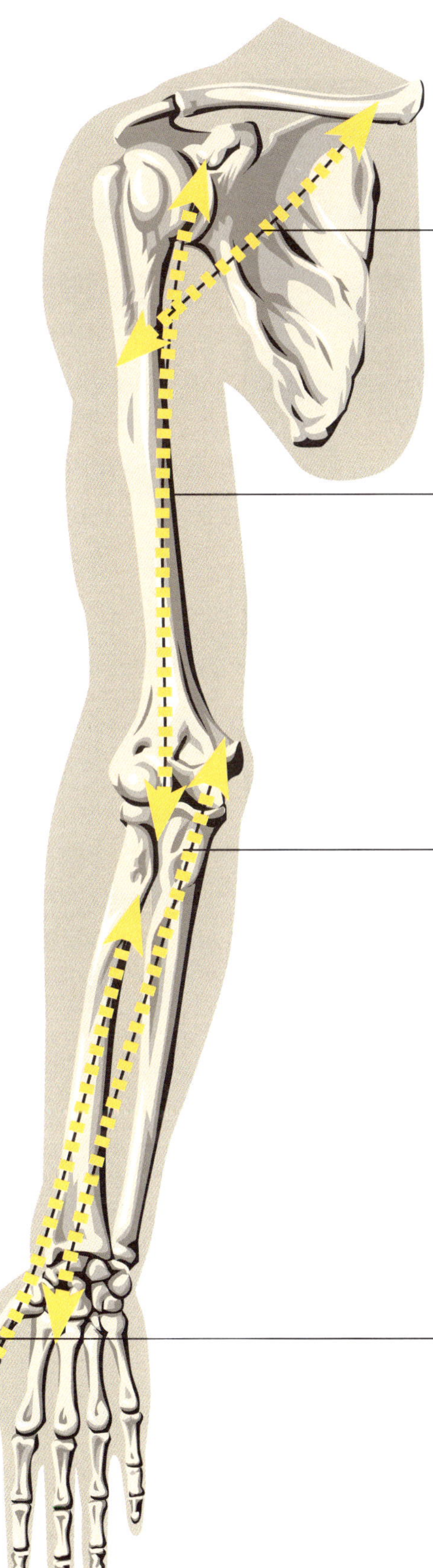

Fig. 2.11. Biarticular muscles for antepulsion in the upper limb.

ACTIVATION OF THE GOLGI TENDON ORGANS

Combined action between ante-scapula and ante-humerus
The clavicular fibres of the pectoralis major muscle act upon the antepulsion of scapula and humerus. Scapula and humerus form a single functional unit hence antepulsion of one segment is always adapting with the other.

Combined action between ante-humerus and ante-cubitus
The biceps brachii muscle originates from the coracoid process through its short head and inserts on the radial tuberosity. Therefore, it simultaneously acts upon humerus and cubitus.
When the shoulder and elbow are flexed, the Golgi tendon organs of the proximal and distal tendons of biceps brachii must interact together based upon the angular variations of both joints.

Combined action between ante-cubitus and ante-carpus
The flexor carpi radialis muscle originates from the medial epicondyle and inserts on the metacarpals. The Golgi tendon organs of the proximal and distal tendons must progressively inhibit some alpha fibres of the flexor carpi radialis muscle during joint angle variations.

Combined action between ante-carpus and ante-digiti (thumb)
The flexor pollicis longus muscle originates underneath the radial tuberosity and inserts on the base of the distal phalanx of the thumb, therefore acting simultaneously on the wrist and thumb.
When grasping an object and bringing it towards the body, the Golgi tendon organs of the proximal and distal tendons of the flexor pollicis longus muscle must progressively inhibit some alpha fibres. This is determined by the variations in joint angle and by the torsion of the collagen fibres of the tendon.

FASCIAE OF THE ANTEPULSION SEQUENCE IN THE UPPER LIMB

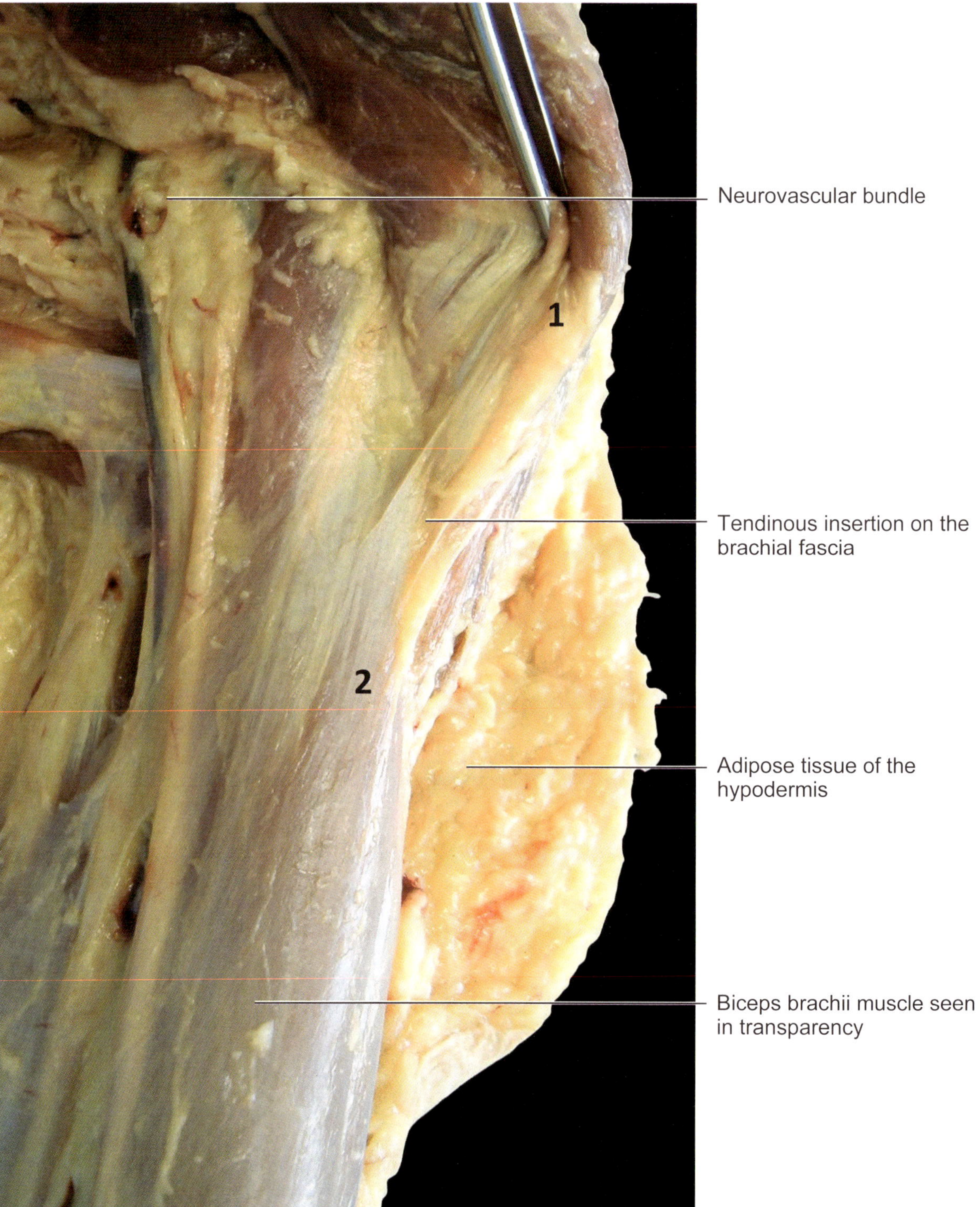

Fig. 2.12. Tendinous expansions of the pectoralis major muscle on the anterior brachial fascia. The forceps (1) proximally tractions the pectoralis major muscle, this traction propagates on the anterior brachial fascia (2).

In the figures horizontal lines indicate anatomical parts whilst numbers (1, 2) indicate the physiology of the fascia. Number 1 indicates a determined action and number 2 indicates its effect.

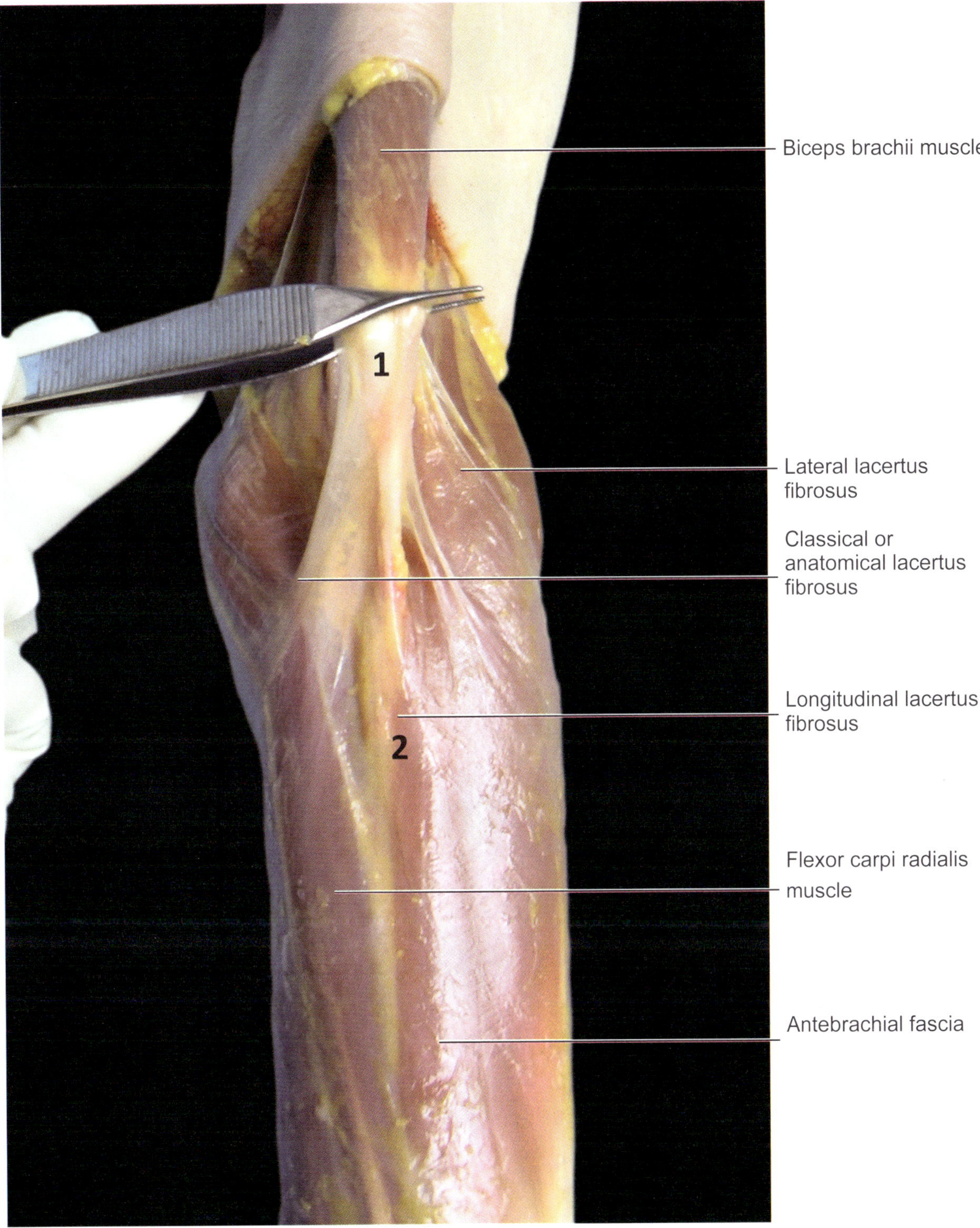

Fig. 2.13. Tendinous expansion of the lacertus fibrosus on the antebrachial fascia. The forceps lifts the lacertus fibrosus (1). The stretch propagates towards the ulnar aspect of the forearm, both longitudinally (2) and laterally towards the radial aspect of the forearm.

FASCIAE OF THE ANTEPULSION SEQUENCE IN THE UPPER LIMB

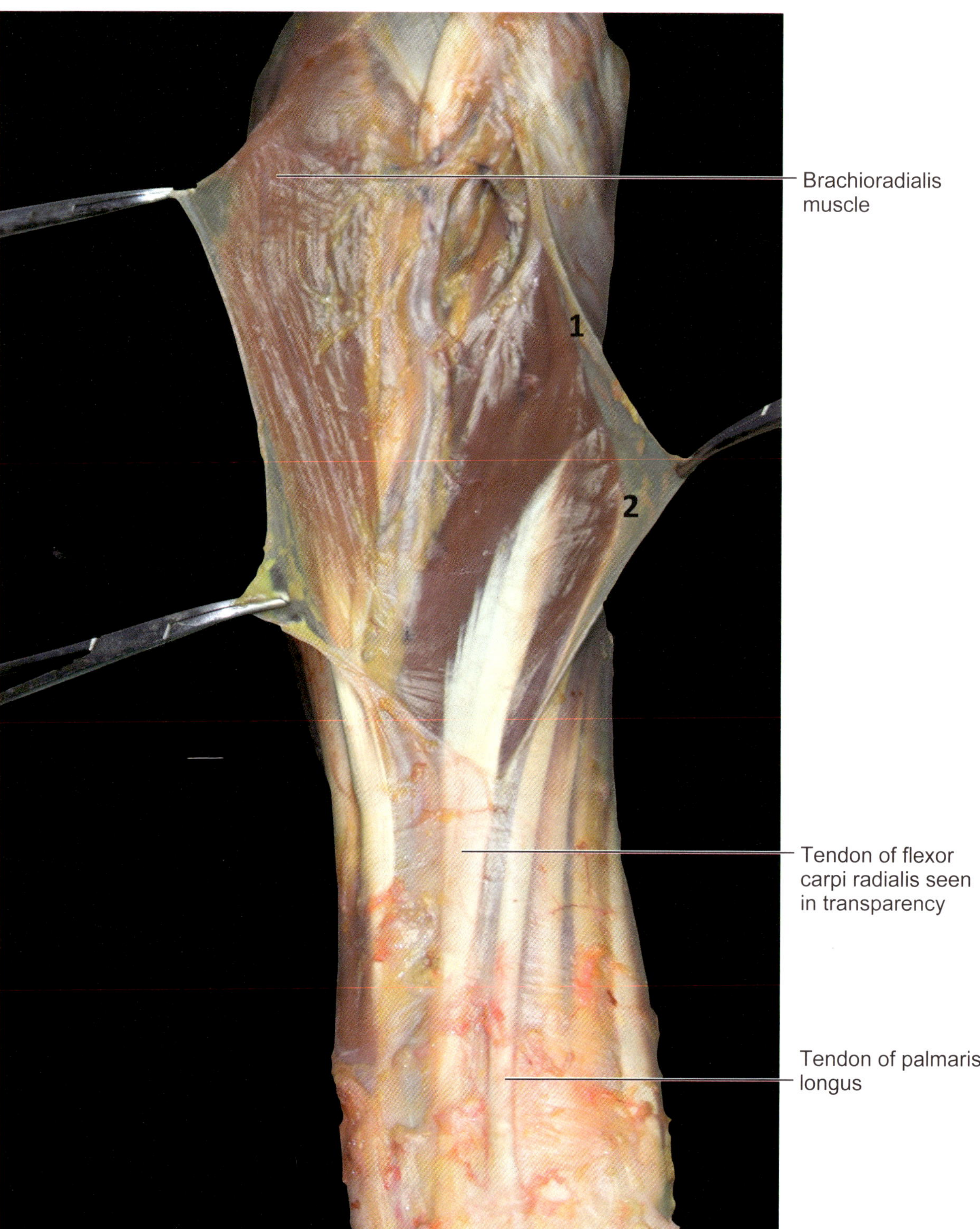

Fig. 2.14. Anterior antebrachial fascia cut and lifted laterally. When lifting the antebrachial fascial laterally up to the area where the lacertus fibrosus is still present (1), it may be observed that many muscle fibres from flexor carpi radialis have their origin (2) on this fascia.

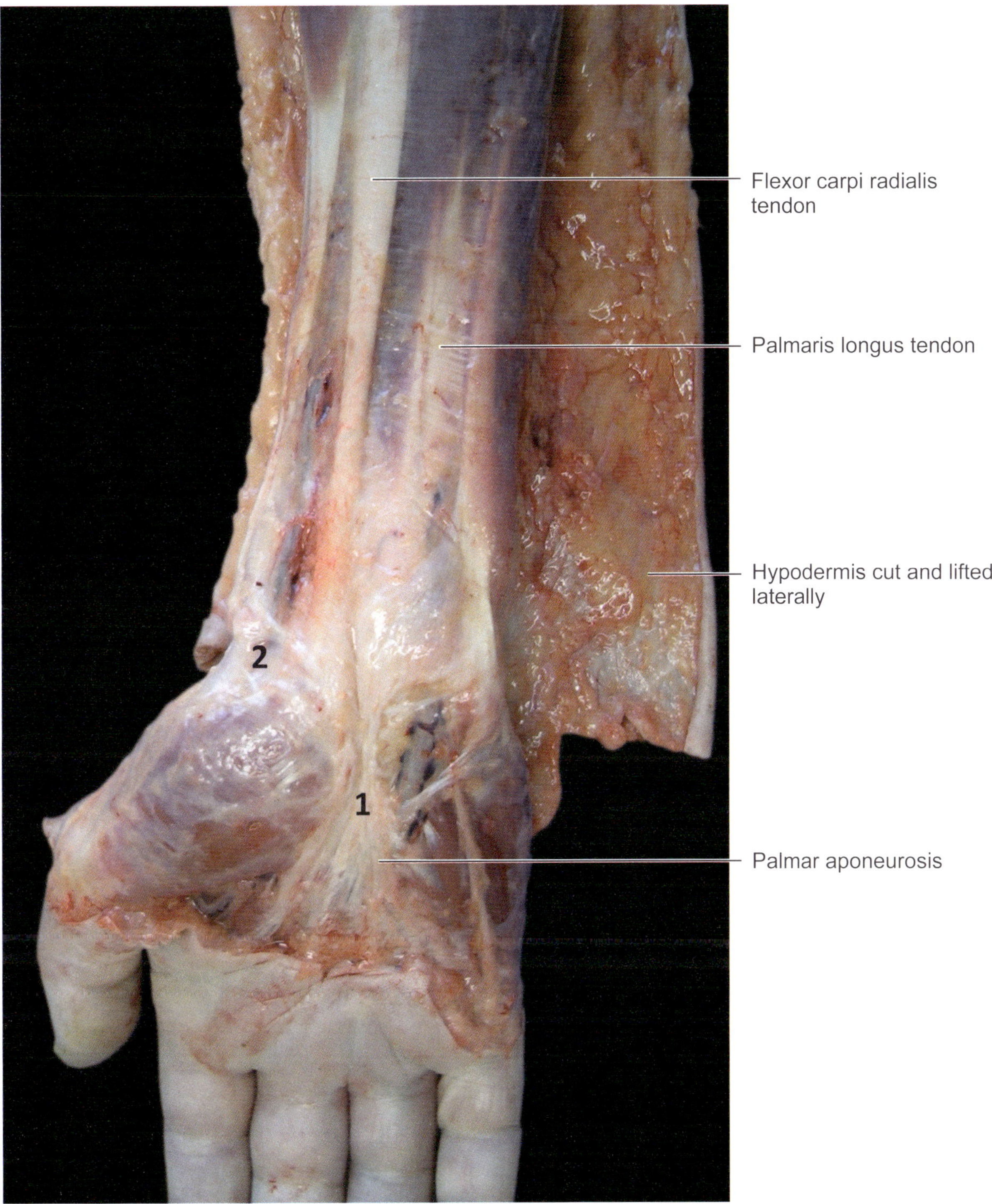

Fig. 2.15. Palmar fascia with palmaris longus aponeurosis. The muscles of the thenar eminence partly take origin from the palmar aponeurosis (1) and from the flexor retinaculum (2), they create a distal traction on these fasciae during their contraction.

POSTERIOR REGION OF THE UPPER LIMB, RETROPULSION SEQUENCE

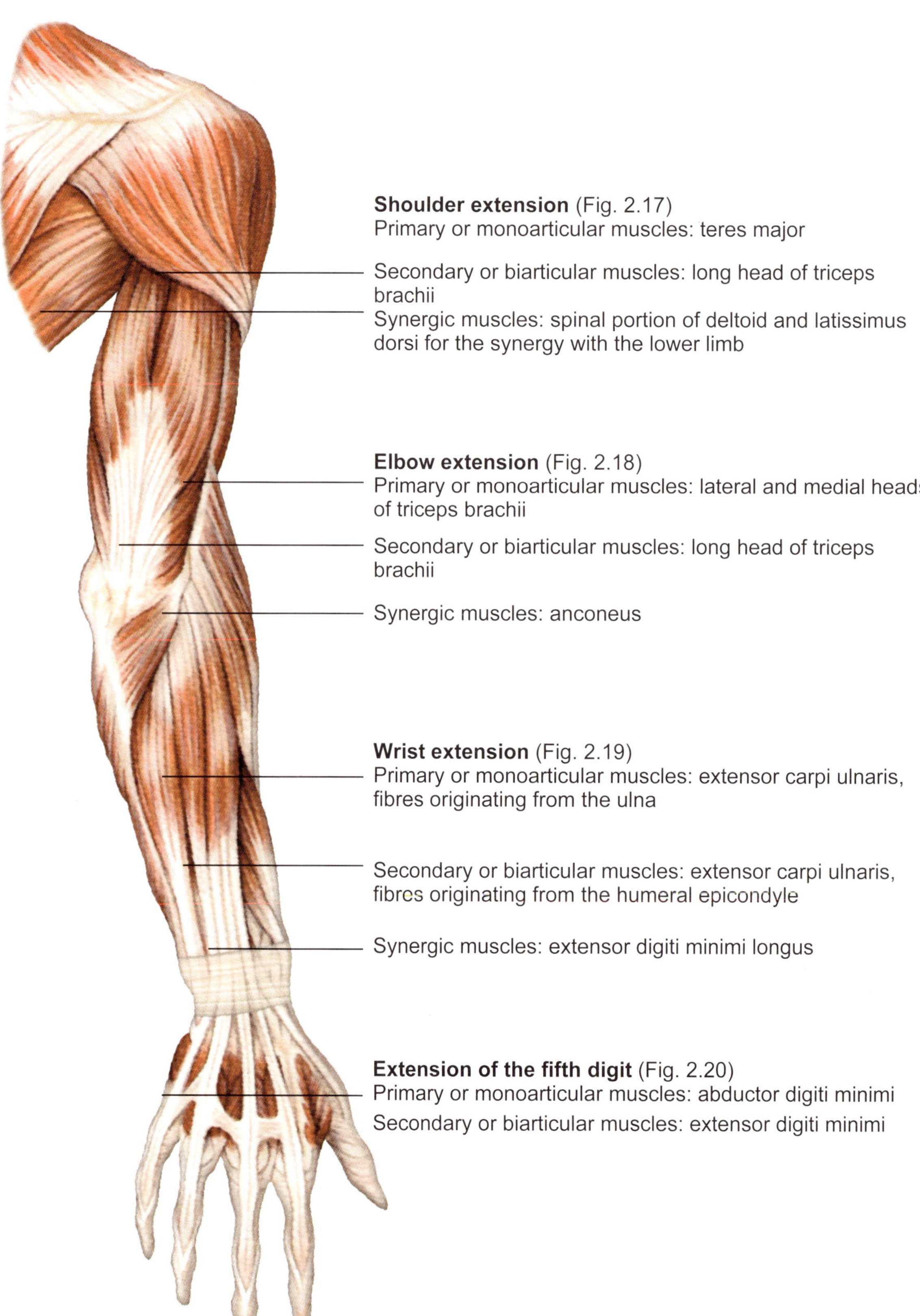

Fig. 2.16. Posterior region of the upper limb.

SEGMENTARY MOVEMENTS IMPLEMENTED BY THE MF UNITS OF RETROPULSION

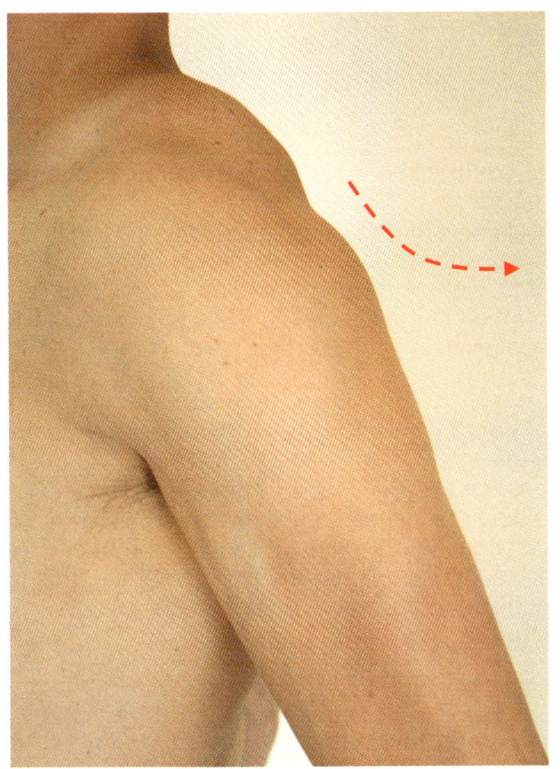

Fig. 2.17. Shoulder extension, managed throughout its range by the myofascial unit of retro-humerus.

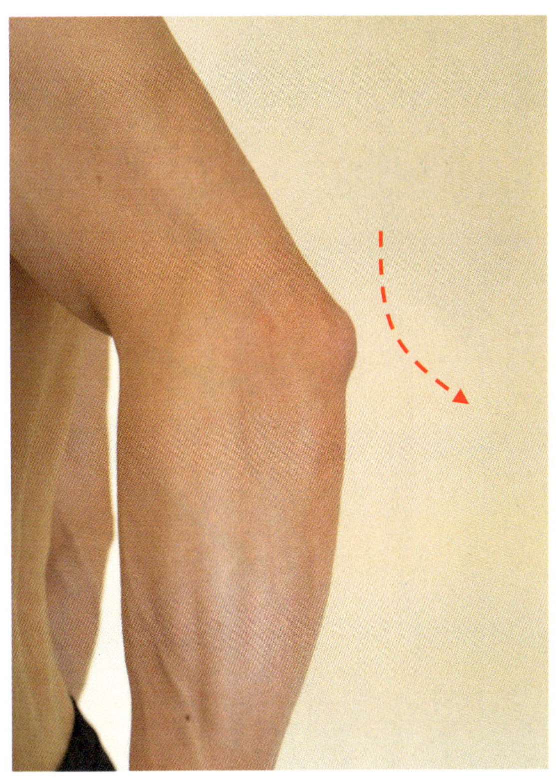

Fig. 2.18. Elbow extension, managed throughout its range by the MF unit of retro-cubitus.

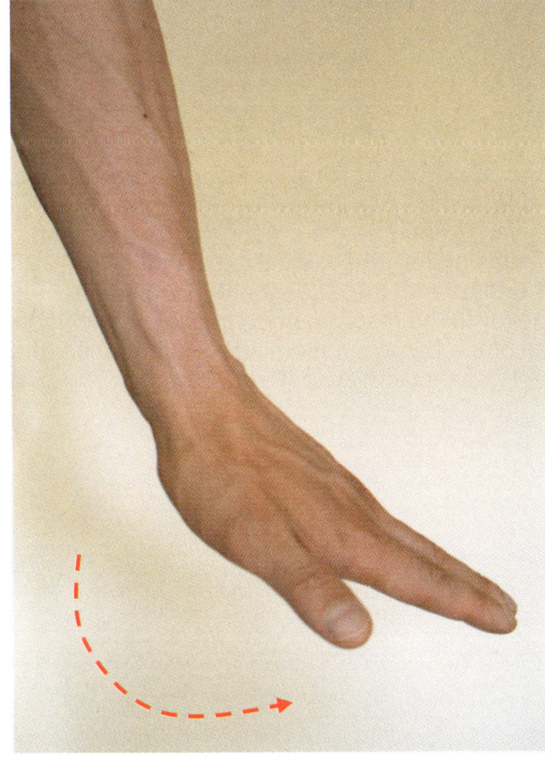

Fig. 2.19. Wrist extension, managed throughout its range by the MF unit of retro-carpus.

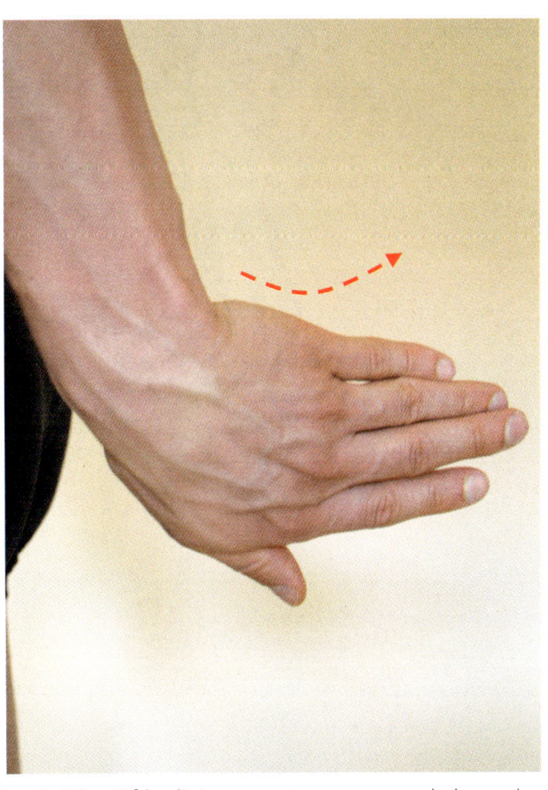

Fig. 2.20. Fifth digit extension, managed throughout its range by the MF unit of retro-digiti (fifth digit).

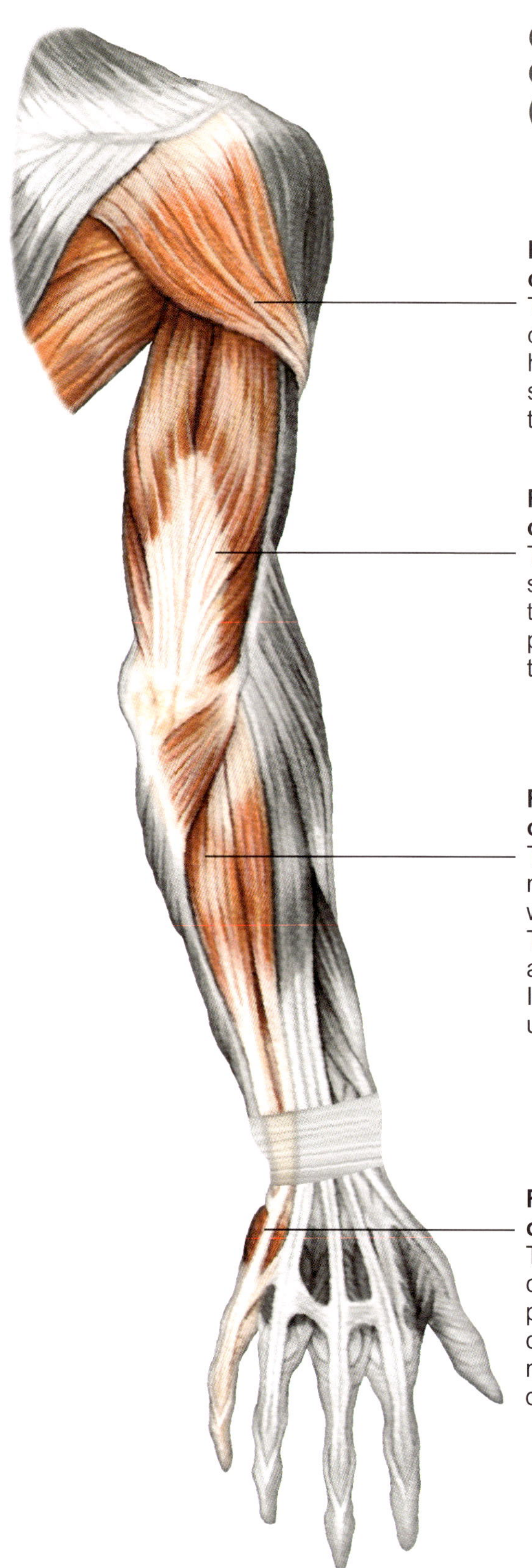

Fig. 2.21. Fascial compartments for retropulsion muscles.

COMPARTMENTS FOR THE MUSCLES OF RETROPULSION, UPPER LIMB (Fig. 2.22)

Fascial compartment for the retropulsion muscles of humerus
The fascia covering the latissimus dorsi muscle is continuous with the fascia of the teres major and long head of triceps brachii muscles. The fascia of the spinal portion of the deltoid muscle also connects with the same fascia.

Fascial compartment for the retropulsion muscles of cubitus
The posterior brachial fascia forms a sheath surrounding the triceps brachii muscle through the medial and lateral septa. It continues with the posterior antebrachial fascia passing over the triceps tendon, the olecranon and the anconeus muscle.

Fascial compartment for the retropulsion muscles of carpus
The muscles extensor carpi ulnaris and extensor digiti minimi take their origin from the lateral epicondyle where the extensor digitorum muscle also inserts. The posterior antebrachial fascia passes over the anconeus muscle and inserts on the ulna (Fig. 2.29). It forms a septum separating the extensor carpi ulnaris and extensor digiti minimi muscles.

Fascial compartment for the retropulsion muscles of digiti V
The fascial compartment surrounding the extensor carpi ulnaris and extensor digiti minimi muscles passes underneath the extensor retinaculum. It continues with the fascial compartment containing the muscles of the hypothenar eminence and the fourth dorsal interosseous muscle (Fig. 2.30).

GLOBAL MOVEMENT IMPLEMENTED BY THE RETROPULSION SEQUENCE

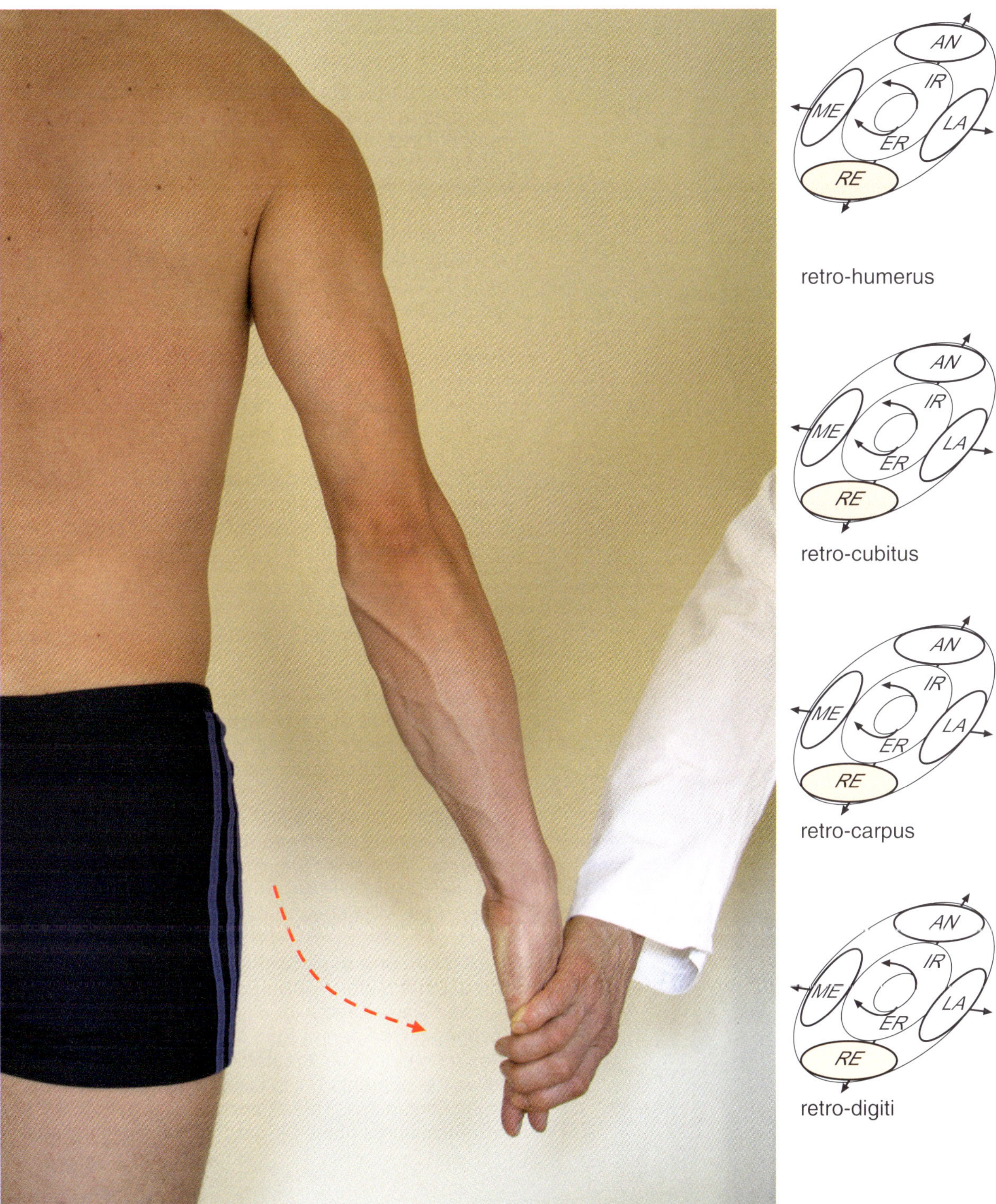

Fig. 2.22. Contraction of the retropulsion sequence bringing the entire upper limb posteriorly.

In order to involve the four MF units of retropulsion, resistance has to be applied to the fifth digit. If resistance were applied at the elbow, only the unit of retro-humerus would be activated. This resistance allows for the recruitment of the four MF units through the stretch reflex.

The fascial stretching of the retropulsion compartments also activate the Paccini and Ruffini receptors giving proprioception for directional movement.

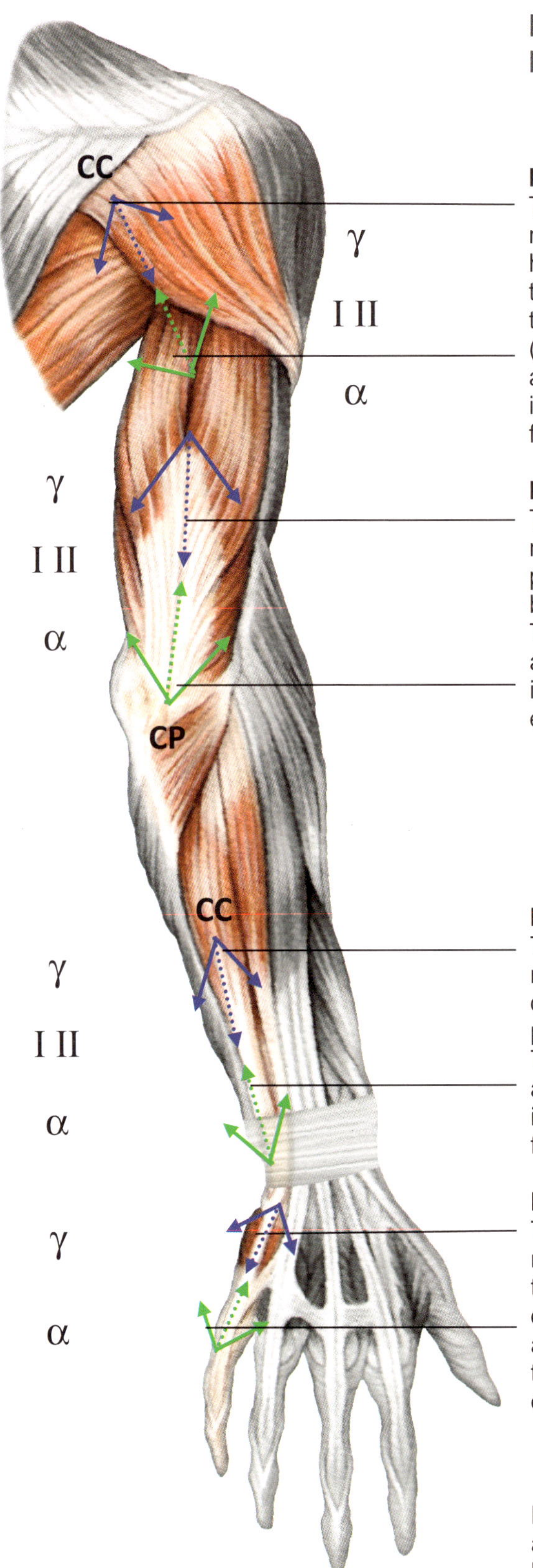

Fig. 2.23. Normal functioning of the gamma circuit.

PHYSIOLOGY OF THE RETROPULSION MF UNITS IN THE UPPER LIMB

Myofascial unit of retro-humerus (re-hu)
The gamma motor neurone stimulates the intrafusal muscle fibres of the spinal portion of deltoid, long head of triceps brachii and latissimus dorsi. The tractions on the perimysium and fascia converge towards the posterior bundles of the deltoid muscle (CC). The adaptability of the perimysium allows the afferents I, II to close the circuit triggering the alpha impulse. This allows the contraction of the extrafusal fibres of the MF unit retro-humerus.

Myofascial unit of retro-cubitus (re-cu)
The gamma motor neurone stimulates the intrafusal muscle fibres of triceps brachii, their tractions on the perimysium converge on the muscle belly of triceps brachii (CC).
The adaptability of the perimysium allows the afferents I, II to close the circuit triggering the alpha impulse. This stimulus causes the contraction of the extrafusal fibres of the MF unit retro-cubitus.

Myofascial unit of retro-carpus (re-ca)
The gamma motor neurone stimulates the intrafusal muscle fibres of extensor carpi ulnaris and extensor digiti minimi longus, where their tractions on the perimysium converge in the centre of coordination. The adaptability of the perimysium allows the afferents I, II to close the circuit triggering the alpha impulse. This allows the contraction of the extrafusal fibres of the MF unit retro-carpus.

Myofascial unit of retro-digiti (re-di)
The gamma motor neurone stimulates the intrafusal muscle fibres of abductor digiti minimi, their tractions on the perimysium converge in the centre of coordination. The adaptability of the perimysium allows the afferents I, II to close the circuit triggering the alpha impulse. This allows the contraction of the extrafusal fibres of the MF unit retro-digiti, fifth finger.

NB. In these figures, the abbreviations CC and CP are not reported for each MF unit due to space limitations. The CC is located in the convergence of the blue vectors, the CP is located in the convergence of the green vectors.

ARTICULAR CONFLICTS IN THE RETROPULSION UNITS IN THE UPPER LIMB

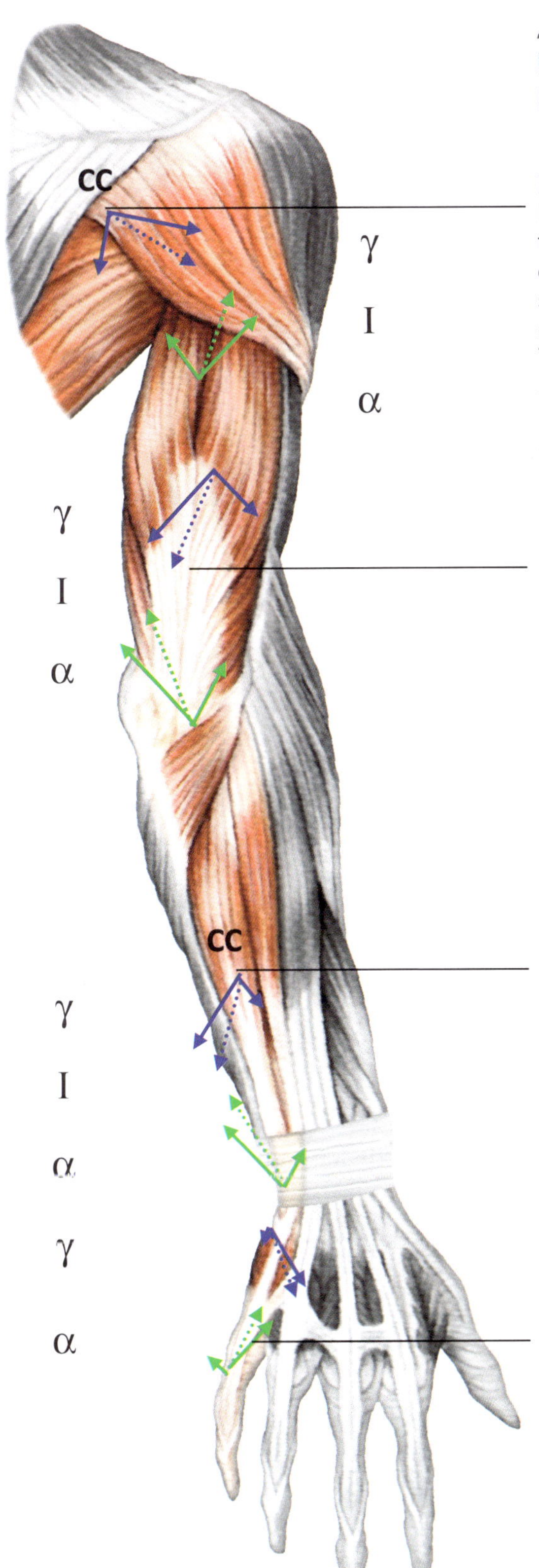

Pain during retropulsion of humerus
If the fascia located at the intersection of the deltoid, triceps brachii and latissimus dorsi muscles (CC) is densified, the afferents from a few neuromuscular spindles are not fired and the alpha circuits are not activated.
The contraction from the extrafusal muscle fibres that are activated shifts the tendinous resultant outside of its physiological axis. Consequently, a conflict occurs at the glenohumeral joint.

Pain during retropulsion of cubitus
If the fascia located midway on the arm over the triceps brachii muscle belly (CC) is densified, the afferents from a few neuromuscular spindles are not fired and their alpha circuits are not activated.
The contraction from the extrafusal muscle fibres that are activated shifts the tendinous resultant outside of its physiological axis. Consequently, a conflict occurs at the elbow joint.

Pain during retropulsion of carpus
If the fascia located over the muscle belly of extensor carpi ulnaris (CC) is densified, the afferents from a few neuromuscular spindles are not fired and the alpha circuits are then not activated.
The contraction from the extrafusal muscle fibres that are activated shifts the tendinous resultant outside of its physiological axis. Consequently, a conflict occurs at the carpal joints with the formation of enthesopathy

Pain during retropulsion of the fifth digit
If the fascia located laterally to the hypothenar eminence (CC) is densified, the afferents from a few neuromuscular spindles are not fired and the alpha circuits are then not activated.
The contraction from the extrafusal muscle fibres that are activated shifts the tendinous resultant outside of its physiological axis. Consequently, a conflict occurs at the metacarpophalangeal of the fifth digit.

Fig. 2.24. Dysfunctions of the gamma circuit.

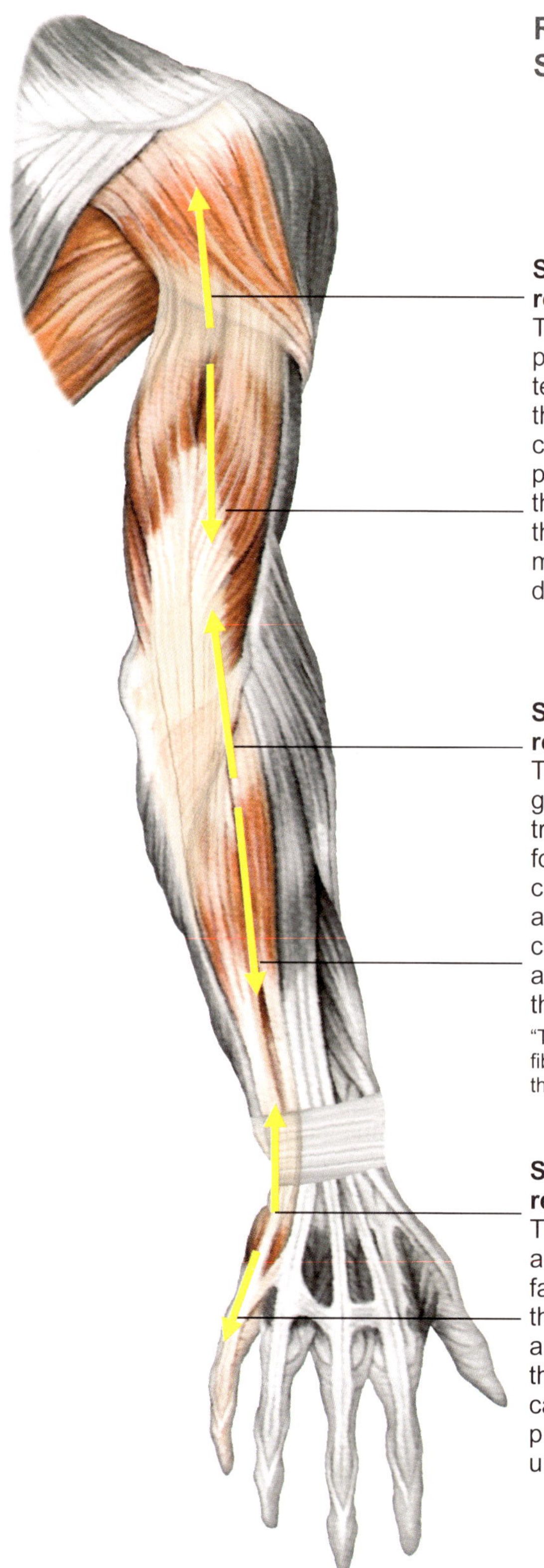

Fig. 2.25. Synergy of the retropulsion sequence in the upper limb.

RETROPULSION SEQUENCE AND STRETCH REFLEX

Synergy between the MF units of retro-humerus and retro-cubitus
The more superficial muscle fibres of the spinal portion of deltoid and latissimus dorsi give origin to a tendinous expansion forming the aponeurotic fascia of the posterior region of the arm (Fig. 2.27). Hence the contraction of the MF unit retro-humerus determines a proximal traction of the posterior brachial fascia. From the medial and lateral intermuscular septa of this fascia, the lateral and medial heads of the triceps brachii muscle originate, and their contraction also determines a distal traction of the brachial fascia.

Synergy between the MF units of retro-cubitus and retro-carpus
The more superficial muscle fibres of triceps brachii give origin to a tendinous expansion (lacertus fibrosus triceps) that inserts into the aponeurotic fascia of the forearm (Fig. 2.28). The contraction of the MF unit retro-cubitus determines a proximal traction of the posterior antebrachial fascia. Many muscle fibres of the extensor carpi ulnaris longus (Fig. 2.29) originate from this fascia, and their contraction also determines a distal traction of the antebrachial fascia.

"The forearm fascia is reinforced on its volar aspect by the lacertus fibrosus of the biceps muscle and dorsally by the lacertus fibrosus of the triceps muscle" (Fumagalli Z. 1974).

Synergy between the MF units of retro-carpus and retro-digiti
The muscle fibres of extensor carpi ulnaris give origin to a tendinous expansion that proceeds and inserts into the fascia of the hypothenar eminence (Fig. 2.30). Hence the contraction of the MF unit retro-carpus determines a proximal traction on the hypothenar fascia from which the muscles of the eminence have their origin. In this case, the neuromuscular spindles are activated by a proximal stretch. If the effort starts in the retro-digiti MF unit then the recruitment becomes disto-proximal.

ACTIVATION OF THE GOLGI TENDON ORGANS

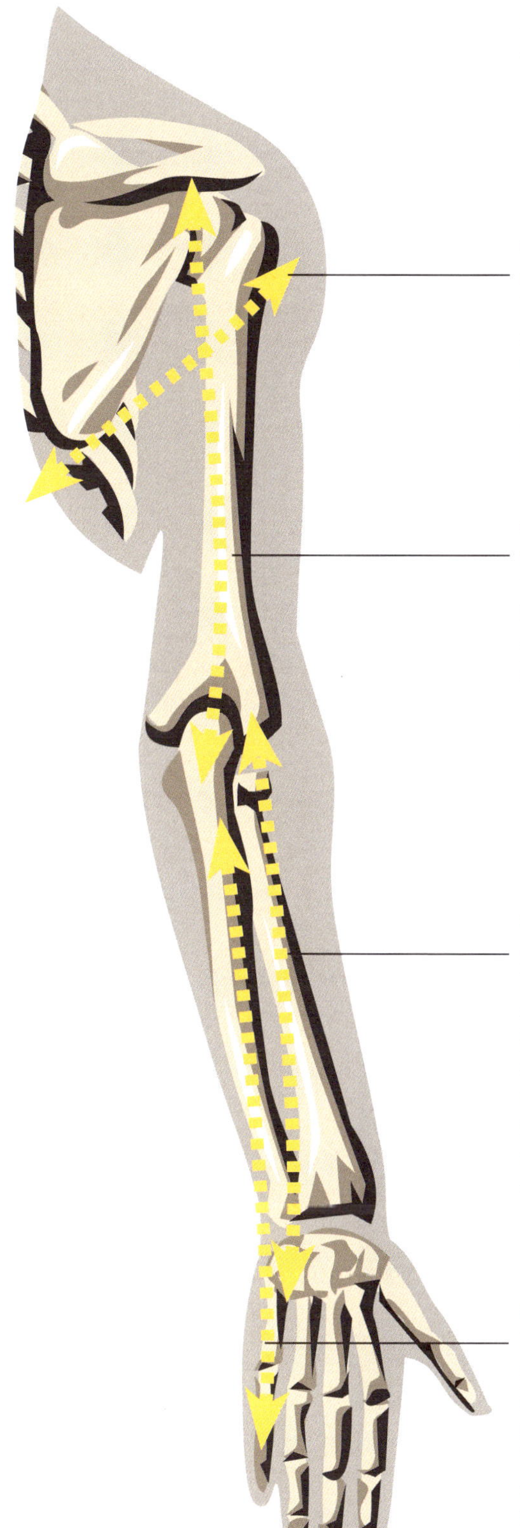

Fig. 2.26. Biarticular muscles for retropulsion in the upper limb.

Combined action between retro-scapula and retro-humerus
The latissimus dorsi muscle inserts on both the inferior angle of the scapula and the humerus, therefore, during retropulsion of the humerus it also acts upon the posterior movement of the scapula. Scapula and humerus form a single functional unit so that when one segment undergoes retropulsion the other also adapts with angular constancy.

Combined action between retro-humerus and retro-cubitus
The long head of the triceps brachii muscle originates from the infraglenoid tubercle of the scapula and inserts onto the olecranon of the ulna, hence it simultaneously acts upon humerus and cubitus.

Combined action between retro-cubitus and retro-carpus
The extensor carpi ulnaris muscle originates from the lateral epicondyle of the humerus and inserts on the base of the fifth metacarpal bone, hence it simultaneously acts upon cubitus and carpus.
During elbow and wrist extension with ulnar deviation, the Golgi tendon organs are activated based upon the variations of joint angles and upon the torsion of the collagen fibres of the tendon.

Combined action between retro-carpus and retro-digiti
The extensor digiti minimi muscle originates from the epicondyle along with the extensor carpi ulnaris muscle and it inserts on the dorsal aponeurosis of the fifth digit, hence it acts simultaneously on the wrist and on the fifth digit.
When opening the hand and simultaneously extending the wrist, the Golgi tendon organs are activated based upon the variations of joint angles and upon the torsion of the collagen fibres belonging to the tendon of the extensor digiti minimi muscle.

FASCIAE OF THE RETROPULSION SEQUENCE IN THE UPPER LIMB

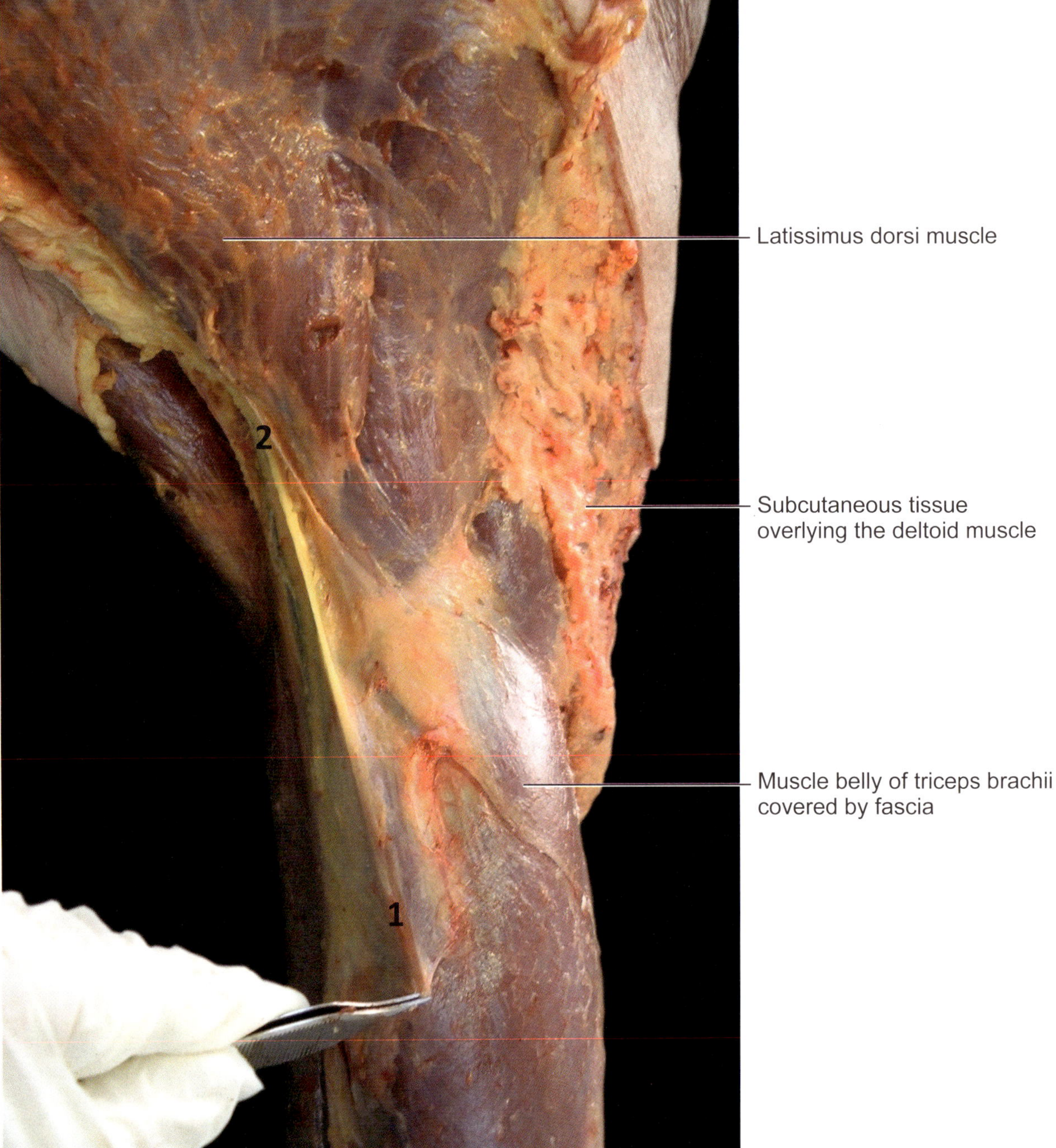

Fig. 2.27. Posterior brachial fascia in continuity with the fascia of the latissimus dorsi and teres major muscles. The distal traction of the posterior brachial fascia (1) propagates up to the fascia of the latissimus dorsi muscle (2).

In the figures horizontal lines indicate anatomical parts, whilst numbers (1, 2) indicate the physiology of the fascia. Number 1 indicates a determined action and number 2 indicates its effect.

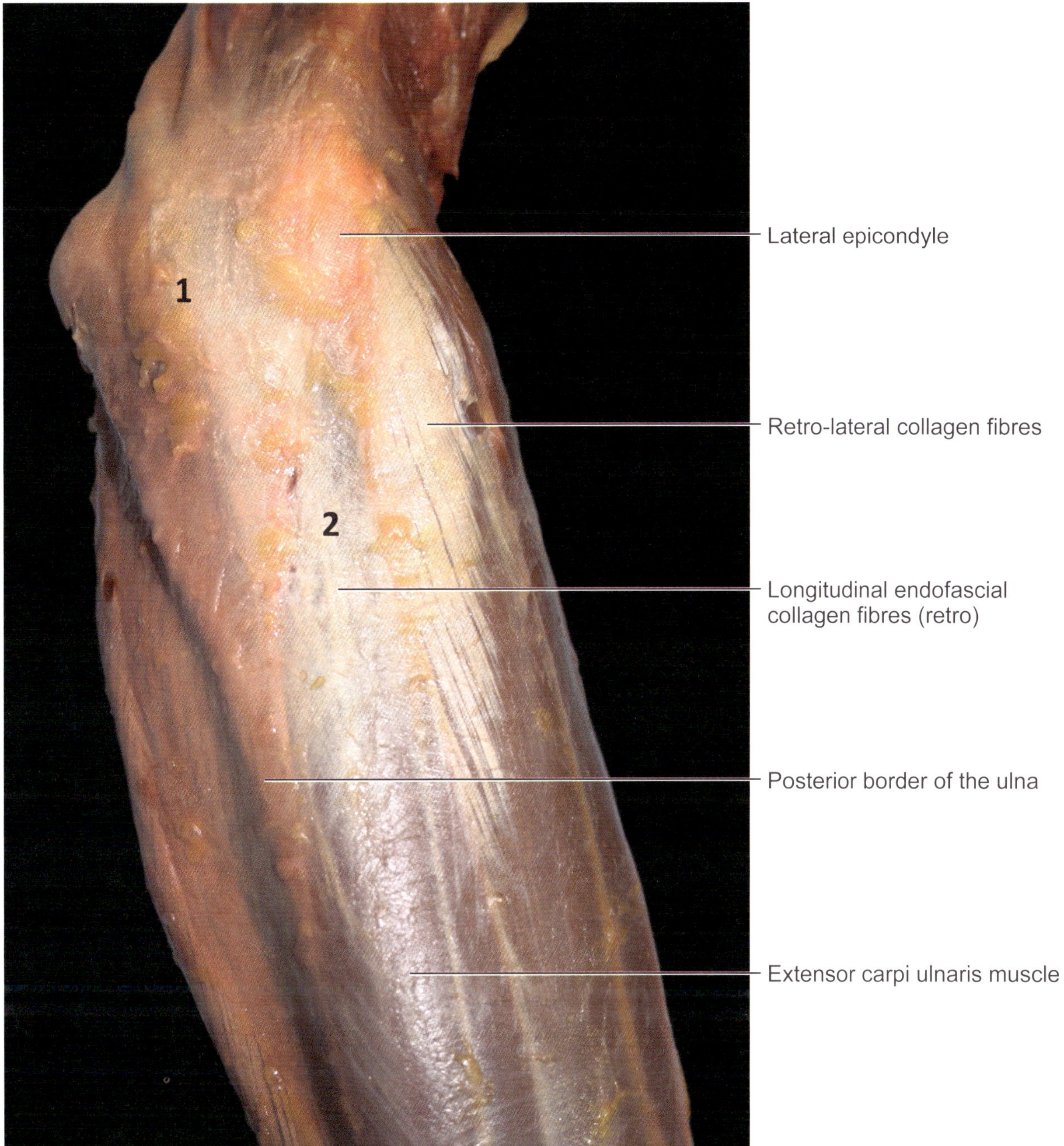

Fig. 2.28. Continuity between the posterior antebrachial fascia and the brachial fascia. The tendon of triceps brachii (1) sends longitudinal and oblique tendinous expansions onto the antebrachial fascia (2), similar to the lacertus fibrosus of the biceps brachii muscle.

FASCIAE OF THE RETROPULSION SEQUENCE IN THE UPPER LIMB

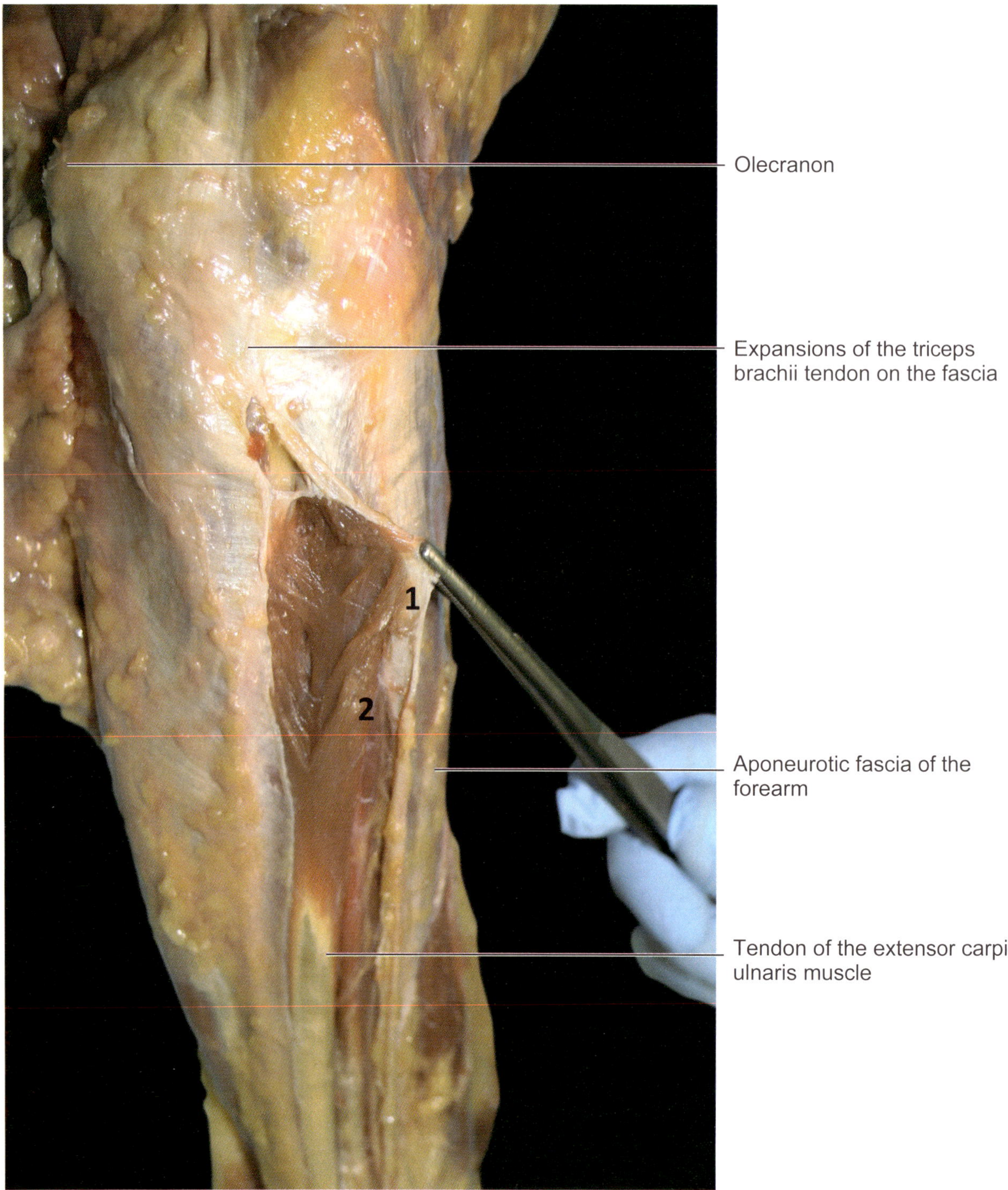

Fig. 2.29. Aponeurotic fascia of the posterior forearm cut and lifted laterally (1). Many muscle fibres of extensor carpi ulnaris take origin from the overlying fascia (2), hence the contraction of extensor carpi ulnaris determines a distal traction on the fascia whilst contraction of triceps pulls it proximally.

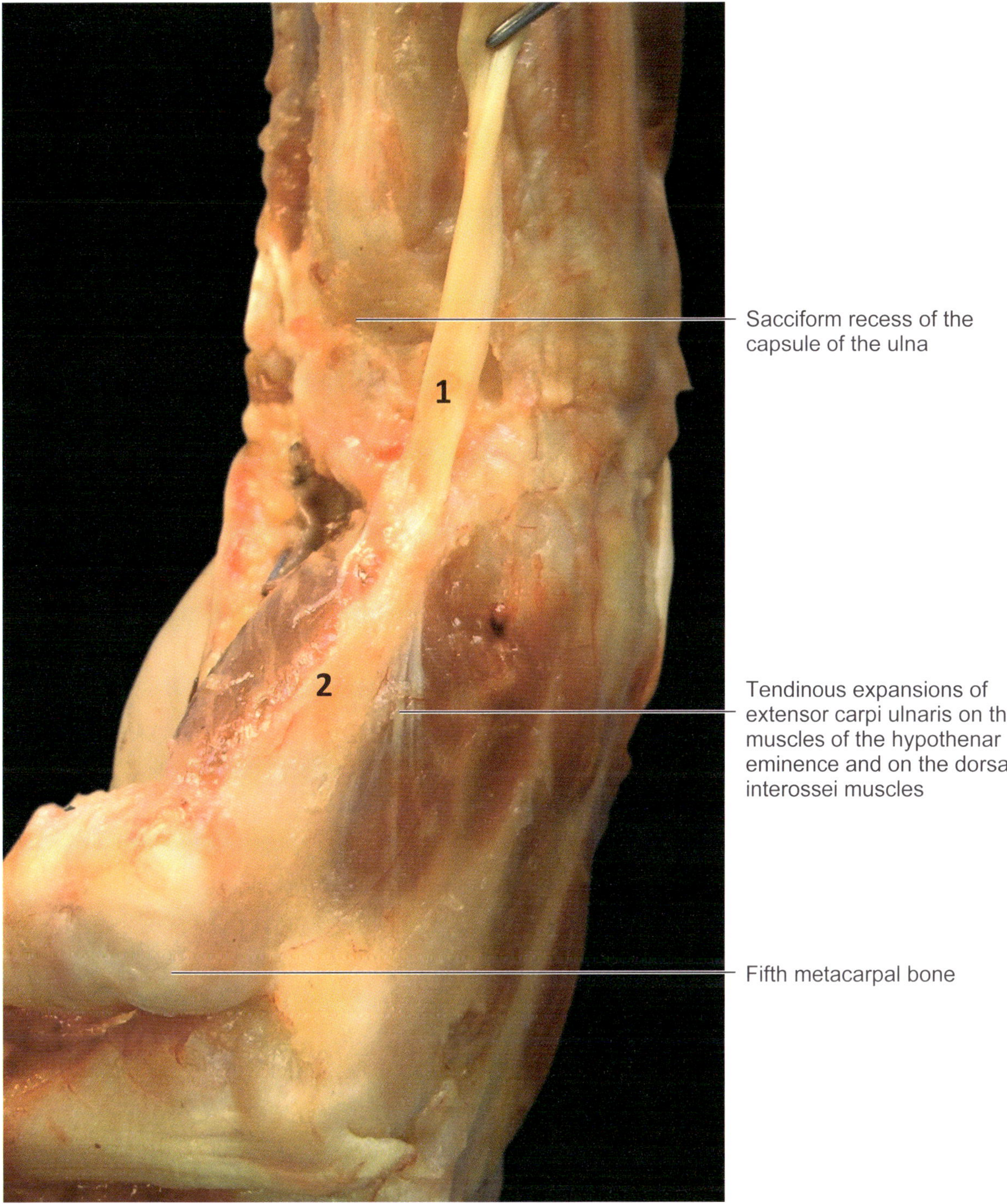

Fig. 2.30. Distal tendon of extensor carpi ulnaris (1). The insertion of the extensor carpi ulnaris muscle is not exclusively attached at the base of the fifth metacarpal. Some tendinous expansions are attached on the dorsal fascia of the hand (2) and others go to the fascia of the hypothenar eminence.

MEDIAL REGION OF THE UPPER LIMB, MEDIOPULSION SEQUENCE

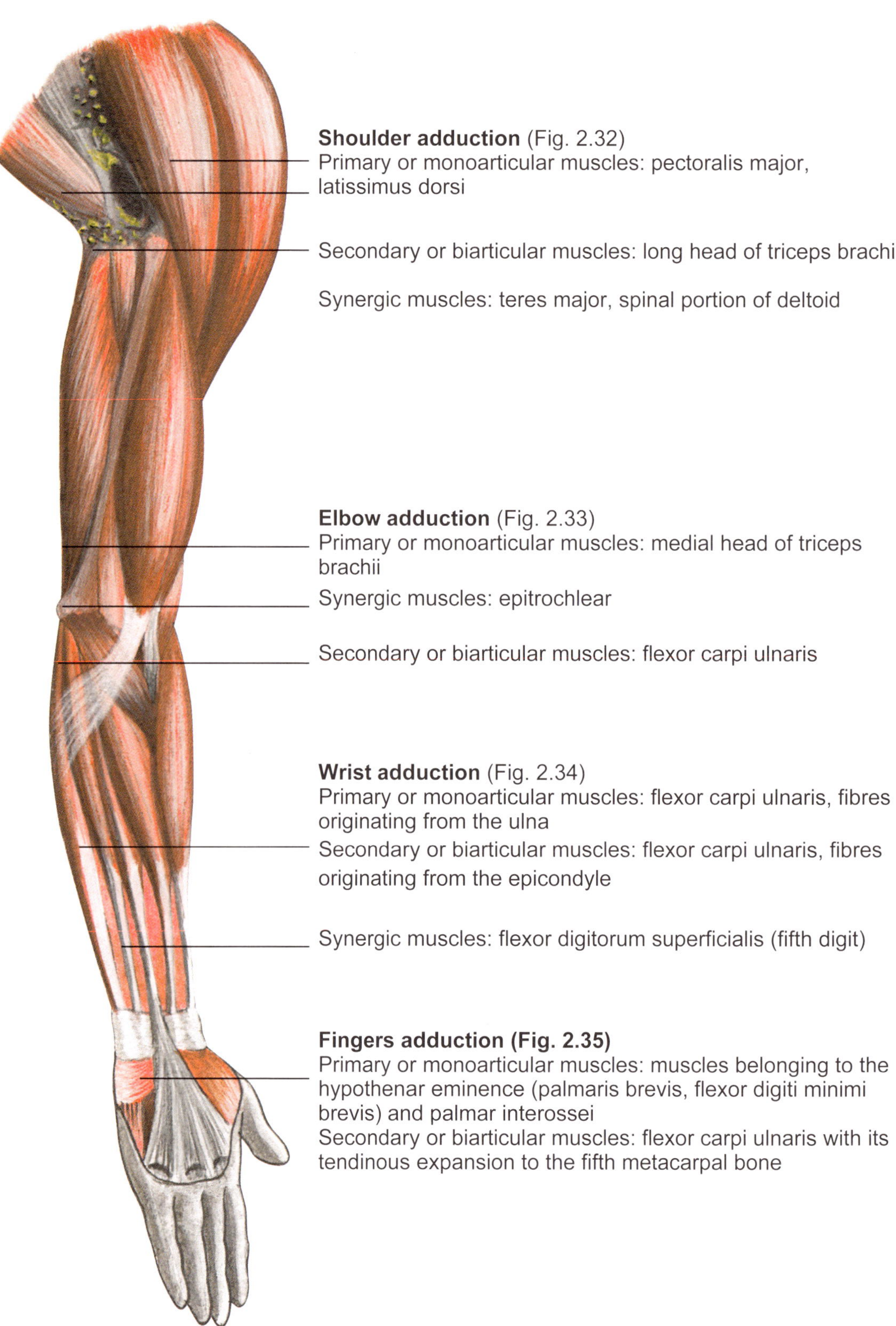

Fig. 2.31. Medial region of the upper limb.

SEGMENTARY MOVEMENTS IMPLEMENTED BY THE MF UNITS OF MEDIOPULSION

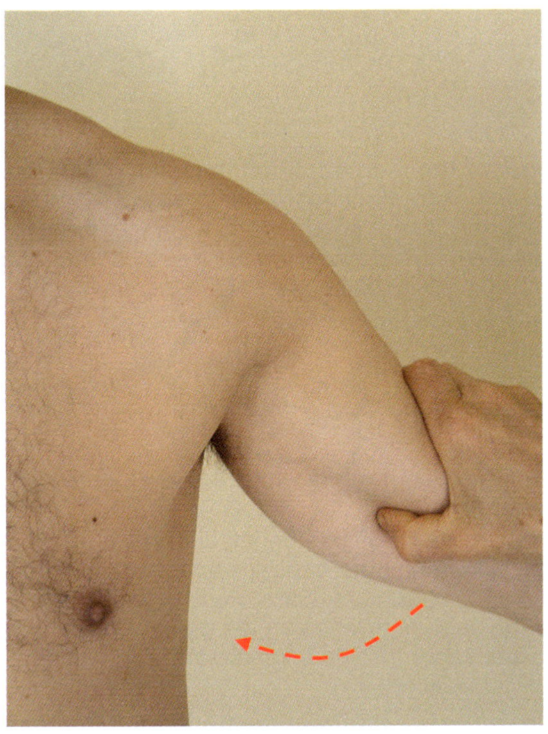

Fig. 2.32. Shoulder adduction against resistance managed by the myofascial unit of medio-humerus.

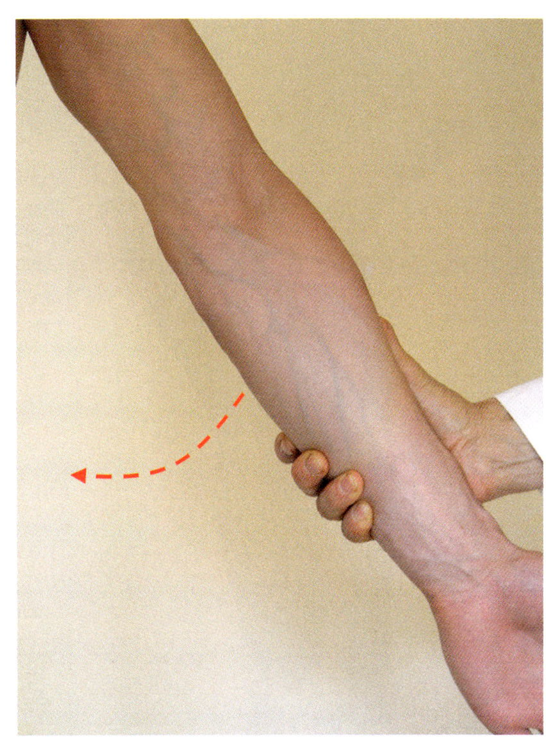

Fig. 2.33. Elbow adduction against resistance stabilised by the MF unit of medio-cubitus.

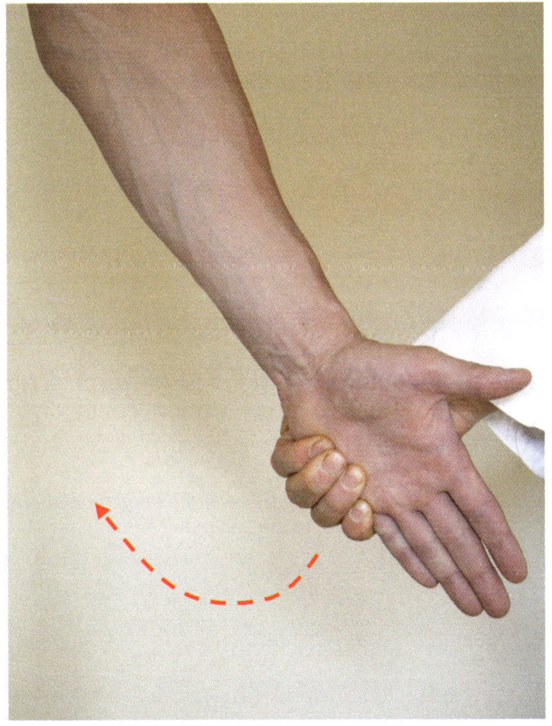

Fig. 2.34. Wrist adduction against resistance managed by the MF unit of medio-carpus.

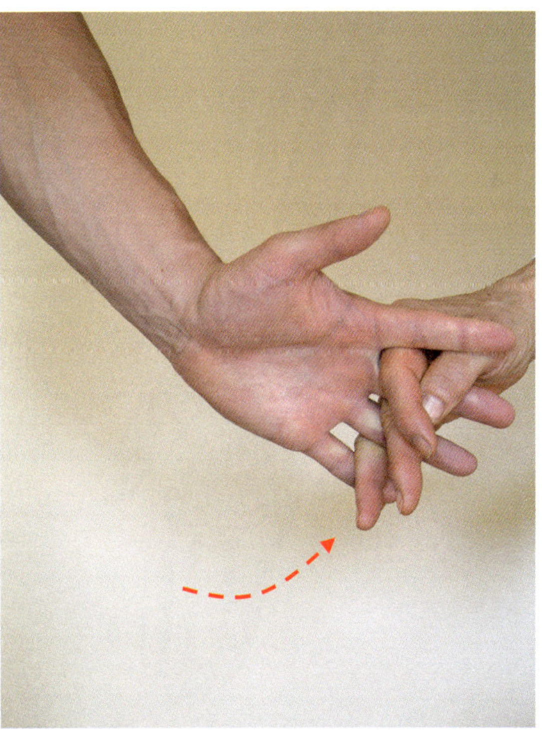

Fig. 2.35. Finger adduction against resistance managed by the MF unit of medio-digiti.

The hand of the operator applies resistance to the movement indicated by the arrow.

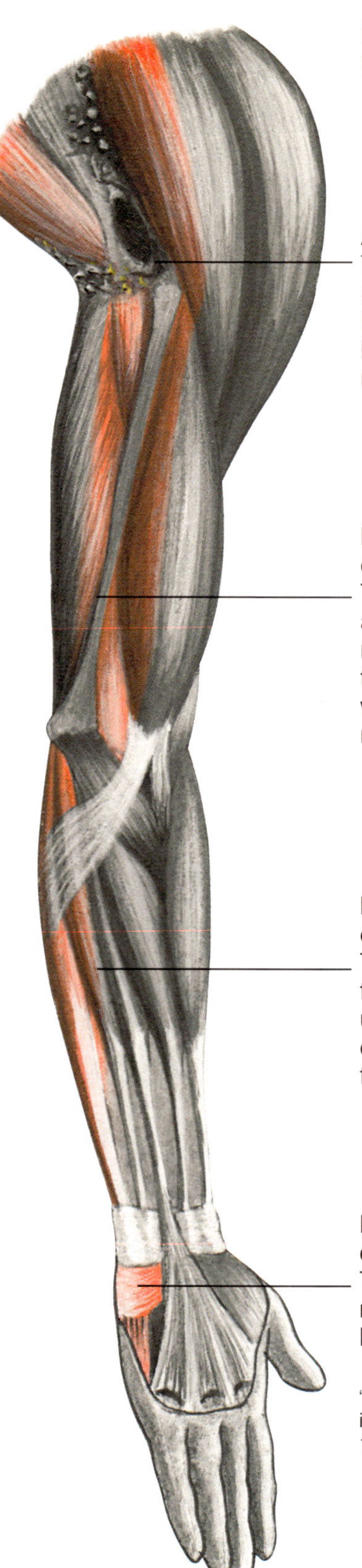

Fig. 2.36. Fascial compartments for mediopulsion muscles.

COMPARTMENTS FOR THE MUSCLES OF MEDIOPULSION, UPPER LIMB (Fig. 2.37.)

Axillary fascia for the mediopulsion muscles of humerus
The fascia covering the axilla has a medial muscular arch uniting the pectoralis major and latissimus dorsi muscles. Laterally it has a second arch uniting the medial border of the biceps brachii with the medial border of the triceps brachii muscles (Fig. 2.43).

Fascial septum between the mediopulsion muscles of cubitus
The axillary fascia continues into the medial region of the arm accompanying the medial intermuscular septum. The medial head of triceps and brachialis muscles take origin on this septum. The septum finishes on the medial epicondyle, where the epitrochlear muscles originate and contribute to medial elbow stabilisation.

Fascial compartment for the mediopulsion muscles of carpus
The flexor carpi ulnaris muscle originates with three heads: from the epitrochlea, from the olecranon and from the ulna. The palmaris longus muscle also originates from the epitrochlea, whilst the palmaris brevis muscle takes origin from its palmar aponeurosis.

Fascial compartment for the mediopulsion muscles of digiti V
The fascial compartment surrounding the flexor carpi ulnaris muscle continues with the fascial compartment containing the hypothenar eminence muscles.

"The flexor carpi ulnaris muscle inserts onto the pisiform bone, from there it continues to the uncinate process and to the fifth metacarpal" (Gray H. 1993).

GLOBAL MOVEMENT IMPLEMENTED BY THE MEDIOPULSION SEQUENCE

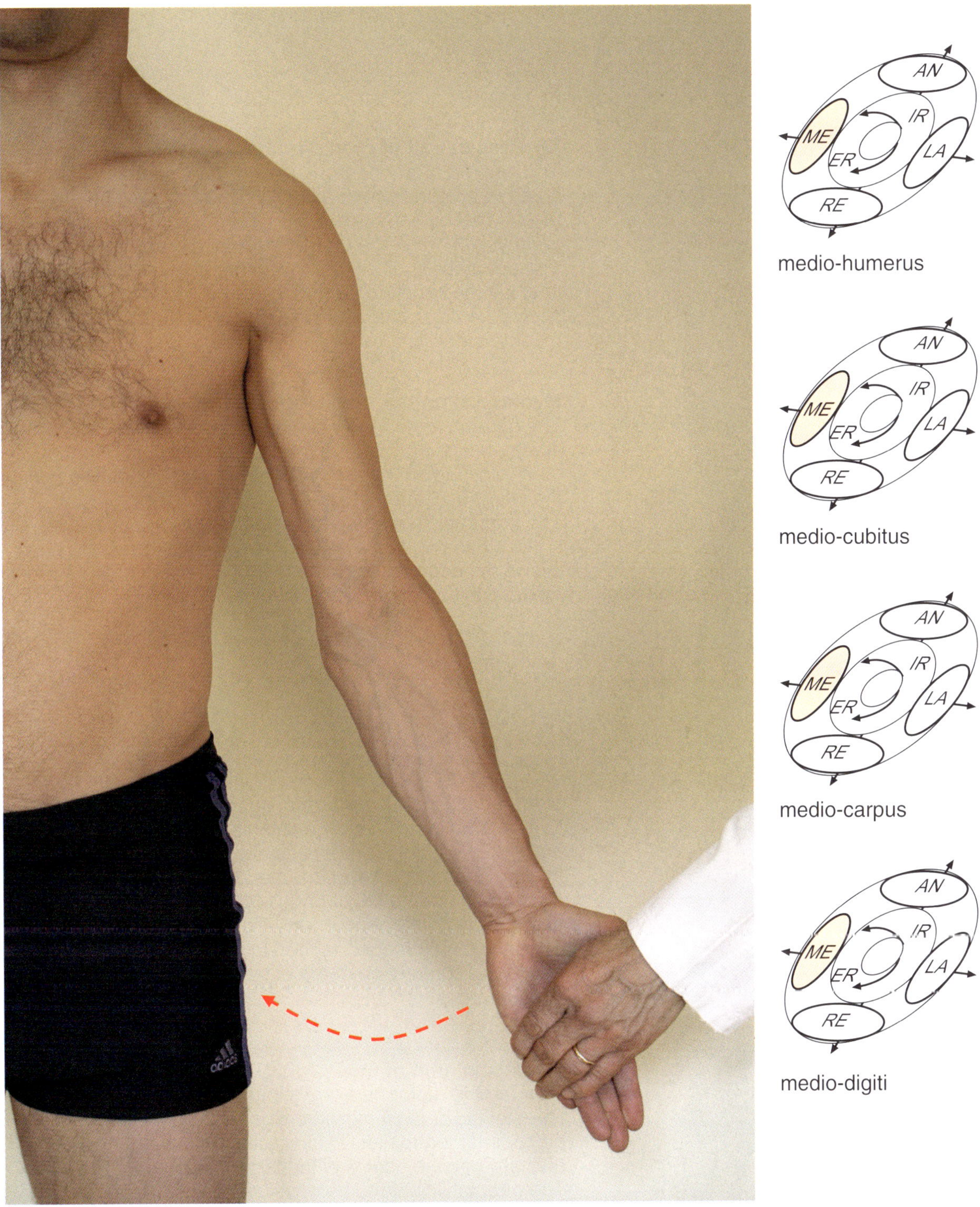

Fig. 2.37. Contraction of the mediopulsion sequence bringing the entire upper limb medially.

Proprioceptors, like the Ruffini and Pacini organs, are identical in the entire body. It is their mapping in a precise fascial architecture that allows them to provide a directional significance to their afferents.
Mediopulsion of the upper limb is perceived as movement towards the inside only because during this movement the fascial compartments containing the adductor muscles are stretched.
Generally, the nerves conducting the motor impulse according to a specific direction also conduct the afferents for that specific movement.

PHYSIOLOGY OF THE MEDIOPULSION MF UNITS IN THE UPPER LIMB

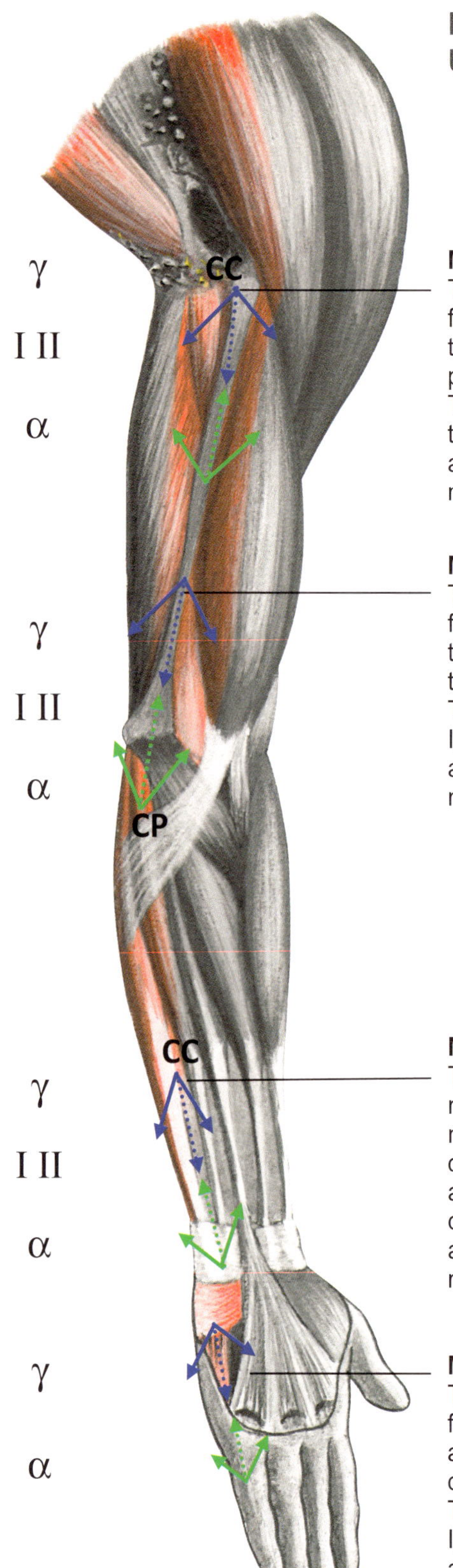

Myofascial unit of medio-humerus (me-hu)
The gamma motor neurone stimulates the intrafusal muscle fibres of pectoralis major, latissimus dorsi, long head of triceps brachii and teres major. Their tractions on the perimysium converge on the external axillary fascia (CC). The adaptability of the perimysium allows the afferents I, II to close the circuit triggering the alpha impulse. This in turn allows the contraction of the extrafusal fibres of the MF unit medio-humerus.

Myofascial unit of medio-cubitus (me-cu)
The gamma motor neurone stimulates the intrafusal muscle fibres originating from the medial intermuscular septum, their tractions on the perimysium converge at midway on the intermuscular septum (CC).
The adaptability of the perimysium allows the afferents I, II to close the circuit triggering the alpha impulse. This allows the contraction of the extrafusal fibres of the MF unit medio-cubitus for stabilisation.

Myofascial unit of medio-carpus (me-ca)
The gamma motor neurone stimulates the intrafusal muscle fibres of flexor carpi ulnaris and flexor digiti minimi. Their tractions on the perimysium converge in the distal region of the flexor carpi ulnaris muscle (CC). The adaptability of the perimysium allows the afferents I, II to close the circuit triggering the alpha impulse. This in turn allows the contraction of the extrafusal fibres of the MF unit medio-carpus.

Myofascial unit of medio-digiti (me-di)
The gamma motor neurone stimulates the intrafusal muscle fibres of flexor digiti minimi brevis, opponens digiti minimi and palmar interossei. Their tractions on the perimysium converge on the centre of the hypothenar eminence (CC).
The adaptability of the perimysium allows the afferents I, II to close the circuit triggering the alpha impulse. This allows the contraction of the extrafusal fibres of the MF unit medio-digiti.

Fig. 2.38. Normal functioning of the gamma circuit.

ARTICULAR CONFLICTS IN THE MEDIOPULSION UNITS IN THE UPPER LIMB

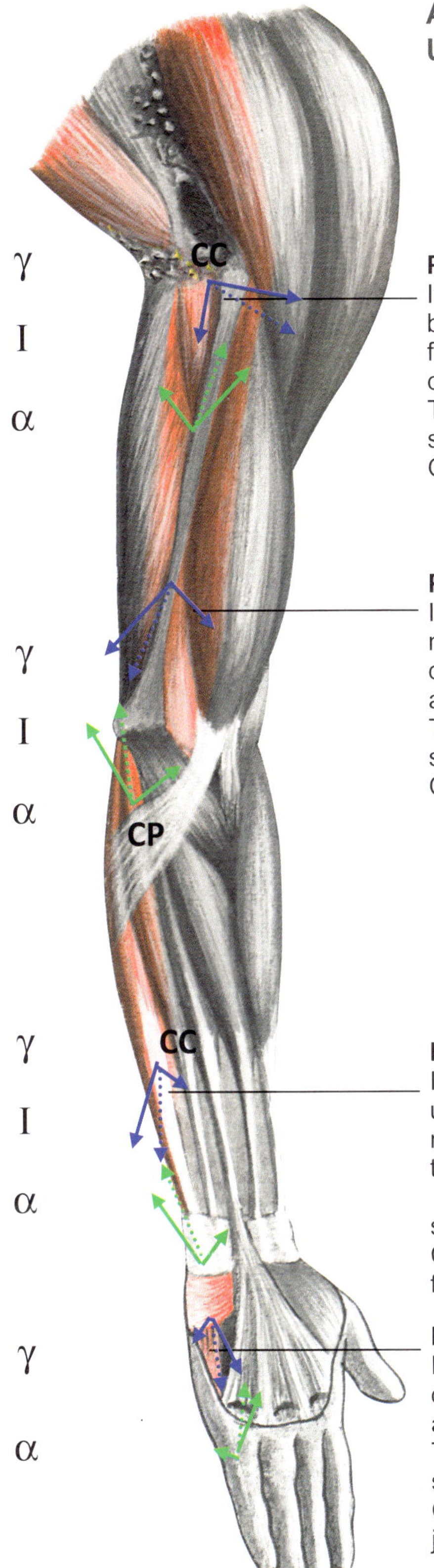

Pain during mediopulsion of humerus
If the fascia located at the intersection of the triceps brachii, biceps brachii and latissimus dorsi muscles (CC) is densified, the afferents from a few neuromuscular spindles is then not fired and the alpha circuits are not activated.
The contraction from the extrafusal muscle fibres that are activated shifts the tendinous resultant outside of its physiological axis. Consequently, a conflict occurs at the glenohumeral joint.

Pain during mediopulsion of cubitus
If the fascia located at midway point on the arm between the medial head of the triceps brachii and brachialis muscles (CC) is densified, then the afferents from a few neuromuscular spindles are not fired and the alpha circuits are then not activated.
The contraction from the extrafusal muscle fibres that are activated shifts the tendinous resultant outside of its physiological axis. Consequently, a conflict occurs at the elbow joint.

Pain during mediopulsion of carpus
If the fascia located over the distal part of the flexor carpi ulnaris muscle (CC) is densified, then the afferents from a few neuromuscular spindles are not fired and the alpha circuits are then not activated.
The contraction from the extrafusal muscle fibres that are activated shifts the tendinous resultant outside of its physiological axis. Consequently, a conflict occurs at the carpal joints with the formation of enthesopathy.

Pain during mediopulsion of digiti V
If the fascia located above the hypothenar eminence (CC) is densified, then the afferents from a few neuromuscular spindles are not fired and hence the alpha circuits are not activated.
The contraction from the extrafusal muscle fibres that are activated shifts the tendinous resultant outside of its physiological axis. Consequently, a conflict occurs at the fifth metacarpophalangeal joint.

Fig. 2.39. Dysfunctions of the gamma circuit.

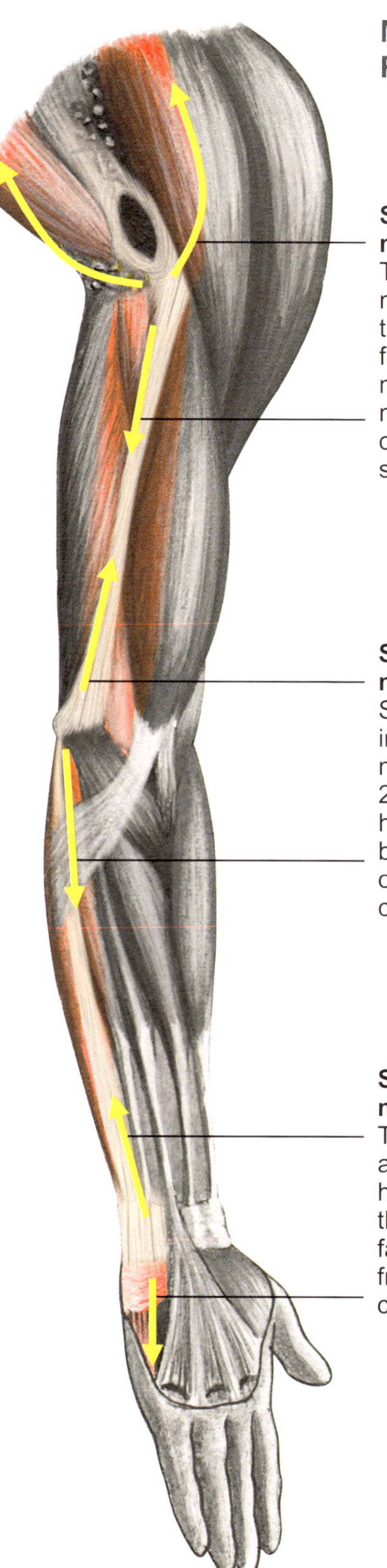

Fig. 2.40. Synergy of the mediopulsion sequence in the upper limb.

MEDIOPULSION SEQUENCE AND STRETCH REFLEX

Synergy between the MF units of medio-humerus and medio-cubitus

The fascia overlying the axilla is united to the pectoralis major and latissimus dorsi muscles, during mediopulsion of the scapula and humerus both muscles traction the axillary fascia proximally. This fascia continues distally into the medial intermuscular septum of the arm on which both the medial head of triceps and brachialis muscles have their origin. The contraction of these muscles determines a distal stretch of the medial septum.

Synergy between the MF units of medio-cubitus and medio-carpus

Some motor units of the coracobrachialis muscle participate in humeral adduction. A part of the distal tendon of this muscle inserts on the medial intermuscular septum (Fig. 2.43). Therefore, the contraction of the MF unit medio-humerus determines a proximal stretch of the medial brachial fascia. The flexor carpi ulnaris muscle (Fig. 2.44) originates from the distal part of the medial septum, its contraction determines the distal stretch of the septum.

Synergy between the MF units of medio-carpus and medio-digiti

The muscle fibres of extensor carpi ulnaris give origin to a tendinous expansion that inserts into the fascia of the hypothenar eminence (Fig. 2.45). Hence the contraction of the MF unit medio-carpus determines a distal stretch of the fascia. The muscles of the hypothenar eminence take origin from the retinaculum that is stretched distally during their contraction.

ACTIVATION OF THE GOLGI TENDON ORGANS

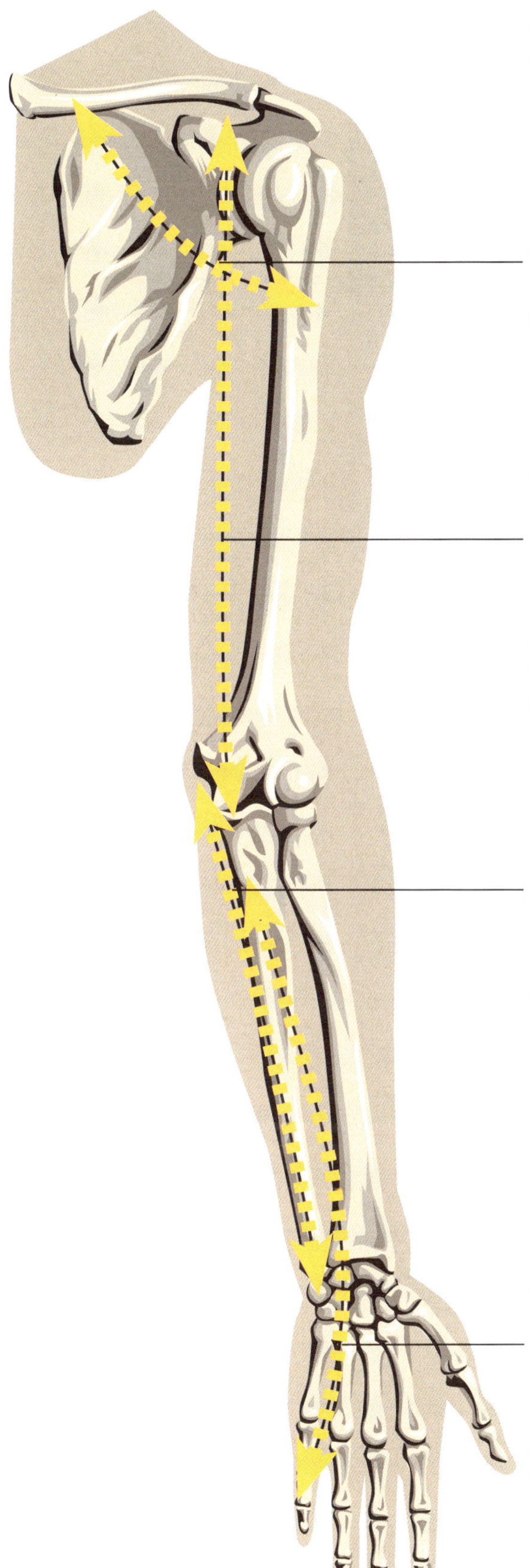

Fig. 2.41. Biarticular muscles for mediopulsion in the upper limb.

Combined action between medio-scapula and medio-humerus
The pectoralis major and latissimus dorsi muscles act on the abduction of both scapula and humerus. Through the axillary fascia both muscles are united to the long head of triceps and the short head of biceps muscles.

Combined action between medio-humerus and medio-cubitus
The triceps brachii muscle originates from the infraglenoid tubercle of the scapula through its long head and inserts on the olecranon of the ulna, hence it simultaneously acts upon humerus and cubitus. When a heavy object is squeezed with both hands, the Golgi tendon organs of the proximal and distal triceps brachii are then activated based upon the various joint angles between the shoulder and elbow.

Combined action between medio-cubitus and medio-carpus
The flexor carpi ulnaris muscle originates from the medial epicondyle of the humerus and inserts onto the pisiform, hence simultaneously acting upon cubitus and carpus. When a heavy object is squeeze with both hands, the Golgi tendon organs of the proximal and distal flexor carpi ulnaris muscle are activated based upon the various joint angles between the elbow and wrist.

Combined action between medio-carpus and medio-digiti
The flexor digiti minimi longus muscle originates from the epicondyle along with the flexor carpi ulnaris muscle, it inserts on the pisiform and the hypothenar and palmar fasciae. Hence it acts simultaneously upon the wrist and the fifth digit.
When squeezing a heavy object with both hands, the Golgi tendon organs of the flexor digiti minimi longus muscle are then activated based upon the various joint angles and upon the variations of forces that the fingers must perform when grasping.

FASCIAE OF THE MEDIOPULSION SEQUENCE IN THE UPPER LIMB

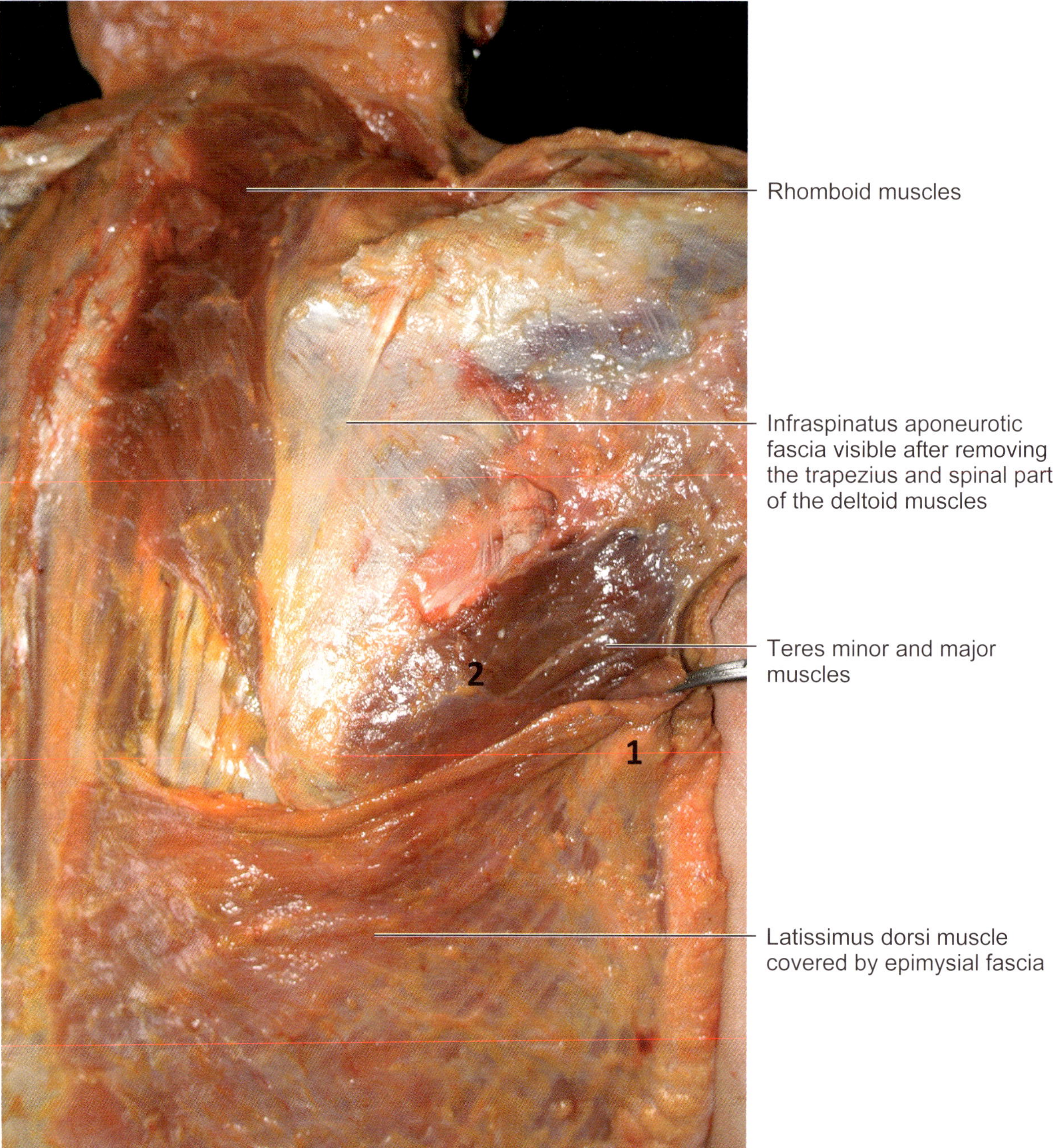

Fig. 2.42. Infraspinatus aponeurotic fascia. The forceps tractions the latissimus dorsi muscle inferiorly (1) to highlight its insertions on the inferior angle of the scapula and the fascia of the teres major and minor muscles (2).

In the figures horizontal lines indicate anatomical parts whilst numbers (1, 2) indicate the physiology of the fascia. Number 1 indicates a determined action and number 2 indicates its effect.

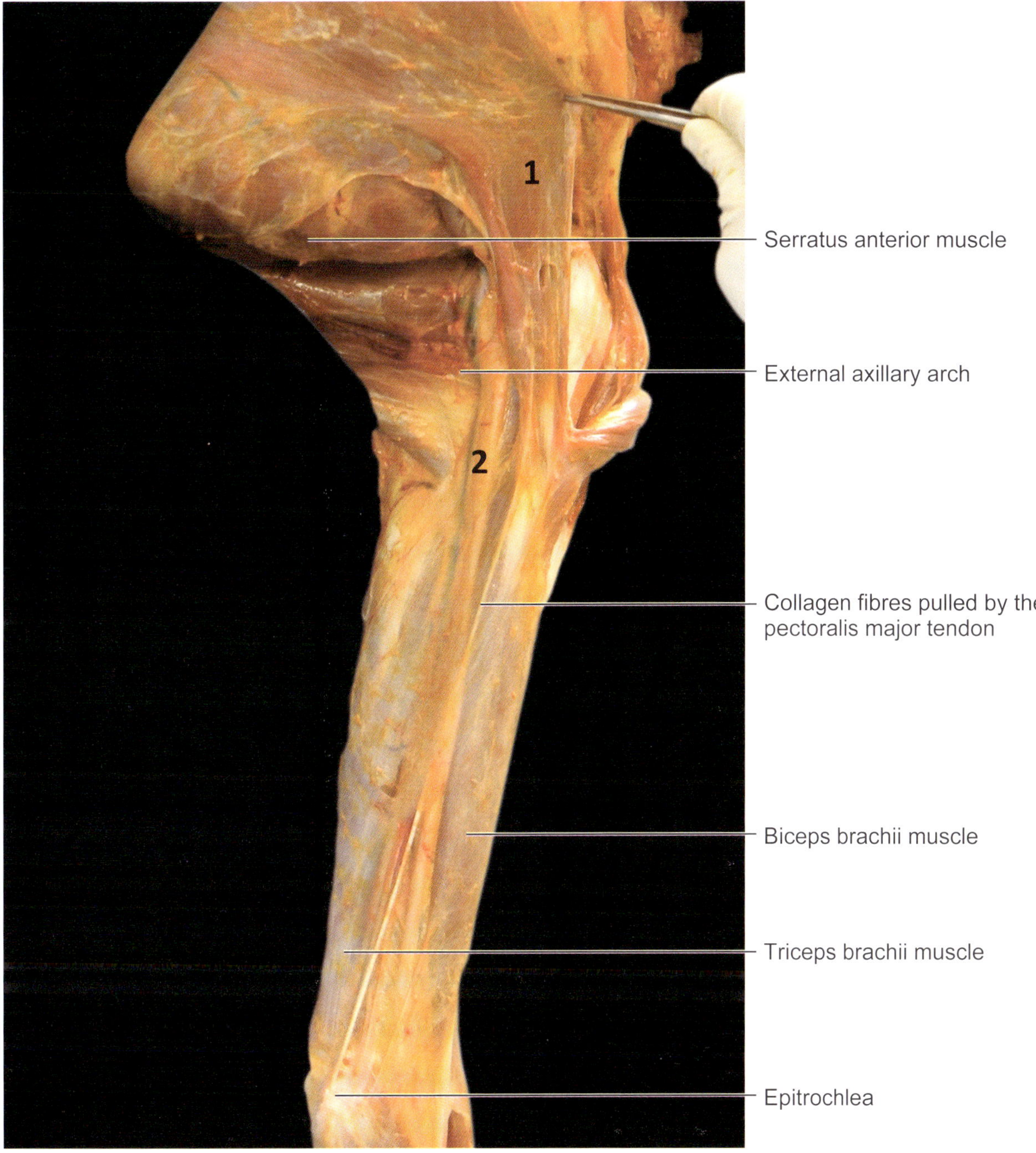

Fig. 2.43. Medial intermuscular septum of the arm with the neurovascular bundle. The forceps lifts the pectoralis major muscle (1) to highlight the proximal part of the neurovascular bundle (2).

FASCIAE OF THE MEDIOPULSION SEQUENCE IN THE UPPER LIMB

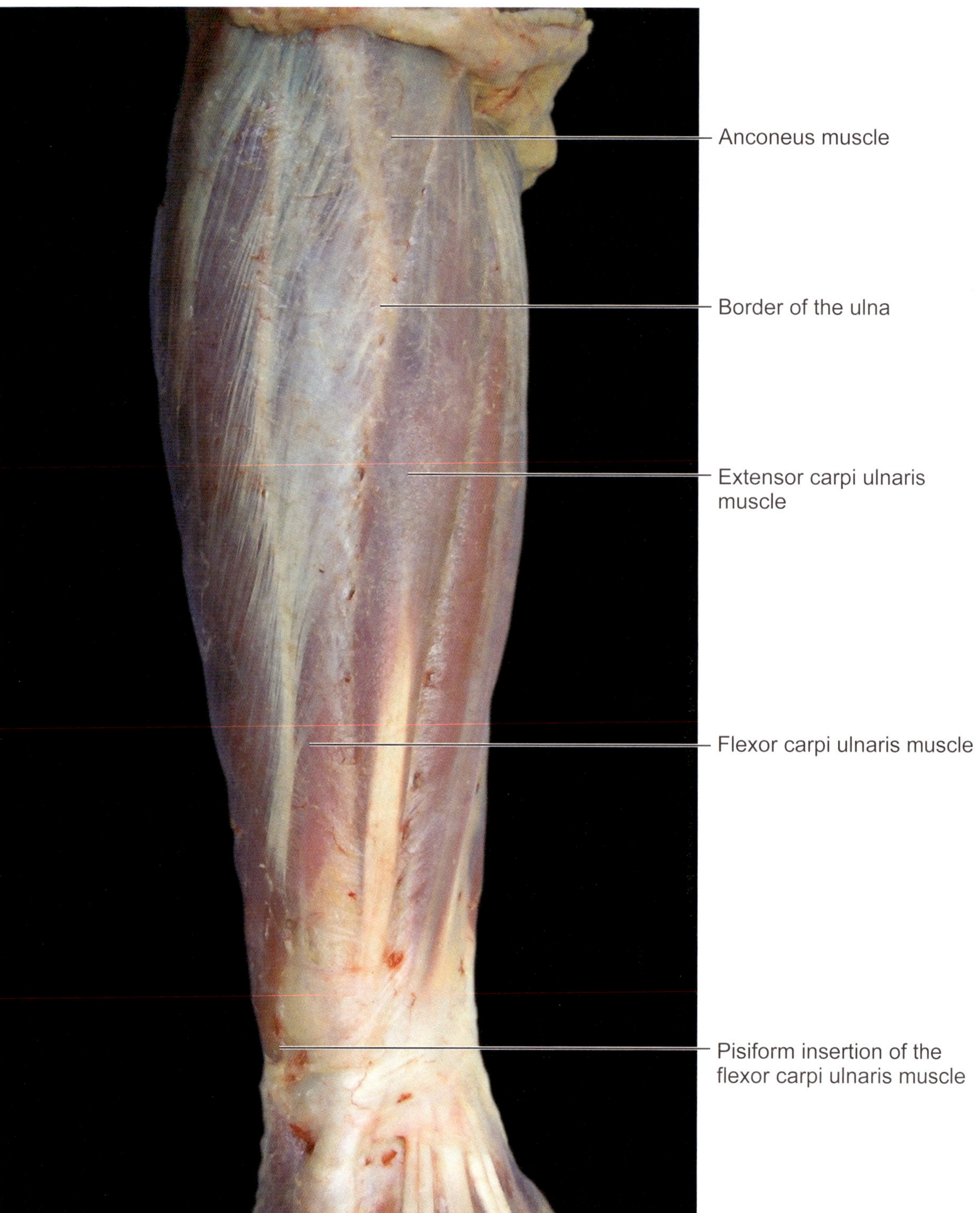

Fig. 2.44. Aponeurotic fascia of the medial forearm. The muscles and intrafascial collagen fibres are seen in transparency underneath the aponeurotic fascia.

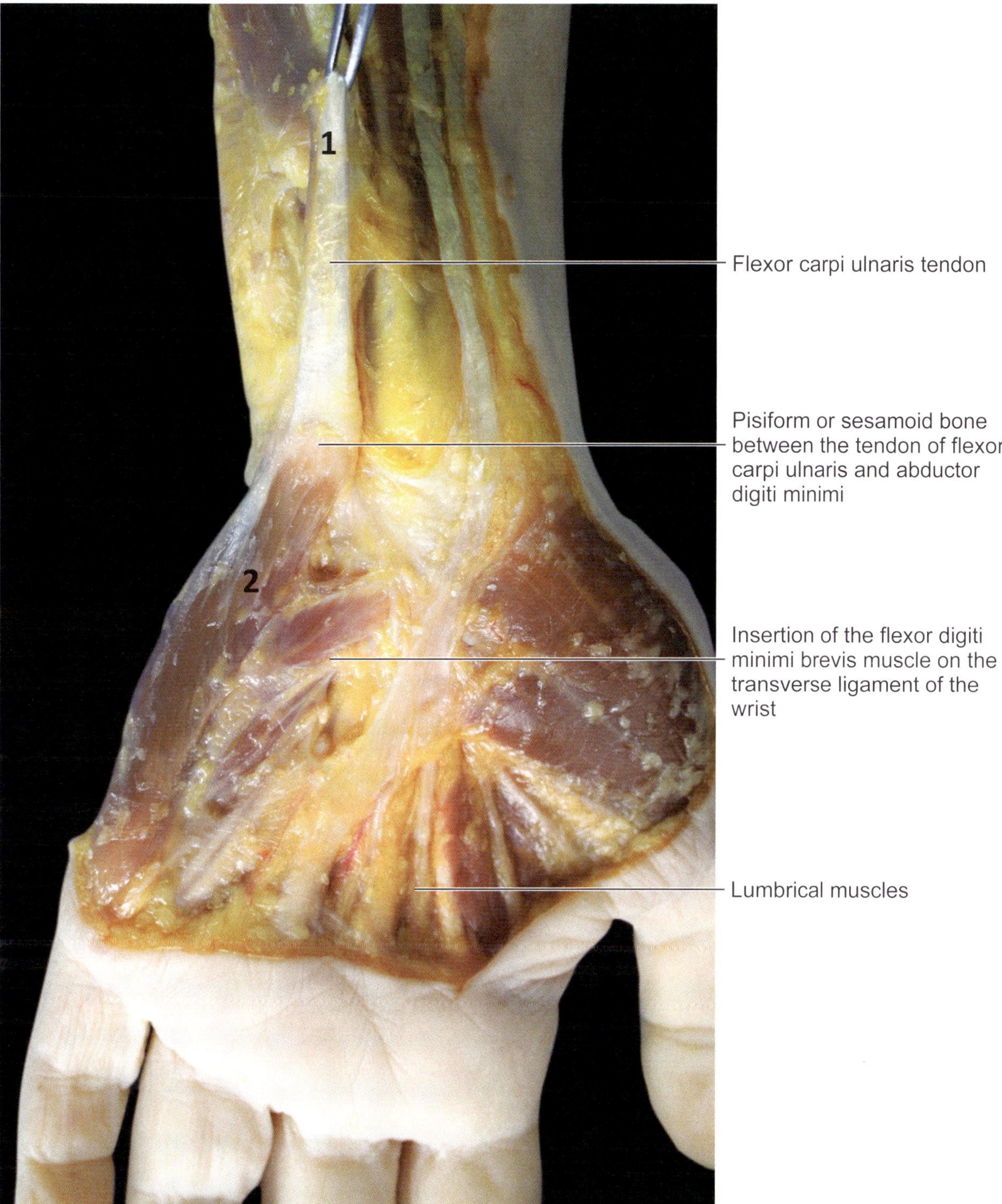

Fig. 2.45. Epimysial fasciae of the thenar and hypothenar eminences. The traction on the tendon of flexor carpi ulnaris (1) propagates to the muscles of the hypothenar eminence (2).

LATERAL REGION OF THE UPPER LIMB, LATEROPULSION SEQUENCE

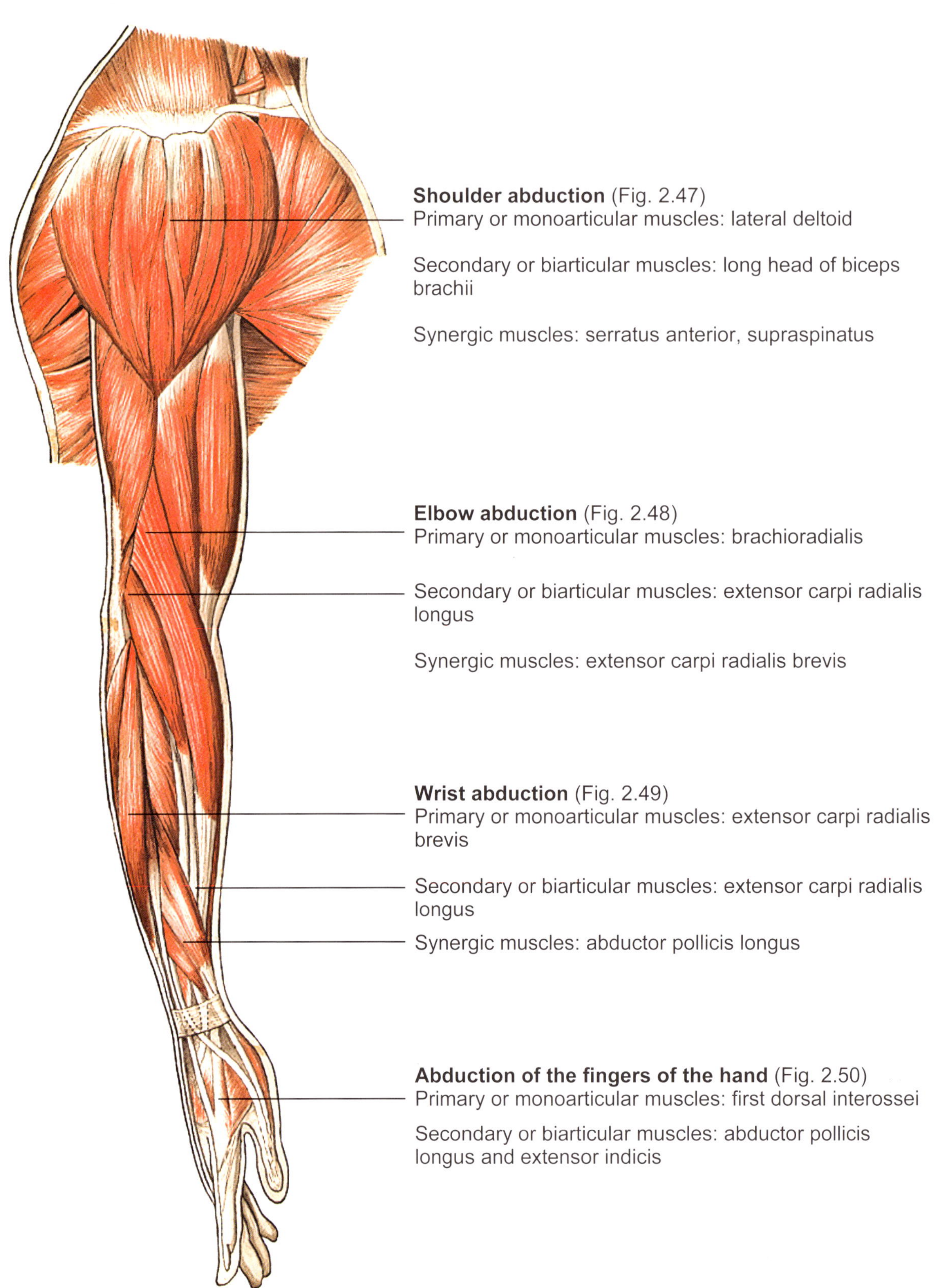

Fig. 2.46. Lateral region of the upper limb.
(From G. Chiarugi and L. Bucciante, Istituzioni di anatomia dell'uomo. Piccin Nuova Libraria, Padova 1983, modified).

SEGMENTARY MOVEMENTS IMPLEMENTED BY THE MF UNITS OF LATEROPULSION

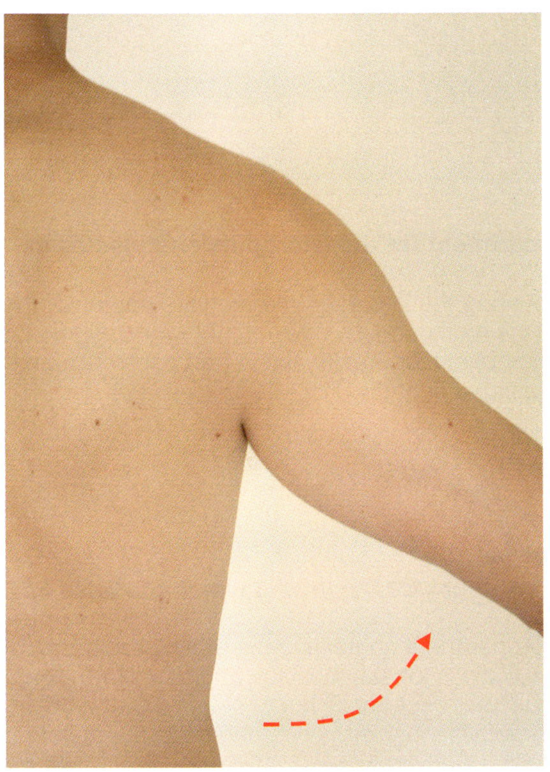

Fig. 2.47. Shoulder abduction, managed throughout the range by the myofascial unit of latero-humerus.

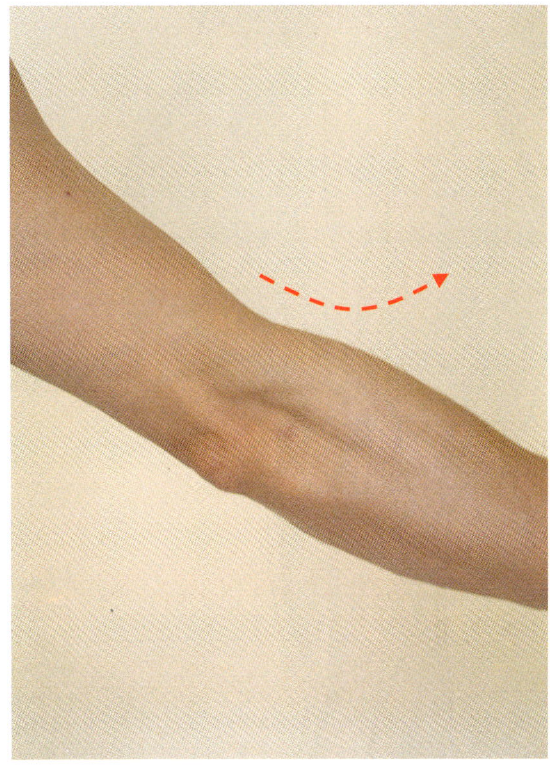

Fig. 2.48. Elbow abduction, stabilised by the MF unit of latero-cubitus.

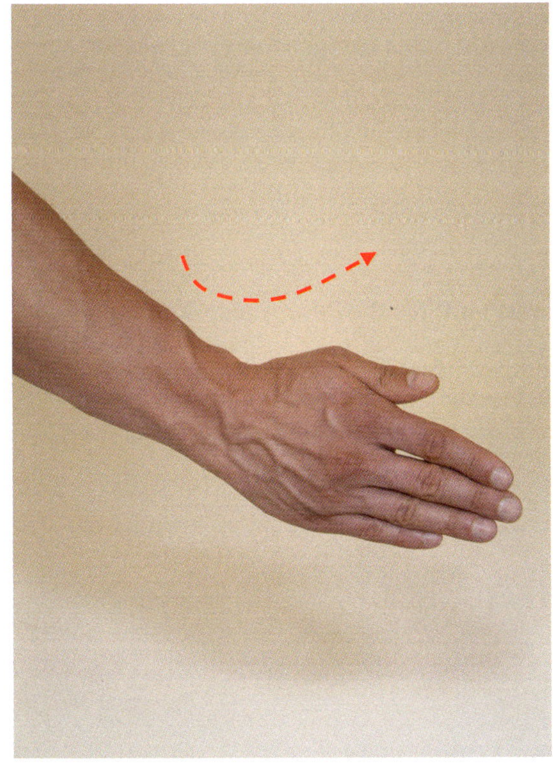

Fig. 2.49. Wrist abduction, managed throughout the range by the MF unit of latero-carpus.

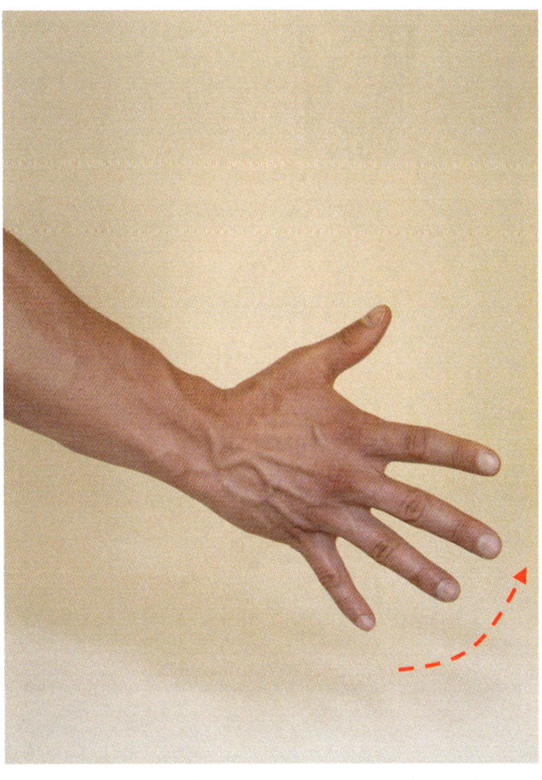

Fig. 2.50. Finger abduction, managed throughout the range by the MF unit of latero-digiti.

COMPARTMENTS FOR THE MUSCLES OF LATEROPULSION, UPPER LIMB (Fig. 2.52)

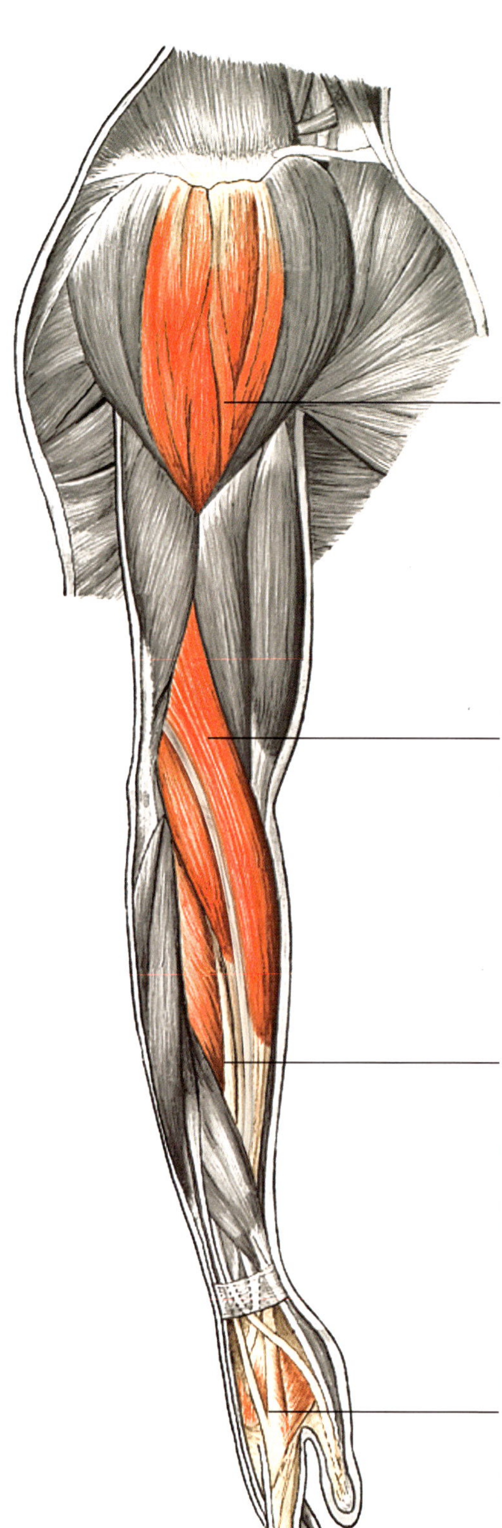

Fascial compartment for the lateropulsion muscles of humerus

The fascia covering the lateral or intermediate portion of the deltoid muscle is multipennate. The four intermuscular septa go towards the deltoid tuberosity and in part continue with the lateral intermuscular septum.

Fascial compartment for the lateropulsion muscles of cubitus

The fascial compartment containing the brachioradialis and extensor carpi radialis longus muscles originates from the lateral intermuscular septum. Chiarugi states that the origin of the brachioradialis muscle may extend up to the deltoid tuberosity.

Fascial compartment for the lateropulsion muscles of carpus

The radial collateral ligament of the elbow is partly a tendinous expansion of the extensor carpi radialis brevis muscle.

"The extensor carpi radialis brevis muscle originates from the epicondyle, from the aponeurosis covering it, from the adjacent intermuscular septa and from the radial collateral ligament of the elbow" (Chiarugi G. 1975).

Fascial compartment for the lateropulsion muscles of digiti

The fascial compartment of the first dorsal interossei continues with the deep dorsal fascia of the hand.

"The distal tendon of extensor carpi radialis longus contributes to the formation of the intermetacarpal ligaments" (Gray H. 1993).

Fig. 2.51. Fascial compartments for the lateropulsion muscles.

(From G. Chiarugi and L. Bucciante, Istituzioni di anatomia dell'uomo. Piccin Nuova Libraria, Padova 1983, modified).

GLOBAL MOVEMENT IMPLEMENTED BY THE LATEROPULSION SEQUENCE

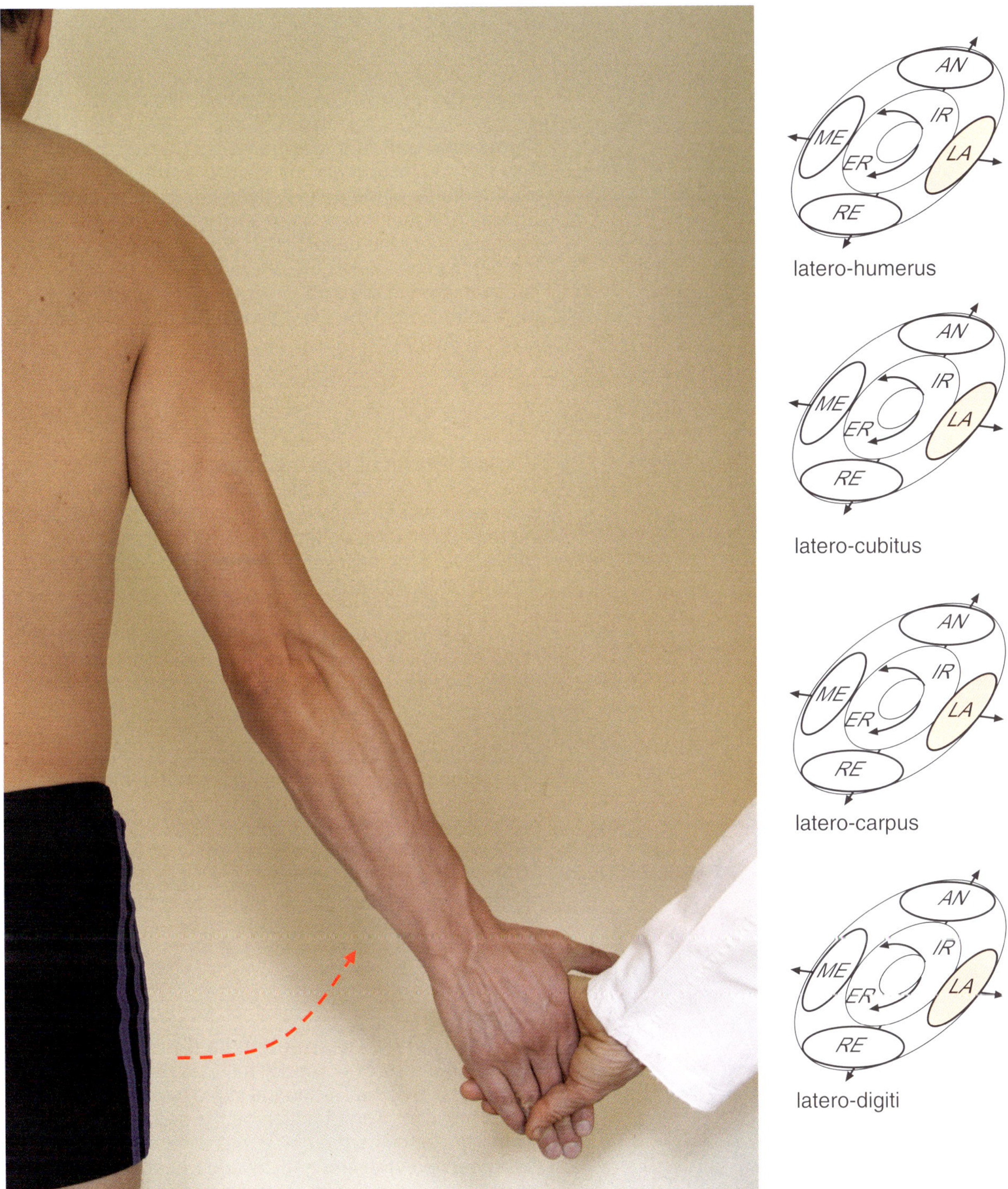

Fig. 2.52. Contraction of the lateropulsion sequence bringing the entire upper limb laterally.

Stabilisation of the elbow was the consideration for movements in mediopulsion for the elbow. Similarly, the same is true for the lateropulsion of cubitus where lateral stability is the movement considered. Lateropulsion of humerus is commonly called abduction whereas in the wrist it is called radial deviation. This confusion in terminology does not exist for the brain: it programmes for lateral movement and the fascial sequence conveys the afferents to the brain for the executed movement.

PHYSIOLOGY OF THE LATEROPULSION MF UNITS IN THE UPPER LIMB

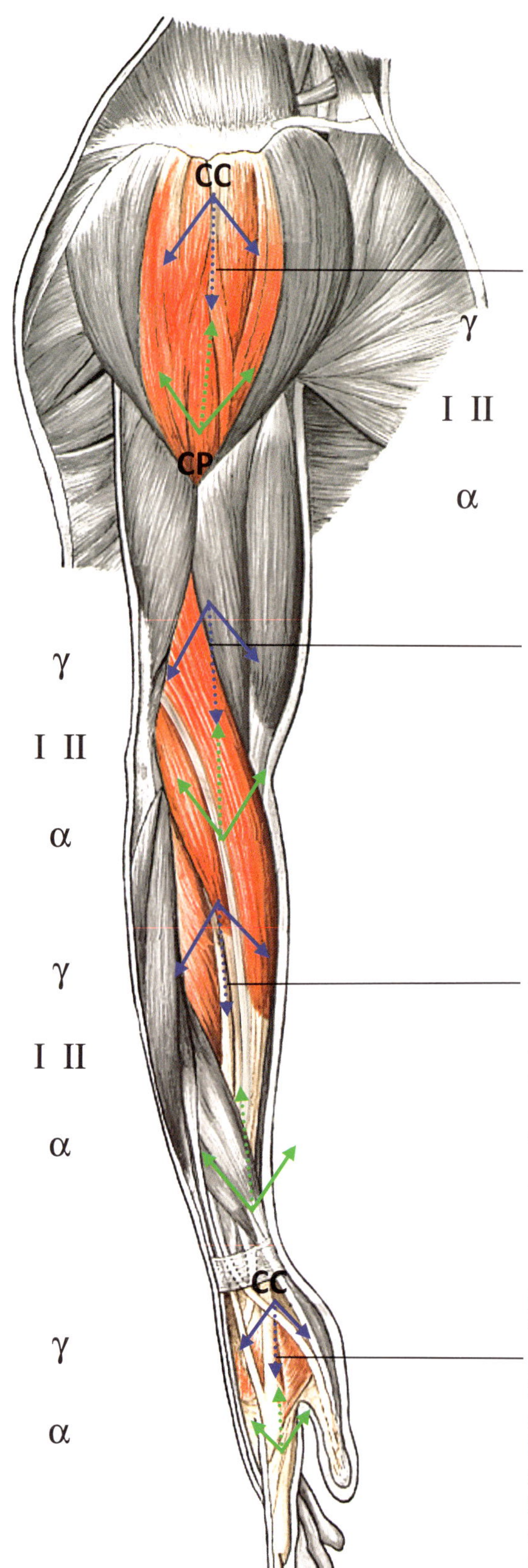

Myofascial unit of latero-humerus (la-hu)
The gamma motor neurone stimulates the intrafusal muscle fibres of the deltoid and long head of biceps brachii, and their tractions on the perimysium converge on the apex of the deltoid (CC). The adaptability of the perimysium allows the afferents I, II to close the circuit triggering the alpha impulse. This in turn allows the contraction of the extrafusal fibres of the MF unit latero-humerus.

Myofascial unit of latero-cubitus (la-cu)
The gamma motor neurone stimulates the intrafusal muscle fibres of the muscles originating from the lateral intermuscular septum, their tractions on the perimysium converge on the epimysium of the brachioradialis muscle (blue vectors).
The adaptability of the perimysium allows the afferents I, II to close the circuit triggering the alpha impulse. This stimulus causes the contraction of the extrafusal fibres for the stabilising action of the MF unit latero-cubitus.

Myofascial unit of latero-carpus (la-ca)
The gamma motor neurone stimulates the intrafusal muscle fibres of the extensor carpi radialis longus and brevis muscles, their tractions on the perimysium converge on the septum located between both muscles (CC). The adaptability of the perimysium allows the afferents I, II to close the circuit triggering the alpha impulse. This allows the contraction of the extrafusal fibres of the MF unit latero-carpus.

Myofascial unit of latero-digiti (la-di)
The gamma motor neurone stimulates the intrafusal muscle fibres of the first dorsal interossei and extensor indicis muscles. Their traction on the perimysium converges in the centre of the intercommissural fascia between the first and second metacarpals. The adaptability of the perimysium allows the afferents I, II to close the circuit triggering the alpha impulse. This allows the contraction of the extrafusal fibres of the MF unit latero-digiti.

Fig. 2.53. Normal functioning of the gamma circuit.
(From G. Chiarugi and L. Bucciante, Istituzioni di anatomia dell'uomo. Piccin Nuova Libraria, Padova 1983, modified).

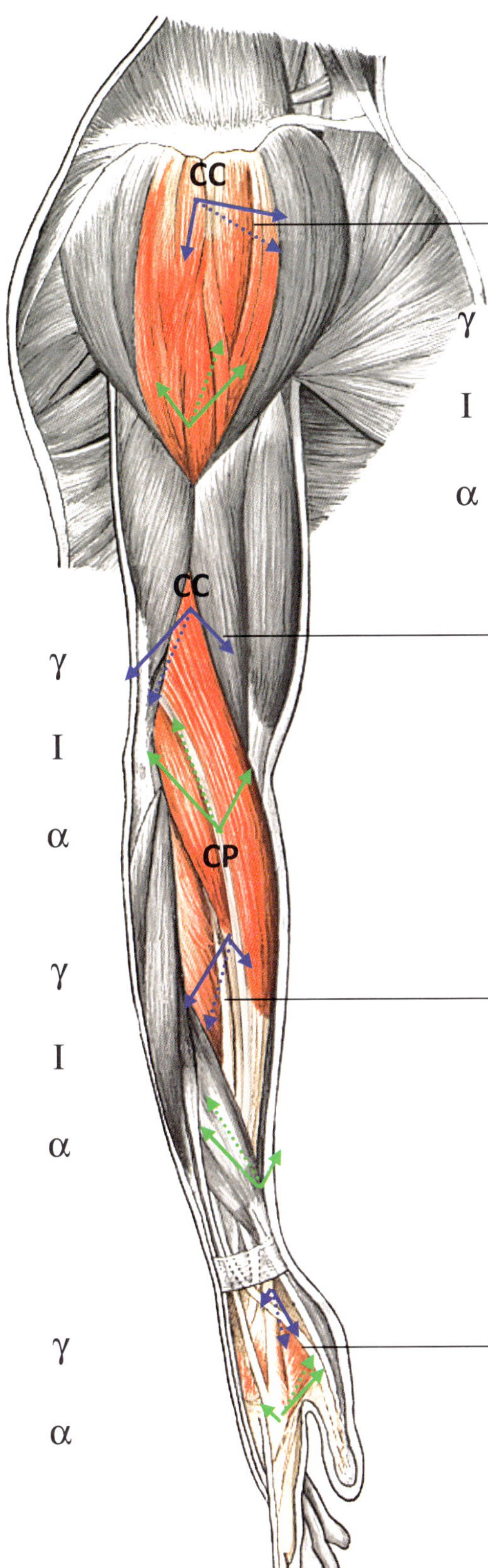

ARTICULAR CONFLICTS IN THE LATEROPULSION UNITS IN THE UPPER LIMB

Pain during lateropulsion of humerus
If the fascia located on the subacromial deltoid corresponding to the long head of the biceps brachii muscle (CC) is densified, then the afferents from a few neuromuscular spindles are not fired. Therefore, the alpha circuits for some extrafusal fibres of the MF unit of la-hu are not activated. The contraction from the extrafusal muscle fibres that are activated shifts the tendinous resultant outside of its physiological axis. Consequently, a conflict occurs at the glenohumeral joint.

Pain during lateropulsion of cubitus
If the fascia located in the distal third of the arm over the lateral intermuscular septa (CC) is densified, the afferents from a few neuromuscular spindles are not fired to close the alpha circuit.
The contraction from the extrafusal muscle fibres that are activated shifts the tendinous resultant outside of its physiological axis. Consequently, a conflict occurs at the lateral elbow joint.

Pain during lateropulsion of carpus
If the fascia located between the muscle bellies of extensor carpi radialis longus and brevis (CC) is densified, the afferents from a few neuromuscular spindles are not fired and the alpha circuits are not activated for those extrafusal fibres of the MF unit. The contraction from the extrafusal muscle fibres that are activated shifts the tendinous resultant outside of its physiological axis. Consequently, a conflict occurs at the carpal joints with formation of tendinopathies.

Pain during lateropulsion of digiti II
If the fascia located over the intercommissural compartment (CC) is densified, the afferents from a few neuromuscular spindles are not fired; the alpha circuits are then not activated for those extrafusal fibres of the MF unit.
The contraction from the extrafusal muscle fibres that are activated shifts the tendinous resultant outside of its physiological axis. Consequently, a conflict occurs at the second metacarpophalangeal joint.

Fig. 2.54. Dysfunctions of the gamma circuit.
(From G. Chiarugi and L. Bucciante, Istituzioni di anatomia dell'uomo. Piccin Nuova Libraria, Padova 1983, modified).

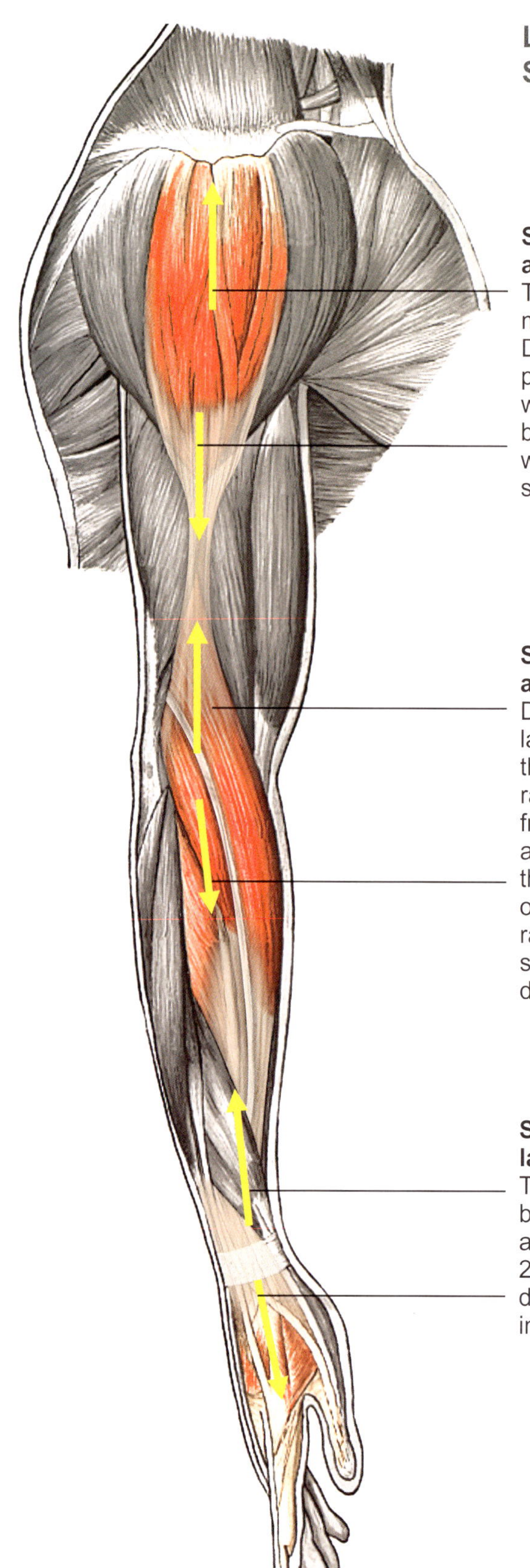

LATEROPULSION SEQUENCE AND STRETCH REFLEX

Synergy between the MF units of latero-humerus and latero-cubitus
The fascia covering the lateral deltoid muscle forms many intermuscular septa uniting it to the perimysium. During lateropulsion of humerus, the septa proximally pull on the deltoid fascia. This fascia continues distally with the lateral intermuscular septum (Fig. 2.57). The brachioradialis muscle originates from this septum, where its contraction determines a distal traction of the septum.

Synergy between the MF units of latero-humerus and latero-carpus
During shoulder abduction, the contraction of the lateral deltoid muscle determines a proximal pull on the lateral intermuscular septum. The extensor carpi radialis longus and brevis muscles (Fig. 2.58) originate from the distal part of the lateral septum and from the antebrachial fascia. Their spindles are activated by the contraction of the deltoid muscle and by stretching of the septum. The contraction of the extensor carpi radialis longus muscle in turn determines a pull on the septum and the activation of the muscle spindles of the deltoid.

Synergy between the MF units of latero-carpus and latero-digiti
The muscle fibres of extensor carpi radialis longus and brevis give origin to tendinous expansions that proceed and insert into the deep dorsal fascia of the hand (Fig. 2.59, 2.60). The contraction of the latero-carpus MF unit determines a proximal traction of the fascia of the dorsal interossei muscles.

Fig. 2.55. Synergy of the lateropulsion sequence in the upper limb.
(From G. Chiarugi and L. Bucciante, Istituzioni di anatomia dell'uomo. Piccin Nuova Libraria, Padova 1983, modified).

ACTIVATION OF THE GOLGI TENDON ORGANS

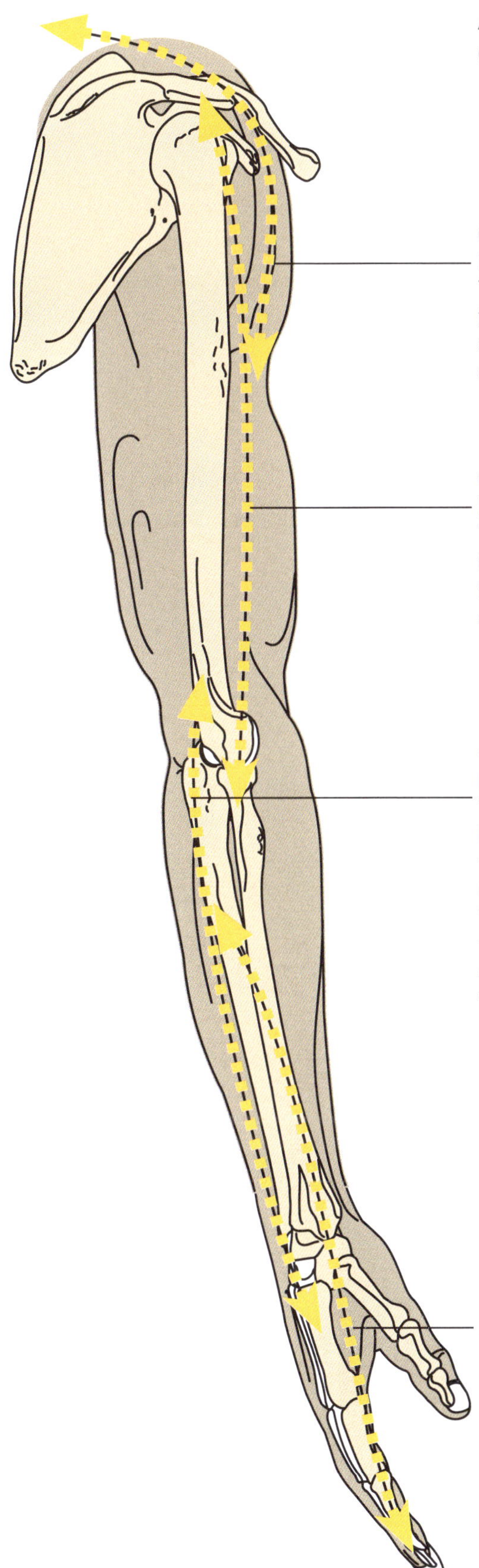

Combined action between latero-scapula and latero-humerus
The lateral deltoid fascia is the continuation of the fascia of the trapezius muscle inserted on the acromion. The trapezius acts on the acromioclavicular and the sternoclavicular joints during scapular elevation and abduction of the arm.

Combined action between latero-humerus and latero-cubitus
The biceps brachii muscle originates from the glenoid of the scapula through its long head and inserts on the radial tuberosity, hence it simultaneously acts upon humerus and cubitus.

Combined action between latero-cubitus and latero-carpus
The extensor carpi radialis longus muscle originates from the lateral intermuscular septum of the humerus and inserts on the second metacarpal bone, hence it simultaneously acts upon cubitus and carpus.
When an object is brought superiorly and laterally, the Golgi tendon organs of the proximal and distal tendons of extensor carpi radialis longus are then activated based upon the various joint angles.

Combined action between latero-carpus and latero-digiti
The abductor pollicis longus and extensor indicis muscles originate from the ulna and the interosseous membrane; they insert either on the thumb or index finger, hence they act simultaneously on the wrist and on the first two digits.
When the hand lifts up a heavy object, the Golgi tendon organs are activated based upon the various joint angles of the wrist and upon the force variations that the fingers (thumb-index) must perform when grasping.

Fig. 2.56. Biarticular muscles for lateropulsion in the upper limb.

FASCIAE OF THE LATEROPULSION SEQUENCE IN THE UPPER LIMB

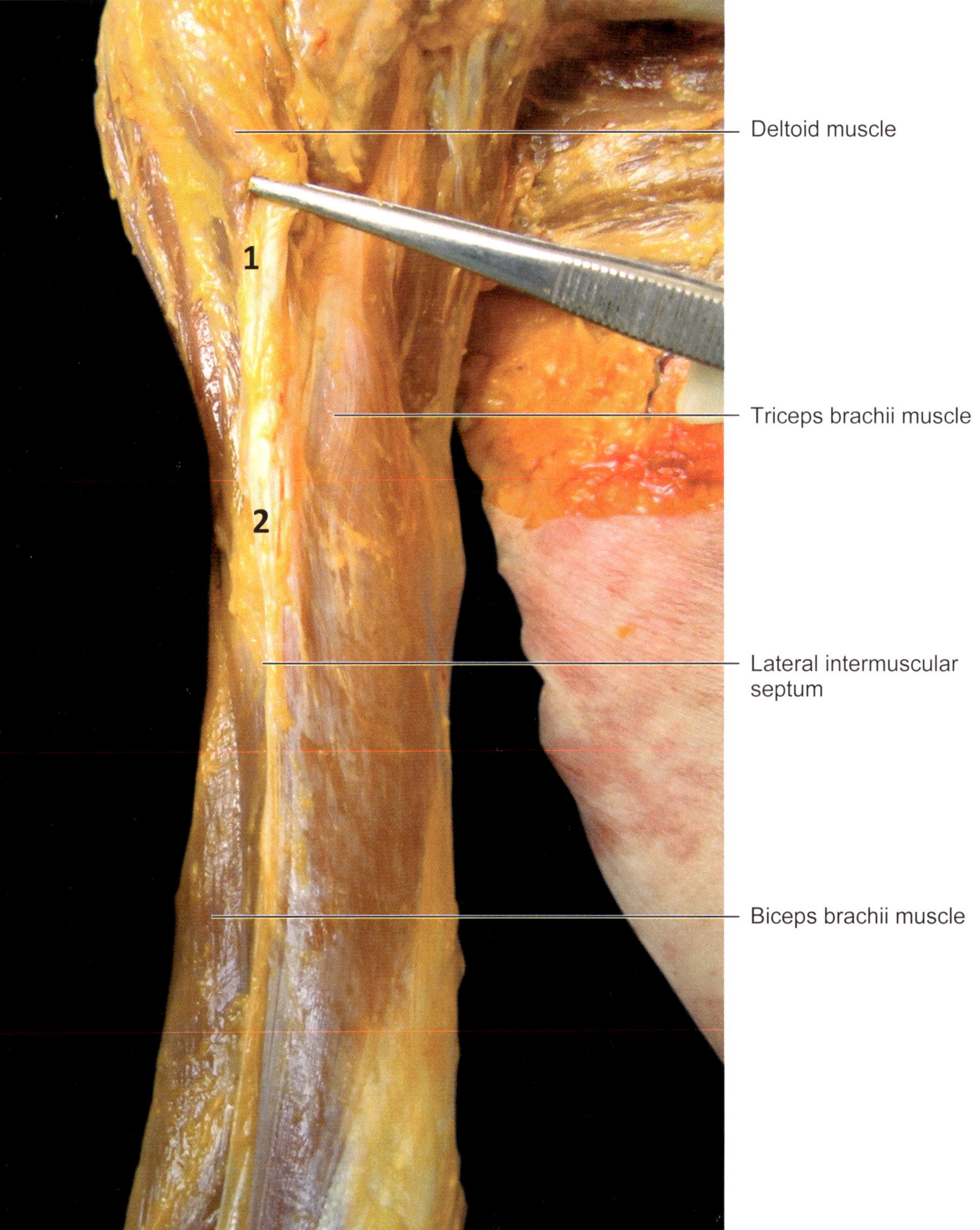

Fig. 2.57. Lateral intermuscular septum of the arm. The forceps proximally tractions the deltoid muscle (1), with subsequent stretching of the lateral septum (2).

In the figures horizontal lines indicate anatomical parts whilst numbers (1, 2) indicate the physiology of the fascia. Number 1 indicates a determined action and number 2 indicates its effect.

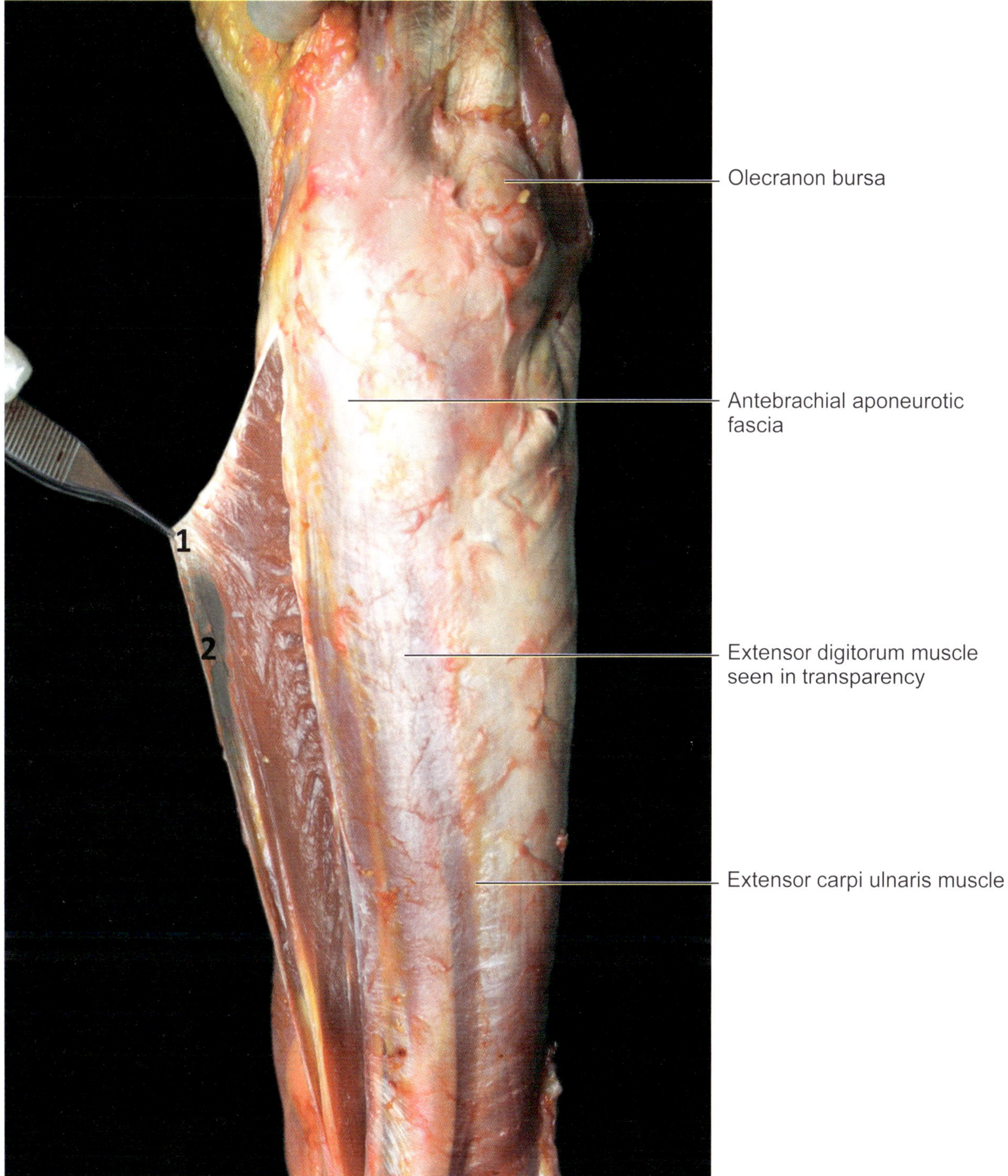

Fig. 2.58. Lateral antebrachial fascia cut along the extensor carpi radialis brevis muscle. The traction on the antebrachial fascia (1) highlights the origin of the extensor radialis muscle on the overlying fascia (2).

FASCIAE OF THE LATEROPULSION SEQUENCE IN THE UPPER LIMB

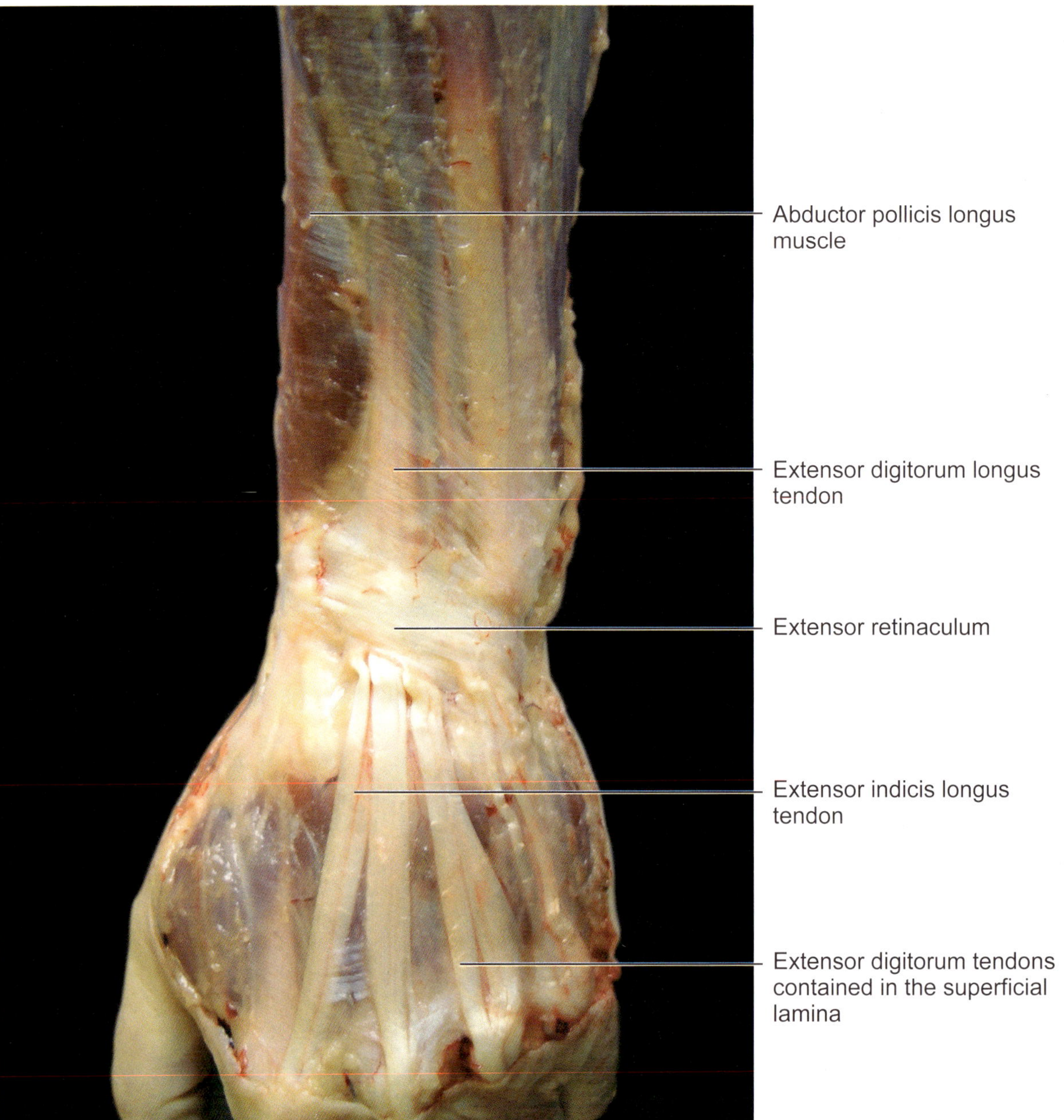

Fig. 2.59. Dorsal fascia of the hand, superficial lamina. The skin was removed, underneath a thin layer of loose connective tissue is present, the next layer is the superficial lamina that contains the tendons of the extensor digitorum muscle.

FASCIAE OF THE LATEROPULSION SEQUENCE IN THE UPPER LIMB

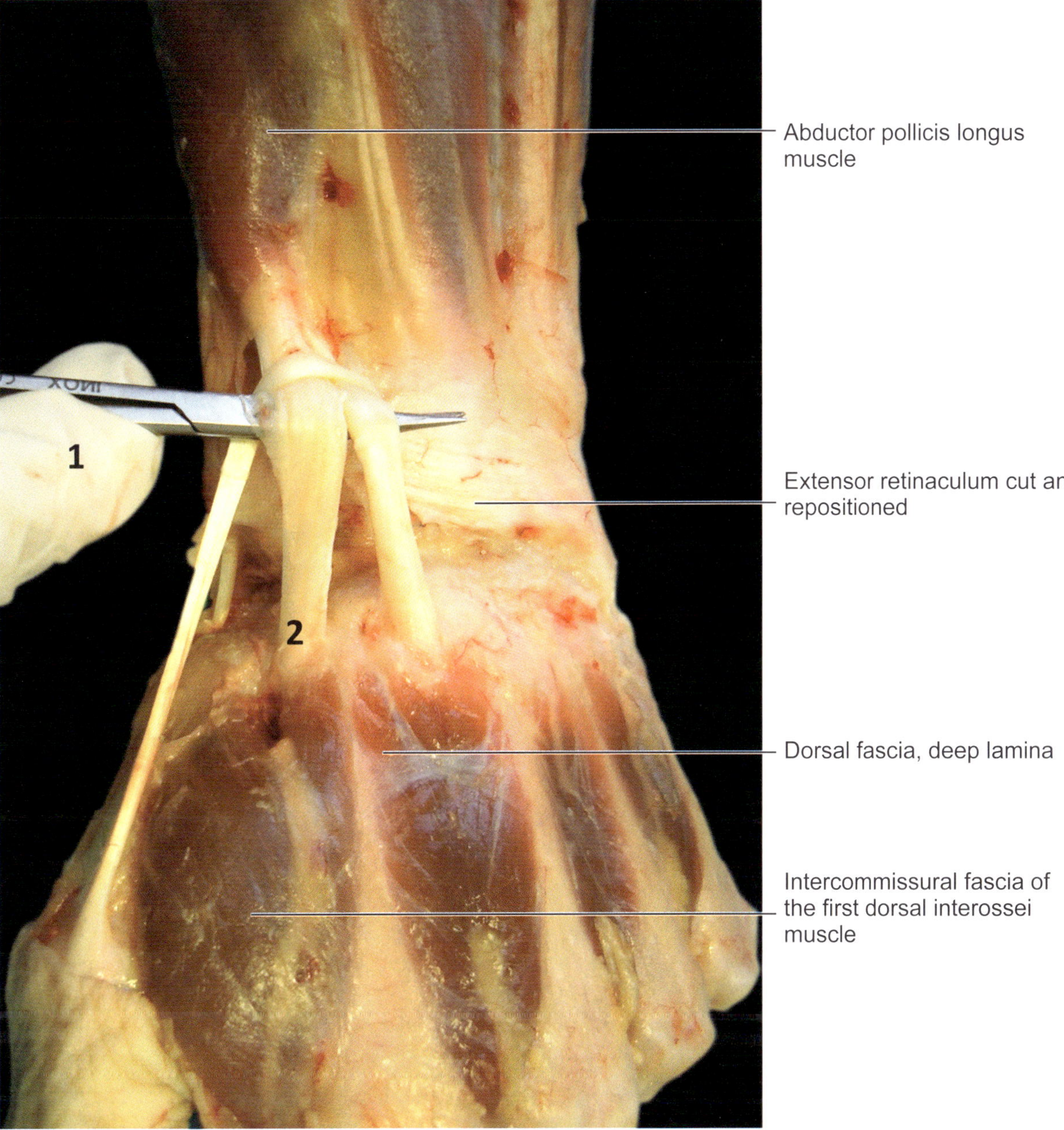

Fig. 2.60. Dorsal fascia of the hand, deep lamina. The extensor retinaculum was cut and the tendons of the extensor carpi radialis brevis and longus muscles (2) were forcefully lifted (1). It is observed that the osseous insertions and the tendon of extensor pollicis longus held these tendons in place and not the retinaculum.

DEEP ANTERIOR REGION OF THE UPPER LIMB, INTRAROTATION SEQUENCE

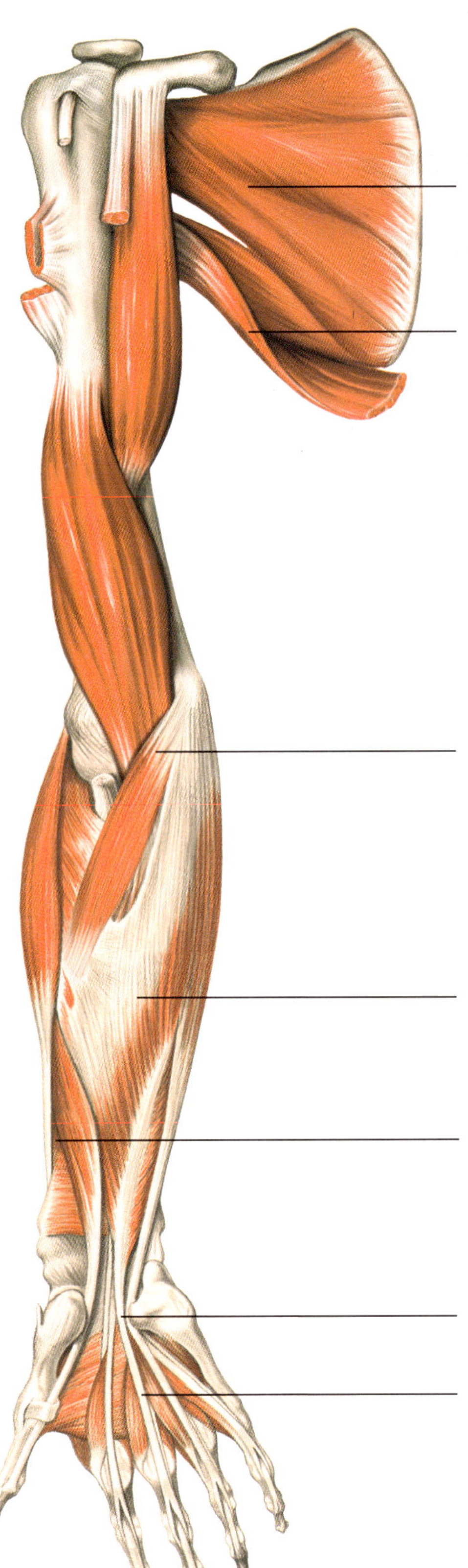

Shoulder internal rotation (Fig. 2.62)
Primary or monoarticular muscles: subscapularis

Secondary or biarticular muscles: long head of biceps brachii

Synergic muscles: teres major, latissimus dorsi, pectoralis major and clavicular portion of the deltoid

Elbow internal rotation (Fig. 2.63)
Secondary or biarticular muscles: flexor carpi radialis

Synergic muscles: palmaris longus

Primary or monoarticular muscles: pronator teres

Wrist pronation (Fig. 2.64)
Secondary or biarticular muscles: flexor digitorum

Synergic muscles: palmaris longus

Primary or monoarticular muscles: pronator quadratus

Finger closure (Fig. 2.65)
Secondary or biarticular muscles: flexor digitorum superficialis and profundus

Primary or monoarticular muscles: lumbrical

Fig. 2.61. Deep anterior region of the upper limb.
(From G. Chiarugi and L. Bucciante, Istituzioni di anatomia dell'uomo. Piccin Nuova Libraria, Padova 1983, modified)

SEGMENTARY MOVEMENTS IMPLEMENTED BY THE MF UNITS OF INTRAROTATION

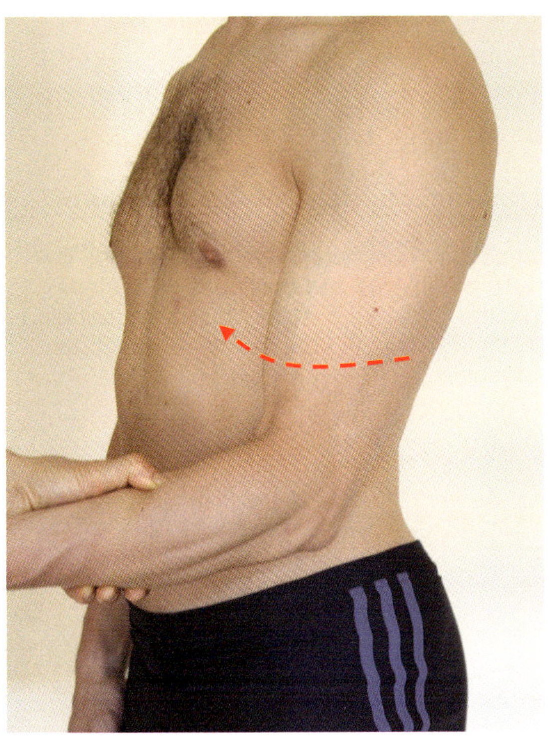

Fig. 2.62. Shoulder internal rotation, managed throughout the range by the myofascial unit of intra-humerus.

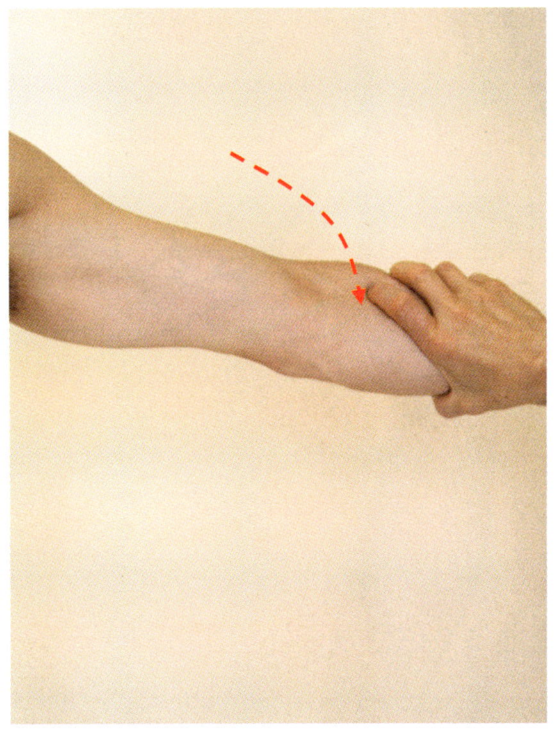

Fig. 2.63. Radio-ulnar pronation, managed throughout the range by the MF unit of intra-cubitus.

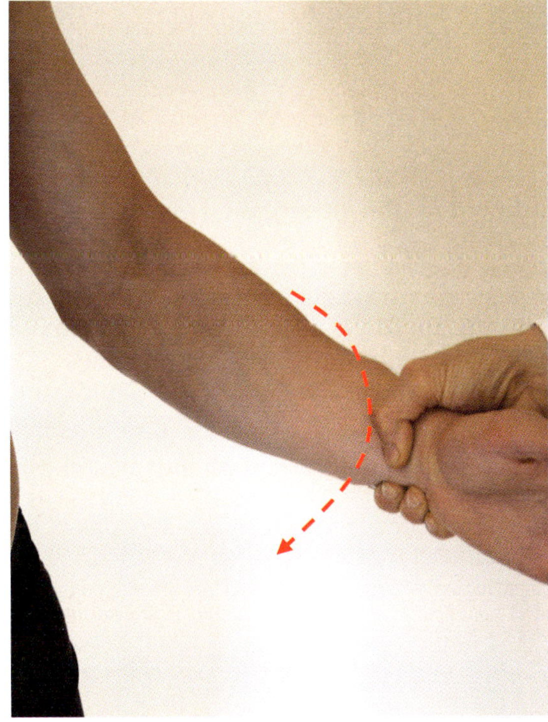

Fig. 2.64. Radio-carpal pronation, managed throughout the range by the MF unit of intra-carpus.

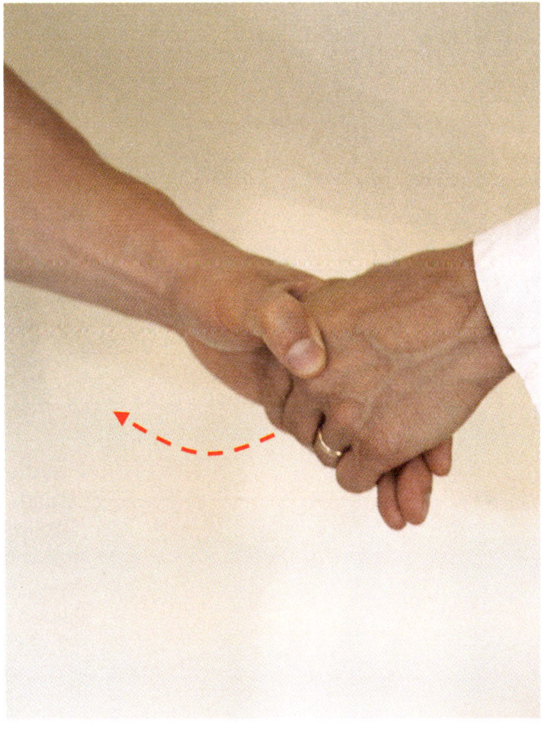

Fig. 2.65. Internal rotation of the fingers, managed throughout the range by the MF unit of intra-digiti.

The hand of the operator provides resistance to the movement indicated by the arrow.

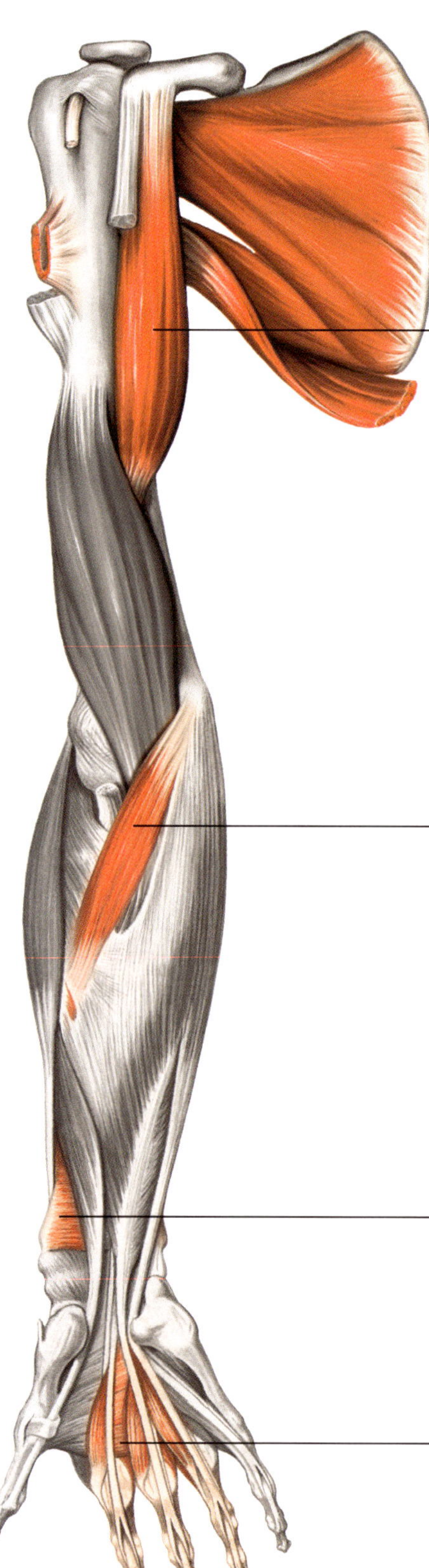

Fig. 2.66. Fascial compartments for intrarotation muscles.

(From G. Chiarugi and L. Bucciante, Istituzioni di anatomia dell'uomo. Piccin Nuova Libraria, Padova 1983, modified)

COMPARTMENTS FOR THE MUSCLES OF INTRAROTATION, UPPER LIMB (Fig. 2.67)

Fascial compartment for the intrarotation muscles of humerus

The fascia covering the subscapularis muscle reaches the lesser tubercle of the humerus and continues with: the fascia of the rotator cuff, the clavicoracoaxillary fascia surrounding the coracobrachialis muscle, and both pectoralis major and latissimus dorsi fasciae.

Fascial compartment for the intrarotation muscles of cubitus

The clavicoracoaxillary fascia surrounds the coracobrachialis muscle and accompanies it along the medial intermuscular septum. This septum reaches the epicondyle and forms the fascia of the pronator teres and palmaris longus muscles.

Fascial compartment for the intrarotation muscles of carpus

The palmaris longus muscle forms the superficial continuity between the medial septum and the palm of the hand whilst the pronator quadratus forms the deep continuity between the interosseous membrane and the joint capsule of carpus.

"Some fibres of the pronator quadratus reach the synovial capsule of the wrist joint" (Chiarugi G. 1975).

Fascial compartment for the intrarotation muscles of digiti (third, fourth digit)

The lumbrical muscles originate from the distal tendons of the flexor digitorum profundus muscle.

"The lumbrical muscles for the index and the fifth digit are innervated by the median nerve; the two lumbrical for the third and fourth digit are innervated by the ulnar nerve" (Platzer W. 2009).

GLOBAL MOVEMENT IMPLEMENTED BY THE INTRAROTATION SEQUENCE

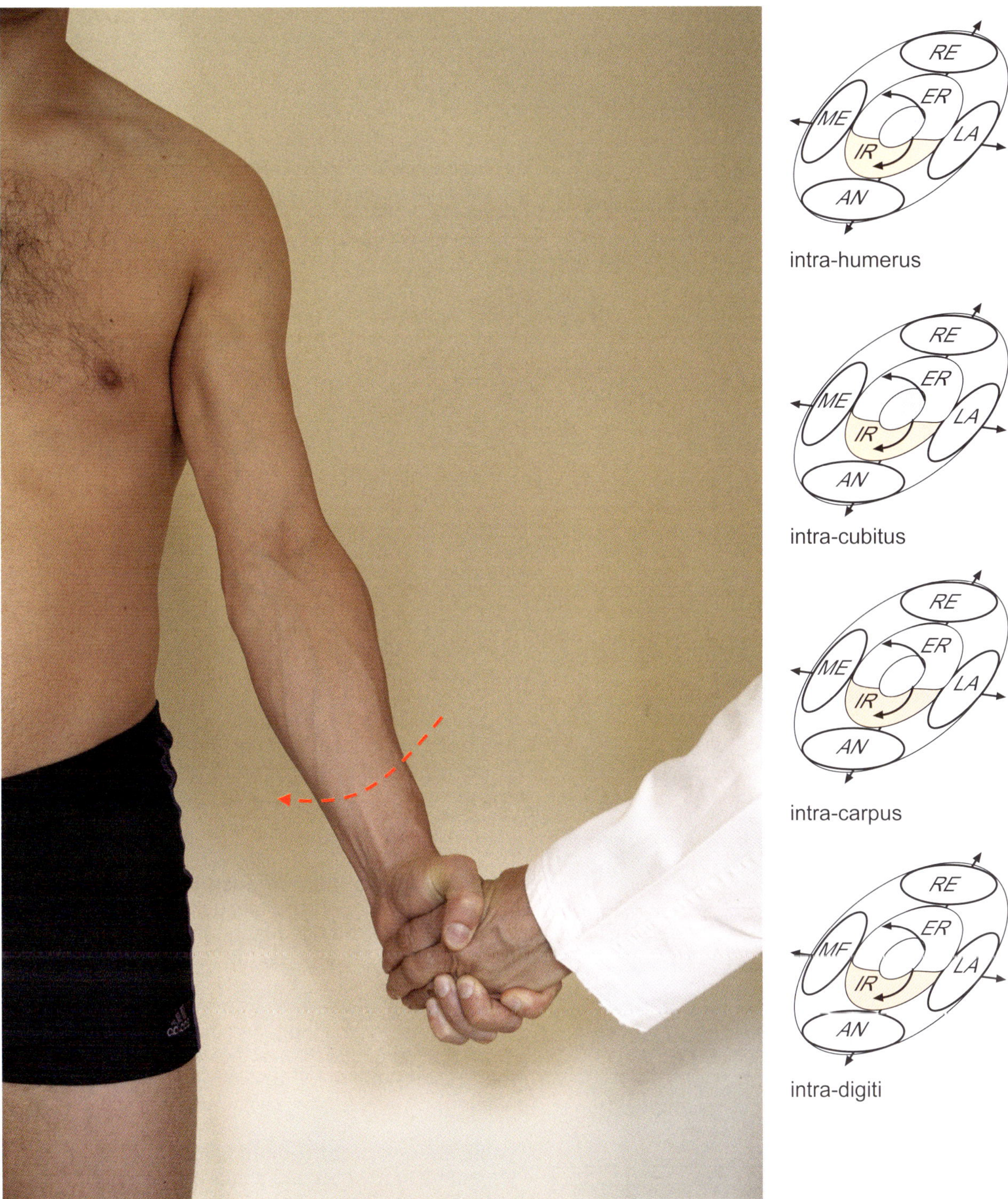

Fig. 2.67. Contraction of the intrarotation sequence rotating the entire upper limb internally.

The muscles carrying out intrarotation of the humerus (subscapularis muscle), of cubitus (pronator teres muscle), of carpus (pronator quadratus muscle), and of digiti (lumbrical muscles) are contained in their fascia of contention (epimysial fascial compartments). Their continuity along the sequence of intrarotation is more readily understandable when also taking into consideration the intermuscular septa and the fascial compartment of the flexor digitorum superficialis muscle. During movements of intrarotation the septa are stretched differently compared to adduction movements hence these movements also activate different proprioceptors.

PHYSIOLOGY OF THE INTRAROTATION MF UNITS IN THE UPPER LIMB

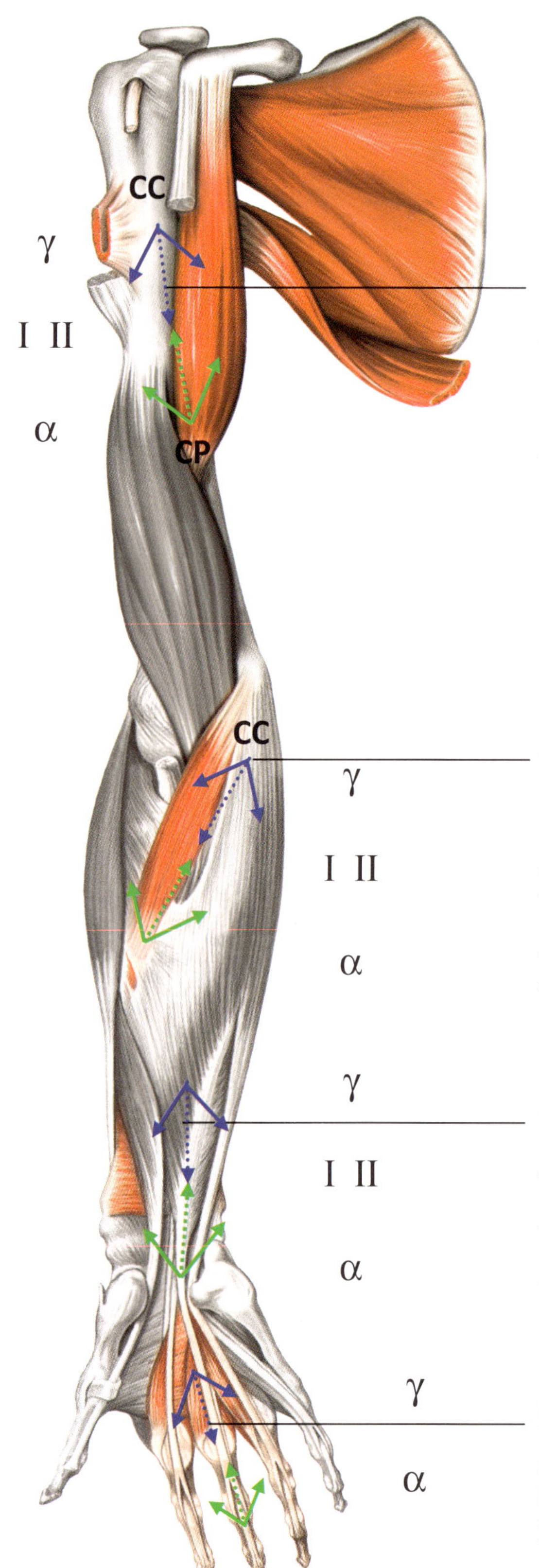

Fig. 2.68. Normal functioning of the gamma circuit. *(From G. Chiarugi and L. Bucciante, Istituzioni di anatomia dell'uomo. Piccin Nuova Libraria, Padova 1983, modified)*

Myofascial unit of intra-humerus (ir-hu)
The gamma motor neurone stimulates the intrafusal muscle fibres of the motor units for intrarotation, their tractions on the perimysium converge on the tendon of the pectoralis major muscle (CC). The adaptability of the perimysium allows the afferents I, II to close the circuit triggering the alpha impulse, which in turn allows the contraction of the extrafusal fibres of the MF unit intra-humerus.

Myofascial unit of intra-cubitus (ir-cu)
The gamma motor neurone stimulates the intrafusal muscle fibres of muscles originating from the motor units for intrarotation, their tractions on the perimysium converge on the muscle belly of pronator teres (blue vectors).
The adaptability of the perimysium allows the afferents I, II to close the circuit triggering the alpha impulse. This stimulus causes the contraction of the extrafusal fibres of the MF unit intra-cubitus (radio-ulnar pronation).

Myofascial unit of intra-carpus (ir-ca)
The gamma motor neurone stimulates the intrafusal muscle fibres of pronator quadratus; their tractions on the perimysium converge on the centre of coordination (CC).
The adaptability of the perimysium allows the afferents I, II to close the circuit triggering the alpha impulse. This allows the contraction of the extrafusal fibres (green vectors) of the MF unit intra-carpus (wrist pronation).

Myofascial unit of intra-digiti (ir-di)
The gamma motor neurone stimulates the intrafusal muscle fibres of the lumbricals, their tractions on the perimysium converges in the centre of the palmar aponeurosis.
The adaptability of the perimysium allows the afferents I, II to close the circuit triggering the alpha impulse. This allows the contraction of the extrafusal fibres of the MF unit intra-digiti.

ARTICULAR CONFLICTS IN THE INTRAROTATION UNITS IN THE UPPER LIMB

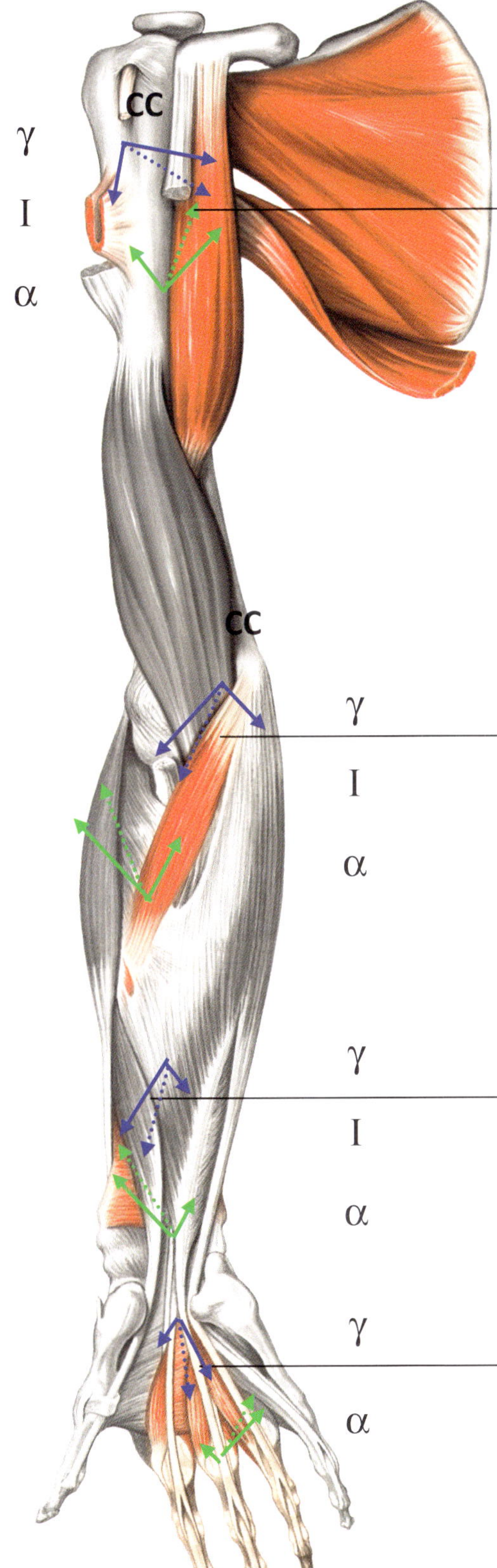

Pain during intrarotation of humerus
If the fascia located on the intersection between the tendon of subscapularis and pectoralis major (CC) is densified, then the afferents from a few neuromuscular spindles are not fired. Hence the alpha circuits for those extrafusal fibres of the MF unit of ir-hu are not activated. The contraction from the extrafusal muscle fibres that are activated shifts the tendinous resultant outside of its physiological axis. Consequently, a conflict occurs at the glenohumeral joint.

Pain during intrarotation of cubitus
If the fascia located in the elbow crease below the epitrochlea (CC) is densified, then the afferents from a few neuromuscular spindles are not fired to close the alpha circuit.
The contraction from the extrafusal muscle fibres that are activated shifts the tendinous resultant of these vectors outside of its physiological axis. Consequently, a conflict occurs at the medial elbow joint and in the forearm.

Pain during intrarotation of carpus
If the fascia located proximally to the muscle belly of pronator quadratus (CC) is densified, then the afferents from a few neuromuscular spindles are not fired, hence the alpha circuits for those extrafusal fibres of the MF unit are not activated.
The contraction from the extrafusal muscle fibres that are activated shifts the tendinous resultant of these vectors outside of its physiological axis. Consequently, a conflict occurs at the carpal joint.

Pain during intrarotation of digiti III
If the fascia located over the lumbrical muscles (CC) is densified, then the afferents from a few spindles are not fired, hence the alpha circuit for those extrafusal fibres of the MF unit is not activated.
The contraction from the extrafusal muscle fibres that are activated shifts the tendinous resultant of these vectors outside of its physiological axis. Consequently, a conflict occurs at the joints of digiti.

Fig. 2.69. Dysfunctions of the gamma circuit.
(From G. Chiarugi and L. Bucciante, Istituzioni di anatomia dell'uomo. Piccin Nuova Libraria, Padova 1983, modified)

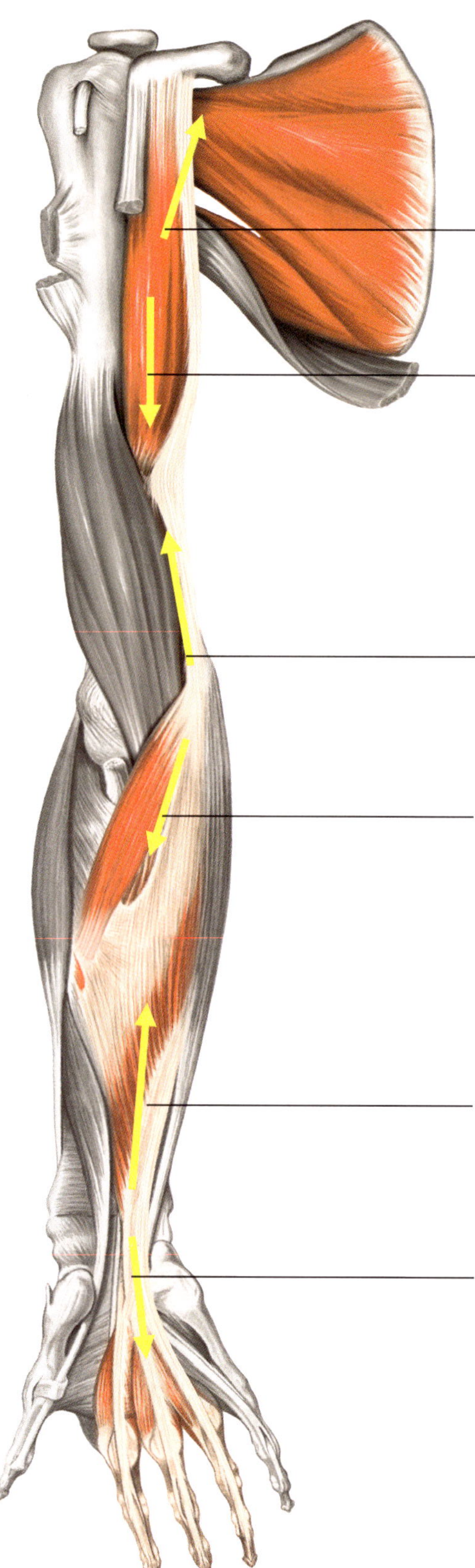

INTRAROTATION SEQUENCE AND STRETCH REFLEX

Synergy between the MF units of intra-humerus and intra-cubitus
The fascia covering the subscapularis muscle is connected to the clavicoracoaxillary fascia that is united with the coracobrachialis muscle (Fig. 2.72). The ensemble of these fasciae is maintained into a basal tone through the proximal traction of the subscapularis muscle and the distal traction of the coracobrachialis muscle.

Synergy between the MF units of intra-humerus and intra-carpus
When the effort of screwing a bolt is performed, the intrarotation tension of the shoulder muscles must be synchronised with the muscular force of cubitus, carpus and digiti. The medial intermuscular septum is pulled: proximally by the coracobrachialis, distally by the pronator teres (Fig. 2.73), and by the flexor digitorum muscles that are in continuity with the pronator teres fascia.

Synergy between the MF units of intra-carpus and intra-digiti
The palmaris longus muscle participates in the pronation of the forearm and forms the palmar aponeurosis (Fig. 2.75), where its longitudinal bundles spread out to the tendons of flexor digitorum. Both the pronator quadratus (Fig. 2.74) and flexor digitorum profundus muscles are located in the third musculo-fascial layer, the distal tendons of the latter give insertions to the lumbrical muscles. The contraction of the flexor digitorum profundus muscle creates a proximal traction on the deep aponeurosis whilst the contraction of the lumbrical muscles creates a distal traction.

Fig. 2.70. Synergy of the intrarotation sequence in the upper limb.
(From G. Chiarugi and L. Bucciante, Istituzioni di anatomia dell'uomo. Piccin Nuova Libraria, Padova 1983, modified)

ACTIVATION OF THE GOLGI TENDON ORGANS

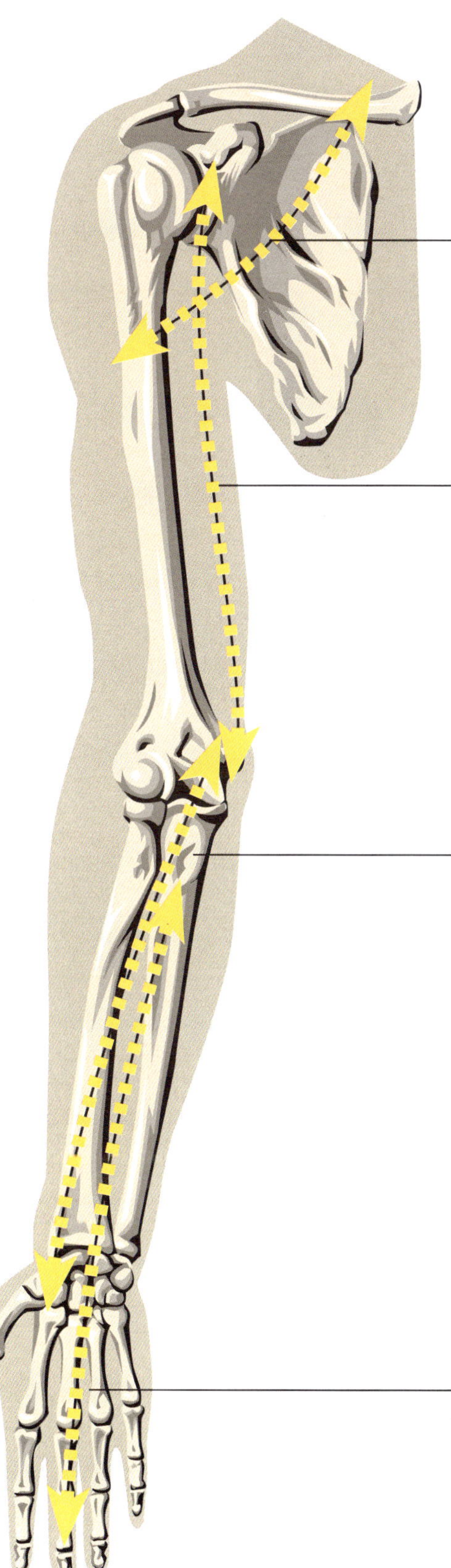

Combined action between intra-scapula and intra-humerus

The pectoralis major muscle participates in intrarotation of humerus through its distal tendon and participates in intrarotation of scapula through it clavicular origin (when acting as a lever on the humerus).

Combined action between intra-humerus and intra-cubitus

Some fibres of the pronator teres muscle may extend upwards and connect to the coracobrachialis muscle.

"The long muscle coracobrachialis is a supernumerary bundle stretched between the coracoid process and the medial epicondyle. It rotates the humerus internally" (Chiarugi G. 1975).

Combined action between intra-cubitus and intra-carpus

The flexor carpi radialis muscle originates from the medial intermuscular septum of the humerus and inserts on the second and third metacarpal bones, hence it acts simultaneously on the intrarotation of cubitus and carpus.

When bringing a glass to the mouth, the flexor carpi radialis muscle must scale its force in the elbow and the wrist based upon the variations of the liquid contained in the glass itself.

Combined action between intra-carpus and intra-digiti

The flexor digitorum profundus muscle originates from the proximal two thirds of the ulna and the interosseous membrane. This muscle simultaneously performs a slight internal rotation and flexion of the wrist, metacarpals and phalanges.

When an object is grasped, the grip is stronger if the fingers and wrist are placed in intrarotation or pronation.

Fig. 2.71. Biarticular muscles for intrarotation in the upper limb.

FASCIAE OF THE INTRAROTATION SEQUENCE IN THE UPPER LIMB

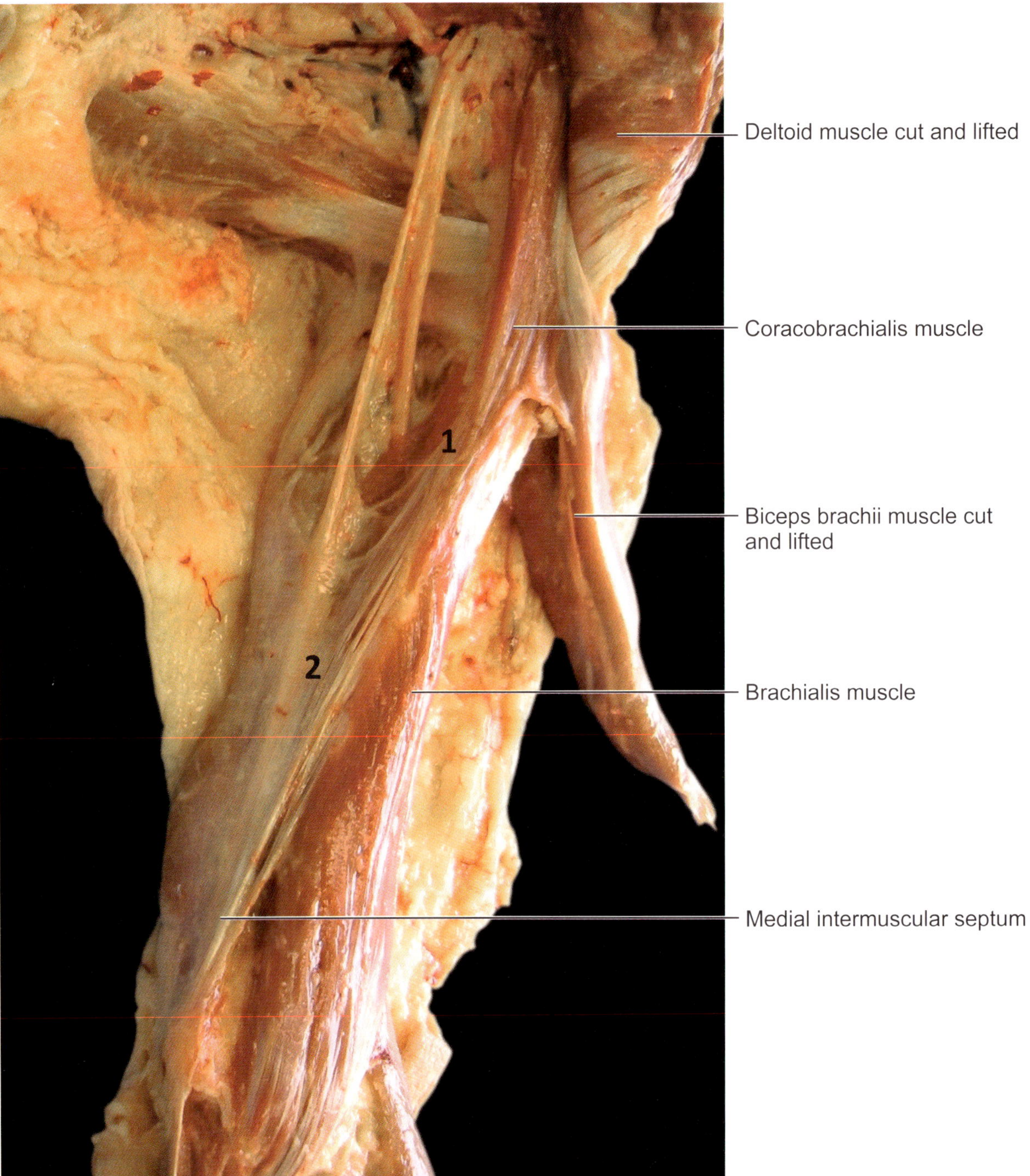

Fig. 2.72. Axilla with the origin of the medial septum. Contraction of the coracobrachialis muscle (1) propagates along the medial intermuscular septum (2).

In the figures horizontal lines indicate anatomical parts whilst numbers (1, 2) indicate the physiology of the fascia. Number 1 indicates a determined action and number 2 indicates its effect.

FASCIAE OF THE INTRAROTATION SEQUENCE IN THE UPPER LIMB

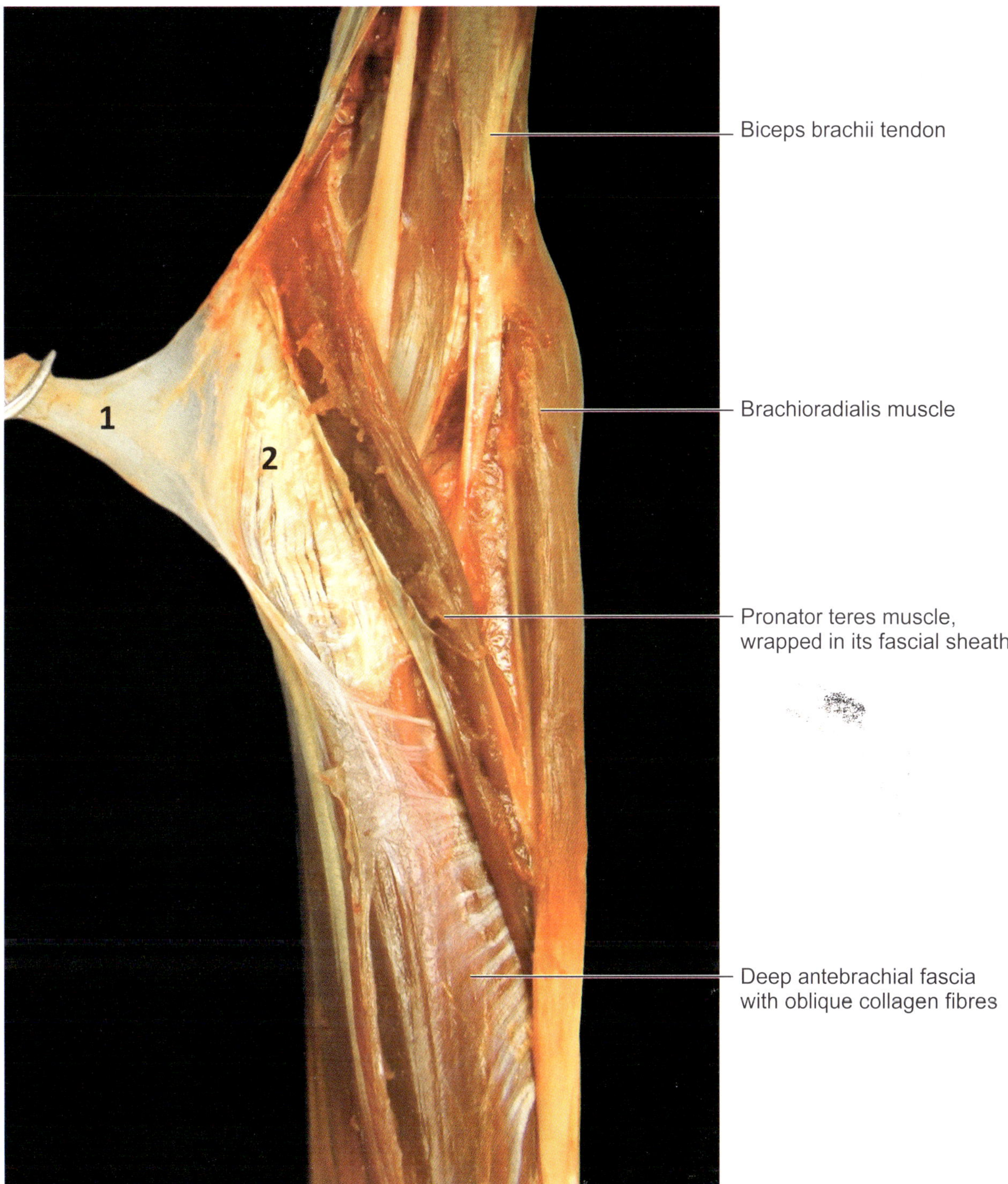

Fig. 2.73. Antebrachial fascia cut and lifted laterally (1) to highlight the pronator teres and flexor carpi radialis (2) muscles.

FASCIAE OF THE INTRAROTATION SEQUENCE IN THE UPPER LIMB

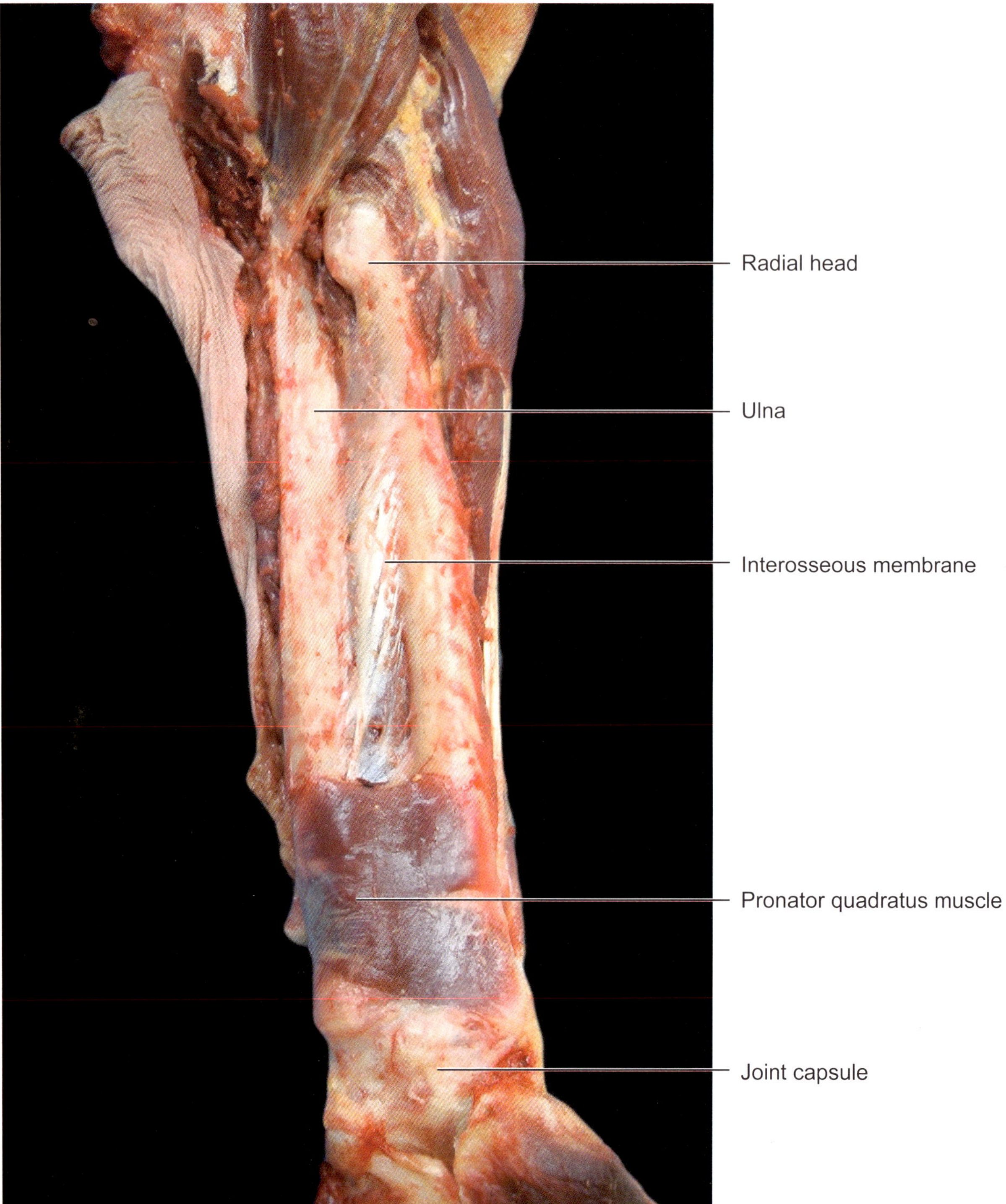

Fig. 2.74. Interosseous membrane of the forearm. This membrane passes underneath the pronator quadratus muscle, its fascia forming a whole with the joint capsule of the wrist.

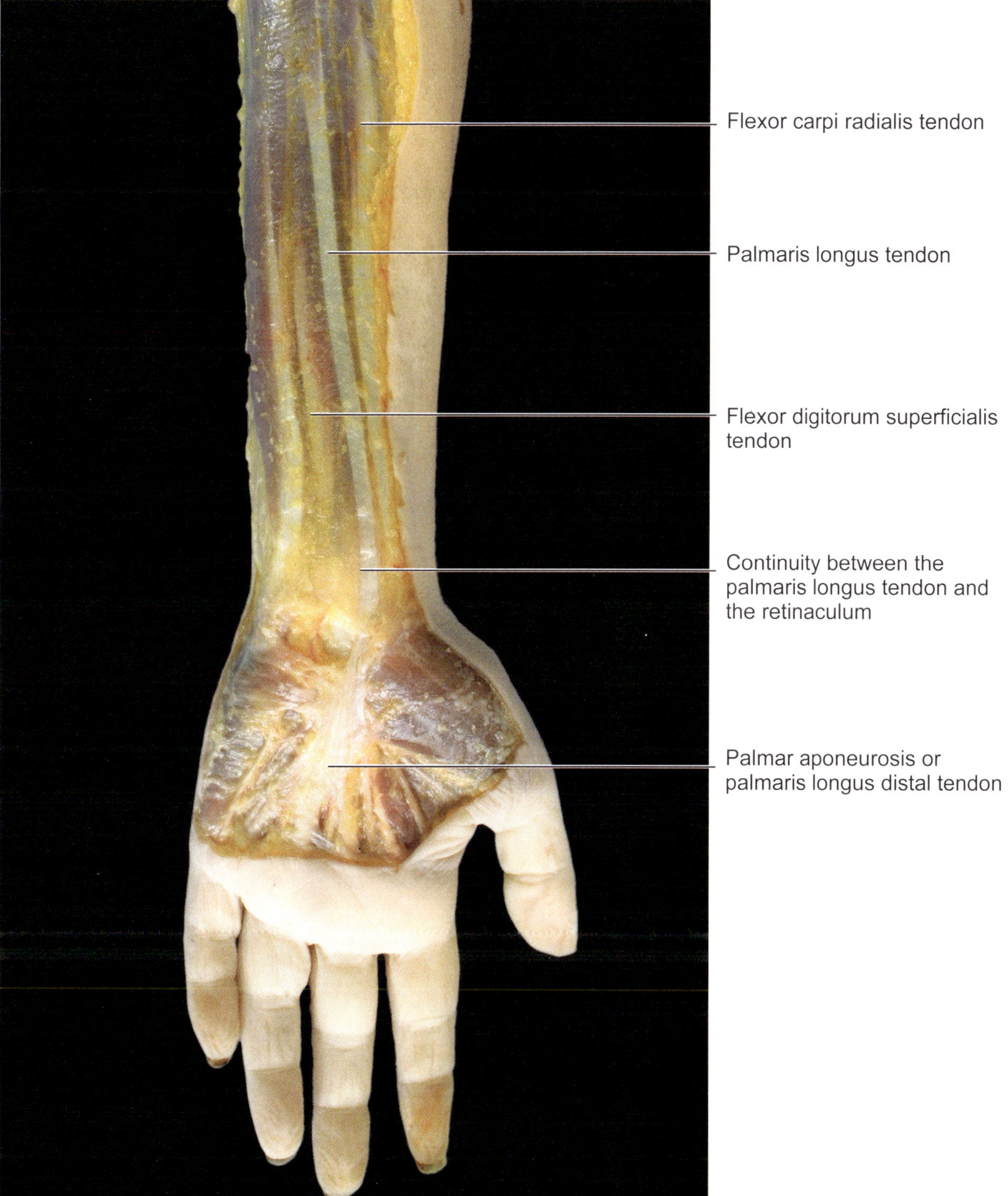

Fig. 2.75. Palmar aponeurosis and medial antebrachial fascia. In this photograph, the flexor retinaculum appears like a slight thickening of the antebrachial fascia.

DEEP POSTERIOR REGION OF THE UPPER LIMB, EXTRAROTATION SEQUENCE

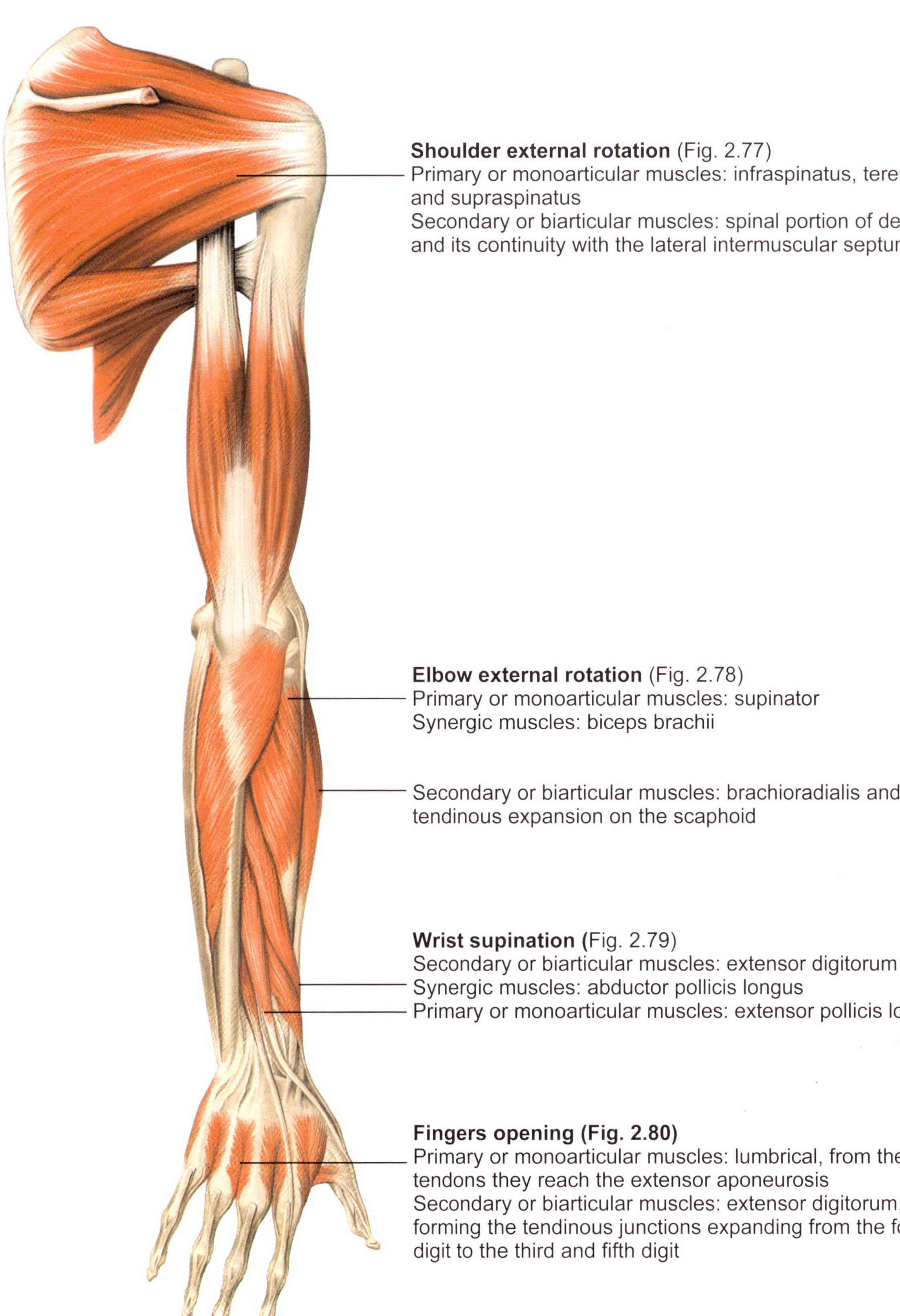

Fig. 2.76. Deep posterior region of the upper limb.
(From G. Chiarugi and L. Bucciante, Istituzioni di anatomia dell'uomo. Piccin Nuova Libraria, Padova 1983, modified)

SEGMENTARY MOVEMENTS IMPLEMENTED BY THE MF UNITS OF EXTRAROTATION

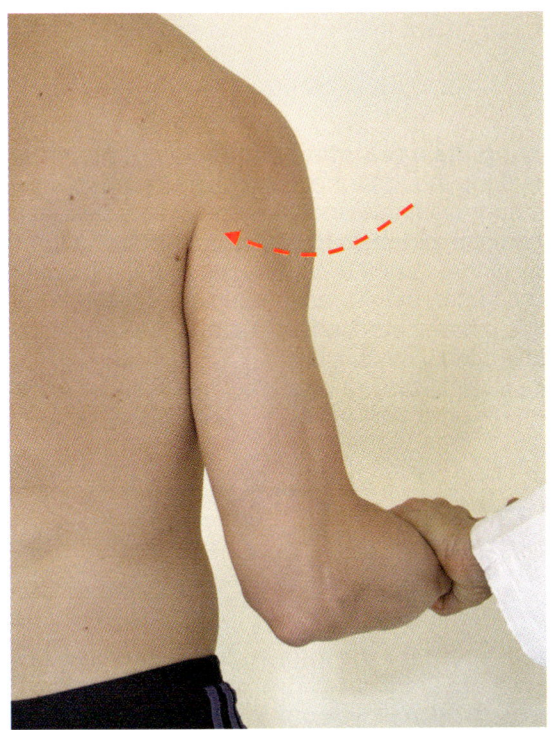

Fig. 2.77. Shoulder external rotation, managed throughout the range by the myofascial unit of extra-humerus.

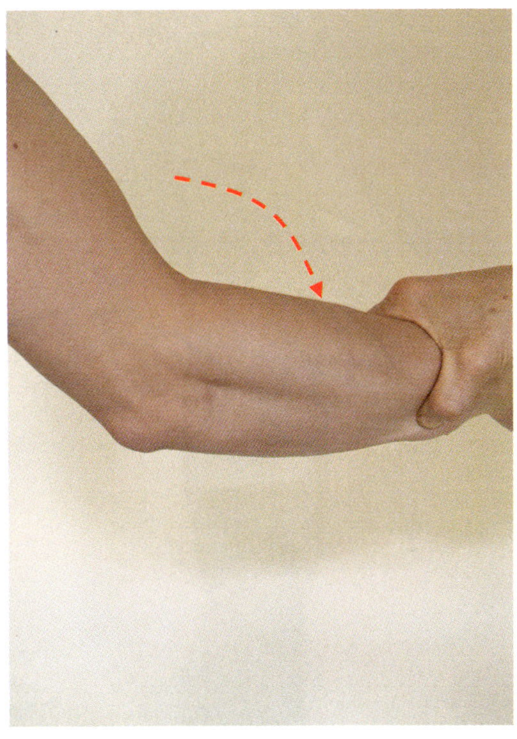

Fig. 2.78. Radio-ulnar supination, managed throughout the range by the MF unit of extra-cubitus.

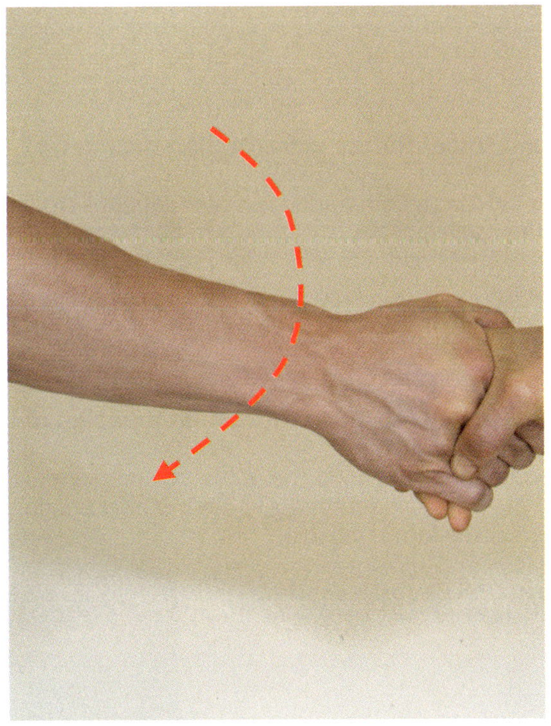

Fig. 2.79. Radio-ulnar supination, managed throughout the range by the MF unit of extra-carpus.

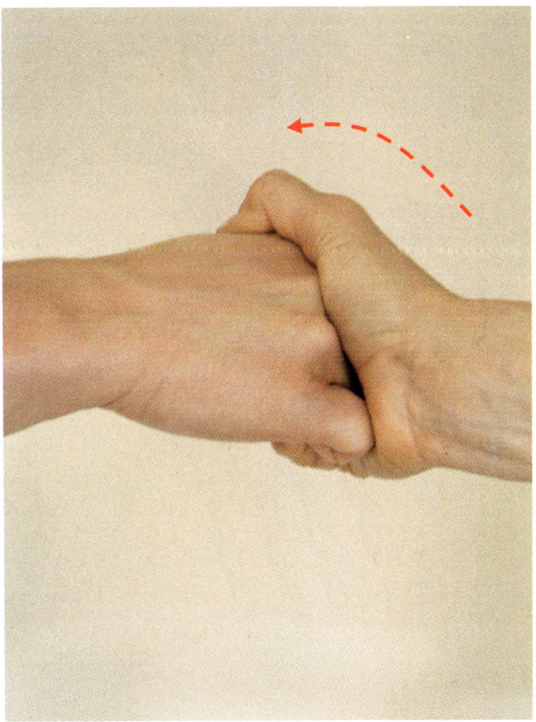

Fig. 2.80. Opening external rotation of the fingers, managed by the MF unit of extra-digiti.

The hand of the operator provides resistance to the direction of movement indicated by the arrow.

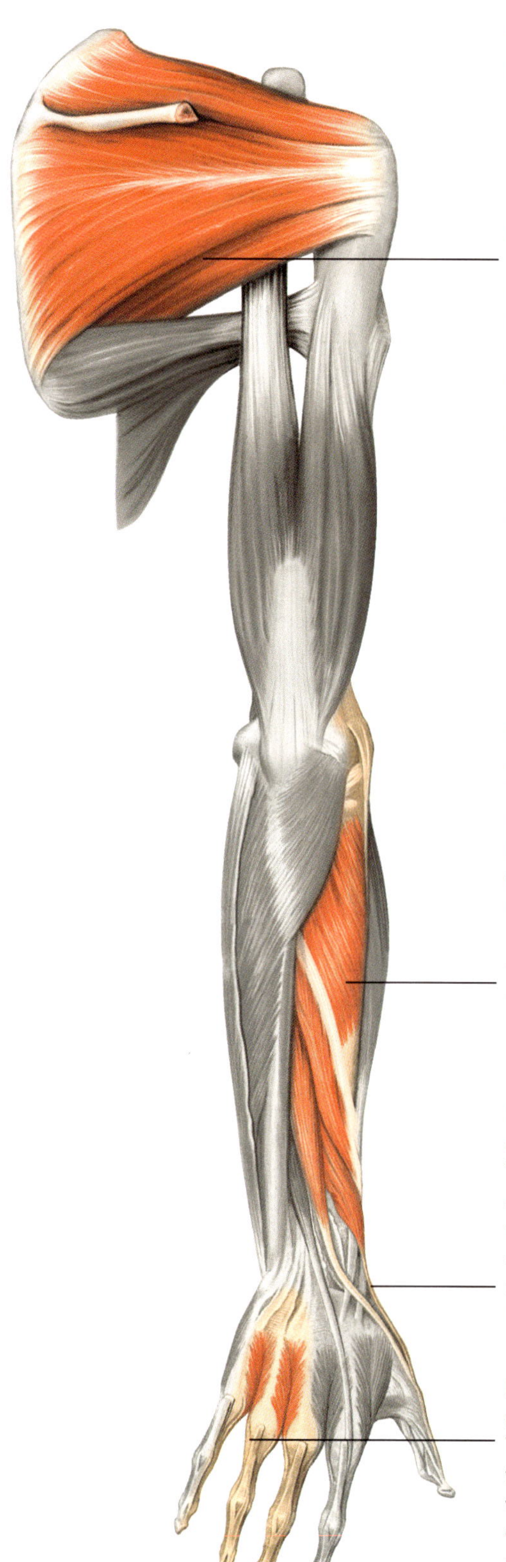

Fig. 2.81. Fascial compartments for the extrarotation muscles.

(From G. Chiarugi and L. Bucciante, Istituzioni di anatomia dell'uomo. Piccin Nuova Libraria, Padova 1983, modified)

COMPARTMENTS FOR THE MUSCLES OF EXTRAROTATION, UPPER LIMB (Fig. 2.82)

Fascia overlying the extrarotation muscles of humerus

The fascia covering the rotator cuff is continuous with the infraspinatus, supraspinatus and teres minor muscles. At the level of the spine of the scapula it is connected to the subdeltoid fascia that in turn is continuous with the lateral intermuscular septum. In this case, no unique fascial compartment is present but the fascia forms the continuity between ipsidirectional motor units.

"The infraspinatus fascia converts the infraspinatus fossa of the scapula in a compartment. The supraspinatus and the infraspinatus compartments communicate between them" (Fumagalli Z. 1974).

Fascial compartment for the extrarotation muscles of cubitus

The brachioradialis muscle was previously called the "supinator longus", it originates from the lateral border of the humerus starting from the groove of the radial nerve and from the anterior aspect of the lateral intermuscular septum. Its origins may ascend up to the deltoid tuberosity.

"The supinator muscle takes origin from the epicondyle, from the radial collateral ligament and from the annular radio-ulnar ligament" (Chiarugi G. 1975).

Fascial compartment for the extrarotation muscles of carpus

The extensor digitorum communis muscle originates from the epicondyle, the radial collateral ligament of the elbow and from the deep aspect of the fascia.

"The abductor pollicis longus muscle takes origin from below the supinator muscle, from the ulna and from the interosseous membrane" (Chiarugi G. 1975).

Fascial compartment for the extrarotation muscles of digiti (third, fourth digit)

The thumb, index and little finger have their own extensor tendon. Only the third and fourth digits are in direct continuity with the extensor digitorum muscle.

"The dorsal interossei muscles are more robust than the palmar interossei muscles. Their tendon is fixed partly on the base of the first phalanx and partly on the tendons of the extensor digitorum communis muscle" (Chiarugi G. 1975).

GLOBAL MOVEMENT IMPLEMENTED BY THE EXTRAROTATION SEQUENCE

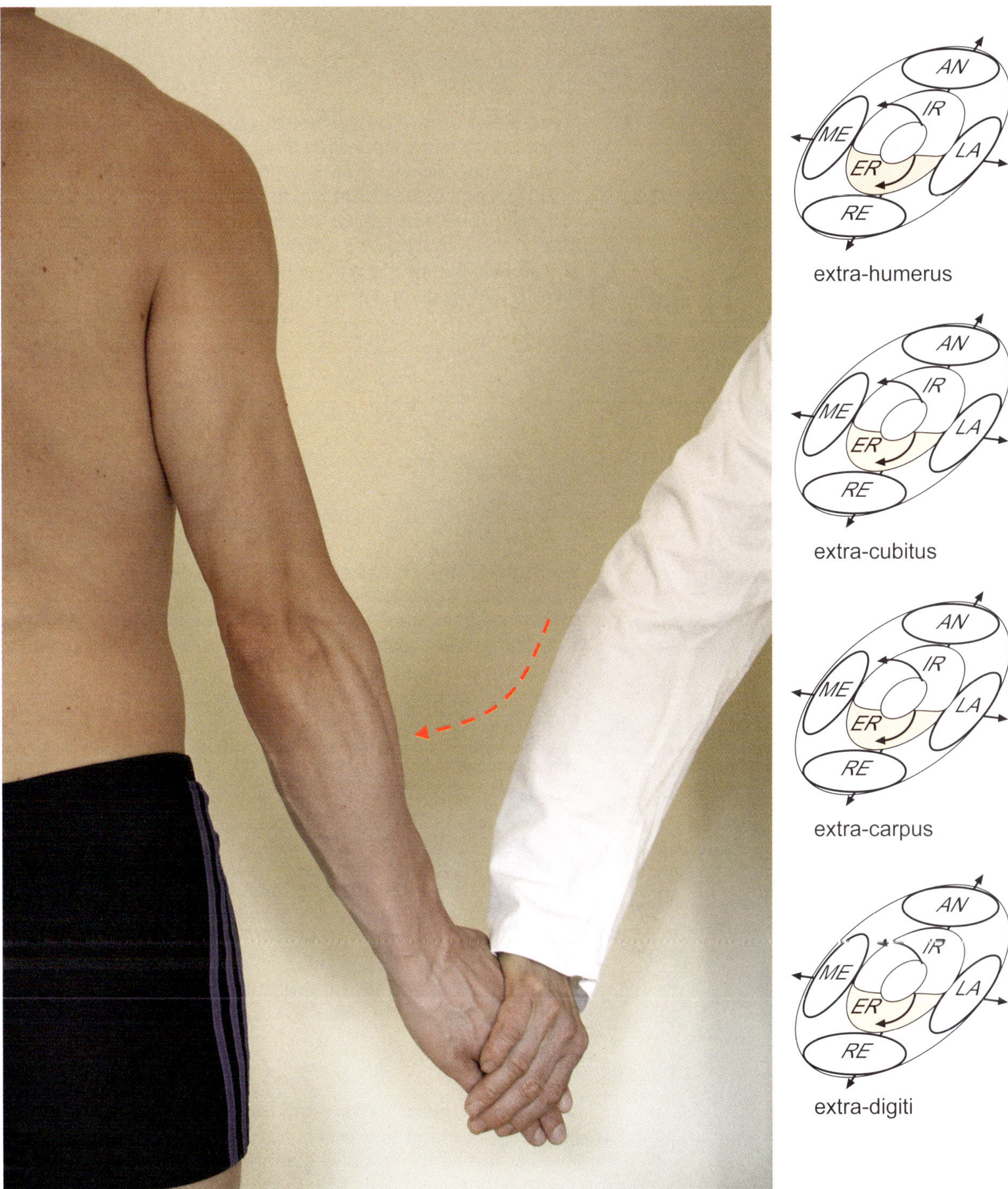

Fig. 2.82. Contraction of the extrarotation sequence rotating the entire upper limb externally.

The dashed red arrow indicates the movement implemented by the entire sequence. When the operator offers resistance to the most distal MF unit, or extrarotation unit of digiti, then there is major recruitment of the four MF units. The interaction between the MF units of extrarotation is more or less intense based upon the effort.

PHYSIOLOGY OF THE EXTRAROTATION MF UNITS IN THE UPPER LIMB

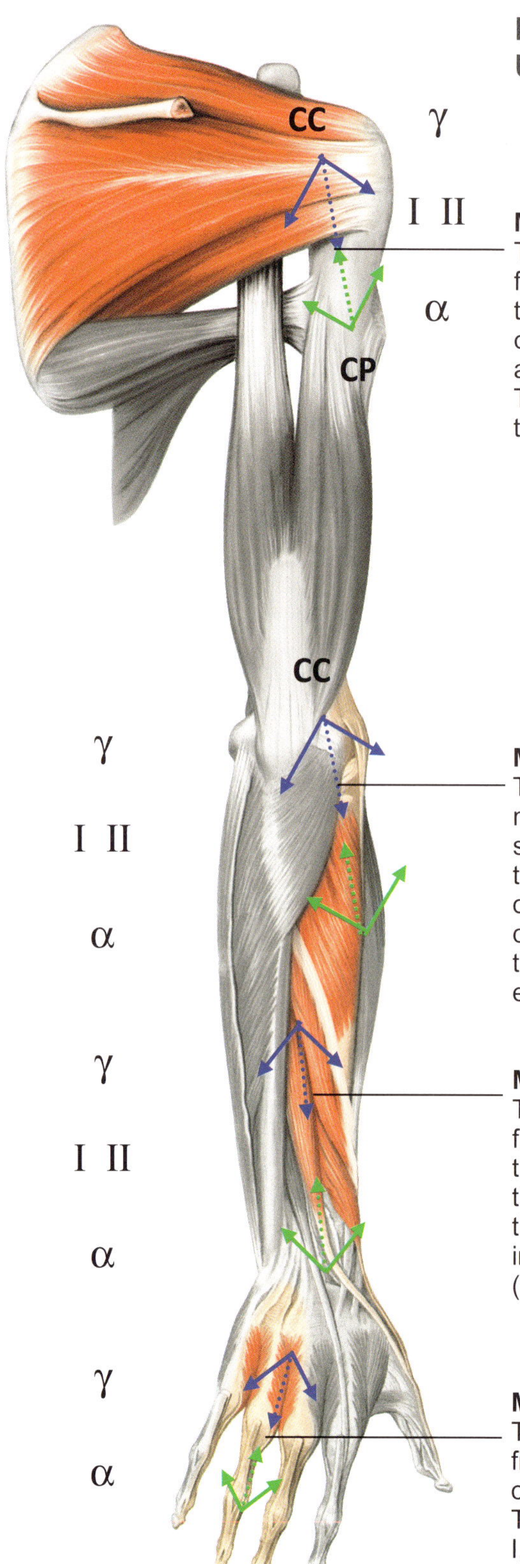

Myofascial unit of extra-humerus (er-hu)
The gamma motor neurone stimulates the intrafusal muscle fibres of the infraspinatus and teres minor motor units, their tractions on the perimysium converge on the rotator cuff (CC). The adaptability of the perimysium allows the afferents I, II to close the circuit triggering the alpha impulse. This in turn allows the contraction of the extrafusal fibres for the MF unit extra-humerus.

Myofascial unit of extra-cubitus (er-cu)
The gamma motor neurone stimulates the intrafusal muscle fibres of long supinator (brachioradialis) and short supinator, their tractions on the perimysium converge on the centre of coordination (blue vectors). The adaptability of the perimysium allows the afferents I, II to close the circuit triggering the alpha impulse. This stimulus causes the contraction of the extrafusal fibres for the MF unit extra-cubitus.

Myofascial unit of extra-carpus (er-ca)
The gamma motor neurone stimulates the intrafusal muscle fibres of abductor pollicis longus and extensor digitorum, their tractions on the perimysium converge on the fascia of this muscle (CC). The adaptability of the perimysium allows the afferents I, II to close the circuit triggering the alpha impulse. This allows the contraction of the extrafusal fibres (green arrows) for the MF unit extra-carpus.

Myofascial unit of extra-digiti (er-di)
The gamma motor neurone stimulates the intrafusal muscle fibres of the lumbricals and dorsal interossei, their tractions on the perimysium converge in the centre of coordination. The adaptability of the perimysium allows the afferents I, II to close the circuit triggering the alpha impulse. This allows the contraction of the extrafusal fibres for the MF unit extra-digiti.

Fig. 2.83. Normal functioning of the gamma circuit.

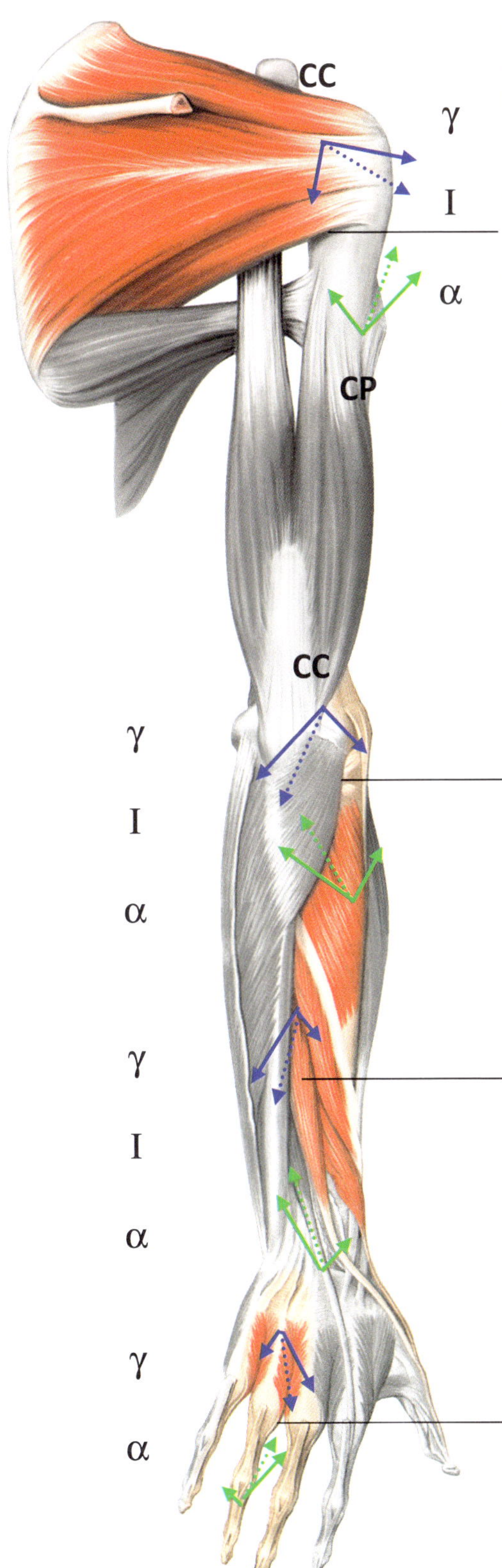

Fig. 2.84. Dysfunctions of the gamma circuit.
(From G. Chiarugi and L. Bucciante, Istituzioni di anatomia dell'uomo. Piccin Nuova Libraria, Padova 1983, modified)

ARTICULAR CONFLICTS IN THE EXTRAROTATION UNITS IN THE UPPER LIMB

Pain during extrarotation of humerus
If the fascia located over the rotator cuff (CC) is densified, then the afferents (II) from a few muscle spindles are not fired. Hence the alpha circuit for those extrafusal fibres of the MF unit of er-hu is not activated. The contraction from the extrafusal muscle fibres that are activated shifts the tendinous resultant outside of its physiological axis. Consequently, a conflict occurs at the glenohumeral joint.

Pain during extrarotation of cubitus
If the fascia located behind the elbow on the origin of the supinator muscle (CC) is densified, then the afferents from a few neuromuscular spindles are not fired to close the alpha circuit.
The contraction from the extrafusal muscle fibres that are activated shifts the tendinous resultant of these vectors outside of its physiological axis. Consequently, a conflict occurs at the lateral elbow joint.

Pain during extrarotation of carpus
If the fascia overlying the muscle belly of abductor pollicis and extensor digitorum communis (CC) is densified, then the afferents from a few neuromuscular spindles will not trigger the alpha circuit for those extrafusal fibres of the MF unit (blue vectors).
The contraction from the extrafusal muscle fibres that are activated shifts the tendinous resultant of these vectors outside of its physiological axis. Consequently, a conflict occurs at the carpal joint (green vectors).

Pain during extrarotation of digiti
If the fascia located over the dorsal interossei muscles (CC) is densified, then the afferents from a few neuromuscular spindles are not activated and do not trigger the alpha circuit for those extrafusal fibres of the MF unit.
The contraction from the extrafusal muscle fibres that are activated shifts the tendinous resultant of these vectors outside of its physiological axis. Consequently, a conflict occurs at the joints of digiti (especially third and fourth digit).

EXTRAROTATION SEQUENCE AND STRETCH REFLEX

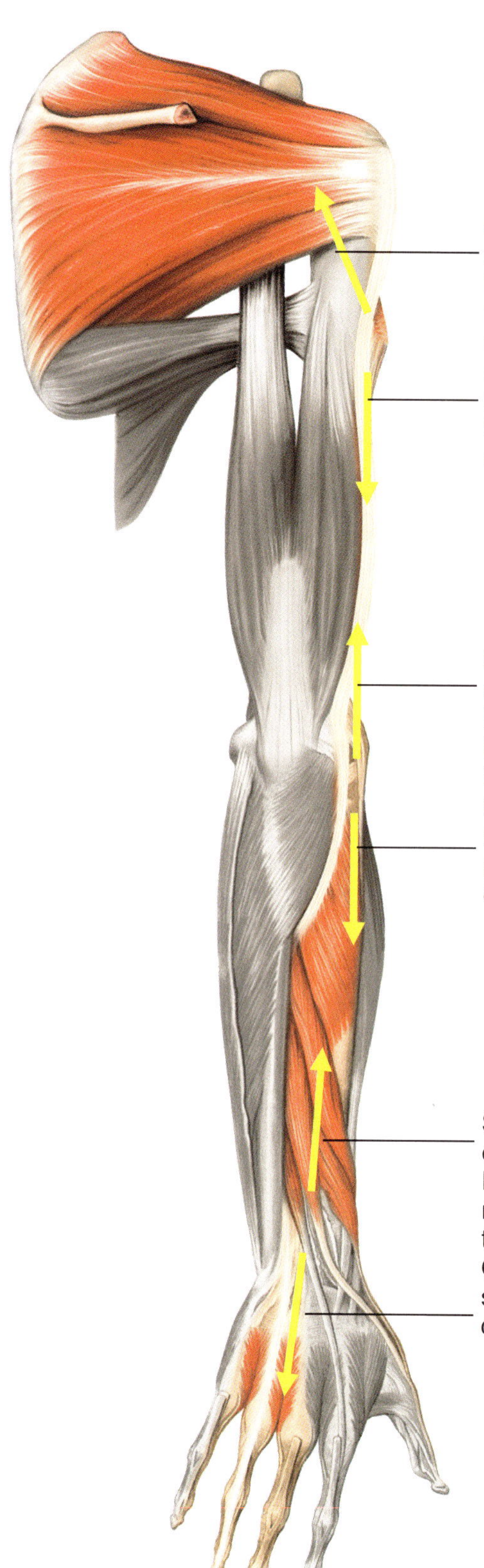

Fig. 2.85. Synergy of the extrarotation sequence in the upper limb.

(From G. Chiarugi and L. Bucciante, Istituzioni di anatomia dell'uomo. Piccin Nuova Libraria, Padova 1983, modified)

Synergy between the MF units of extra-humerus and extra-cubitus

When opening a jar, the entire upper limb is implicated in the extrarotation effort. In this case, the fascia covering the infraspinatus (Fig. 2.87) and the posterior deltoid muscles is pulled proximally. The fascia of the deltoid muscle continues with the lateral intermuscular septum. In turn, this septum is stretched distally by the simultaneous contraction of the brachioradialis and supinator muscles.

Synergy between the MF units of extra-humerus and extra-carpus

During the effort in extrarotation of the arm, the lateral head of the triceps muscle fixes the lateral septum (Fig. 2.88), whilst the supinator muscle distally tractions this septum. Through the effect of the stretch reflex, the neuromuscular spindles of the extensor digitorum muscle partly originating from the antebrachial fascia (Fig. 2.89) are also activated.

Synergy between the MF units of extra-carpus and extra-digiti

During an effort in extrarotation of the upper limb, the musculature of the hand (Fig. 2.90) must adapt its force to that of the forearm and arm muscles.

Only the continuity of the fascia can coordinate and synchronise the operation of all the myofascial units distributed along the extrarotation sequence.

ACTIVATION OF THE GOLGI TENDON ORGANS

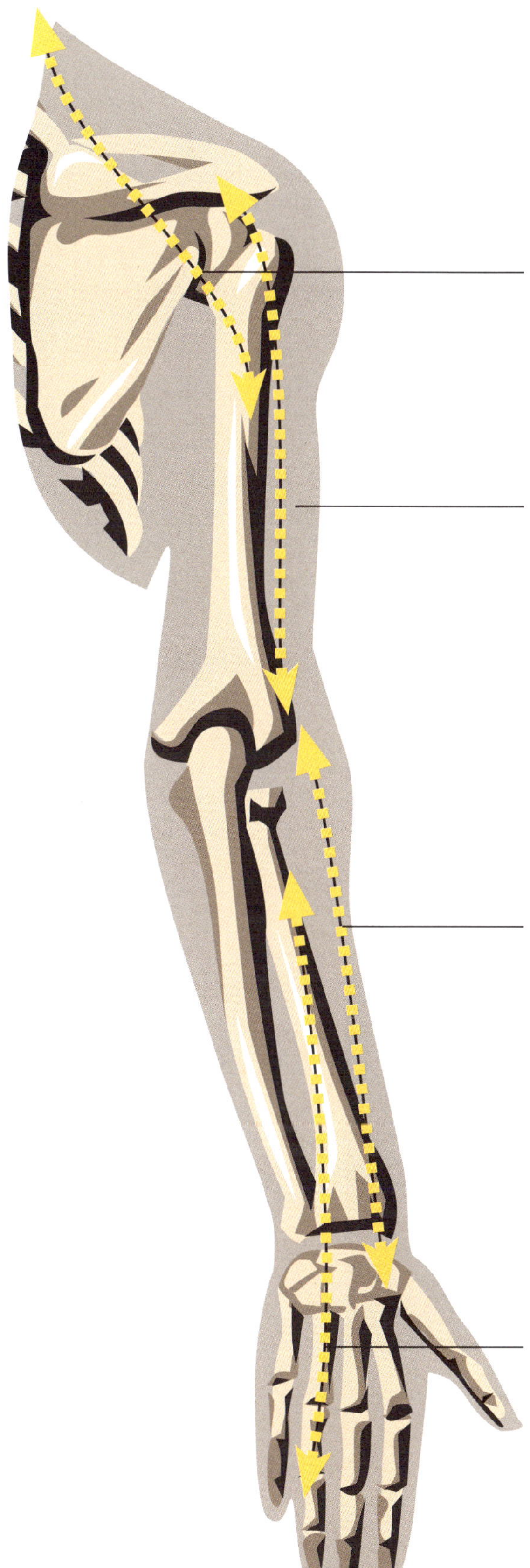

Fig. 2.86. Biarticular muscles for extrarotation in the upper limb.

Combined action between extra-scapula and extra-humerus
The fascia of the spinal portion of the deltoid muscle continues with the fascia overlying the trapezius muscle. During extrarotation of the humerus, the scapula is pulled posteriorly by the trapezius muscle.

Combined action between extra-humerus and extra-cubitus
During extrarotation of the humerus without resistance, only the specific muscles for the MF unit of er-hu intervene. However if the movement is performed against resistance as when unscrewing a bolt, then the triceps, the spinal portion of the deltoid, the brachioradialis and the supinator muscles are activated. The lateral intermuscular septum unites these forces into a single mass in order to adapt them to the variations in joint angles of humerus and cubitus.

Combined action between extra-cubitus and extra-carpus
The extensor carpi radialis muscle participates in the extrarotation of the carpus. It originates from the lateral intermuscular septum and proceeds up to the hand. The brachioradialis muscle also originates from the lateral septum, where distally it inserts on: the styloid process of the radius, the scaphoid through tendinous expansions, and the radial collateral carpal ligament. The Golgi tendon organs of this ligament coordinate the movement of the wrist with that of the elbow.

Combined action between extra-carpus and extra-digiti
The extensor digitorum muscle does not only end with tendons, but its tendons connect with the juncturae tendinum at the level of the metacarpals. At the metacarpo-phalangeal level, each tendon sends out expansions to the joint capsules and receives expansions from the tendons of the lumbricals and interossei muscles.

FASCIAE OF THE EXTRAROTATION SEQUENCE IN THE UPPER LIMB

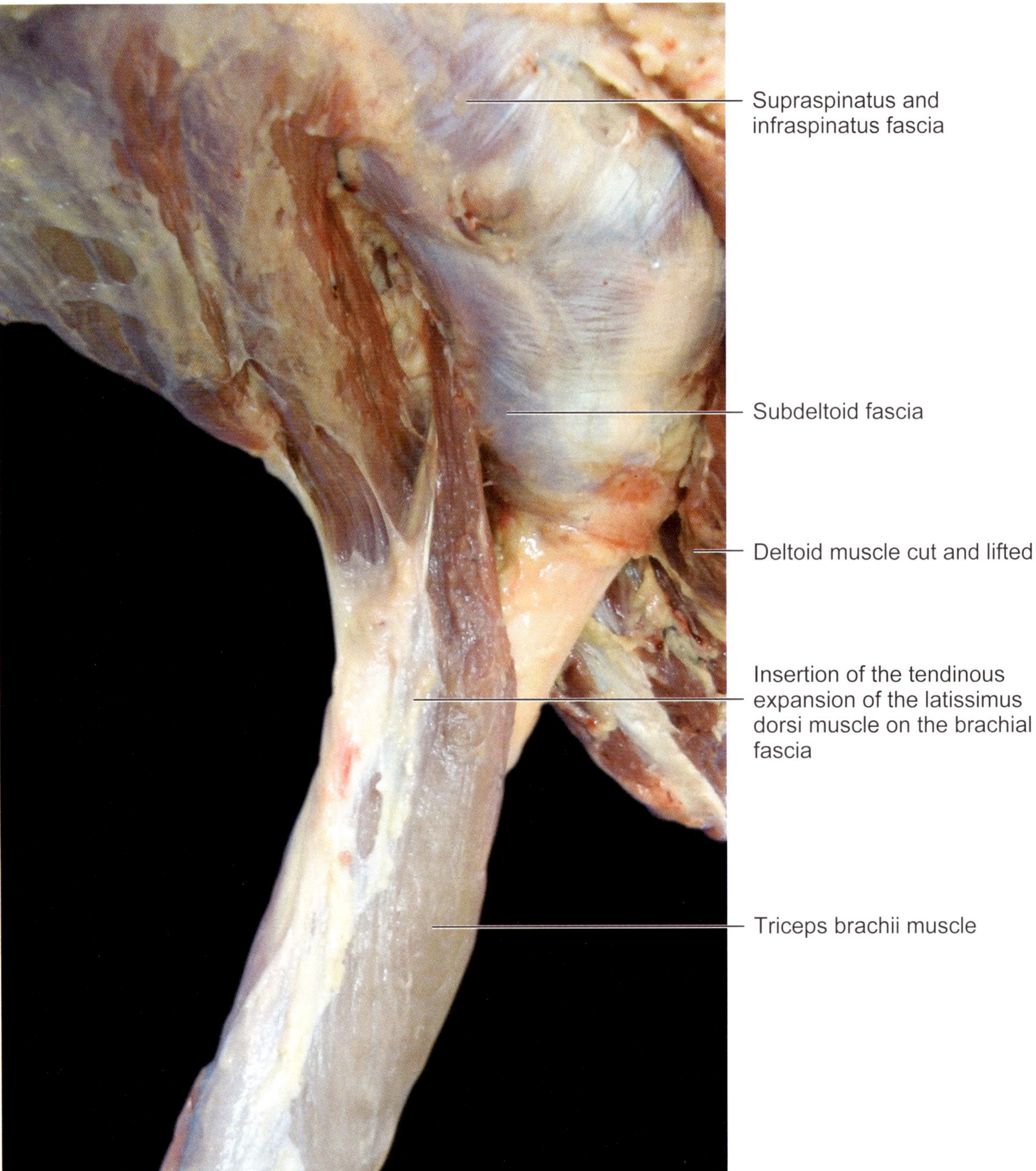

Fig. 2.87. Infraspinatus fascia is visible after lifting the deltoid muscle cranially. The infraspinatus fascia continues with the subdeltoid fascia covering the external rotator cuff, it then continues with the fascia covering the internal rotators.

In the figures horizontal lines indicate anatomical parts whilst numbers (1, 2) indicate the physiology of the fascia. Number 1 indicates a determined action and number 2 indicates its effect.

FASCIAE OF THE EXTRAROTATION SEQUENCE IN THE UPPER LIMB

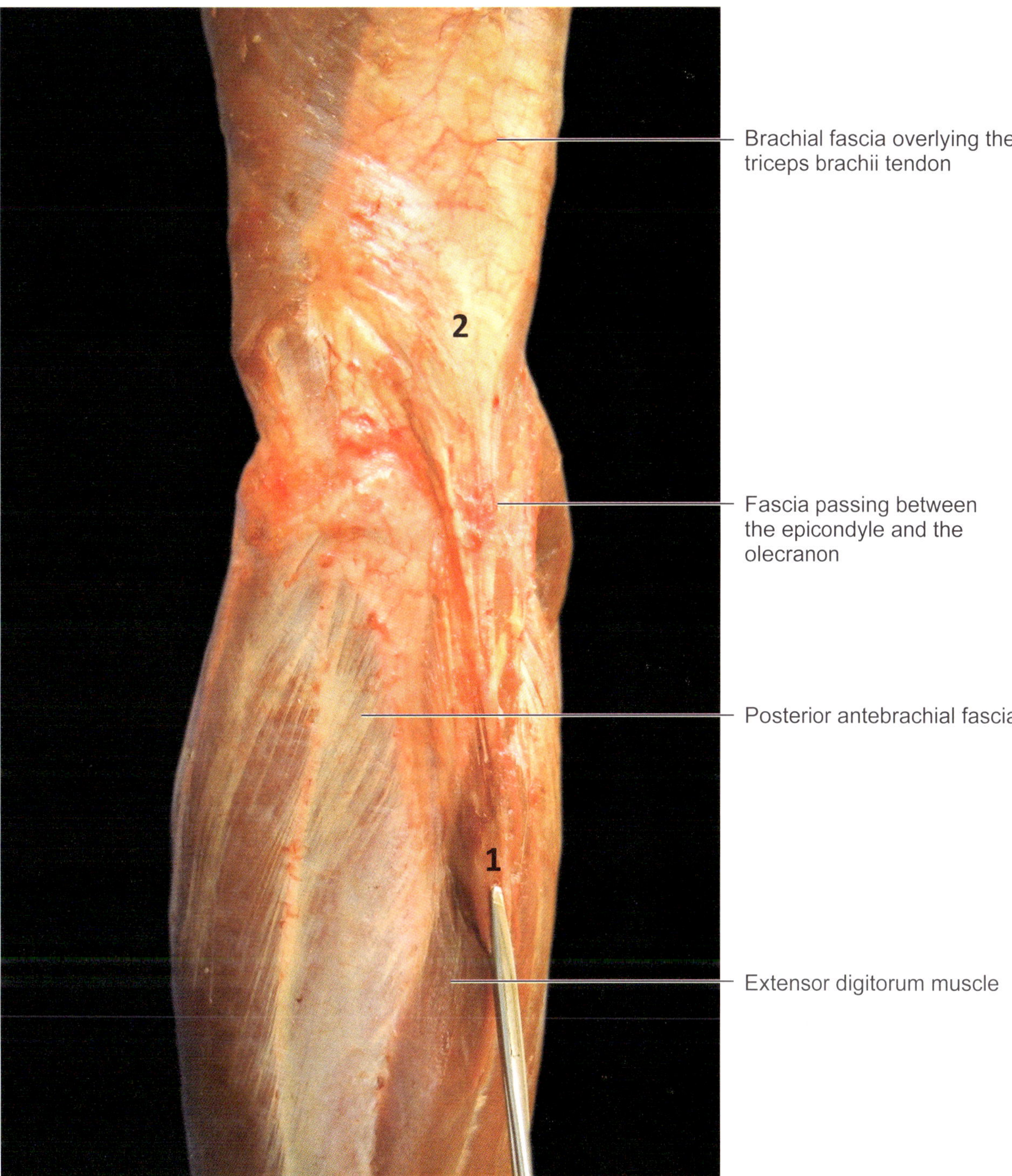

Fig. 2.88. Posterior antebrachial fascia. The forceps imitate the action of the extensor digitorum muscle inserted on the fascia, it tractions the antebrachial fascia (1) distally, this stretch propagates up to the triceps brachii muscle (2).

FASCIAE OF THE EXTRAROTATION SEQUENCE IN THE UPPER LIMB

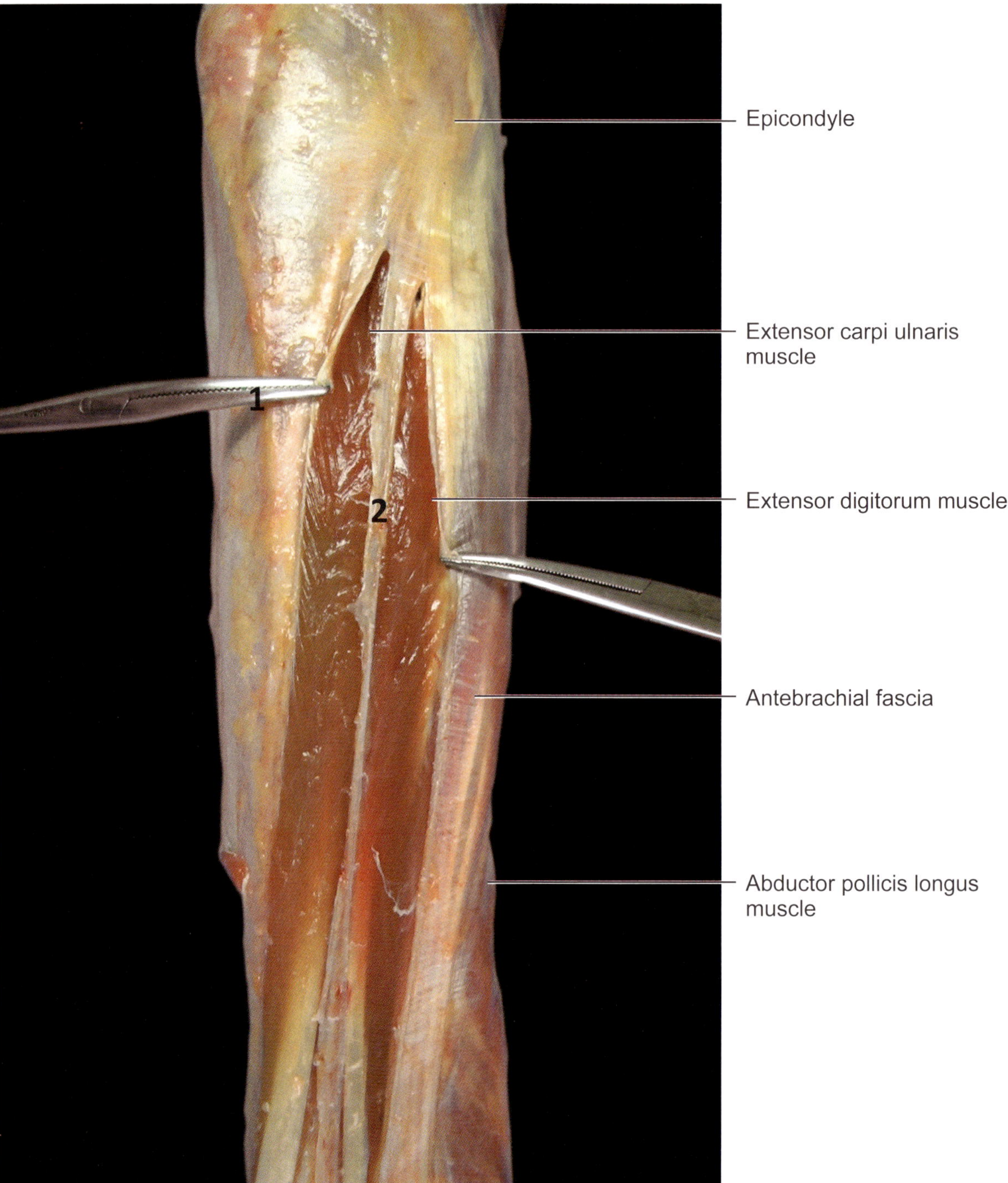

Fig. 2.89. Aponeurotic fascia of the postero-lateral forearm. The fascia overlying the extensor carpi ulnaris and extensor digitorum muscles (1) was cut to show their insertions on the fascia and on the septum that divides them (2).

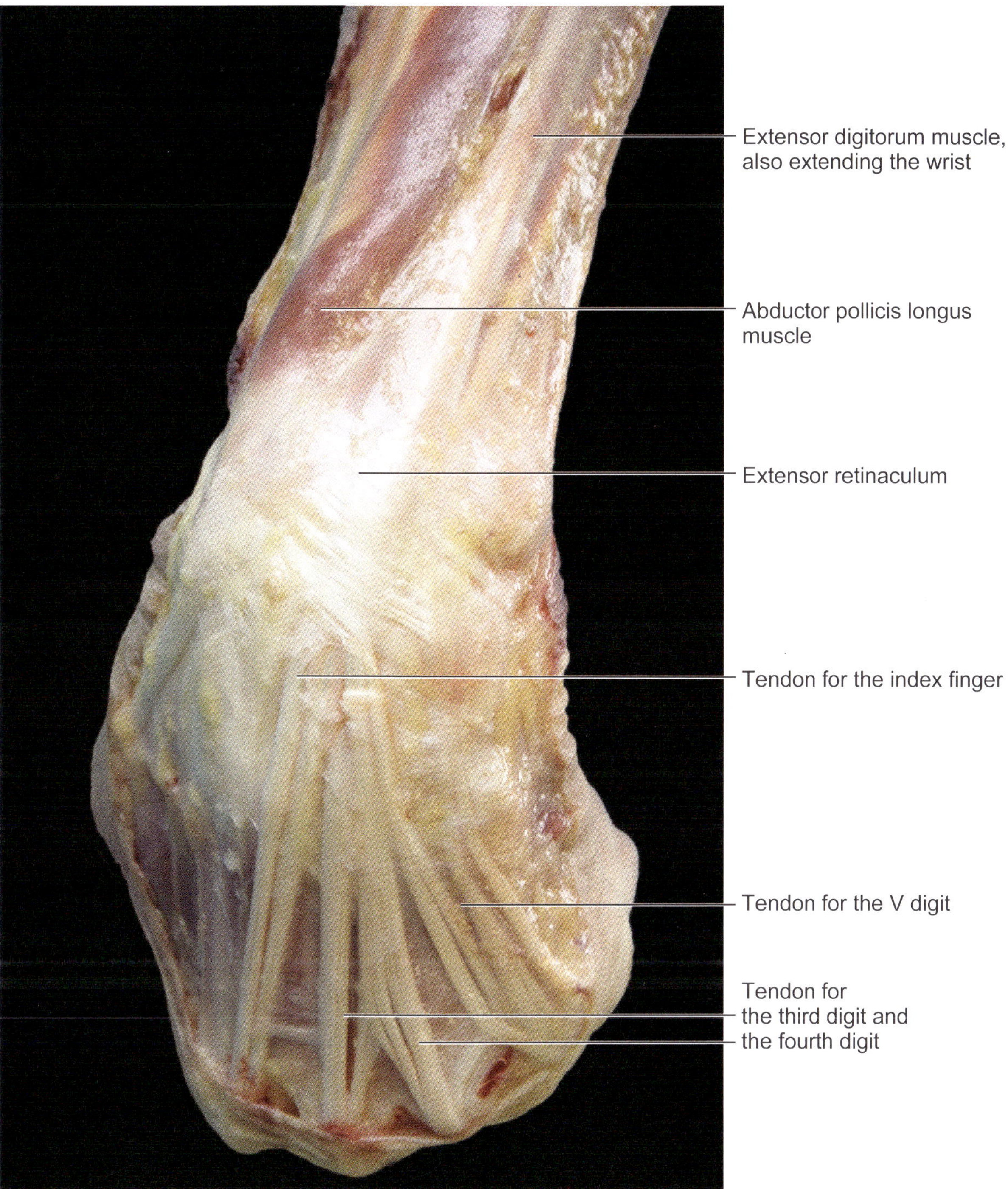

Fig. 2.90. Fascia of the dorsum of the hand, superficial lamina. The disposition of the extensor tendons is such that their contraction imbeds an external rotation on the wrist and hand. Vesalius gave to the retinacula the function of containing tendons. Since 1543, anatomical drawings have represented the retinacula as a strip of contention (Fig. 2.16). From anatomical dissections the course of retinacula results different, therefore their function must also be different.

CHAPTER 3

CENTRES OF COORDINATION AND SEQUENCES OF THE TRUNK

MYOFASCIAL UNITS AND UNIDIRECTIONAL MOVEMENTS OF THE TRUNK (TR)

The four segments of the trunk (collum, thorax, lumbi and pelvis) often move together in series as a single segment, nevertheless each segment is able to move independently when using a single myofascial unit.

Electromyography has demonstrated (Weisman M.H.S. 2014) that muscles belonging to the retropulsion sequence often work in synergy. For instance, contraction of the back activates the entire myofascial sequence or kinematic chain. This cannot be explained without considering the connections provided by the fascia to all the muscle fibres of retropulsion.

The assessment of retropulsion may be realised concentrically, when hyperextending the back from a standing or prone position, or eccentrically, when bending forward.

Not only are there connections between paravertebral muscles in retropulsion, there are also connections between muscles implicated in trunk antepulsion[1]. Antepulsion may be realised concentrically, when bending forward from a standing or supine position, or eccentrically when hyperextending the trunk backward from a standing position.

The anterior trunk musculature is derived from hypaxial muscles that, through evolution, were divided into prevertebral and thoraco-abdominal muscles. The cavity holding the internal organs was formed inside both layers.

Lateropulsion refers to lateral flexion of the trunk. This movement is achieved through eccentric contraction of the side lengthening and through concentric contraction of the contralateral side.

Mediopulsion does not refer to a specific trunk movement, rather it refers to the fascial structures (linea alba and interspinous ligaments) providing a reference point for the lateropulsion muscles when bringing the trunk back to the midline.

Trunk torsion is a movement implemented on the horizontal plane. When the body turns, forces are generated: internal rotation on one side and external rotation on the opposite side. Intrarotation muscles are distributed in the anterior wall of the trunk since the brain organises movement as the displacement of one half of the body forward. In the same manner extrarotation muscles are distributed in the posterior wall of the trunk since the brain organises movement as the displacement of one half of the body backward.

To facilitate longitudinal recruitment of all four MF units belonging to each single sequence, movement must be carried out against resistance. Hence if resistance is applied to the head during antepulsion of the neck, consequently the effort will implicate the following MF units: ante-collum, ante-thorax, ante-lumbi, ante-pelvis.

The various displays of pain in the trunk appear according to the organization of the fascial sequences. As a matter of fact, isolated neck pain may occur but often patients present with cervico-thoracic pain, also a simple low back pain may be encountered but often patients also present with pain in both the lumbar and pelvic regions. All this is also caused by motor interdependency: the neck musculature extends into the trunk and lumbar region is anchored in the pelvis and sacrum.

In the trunk, pain connected to the locomotor apparatus will mainly manifest along the spine since the spinal column is where articular conflicts stemming from motor incoordination are encountered.

Neck, thoracic, lumbar and sacro-iliac pain are often caused by densifications of the fasciae of paravertebral muscles but these may sometimes also be caused by incoordination of the myofascial units of antepulsion, lateropulsion, intrarotation and extrarotation.

[1] The spinocostal muscles include the anterior, medial and posterior scalenes along with the elevators of the ribs. All are derivatives of the external intercostal muscles.
The sternalis muscle is found before the sternal origin of the pectoralis major muscle. Typically, it connects superiorly with the sternal tendon of the sternocleidomastoid muscle, inferiorly it attaches to the cartilages from rib 5 to 7. (Chiarugi G. 1975)

ANTERIOR REGION OF THE TRUNK, ANTEPULSION SEQUENCE

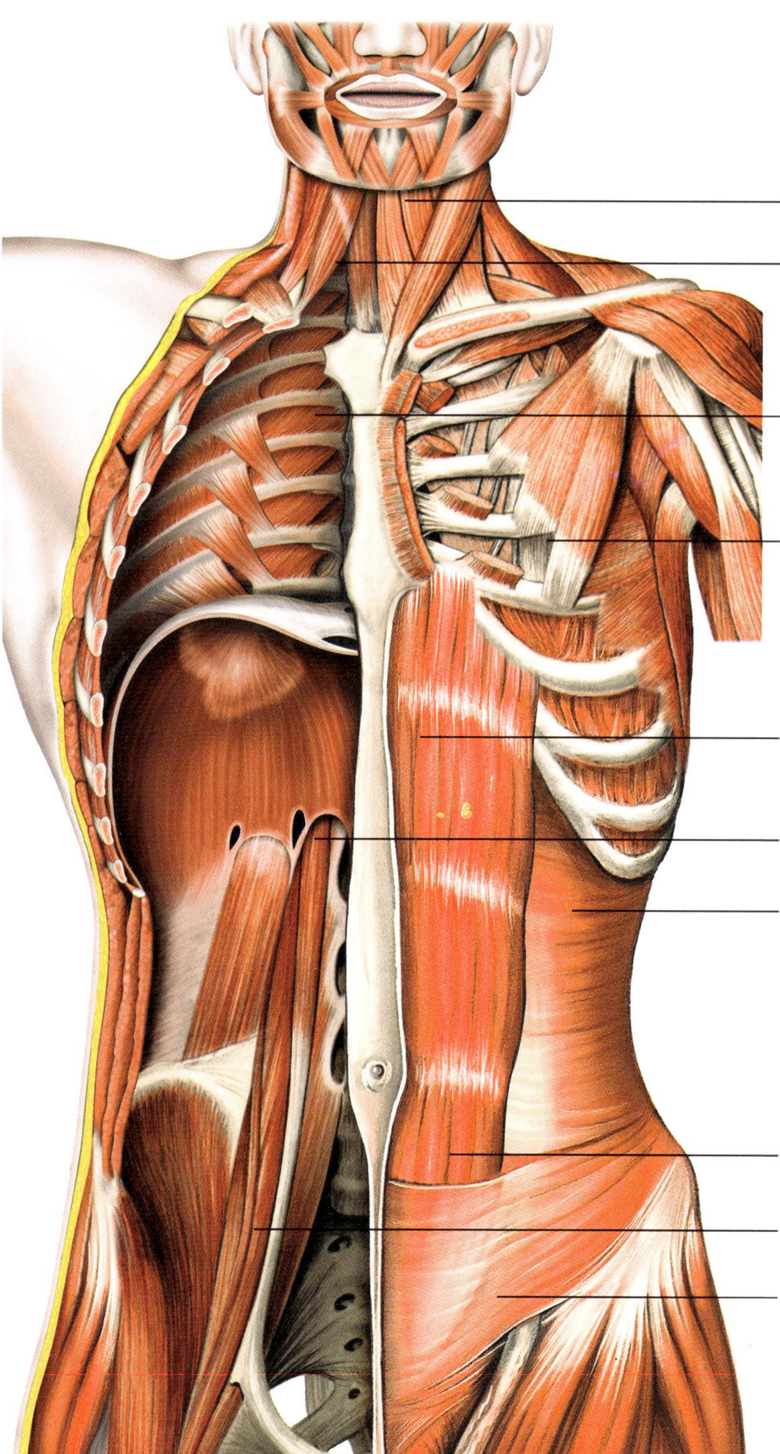

Fig. 3.1. Muscles of the anterior region of the trunk.

SEGMENTARY MOVEMENTS IMPLEMENTED BY THE MF UNITS OF ANTEPULSION

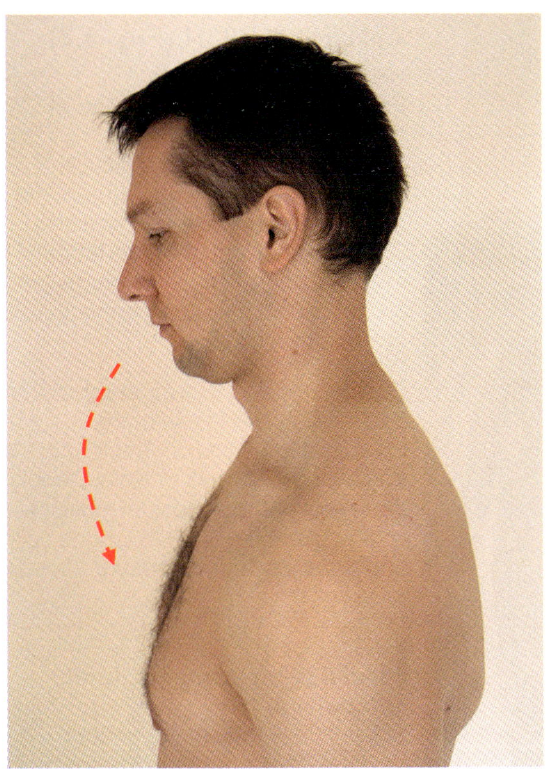

Fig. 3.2. Cervical flexion managed by the MF unit of ante-collum.

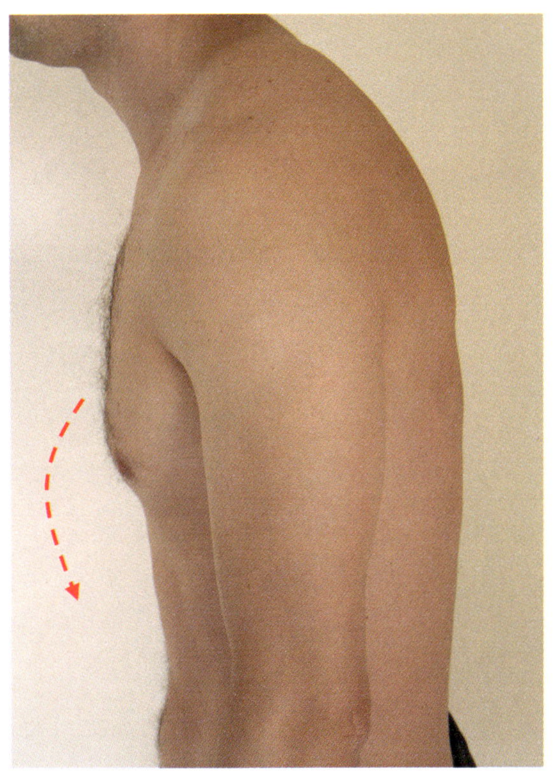

Fig. 3.3. Thoracic flexion implemented by the MF unit of ante-thorax.

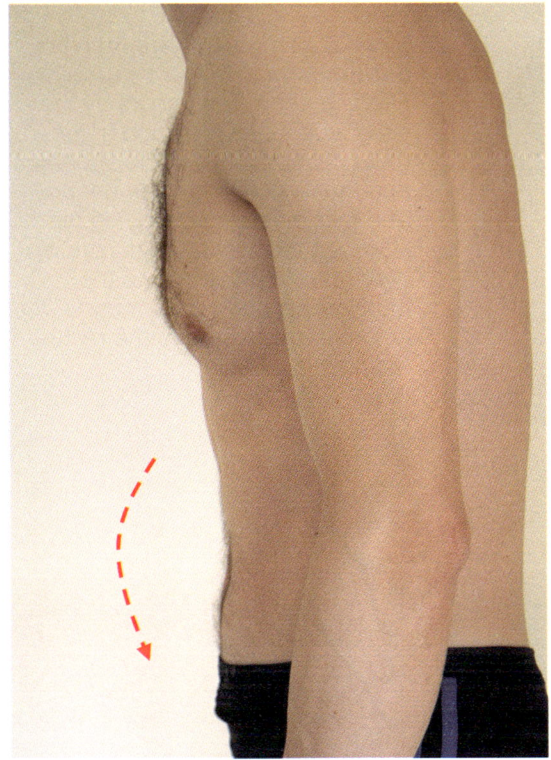

Fig. 3.4. Lumbar flexion implemented by the MF unit of ante-lumbi.

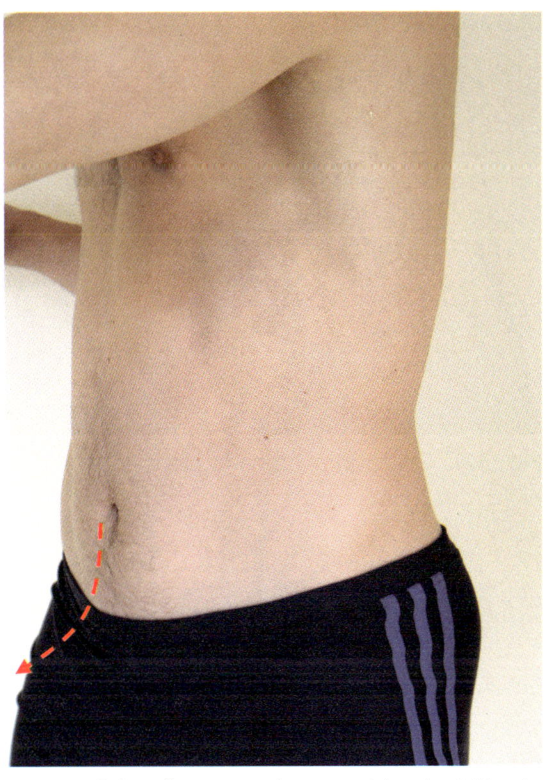

Fig. 3.5. Pelvic flexion implemented by the MF unit of ante-pelvis.

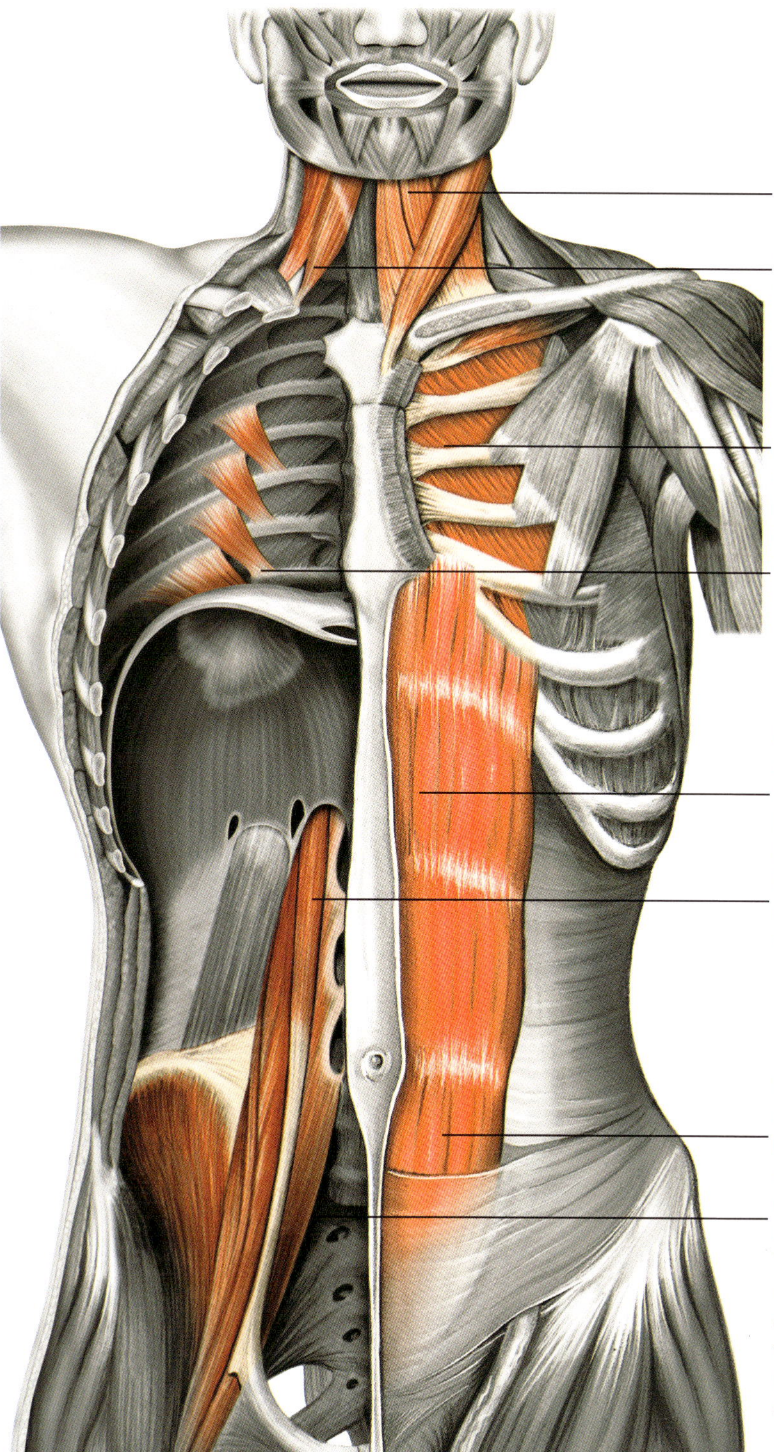

Fig. 3.6. Fascial compartments of the antepulsion muscles of the trunk.

COMPARTMENTS FOR THE MUSCLES OF TRUNK ANTEPULSION (Fig. 3.7)

Fascial lamina, antepulsion of collum
Superficially the cervical fascia contains the infrahyoid, suprahyoid and sternocleidomastoid muscles. Deeply the fascia of prevertebral muscles (longus capitis, longus colli, rectus capitis anterior) connects to the scalene muscles.

Fascial lamina, thorax antepulsion
Superficially the fascia of the intercostal muscles connects with the transversus thoracis muscle. Deeply the fascia of the subcostal muscles connects proximally with longus colli and distally with the iliopsoas muscle.

Fascial compartments, lumbi antepulsion
Superficially the rectus sheath longitudinally connects the fascia of the intercostal muscles to the pubis. Deeply the fascia of the iliopsoas muscle connects the fascia of the subcostal muscles to the iliac fascia.

Fascial compartments, pelvis antepulsion
Pelvis antepulsion occurs by the simultaneous contraction of the rectus abdominis muscle superficially and the iliopsoas muscle deeply. The fascial lamina overlying the iliopsoas muscle is the continuity of the fascia belonging to the transversus abdominis muscle, that in turn is connected to the rectus abdominis muscle.

GLOBAL MOVEMENT IMPLEMENTED BY THE ANTEPULSION SEQUENCE

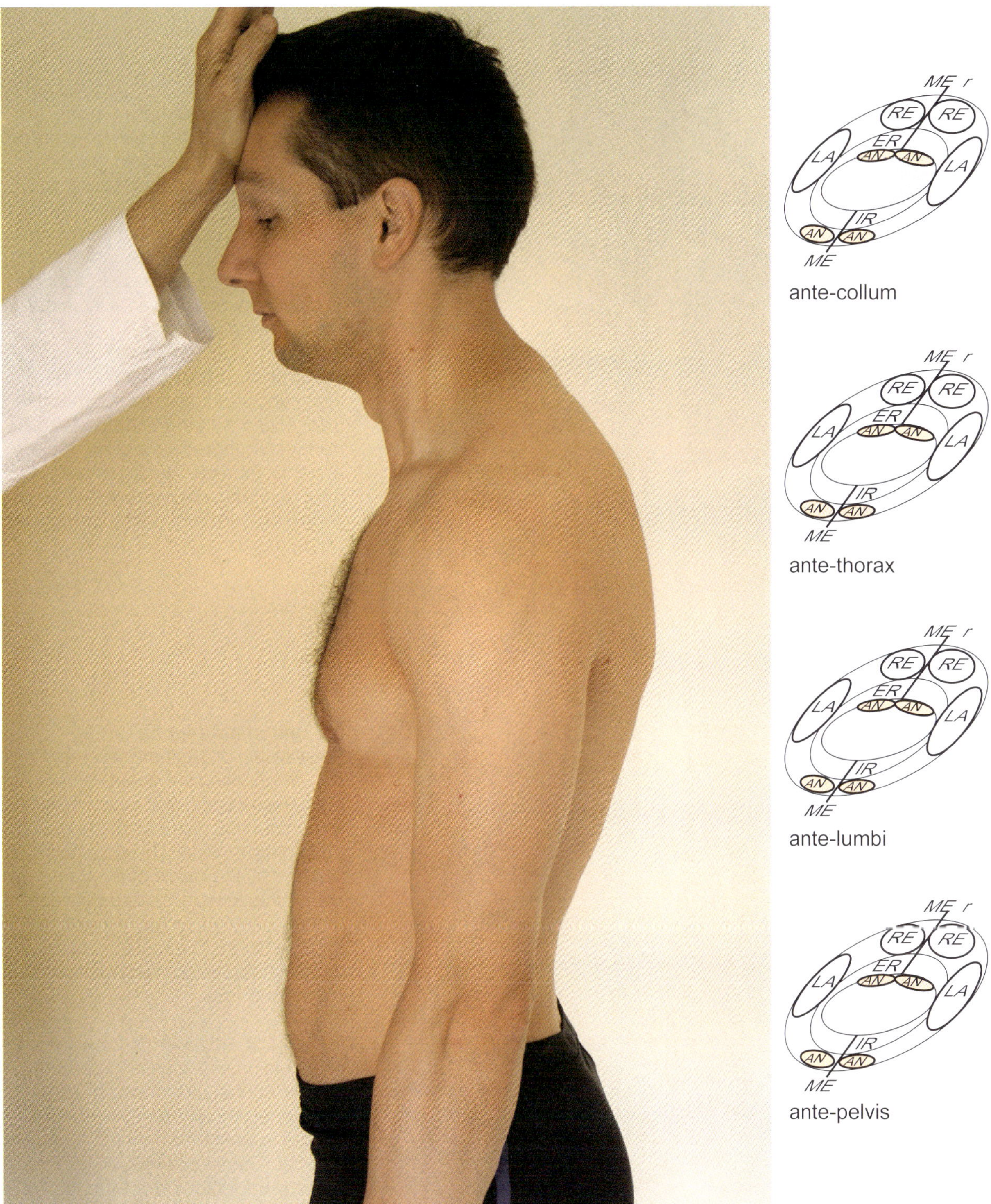

Fig. 3.7. Contraction of the antepulsion sequence brings the entire trunk anteriorly.

Antepulsion of the trunk involves the synergy of four myofascial compartments:

- right and left compartments of the anterior superficial trunk wall (hyoids, sternocleidomastoid, sternalis, rectus abdominis muscles);
- right and left compartments of the prevertebral muscles of the trunk (prevertebrals of the neck and thorax, iliopsoas in lumbi and pelvis).

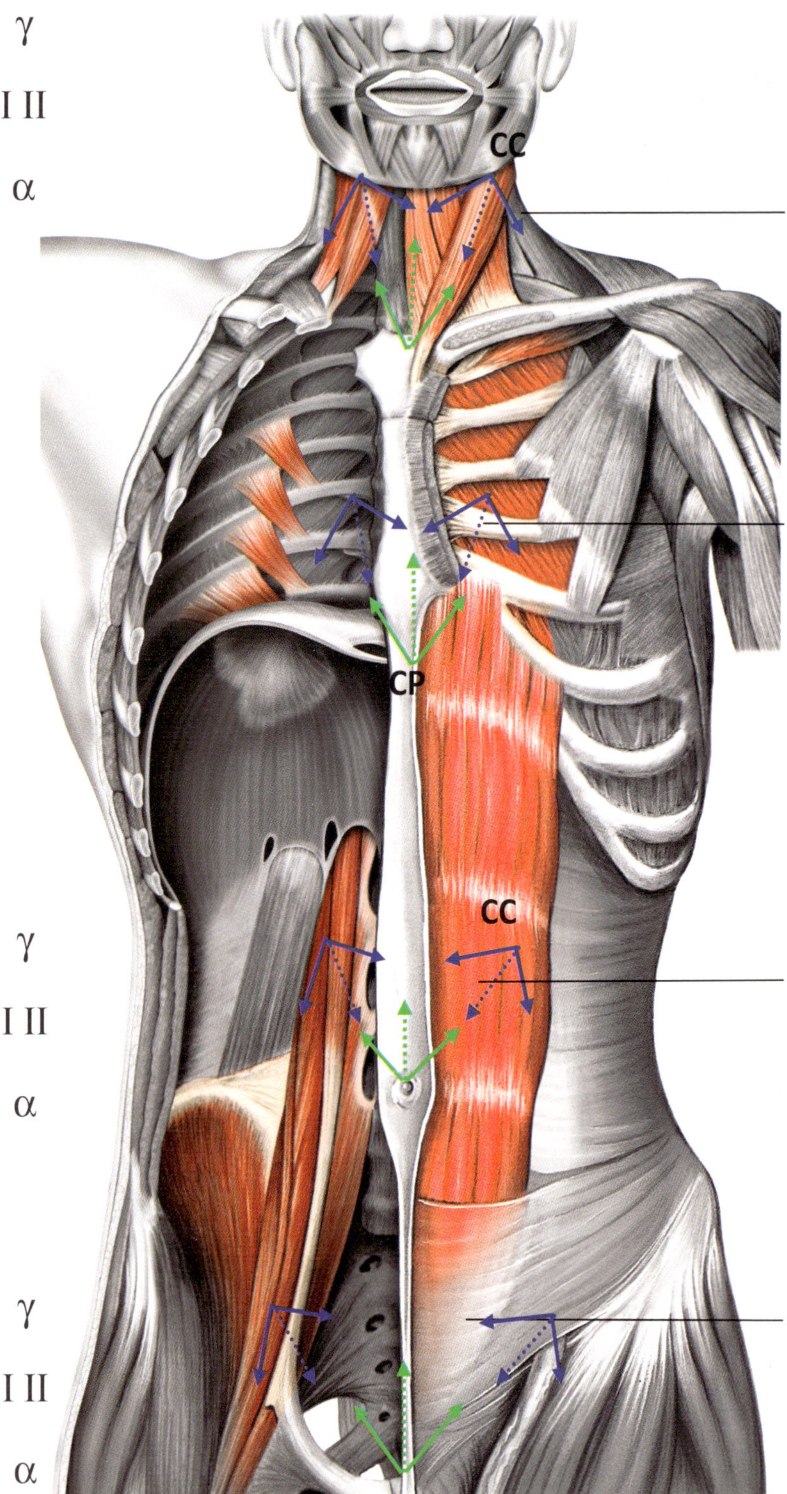

Fig. 3.8. Normal function of the gamma circuit.

PHYSIOLOGY OF THE ANTEPULSION MF UNITS TRUNK

MF unit of ante-collum (an-cl)
The prevertebral muscles synchronise their action with the hyoid muscles. Indeed, the prevertebral fascia is connected to the antagonists (erector spinae muscles), the supra and infra-hyoid muscles, and the sternocleido-mastoid muscle. All these tendinous vectors converge towards the sternal notch (green vectors).

MF unit of ante-thorax (an-th)
The subcostal muscles synchronise their action with the intercostal and transverse thoracis muscles. Indeed, the endothoracic fascia connects the right and left muscles together as well as the anterior and posterior muscles of the thorax.

MF unit of ante-lumbi (an-lu)
Antepulsion of the lumbar spine occurs following the contraction of the psoas muscle that synchronises its contribution with that of the rectus abdominis muscle. This connection is realised by the fascia of the transverse abdominis muscle located between the anterior and posterior muscles (blue vectors). The resultant of these muscular forces converge at the level of the umbilicus.

MF unit of ante-pelvis (an-pv)
Antepulsion of the pelvis implicates the abdominal muscles in a different manner since all their aponeuroses course in front of the rectus abdominis muscle. The iliacus muscle located in the retroperitoneal area is implicated in moving the right and left CCs laterally. The resultant has its fulcrum over the pubis.

ARTICULAR CONFLICTS IN TRUNK ANTEPULSION

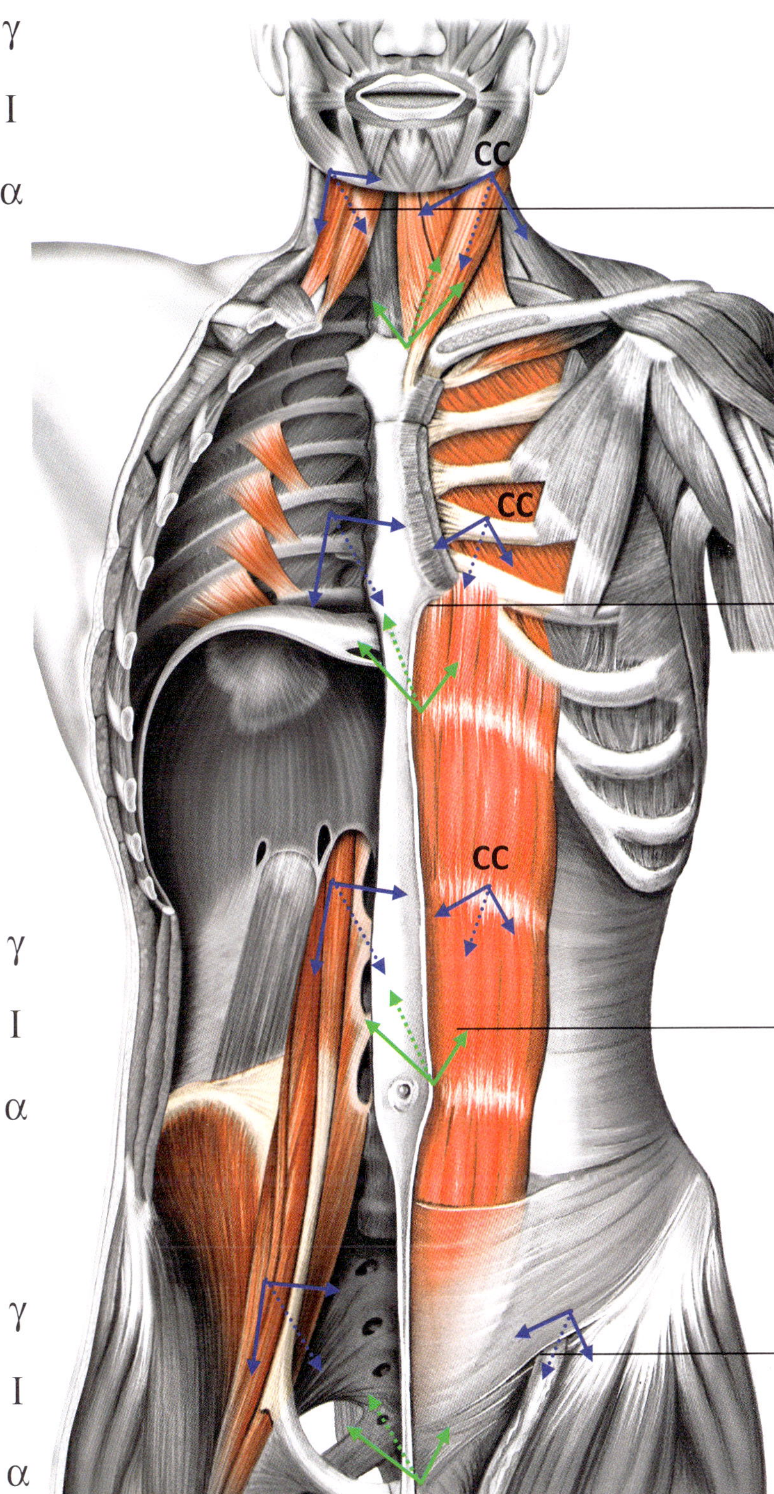

Fig. 3.9. Dysfunctions of the gamma circuit.

Pain during antepulsion of collum
If the right cervical fascia (CC) is densified, then the afferents (II) from a few spindles are not triggered, and their alpha circuits are not activated. The predominance of the muscles on the left shifts the tendinous resultant outside its physiological axis. Consequently, a conflict occurs at the cervical vertebrae.

Pain during antepulsion of thorax
If the transverse fascia of the left thorax (where it connects with the rectus abdominis muscle) is densified, then the force of the right musculature prevails. This results in a shift of the resultant with an alteration of body perception.

Pain during antepulsion of lumbi
If the fascia overlying the left muscle belly of the rectus abdominis is densified, then the underlying muscles intervene with minor force compared to the contralateral ones. This imbalance may manifest over the lumbar vertebrae during antepulsion.

Pain during antepulsion of pelvis
If the fascia of the left iliacus muscle (CC) is densified, the alpha-gamma circuit does not operate and the forces of the right side prevail. The iliacus muscle also originates from the sacroiliac ligaments, hence its contraction outside of the normal axis results in a conflict in the pubic or sacroiliac joints.

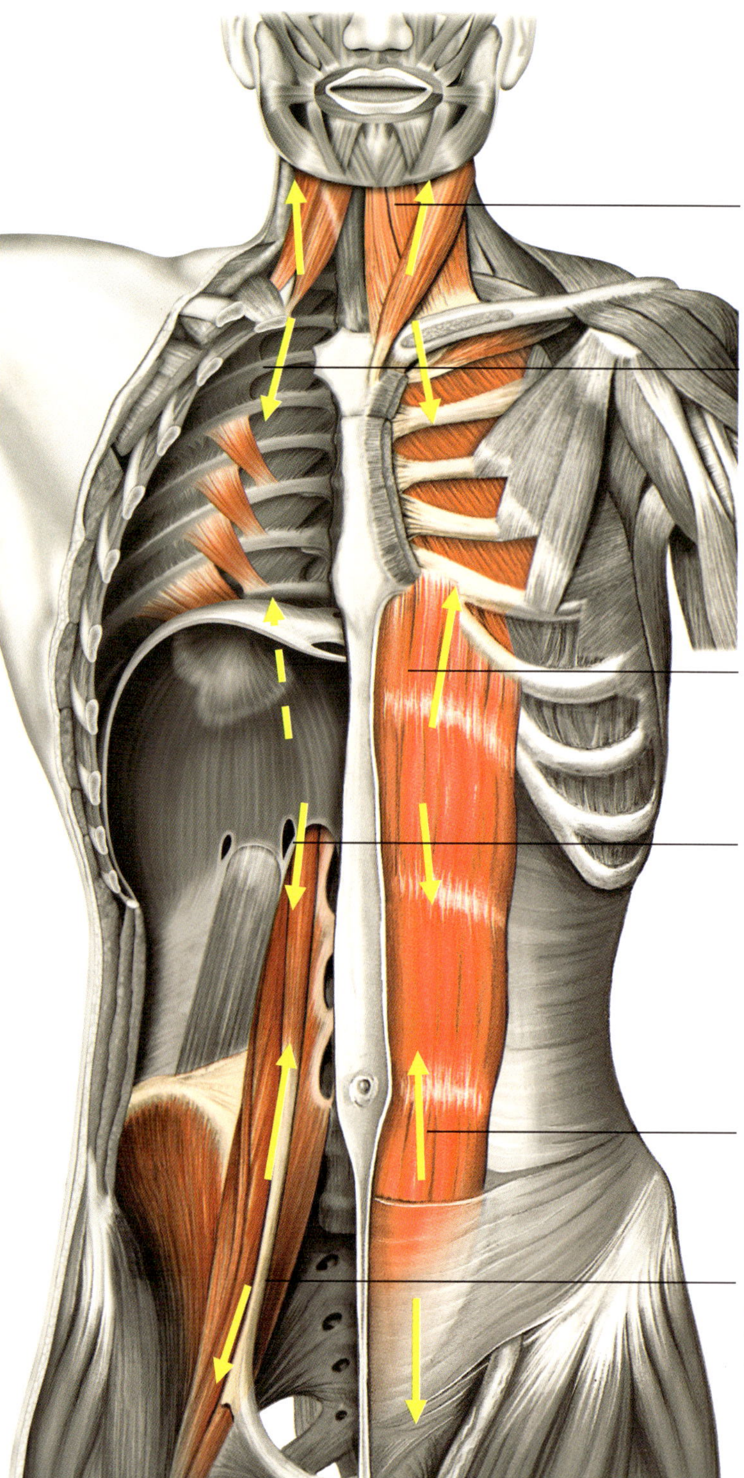

Fig. 3.10. Synergy along the antepulsion sequence of the trunk.

TR ANTEPULSION SEQUENCE AND STRETCH REFLEX

Synergy between an-cl and an-th
Superficially the contraction of the hyoid muscles (Fig. 3.12) act upon the fascia of the anterior intercostal muscles. Their activation determines a tension in the caudal direction.
Deeply the scalene muscles pull the prevertebral fascia cranially and the subcostal muscles determine a tension in the opposite direction.

Synergy between an-th and an-lu
Superficially the pectoralis major (Fig. 3.13), minor and intercostal muscles (Fig. 3.14) create a cranial traction that is counterbalanced by the tension of the rectus abdominis muscle.
Deeply the subcostal muscles pull the prevertebral fascia superiorly whilst the psoas muscle pulls it inferiorly.

Synergy between an-lu and an-pv
In the abdominal wall, the rectus and oblique muscles above the umbilicus create a cranial tension on the pelvic fascia whilst the distal portion of the same muscles creates tension caudally.
Deeply the iliacus, psoas major and minor muscles (Fig. 3.15) pull their fascia cranially, the pectineus and tensor fascia lata muscles create a caudal tension.

ACTIVATION OF THE GOLGI TENDON ORGANS

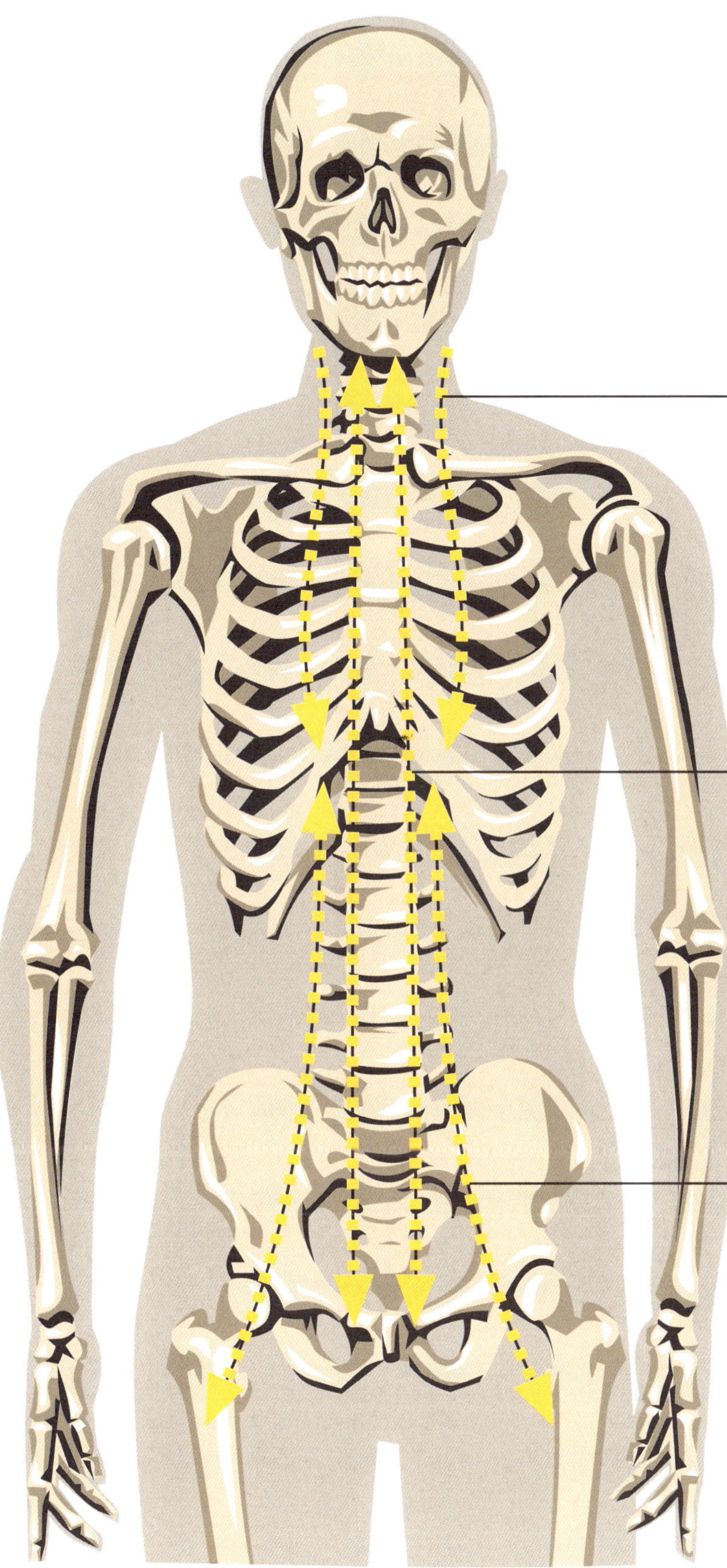

Muscles and fasciae acting upon ante-collum and ante-thorax
Deep connection: the scalenes and prevertebral muscles are continuous with the prevertebral fascia and with the subcostal muscles. This creates a motor bond between collum and thorax above the diaphragm.

Muscles and fasciae acting upon ante-collum, thorax, lumbi and pelvis
Superficial connection: a motor continuity of the entire trunk is present during antepulsion. This continuity is guaranteed by the sternocleidomastoids, sternal ligaments and rectus abdominis muscles.

Muscles and fasciae acting upon ante-lumbi and ante-pelvis
The connection between antepulsion of lumbi and pelvis is so strong that is it impossible to execute the movement of one segment without implicating the other.
The iliopsoas is the biarticular muscle acting deeply for the antepulsion of lumbi and pelvis. The tendon organs of this muscle interact during the antepulsion of lumbi and pelvis.

Fig. 3.11. Biarticular muscles for the antepulsion sequence of the trunk.

FASCIAE OF THE ANTEPULSION SEQUENCE OF THE TRUNK

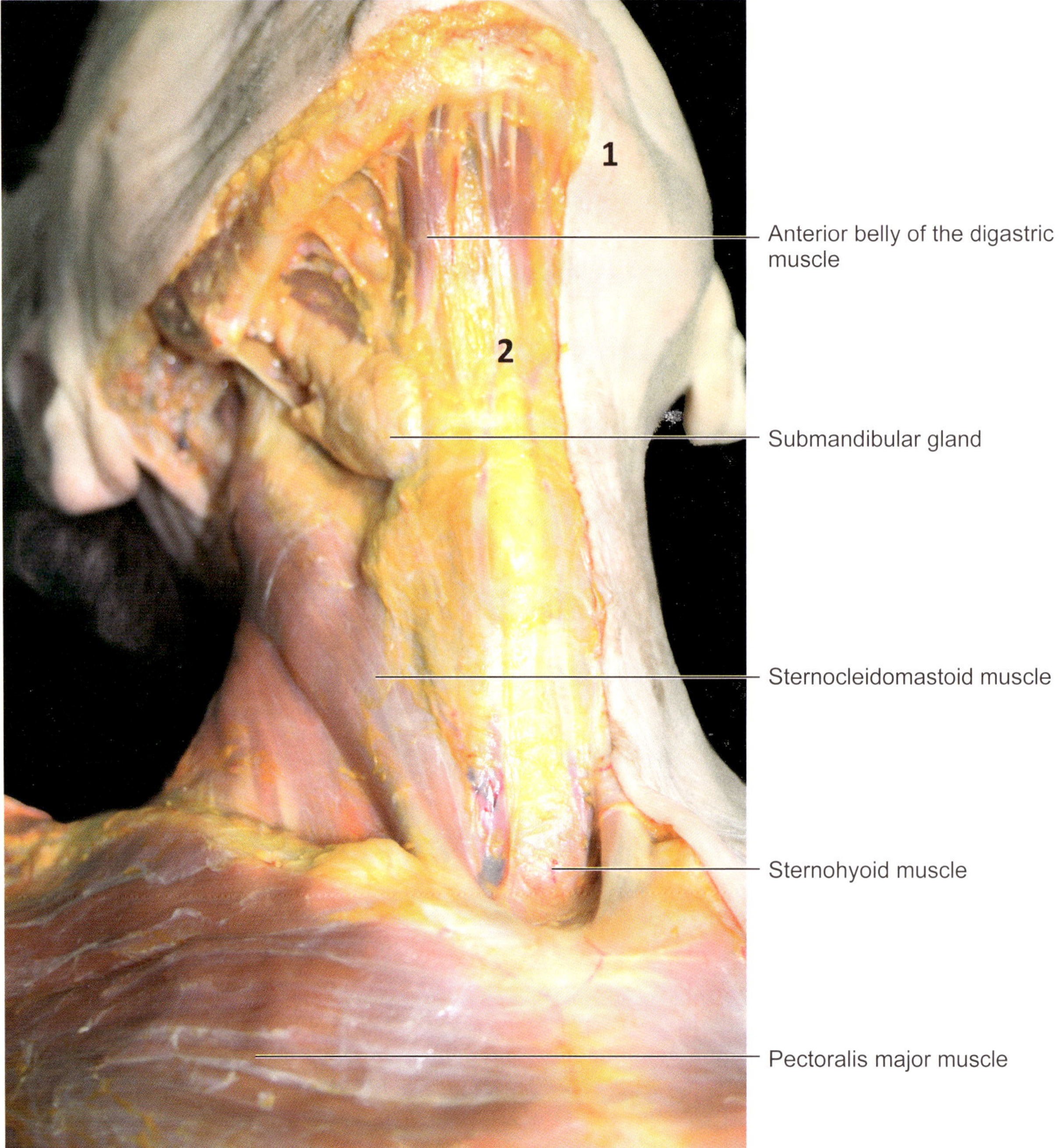

Fig. 3.12. Anterior cervical fascia, superficial lamina. The superficial lamina surrounds the trapezius muscle posteriorly, the sternocleidomastoid muscle laterally and the hyoid muscles anteriorly. When extending the head (1), the fasciae connecting the chin to the sternum are put under tension (2) whilst the lateral and posterior fasciae are relaxed.

The lines indicate anatomical parts whilst the numbers (1, 2) indicate the physiology of the fascia. Number one indicates a determined action and number two indicates its effect.

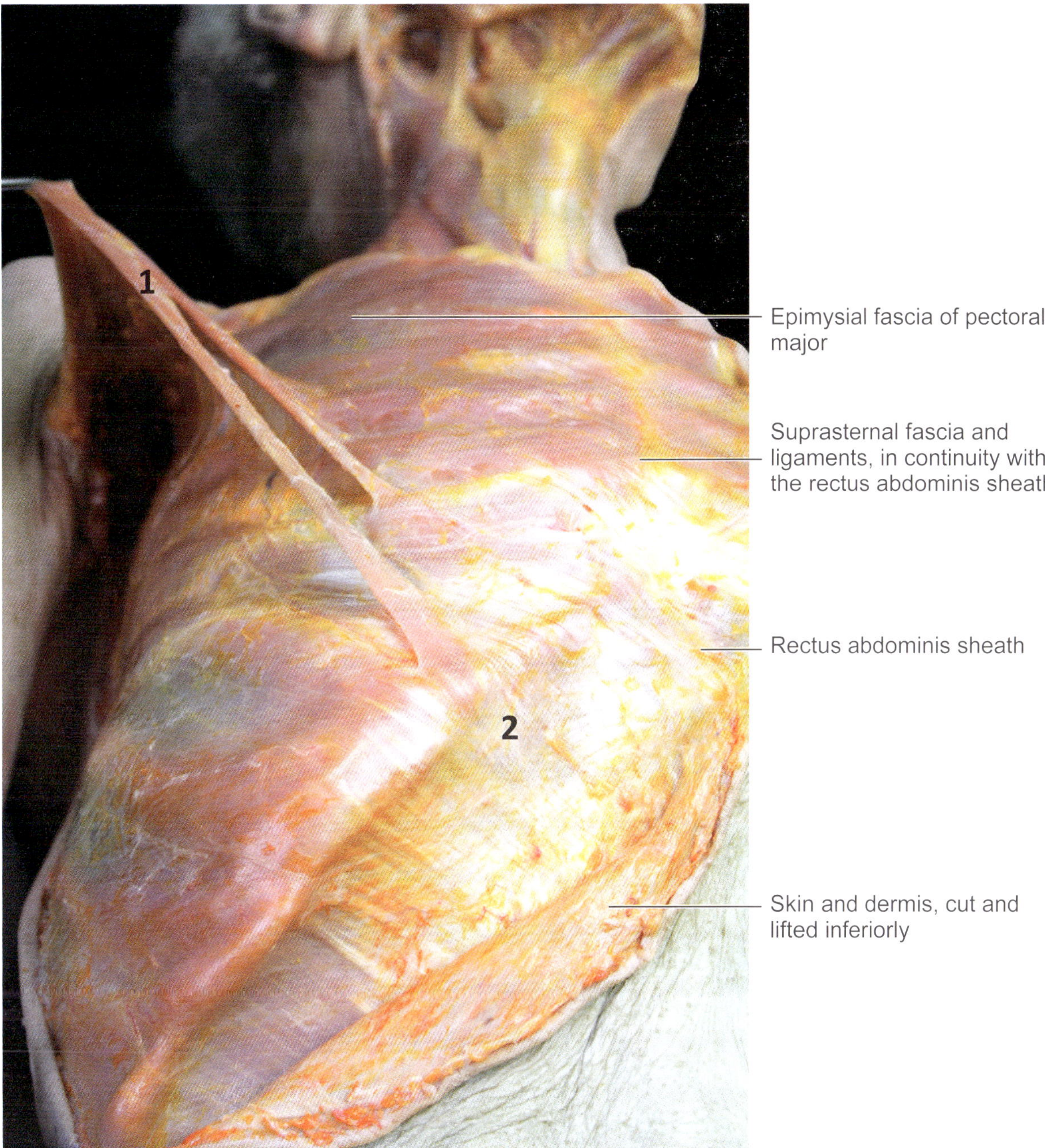

Fig. 3.13. Fascia of the pectoralis major muscle. The pectoralis major muscle was cut and lifted superiorly (1). The distal fibres are shown in continuity with the aponeurotic fascia or the contention sheath of the rectus abdominis muscle (2).

FASCIAE OF THE ANTEPULSION SEQUENCE OF THE TRUNK

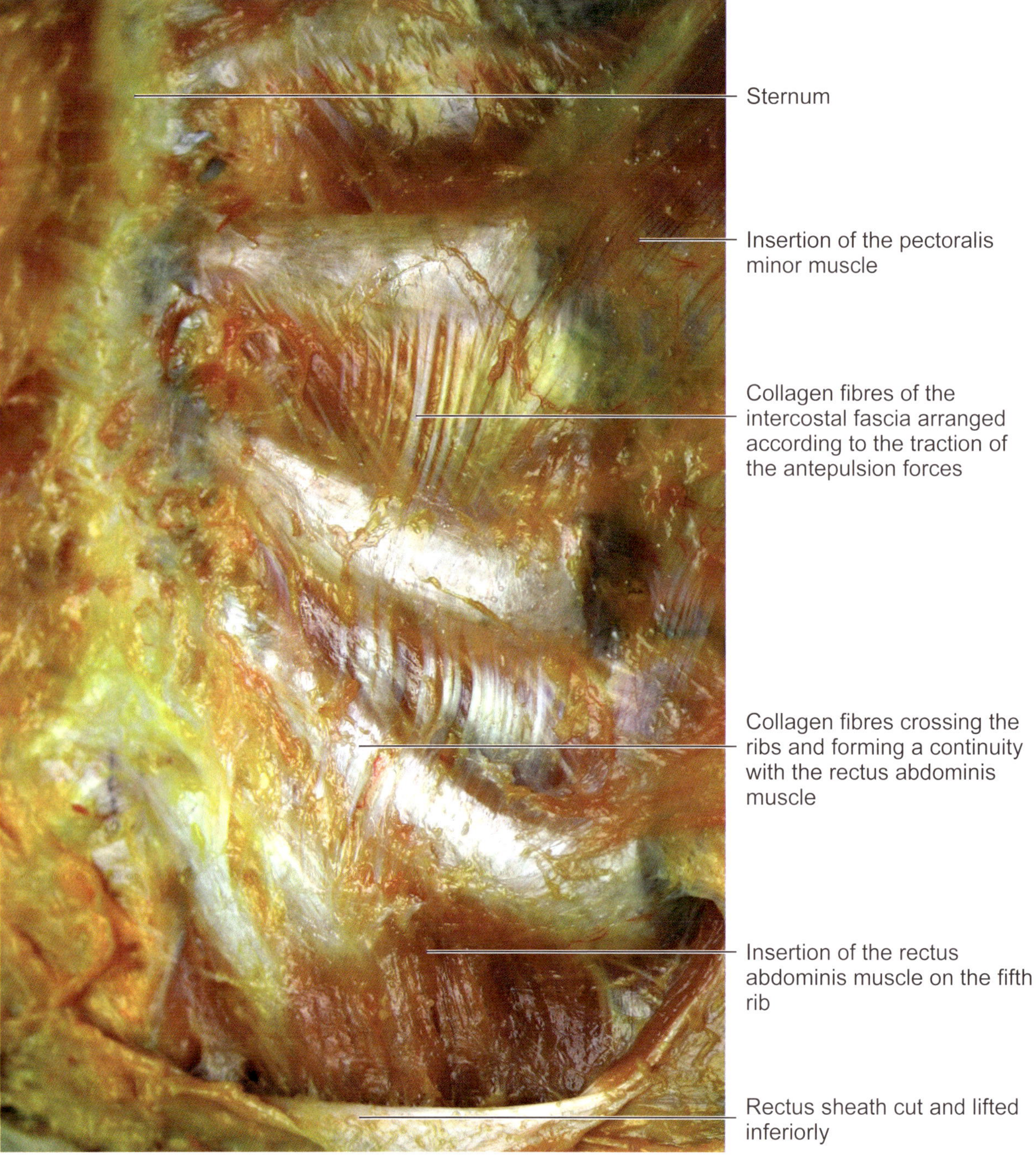

Fig. 3.14. Intercostal fascia on the left side of the sternum. The collagen fibres of the fascia are arranged longitudinally and in continuity to the arrangement of the muscle fibres of rectus abdominis. Hence the intercostal muscles and overlying fascia also participate in antepulsion of the thorax.

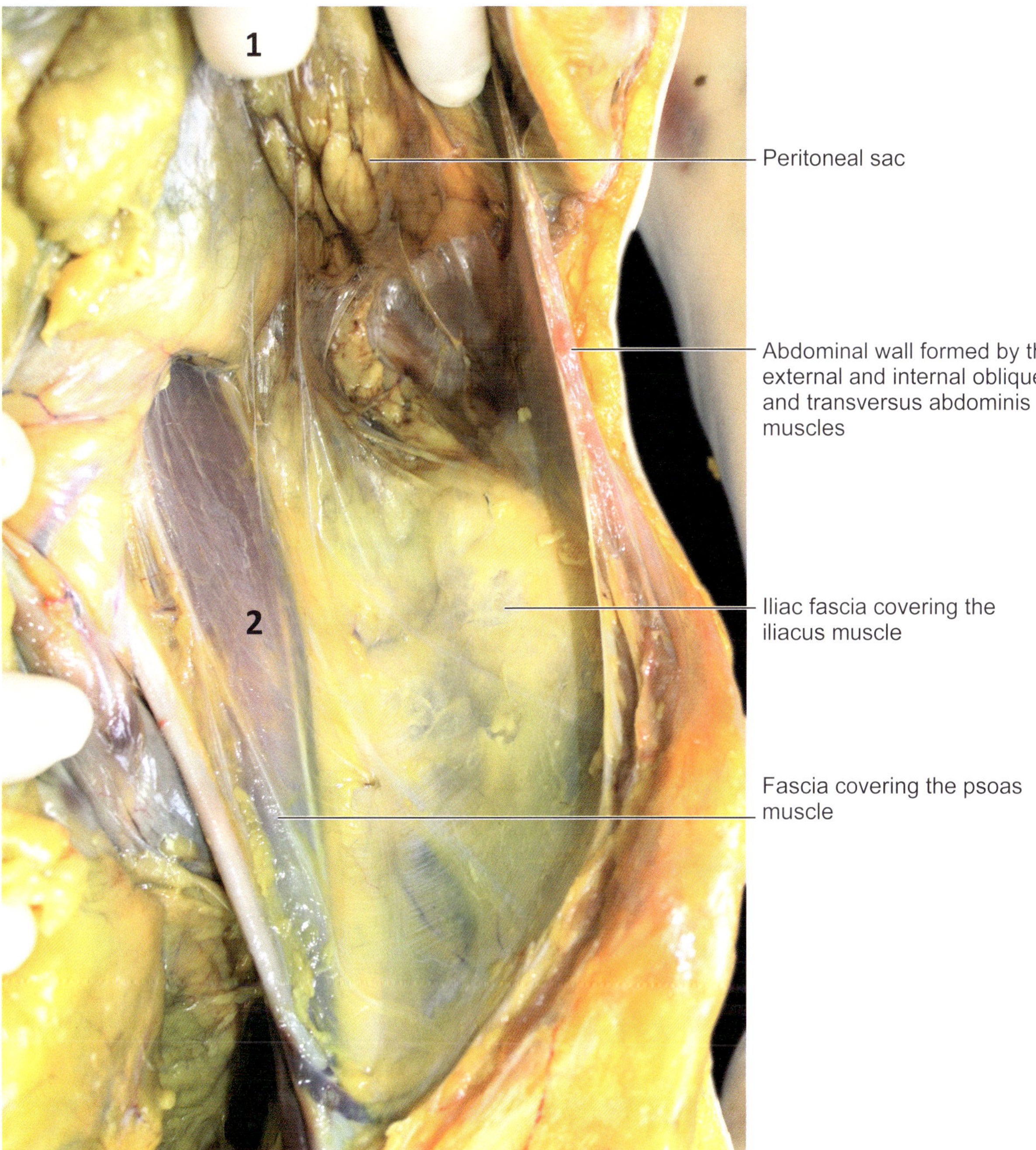

Fig. 3.15. Fascia of the psoas and iliacus muscles. After cutting the abdominal wall and lifting the peritoneal sac containing the viscera (1), the psoas (2) and iliacus muscles may be observed.

POSTERIOR REGION OF THE TRUNK, RETROPULSION SEQUENCE

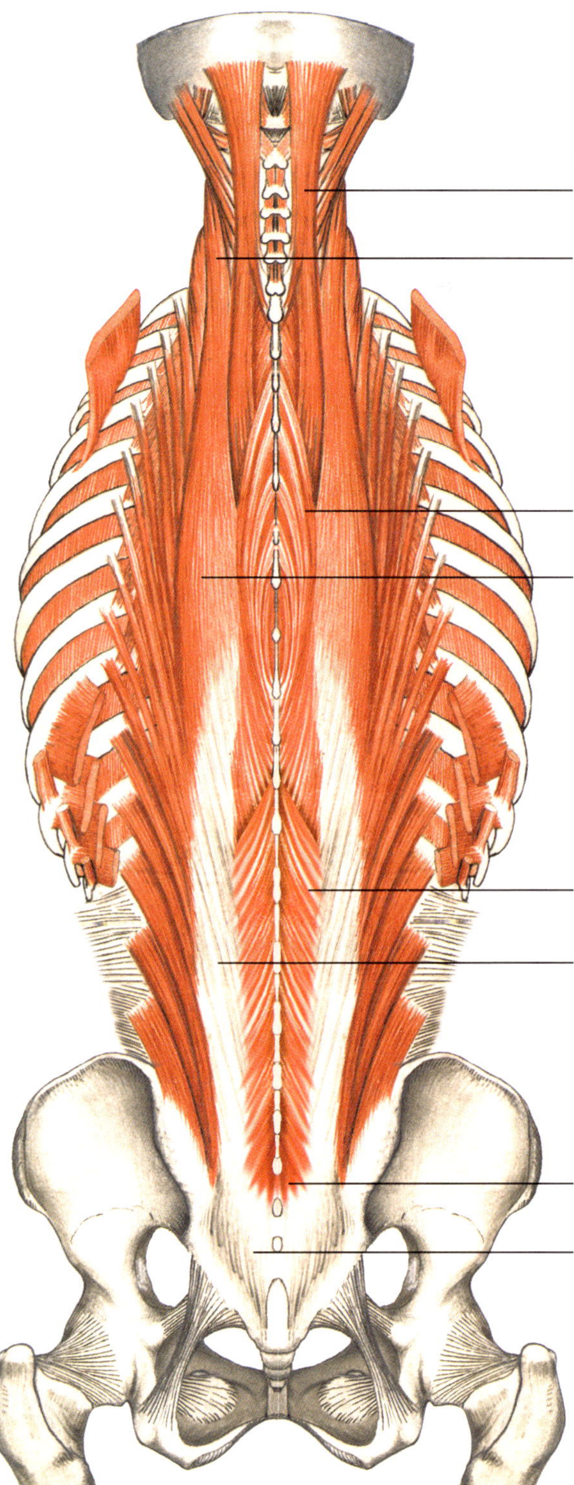

Cervical extension (Fig. 3.17)
Primary or monoarticular muscles: semispinalis cervicis and capitis
Secondary or biarticular muscles: longissimus cervicis and capitis
Synergic or scheme muscles: trapezius

Thoracic extension (Fig. 3.18)
Primary or monoarticular muscles: spinalis thoracis
Secondary or biarticular muscles: longissimus thoracis

Lumbar extension (Fig. 3.19)
Primary or monoarticular muscles: multifidus
Secondary or biarticular muscles: longissimus thoracis
Synergic muscles: rotatores

"Oblique muscles (rotatores brevis and longus, multifidus, semispinalis) function as rotators when activated unilaterally and as extensors when activated bilaterally" (Platzer W. 2009).

Pelvic extension (Fig. 3.20)
Primary or monoarticular muscles: multifidus
Secondary or biarticular muscles: erector spinae

"The straight muscles (interspinalis, spinalis, intertranversarii lumborum) function as extensors when both sides are activated and unilaterally as lateral flexors when only one side is activated (Platzer W. 2009).

Fig. 3.16. Posterior trunk region, erector spinae muscles.
(From G. Chiarugi and L. Bucciante, Istituzioni di anatomia dell'uomo. Piccin Nuova Libraria, Padova 1983, modified)

SEGMENTARY MOVEMENTS IMPLEMENTED BY THE MF UNITS OF RETROPULSION

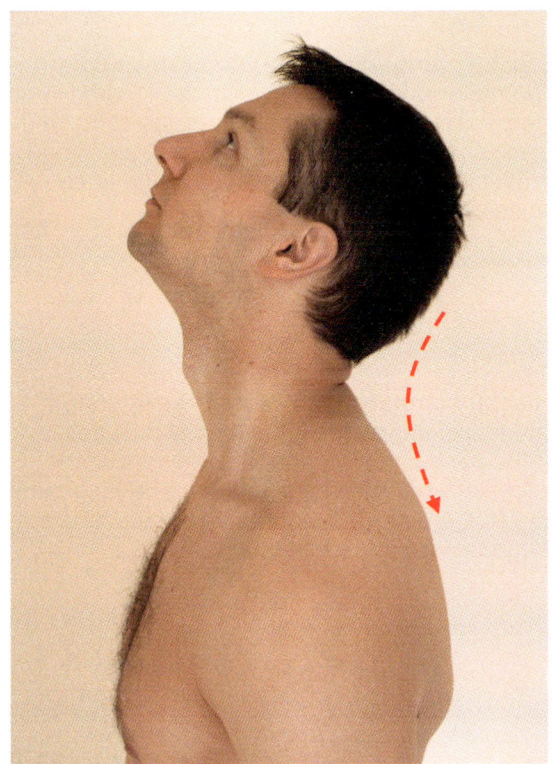

Fig. 3.17. Cervical extension managed by the MF unit of retro-collum.

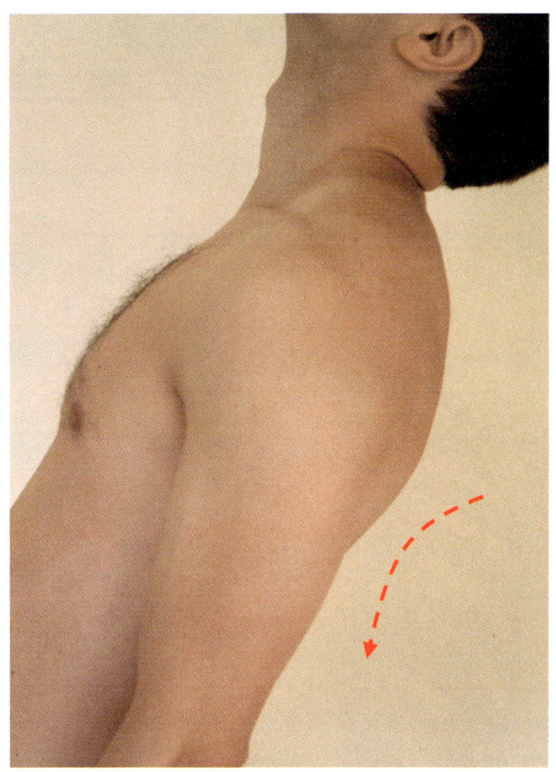

Fig. 3.18. Thoracic extension managed by the MF unit of retro-thorax.

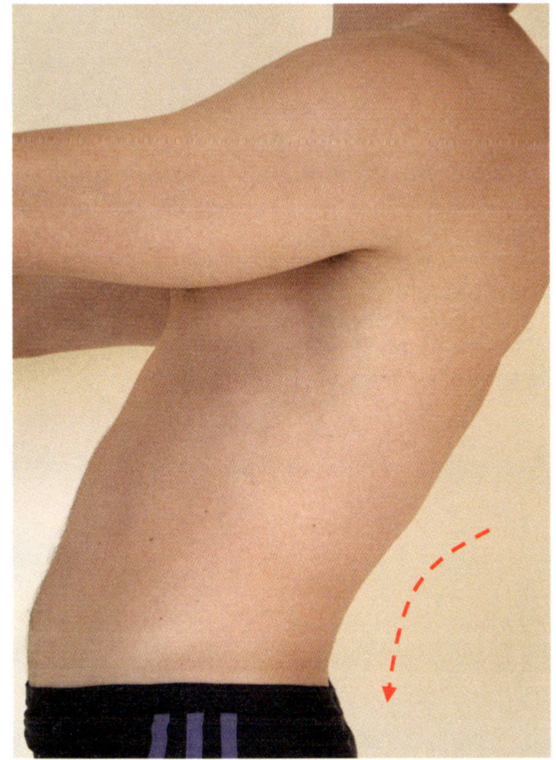

Fig. 3.19. Lumbar extension managed by the MF unit of retro-lumbi.

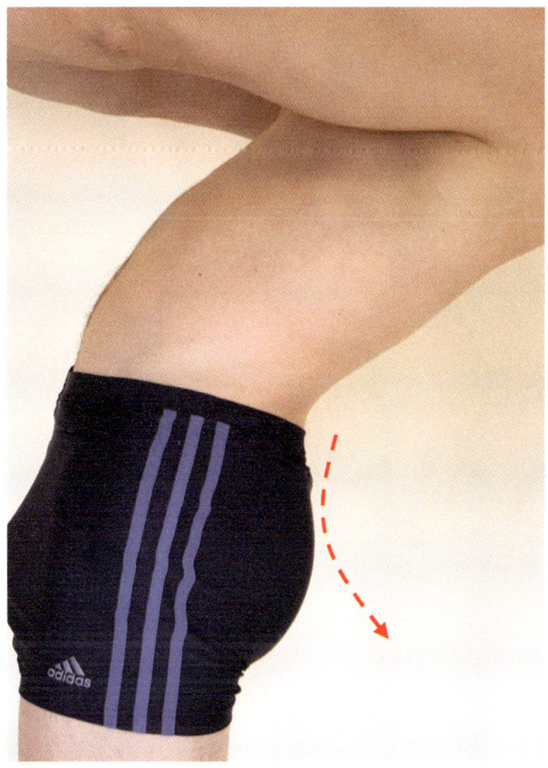

Fig. 3.20. Pelvic extension managed by the MF unit of retro-pelvis.

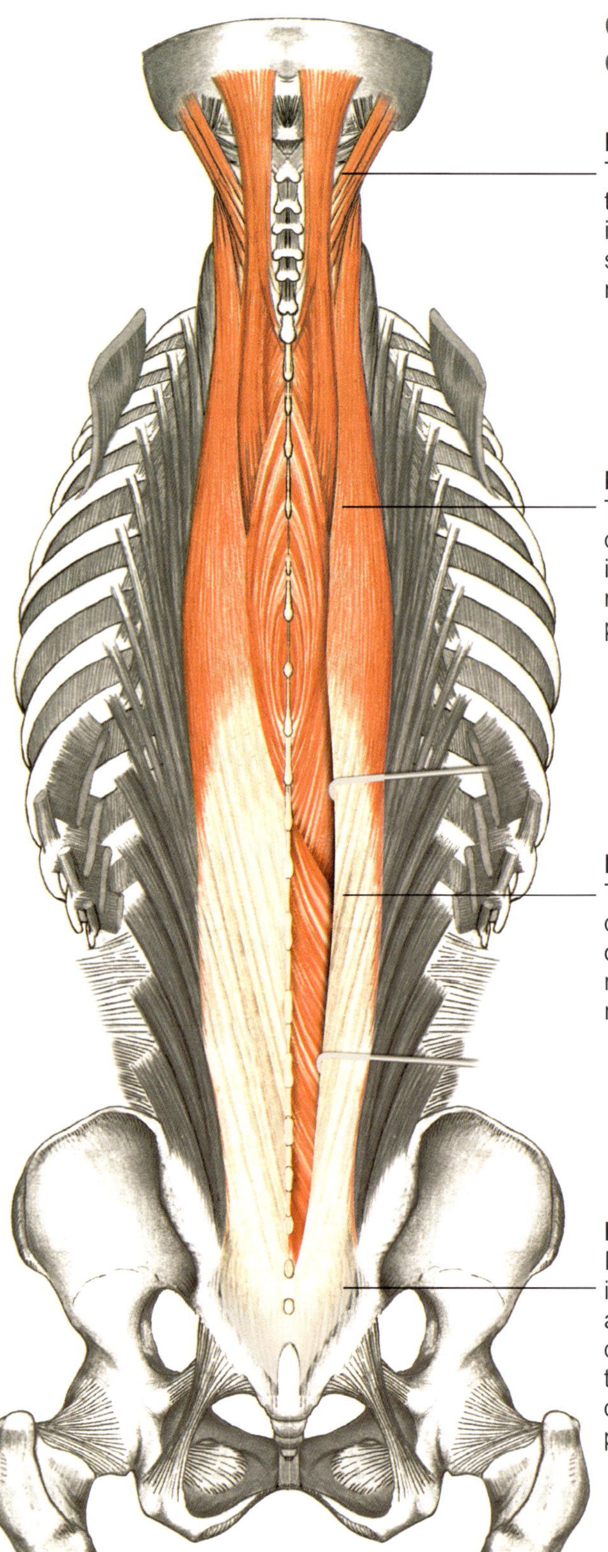

Fig. 3.21. Fascial compartments for the retropulsion muscles of the trunk.

(From G. Chiarugi and L. Bucciante, Istituzioni di anatomia dell'uomo. Piccin Nuova Libraria, Padova 1983, modified)

COMPARTMENTS FOR THE MUSCLES OF TRUNK RETROPULSION (Fig. 3.22)

Fascial compartment, collum retropulsion
The motor units of retropulsion are located in both the trapezius and rhomboid muscles contained in the superficial lamina, and in the splenii and semispinalis muscles contained in the deep muscular lamina.

Fascial compartment, thorax retropulsion
The fascia surrounding the medial muscles of the back partially separates them from the iliocostalis muscles by a septum. The long medial muscles are divided in three layers each being progressively more metameric.

Fascial compartment, lumbi retropulsion
The thoracolumbar fascia forms a superficial and deep sheet surrounding all the erector muscles of the spinal column (erector spinae). All these muscles contain motor units participating in retropulsion, lateropulsion and rotation.

Fascial compartment, pelvis retropulsion
It is the fascia that synchronises the motor units in each direction. For instance, the thoracolumbar aponeurosis through its longitudinal fibres inserts on the sacrotuberous ligament. It synchronises the retropulsion of the gluteus maximus muscle during the righting action implemented by the paravertebral muscles of the trunk.

GLOBAL MOVEMENT IMPLEMENTED BY THE RETROPULSION SEQUENCE

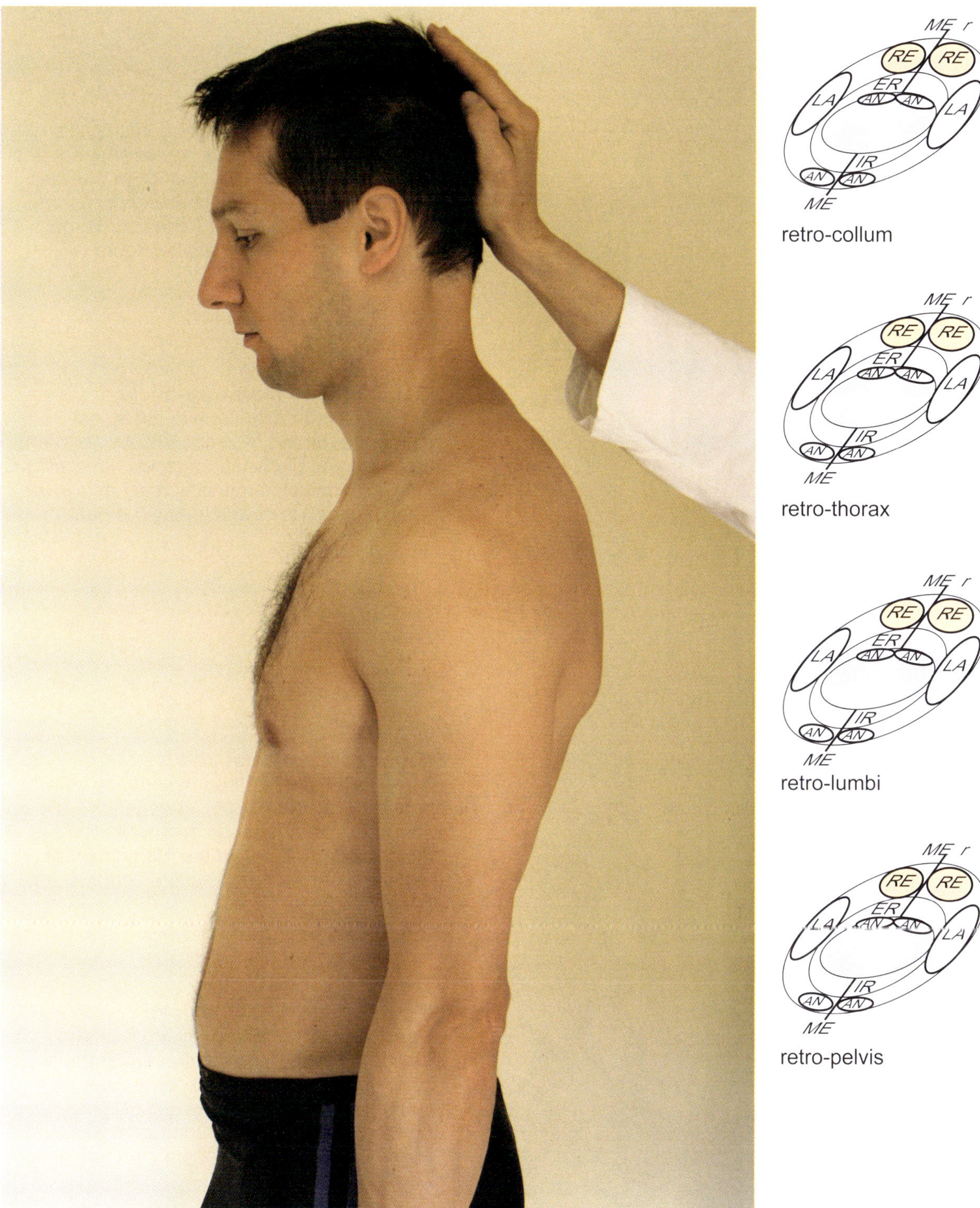

Fig. 3.22. Contraction of the retropulsion sequence brings the entire trunk posteriorly.

Platzer's anatomical textbook states that when activated unilaterally rotator muscles act as rotators and the inter-tranversarii muscles act as lateral flexors; whilst they act as erectors when activated bilaterally. It might be more correct to state that within the paravertebral muscles there are motor units that are activated via impulses for righting, and others are activated for torsion and lateral flexion. The neuromuscular spindles of the motor units dedicated to righting are activated when the myofascial stretch occurs in a longitudinal direction.

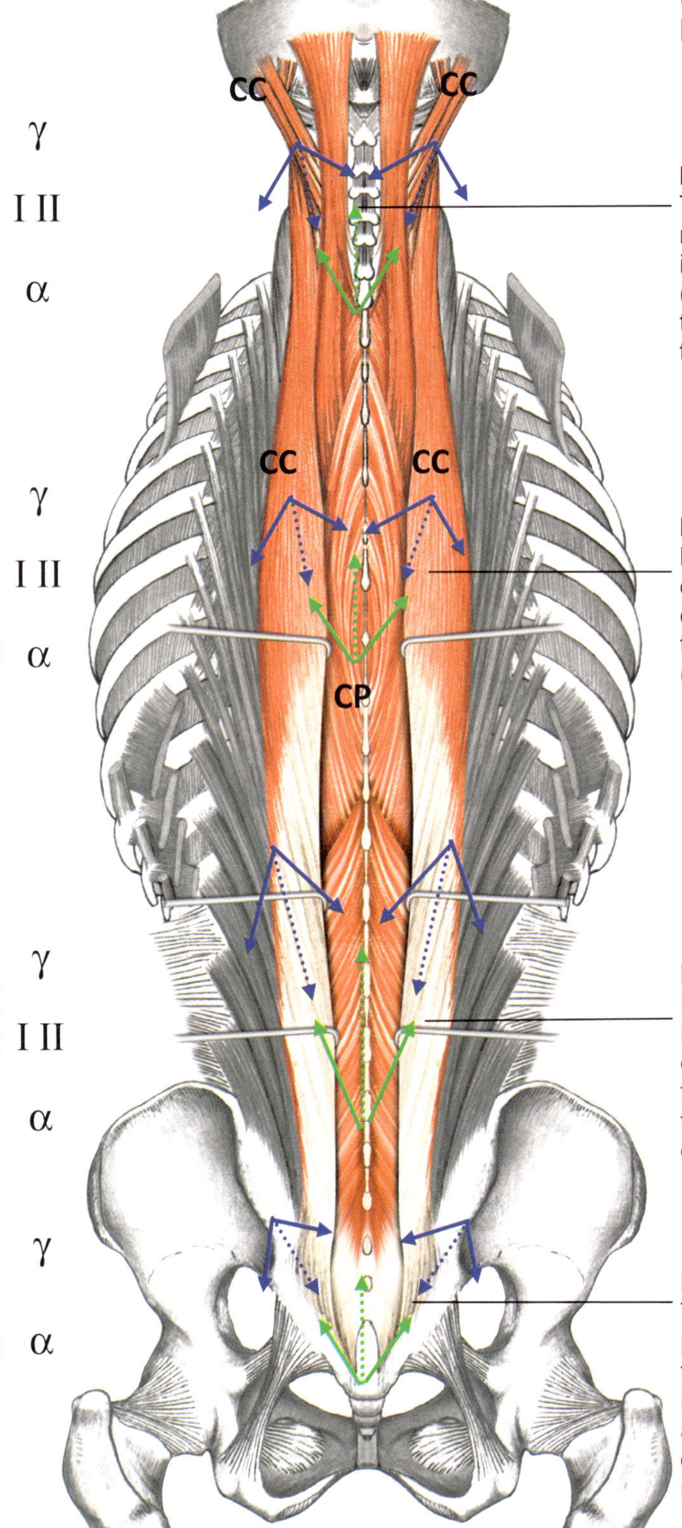

Fig. 3.23. Normal function of the alpha-gamma circuit.
(From G. Chiarugi and L. Bucciante, Istituzioni di anatomia dell'uomo. Piccin Nuova Libraria, Padova 1983, modified)

PHYSIOLOGY OF THE RETROPULSION MF UNITS TRUNK

MF unit of retro-collum (re-cl)
The monoarticular muscles (rectus capitis major and minor, obliquus capitis superior and inferior) together with the biarticular muscles (semispinalis and longissimus cervicis) form two parallelograms. Their forces converge towards the seventh cervical vertebra.

MF unit of retro-thorax (re-th)
Both parallelograms lateral to the spinal column are formed by monoarticular (levatores costarum) and biarticular muscles (longissimus thoracis). Their synergic action act as a lever (green vectors) to straighten up the back.

MF unit of retro-lumbi (re-lu)
Retropulsion of the lumbar spine may be implemented eccentrically or concentrically. In either case the stretch on the thoracolumbar fascia is different, hence the recruitment of the respective neuromuscular spindles is also different.

MF unit of retro-pelvis (re-pv)
The multifidus muscles originate from the posterior aspect of the sacrum and from the transverse processes of the vertebrae, they insert on the spinous processes of the lumbar and thoracic vertebrae. During retropulsion of pelvis, motor units belonging to the gluteal muscles also intervene.

ARTICULAR CONFLICTS IN RETROPULSION OF THE TRUNK

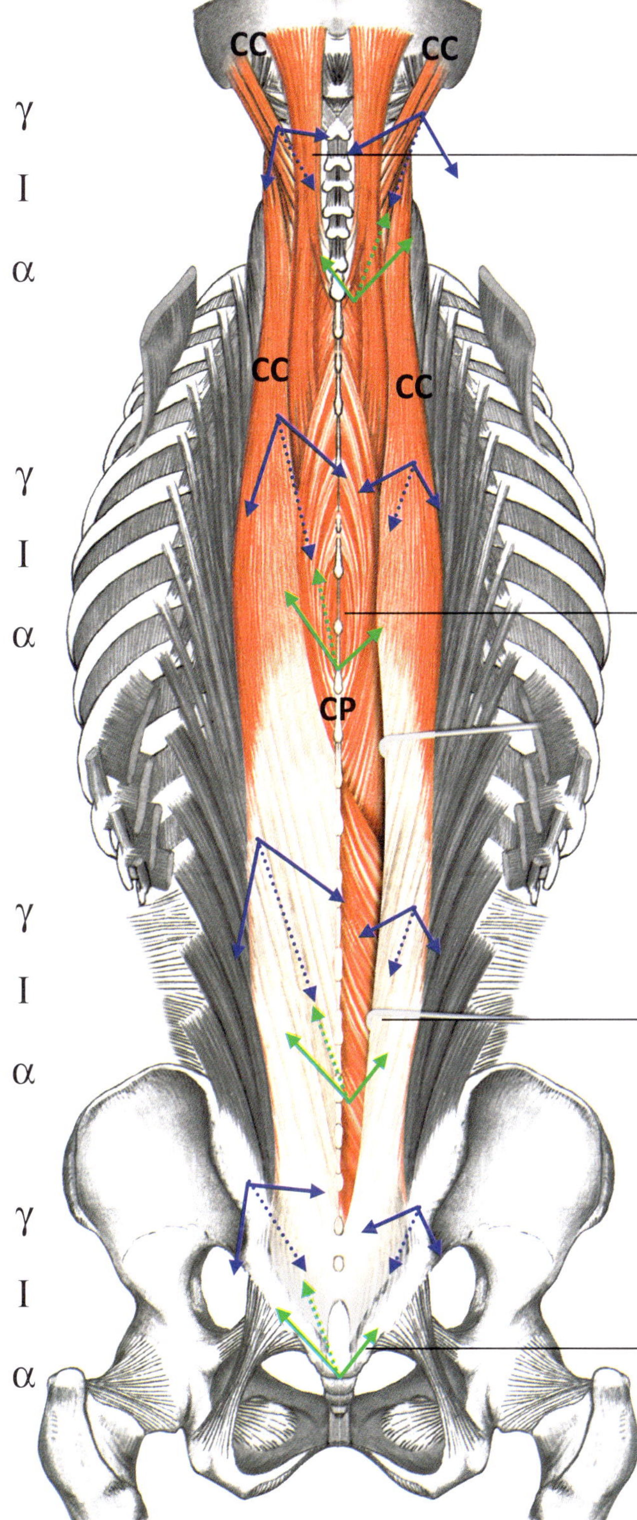

Pain during retropulsion of collum
If the left nuchal fascia (CC) is densified then the afferents (II) from a few spindles are not triggered, therefore the alpha circuits are not activated. The predominance in the muscles on the right shifts the tendinous resultant outside its physiological axis. Consequently, a conflict is created at the cervical vertebrae (resulting in neck pain).

Pain during retropulsion of thorax
If the fascia of the right thoracic erector spinae is densified, then the force of the muscles on the left of that hemi thorax prevails. This results in a shift of the resultant with an alteration of body perception and zygapophyseal joints conflicts.

Pain during retropulsion of lumbi
If the thoracolumbar fascia on one or both sides is densified, then the underlying muscles intervene with minor force. This imbalance may manifest over the lumbar vertebrae or more often between the fifth lumbar and first sacral vertebrae.

Pain during retropulsion of pelvis
If the fascia overlying the sacrum (CC) is densified, then the alpha-gamma circuit does not operate and the sacroiliac ligaments are not stretched physiologically. The receptors embedded in these ligaments then start changing their behaviour from proprioceptors to nociceptors.

Fig. 3.24. Dysfunctions of the alpha-gamma circuit.
(From G. Chiarugi and L. Bucciante, Istituzioni di anatomia dell'uomo. Piccin Nuova Libraria, Padova 1983, modified)

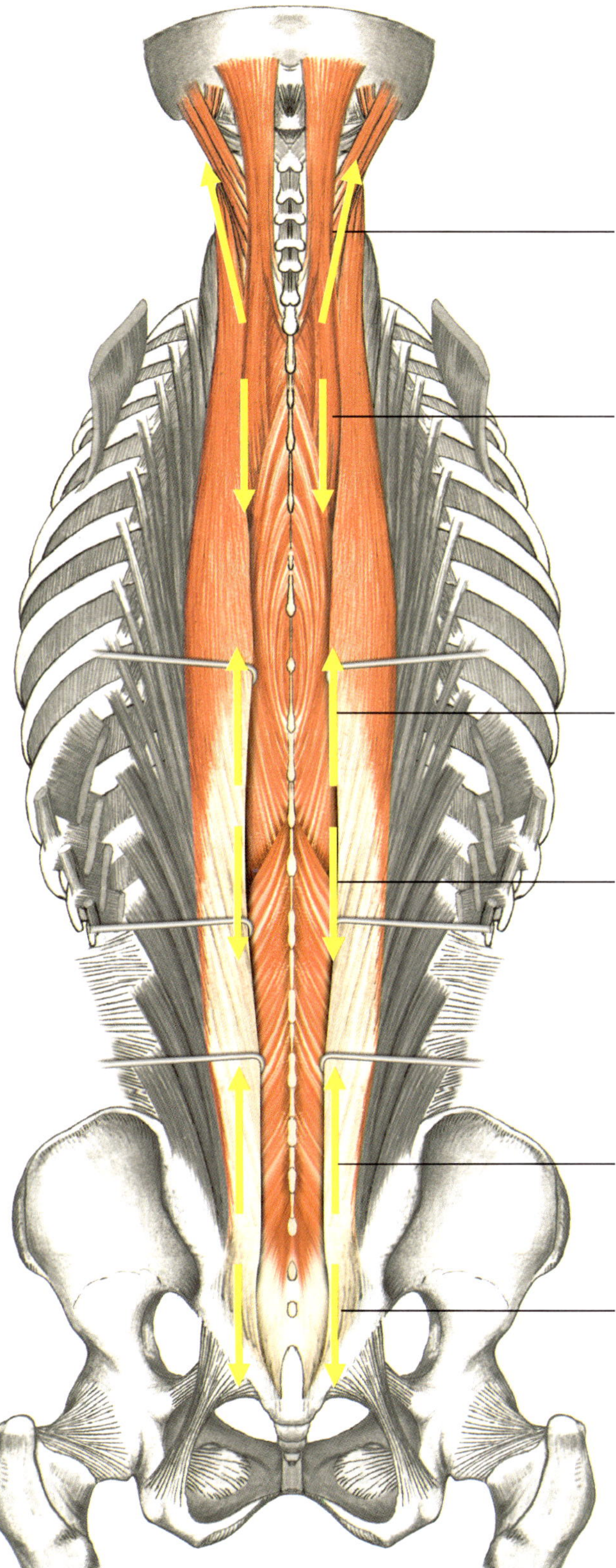

Fig. 3.25. Synergy along the retropulsion sequence of the trunk.
(From G. Chiarugi and L. Bucciante, Istituzioni di anatomia dell'uomo. Piccin Nuova Libraria, Padova 1983, modified)

TR RETROPULSION SEQUENCE AND STRETCH REFLEX

Synergy between re-cl and re-th
The splenii (Fig. 3.27) and semispinalis capitis muscles cranially pull on the erector spinae fascia.

The spinalis thoracis muscles pull on their perimysium and the overlying fascia caudally.

Synergy between re-th and re-lu
During their contraction the semispinalis and spinalis thoracis muscles create a cranial traction on the lumbar fascia.
The longissimus lumborum muscle determines a caudal traction on the thoracolumbar fascia during righting.
The longissimus muscle originates from the sacrum and the spinous processes of all lumbar vertebrae, where its medial bundles anchor on the costal processes of the first two lumbar vertebrae. Consequently, it is a muscle acting upon lumbar movements hence the terminology longissimus lumborum may also be opportune. This facilitates reference when describing distal tractions of the thoracolumbar fascia along the retropulsion sequence.

Synergy between re-lu and re-pv
In the sacral area the thoracolumbar and erector spinae fasciae adhere together (Fig. 3.29). This union is only apparent since each layer of collagen fibres maintains its independent gliding. The longitudinal fibres (Fig. 3.30) when reaching the sacrotuberous ligament connect with the deep muscle fibres of gluteus maximus (coxa retropulsion).

ACTIVATION OF THE GOLGI TENDON ORGANS

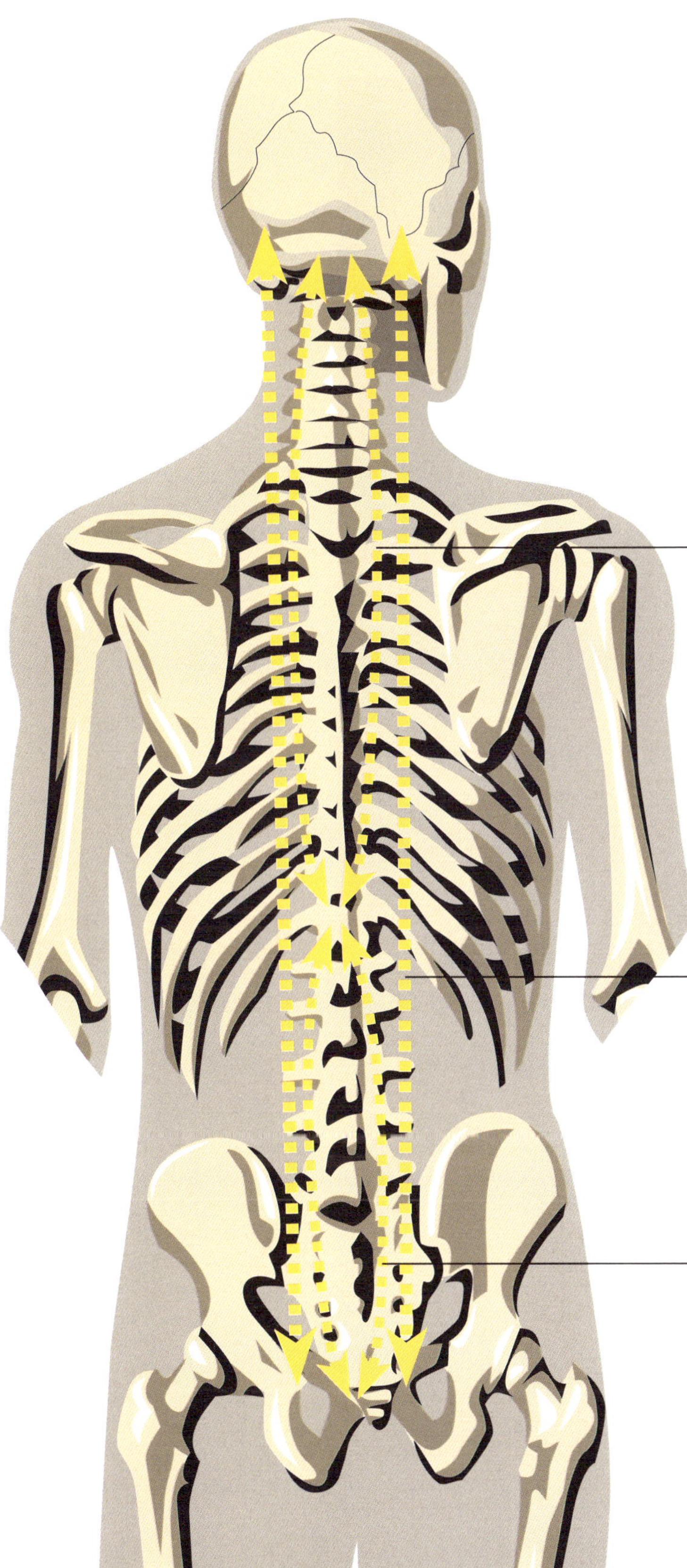

Fig. 3.26. Biarticular muscles for the retropulsion sequence of the trunk.

Myo-kinetic chain between collum and thorax
The semispinalis thoracis, cervicis and capitis muscles form a secondary fascial sequence connecting the neck to the thorax. The semispinalis muscle originates from the transverse processes of all the thoracic vertebrae and inserts on the cervical vertebrae and the occiput. The fascia of this muscle unites the movement of the neck and thorax together.

Global myo-kinetic chain
The longissimus lumborum, thoracis and cervicis muscles are the anatomical substrate for global myofascial retropulsion sequence of the trunk. When lifting a weight from the floor, the entire retropulsion sequence is activated but muscular implication varies based upon the degrees of straightening and upon the particular involvement of the Golgi tendon organs.

Myo-kinetic chain between lumbi and pelvis
This secondary sequence connects the movements of lumbi and pelvis together. It is formed by the common mass of the erector spinae muscles, in particular by muscles reaching from the sacrum to the twelfth thoracic vertebra and twelfth rib.

FASCIAE OF THE RETROPULSION SEQUENCE OF THE TRUNK

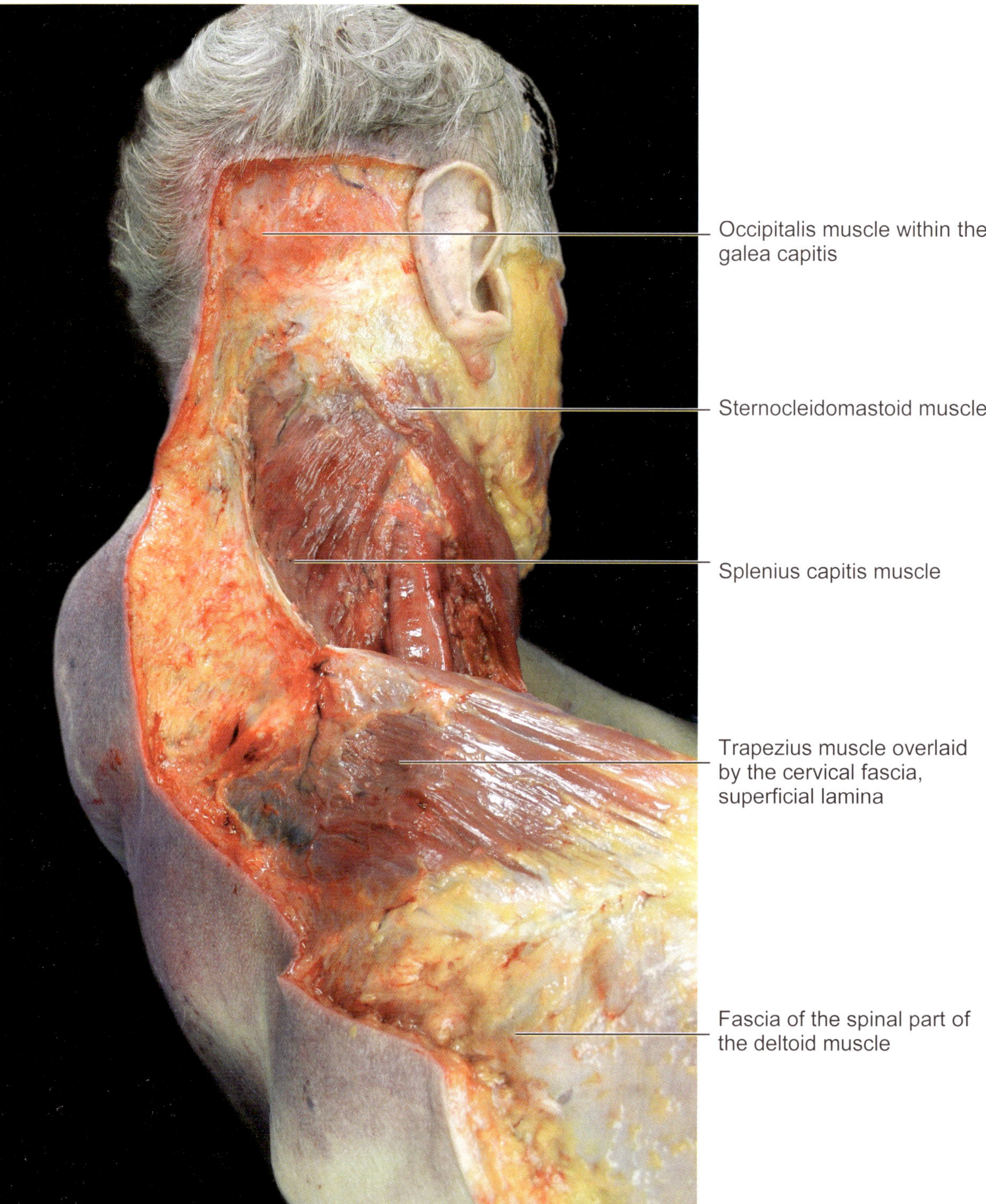

Fig. 3.27. Posterior fasciae of the neck and trapezius muscle. The trapezius together with the sternocleidomastoid muscle are included in the superficial lamina of the deep fascia. Deeper the intermediate lamina covers the splenii muscles, deeper still the deep lamina covers the erector spinae muscles.

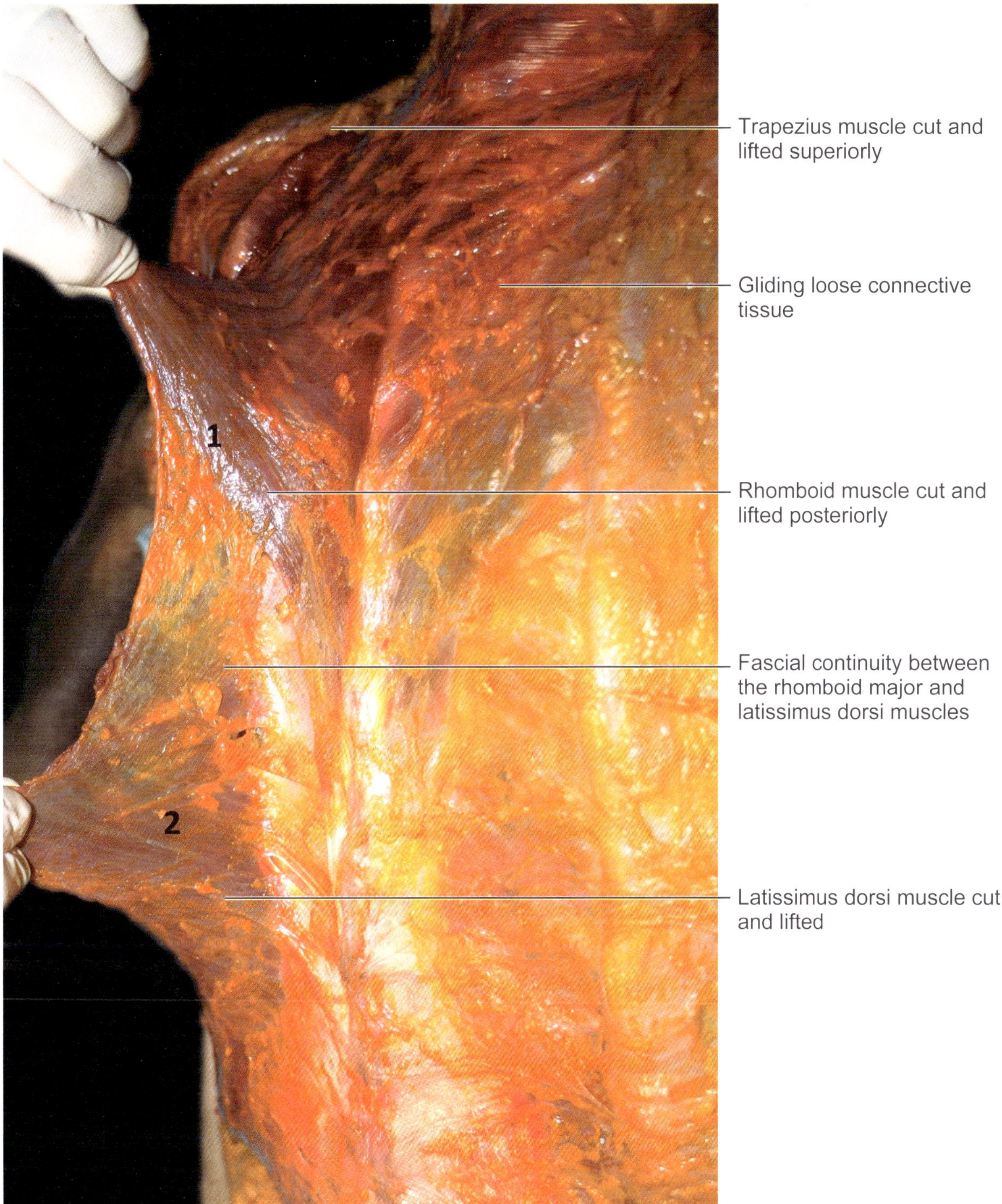

Fig. 3.28. Epimysial fascia of the rhomboid major and latissimus dorsi muscles cut and lifted laterally. The superficial lamina of the deep fascia covers the rhomboid muscles (1) and continues without interruption with the fascia covering the latissimus dorsi muscle (2).

FASCIAE OF THE RETROPULSION SEQUENCE OF THE TRUNK

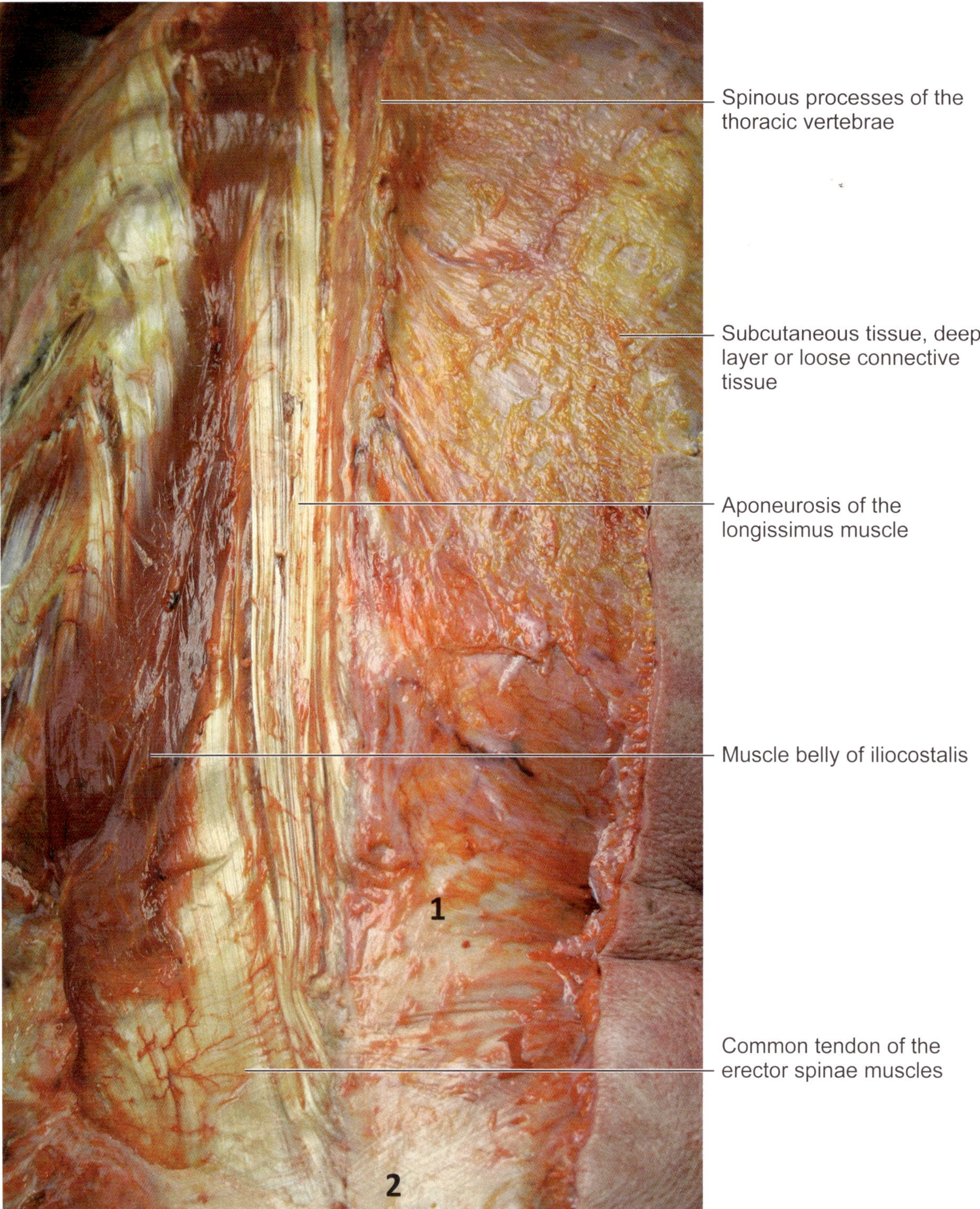

Fig. 3.29. Common tendon of the erector spinae muscles. The thoracolumbar fascia (1) intimately adheres to the tendons of the erector spinae muscles over the sacrum (2).

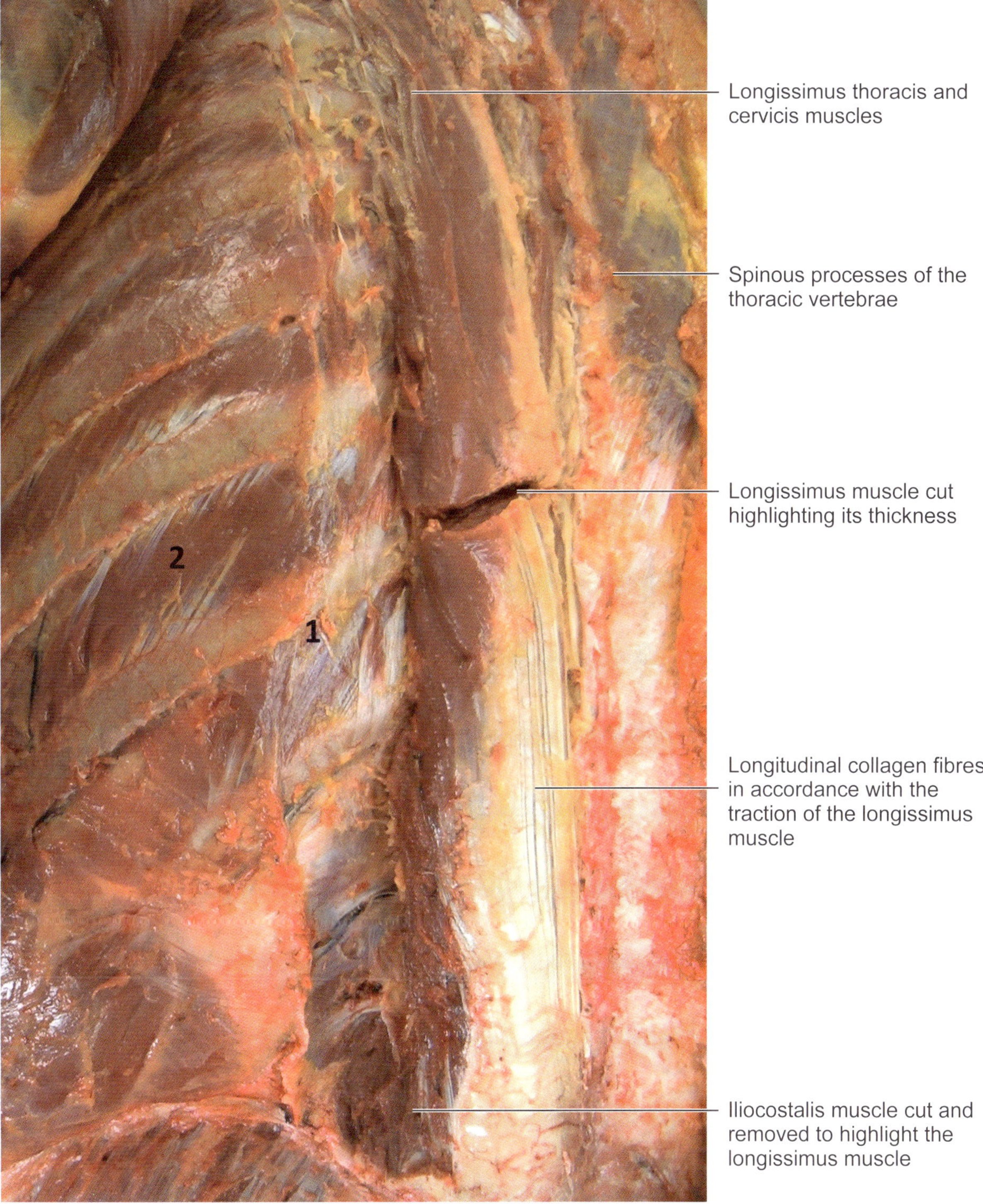

Fig. 3.30. Fascial compartment of the longissimus lumborum muscle. The iliocostalis muscle (1) was cut and removed, the external intercostal muscles (2) become visible.

SUPERFICIAL REGION OF THE TRUNK, MEDIOPULSION SEQUENCE

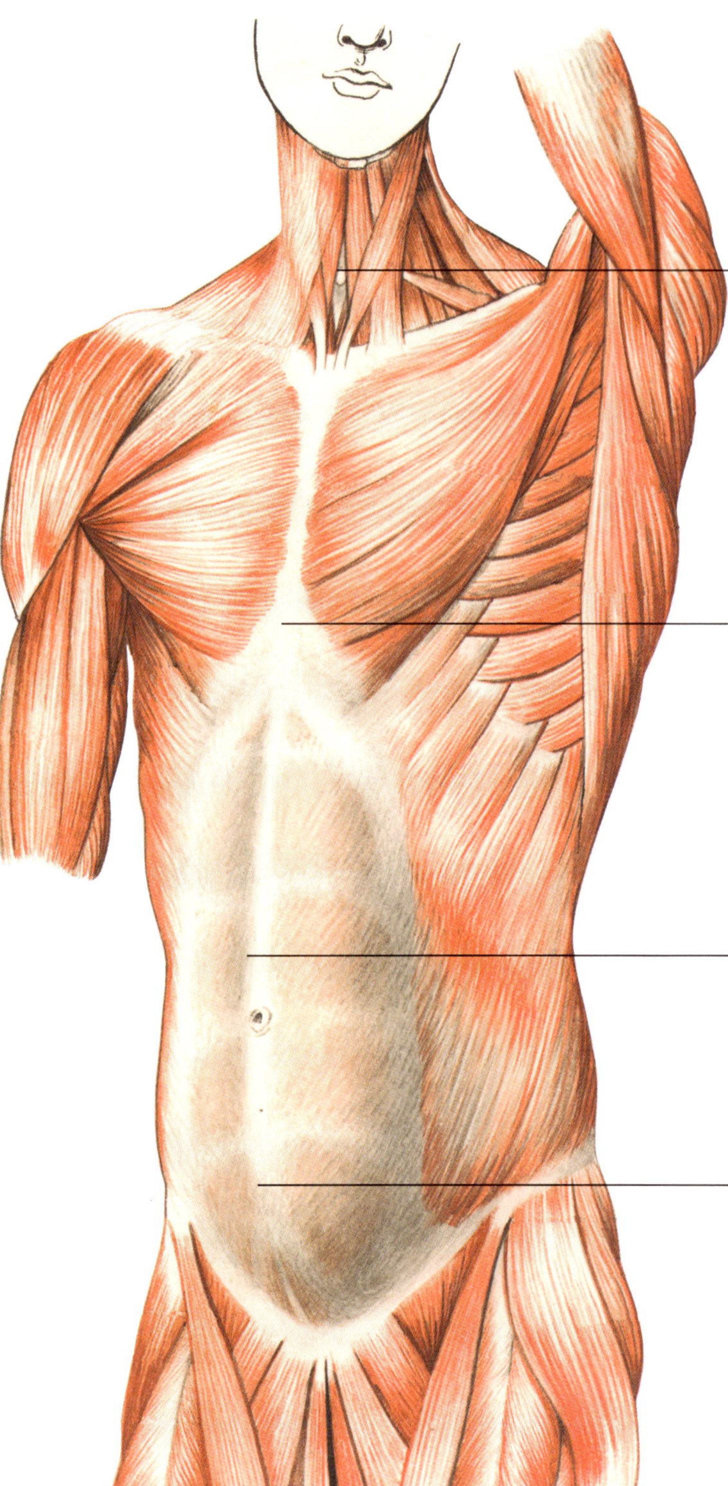

Fig. 3.31. Anterior superficial region of the trunk.
(From G. Chiarugi and L. Bucciante, Istituzioni di anatomia dell'uomo. Piccin Nuova Libraria, Padova 1983, modified)

MEDIOPULSION SEQUENCE OF THE TRUNK

Cervical mediopulsion (Fig. 3.32)
The mediopulsion sequence is not supported by muscles in the trunk, therefore the term myofascial unit should not be used. The longitudinal collagen fibres located over the median line of the anterior and posterior trunk serve in:
- the motor organisation of the muscles of the right body half with the muscles on the left,
- the perception of return to the midline after lateral flexion on the right or left.

Thoracic mediopulsion
The anterior median line of the thorax is formed by the fascia connecting both pectoralis major muscles and by the longitudinal collagen fibres over the sternum.

Lumbar mediopulsion
Above the umbilicus the aponeuroses of the three abdominal muscles are distributed equally in front and behind the rectus abdominis muscle.

Pelvic mediopulsion
Below the umbilicus the aponeuroses fuse together in front of the rectus abdominis muscle. Underneath the rectus abdominis, below the Douglas' line, the connective lining is formed by the transverse fascia united to the parietal peritoneum.

PROPRIOCEPTION OF THE POSTURE BY THE SEQUENCE OF MEDIOPULSION AN

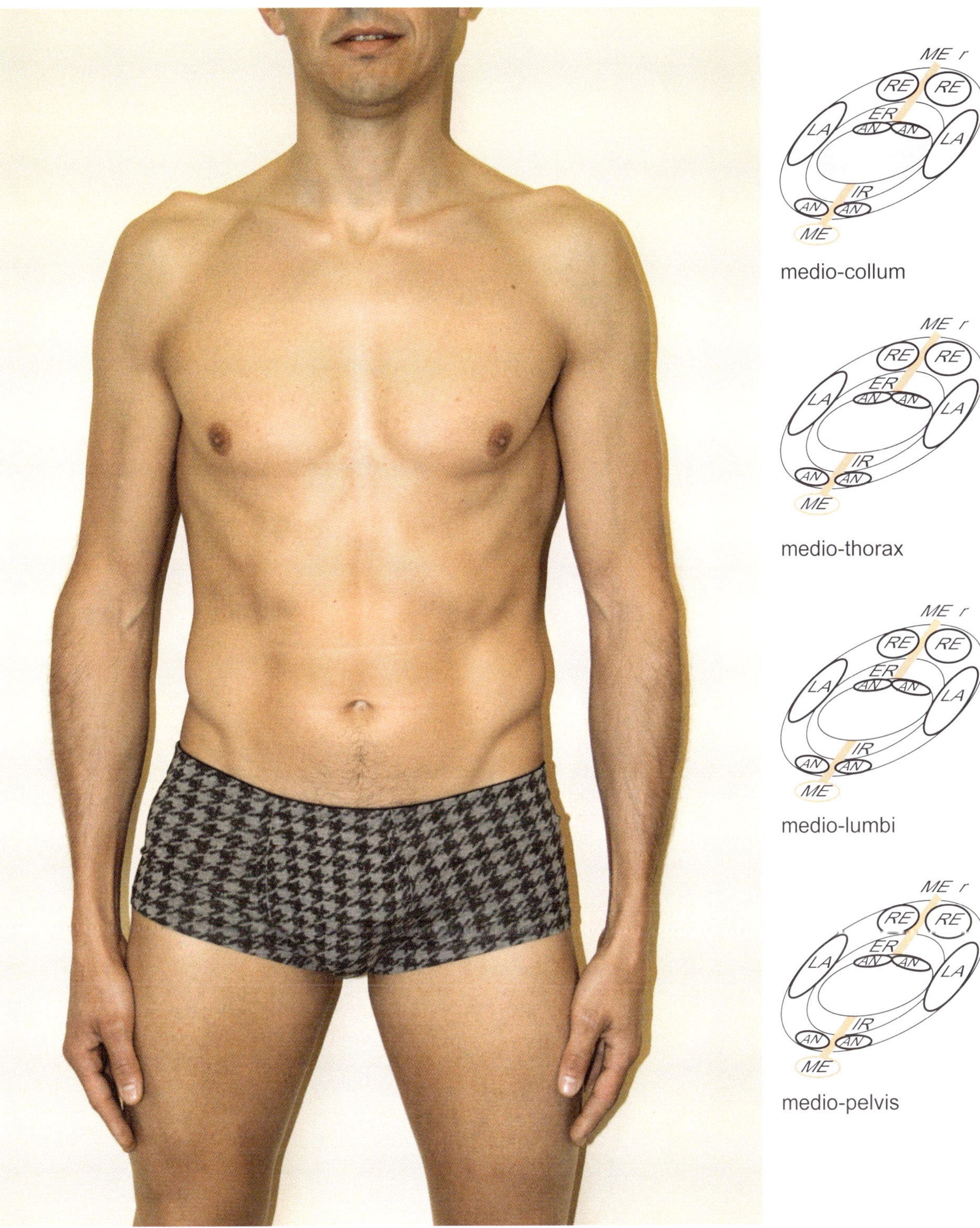

Fig. 3.32. The median line of the trunk corresponds to the plumb line for the centre of gravity.

The anterior median (ME) line is formed by the cervical linea alba, by the sternum and by the abdominal linea alba. This collagenous fascial septum divides all the musculature of the anterior trunk in two symmetrical parts. This septum serves as a reference point for the anterior muscles when balancing lateral flexion forces between the right and left body halves. Trunk mediopulsion does not have specific muscles and hence the figures showing the myofascial units of collum, thorax, lumbi and pelvis are not reported.

MEDIOPULSION SEQUENCE OF THE TRUNK RETRO (R)

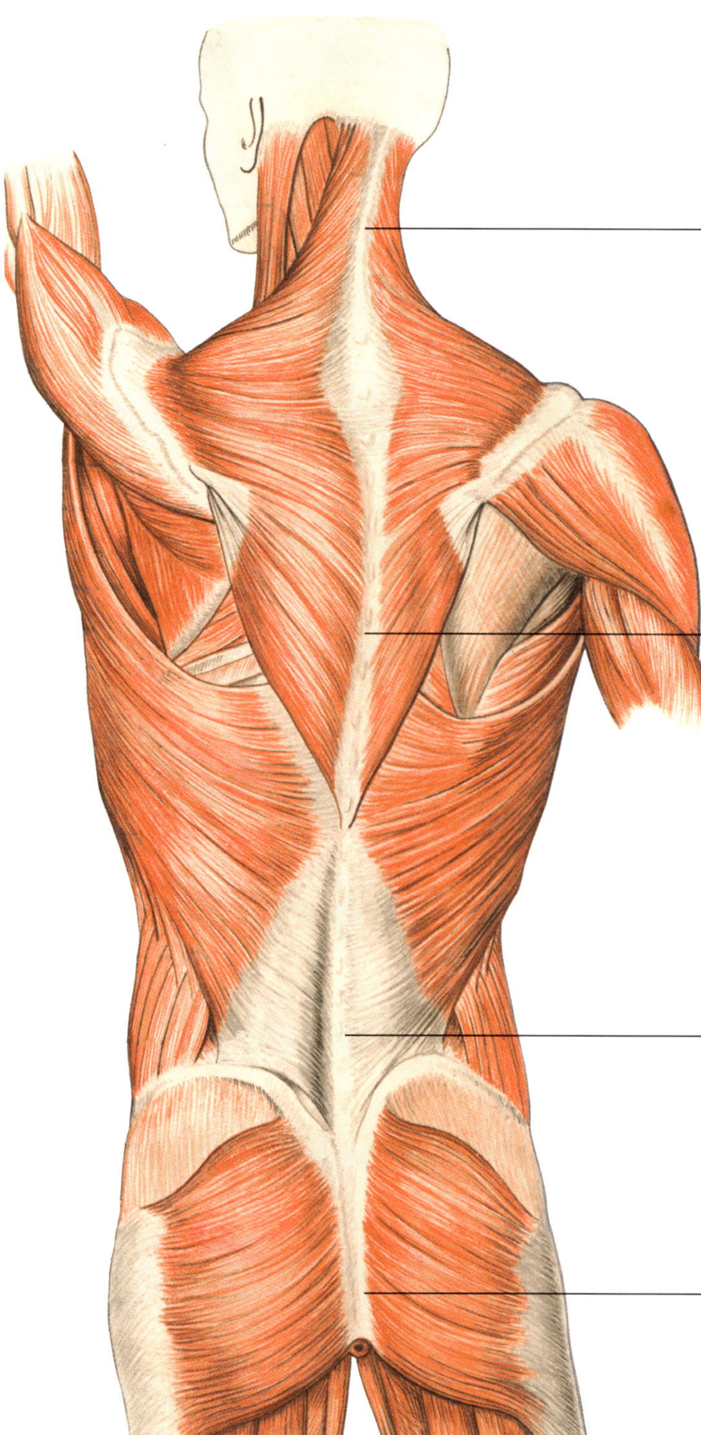

Fig. 3.33. Posterior superficial region of the trunk.
(From G. Chiarugi and L. Bucciante, Istituzioni di anatomia dell'uomo. Piccin Nuova Libraria, Padova 1983, modified)

Cervical mediopulsion retro (Fig. 3.34)
The nuchal ligament forms the start of the medio sequence (retro).

"The posterior margin of the nuchal ligament blends with the tendinous fibres of the trapezius muscle. Its right and left faces are connected to the muscles of the head and neck having numerous insertions on it" (Testut L. 1987).

Thoracic mediopulsion retro
The supraspinous ligament is a robust fibrous chord holding the apices of the spinous processes together from the seventh cervical vertebra to the sacrum, it is intimately fused with the adjacent fasciae. The most superficial fascicles extend over three to four vertebrae whilst the deeper one unite the spinous processes of the adjacent vertebrae and are in continuity with the interspinous ligaments.

Lumbar mediopulsion retro
The lumbar and sacral supraspinous ligaments form the distal part of the sequence.

"A discopathy, often considered a fashionable disease, is erroneously connected to discs and spinal column dysfunctions. Vice versa, experts confirm that many patients, even when presenting significant radiologically visible alterations do not present any disorder" (Benninghoff H. 1978).

Pelvic mediopulsion retro
The gluteus maximus through its most superficial fibres originates from the ligamentous mass overlying the spinous apophyses of the sacrum and coccyx.

PROPRIOCEPTION OF THE POSTURE BY THE SEQUENCE OF MEDIOPULSION RE

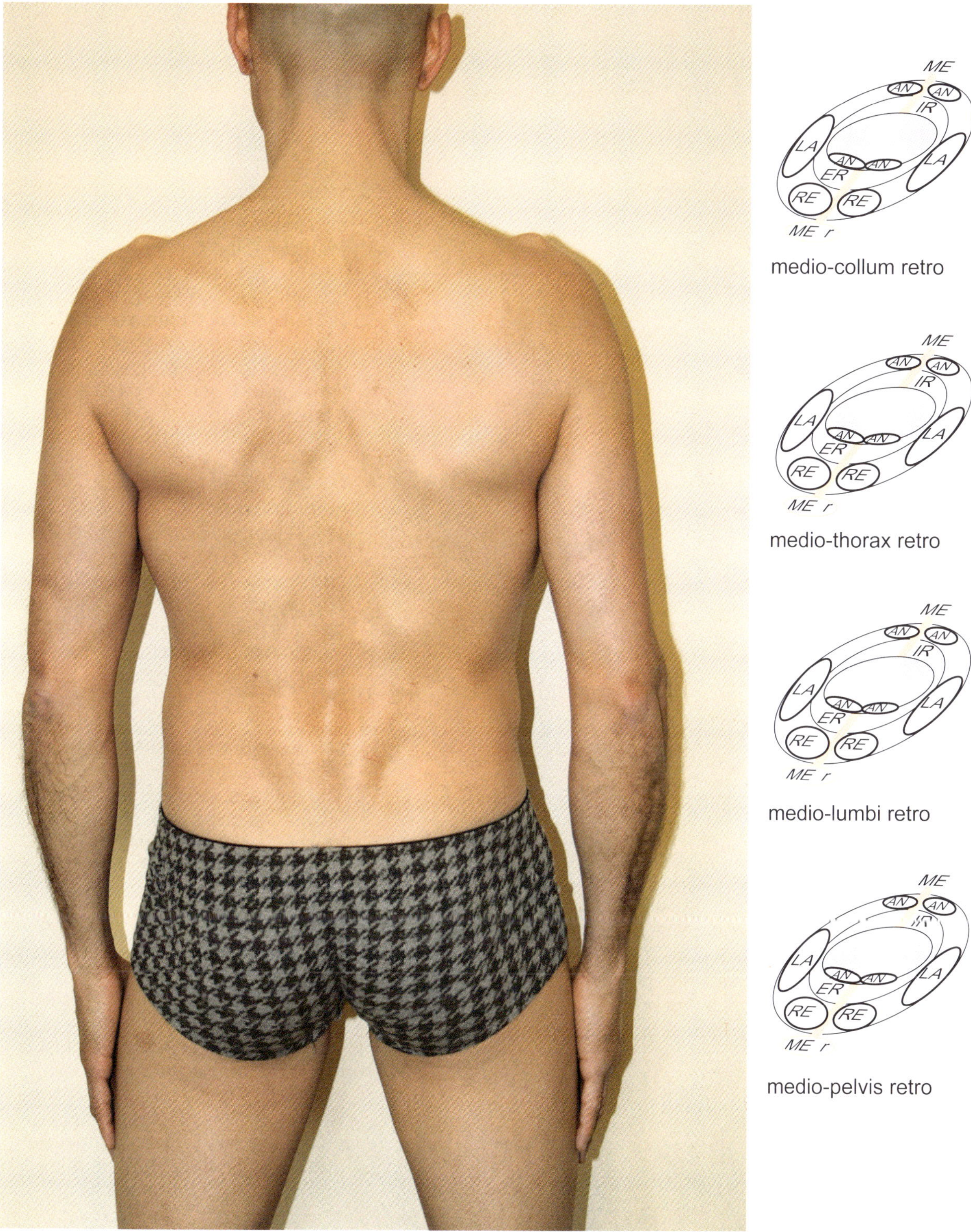

Fig. 3.34. The supraspinous ligaments correspond to the plumb line for the centre of gravity.

In the pictures of mediopulsion no hand is offering resistance since there are no muscles activated according to this motor direction. The anterior median line of separation is divided from the median (ME) retro (r) line since the cavity holding the viscera is located in the centre of the trunk.

PHYSIOLOGY OF THE LINEA ALBA

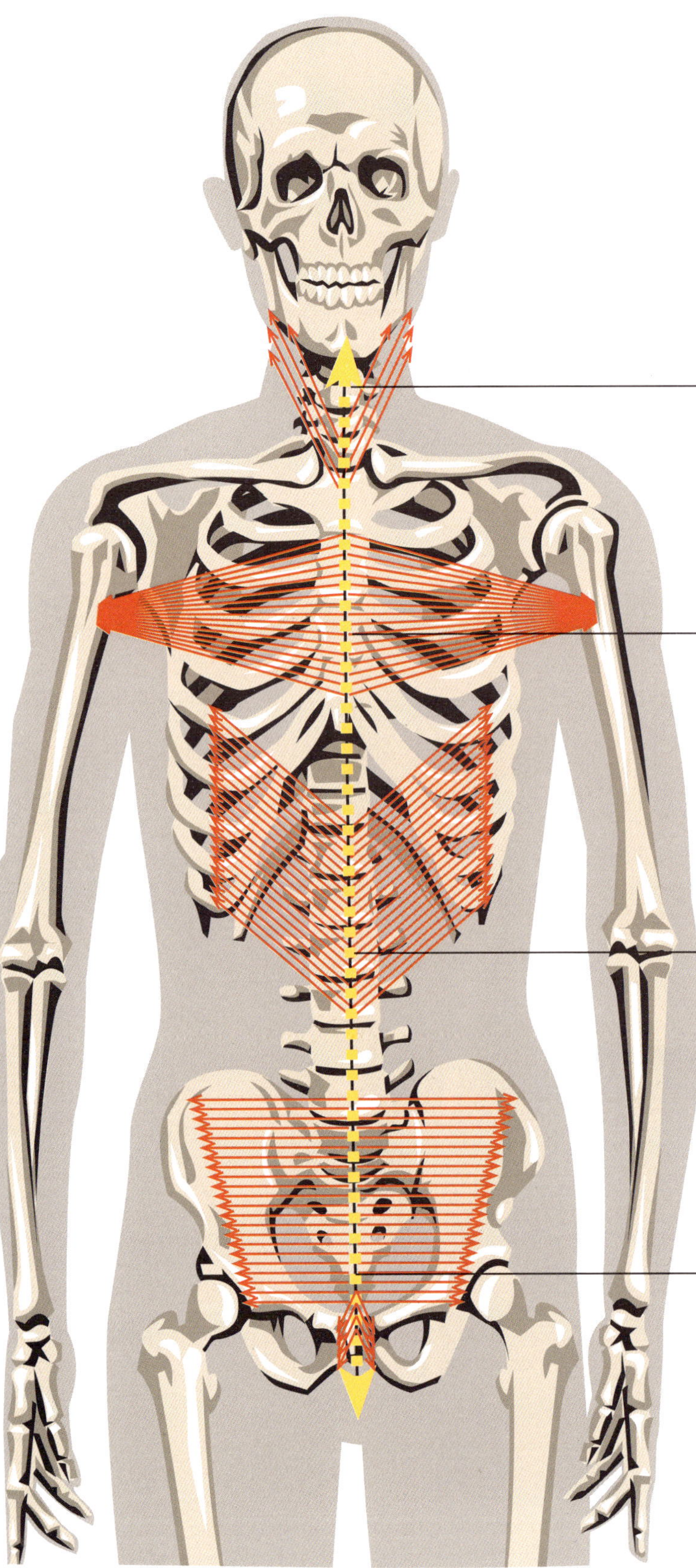

Fig. 3.35. Median convergence of the large muscles of the anterior trunk.

MF insertions for collum mediopulsion
The cervical linea alba is pulled proximally by the muscles belonging to the superficial and intermediate laminae of the neck (Fig. 3.37). The cervical linea alba signals the tensional equilibrium to the lateropulsion muscles of the neck.

MF insertions for thorax mediopulsion
The sternal division of the pectoralis major muscle contracts when both arms perform an effort in adduction. The pectoralis fascia crosses over the sternum (Fig. 3.38) and synchronises the force of both pectoralis muscles through the stretch reflex.

MF insertions for lumbi mediopulsion
Above the umbilicus the abdominal oblique muscles form fibrous meshes along the linea alba, this allows a mutual information on their respective tension towards both body halves.

MF insertions for pelvis mediopulsion
The transversus abdominis muscle, below the umbilicus, greatly contributes to the formation of the linea alba. This fibrous chord is pulled caudally by the pyramidalis muscle originating from the pubis and inserting on the linea alba.

PHYSIOLOGY OF THE SUPRASPINOUS LIGAMENTS

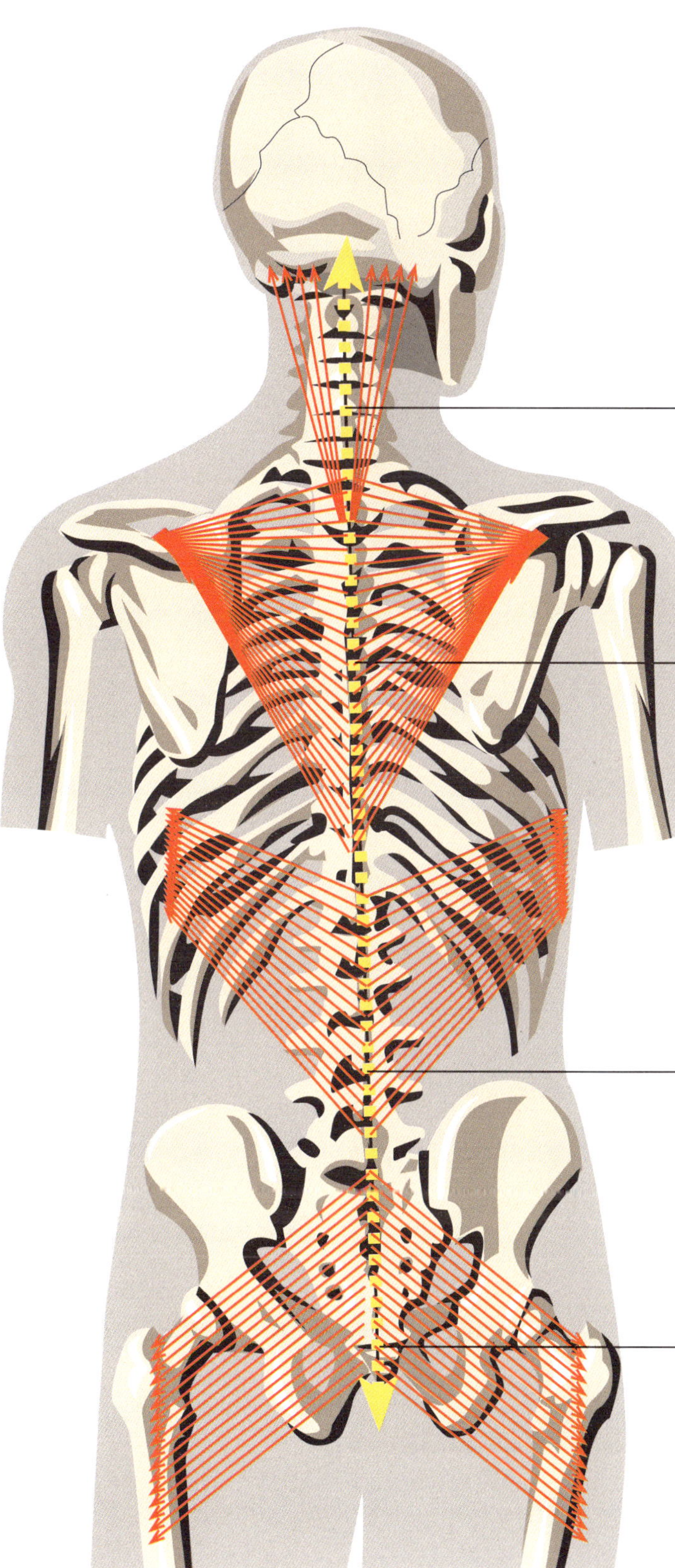

Fig. 3.36. Median posterior convergence of the large muscles of the trunk.

MF insertions for collum mediopulsion
The splenius capitis muscle, or transversal spinal system, originates from the nuchal ligament and terminates on the superior nuchal line up to the mastoid process of the temporal bone. Hence this muscle pulls the nuchal and supraspinous ligaments cranially.

MF insertions for thorax mediopulsion
All the muscles of the back held within the superficial, intermediate and deep laminae are connected to the interspinous ligament.

"The medial horizontal fascicles of the trapezius bring the scapula near to the spinal column, as is the case when attempting to pull apart both hands that are forcibly held together at chest level" (Benninghoff H. 1978).

MF insertions for lumbi mediopulsion
The latissimus dorsi muscle originates from the spinous processes, the interspinous ligaments of the lower six thoracic vertebrae and from all the lumbar vertebrae. The inferior part of this muscle fuses with the thoracolumbar aponeurosis that descends over the sacrum (Fig. 3.40).

MF insertions for pelvis mediopulsion
The lateropulsion tractions of the most superficial fibres of the gluteus maximus muscle converge on the thoracolumbar fascia overlying the sacrum (Fig. 3.39). This muscle becomes the caudal tensor of the supraspinous ligaments.

FASCIAE OF THE MEDIOPULSION SEQUENCE OF THE TRUNK

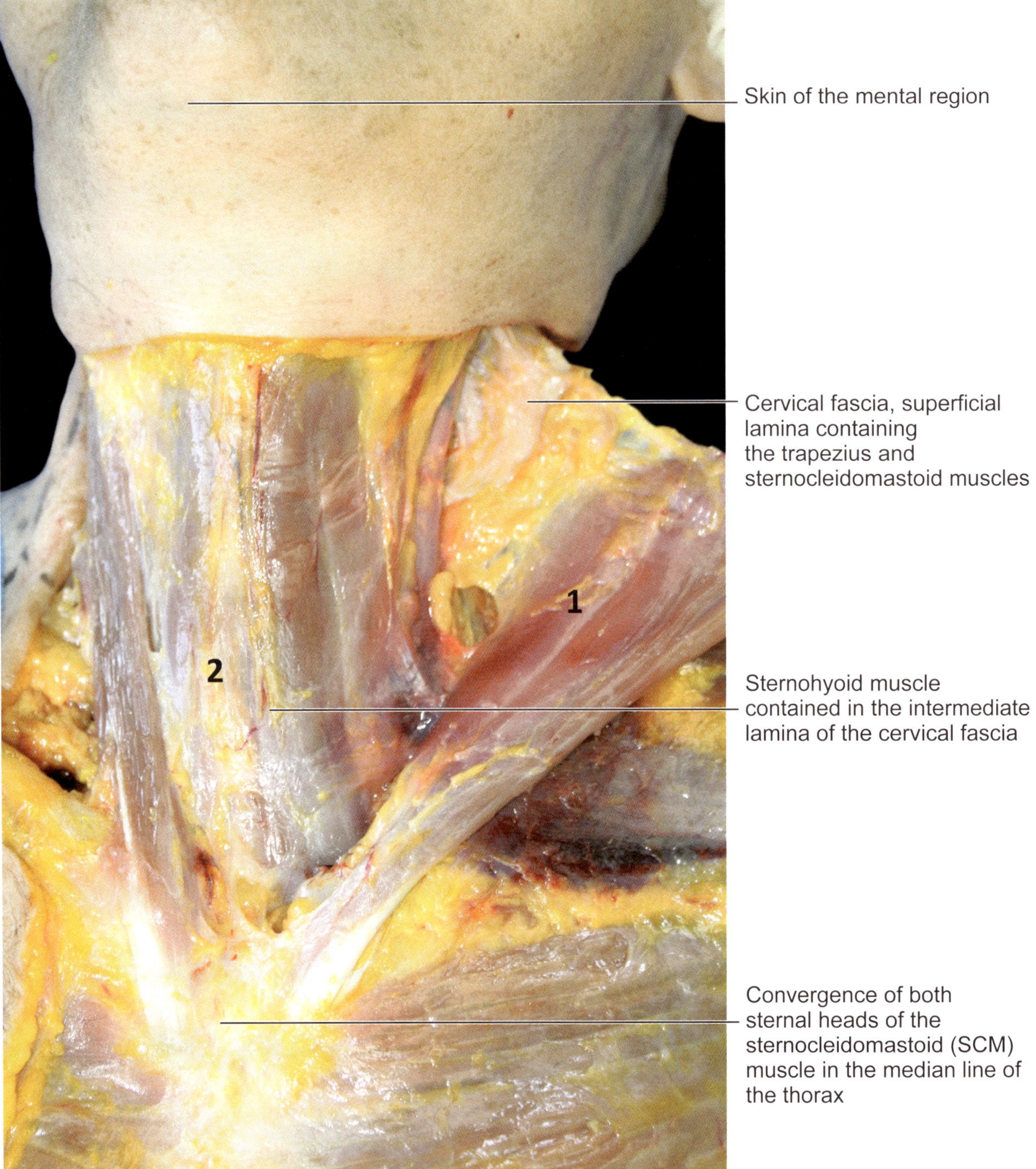

Fig. 3.37. Anterior cervical fascia, intermediate lamina. The sternocleidomastoid muscle (1) was cut and lifted inferiorly, the cervical linea alba (2) becomes visible and is continuous with the suprasternal ligaments.

The lines indicate anatomical parts whilst the numbers (1, 2) indicate the physiology of the fascia. Number one indicates a determined action and number two indicates its effect.

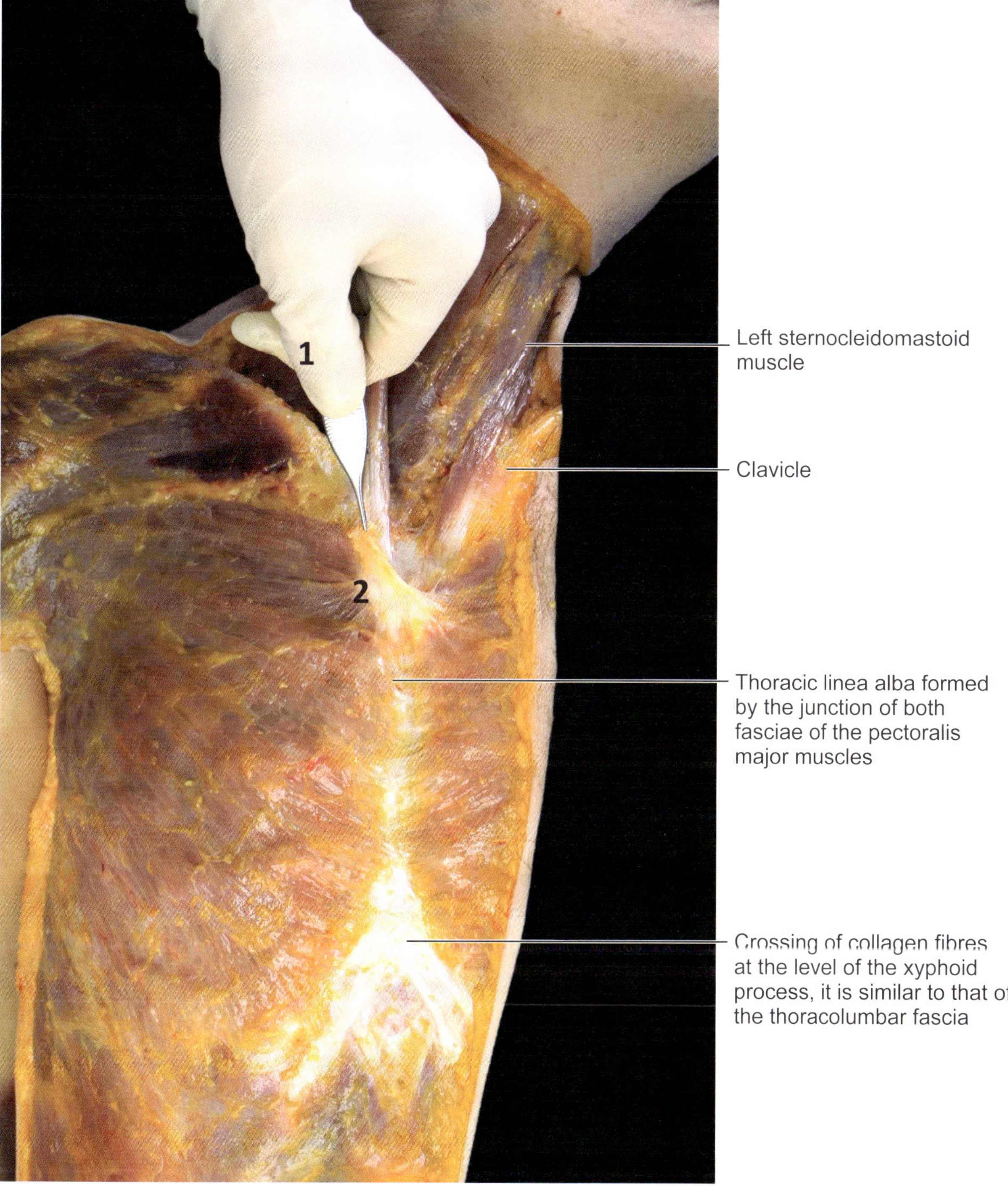

Fig. 3.38. Epimysial fascia of the pectoralis major muscle. The superficial fascia was removed, the forceps (1) pulls on the external lamina of the pectoralis major fascia, it is visible that it courses over the sternum (2).

FASCIAE OF THE MEDIOPULSION SEQUENCE OF THE TRUNK

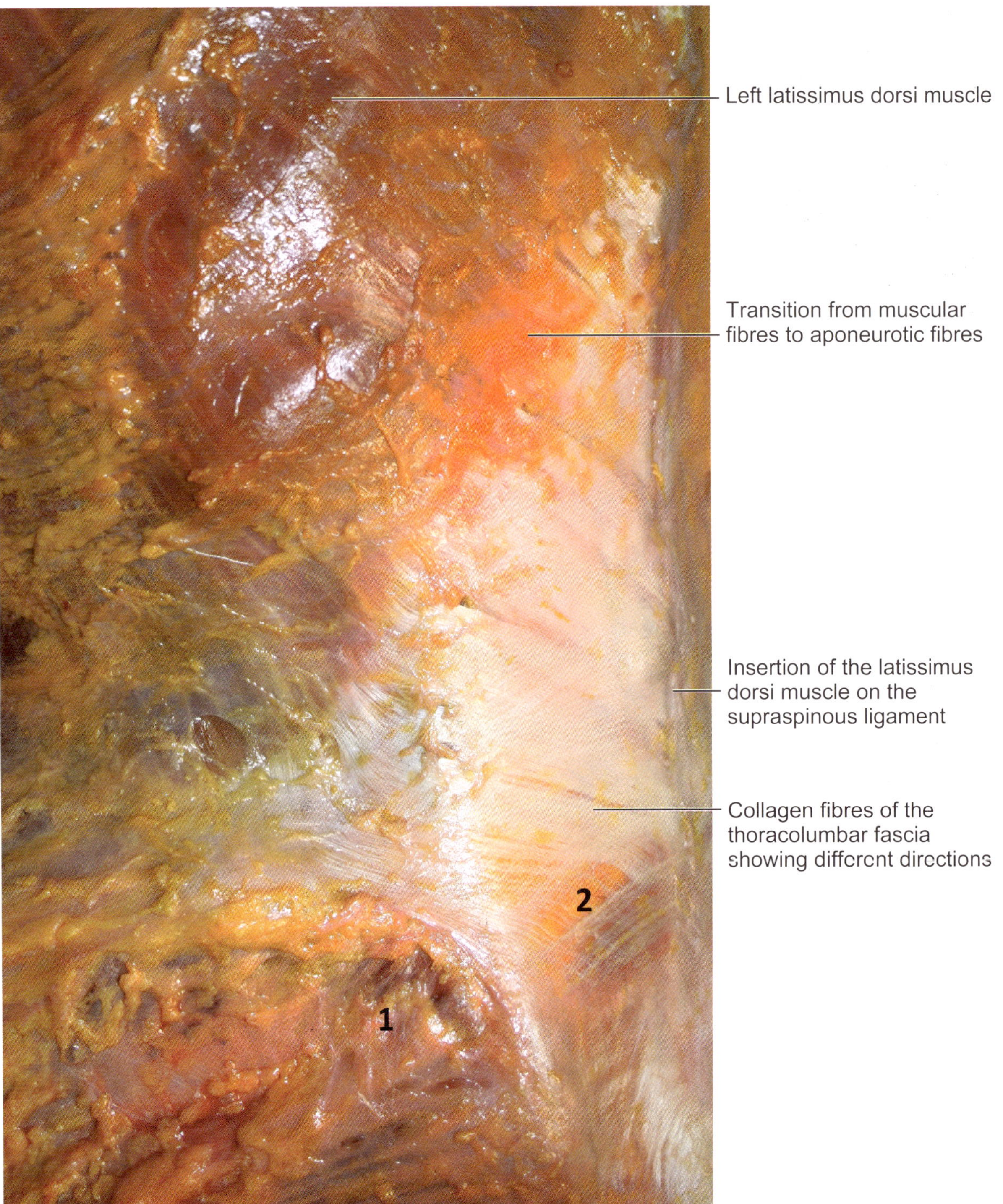

Fig. 3.39. Thoracolumbar aponeurosis and its insertions on the supraspinous ligament. The superficial fibres (1) of the gluteus maximus muscle create a disto-proximal tension on the supraspinous ligament (2).

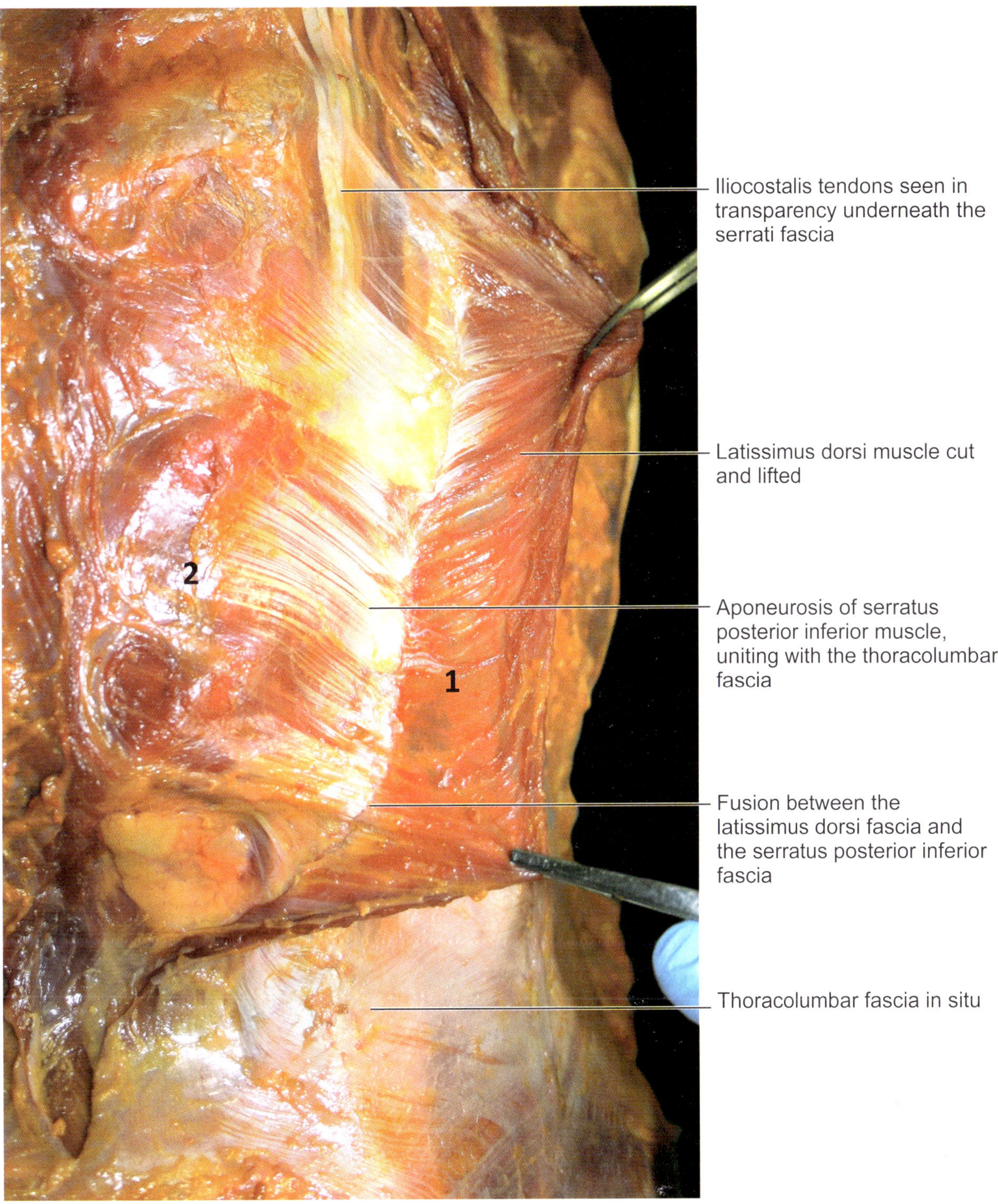

Fig. 3.40. Latissimus dorsi muscle cut and lifted medially. The thoracolumbar fascia is formed by the aponeurosis or flat tendon of the latissimus dorsi (1) and serratus posterior inferior muscles (2). The serratus posterior inferior muscle is contained within the intermediate lamina of the deep fascia.

POSTERIOR REGION OF THE TRUNK, LATEROPULSION SEQUENCE

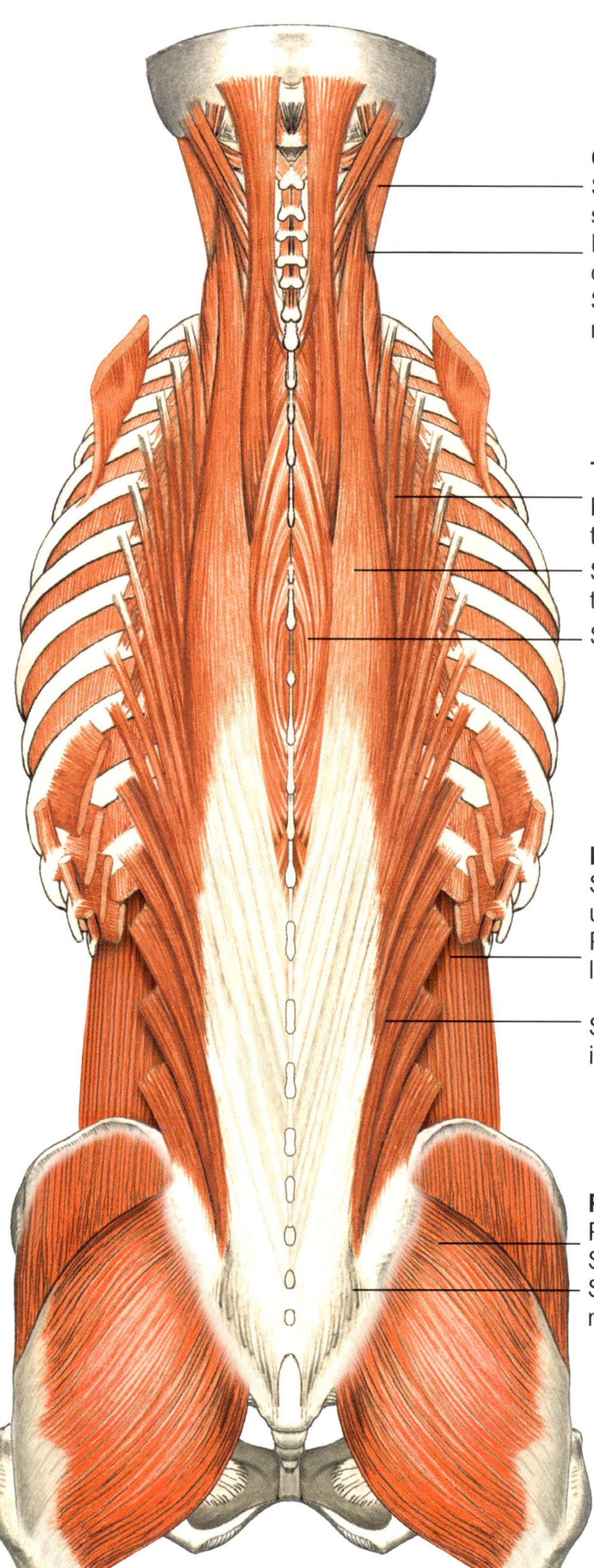

Cervical lateral flexion (Fig. 3.42)
Secondary or biarticular muscles: trapezius and sternocleidomastoid
Primary or monoarticular muscles: iliocostalis cervicis
Synergic or scheme muscles: deep paravertebral muscles of one side only

Thoracic lateral flexion (Fig. 3.43)
Primary or monoarticular muscles: iliocostalis thoracis
Secondary or biarticular muscles: longissimus thoracis
Synergic muscles: deep unilateral paravertebral

Lumbar lateral flexion (Fig. 3.44)
Synergic muscles: interspinalis with the motor units arranged so as to act as lateral flexors
Primary monoarticular muscles: quadratus lumborum
Secondary biarticular or secondary muscles: iliocostalis lumborum

Pelvic lateral flexion (Fig. 3.45)
Primary monoarticular muscles: gluteus maximus
Secondary or biarticular muscles: erector spinae
Synergic muscles: posterior part of the gluteus medius

Fig. 3.41. Posterior trunk region, lateral flexor muscles.
(From G. Chiarugi and L. Bucciante, Istituzioni di anatomia dell'uomo. Piccin Nuova Libraria, Padova 1983, modified)

SEGMENTARY MOVEMENTS IMPLEMENTED BY THE MF UNITS OF LATEROPULSION

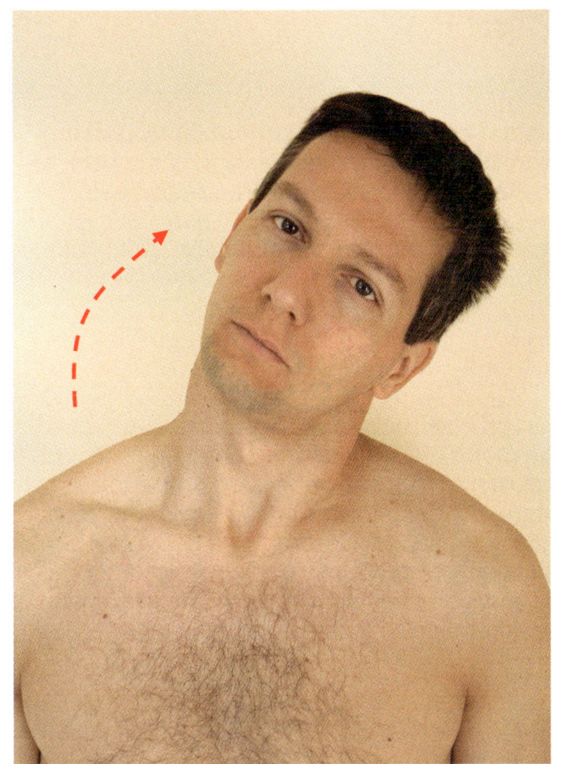

Fig. 3.42. Cervical lateral flexion coordinated by the MF unit of latero-collum (in elongation on the right).

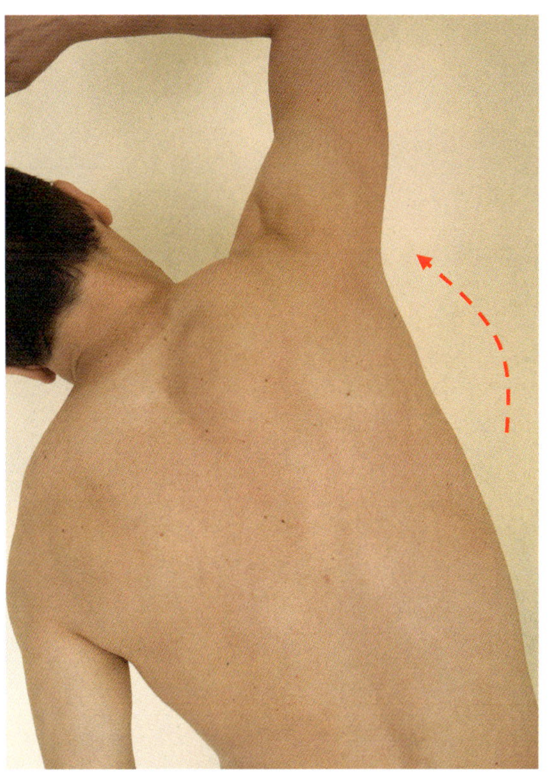

Fig. 3.43. Thoracic lateral flexion managed by the MF unit of latero-thorax (in elongation on the right).

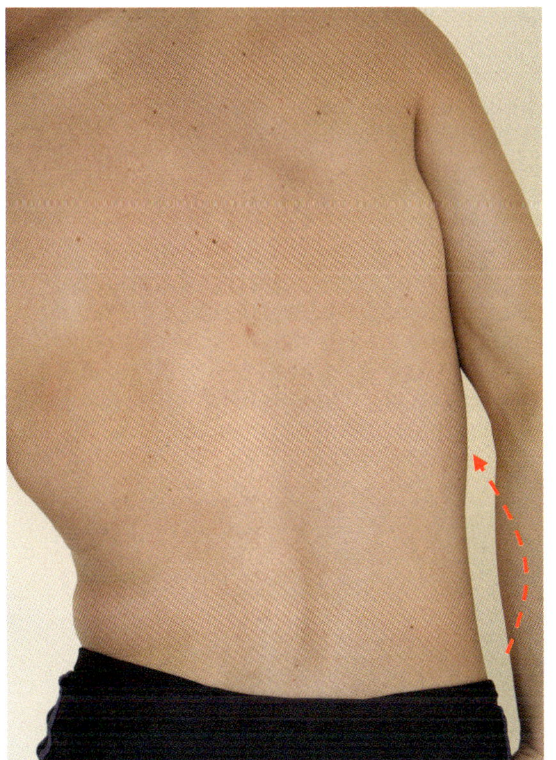

Fig. 3.44. Lumbar lateral flexion managed by the MF unit of latero-lumbi (in elongation or eccentrically on the right).

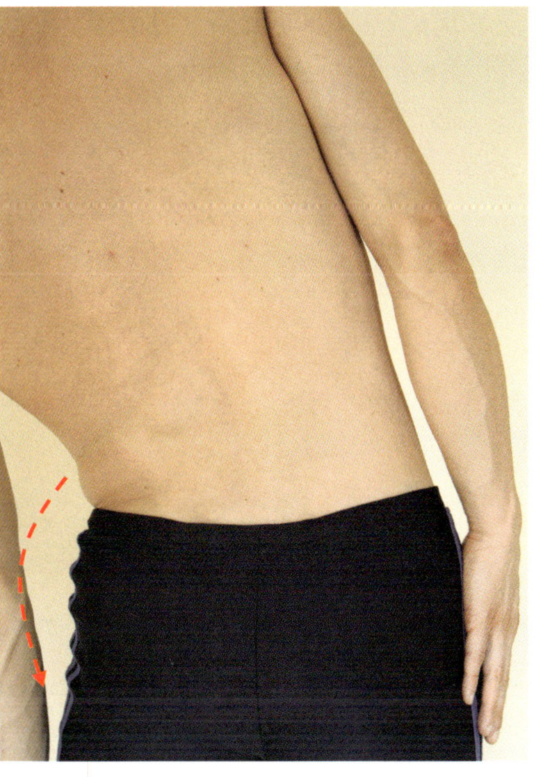

Fig. 3.45. Pelvic lateral flexion managed by the MF unit of latero-pelvis (weight bearing and in shortening on the left).

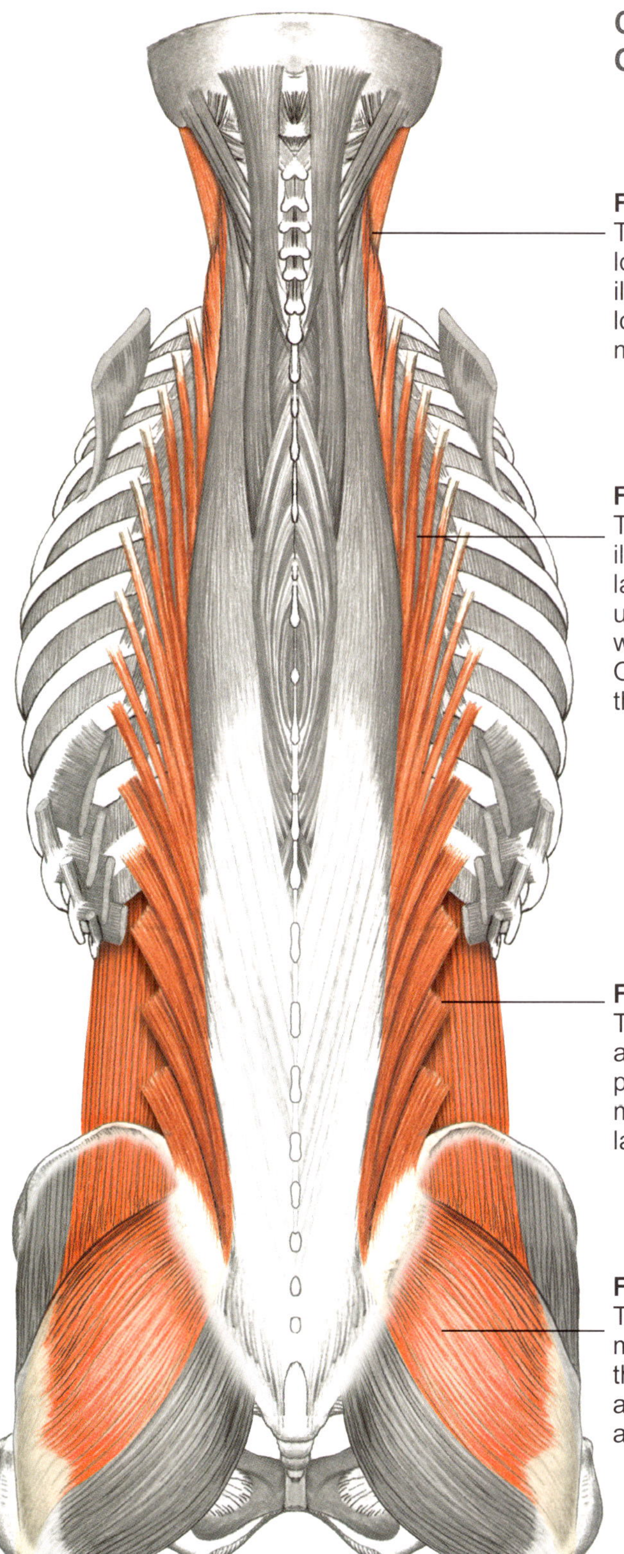

Fig. 3.46. Fascial compartments for the lateropulsion muscles of the trunk.

(From G. Chiarugi and L. Bucciante, Istituzioni di anatomia dell'uomo. Piccin Nuova Libraria, Padova 1983, modified)

COMPARTMENTS FOR THE MUSCLES OF TRUNK LATEROPULSION (Fig. 3.47)

Fascial compartment, collum lateropulsion
The motor units for lateropulsion of the neck are located in the trapezius, sternocleidomastoid and iliocostalis cervicis muscles. These muscles are located in the superficial and deep lamina of the muscular fascia.

Fascial compartment, thorax lateropulsion
The motor units of the deep paravertebral and iliocostalis muscles are located between the two laminae of the thoracolumbar fascia. Some motor units of these muscles participate in retropulsion whilst other motor units participate in lateropulsion. On one side they act with eccentric forces and on the other side with concentric forces.

Fascial compartment, lumbi lateropulsion
The thoracolumbar fascia forms two sheets: a superficial and a deep one surrounding the paravertebral muscles. The motor units located more laterally are mostly implicated in the lateropulsion of lumbi.

Fascial compartment, pelvis lateropulsion
The motor units for lateropulsion of the gluteus maximus and medius muscles are connected through the erector spinae or thoracolumbar aponeuroses with the latissimus dorsi, iliocostalis and quadratus lumborum muscles.

GLOBAL MOVEMENT IMPLEMENTED BY THE LATEROPULSION SEQUENCE

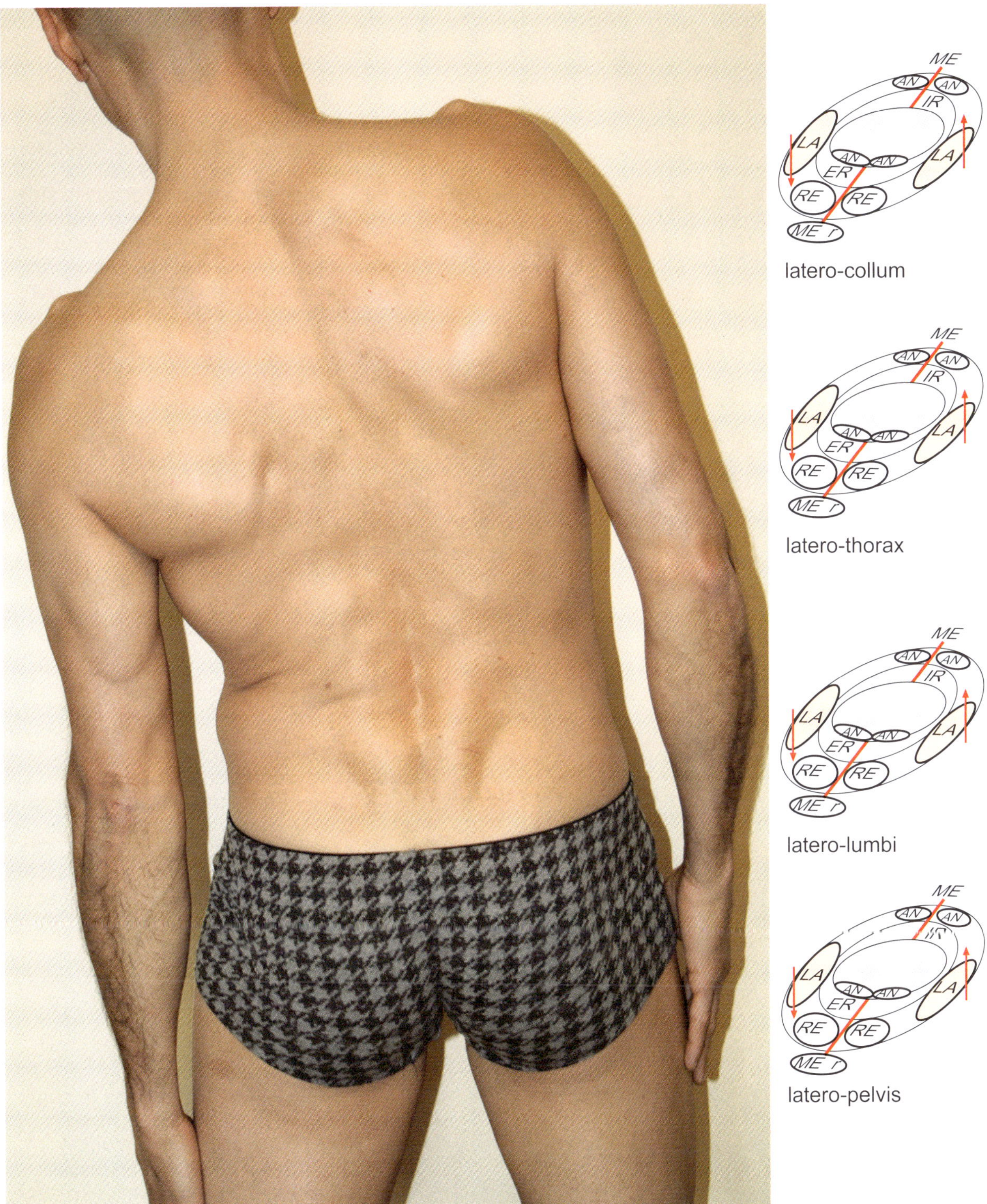

Fig. 3.47. The left lateropulsion sequence works in shortening or concentrically and the right one works in lengthening or eccentrically.

During lateropulsion both the postero-lateral muscles and antero-lateral muscles of the trunk intervene. The images on the side of the figure show this muscle arrangement.
In this section of the chapter the posterior muscles are described since they are mostly implicated in lateral flexion, whilst the anterior lateral muscles will be presented when covering the diagonals.

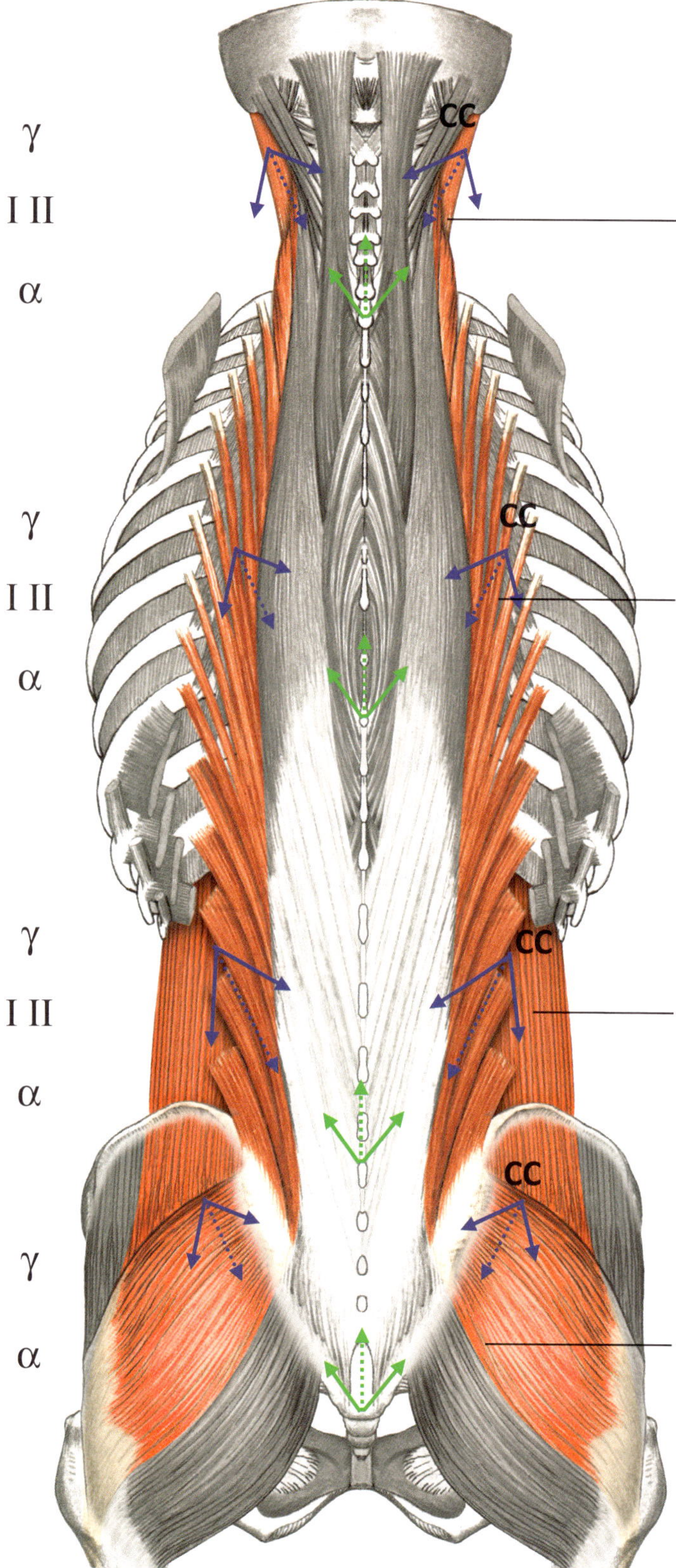

Fig. 3.48. Normal function of the gamma circuit.
(From G. Chiarugi and L. Bucciante, Istituzioni di anatomia dell'uomo. Piccin Nuova Libraria, Padova 1983, modified)

PHYSIOLOGY OF THE MF UNITS, TRUNK LATEROPULSION

MF unit of latero-collum (la-cl)
The gamma neuron stimulates the intrafusal muscle fibres of the motor units that are located in the compartment on only one side of the neck. Through the stretch reflex the motor units on the opposite side activate with a braking effect. The cervical vertebrae (me-cl, green vectors) are the needle of the scale between both MF units of la-cl.

MF unit of latero-thorax (la-th)
The gamma neuron stimulates the intrafusal muscle fibres of the motor units located in the lateral compartment of the back. The adaptability of the perimysium (CC) allows the fibres I, II to close the circuit and to contract the extrafusal fibres of the MF unit la-th.

MF unit of latero-lumbi (la-lu)
The gamma neuron stimulates the intrafusal muscle fibres of the motor units located in the lateral compartment of the low back. The adaptability of the perimysium (CC) allows the fibres I, II to close the circuit and to contract the extrafusal fibres of the MF unit la-lu.

MF unit of latero-pelvis (la-pv)
The central nervous impulse arrives through the gamma fibres to the intrafusal muscles located in the lateral compartment of the pelvis (CC). The adaptability of the fascia allows the closure of the circuit and excitation, through alpha fibres, of all the motor units of lateropulsion in the pelvis.

ARTICULAR CONFLICTS IN LATEROPULSION OF THE TRUNK

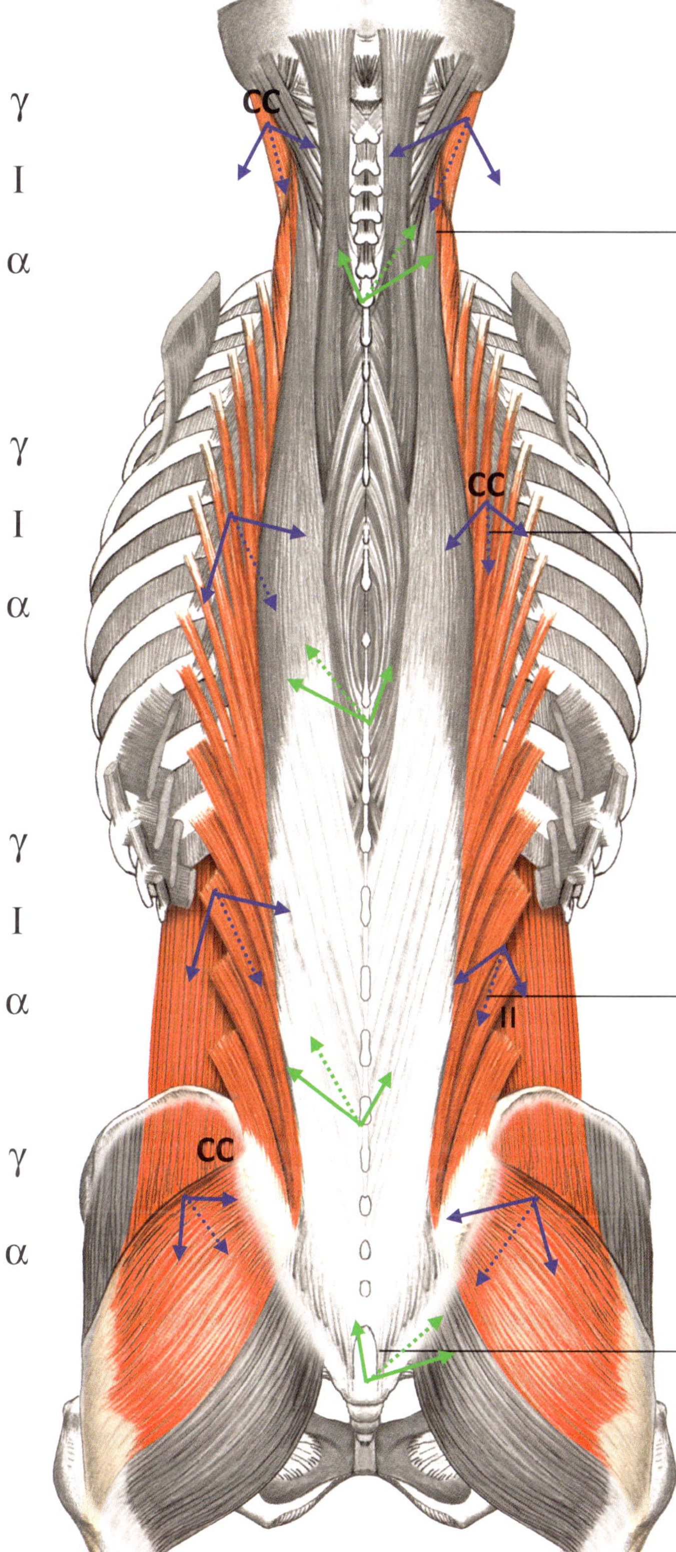

Fig. 3.49. Dysfunctions of the gamma circuit.

(From G. Chiarugi and L. Bucciante, Istituzioni di anatomia dell'uomo. Piccin Nuova Libraria, Padova 1983, modified)

Pain during lateropulsion of collum
If during the lateropulsion of collum one of the two fascial compartments is densified, then in that MF unit the gamma circuit does not allow the physiological contraction of the motor units. This results in a conflict in the cervical vertebrae.

Pain during lateropulsion of thorax
If during the lateropulsion of thorax one of the two fascial compartments is densified, then in that MF unit the gamma circuit does not allow the physiological contraction of the motor units. This results in a conflict in the thoracic vertebrae.

Pain during lateropulsion of lumbi
In the presence of chronic dysfunction of the fascia compensations may be created. For instance, a compensation in the left pelvis may move to the right lumbi as well as the contralateral collum. All this helps in maintaining verticality of the body.

Pain during lateropulsion of pelvis
If during the lateropulsion of collum one of the two fascial compartments is densified, then in that MF unit the gamma circuit does not allow the physiological contraction of the motor units. This results in a conflict in the sacroiliac joint.

TR LATEROPULSION SEQUENCE AND STRETCH REFLEX

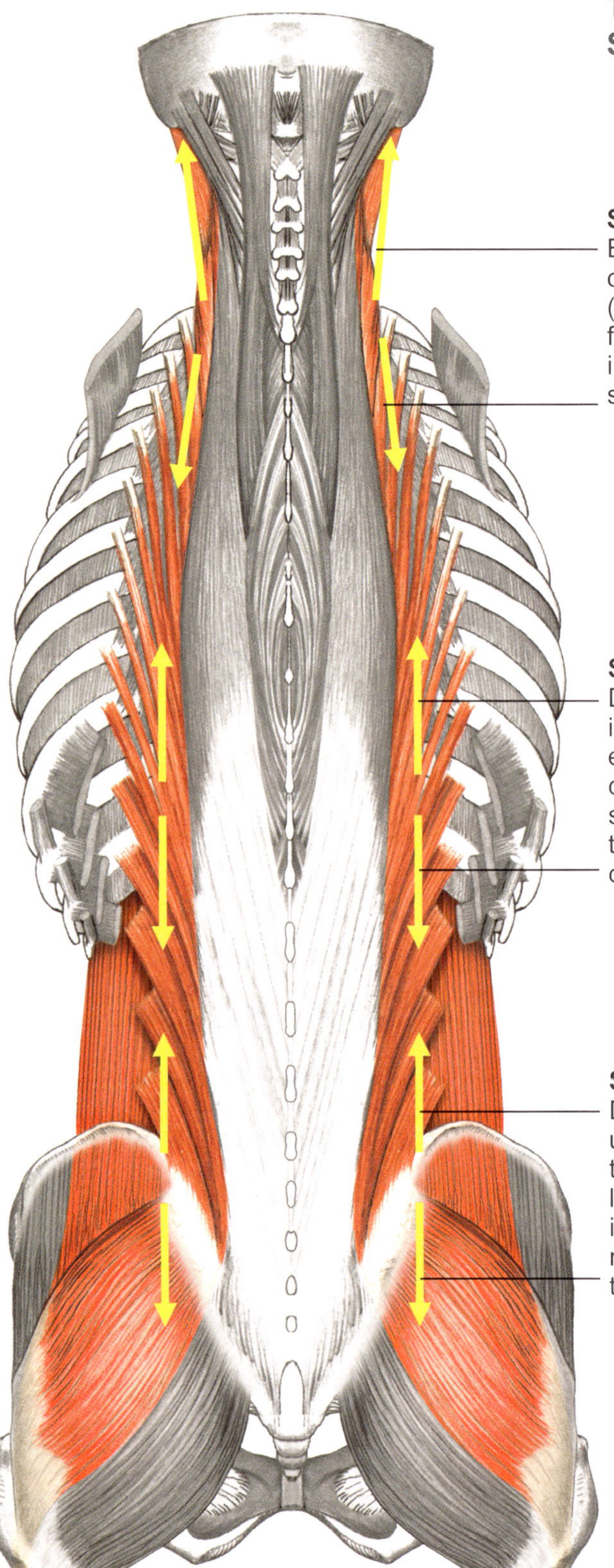

Synergy between la-cl and la-th
Eccentric lateral flexion of the neck requires the contraction of the sternocleidomastoid muscle (Fig. 3.52) that in turn stretches the cervical fascia cranially. To control the movement, the iliocostalis cervicis muscle is also activated, it stretches the cervical fascia caudally.

Synergy between la-th and la-lu
During the lateral flexion of the thorax the iliocostalis muscle (Fig. 3.53) must contract eccentrically to control the movement. The contraction of the iliocostalis thoracis muscle stretches its fascia cranially (Fig. 3.54), whilst the quadratus lumborum muscle stretches it caudally.

Synergy between la-lu and la-pv
During the left lateral flexion of lumbi, the right MF unit of la-lu must contract eccentrically to control the movement. The contraction of the quadratus lumborum muscle stretches its fascia which is in turn stretched by the gluteus maximus and medius muscles (Fig. 3.55). These are activated through the stretch reflex.

Fig. 3.50. Synergy along the lateropulsion sequence of the trunk.
(From G. Chiarugi and L. Bucciante, Istituzioni di anatomia dell'uomo. Piccin Nuova Libraria, Padova 1983, modified)

ACTIVATION OF THE GOLGI TENDON ORGANS

During left lateral flexion of the trunk, the right iliocostalis muscles must contract eccentrically to curb the fall. The braking force varies based upon the degrees of flexion of the trunk: as the degrees of lateral flexion increase so does the stretch on the tendons of iliocostalis inserting on the ribs, consequently the stretch on the spindles also increase. The architectural arrangement of the fascia enables the balance between inhibition of forces through the Golgi tendon organs and stimulation of forces through the spindles via the stretch reflex.

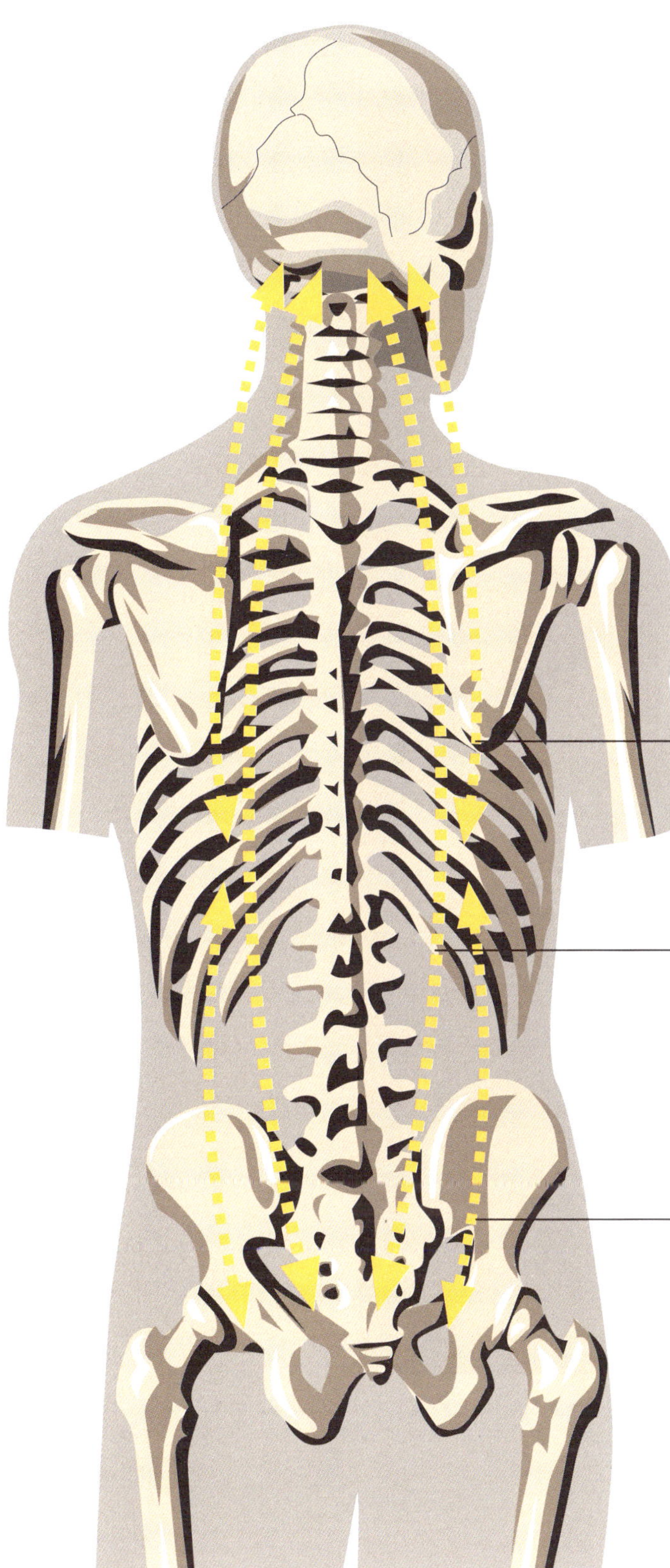

Connection between collum and thorax
The superficial lamina of the fascia of sternocleidomastoid and trapezius muscles synchronises the lateropulsion of the neck and back.

Global sequence connection
This chain corresponds to the myofascial sequence of lateropulsion. The anatomical substrate is found in the continuity of the iliocostalis lumborum, thoracis and cervicis muscles.

Connection between lumbi and pelvis
This chain consolidates the movements of lumbi and pelvis. It is formed by the most lateral muscles (quadratus lumborum and gluteus maximus and medius muscles).

Fig. 3.51. Biarticular muscles for lateropulsion in the trunk.

FASCIAE OF THE LATEROPULSION SEQUENCE OF THE TRUNK

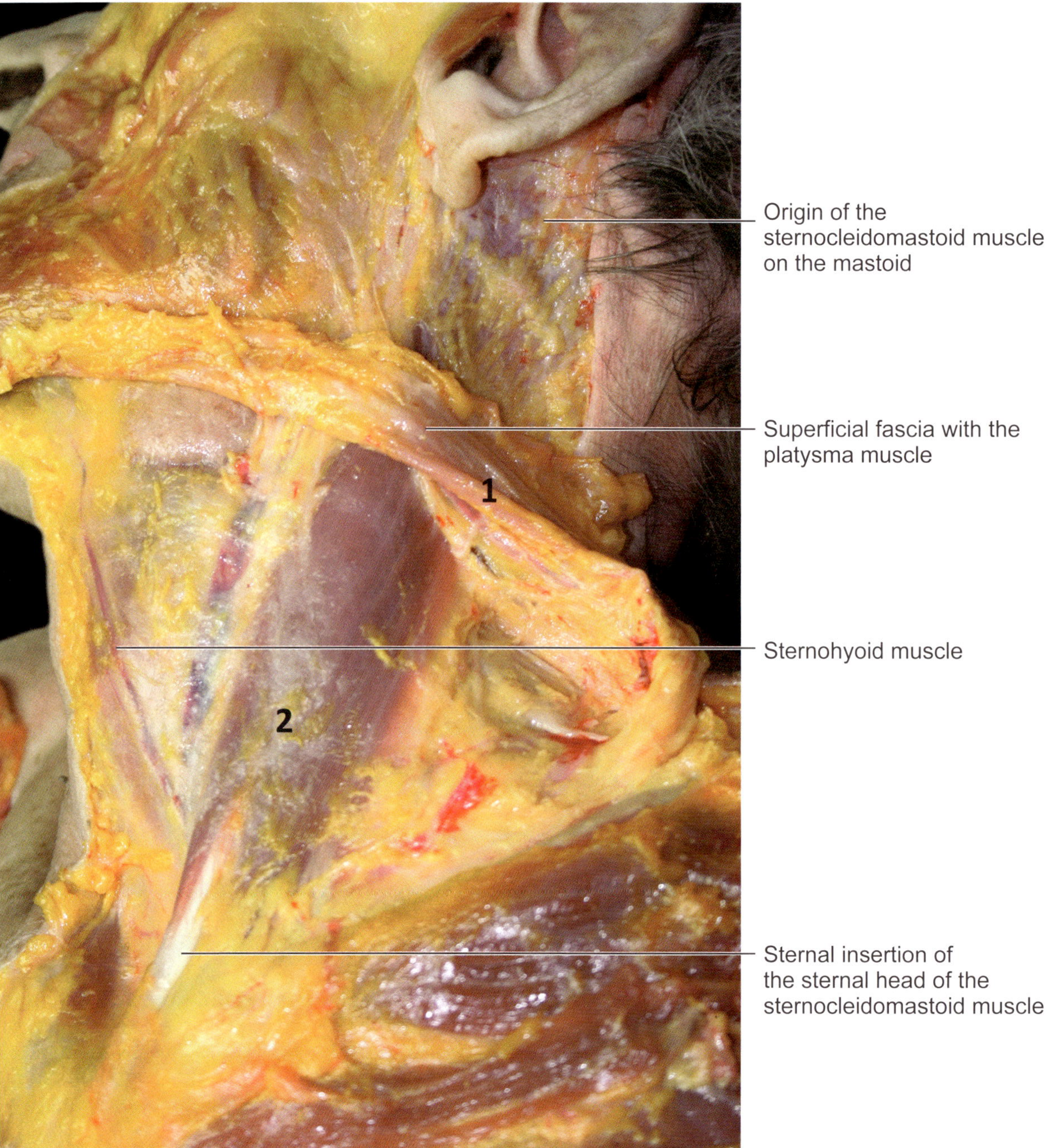

Fig. 3.52. Sternocleidomastoid muscle. The superficial fascia containing the platysma muscles was cut and lifted superiorly (1), the superficial lamina of the deep fascia becomes visible, it contains the sternocleidomastoid muscle (2).

The lines indicate anatomical parts whilst the numbers (1, 2) indicate the physiology of the fascia. Number one indicates a determined action and number two indicates its effect.

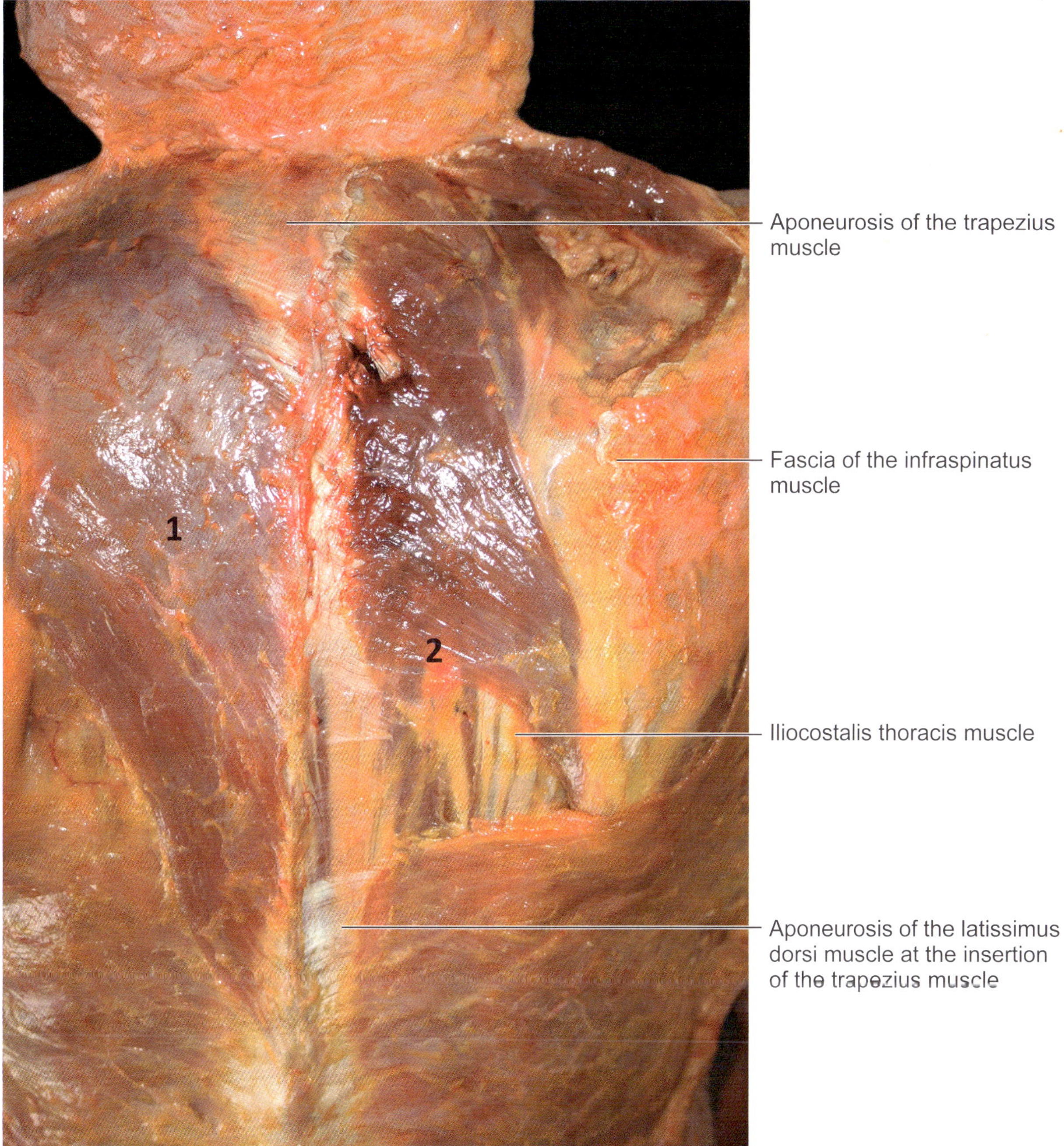

Fig. 3.53. Superficial and intermediate lamina of the fascia of the back. On the left (1) the trapezius muscles is still in situ, on the right the trapezius muscle was removed, the rhomboid muscle (2) becomes visible.

FASCIAE OF THE LATEROPULSION SEQUENCE OF THE TRUNK

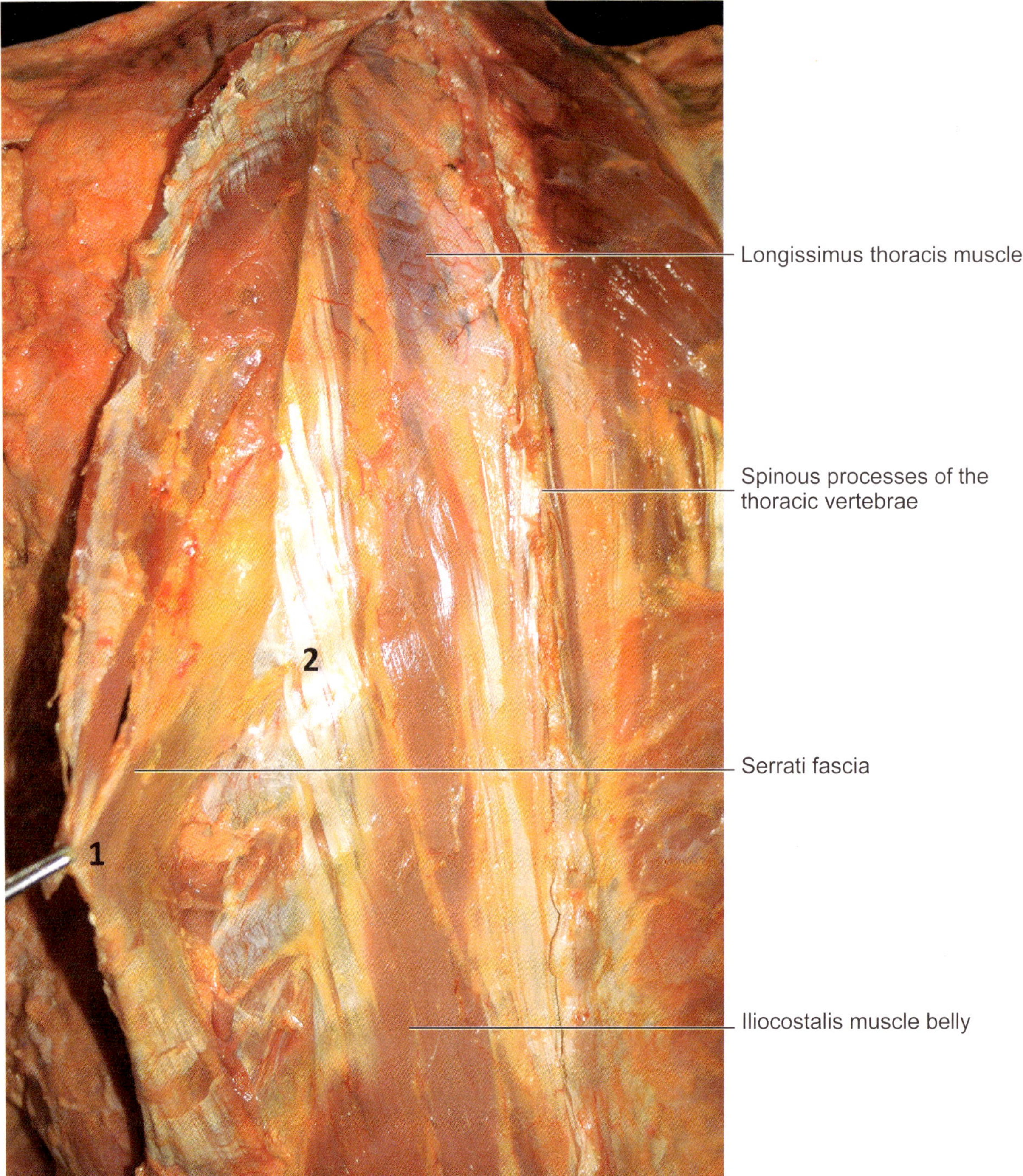

Fig. 3.54. Iliocostalis thoracis and lumborum muscles. The latissimus dorsi muscle and serrati fascia (1) were removed, the tendinous insertions of the iliocostalis muscle (2) become visible.

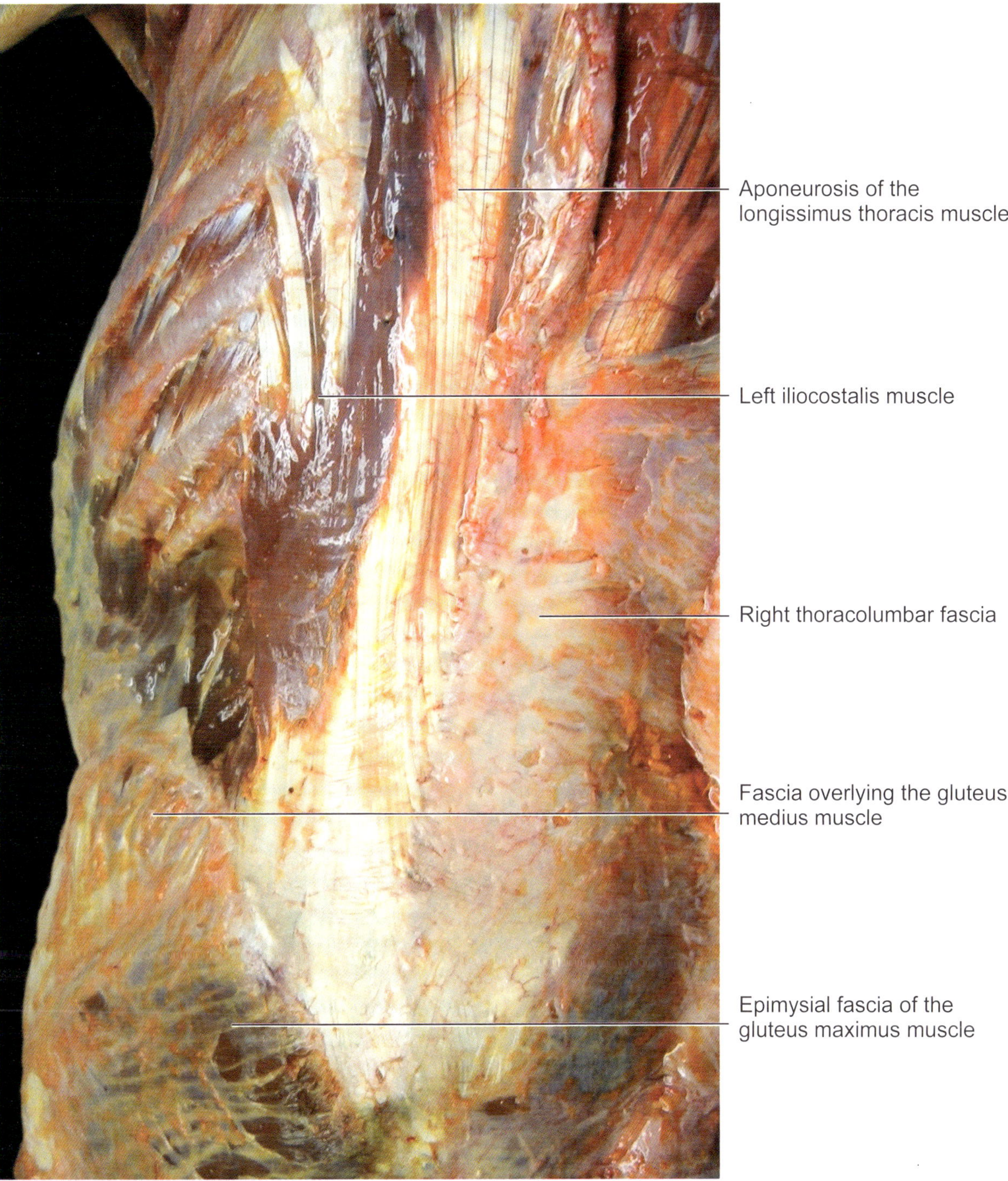

Fig. 3.55. Aponeurotic thoracolumbar fascia. This fascia, like the rectus sheath, realises a double function: it coordinates the various muscles relating to it and it is a flat tendon transmitting the force of the muscles inserting on it.

LATERAL SUPERFICIAL REGION OF THE TRUNK, INTRAROTATION SEQUENCE

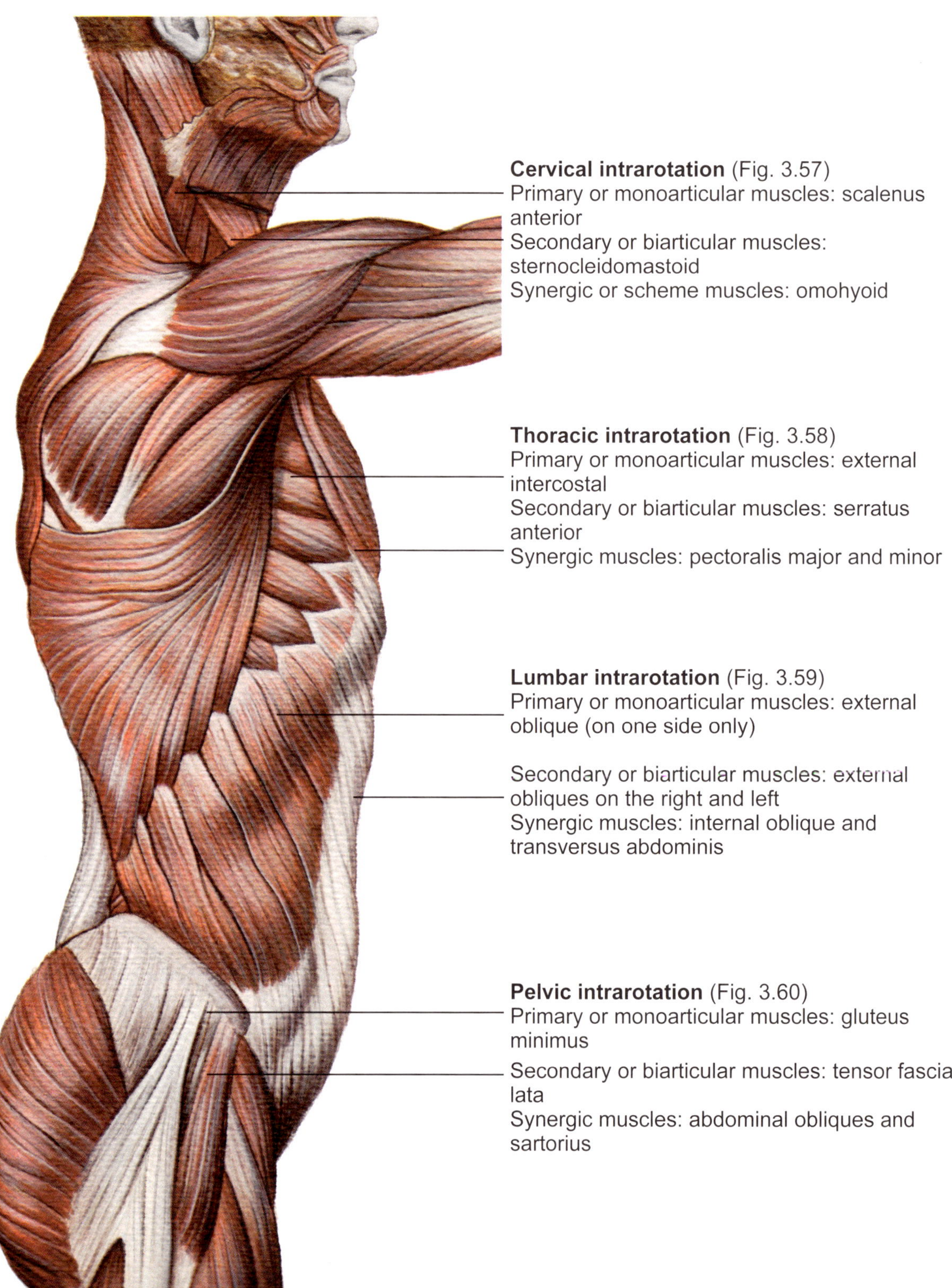

Fig. 3.56. Lateral superficial region of the trunk.

SEGMENTARY MOVEMENTS IMPLEMENTED BY THE MF UNITS OF INTRAROTATION

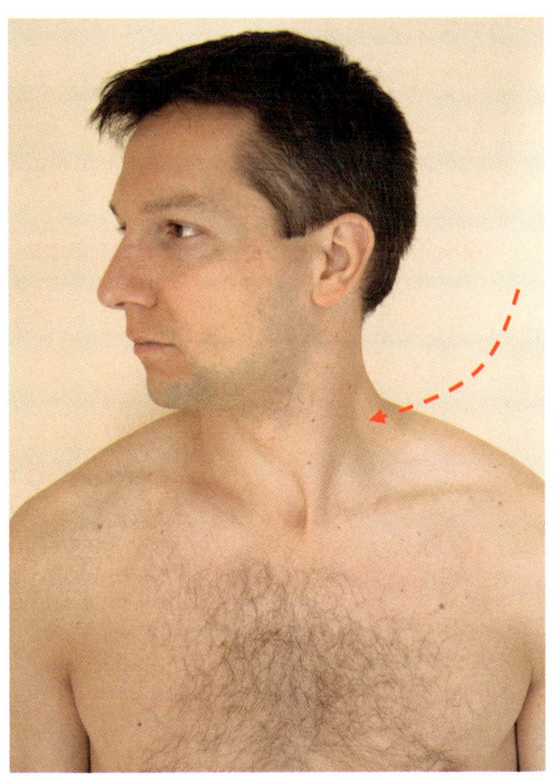

Fig. 3.57. Cervical intrarotation managed by the MF unit of intra-collum.

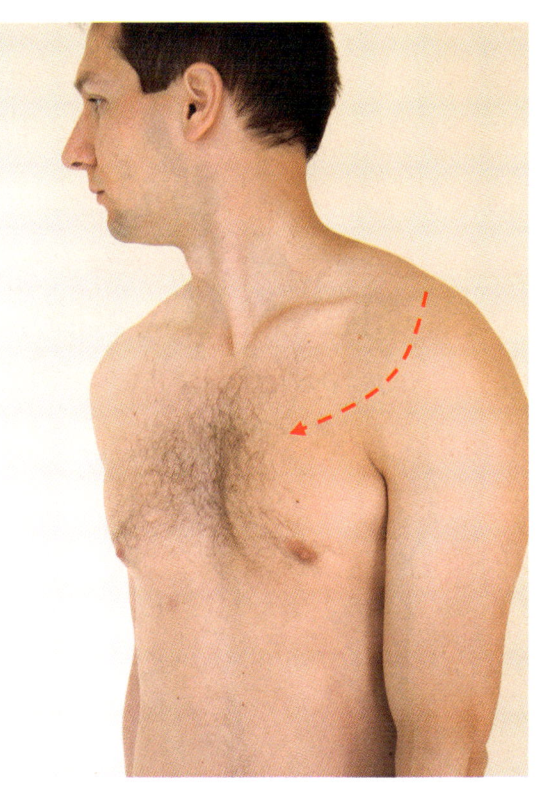

Fig. 3.58. Thoracic intrarotation managed by the MF unit of intra-thorax.

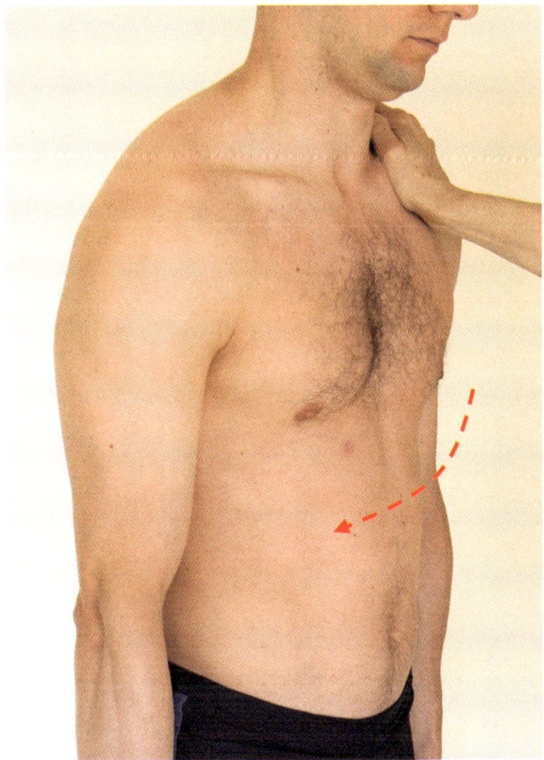

Fig. 3.59. Lumbar intrarotation managed by the MF unit of intra-lumbi.

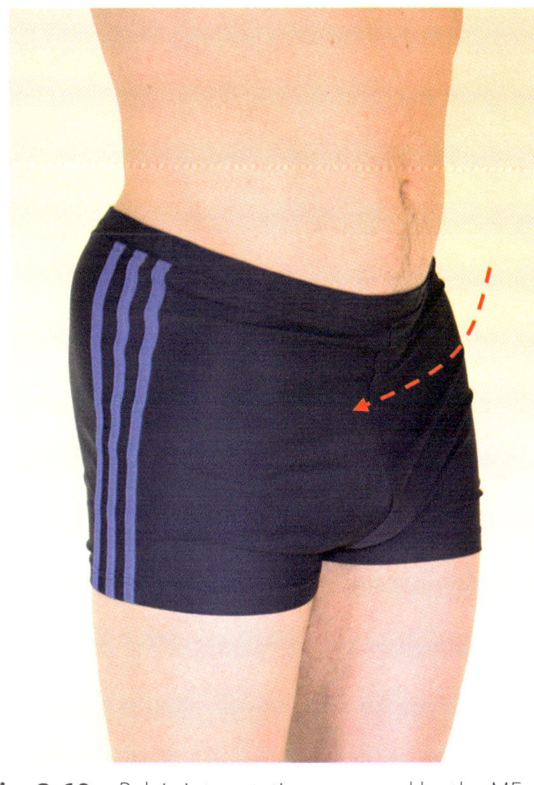

Fig. 3.60. Pelvic intrarotation managed by the MF unit of intra-pelvis.

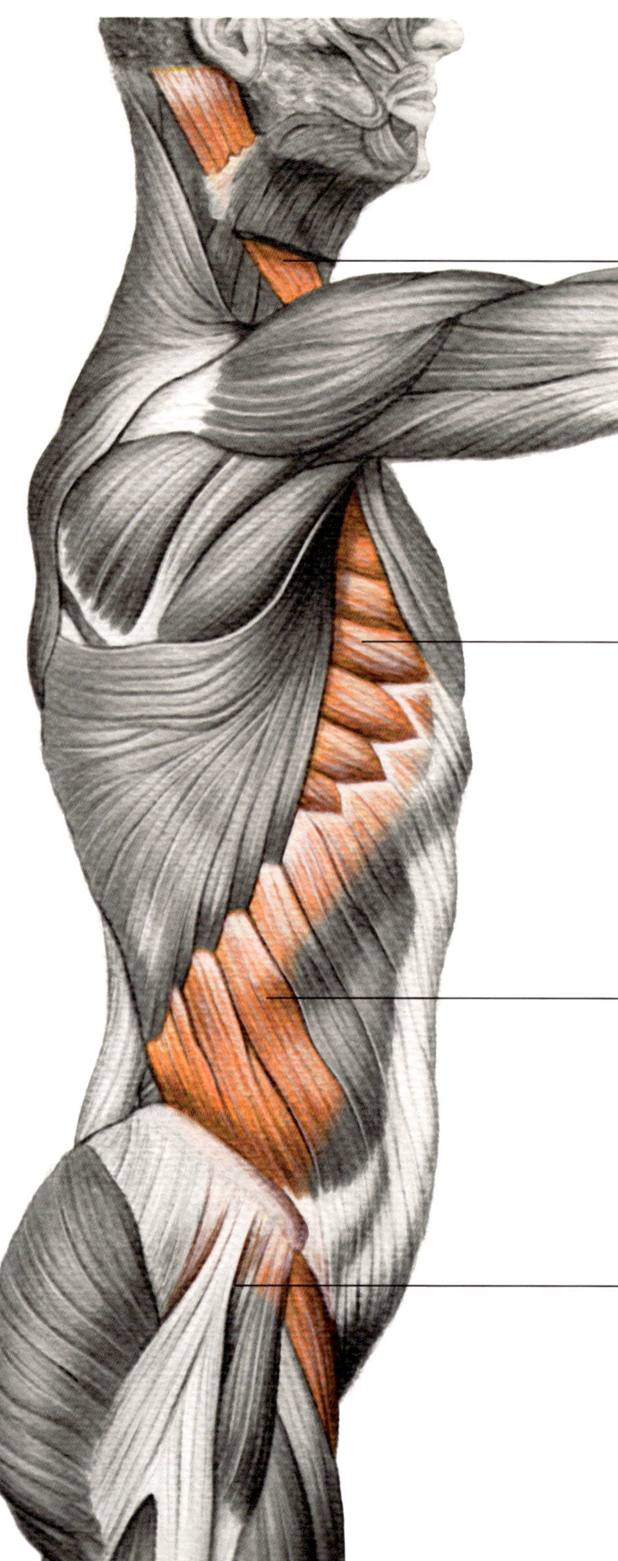

Fig. 3.61. Fascial laminae connected to the intrarotation muscles of the trunk.

COMPARTMENTS FOR THE MUSCLES OF INTRAROTATION OF THE TRUNK (Fig. 3.62)

Fascial compartment, collum intrarotation
The motor units of intrarotation of the neck are located in the scalenus anterior, sternocleidomastoid and omohyoid muscles. The intermediate lamina of the deep fascia connects these motor units together through the septa.

Fascial compartment, thorax intrarotation
The intrarotation motor units of the thorax are located in the serratus anterior, external intercostals and pectoralis muscles. The clavicoracoaxillary lamina of the deep fascia connects these motor units together through strips and septa.

Fascial compartment, lumbi intrarotation
The intrarotation motor units of the low back are located in the external oblique, internal oblique and transversus abdominis muscles. The intermediate lamina of the deep fascia connects these motor units together through various septa.

Fascial compartment, pelvis intrarotation
The intrarotation motor units of the pelvis are located in the gluteus minimus, tensor fascia lata, abdominal obliques and sartorius muscles. The intermediate lamina of the deep fascia connects these motor units together through various septa.

GLOBAL MOVEMENT IMPLEMENTED BY THE MF SEQUENCE OF INTRAROTATION

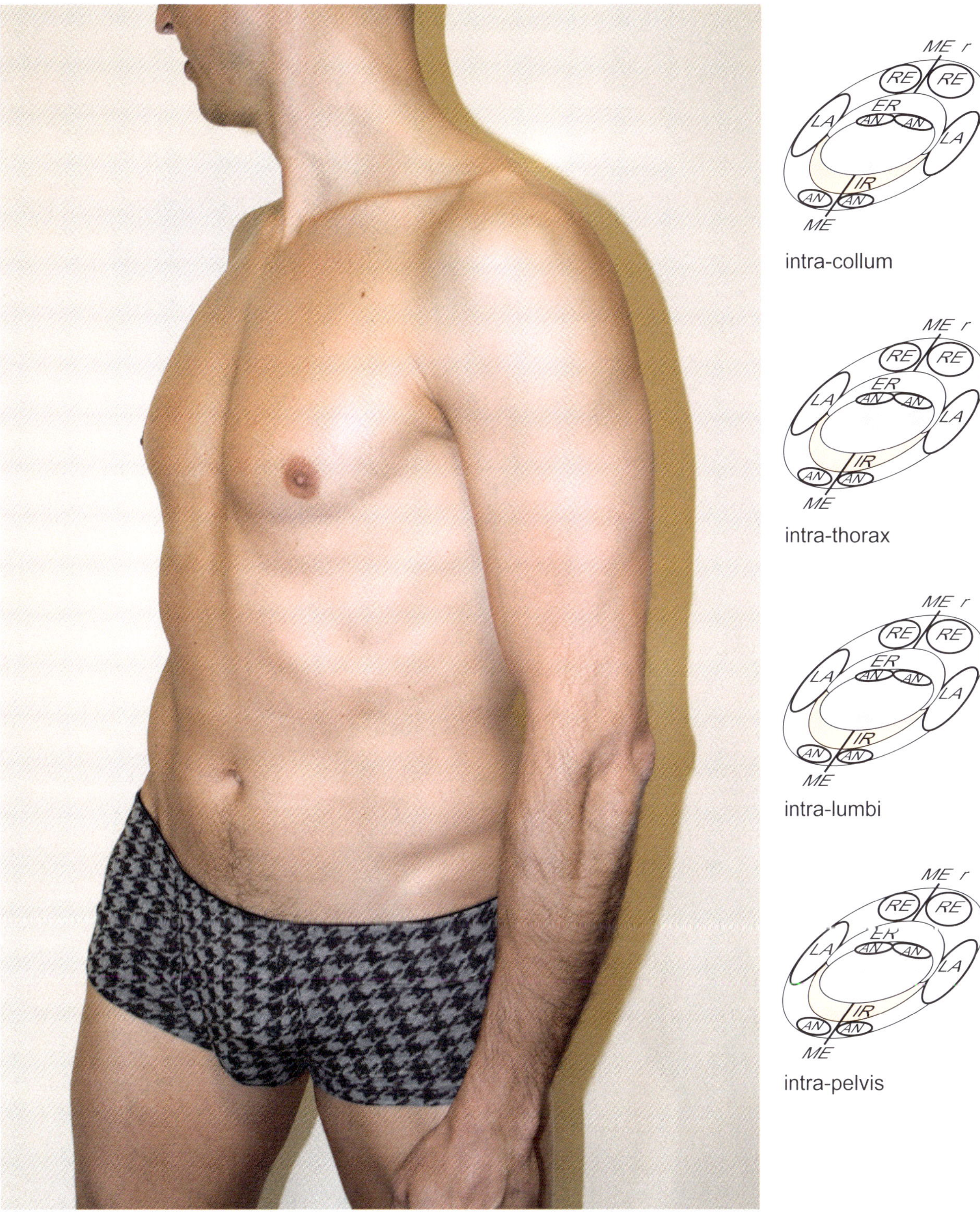

Fig. 3.62. Intrarotation of the trunk occurs when the brains programmes for the movement of one side of the body forward, this entails the activation of the MF units of intrarotation.

Trunk torsion is the result of torsional forces between internal rotation on one side and external rotation on the other side. When bringing the left hemi thorax forward the mind programmes impulses for the MF units of intra-thorax, and the fascial stretch recruits the other synergic MF units. During torsion, the stretching of the fascia activates the colonies of receptors connected to the oblique collagen fibres.

PHYSIOLOGY OF THE MF UNITS, TRUNK INTRAROTATION

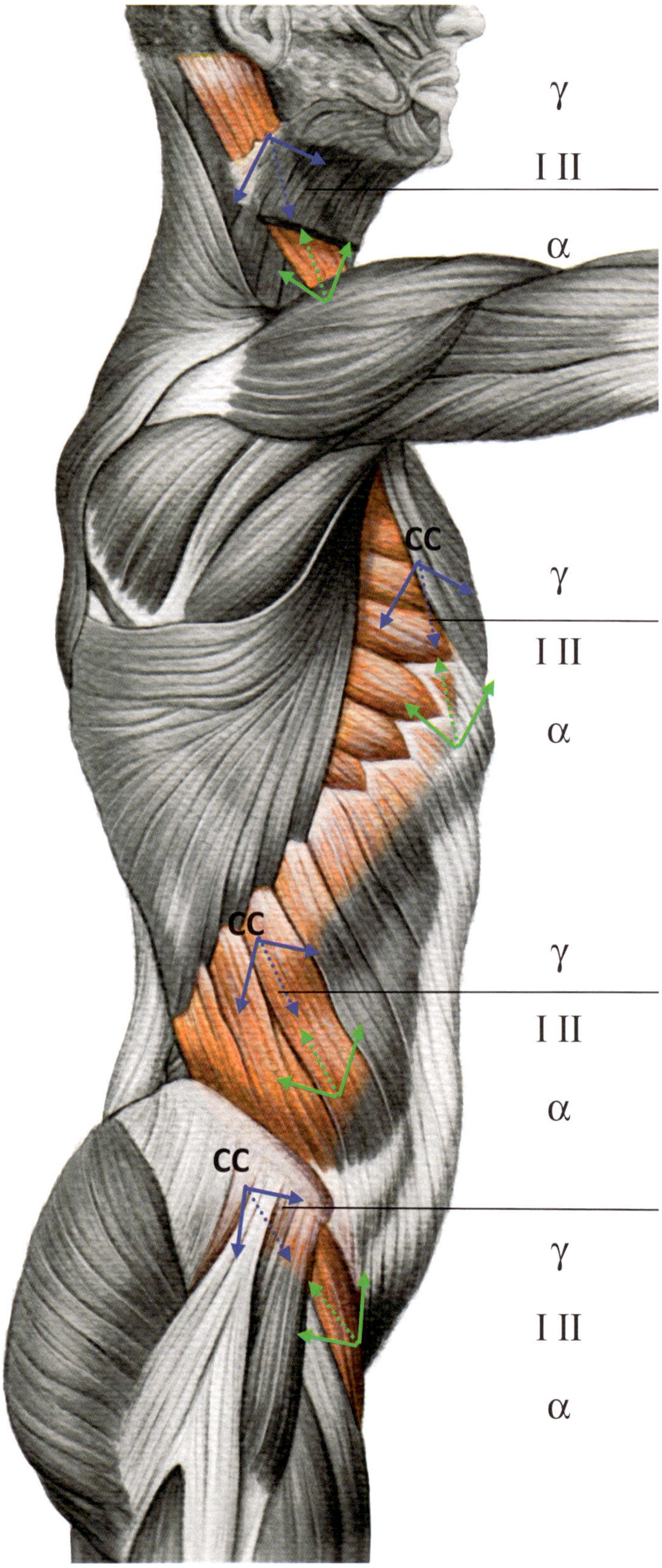

MF unit of intra-collum (ir-cl)
The gamma neuron stimulates the intrafusal muscle fibres of the motor units located in the internal compartment of the neck. The adaptability of the perimysium (CC) allows the fibres I, II to close the circuit and to contract the extrafusal muscles (green vectors) of the MF unit ir-cl.

MF unit of intra-thorax (ir-th)
The gamma neuron stimulates the intrafusal muscle fibres of the motor units located in the intermediate compartment of the thorax. The adaptability of the perimysium (CC) allows the fibres I, II to close the circuit and to contract the extrafusal muscles (green vectors) of the MF unit ir-th.

MF unit of intra-lumbi (ir-lu)
The gamma neuron stimulates the intrafusal muscle fibres of the motor units located in the intrarotation compartment of the low back. The adaptability of the perimysium (CC) allows the fibres I, II to close the circuit and to contract the extrafusal muscles (green vectors) of the MF unit ir-lu.

MF unit of intra-pelvis (ir-pv)
The gamma neuron stimulates the intrafusal muscle fibres of the motor units located in the intrarotation compartment of the pelvis. The adaptability of the perimysium (CC) allows the fibres I, II to close the circuit and to contract the extrafusal muscles (green vectors) of the MF unit ir-pv.

Fig. 3.63. Normal function of the alpha-gamma circuit.

ARTICULAR CONFLICTS IN INTRAROTATION OF THE TRUNK

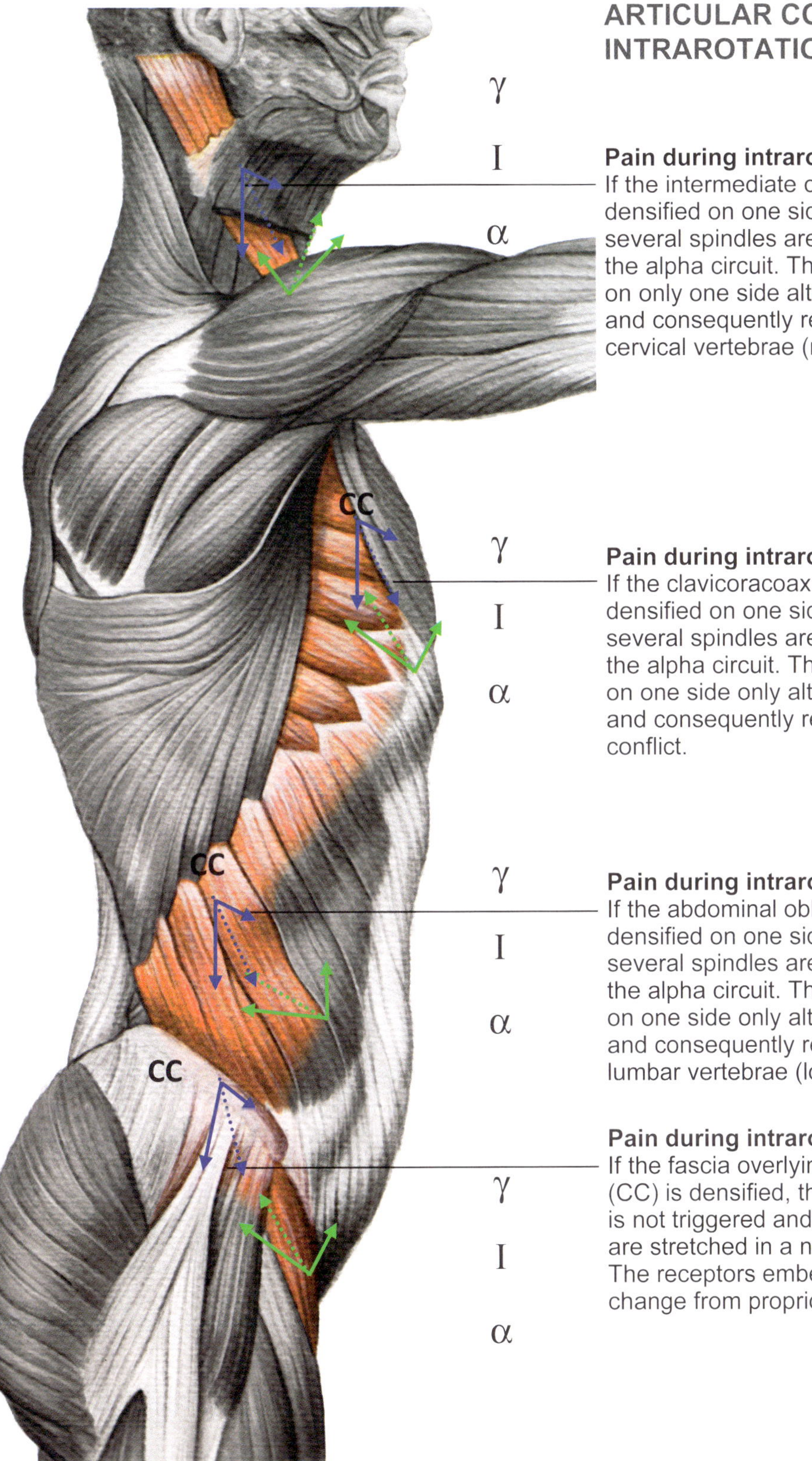

Pain during intrarotation of collum
If the intermediate cervical fascia (CC) is densified on one side, the afferents (II) from several spindles are not triggered to activate the alpha circuit. The prevalence of muscles on only one side alters the torsional forces and consequently results in a conflict in the cervical vertebrae (neck pain).

Pain during intrarotation of thorax
If the clavicoracoaxillary fascia (CC) is densified on one side, the afferents (II) from several spindles are not triggered to activate the alpha circuit. The prevalence of muscles on one side only alters the torsional forces and consequently results in an intercostal conflict.

Pain during intrarotation of lumbi
If the abdominal obliques fascia (CC) is densified on one side, the afferents (II) from several spindles are not triggered to activate the alpha circuit. The prevalence of muscles on one side only alters the torsional forces and consequently results in a conflict in the lumbar vertebrae (low back pain).

Pain during intrarotation of pelvis
If the fascia overlying the gluteus minimus (CC) is densified, the alpha-gamma circuit is not triggered and the sacroiliac ligaments are stretched in a non-physiological manner. The receptors embedded in these ligaments change from proprioceptors to nociceptors.

Fig. 3.64. Dysfunctions of the alpha-gamma circuit.

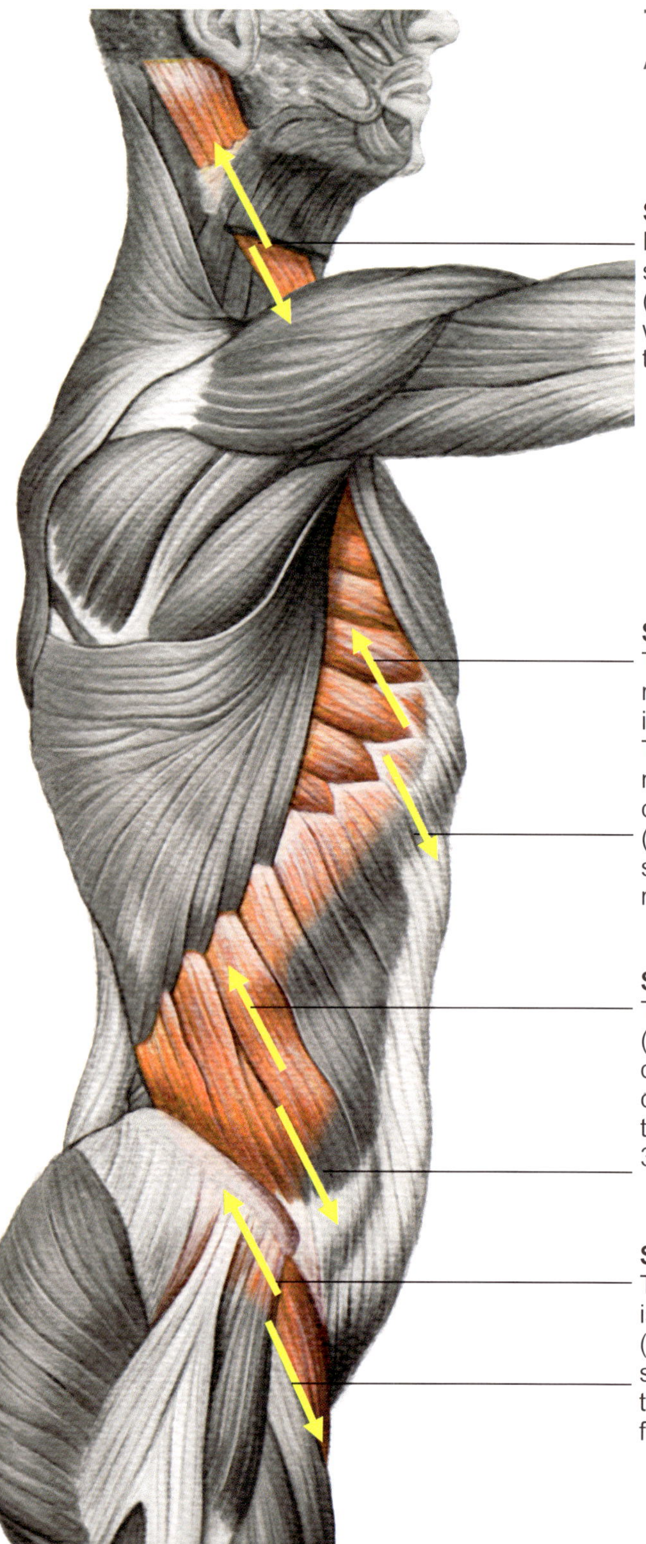

Fig. 3.65. Synergy along the intrarotation sequence of the trunk.

TR INTRAROTATION SEQUENCE AND STRETCH REFLEX

Synergy between ir-cl and ir-th
During internal rotation of the neck, the superficial and intermediate cervical fasciae (Fig. 3.67) are stretched cranially by the SCM whilst the clavicoracoaxillary fascia stretches the cervical fasciae caudally.

Synergy between ir-th and ir-lu
The digitations of the serratus anterior muscle (Fig. 3.68) engage with the costal insertions of the external oblique muscle. The contraction of the serratus anterior muscle stretches its fascia cranially whilst the contraction of the external oblique muscle (ir-th) stretches its fascia caudally. The stretch reflex synchronises the action of both muscles.

Synergy between ir-lu and ir-pv
The fascia of the external oblique muscle (ir-lu) above the umbilicus is pulled cranially during intrarotation whilst the fascia of the contralateral internal oblique muscle below the umbilicus (ir-pv) is pulled caudally (Fig. 3.69).

Synergy between ir-pv and ir-cx
The fascia of the gluteus minimus muscle is continuous with the inguinal ligament (Fig. 3.70) that is connected to the sartorius sheath. These muscles have insertions on their fascia hence during their contraction a fascial stretch occurs cranially and caudally.

ACTIVATION OF THE GOLGI TENDON ORGANS

Despite the appearance of being a single muscle, the external abdominal oblique is formed by many fascicles each originating from a rib or in continuity with a specific digitation of the serratus anterior muscle. Hence the oblique muscle is also progressively contracted and regulated by Golgi tendon organs.

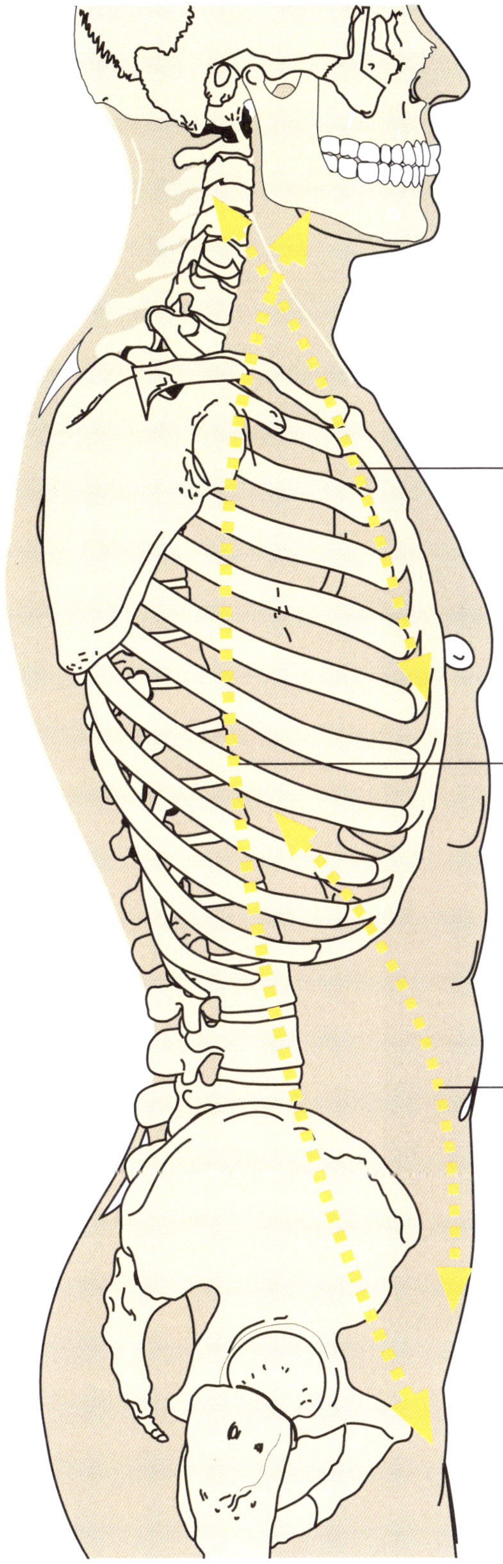

Connection between collum and thorax
When turning the head, the motor units belonging to the sternocleidomastoid and serratus anterior muscles are activated. The latter muscle is a derivative of the external intercostal muscles.

Global sequence connection
The external oblique muscle is the larger biarticular muscle of internal rotation acting on thorax, lumbi and pelvis. Its insertions on the thorax connect it to the clavicoracoaxillary fascia.

Connection between lumbi and pelvis
The internal rotation or forward rotation of the low back is not separable from the contraction of the internal oblique and contralateral external oblique muscles. Hence a functional continuity also exists in intrarotation between lumbi and pelvis.

Fig. 3.66. Biarticular muscles for intrarotation in the trunk.

FASCIAE OF THE INTRAROTATION SEQUENCE OF THE TRUNK

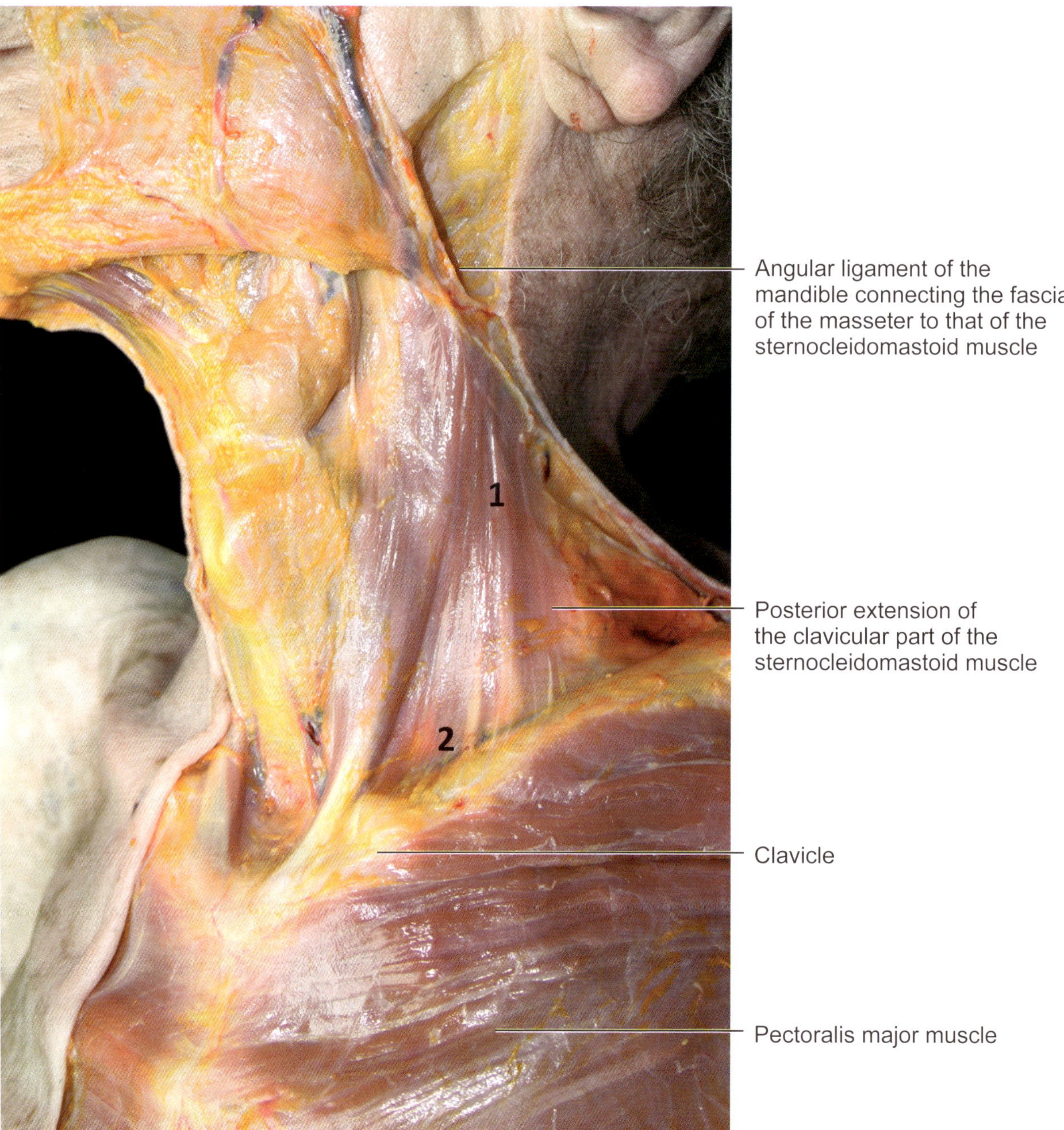

Fig. 3.67. Angular ligament of the mandible. The platysma muscle was cut and removed. The sternocleidomastoid (1) muscle participates in intrarotation of the neck, its clavicular fibres (2) are continuous with the subclavius muscle located underneath the pectoralis major muscle.

The lines indicate anatomical parts whilst the numbers (1, 2) indicate the physiology of the fascia. Number one indicates a determined action and number two indicates its effect.

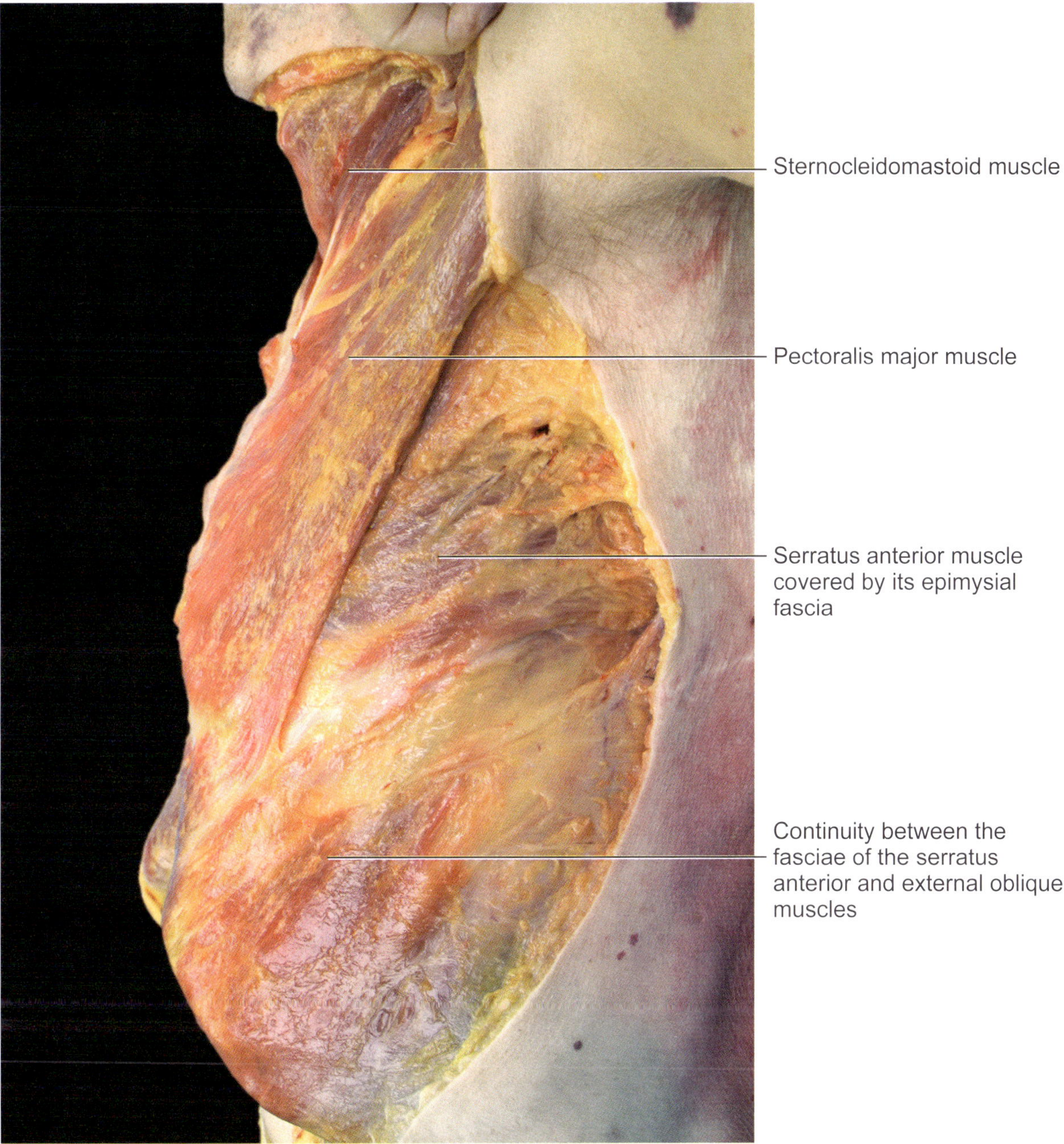

Fig. 3.68. Epimysial fascia of the serratus anterior muscle. All the large muscles of the trunk belong to the superficial lamina of the deep fascia that corresponds to the epimysial fascia.

FASCIAE OF THE INTRAROTATION SEQUENCE OF THE TRUNK

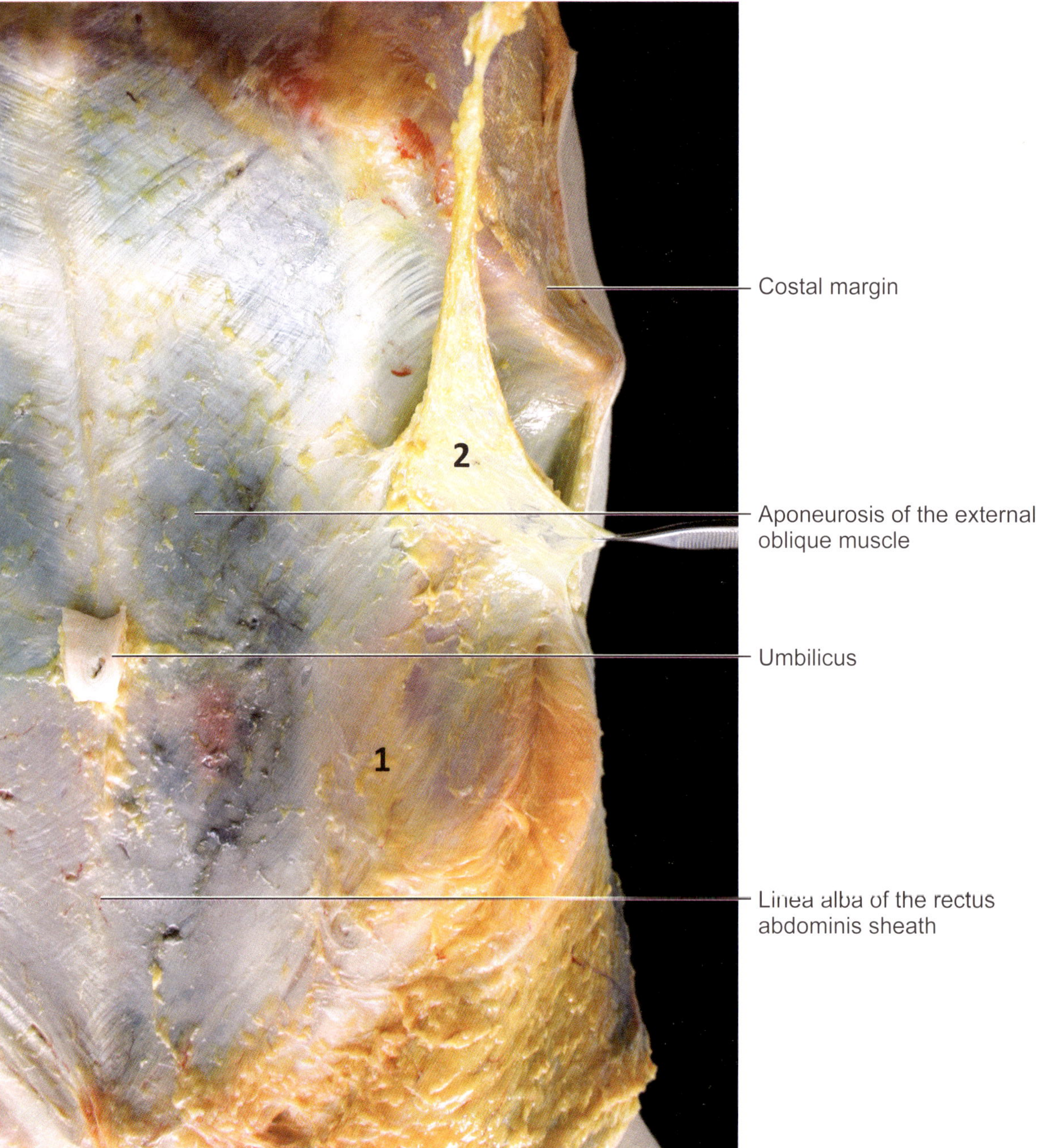

Fig. 3.69. Abdominal fascia parallel to the external abdominal oblique muscle. The abdominal muscles are not only wrapped by the epimysium (1) since a careful dissection may highlight a transparent lamina (2) (elastic receptorial fascia) that accompanies the muscles themselves.

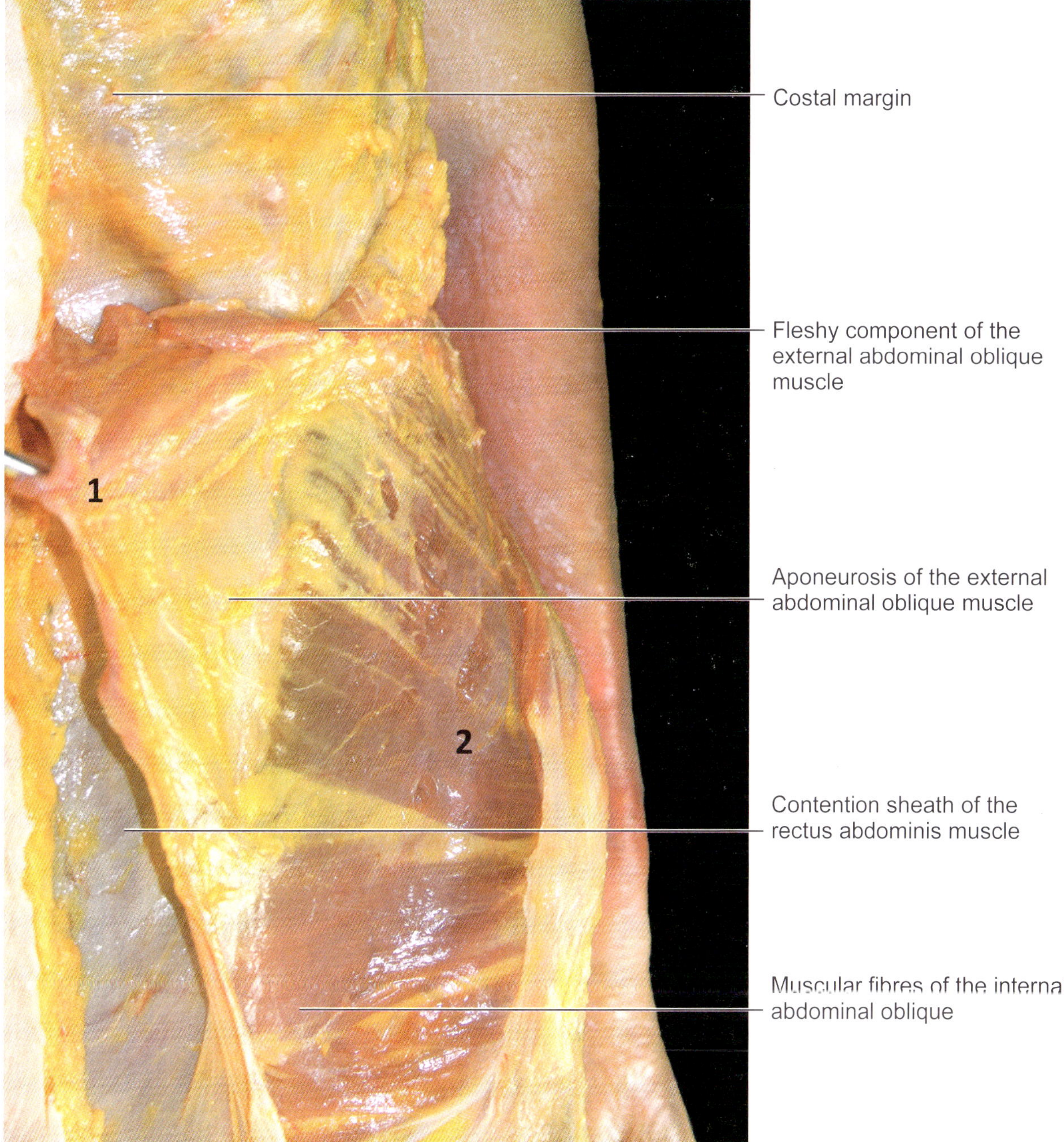

Fig. 3.70. Abdominal fascia of the anterior pelvic region. The forceps pulls the external oblique muscle (1) superiorly in order to highlight the internal oblique muscle (2) and its connection to the aponeurosis of the external oblique.

POSTERIOR INTERMEDIATE REGION OF THE TRUNK, EXTRAROTATION SEQUENCE

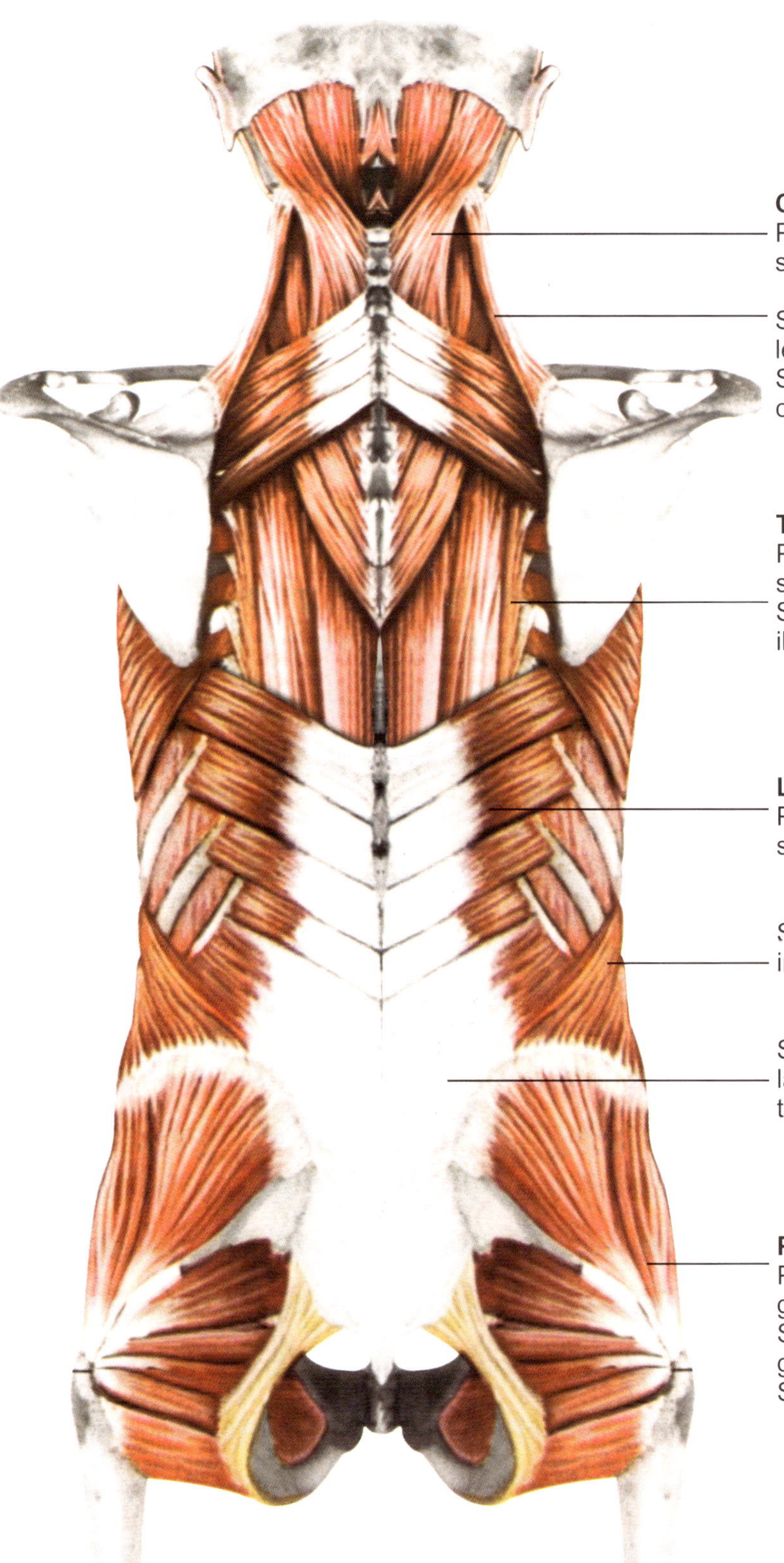

Cervical extrarotation (Fig. 3.72)
Primary or monoarticular muscles: splenius capitis and cervicis

Secondary or biarticular muscles: levator scapula
Synergic or scheme muscles: rectus capitis posterior major

Thoracic extrarotation (Fig. 3.73)
Primary or monoarticular muscles: serratus posterior superior
Secondary or biarticular muscles: iliocostalis

Lumbar extrarotation (Fig. 3.74)
Primary or monoarticular muscles: serratus posterior inferior

Secondary or biarticular muscles: internal abdominal oblique

Synergic or scheme muscles: latissimus dorsi inserting into the thoracolumbar fascia

Pelvic extrarotation (Fig. 3.75)
Primary or monoarticular muscles: gluteus medius and minimus
Secondary or biarticular muscles: gluteus maximus
Synergic muscles: quadratus femoris

Fig. 3.71. Posterior intermediate muscular region of the trunk.
(From G. Chiarugi and L. Bucciante, Istituzioni di anatomia dell'uomo. Piccin Nuova Libraria, Padova 1983, modified)

SEGMENTARY MOVEMENTS IMPLEMENTED BY THE MF UNITS OF EXTRAROTATION

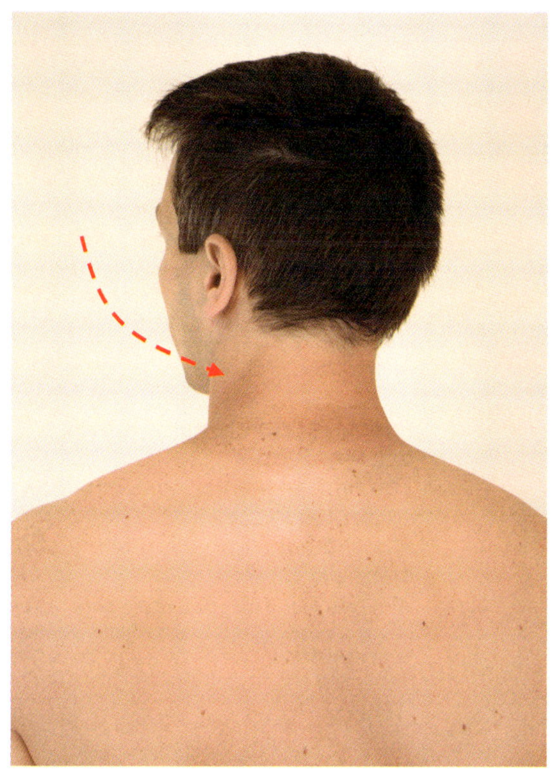

Fig. 3.72. Cervical extrarotation managed by the MF unit of extra-collum.

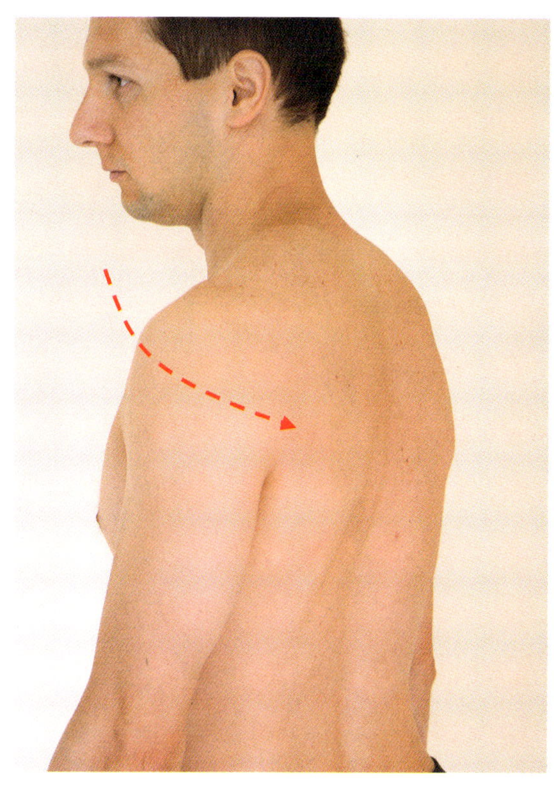

Fig. 3.73. Thoracic extrarotation managed by the MF unit of extra-thorax.

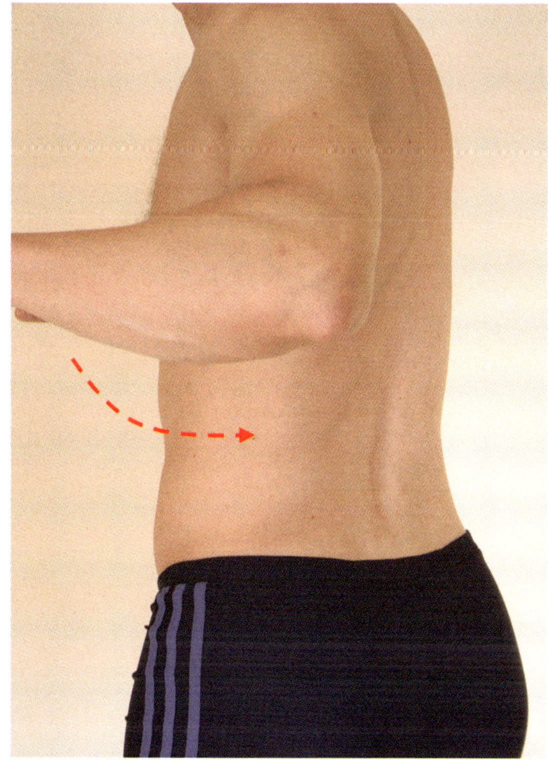

Fig. 3.74. Lumbar extrarotation managed by the MF unit of extra-lumbi.

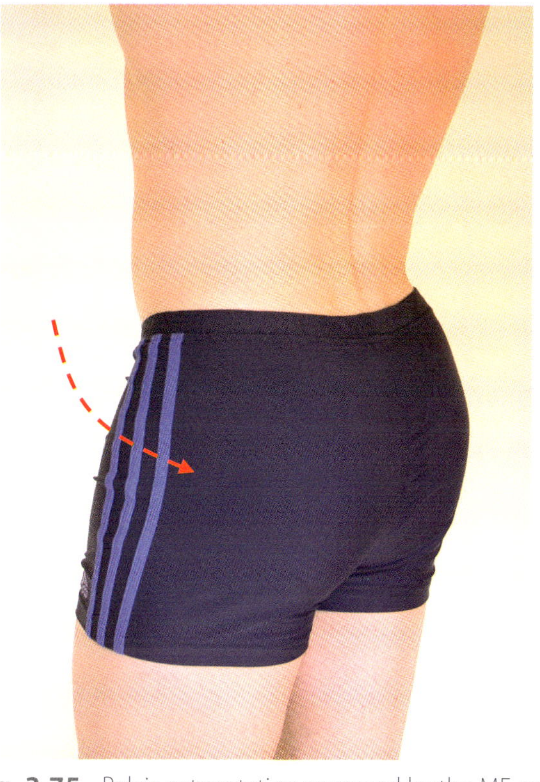

Fig. 3.75. Pelvic extrarotation managed by the MF unit of extra-pelvis.

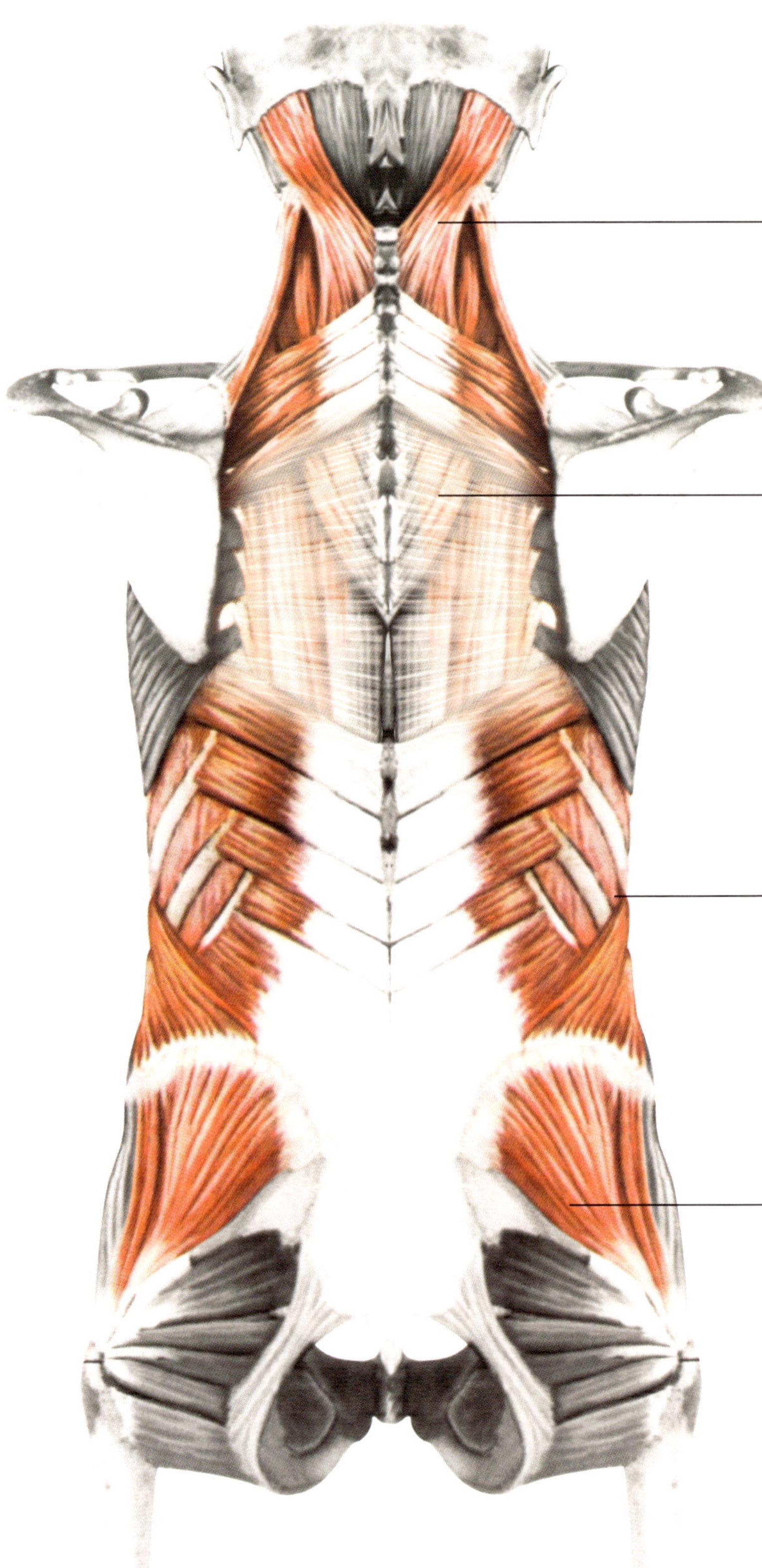

Fig. 3.76. Fascial compartments connected to the extrarotation muscles of the trunk.

(From G. Chiarugi and L. Bucciante, Istituzioni di anatomia dell'uomo. Piccin Nuova Libraria, Padova 1983, modified)

COMPARTMENTS FOR THE MUSCLES OF EXTRAROTATION OF THE TRUNK (Fig. 3.77)

Fascial compartment, collum extrarotation

The principal motor units of neck extrarotation are located in the levator scapula, splenius capitis and cervicis muscles.

"The rhomboid, levator scapula, serratus anterior, subclavius, inferior head of omohyoid muscles constitute a group derived from a myoblastic cluster of the trunk that was pushed towards the scapular girdle" (Chiarugi G. 1975).

Fascial compartment, thorax extrarotation

The principal motor units of thorax extrarotation are located in the serratus posterior superior and paravertebral muscles.

"The third muscular plane of the back holds the serratus posterior superior and inferior muscles. Both muscles are joined by a fibrous, very resistant membrane known as the interdentate aponeurosis" (Testut L. 1987).

Fascial compartment, lumbi extrarotation

The posterior part of the internal abdominal oblique rotates lumbi ipsilaterally (external rotation), whilst the contraction of the external abdominal oblique muscle rotates lumbi contralaterally (internal rotation). Some motor units of the iliocostalis muscle also rotate the spine towards the side upon which they act.

Fascial compartment, pelvis extrarotation

The principal motor units of extrarotation of the pelvis are located in the gluteus medius and minimus.

"The gluteus medius sometimes fuses more or less exactly with the gluteus minimus or with the piriform. The contraction of its posterior bundles determines an external rotation of the thigh. If the muscle has a fixed point on the femur, it extends the pelvis over the thigh, it bends and rotates it ipsilaterally". (Chiarugi G. 1975)

GLOBAL MOVEMENT IMPLEMENTED BY THE MF SEQUENCE OF EXTRAROTATION

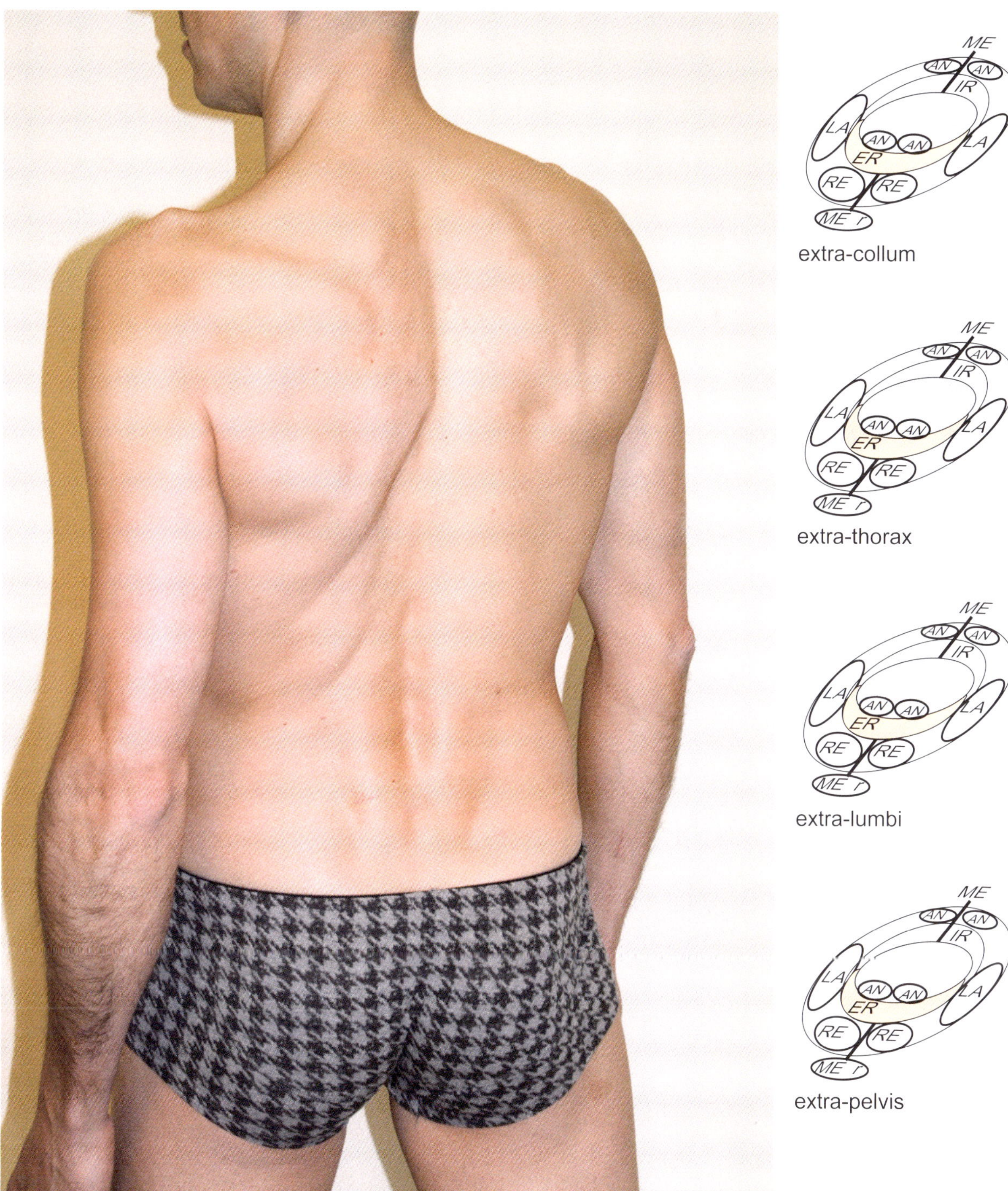

Fig. 3.77. Extrarotation of the trunk is implemented when the brain programmes for the movement of one side of the body backward activating the MF units of extrarotation.

Trunk torsion is the result of the simultaneous torsional forces between internal rotation on one side and external rotation on the other side.
The brain may trigger impulses to two units which may appear antagonists. What more likely happens when movement is completed, is that the brain sends impulses to a primary motor unit and then the secondary MF units are activated through the stretch reflex.
In the above diagrams the colour indicates the intermediate fascia where most rotation occurs. This fascia is also connected to the extrarotation motor units distributed in other muscles.

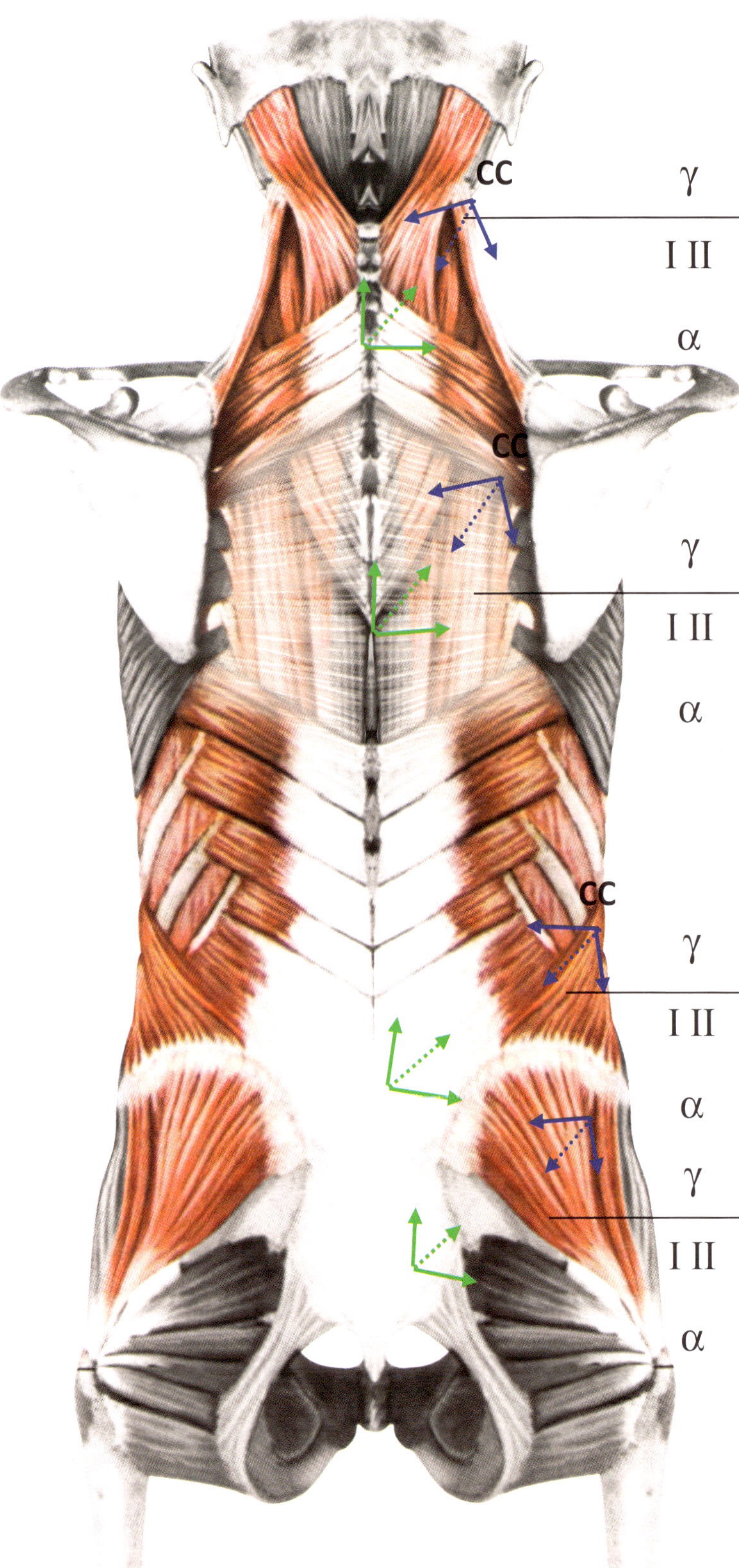

Fig. 3.78. Normal function of the alpha-gamma circuit.
(From G. Chiarugi and L. Bucciante, Istituzioni di anatomia dell'uomo. Piccin Nuova Libraria, Padova 1983, modified)

PHYSIOLOGY OF THE MF UNITS, TRUNK EXTRAROTATION

MF unit of extra-collum (er-cl)
The gamma neuron stimulates the motor units of the intrafusal muscle fibres located in the motor units for external rotation of the neck. The adaptability of the perimysium (CC) allows the fibres Ia and II to close the circuit and to trigger the alpha stimulus for the extrafusal muscles of the MF unit er-cl.

MF unit of extra-thorax (er-th)
The gamma neuron stimulates the intrafusal muscle fibres of the motor units for external rotation of the thorax. The adaptability of the perimysium (CC) allows the fibres I, II to close the circuit and to trigger the alpha stimulus for the extrafusal muscles of the MF unit er-th.

MF unit of extra-lumbi (er-lu)
The gamma neuron stimulates the intrafusal muscle fibres of the motor units for external rotation of the low back. The adaptability of the perimysium (CC) allows the fibres I, II to close the circuit and to trigger the alpha stimulus for the extrafusal muscles of the MF unit er-lu.

MF unit of extra-pelvis (er-pv)
The gamma neuron stimulates the intrafusal muscle fibres of the motor units for external rotation of the pelvis. The adaptability of the perimysium (CC) allows the fibres Ia and II to close the circuit and to trigger the alpha stimulus for the extrafusal muscles of the MF unit er-pv.

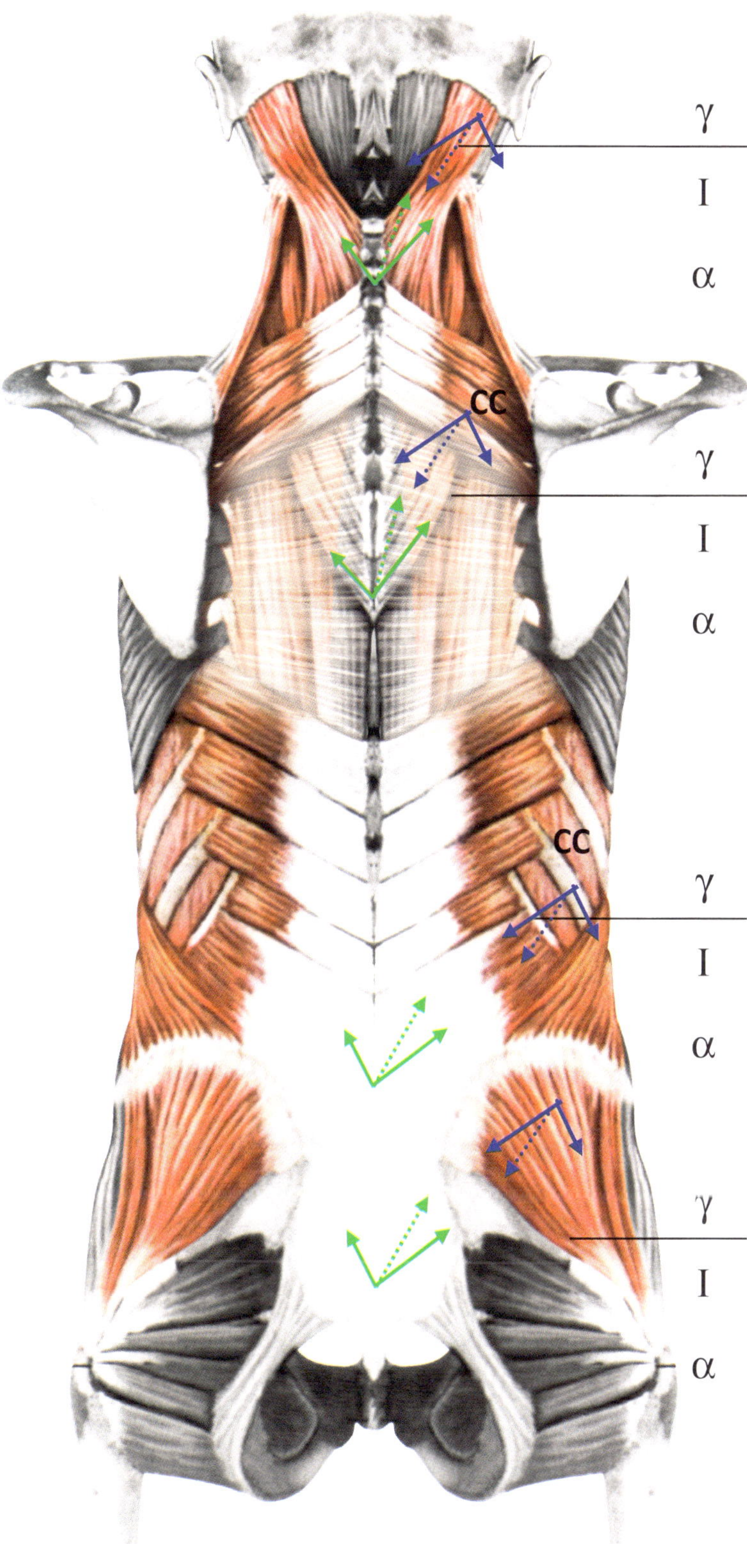

Fig. 3.79. Dysfunctions of the alpha-gamma circuit.
(From G. Chiarugi and L. Bucciante, Istituzioni di anatomia dell'uomo. Piccin Nuova Libraria, Padova 1983, modified)

ARTICULAR CONFLICTS IN EXTRAROTATION OF THE TRUNK

γ
I
α

Pain during extrarotation of collum
If the fascia of the MF unit er-cl is densified, then only some motor units in the gamma circuit are activated. Hence a conflict in the torque forces of intrarotation and extrarotation is created with subsequent pain in the cervical vertebrae.

γ
I
α

Pain during extrarotation of thorax
If the fascia of the MF unit er-th is densified, then only some motor units in the gamma circuit are activated. Hence in the torque forces the contralateral intrarotation forces prevail with subsequent pain in the thorax.

γ
I
α

Pain during extrarotation of lumbi
If the fascia of the MF unit er-lu is densified, then only some motor units in the gamma circuit are activated. Hence in the torque forces the contralateral intrarotation forces prevail with subsequent articular conflict and pain in the low back.

γ
I
α

Pain during extrarotation of pelvis
If the fascia overlying the gluteus medius (CC) is densified, then the alpha-gamma circuit is not triggered and the sacroiliac ligaments are stretched in a non-physiological manner. The receptors embedded in these ligaments change from proprioceptors and become nociceptors.

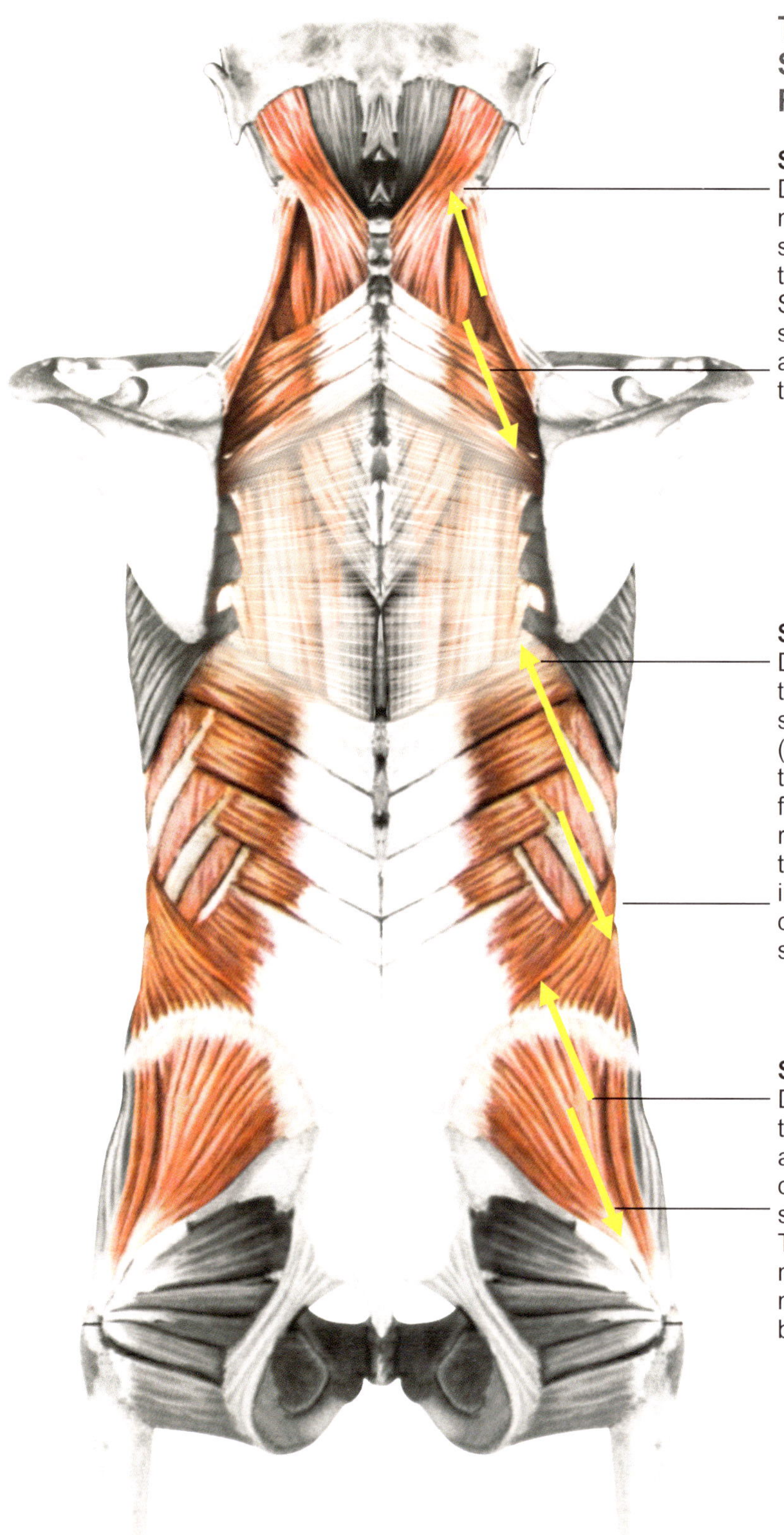

TR EXTRAROTATION SEQUENCE AND STRETCH REFLEX

Synergy between er-cl and er-th
During external rotation of the neck, the levator scapula and splenius muscles contract stretching their fasciae cranially (Fig. 3.82). Simultaneously the posterior superior serratus muscle contracts and consequently creates a caudal tension on its fascia.

Synergy between er-th and er-lu
During external rotation of the thorax, the iliocostalis and posterior superior serratus muscles contract (Fig. 3.83). The contraction of these muscles stretches the serrati fascia cranially. The external rotation of lumbi is implemented by the posterior inferior serratus and internal oblique muscles (Fig. 3.84) causing a caudal stretch of the serrati fascia.

Synergy between er-lu and er-pv
During external rotation of lumbi, the posterior inferior serratus and ipsilateral internal abdominal oblique muscles contract (Fig. 3.83) stretching their fascia cranially. The external rotation of pelvis is managed by the gluteus medius muscles (Fig. 3.85), with its fascia being stretched caudally.

Fig. 3.80. Synergy along the extrarotation sequence of the trunk.
(From G. Chiarugi and L. Bucciante, Istituzioni di anatomia dell'uomo. Piccin Nuova Libraria, Padova 1983, modified)

ACTIVATION OF THE GOLGI TENDON ORGANS

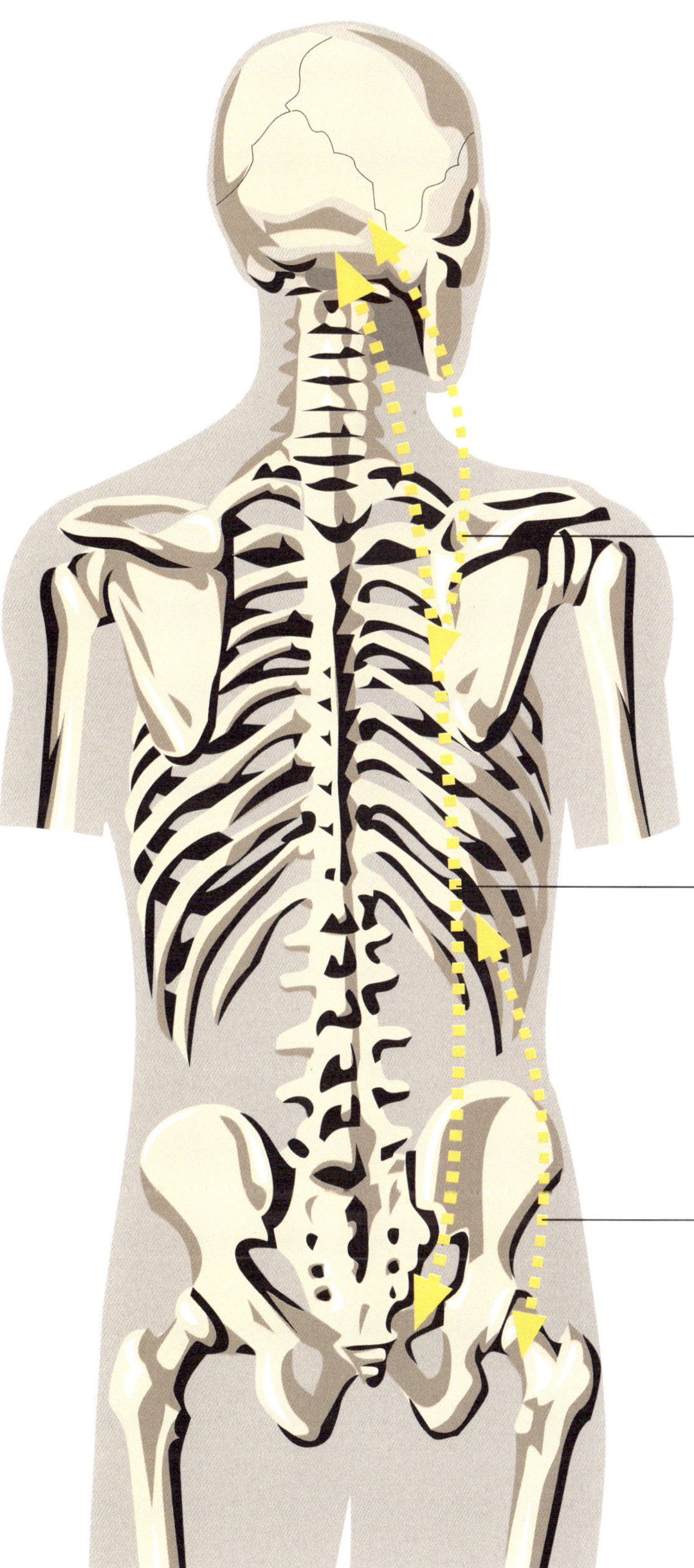

Connection between collum and thorax
The variations in joint degrees of the cervical vertebrae implicate the Golgi tendon organs of the rotator muscles of the neck and levator scapula.

"Some bundles of the levator scapula may arise from the fascia of the posterior superior serratus and from the serratus anterior muscle, in many mammals it forms a unique muscle" (Chiarugi G. 1975).

Global sequence connection
When turning backwards often the entire musculature of the sequence of extrarotation is implicated.
In this case the levator scapula, serrati, internal abdominal oblique and glutei muscles form a single functional unit.

Connection between lumbi and pelvis
The torsion of lumbi leverages the pelvis, pelvic torsion is in part implemented by lumbar muscles.

"The internal oblique muscle originates from the reunited sheaths of the lumbo-dorsal fascia and from the iliac crest. The posterior bundles attach to the inferior margin of the lower three ribs and continues with the internal intercostal muscles" (Chiarugi G. 1975).

Fig. 3.81. Biarticular muscles for extrarotation in the trunk.

FASCIAE OF THE EXTRAROTATION SEQUENCE OF THE TRUNK

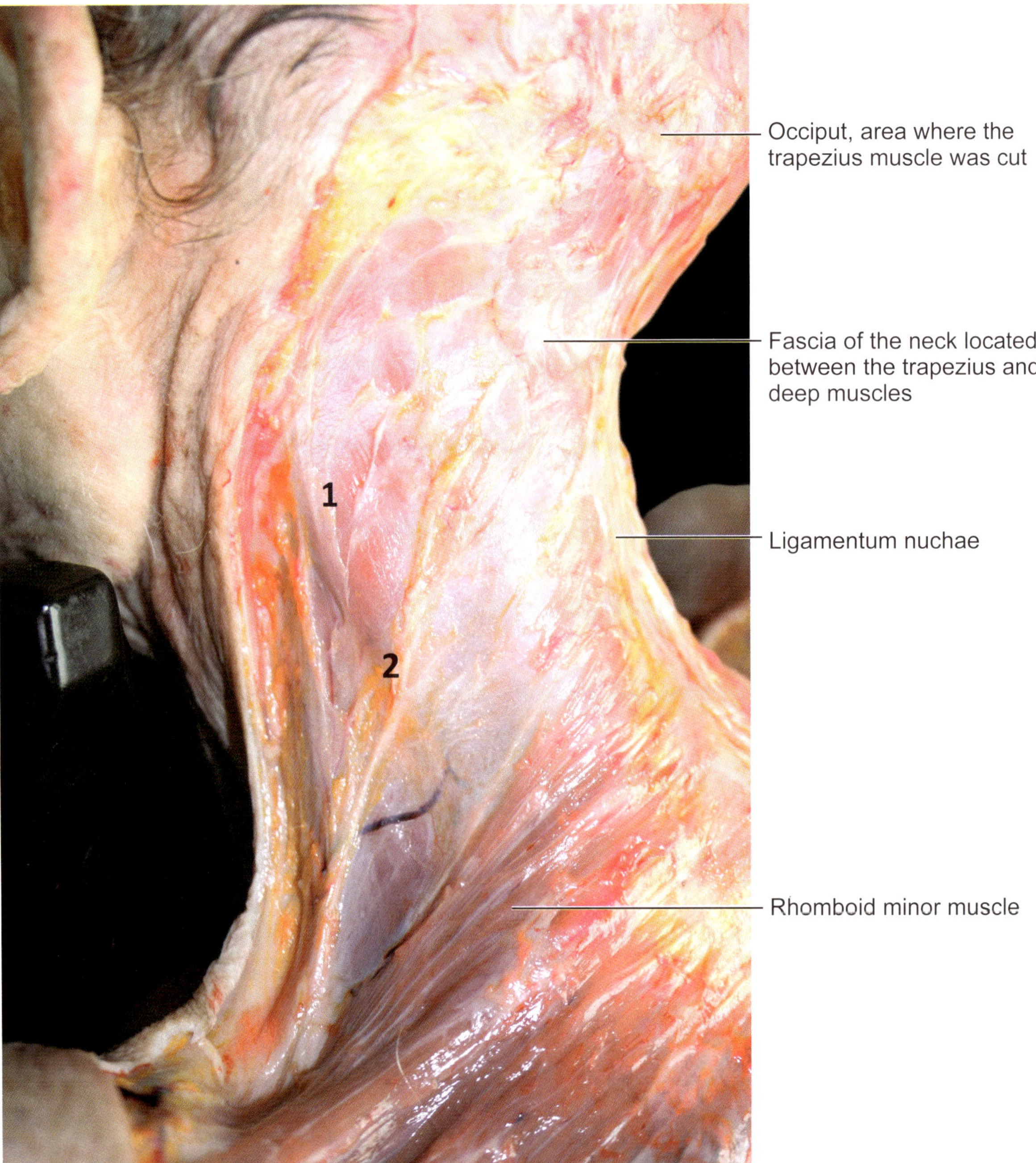

Fig. 3.82. Fascia of the neck or intermediate lamina of the posterior cervical fascia. Underneath the nuchal fascia the splenii muscles (1) are visible and, adjoining the fascia, the course of the lesser occipital nerve (2) is evident.

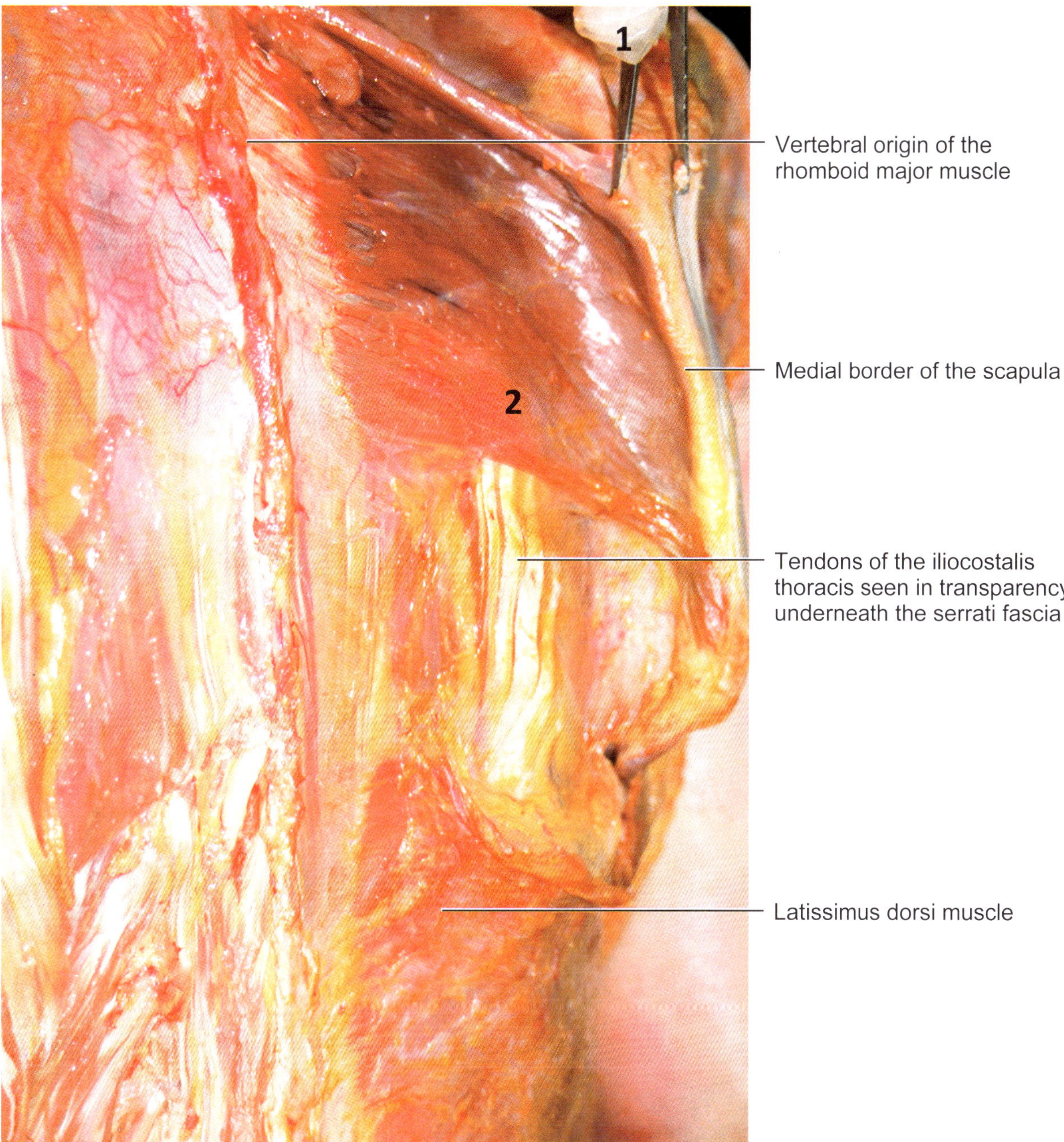

Fig. 3.83. Scapula or bone lever interposed between the motor muscles of the arm. The forceps (1) laterally moves the scapula to highlight the thin rhomboid muscles (2) that from the spinous processes insert onto the scapula.

FASCIAE OF THE EXTRAROTATION SEQUENCE OF THE TRUNK

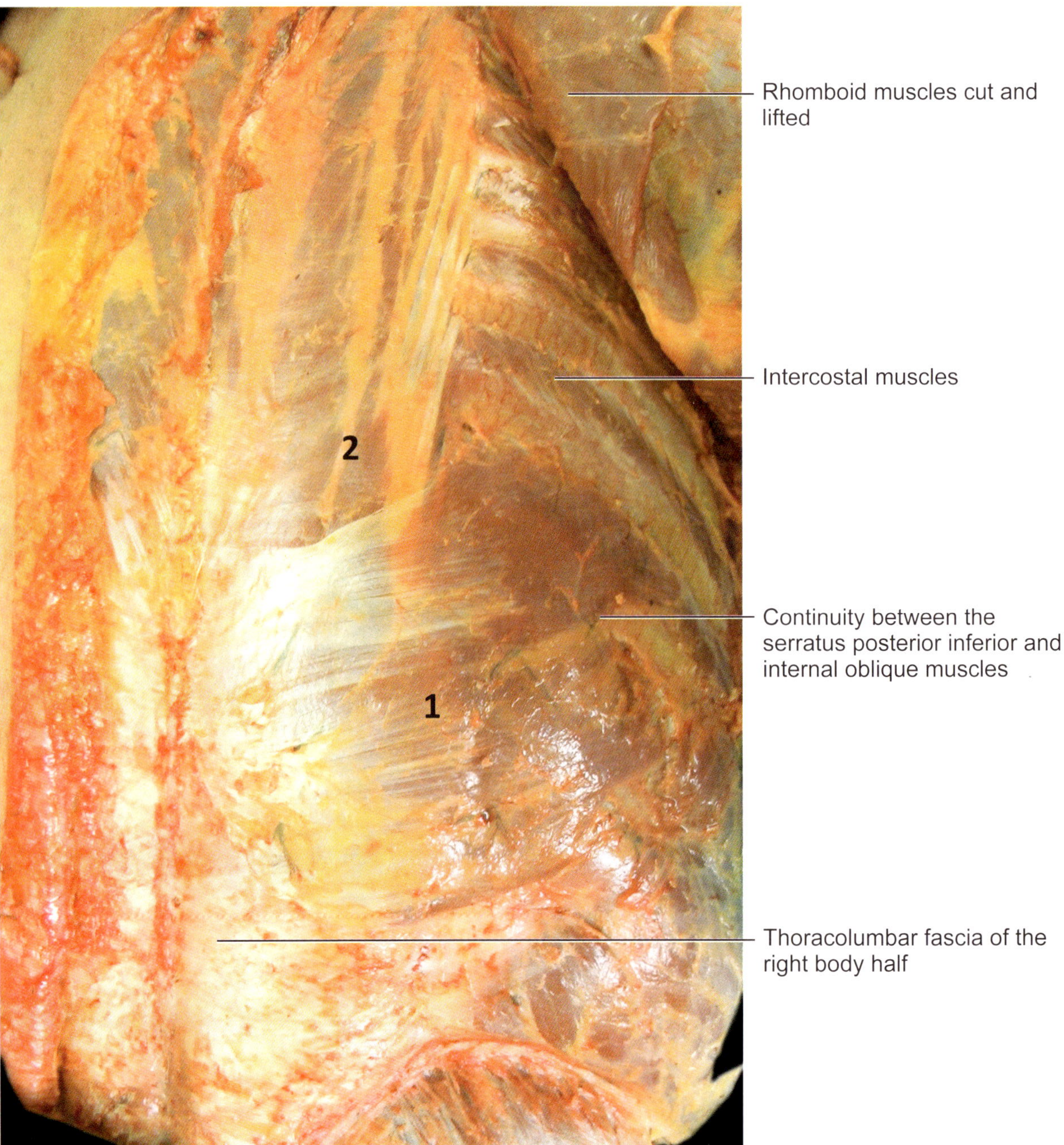

Fig. 3.84. The serratus posterior inferior muscle. The thoracolumbar fascia forms the first layer together with the latissimus dorsi muscle, the serrati fascia forms the second layer (1), the fascia of the erector spinae forms the third layer (2).

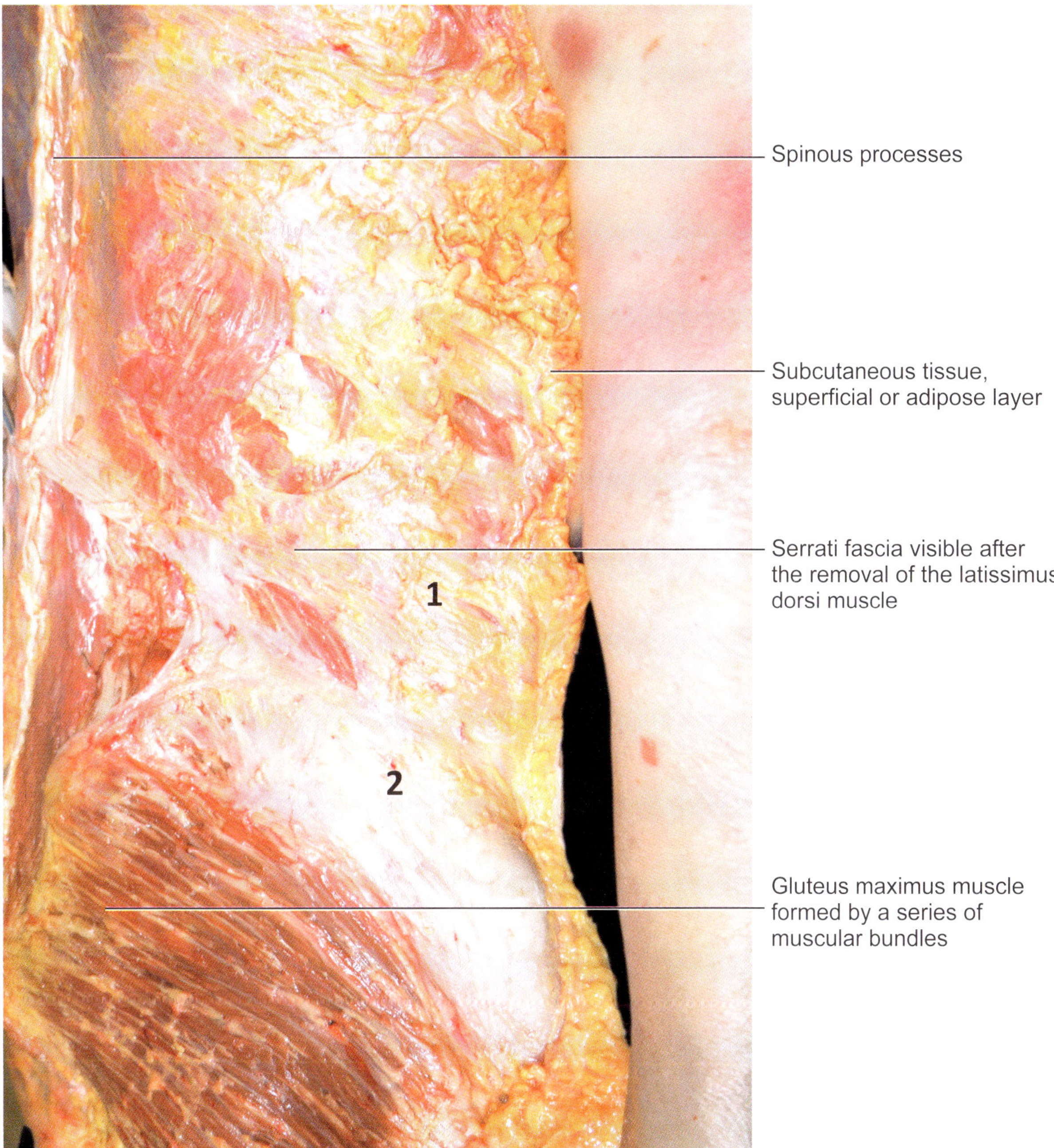

Fig. 3.85. Aponeurotic fascia of the gluteus medius and epimysial fascia of the gluteus maximus muscles. The superficial fascia was removed, the fascia covering the internal (1) and external oblique muscles is visible. The fascia of these muscles is continuous with the fascia of the gluteus medius muscle (2).

CHAPTER 4

CENTRES OF COORDINATION AND SEQUENCES OF THE LOWER LIMB

MYOFASCIAL UNITS AND UNIDIRECTIONAL MOVEMENTS OF THE LOWER LIMB (LL)

The lower limb is the principal agent of locomotion, it must offer support to the body in both the upright posture and when walking.

Chiarugi subdivides the lower limb musculature into the muscles of the hip, thigh, leg and foot, and subdivides the upper limb musculature into the muscles of the shoulder, arm, forearm and hand. This subdivision is in agreement with the topography of the myofascial units of the limbs.

The foot is composed of several bones, its movements on the three spatial planes are not managed by the brain separately for each joint, rather, they are organised from a motor point of view as two entities: the forefoot (metatarsals and toes) and the hind foot (tarsus).

The foot, like the hand, is moved by intrinsic muscles and by tendons originating from the leg.

Each finger of the hand has perfect motor independence whilst in the foot the hallux and fifth toe have a partial independence and the three central toes move together.

The various parts of the foot are reached by leg muscles in a slightly different manner to what occurs in the hand. The muscles moving the talus and navicular bones in the three spatial planes do not connect with each toe but rather with the following parts of the foot:

- flexor digitorum longus muscle connects with the muscles of the intermediate compartment of the foot (mediopulsion);
- peroneus brevis muscle extends into the superior lateral part of the foot[1] (extrarotation);
- triceps surae muscle continues into the inferior lateral compartment of the foot (retropulsion);
- tibialis anterior muscle connects to the fascia of the extensor hallucis longus muscle (antepulsion);
- tibialis posterior muscle connects to the compartment of the abductor hallucis muscle (intrarotation);
- extensor digitorum longus muscle has its tendons included in the dorsal fascia of the foot (lateropulsion).

The myofascial sequences of the trunk and limbs extend themselves into the extremities so that the afferents from the most distal points of the body arrive to the brain perfectly structured according to the spatial directions.

Each MF unit may act independently however, when the effort in one MF unit increases the local muscular contraction will propagate both proximally and distally[2], implicating the ipsidirectional MF units of the entire MF sequence. Each MF unit coordinates the motor units included in its fascial compartment.

The brain programmes a directional movement and the fascia coordinates the variations of motor unit recruitment based upon joint range or the recruitment of myofascial units along a sequence. The biarticular muscles act as a bridge between two myofascial units; the Golgi tendon organs of these muscles regulate muscle strength based upon variations in range of the proximal joint with respect to the distal one. This coordination is only implemented if the fascia is fluid, when its ground substance is densified then motor incoordination and articular pain appear.

The movements implemented according to the three spatial planes presented in the initial chapters, mirror the evolution of the locomotor apparatus. Namely first unidirectional movements, then those associated with rotational movements (motor schemes) and finally motor gestures.

Only by breaking down body movement according to the progressive motor conquests can its physiology be better understood and a better therapy for its dysfunctions implemented.

[1] An additional tendon may arise from both the musculature or tendon of peroneus brevis and insert on the fifth toe, or on the fourth metatarsal, or even on the abductor digiti minimi muscle. (Chiarugi G. 1975)

[2] The active contraction without resistance of the muscles of a segment did not produce, through surface electromyography, any activation along the kinetic chain. With increased effort in a district the activation of other muscles along the kinetic chain was increase both cranially and caudally. (Weissmann M.H.S. 2014)

ANTERIOR REGION OF THE LOWER LIMB, ANTEPULSION SEQUENCE

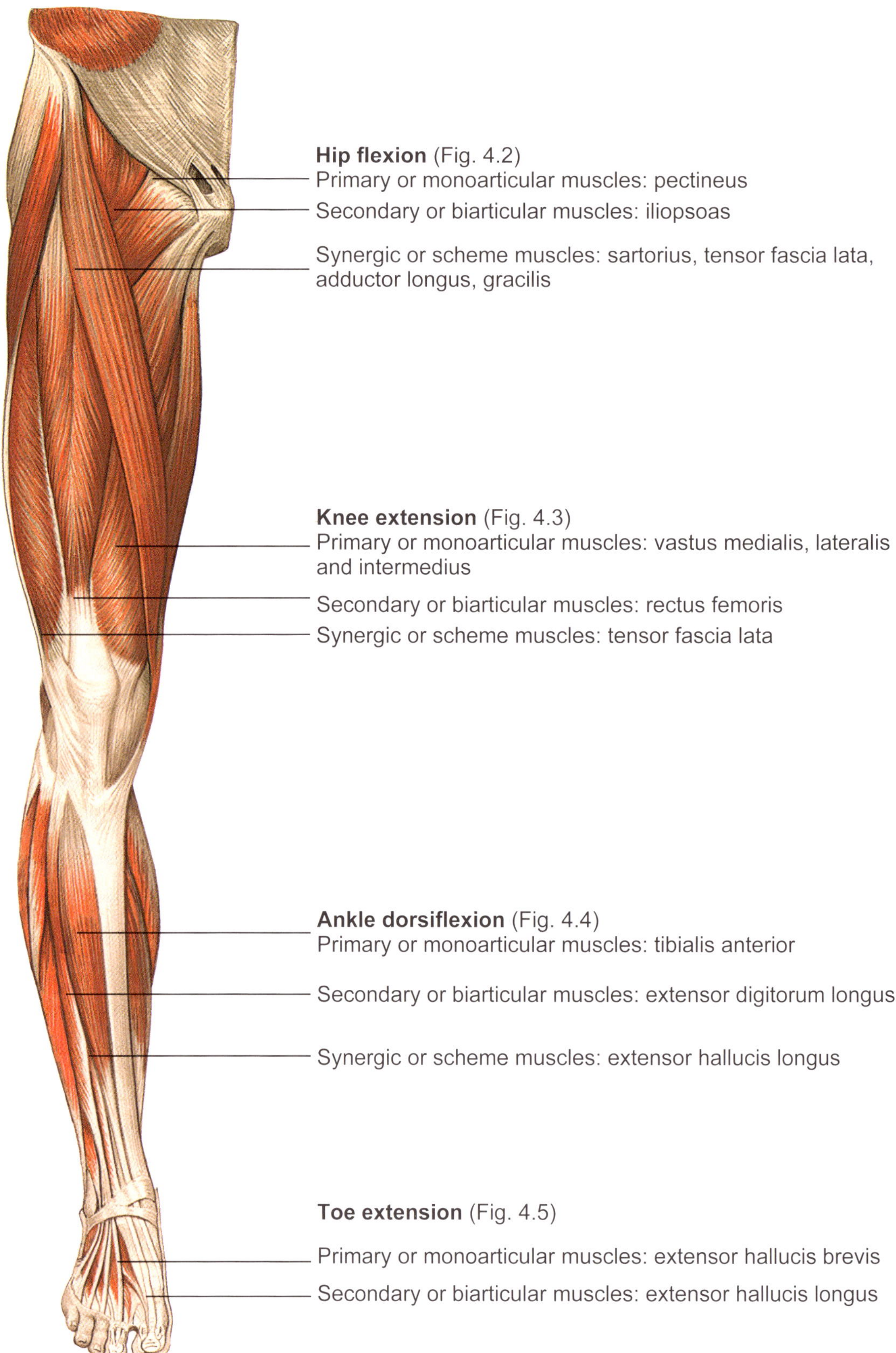

Fig. 4.1. Anterior region of the lower limb.
(From G. Chiarugi and L. Bucciante, Istituzioni di anatomia dell'uomo. Piccin Nuova Libraria, Padova 1983, modified)

SEGMENTARY MOVEMENTS IMPLEMENTED BY THE MF UNITS OF ANTEPULSION

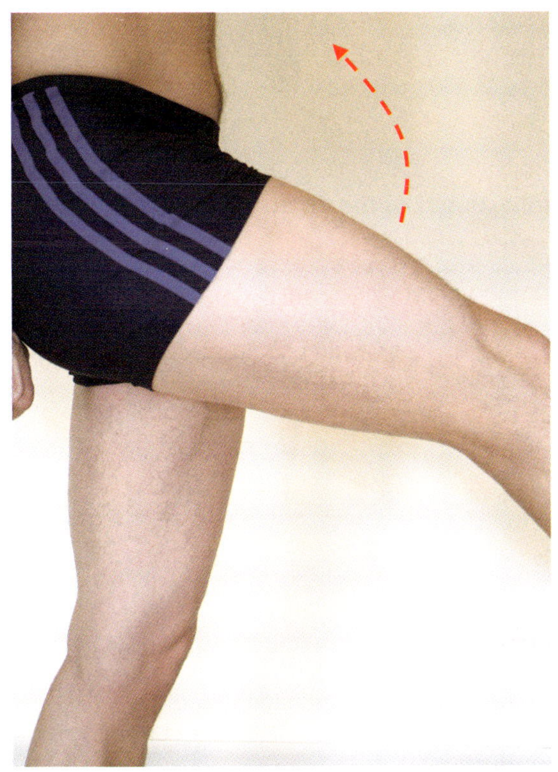

Fig. 4.2. Thigh flexion managed throughout its range by the myofascial unit of ante-coxa.

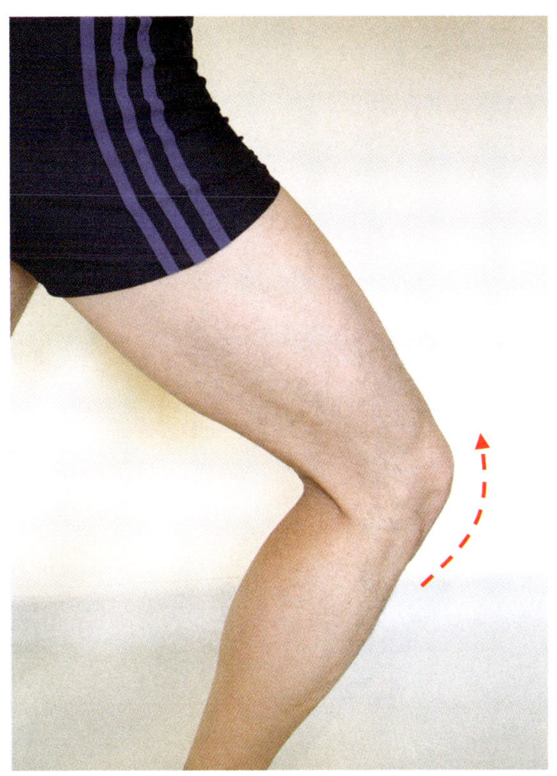

Fig. 4.3. Knee extension managed throughout its range by the myofascial unit of ante-genu.

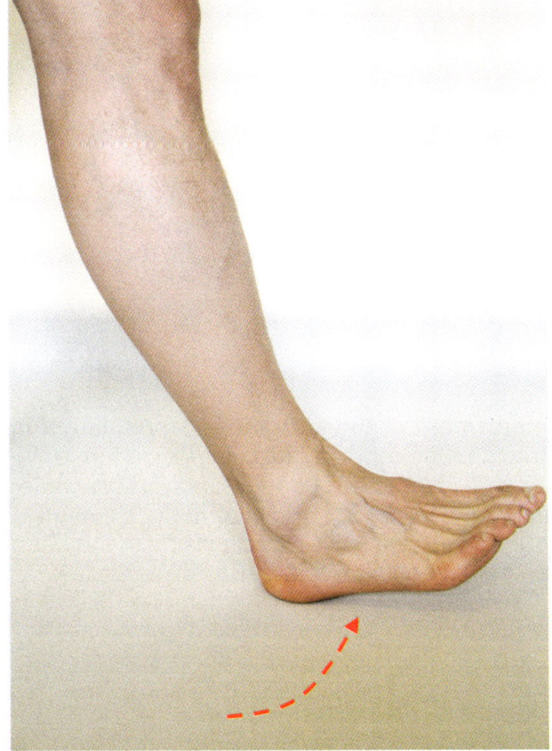

Fig. 4.4. Ankle dorsiflexion managed throughout its joint range by the MF unit of ante-talus.

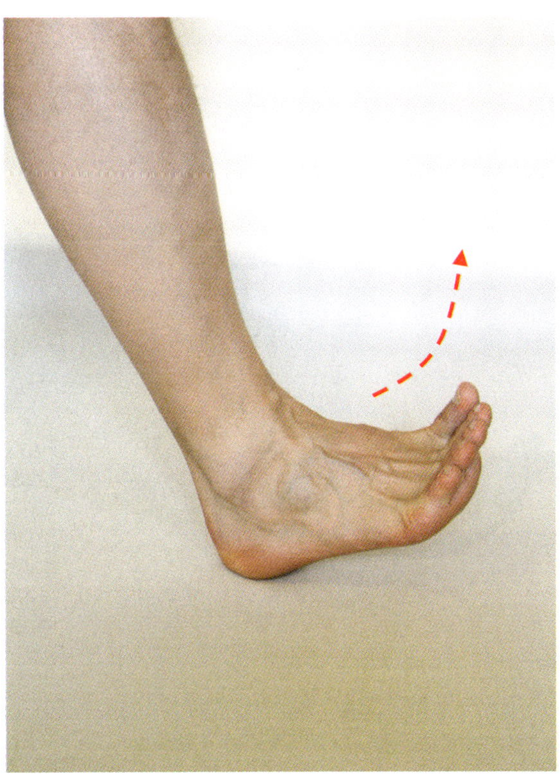

Fig. 4.5. Dorsiflexion of the big toe managed throughout its joint range by the MF unit of ante-pes.

COMPARTMENTS FOR THE MUSCLES OF ANTEPULSION, LOWER LIMB (Fig. 4.7)

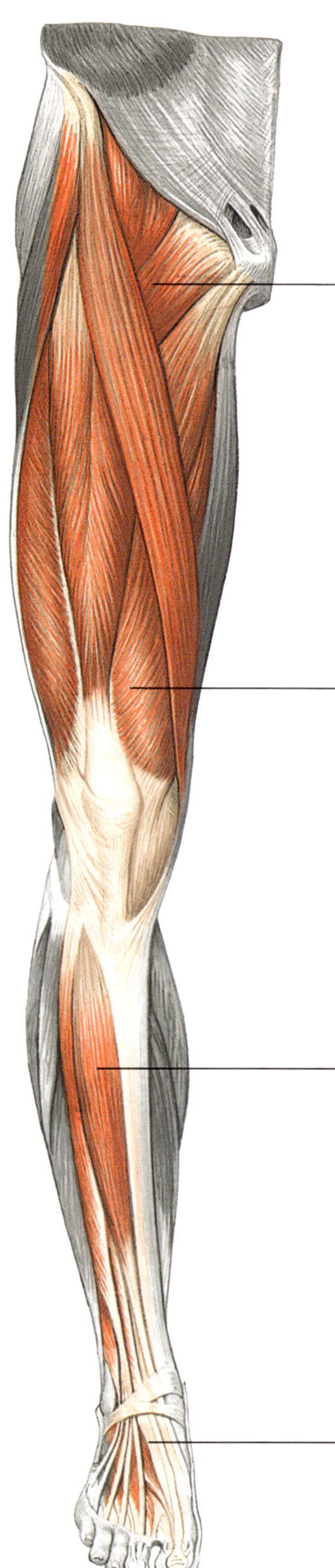

Fascial compartment of the antepulsion muscles of coxa
The iliopectineal fascia covers the psoas, iliacus, pectineus and adductor longus muscles, and connects through numerous septa to the motor units responsible for the antepulsion of coxa. This fascia continues seamlessly over the vastus medialis of the quadriceps muscle.

Fascial compartment of the antepulsion muscles of genu
The fascia for antepulsion of genu is formed by:
- the superficial lamina continued from the abdominal and cribriform fasciae;
- the deep lamina continued from the iliopectineal fascia; this deep lamina continues over the vastus medialis muscle and then offers insertion through its septa to the motor units included in the vastus intermedius and vastus lateralis of the quadriceps muscle.

Fascial compartment of the antepulsion muscles of talus
The anterior crural fascia forms the compartment of the extensor muscles, this compartment contains the motor units responsible for the antepulsion of talus. Many muscle fibres of extensor digitorum originate from the overlying fascia.

Fascial compartment of the antepulsion muscles of pes
Over the dorsum of the foot the muscular fascia forms three superposing layers: the superficial lamina continuing from the cruciform retinaculum, the intermediate lamina containing the extensor hallucis muscle inside it, the deep lamina covering and uniting with the dorsal interossei muscles.

Fig. 4.6. Fascial compartments for antepulsion muscles.
(From G. Chiarugi and L. Bucciante, Istituzioni di anatomia dell'uomo. Piccin Nuova Libraria, Padova 1983, modified)

GLOBAL MOVEMENT IMPLEMENTED BY THE ANTEPULSION MF SEQUENCE

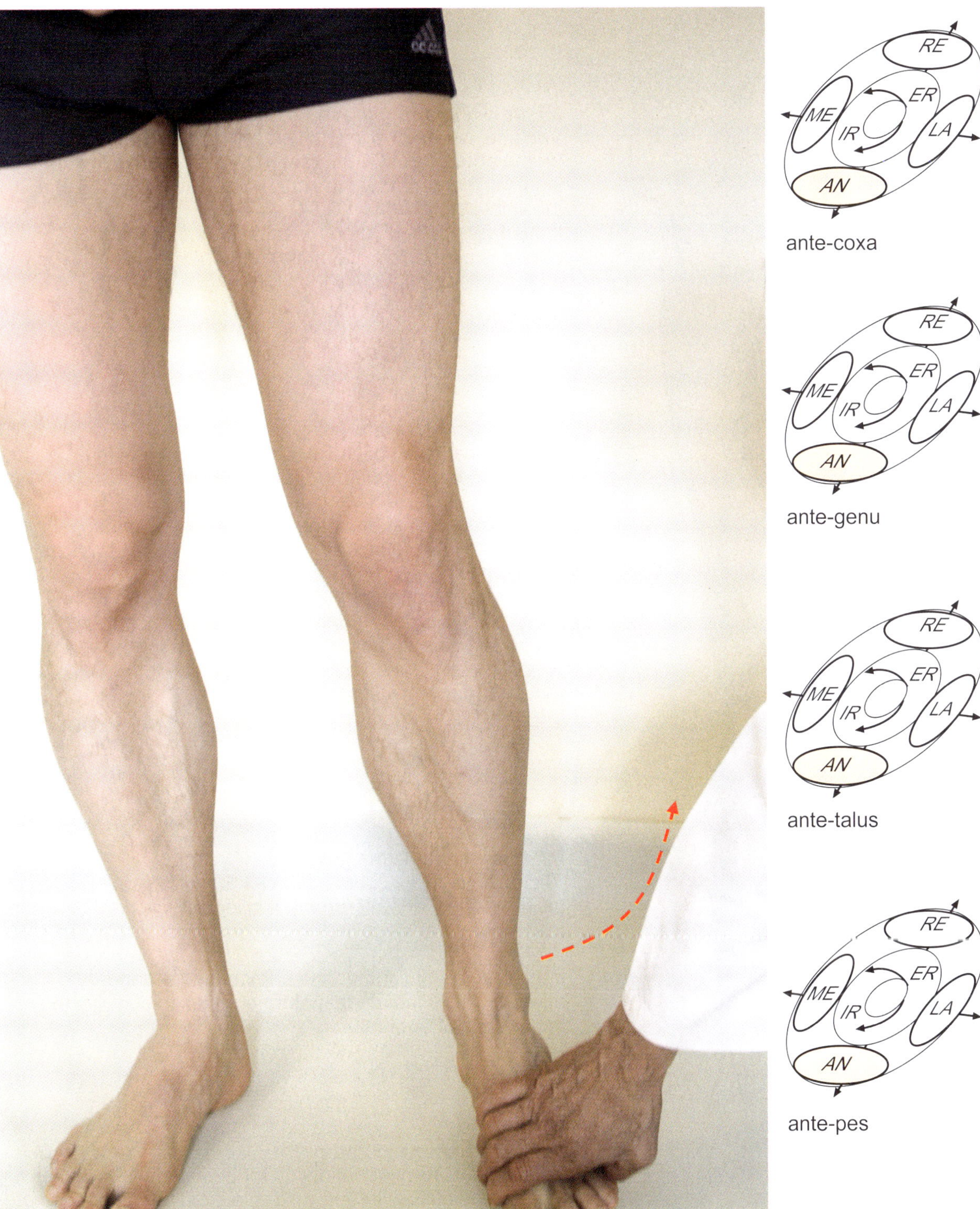

Fig. 4.7. Contraction of the antepulsion sequence bringing the entire lower limb anteriorly.

When the brain programmes for forward lower limb movement, the ipsidirectional motor units included in the fascial compartments of the anterior region of the limb are then activated.
The contraction of the antepulsion motor units included in the anterior fascial compartments determines the stretch of the overlying fascia and the activation of proprioceptors. The afferents from the antepulsion sequence return to the brain confirming the occurrence of the movement according to the programmed direction.

PHYSIOLOGY OF THE ANTEPULSION MF UNITS, LOWER LIMB

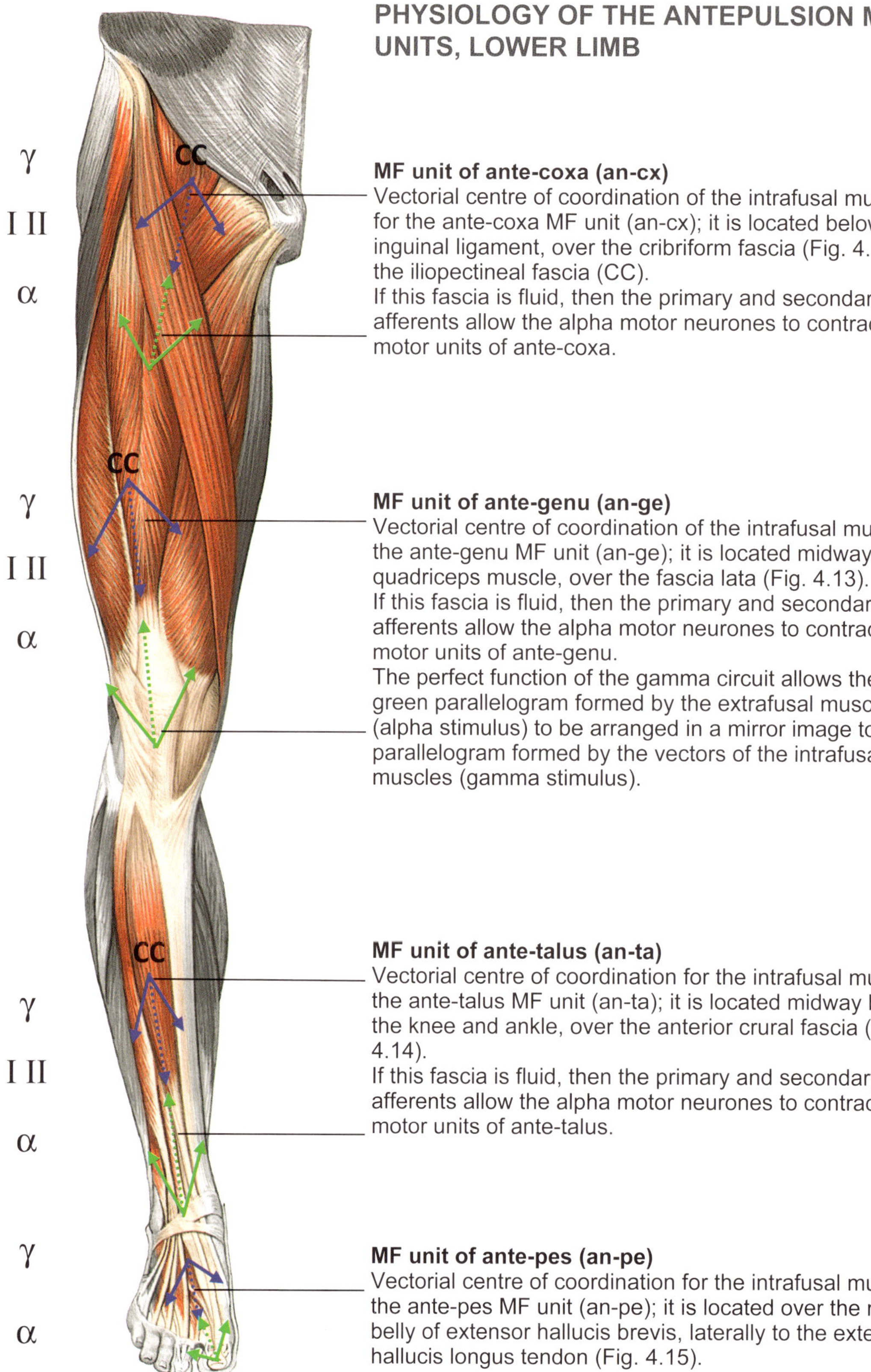

MF unit of ante-coxa (an-cx)
Vectorial centre of coordination of the intrafusal muscles for the ante-coxa MF unit (an-cx); it is located below the inguinal ligament, over the cribriform fascia (Fig. 4.12) and the iliopectineal fascia (CC).
If this fascia is fluid, then the primary and secondary afferents allow the alpha motor neurones to contract the motor units of ante-coxa.

MF unit of ante-genu (an-ge)
Vectorial centre of coordination of the intrafusal muscles for the ante-genu MF unit (an-ge); it is located midway over the quadriceps muscle, over the fascia lata (Fig. 4.13).
If this fascia is fluid, then the primary and secondary afferents allow the alpha motor neurones to contract the motor units of ante-genu.
The perfect function of the gamma circuit allows the green parallelogram formed by the extrafusal muscles (alpha stimulus) to be arranged in a mirror image to the parallelogram formed by the vectors of the intrafusal muscles (gamma stimulus).

MF unit of ante-talus (an-ta)
Vectorial centre of coordination for the intrafusal muscles for the ante-talus MF unit (an-ta); it is located midway between the knee and ankle, over the anterior crural fascia (Fig. 4.14).
If this fascia is fluid, then the primary and secondary afferents allow the alpha motor neurones to contract the motor units of ante-talus.

MF unit of ante-pes (an-pe)
Vectorial centre of coordination for the intrafusal muscles for the ante-pes MF unit (an-pe); it is located over the muscle belly of extensor hallucis brevis, laterally to the extensor hallucis longus tendon (Fig. 4.15).

Fig. 4.8. Normal functioning of the gamma circuit.
(From G. Chiarugi and L. Bucciante, Istituzioni di anatomia dell'uomo. Piccin Nuova Libraria, Padova 1983, modified)

ARTICULAR CONFLICTS IN THE ANTEPULSION UNITS, LOWER LIMB

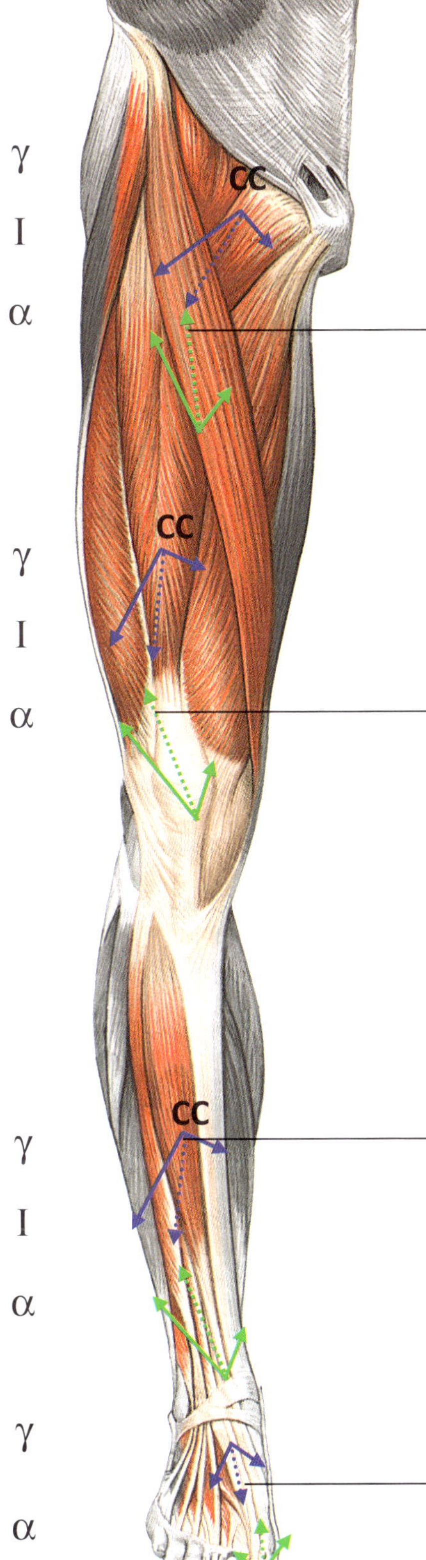

Pain during antepulsion of coxa
If the iliopectineal fascia is densified, then some intrafusal fibres are not able to contract and to activate all the extrafusal fibres of the an-cx MF unit.
For instance, if only the lateral fibres of the iliopsoas muscle are activated then a conflict occurs in the hip joint with pain in the groin.

Pain during antepulsion of genu
If the fascia corresponding to the CC is densified, then some intrafusal fibres are not able to contract and to activate all the extrafusal fibres of the an-ge MF unit.
For instance, the predominance in the lateral fibres of the quadriceps muscle results in a lateral subluxation of the patella and patellofemoral conflict.
Densification of the fascia does not determine the blockage of the gamma circuit but only its dysfunction. Both parallelograms have the same position but their resultant is no longer aligned with the joint axis.

Pain during antepulsion of talus
If the anterior crural fascia is densified, then some intrafusal fibres are not able to contract and to activate all the extrafusal fibres of the an-ta MF unit.
For instance, if only the muscular fibres of the extensor digitorum muscle are activated then a conflict is developed in the talar joint with consequent tendinosis and pain.

Pain during antepulsion of pes
If the fascia of the extensor hallucis brevis muscle is densified, then some intrafusal fibres are not able to contract and to activate all the extrafusal fibres of the an-pe MF unit.
This results in pain in the first metarsal joint and the big toe.

Fig. 4.9. Dysfunction of the gamma circuit.
(From G. Chiarugi and L. Bucciante, Istituzioni di anatomia dell'uomo. Piccin Nuova Libraria, Padova 1983, modified)

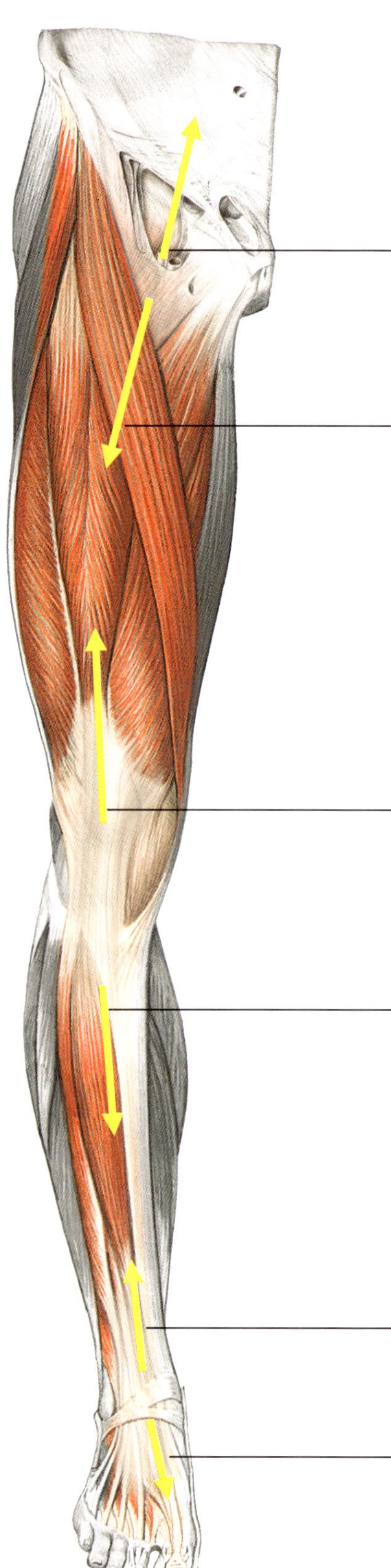

Fig. 4.10. Synergy of the antepulsion sequence in the lower limb.
(From G. Chiarugi and L. Bucciante, Istituzioni di anatomia dell'uomo. Piccin Nuova Libraria, Padova 1983, modified)

ANTEPULSION SEQUENCE AND STRETCH REFLEX

Synergy between the MF unit of ante-coxa and ante-genu
Superficially the cribriform fascia, spread over the triangle of Scarpa (Fig. 4.12), is stretched proximally by the abdominal oblique muscles (an-pv) and distally by the sartorius muscle (an-cx). Deeply the psoas minor muscle stretches the iliopectineal ligament (an-cx) proximally and the vastus medialis muscle (an-ge) creates a distal traction.

Synergy between the MF unit of ante-genu and ante-talus
The distal tendon of the rectus femoris muscle continues beyond the patella to form the patellar tendon and the quadriceps expansion that extends into the anterior crural fascia. During knee antepulsion the quadriceps expansion pulls the crural fascia proximally.
The dorsiflexion muscles of the talus take origin from the internal proximal aspect of the crural fascia, during their contraction they stretch the fascia distally (Fig. 4.14).

Synergy between the MF unit of ante-talus and ante-pes
The extensor retinaculum is not implicated in the continuity of the antepulsion sequence. Instead it is the insertions of the foot muscles on the tendons of the leg muscles that are synchronising the action of ankle antepulsion with that of the foot. The lumbrical muscles are inserted into the dorsal aponeurosis of the foot inside which the extensor tendons are located.

ACTIVATION OF THE GOLGI TENDON ORGANS

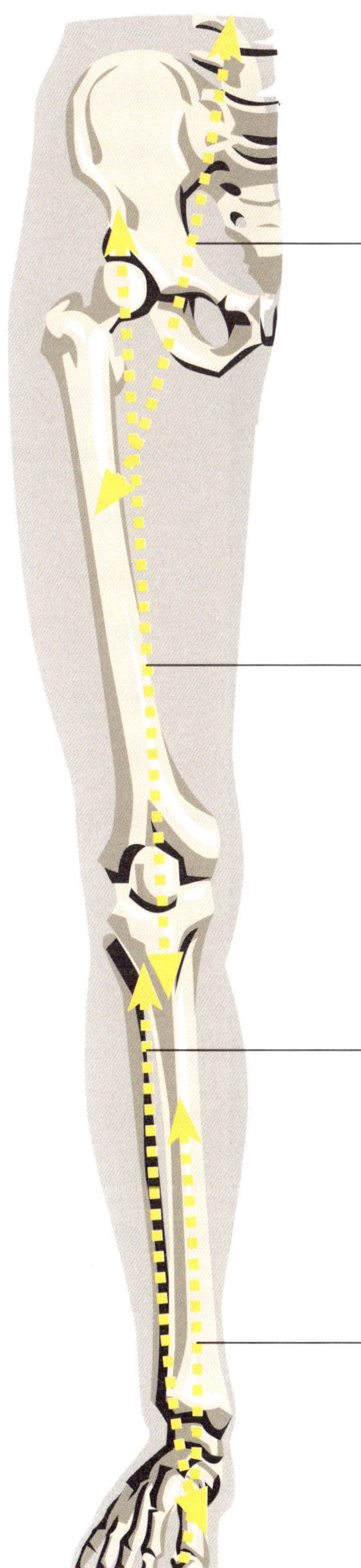

Fig. 4.11. Biarticular muscles for antepulsion in the lower limb.

Connection between pelvis and coxa
The iliopsoas is a biarticular muscle intervening in pelvis antepulsion if coxa is in closed kinematic chain; whilst intervening in thigh antepulsion if it is free to move. Pelvis and coxa form a functional unit; the iliacus and psoas muscles flex pelvis and coxa throughout the range with constant degrees.

Connection between coxa and genu
Biarticular fibres of the rectus femoris muscle which Golgi tendon organs manage the joint range of coxa and genu during their simultaneous movement in antepulsion.

"The distal tendon of the rectus femoris muscle continues beyond the patella participating to the formation of the patellar ligament that inserts onto the tibial tuberosity" (Chiarugi G. 1975).

Connection between genu and talus
Biarticular fibres of the tibialis anterior muscle which Golgi tendon organs manage the joint range of genu and talus during their simultaneous movement in antepulsion.

"The tibialis anterior muscle originates from the lateral condyle of the tibia and from the fascia covering it. An expansion of the patellar tendon of the quadriceps and biceps femoris muscle terminate on this fascia" (Chiarugi G. 1975).

Connection between talus and pes
Biarticular fibres of the extensor hallucis longus muscle which Golgi tendon organs manage the joint range of talus and pes during their simultaneous movement in antepulsion. At the level of the ankle, the angle of reflexion (equal to the angle of incidence) of the tendon passing underneath the cruciate retinaculum stimulates the Golgi tendon organs.

FASCIAE OF THE ANTEPULSION SEQUENCE IN THE LOWER LIMB

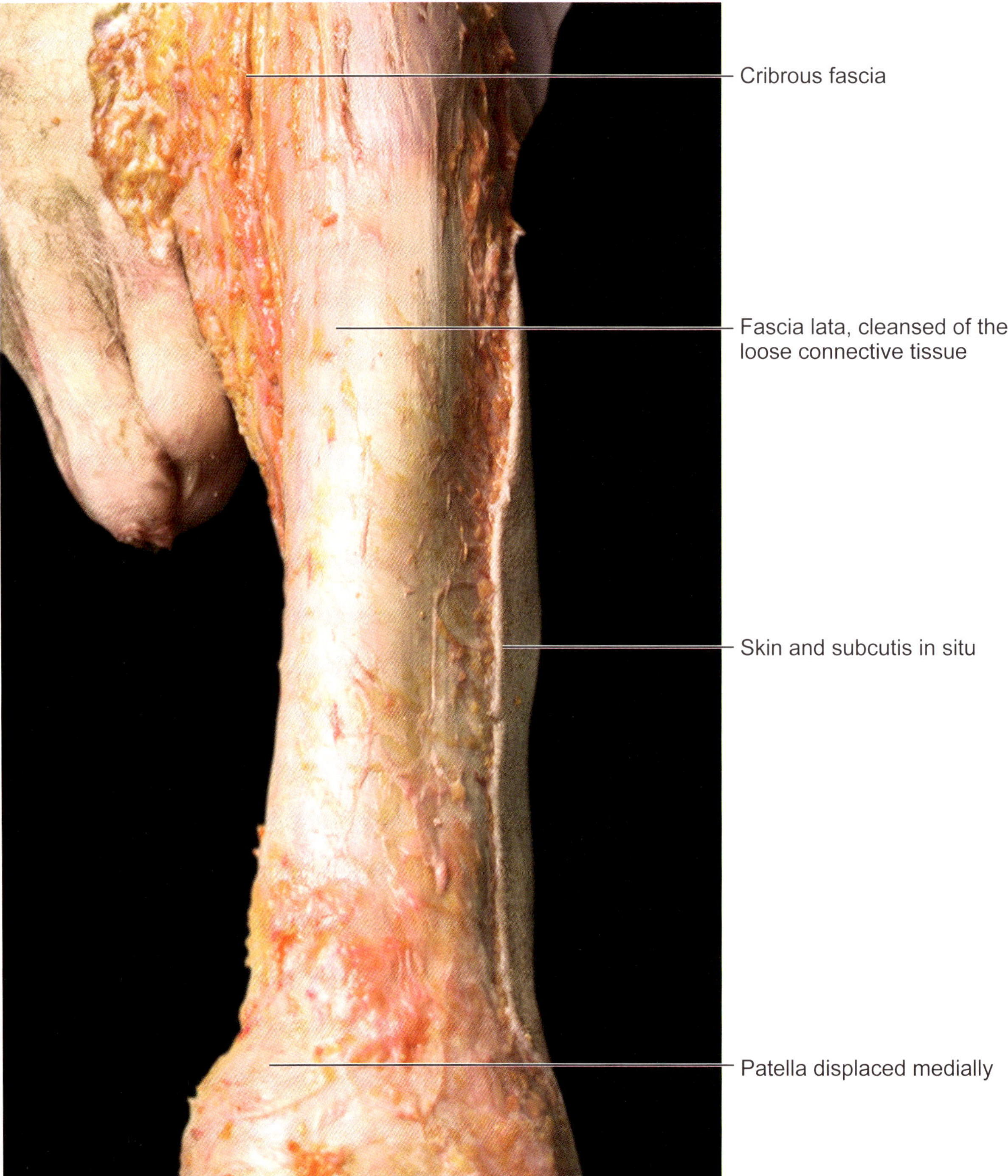

Fig. 4.12. Fascia lata of the anterior region of the thigh. The fascia lata is partially free to glide over the underlying musculature.

The lines indicate anatomical parts whilst numbers (1, 2) indicate the physiology of the fascia. Number one indicates a determined action and number two indicates its effect.

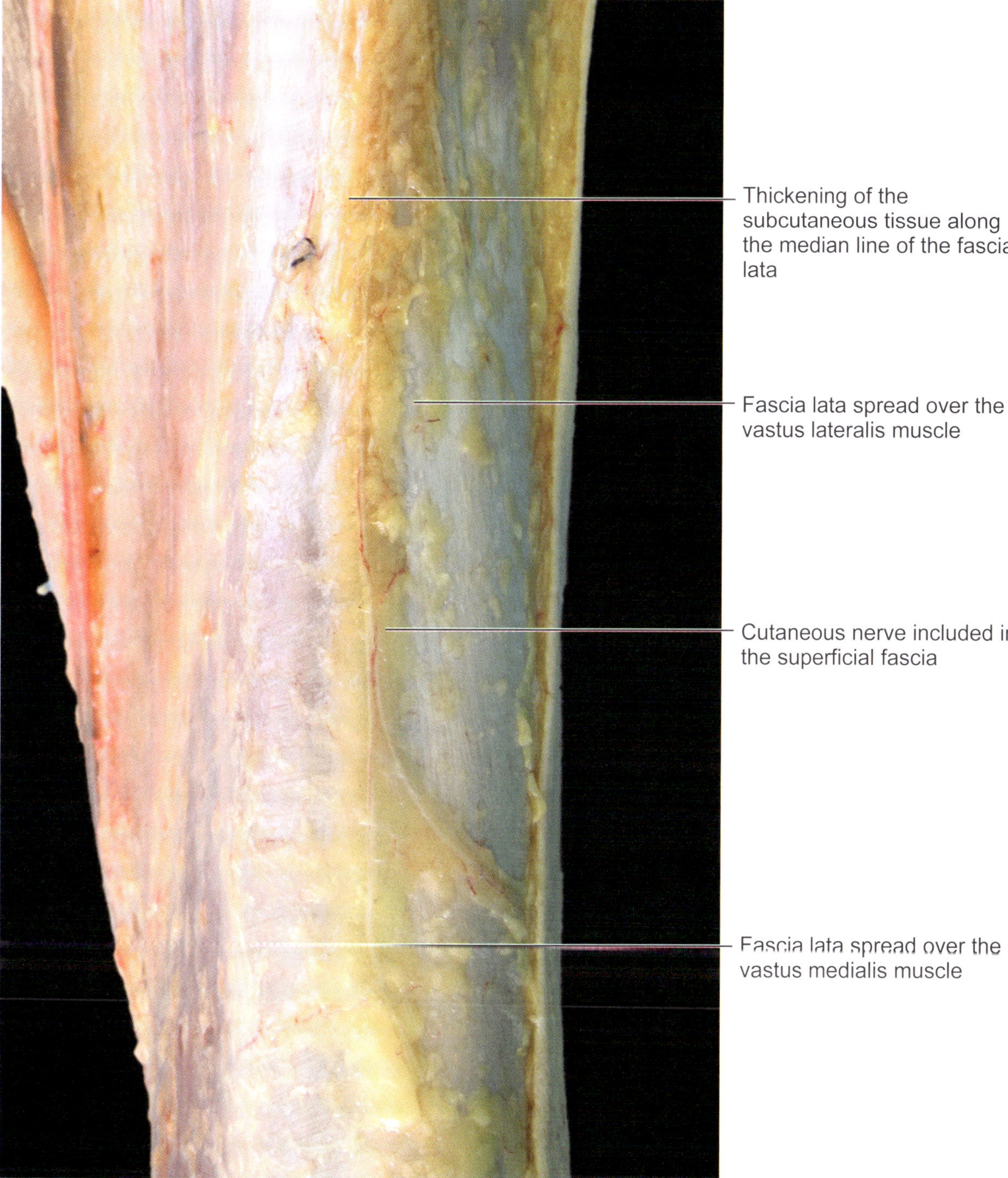

Fig. 4.13. Fascia lata of the proximal region of the knee. The fascia lata included between the medial and lateral septa reunites the four heads of the quadriceps muscle to coordinate their intervention during antepulsion.

FASCIAE OF THE ANTEPULSION SEQUENCE IN THE LOWER LIMB

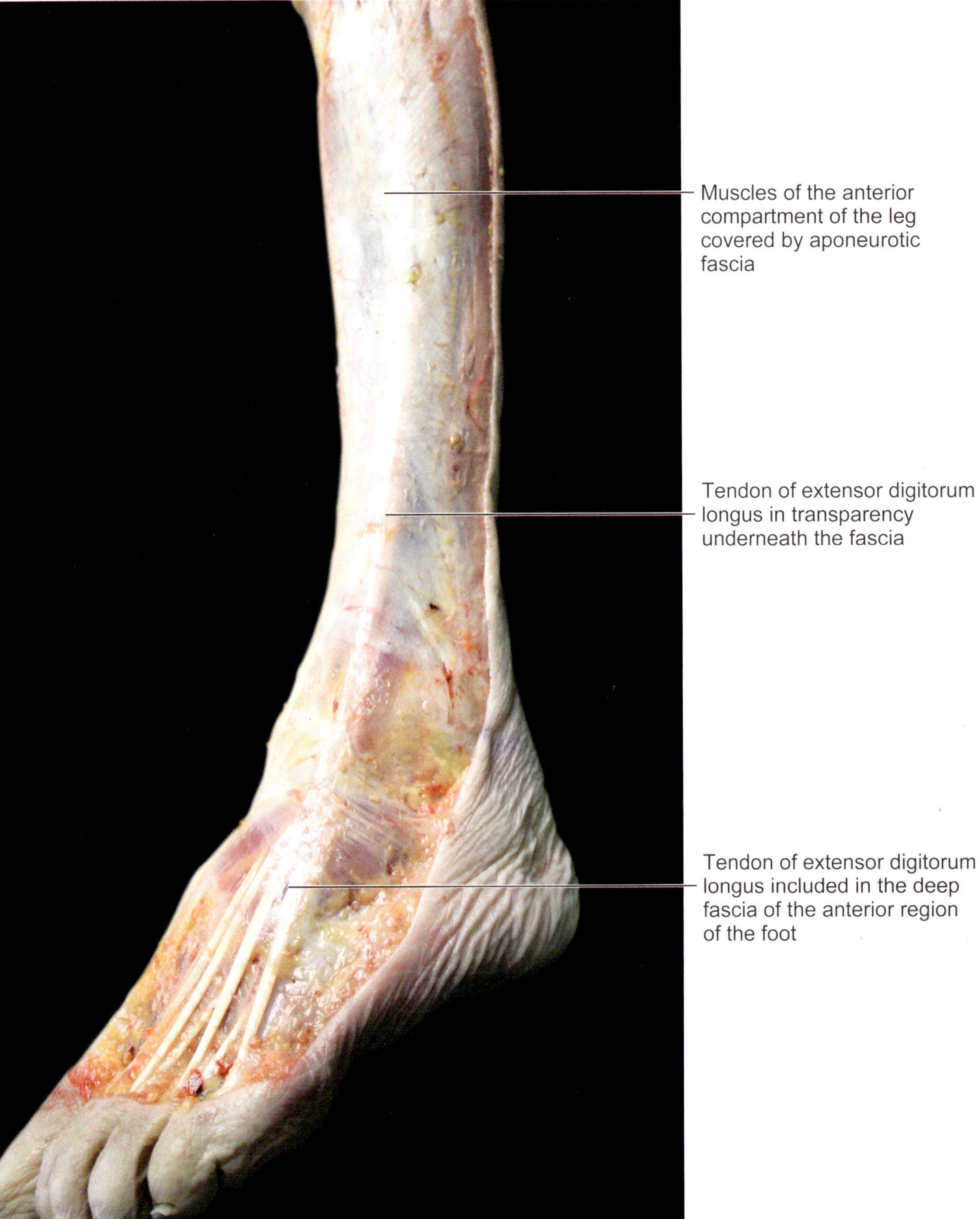

Fig. 4.14. Aponeurotic fascia of the anterior leg and foot regions. The fascia of the leg continues seamlessly with the fascia of the anterior region of the foot.

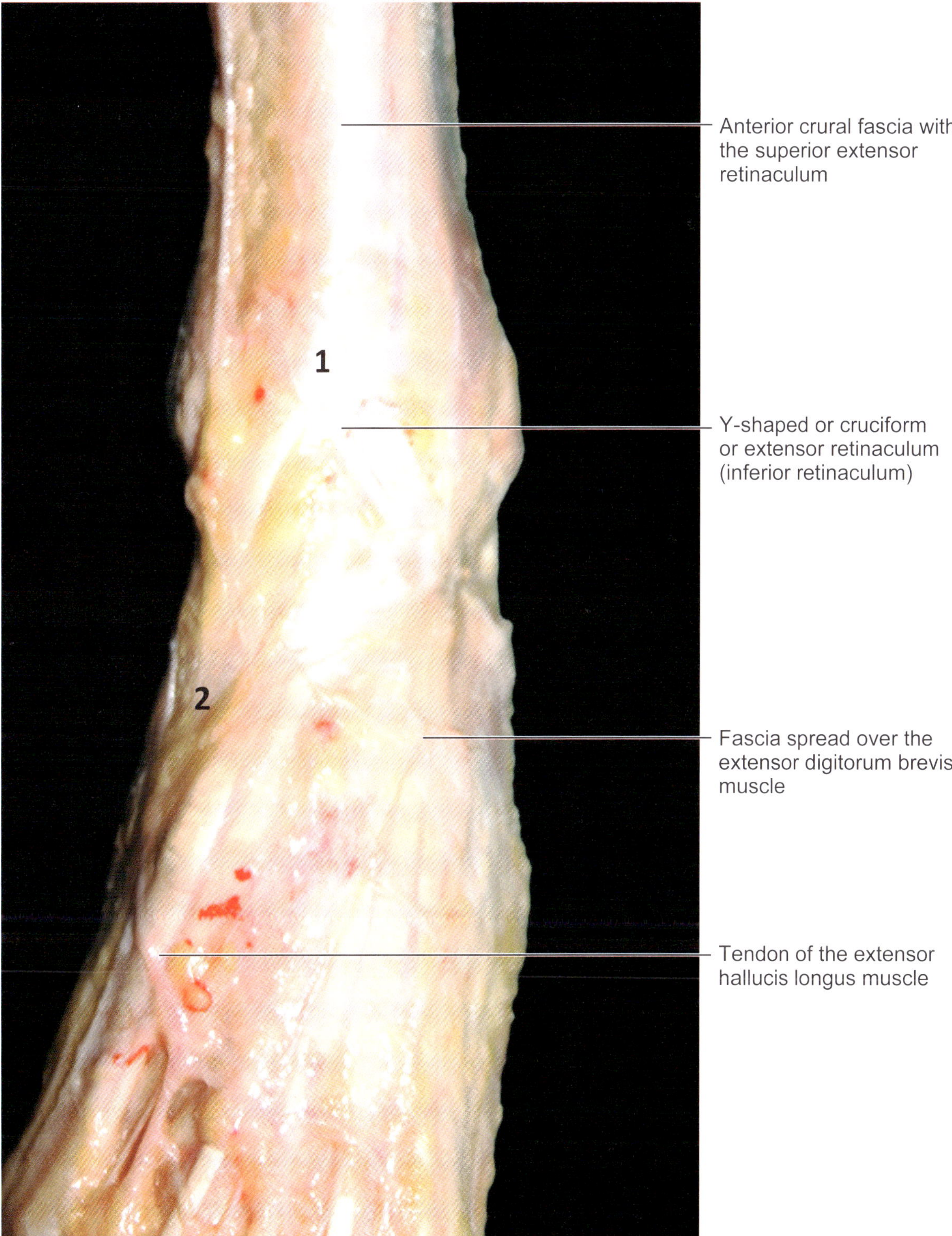

Fig. 4.15. Deep fascia of the dorsum of the foot, superficial lamina. The hypodermis was cut, the cruciform retinaculum (1) becomes visible, it continues inferiorly with other spiral collagen fibres (2).

POSTERIOR REGION OF THE LOWER LIMB, RETROPULSION SEQUENCE

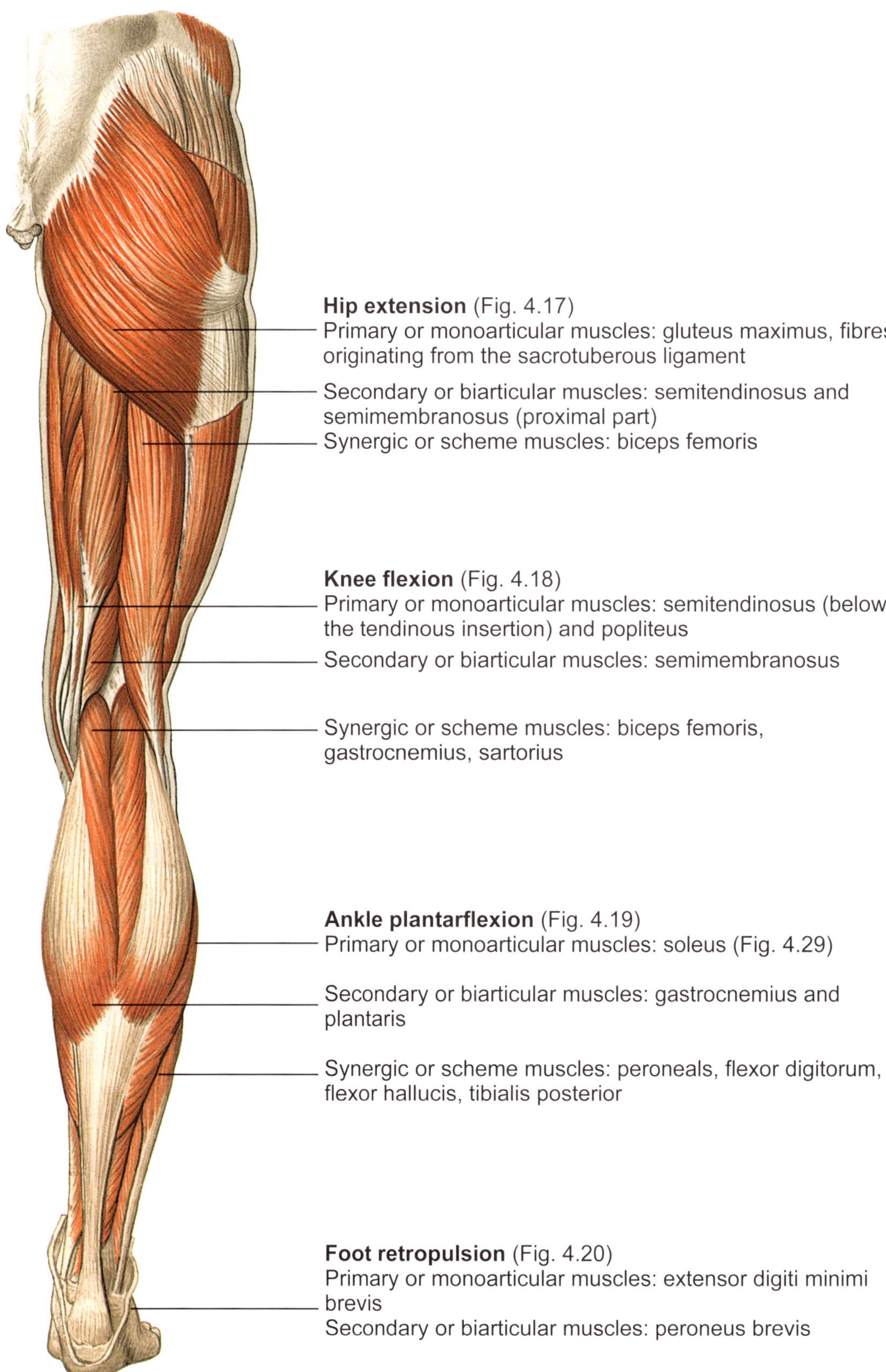

Fig. 4.16. Posterior region of the lower limb.
(From G. Chiarugi and L. Bucciante, Istituzioni di anatomia dell'uomo. Piccin Nuova Libraria, Padova 1983, modified)

SEGMENTARY MOVEMENTS IMPLEMENTED BY THE MF UNITS OF RETROPULSION

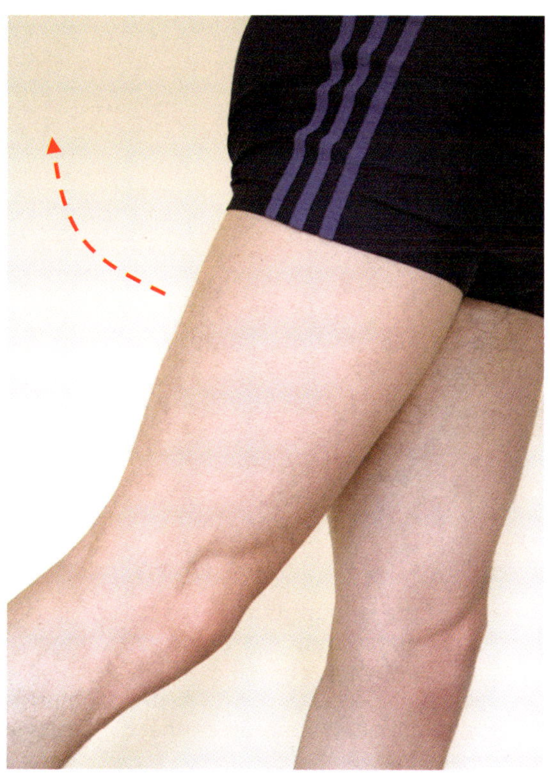

Fig. 4.17. Hip extension managed throughout its range by the myofascial unit of retro-coxa.

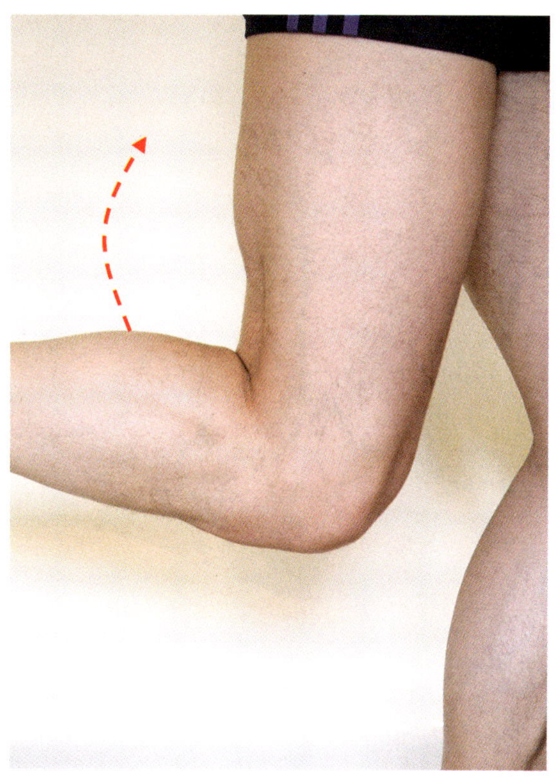

Fig. 4.18. Knee flexion managed throughout its joint range by the MF unit of retro-genu.

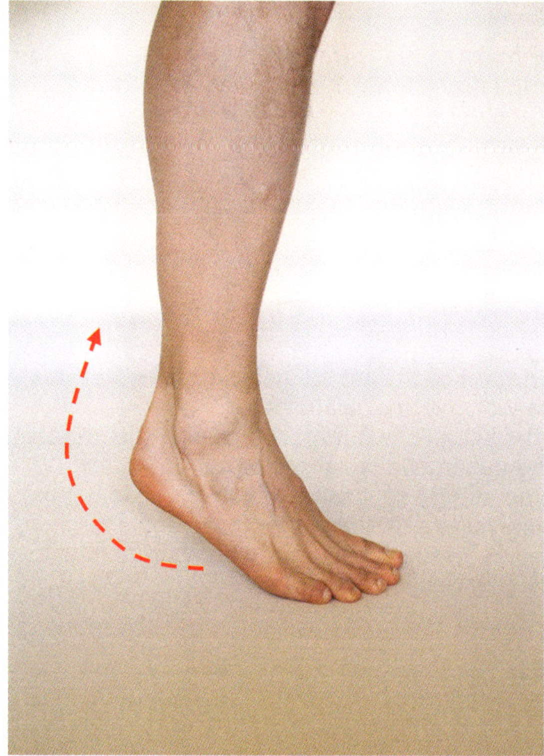

Fig. 4.19. Ankle plantarflexion managed throughout its joint range by the MF unit of retro-talus.

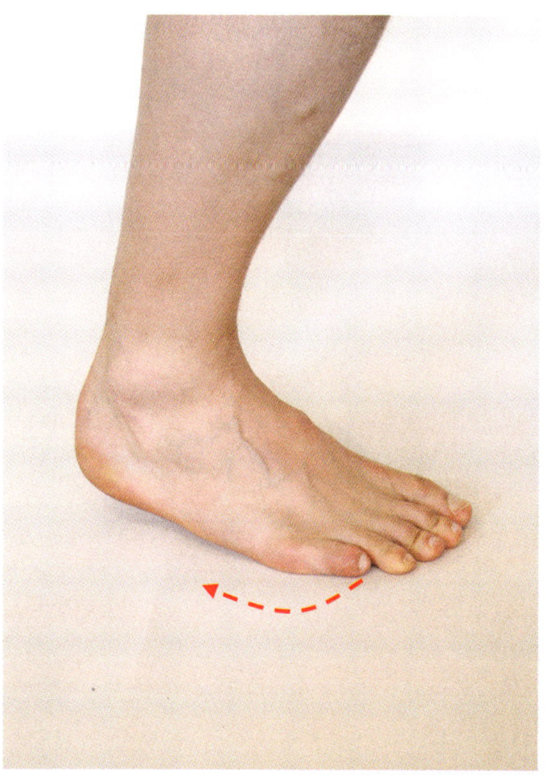

Fig. 4.20. Plantar push of the forefoot managed throughout its joint range by the MF unit of retro-pes.

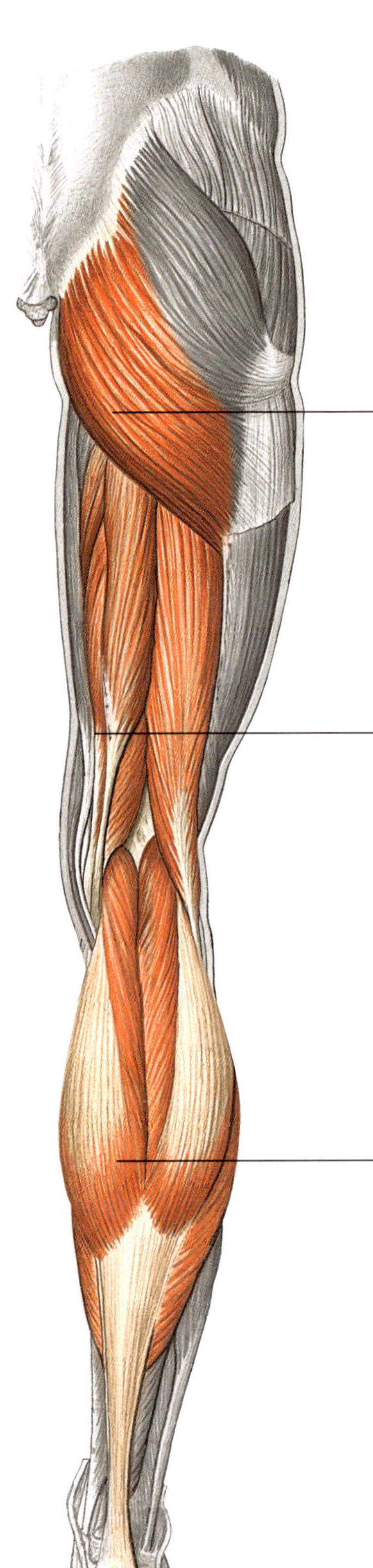

Fig. 4.21. Fascial compartments for retropulsion muscles.
(From G. Chiarugi and L. Bucciante, Istituzioni di anatomia dell'uomo. Piccin Nuova Libraria, Padova 1983, modified)

COMPARTMENTS FOR THE MUSCLES OF RETROPULSION, LOWER LIMB (Fig. 4.22)

Fascial compartment of the retropulsion muscles of coxa
The fascia of the gluteus maximus muscle, like that of the deltoid muscle, sends numerous septa between the muscle fibres. These form the following bundles: proximal muscle fibres (lateropulsion motor units), superficial fibres in continuity with the thoracolumbar fascia (scheme unit), fibres in continuity with the fascia of the gluteus medius muscle (extrarotation motor units), and deep fibres inserted on the sacrotuberous ligament (retropulsion motor units).

Fascial compartment of the retropulsion muscles of genu
The posterior fascia lata, spread from the lateral to the medial intermuscular septa, forms a compartment in which the hamstring muscles are found. The fascia lata partly courses over these muscles and partly connects through connective septa to the motor units of knee retropulsion.

Fascial compartment of the retropulsion muscles of talus
The posterior crural fascia forms a compartment (Fig. 4.27) inside which the motor units responsible for talus retropulsion are included. As with all fascial compartments, some muscle fibres originate from the overlying fascia and others are free to glide underneath it in order for tractions to converge towards the vectorial centre.

Fascial compartment of the retropulsion muscles of pes
In the sole of the foot, the muscular fascia forms three compartments: the lateral compartment including the muscles for the fifth toe (abductor and flexor brevis muscles); the intermediate compartment containing the flexor digitorum brevis muscle; the medial compartment wrapping the abductor and flexor hallucis brevis muscles. Deeply the compartment of the plantar interossei muscles is found.

GLOBAL MOVEMENT IMPLEMENTED BY THE RETROPULSION MF SEQUENCE

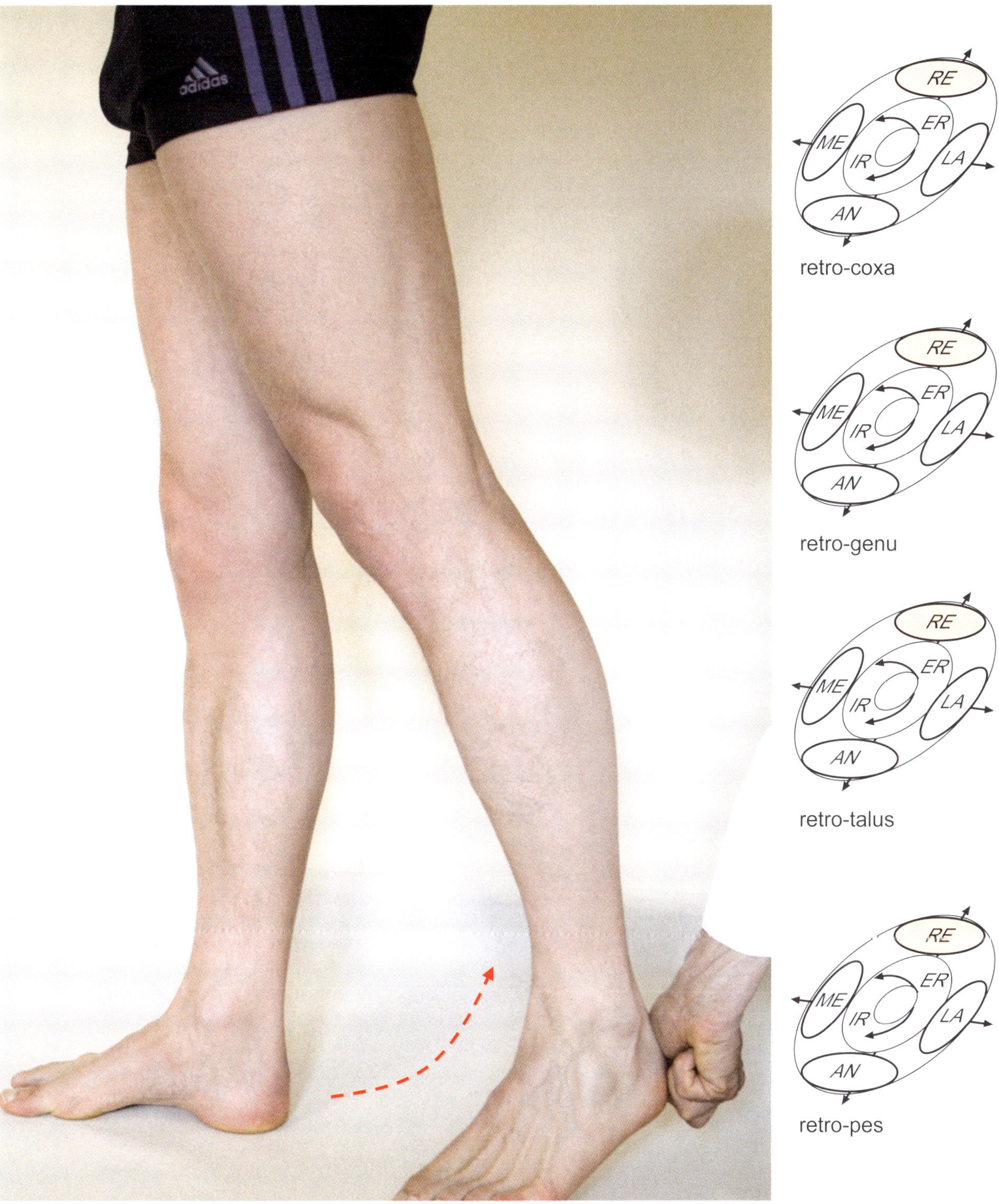

Fig. 4.22. Contraction of the retropulsion sequence bringing the entire lower limb posteriorly.

When the brain programmes for backwards lower limb movement, the ipsidirectional motor units included in the fascial compartments of the posterior region of the limb are then activated.
The contraction of the retropulsion motor units included in the posterior fascial compartments determines the stretch of the overlying fascia and the activation of proprioceptors embedded in it. Hence, mapped afferents reach the brain according to a specific motor direction.

PHYSIOLOGY OF THE RETROPULSION MF UNITS, LOWER LIMB

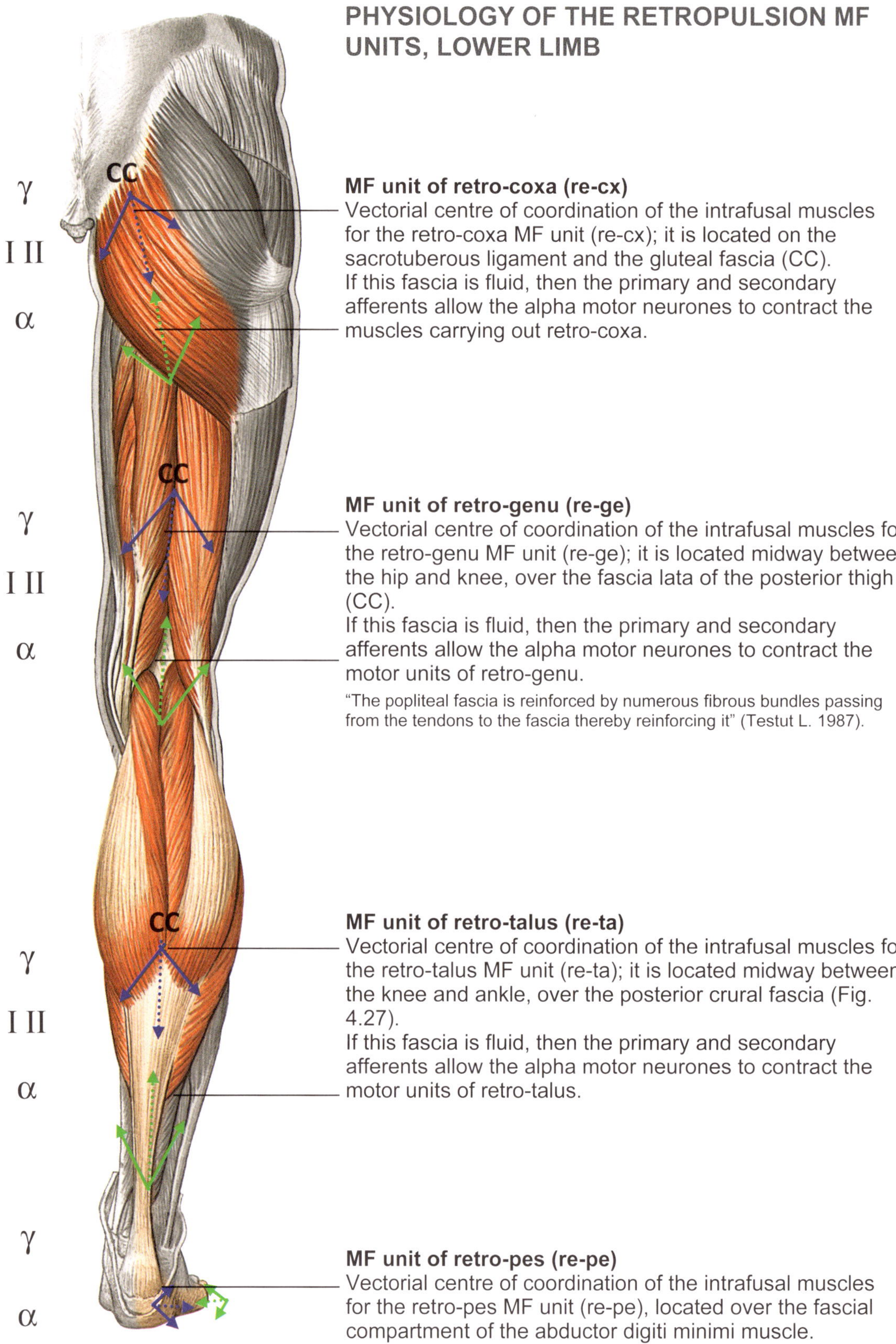

MF unit of retro-coxa (re-cx)
Vectorial centre of coordination of the intrafusal muscles for the retro-coxa MF unit (re-cx); it is located on the sacrotuberous ligament and the gluteal fascia (CC).
If this fascia is fluid, then the primary and secondary afferents allow the alpha motor neurones to contract the muscles carrying out retro-coxa.

MF unit of retro-genu (re-ge)
Vectorial centre of coordination of the intrafusal muscles for the retro-genu MF unit (re-ge); it is located midway between the hip and knee, over the fascia lata of the posterior thigh (CC).
If this fascia is fluid, then the primary and secondary afferents allow the alpha motor neurones to contract the motor units of retro-genu.

"The popliteal fascia is reinforced by numerous fibrous bundles passing from the tendons to the fascia thereby reinforcing it" (Testut L. 1987).

MF unit of retro-talus (re-ta)
Vectorial centre of coordination of the intrafusal muscles for the retro-talus MF unit (re-ta); it is located midway between the knee and ankle, over the posterior crural fascia (Fig. 4.27).
If this fascia is fluid, then the primary and secondary afferents allow the alpha motor neurones to contract the motor units of retro-talus.

MF unit of retro-pes (re-pe)
Vectorial centre of coordination of the intrafusal muscles for the retro-pes MF unit (re-pe), located over the fascial compartment of the abductor digiti minimi muscle.

Fig. 4.23. Normal functioning of the gamma circuit.
(From G. Chiarugi and L. Bucciante, Istituzioni di anatomia dell'uomo. Piccin Nuova Libraria, Padova 1983, modified)

ARTICULAR CONFLICTS IN THE RETROPULSION UNITS, LOWER LIMB

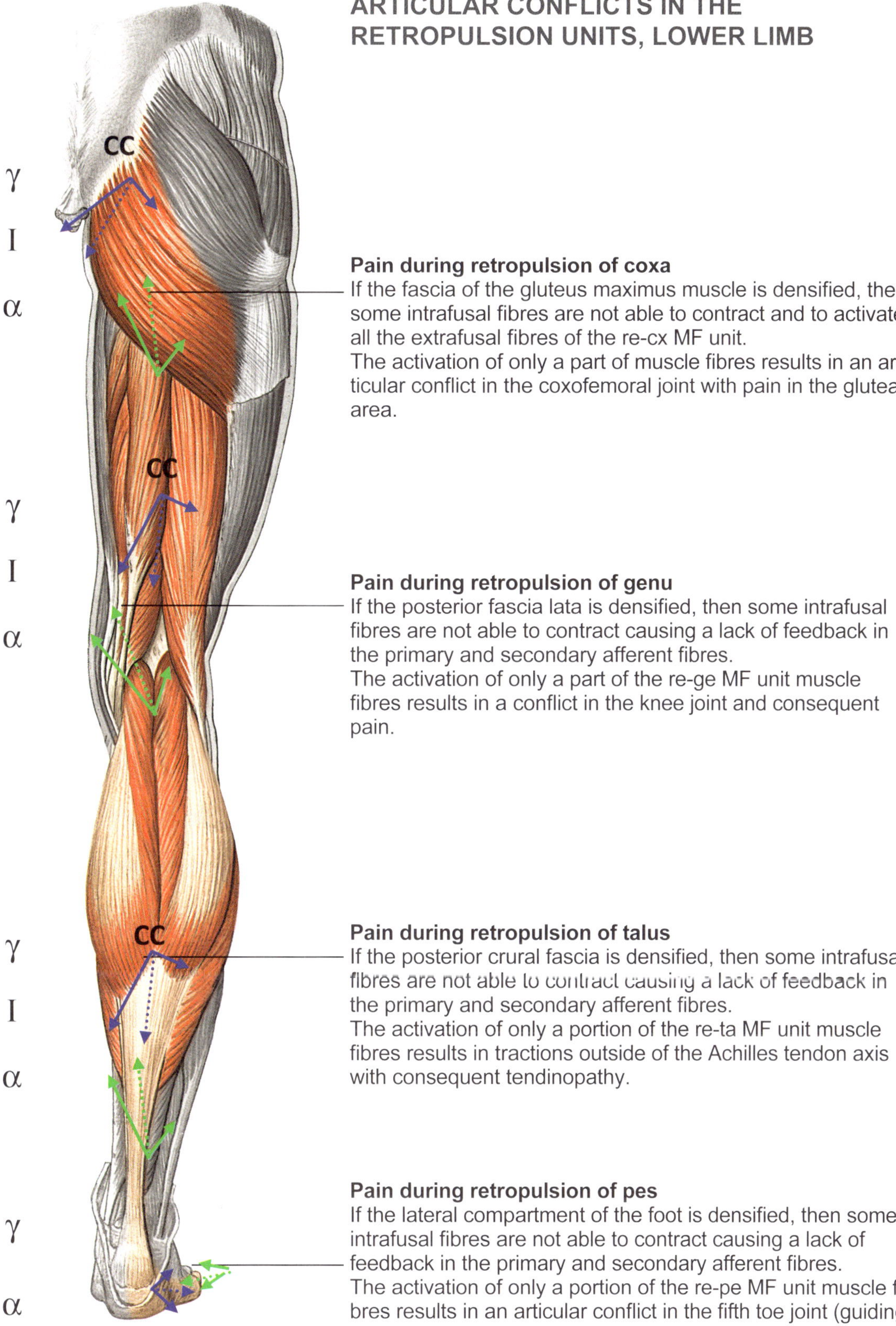

Pain during retropulsion of coxa
If the fascia of the gluteus maximus muscle is densified, then some intrafusal fibres are not able to contract and to activate all the extrafusal fibres of the re-cx MF unit.
The activation of only a part of muscle fibres results in an articular conflict in the coxofemoral joint with pain in the gluteal area.

Pain during retropulsion of genu
If the posterior fascia lata is densified, then some intrafusal fibres are not able to contract causing a lack of feedback in the primary and secondary afferent fibres.
The activation of only a part of the re-ge MF unit muscle fibres results in a conflict in the knee joint and consequent pain.

Pain during retropulsion of talus
If the posterior crural fascia is densified, then some intrafusal fibres are not able to contract causing a lack of feedback in the primary and secondary afferent fibres.
The activation of only a portion of the re-ta MF unit muscle fibres results in tractions outside of the Achilles tendon axis with consequent tendinopathy.

Pain during retropulsion of pes
If the lateral compartment of the foot is densified, then some intrafusal fibres are not able to contract causing a lack of feedback in the primary and secondary afferent fibres.
The activation of only a portion of the re-pe MF unit muscle fibres results in an articular conflict in the fifth toe joint (guiding toe for forefoot retropulsion).

Fig. 4.24. Dysfunction of the gamma circuit.
(From G. Chiarugi and L. Bucciante, Istituzioni di anatomia dell'uomo. Piccin Nuova Libraria, Padova 1983, modified)

RETROPULSION SEQUENCE AND STRETCH REFLEX

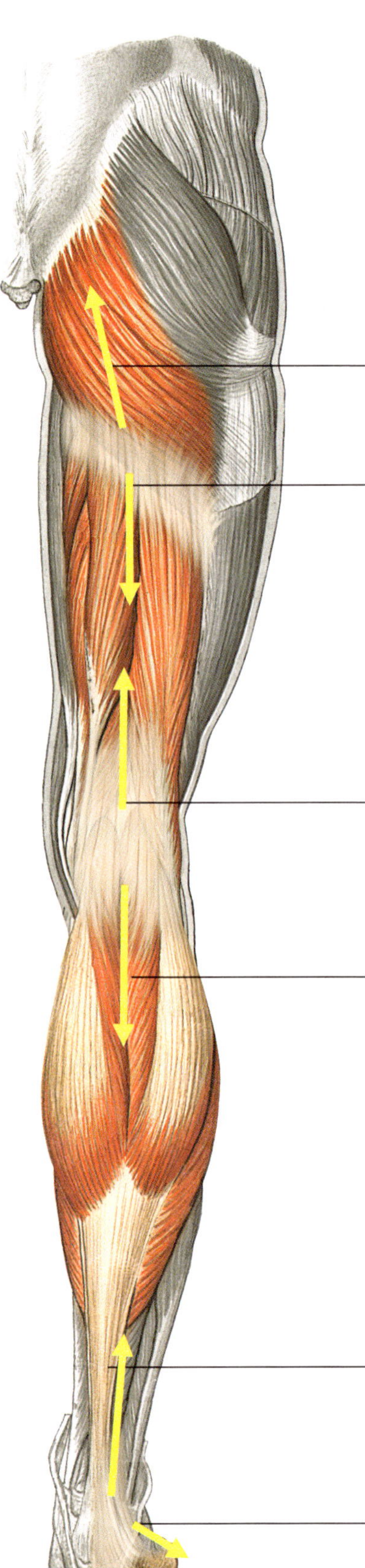

Synergy between the MF unit of retro-coxa and retro-genu

The gluteus maximus muscle, by inserting through its deep fibres on the sacrotuberous ligament and on the gluteal fold, determines a proximal traction on this fascia. The hamstring muscles originating from the ischium and sacrotuberous ligament determine a distal traction.

Synergy between the MF unit of retro-genu and retro-talus

The distal tendon of the semimembranosus muscle forms the deep pes anserinus. Indeed, it is subdivided into three parts: one expansion going to the medial condyle of the tibia, one going in the popliteal fascia and the third part irradiating into the joint capsule (oblique popliteal ligament). The contraction of this muscle tractions the popliteal fascia proximally whilst the gastrocnemius muscles through their insertions traction it distally.

"Some bundles of the gastrocnemius muscle arise directly from the popliteal plane and from the fibrous shell of the joint capsule; these may receive additional bundles from the biceps and semitendinosus muscles" (Chiarugi G. 1975).

Synergy between the MF unit of retro-talus and retro-pes

The peroneus brevis muscle proximally tractions the lateral compartment whilst the abductor digiti minimi muscle, through its fibres inserting on the above compartment, tractions it distally.

"Frequently an additional tendon may arise either from the musculature or from the tendon of peroneus brevis and inserts on the fifth toe or on the abductor digiti minimi muscle" (Chiarugi G. 1975).

Fig. 4.25. Synergy of the retropulsion sequence in the lower limb.

(From G. Chiarugi and L. Bucciante, Istituzioni di anatomia dell'uomo. Piccin Nuova Libraria, Padova 1983, modified)

ACTIVATION OF THE GOLGI TENDON ORGANS

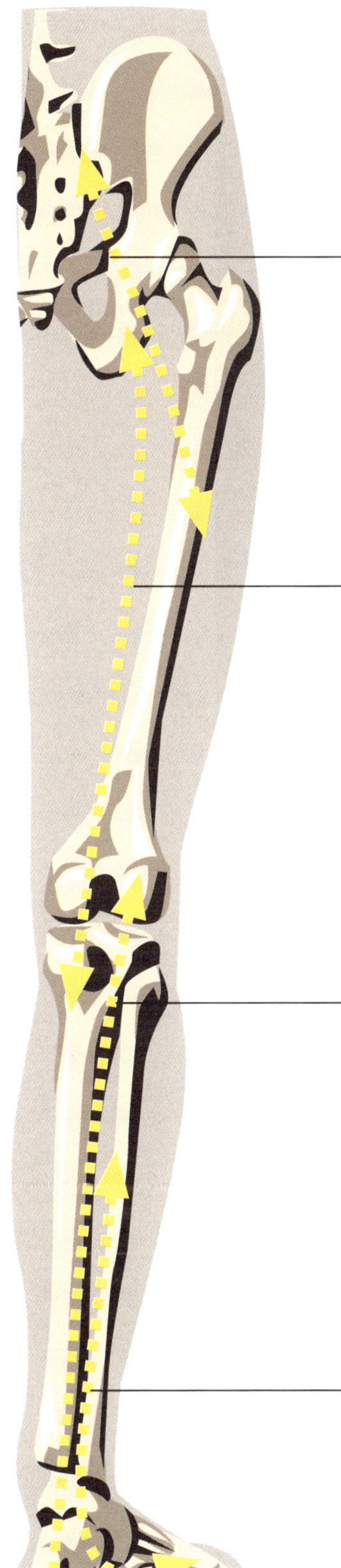

Fig. 4.26. Biarticular muscles for retropulsion sequence in the lower limb.

Connection between pelvis and coxa
The biarticular fibres of the gluteus maximus muscle manage the joint range of pelvis and coxa during their simultaneous movement of retropulsion. Pelvis and coxa form a functional unit since they are moved by the same muscle (gluteus maximus).

Connection between coxa and genu
The biarticular fibres of the semimembranosus, semitendinosus and biceps femoris muscles, through their Golgi tendon organs, manage the joint range of the hip and knee during their simultaneous movement in retropulsion.

Connection between genu and talus
The Golgi tendon organs of both gastrocnemius muscles manage the joint range of the knee and ankle during their simultaneous movement in retropulsion.
The triceps surae muscle is formed by both gastrocnemius and soleus muscles; the latter is monoarticular and hence develops force specifically for the talus whilst the gastrocnemii, being biarticular, synchronise ankle movements with those of the knee.

Connection between talus and pes
Biarticular fibres of the peroneus brevis muscle which Golgi tendon organs manage the joint range of the ankle and foot during their simultaneous movement in retropulsion. The fascia of the gastrocnemius muscles has its continuity into the retinaculum of the peroneal muscles and in the lateral compartment of the foot; whilst the flexor digitorum muscles included in the deep fascia of the leg (Fig. 4.30) carry out a scheme of retro-medio.

FASCIAE OF THE RETROPULSION SEQUENCE IN THE LOWER LIMB

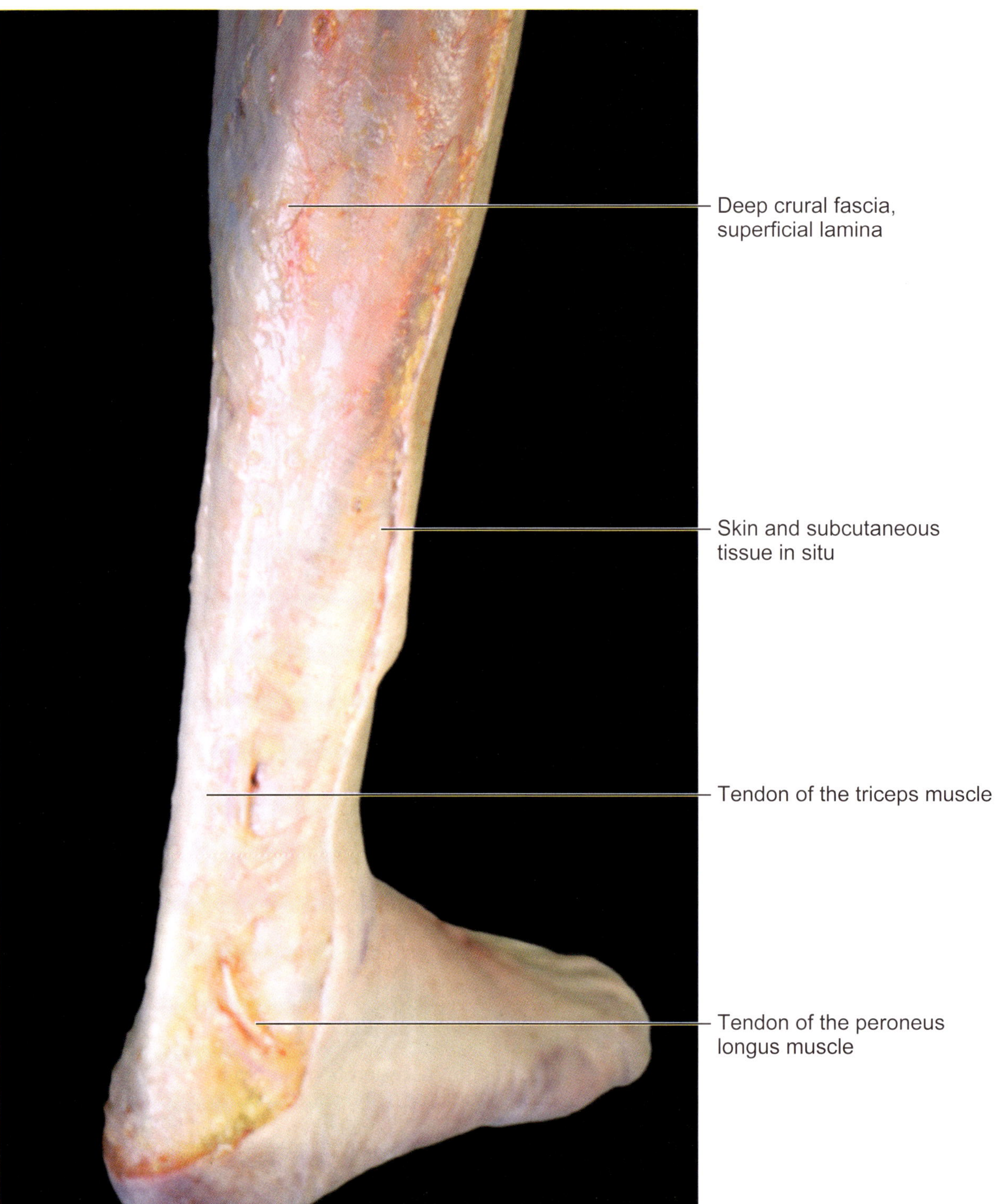

Fig. 4.27. Aponeurotic fascia of the posterior region of the leg, cleansed of loose connective tissue and superficial fascia.

In this sequence it was not deemed opportune to show specific images for the four segments of the lower limb, but rather to highlight the various layers of the deep fascia of the posterior leg.

FASCIAE OF THE RETROPULSION SEQUENCE IN THE LOWER LIMB

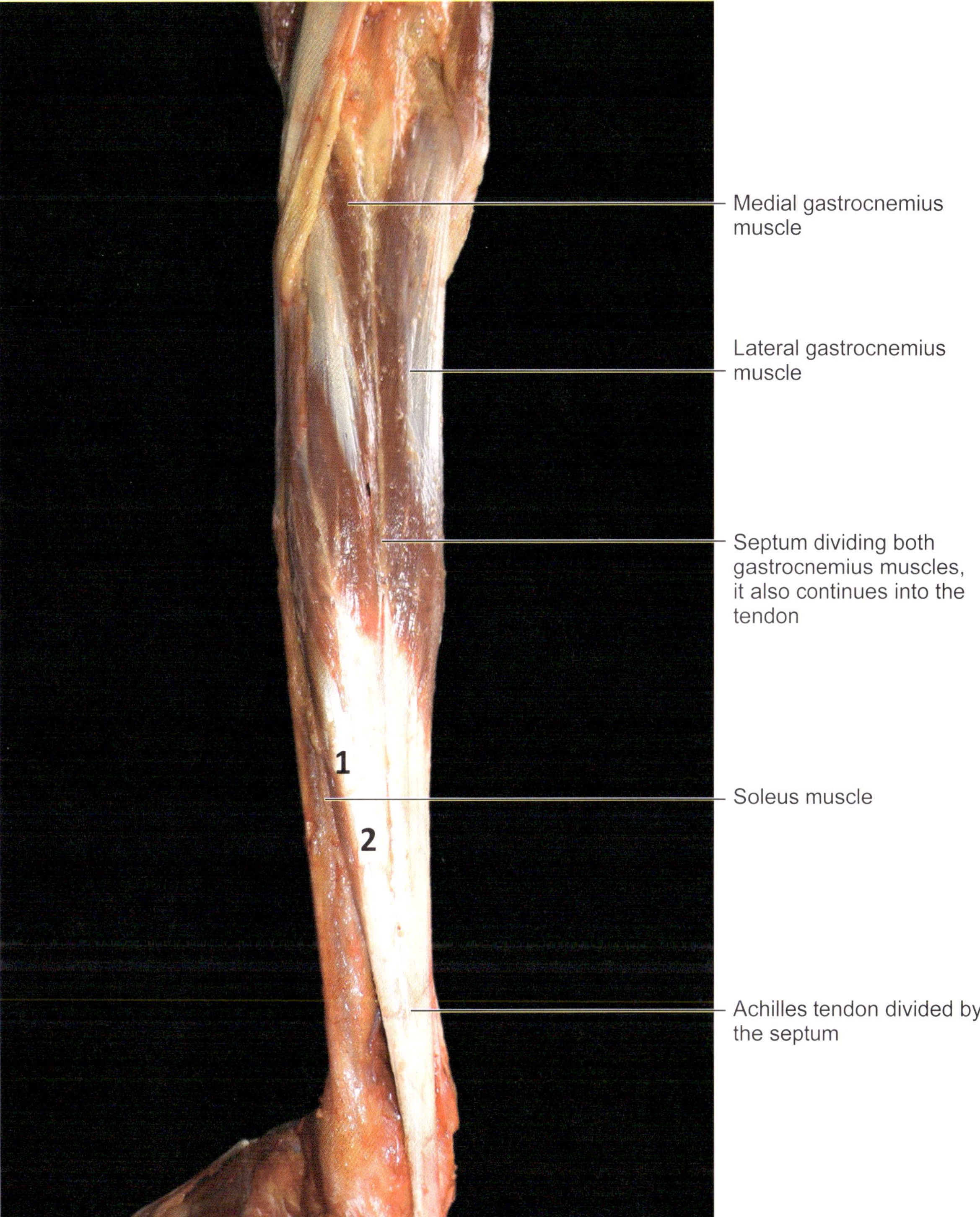

Fig. 4.28. Epimysial fascia of the posterior region of the leg. It becomes visible after cutting and removing the aponeurotic fascia; note how the soleus muscle (1) unites very distally with the Achilles tendon (2).

FASCIAE OF THE RETROPULSION SEQUENCE IN THE LOWER LIMB

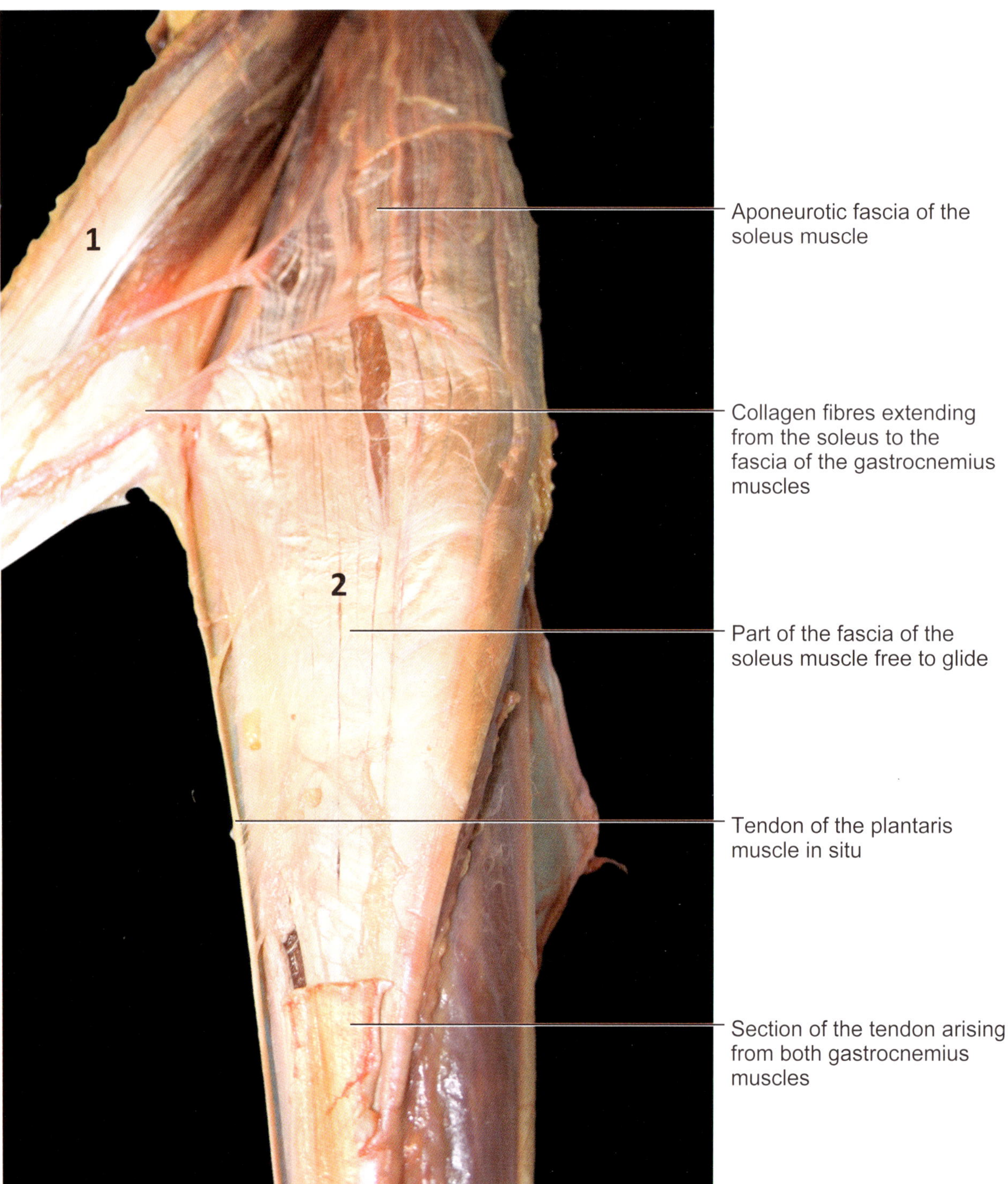

Fig. 4.29. Aponeurotic fascia covering the soleus muscle. Both distal tendons of the gastrocnemius muscles were cut and lifted laterally (1), the muscle belly of the soleus becomes visible, it is covered by its aponeurotic fascia (2).

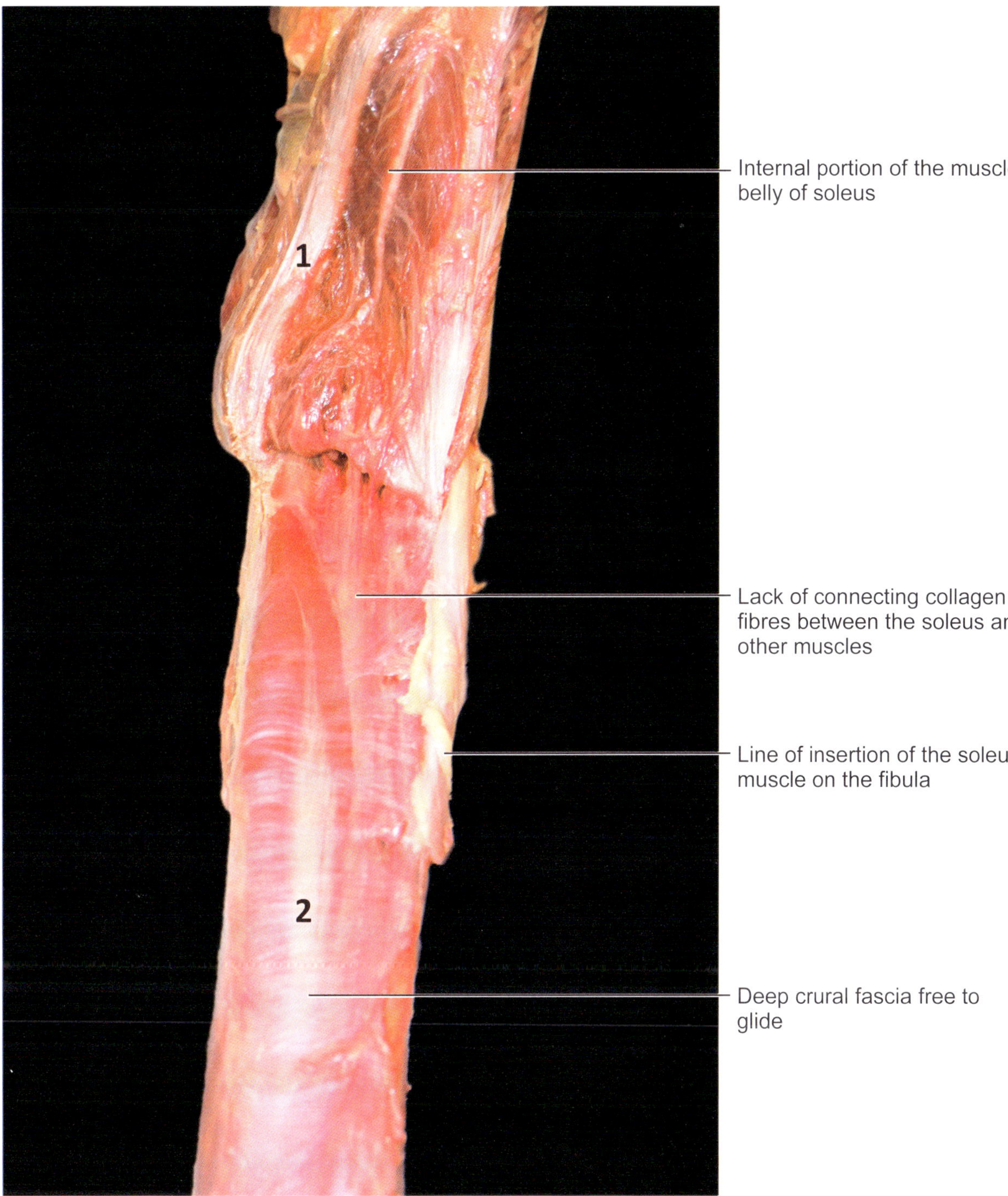

Fig. 4.30. Deep fascia of the leg, deep lamina. The triceps tendon was cut and the soleus muscle (1) was lifted superiorly, the fascial lamina of the deep muscles of the posterior leg is highlighted, it is rich in oblique collagen fibres (2).

MEDIAL REGION OF THE LOWER LIMB, MEDIOPULSION SEQUENCE

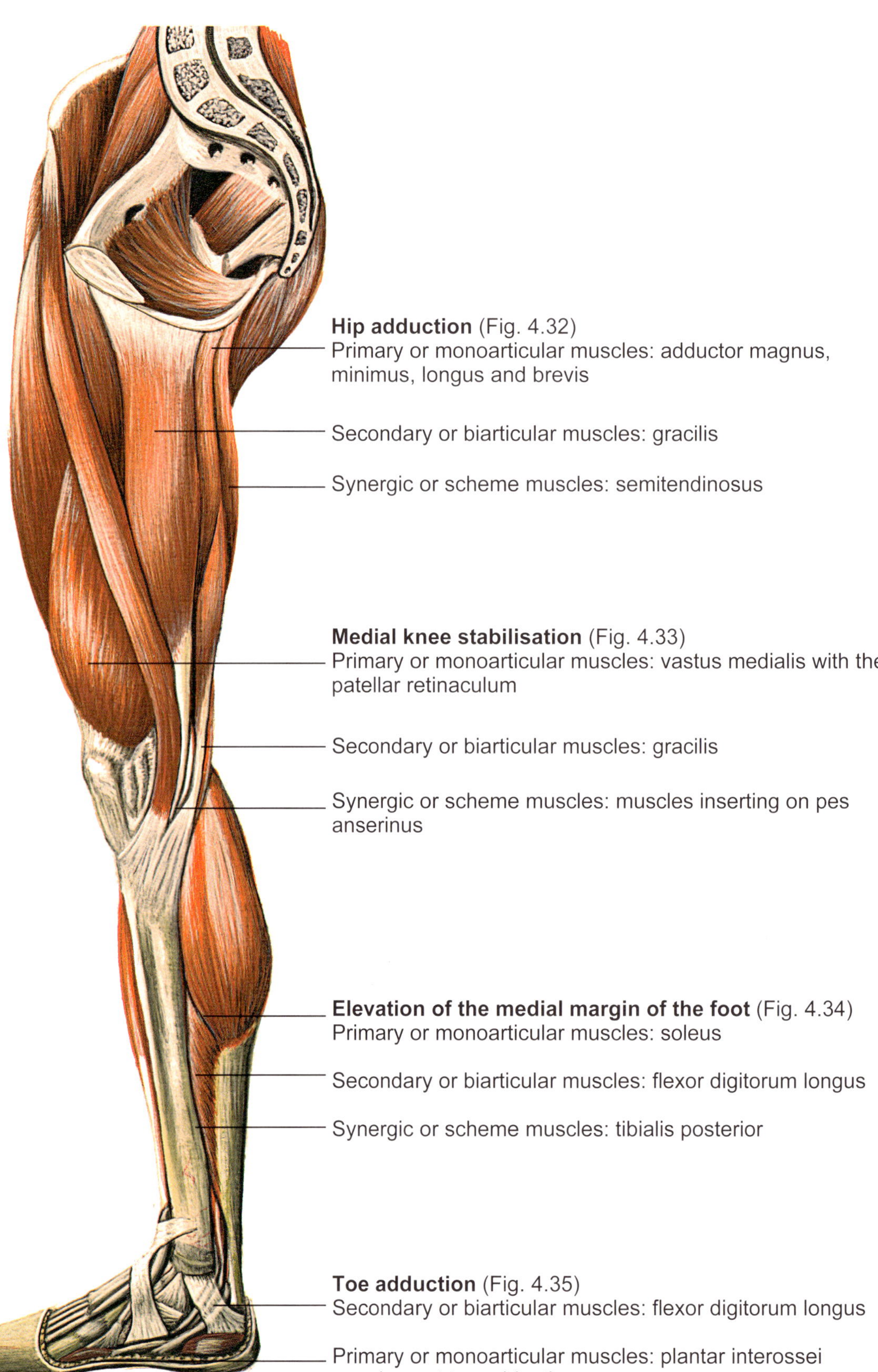

Fig. 4.31. Medial region of the lower limb.

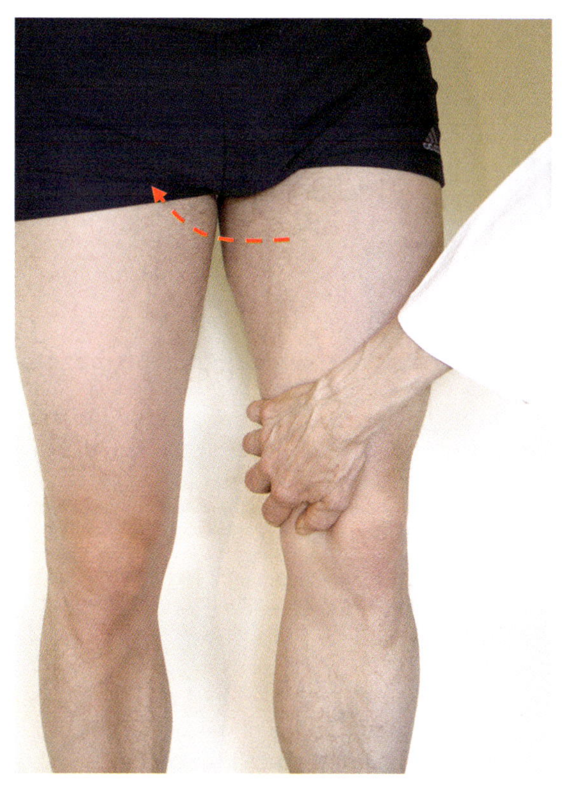

Fig. 4.32. Thigh adduction highlighted by the resistance applied against the myofascial unit of medio-coxa.

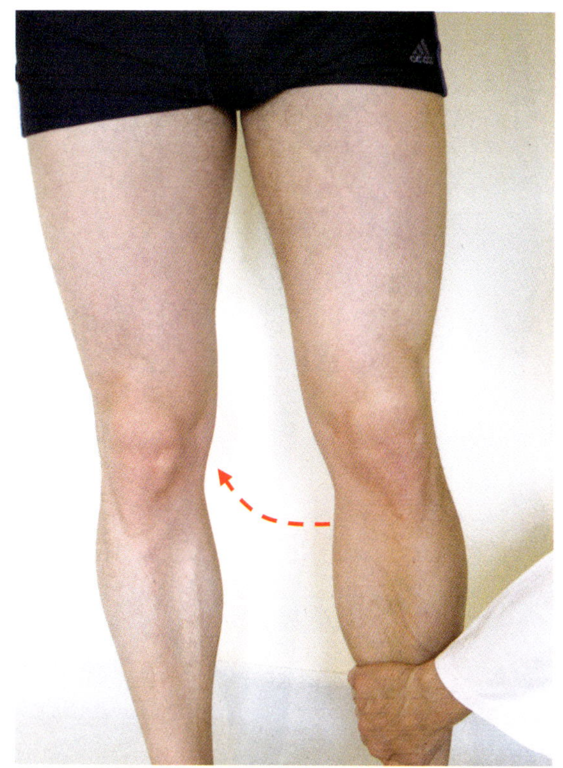

Fig. 4.33. Medial knee stabilisation highlighted by the resistance applied against the myofascial unit of medio-genu.

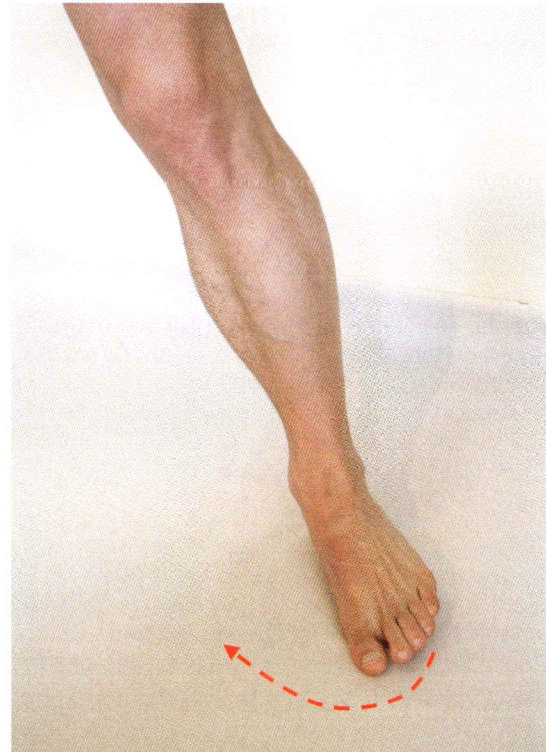

Fig. 4.34. Medial ankle stabilisation highlighted by the push against the floor managed by the myofascial unit of medio-talus.

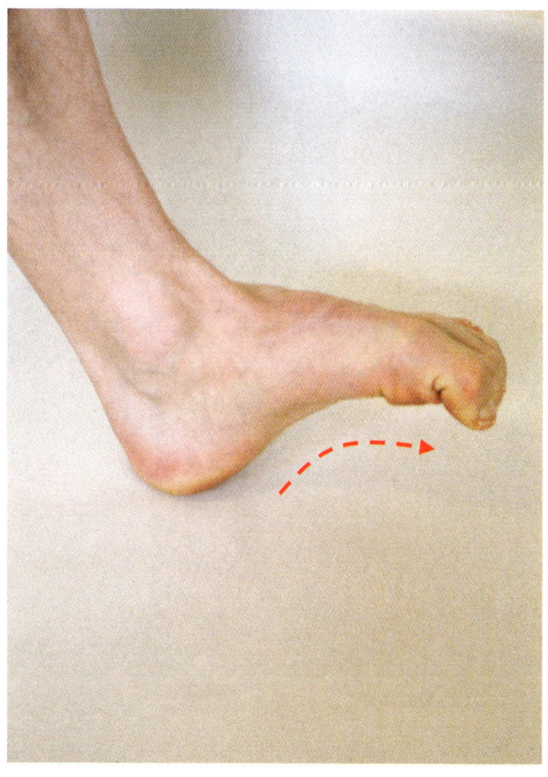

Fig. 4.35. Contraction of the adductor muscles of the foot managed by the myofascial unit of medio-pes.

COMPARTMENTS FOR THE MUSCLES OF MEDIOPULSION, LOWER LIMB (Fig. 4.37)

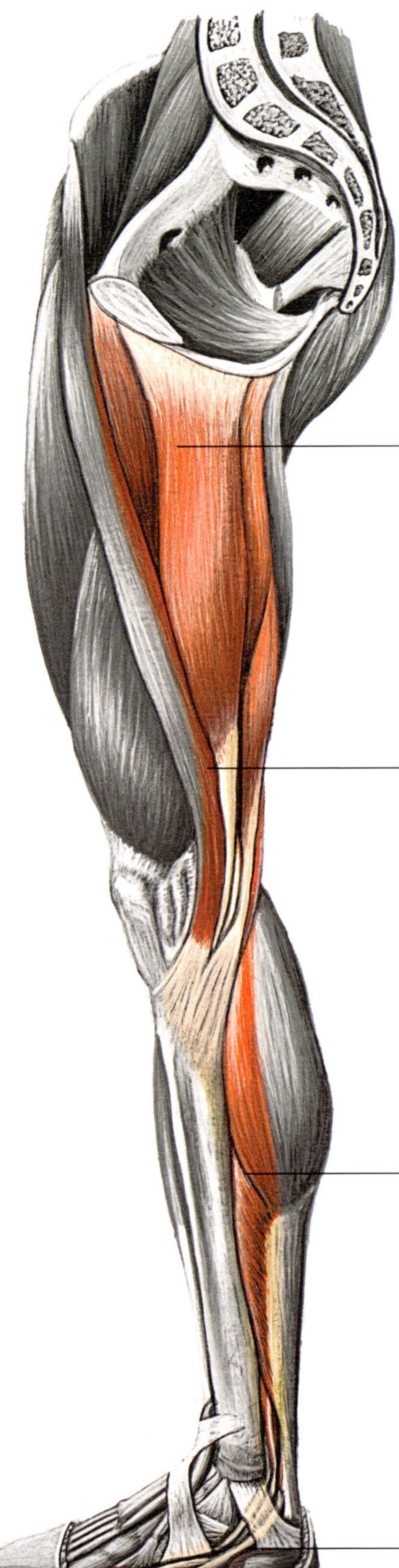

Fig. 4.36. Fascial compartments for mediopulsion muscles.

Fascial compartment for the mediopulsion muscles of coxa

The medial fascia lata forms a compartment for the adductor muscles.

"Connective laminae detach from the fascia lata and merge between the various muscle groups. The most robust laminae merge behind the vastus medialis and lateralis muscles and anchor on the linea aspera. Both these septa delineate two major compartments, an anterior and a posterior one. In the posterior compartment a secondary septum separates the medial muscles from the posterior ones" (Chiarugi G. 1975).

Fascial structures for knee stabilisation

The tendons converging into pes anserinus stabilise the medial knee.

"Pes anserinus is composed of two planes: the superficial plane, represented by the tendon of the sartorius muscle, is widely spread and fused with the fascia to which it sends numerous reinforcing fibres. The deep plane is formed by the tendons of the gracilis and semitendinosus muscles joined together by an aponeurotic lamina arising from the quadriceps expansion that extends to the medial collateral ligament" (Testut L. 1987).

Intermuscular septum for the mediopulsion muscles of talus

The fascia of the leg sends septa forming three compartments: anterior, lateral and posterior compartments. The latter, in the distal portion of the leg, is formed by three layers; a superficial one for the gastrocnemius muscle, a medial one for the soleus muscle and a deep one for the flexor and adductor muscles of the ankle and foot.

Fascia for the mediopulsion muscles of pes

The laciniate ligament or flexor retinaculum is divided into two sheets: the superficial one is the continuity of the superficial lamina of the leg whilst the deep one is the continuity of the deep lamina of the posterior crural fascia.

GLOBAL MOVEMENT IMPLEMENTED BY THE MEDIOPULSION MF SEQUENCE

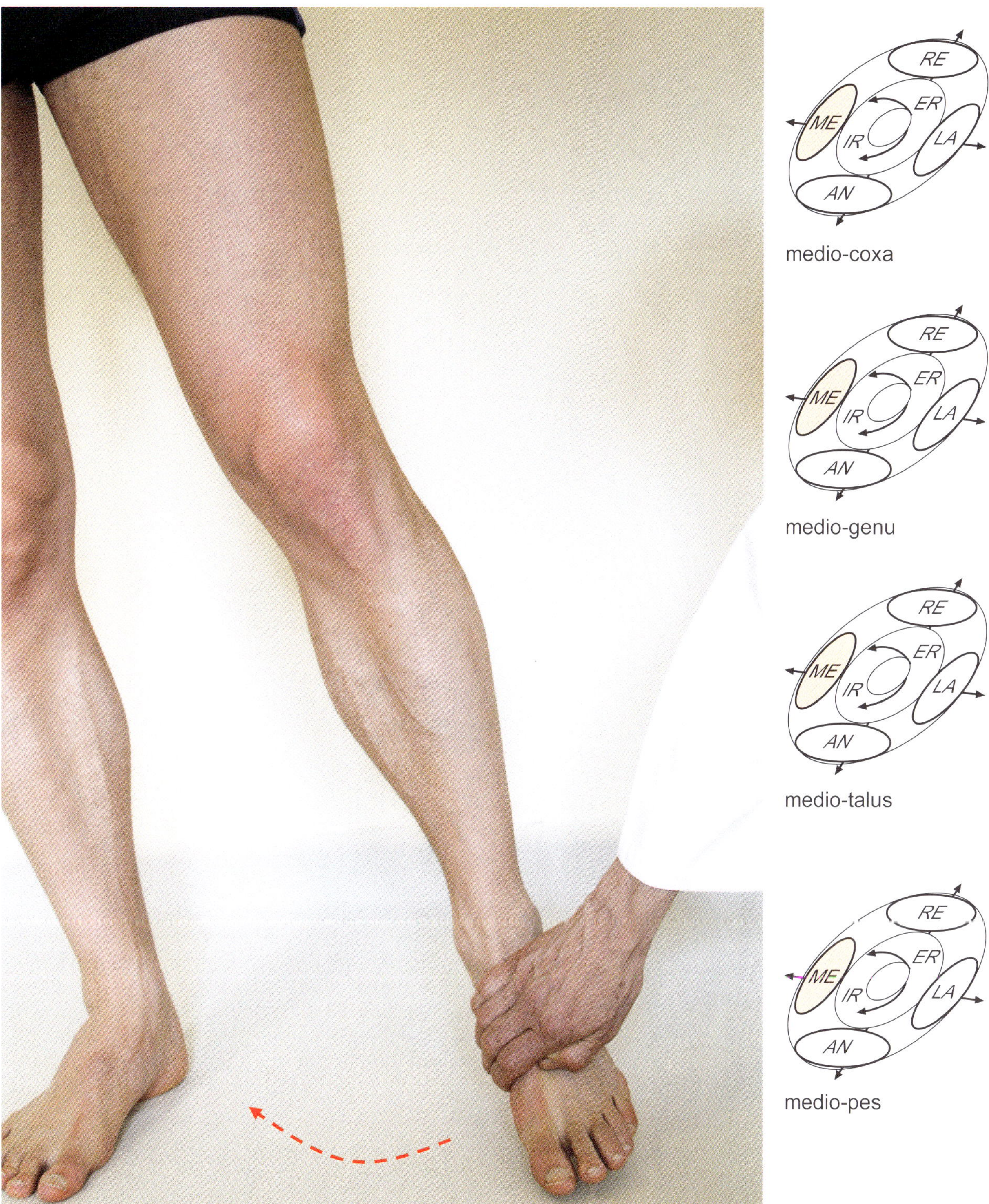

Fig. 4.37. Contraction of the mediopulsion sequence bringing the entire lower limb medially.

When the brain programmes for lower limbs movements towards the midline, the ipsidirectional motor units included in the fascial compartments of the medial region of the limb are then activated.
The contraction against resistance of the mediopulsion motor units included in the medial fascial compartments determines the stretch of the overlying fascia and the activation of proprioceptors embedded in it.
In this way the afferent feedback creates a directional mapping: mediopulsion.

PHYSIOLOGY OF THE MEDIOPULSION MF UNITS, LOWER LIMB

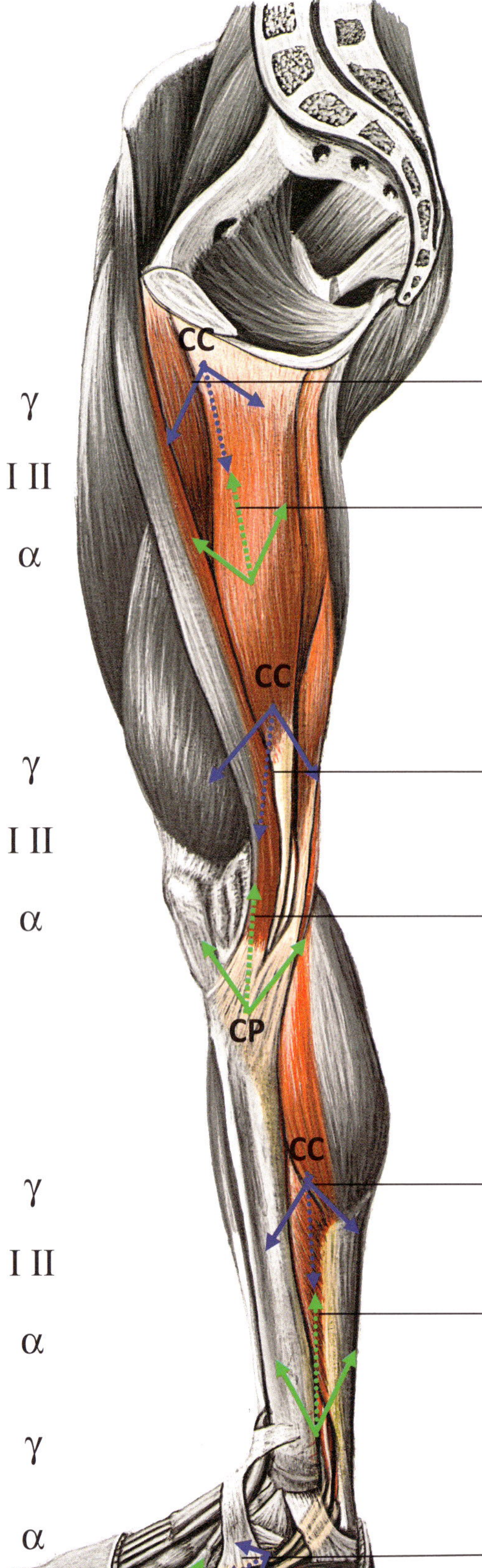

MF unit of medio-coxa (me-cx)
Vectorial centre of coordination of the intrafusal muscles for the medio-coxa MF unit (me-cx); it is located on the fascia containing the proximal gracilis and other adductor muscles (CC).
If this fascia is fluid, then the primary and secondary afferents allow the alpha motor neurones to contract the motor unit of medio-coxa.

MF unit of medio-genu (me-ge)
Vectorial centre of coordination of the intrafusal muscles for the medio-genu MF unit (me-ge); it is located in the distal third of the gracilis sheath (CC).
If this fascia is fluid, then the primary and secondary afferents allow the alpha motor neurones to contract the motor units of medio-genu.

MF unit of medio-talus (me-ta)
Vectorial centre of coordination of the intrafusal muscles for the medio-talus MF unit (me-ta); it is located in the leg, over the medial crural fascia (CC).
If this fascia is fluid, then the primary and secondary afferents allow the alpha motor neurones to contract the motor units of medio-talus.

MF unit of medio-pes (me-pe)
Vectorial centre of coordination of the intrafusal muscles for the medio-pes MF unit (me-pe); it is located in the proximal part of the longitudinal plantar arch (Fig. 4.45).

Fig. 4.38. Normal functioning of the gamma circuit.

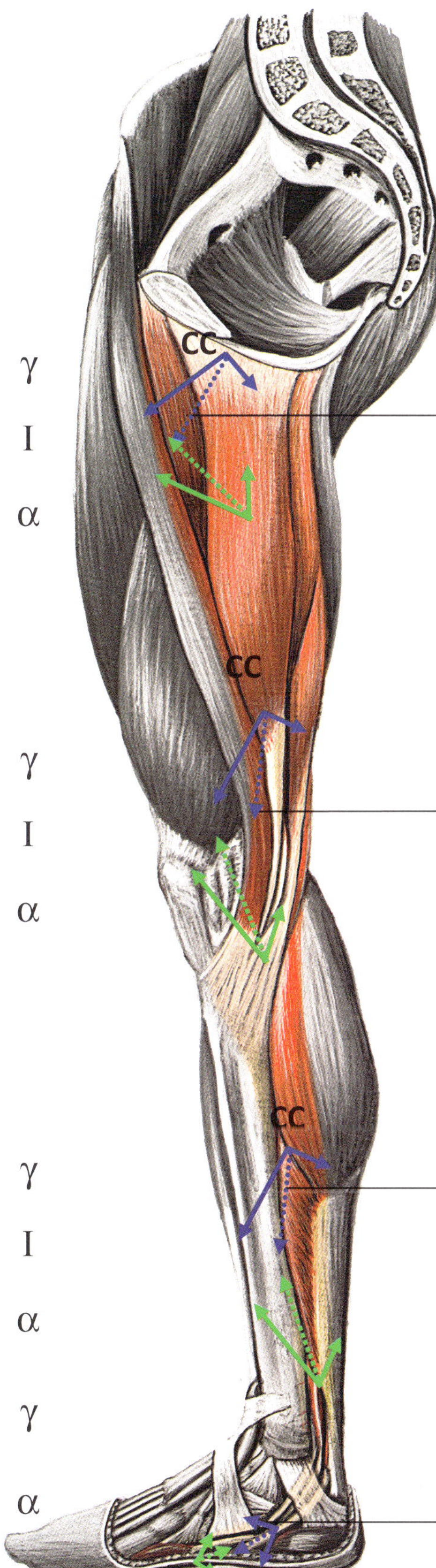

Fig. 4.39. Dysfunction of the gamma circuit.

ARTICULAR CONFLICTS IN THE MEDIOPULSION UNITS, LOWER LIMB

Pain during mediopulsion of coxa
If the fascia of the adductor muscles is densified, then some intrafusal fibres are not able to contract and to activate all the extrafusal fibres of the me-cx MF unit.
The activation of only some motor units results in an abnormal stretching of the insertional tendon with consequent inflammation (tendinopathy, enthesopathy).

Pain during mediopulsion of genu
If the fascia of the stabilising muscles of the knee is densified, then some intrafusal fibres are not able to contract and to activate all the extrafusal fibres of the me-ge MF unit.
The activation of only some motor units results in an abnormal stretching of pes anserinus with consequent inflammation (tendinopathy, enthesopathy, knee pain).

Pain during mediopulsion of talus
If the deep crural fascia is densified, then some intrafusal fibres are not able to contract and to activate all the extrafusal fibres of the me-ta MF unit.
The activation of only some motor units results in an abnormal stretching of the insertional tendon with consequent inflammation (heel pain, plantar fasciitis).

Pain during mediopulsion of pes
If there is no coordination between the intrafusal fibres of the small muscles of the foot, then the traction of the extrafusal muscle of the MF unit of medio-pes (me-pe) creates an articular incoordination.

MEDIOPULSION SEQUENCE AND STRETCH REFLEX

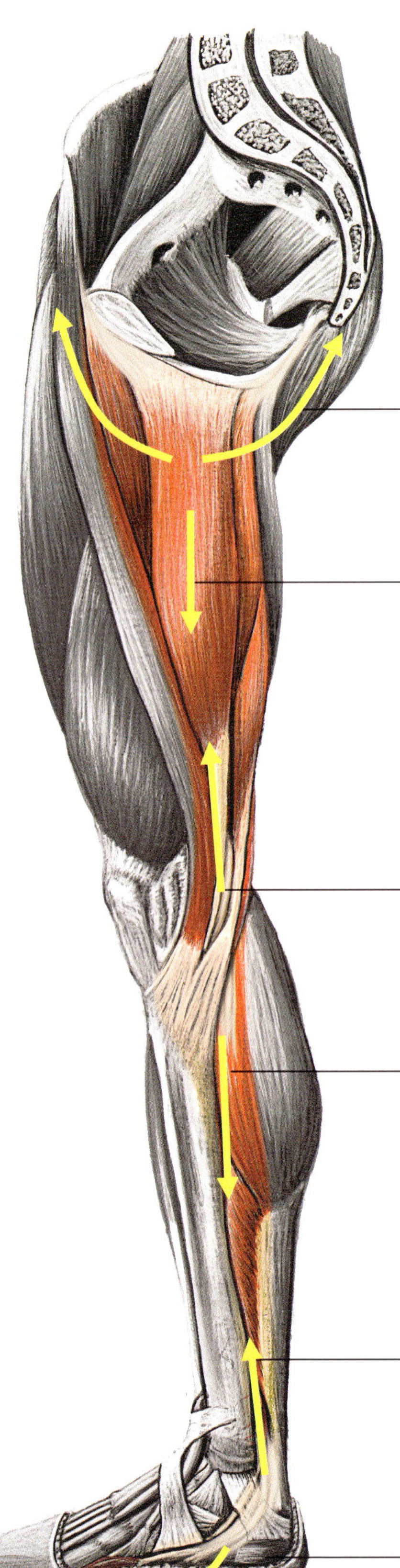

Synergy between the MF unit of medio-coxa and medio-genu
Proximal tractions of the fascia of the gracilis muscle by the rectus abdominis muscle and by the ascending ischial branch of the adductor magnus muscle.

Distal traction of the perineal fasciae by the gracilis muscle (Fig. 4.42).

Synergy between the MF unit of medio-genu and medio-talus
Proximal traction of the deep crural fascia by the gracilis muscle (Fig. 4.43).

Distal traction of the deep crural fascia by the soleus muscle (Fig. 4.44).

Synergy between the MF unit of medio-talus and medio-pes
Proximal traction of the deep plantar fascia of the foot by the flexor hallucis and digitorum longus muscles.

Distal traction of the deep plantar fascia of the foot by the flexor digitorum brevis and plantar interossei muscles carrying out toe adduction.

Fig. 4.40. Synergy of the mediopulsion sequence in the lower limb.

ACTIVATION OF THE GOLGI TENDON ORGANS

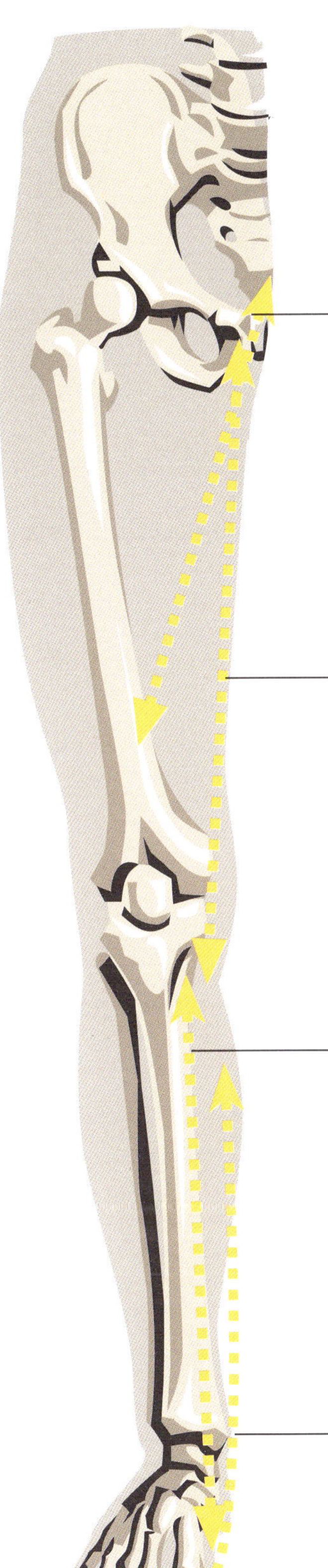

Fig. 4.41. Biarticular muscles for mediopulsion in the lower limb.

Connection between pelvis and coxa
The collagen fibres passing from the rectus abdominis sheath to the adductor longus sheath connect the pelvis to the hip.

"The tendinous fibres of the adductor longus muscle connect with those of the rectus and external oblique abdominal muscles forming the prepubic fibrous complex. The muscular body of the adductor longus muscle ends on the medial intermuscular septum. When having a fixed point on the pelvis it acts as an adductor, when having a fixed point on the femur it acts on the pelvis" (Chiarugi G. 1975).

Connection between coxa and genu
The gracilis muscle is an adductor of the hip and knee. The distal tendon of the adductor magnus muscle ends on the medial septum that in turn is continuous with the medial collateral ligament of the knee. The Golgi tendon organs are also present in this ligament.

Connection between genu and talus
The gracilis muscle inserts on the pes anserinus and on the deep fascia of the leg. This fascia is in relation with the soleus and flexor digitorum muscles that when working together trigger mediopulsion of the ankle and foot.
The tendon of flexor digitorum whilst running on the medial aspect of the calcaneus is forced against the skeleton by the deep layer of the laciniate ligament.

Connection between talus and pes
The flexor digitorum longus muscle connects the movement of the ankle with that of the foot.

"The flexor hallucis longus muscle, like flexor digitorum longus has additional bundles arising from the sural fascia. Its tendon is held in place by the deep layer of the laciniate ligament and inserts on the base of the second phalanx of the big toe; it provides a strip destined to the tendon of the second and third toe" (Chiarugi G. 1975).

FASCIAE OF THE MEDIOPULSION SEQUENCE IN THE LOWER LIMB

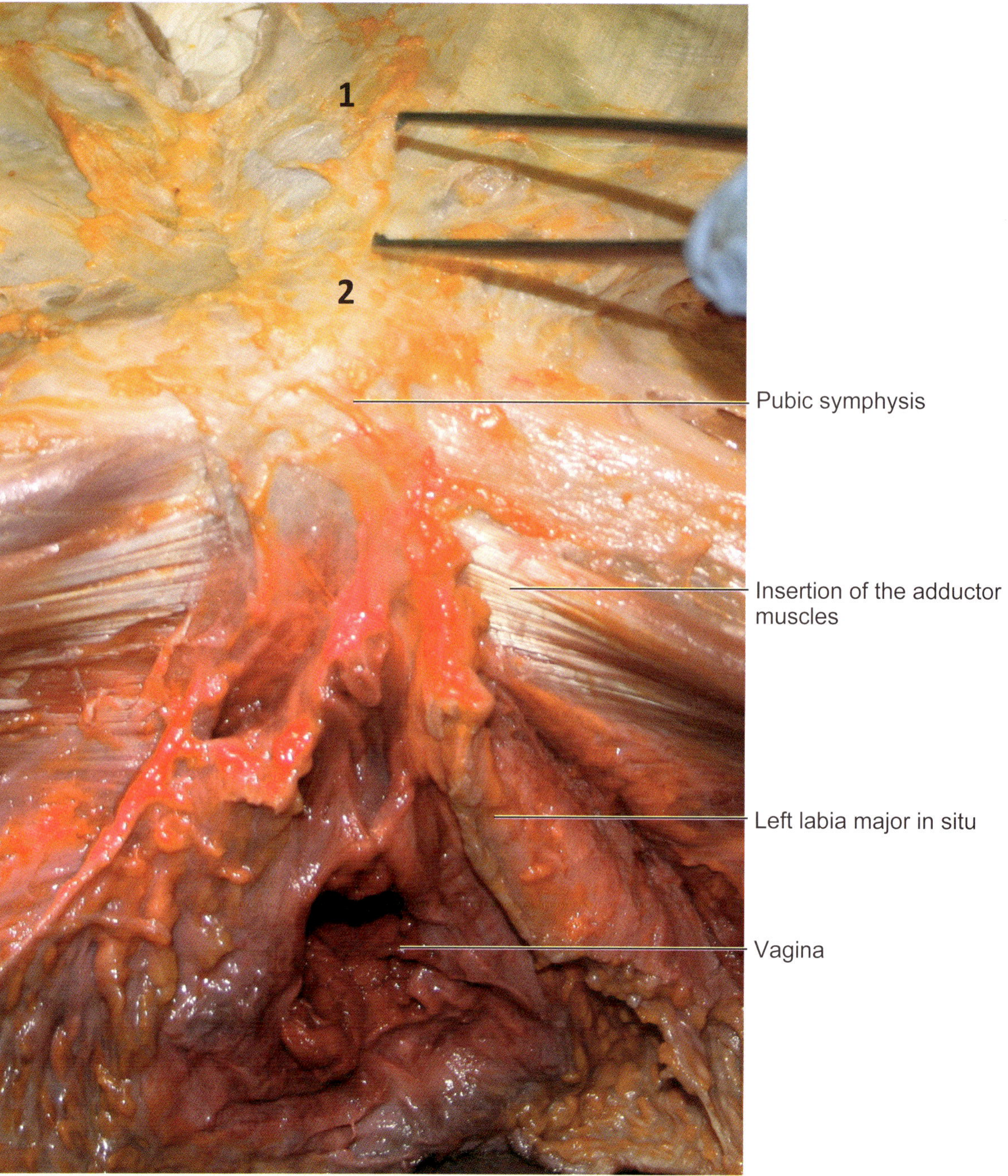

Fig. 4.42. Abdominal fascia and adductor fasciae. The upper tip of the forceps indicates the linea alba (1) whilst the lower tip indicates mons veneris above the pubis (2).

FASCIAE OF THE MEDIOPULSION SEQUENCE IN THE LOWER LIMB

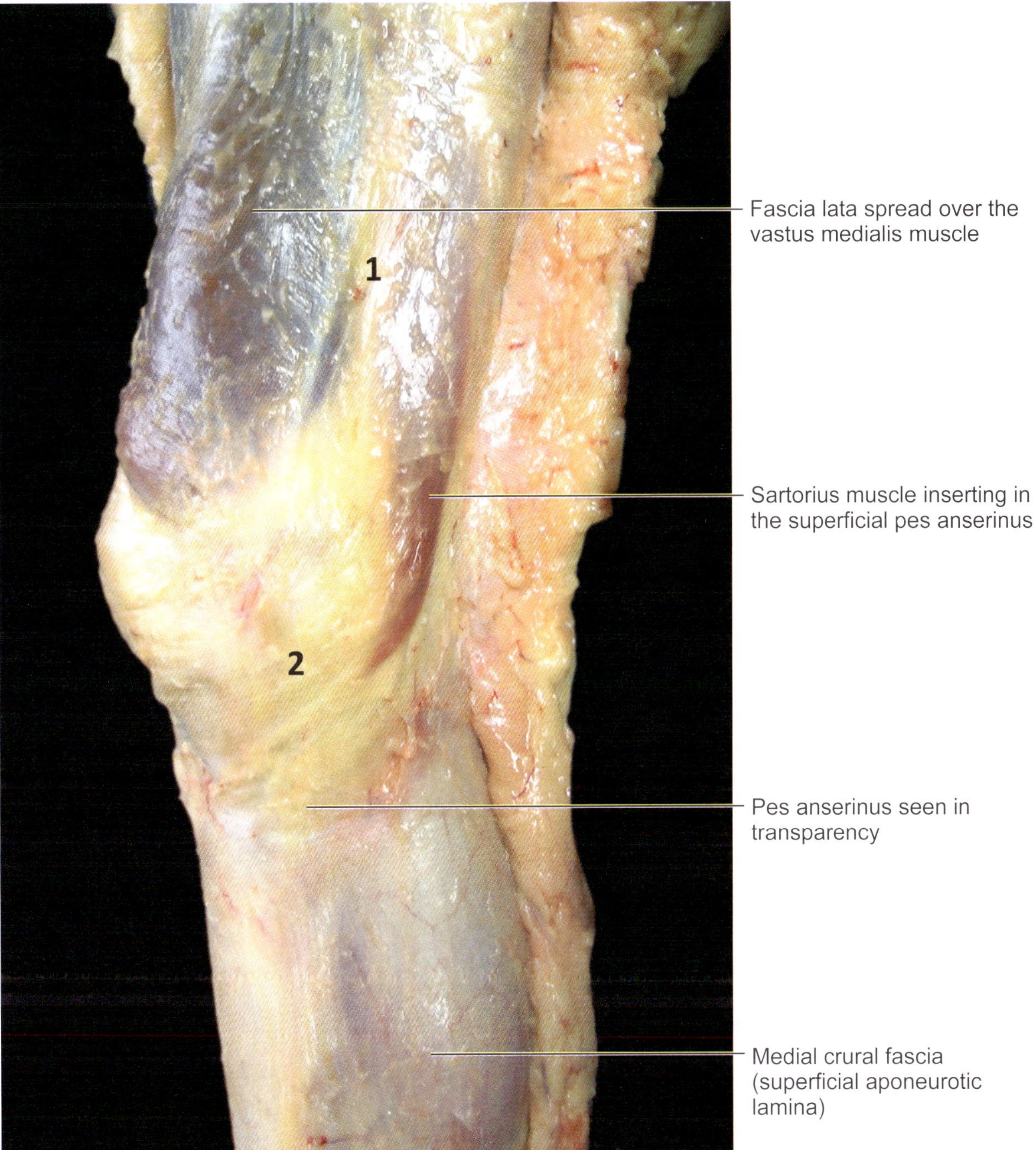

Fig. 4.43. Fascia lata and crural fascia of the medial region of the knee. The medial intermuscular septum (1) continues with the medial collateral ligament of the knee (2).

FASCIAE OF THE MEDIOPULSION SEQUENCE IN THE LOWER LIMB

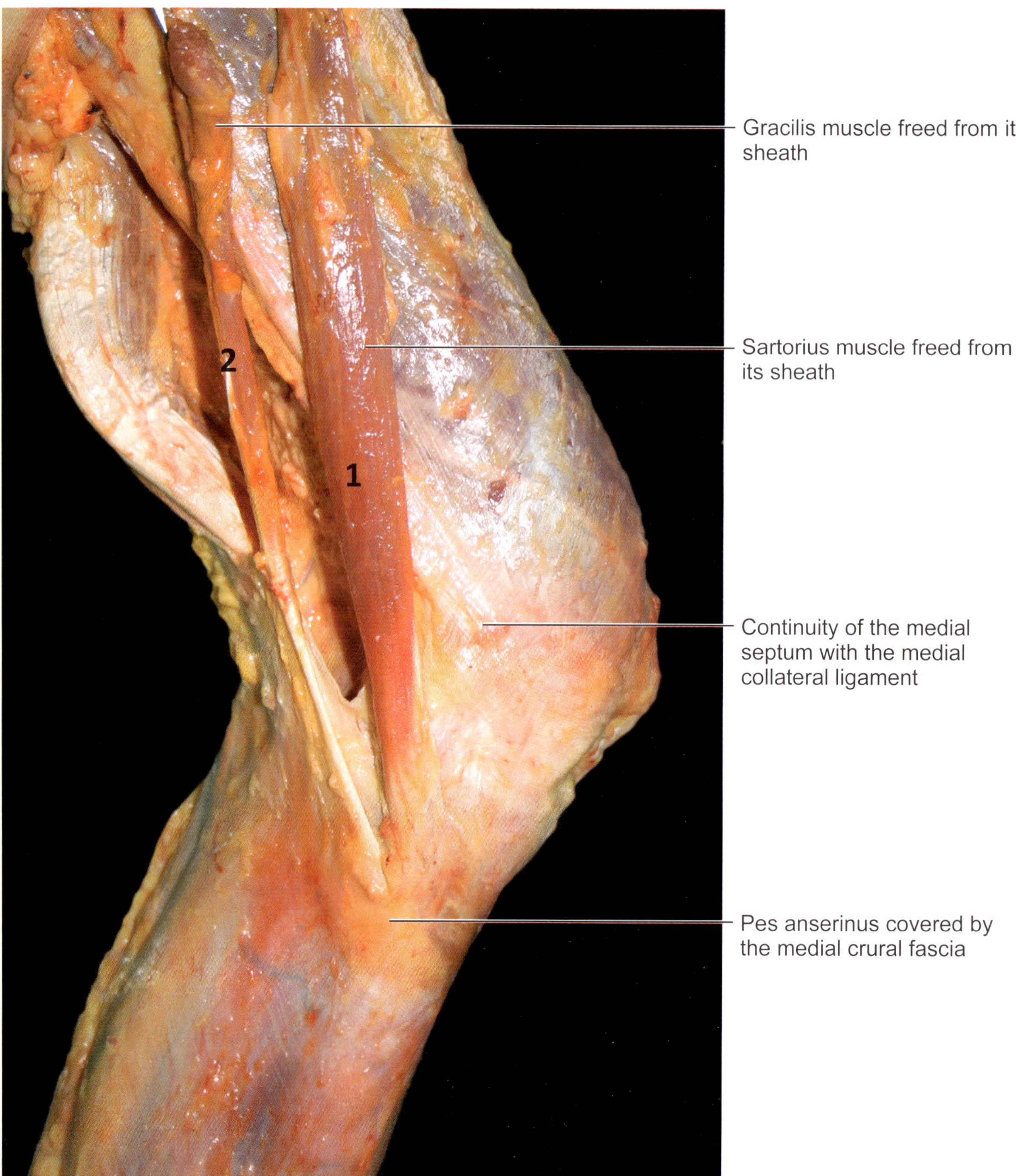

Fig. 4.44. Pes anserinus of the medial knee region. The sartorius (1) and gracilis (2) muscles are freed from their sheaths highlighting their insertions on the medial crural fascia. The sartorius muscle inserts on the aponeurotic fascia (spiral) whilst the gracilis muscle inserts on the deep lamina of the crural fascia (mediopulsion sequence).

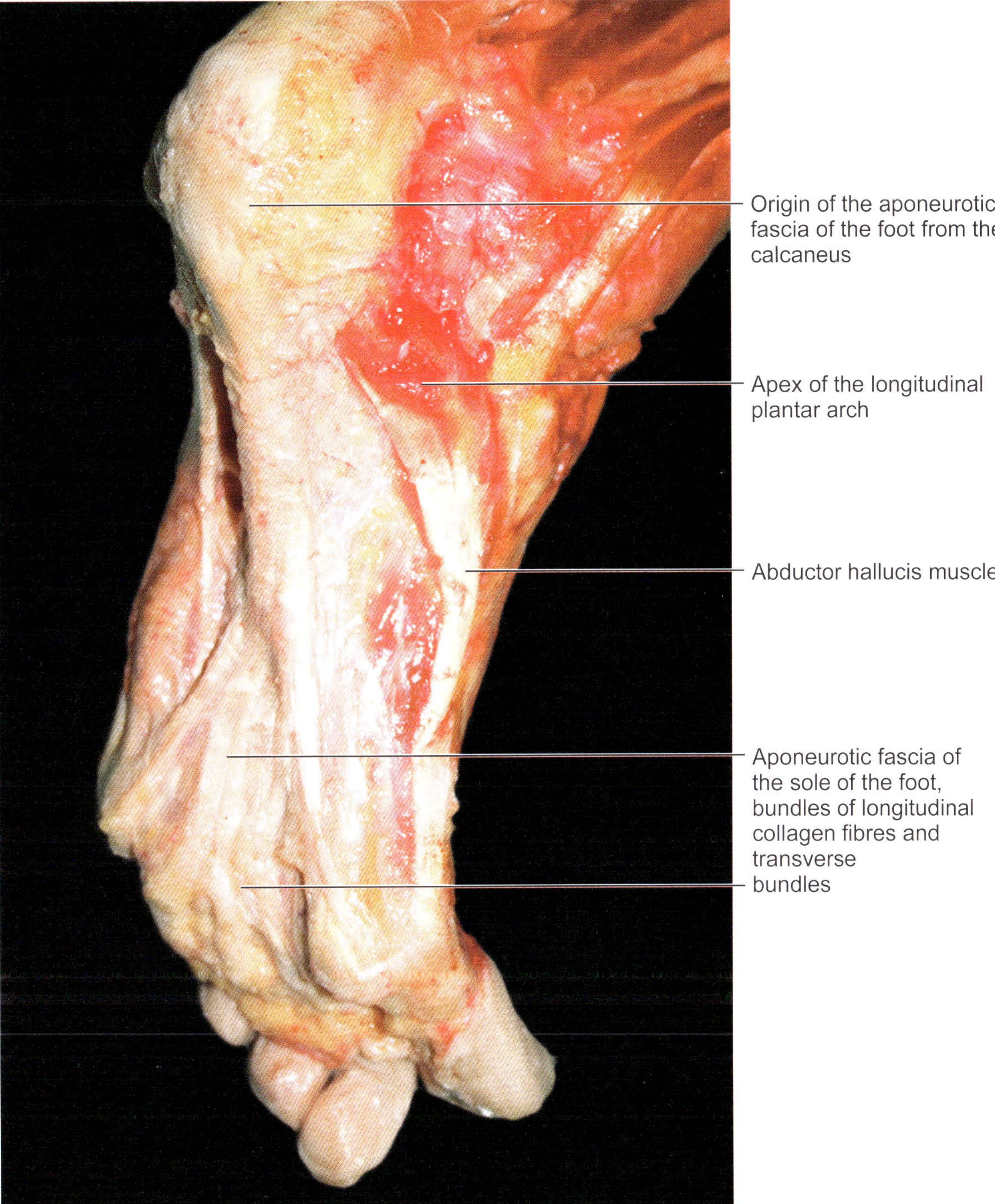

Fig. 4.45. Aponeurotic fascia of the sole of the foot. It is formed by bundles of longitudinal collagen fibres originating from the calcaneal tuberosity and irradiating up to the tendons of the toes.

LATERAL REGION OF THE LOWER LIMB, LATEROPULSION SEQUENCE

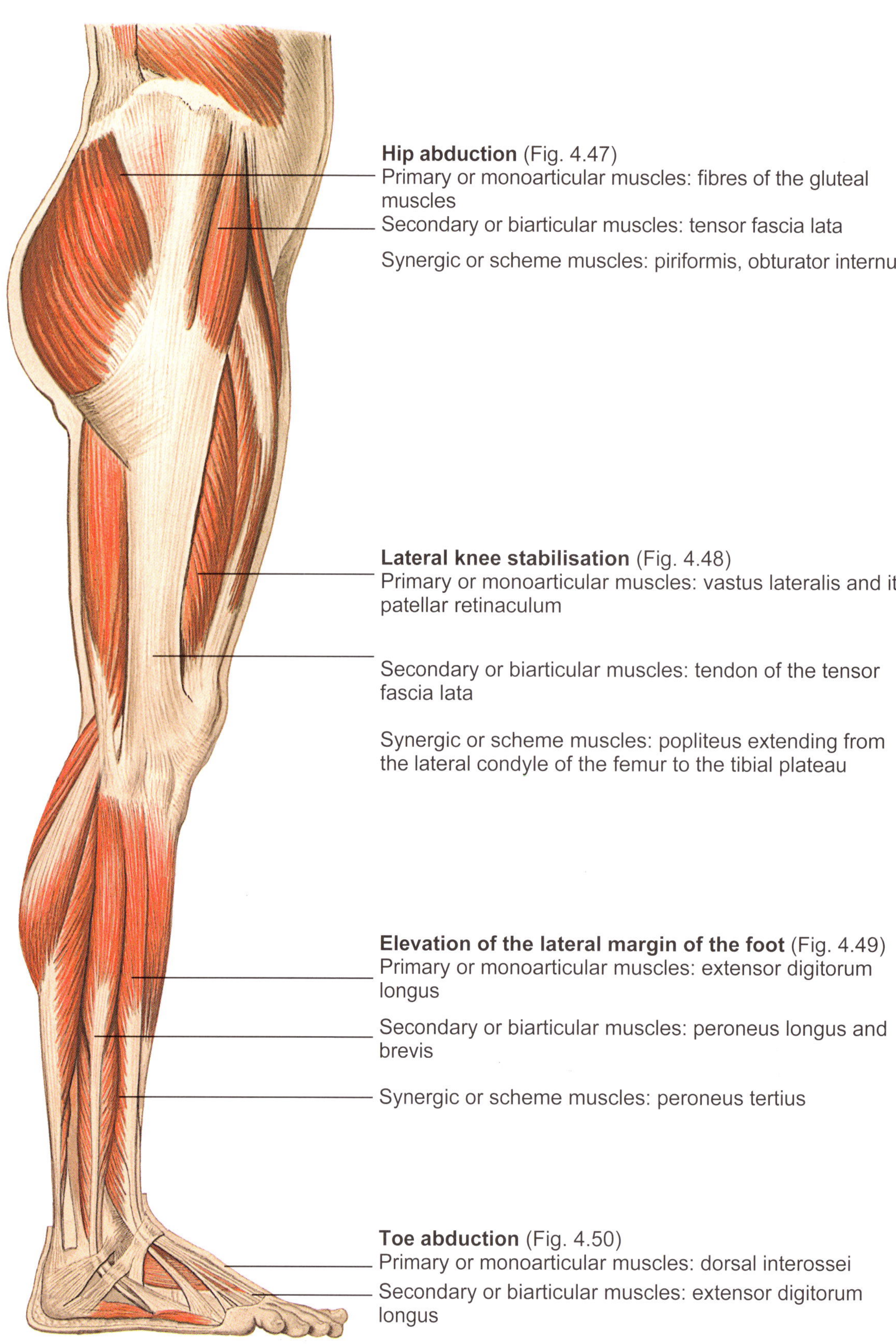

Fig. 4.46. Lateral region of the lower limb.
(From G. Chiarugi and L. Bucciante, Istituzioni di anatomia dell'uomo. Piccin Nuova Libraria, Padova 1983, modified)

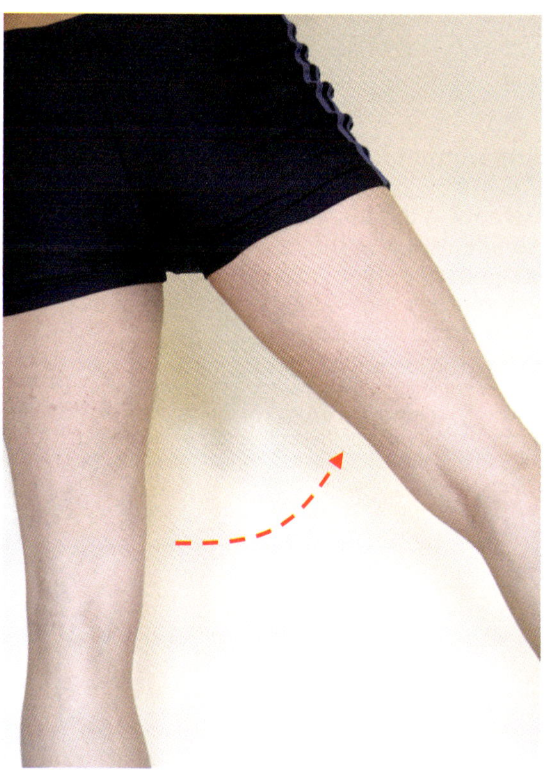

Fig. 4.47. Thigh abduction managed throughout its range by the myofascial unit of latero-coxa.

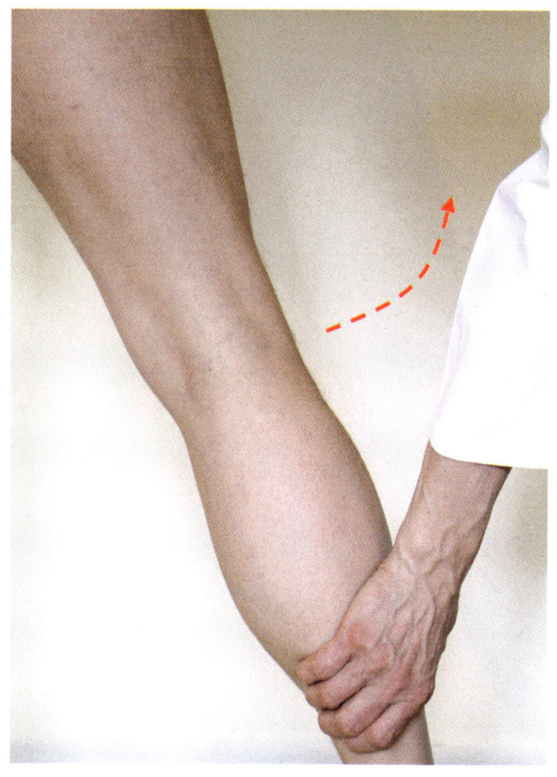

Fig. 4.48. Lateral knee stabilisation managed by the myofascial unit of latero-genu.

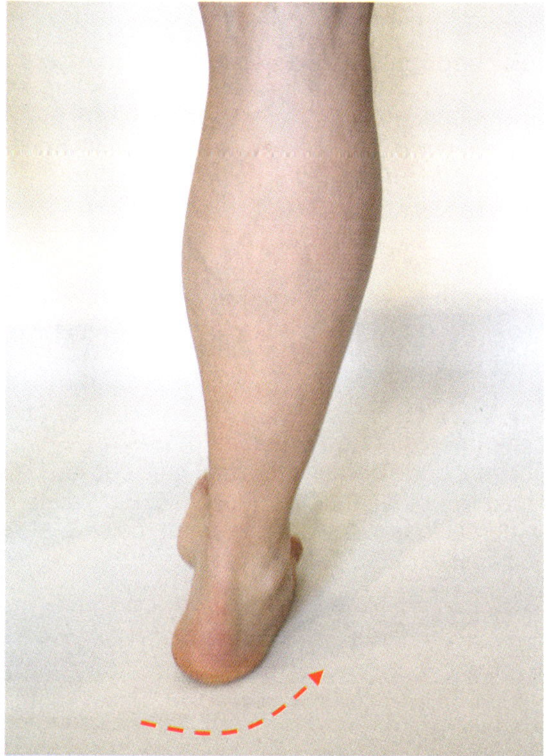

Fig. 4.49. Lateral ankle stabilisation managed throughout its joint range by the MF unit of latero-talus.

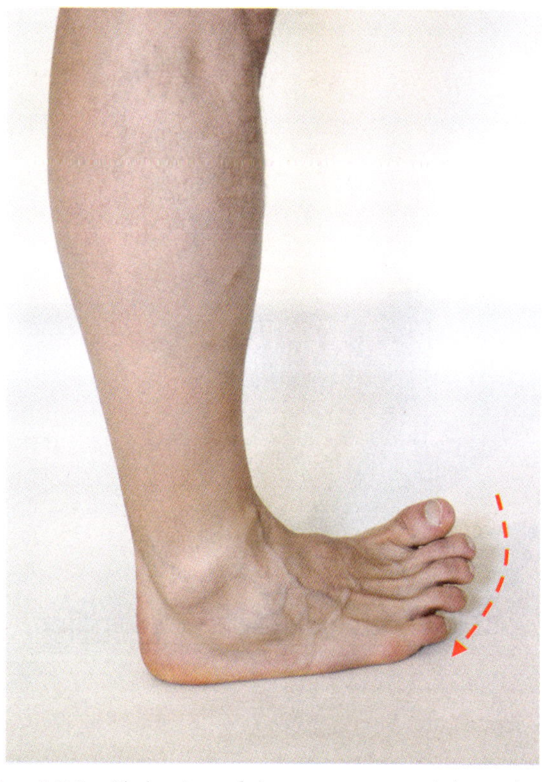

Fig. 4.50. Abduction of the toes managed throughout its joint range by the MF unit of latero-pes.

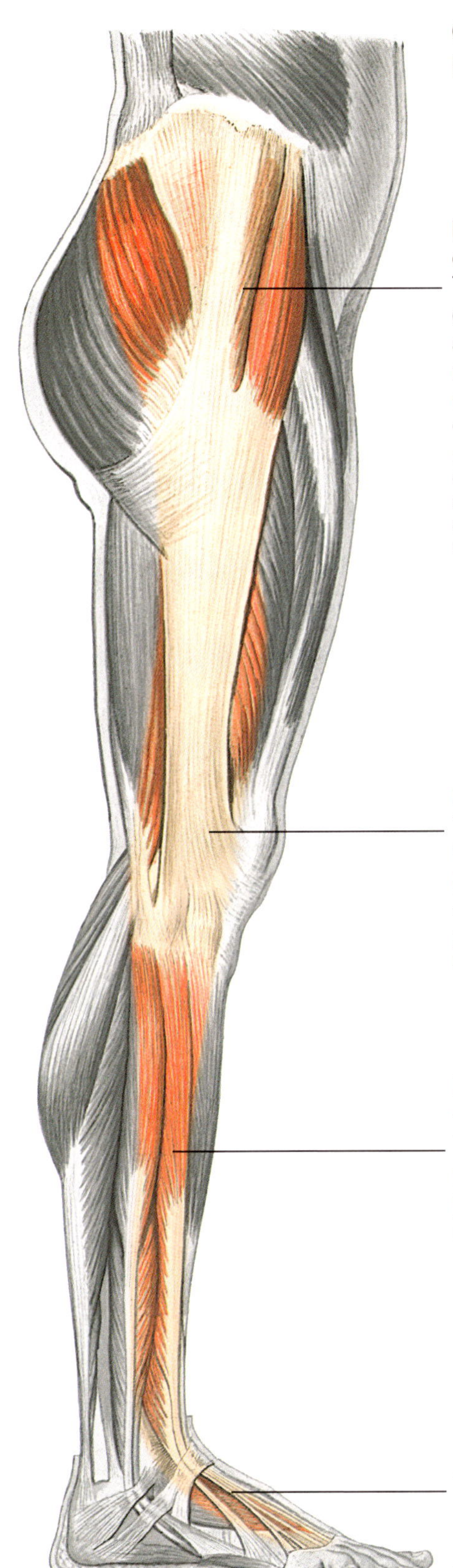

Fig. 4.51. Fascial compartments for lateropulsion muscles.

(From G. Chiarugi and L. Bucciante, Istituzioni di anatomia dell'uomo. Piccin Nuova Libraria, Padova 1983, modified)

COMPARTMENTS FOR THE MUSCLES OF LATEROPULSION, LOWER LIMB (Fig. 4.52)

Fascial compartment for the lateropulsion muscles of coxa

The fascia wrapping the tensor fascia lata muscle continues seamlessly over the fascia of the gluteus medius and maximus muscles (Fig. 4.57). The iliotibial tract is reached by numerous tendinous fibres of the gluteus medius and maximus muscles.

"The gluteal fascia when reaching the superior margin of the gluteus maximus muscle is divided into three sheets: the superficial sheet covering the external aspect of the gluteus maximus; the intermediate sheet covering the deep aspect of the muscle and uniting with the sacrotuberous ligament; the deep sheet continuing to cover the gluteus medius up to the piriformis" (Testut L. 1987).

Fascial structures for knee stabilisation

The iliotibial tract extends, together with its fascia, onto the lateral condyle of the tibia, the fibular head and the ligaments stabilising the knee laterally.

"Proximally the lateral collateral ligament covers the tendon of the popliteus muscle, distally it is sheathed by the tendon of the biceps femoris muscle" (Testut L. 1987).

Intermuscular septum for the lateropulsion muscles of talus

The septum separating the extensor digitorum from the peroneus longus and brevis muscles is the fascial structure providing insertion to all the motor units implicated in bringing the ankle outwards.

Fascia for the lateropulsion muscles of pes

The fascia covering the dorsal interossei muscles is connected distally to the tendons of extensor digitorum longus. The dorsal interossei muscles bring the toes away from the median line of the foot.

GLOBAL MOVEMENT IMPLEMENTED BY THE LATEROPULSION MF SEQUENCE

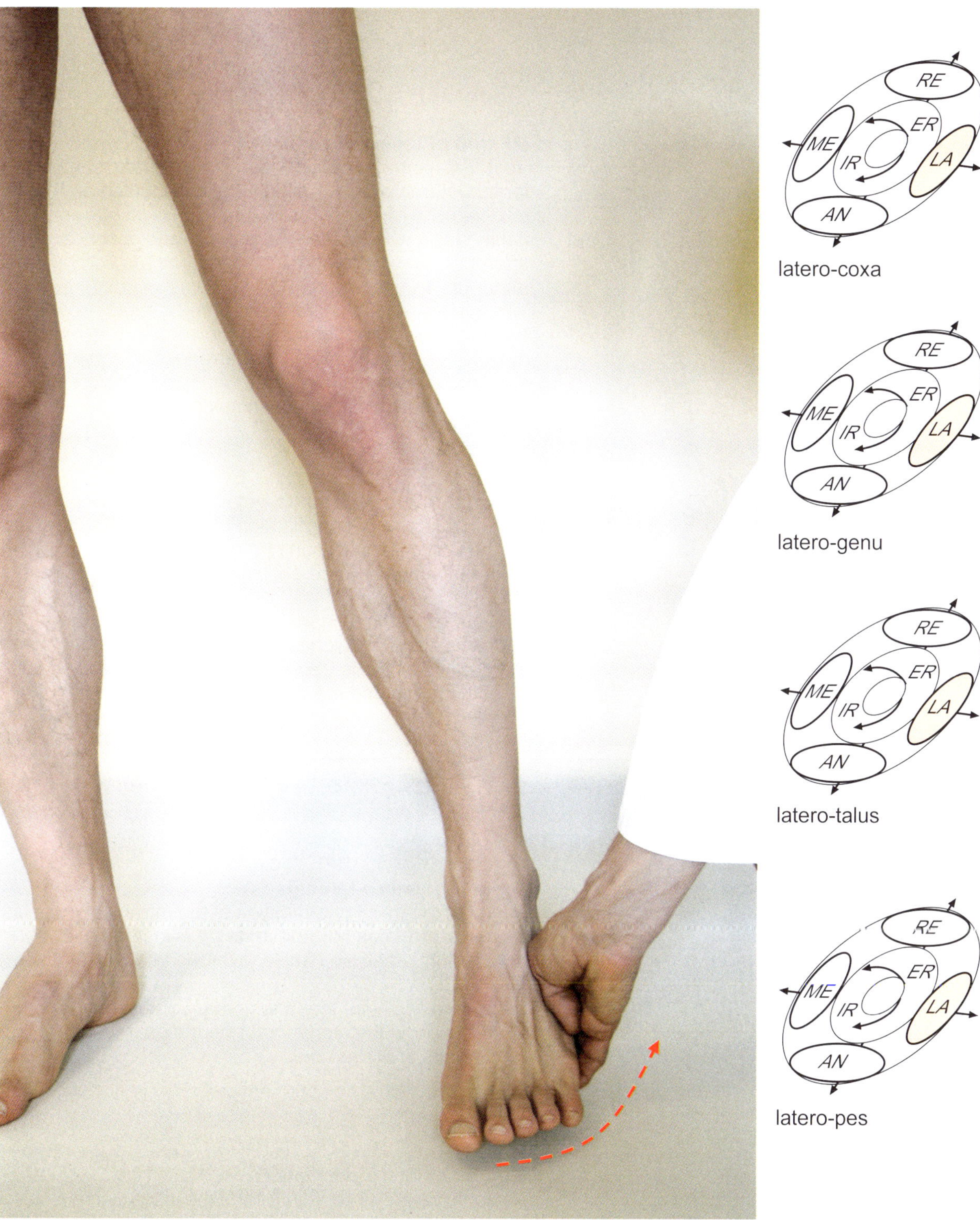

Fig. 4.52. Contraction of the lateropulsion sequence bringing the entire lower limb laterally.

Within the entire sequence of lateropulsion, the latero-talus MF unit is most frequently subject to sprains. To test the stability of this MF unit, the calisthenic abduction of talus is not very significant whereas walking on the external border of the foot is (Fig. 4.49). In the outcomes of a sprain this exercise immediately awakens latent pain even months after the traumatic event.

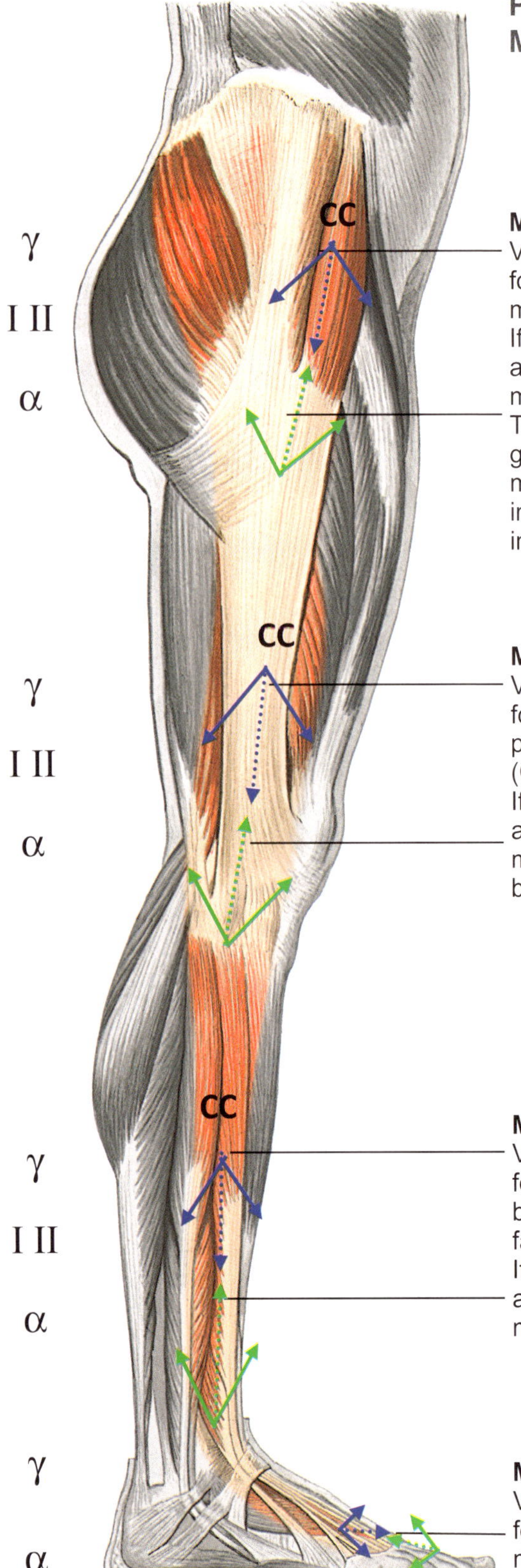

PHYSIOLOGY OF THE LATEROPULSION MF UNITS, LOWER LIMB

MF unit of latero-coxa (la-cx)
Vectorial centre of coordination of the intrafusal muscles for the latero-coxa MF unit (la-cx); it is located on the muscle belly of tensor fascia lata (CC).
If this fascia is fluid, then the primary and secondary afferents allow the alpha motor neurones to contract the motor units of latero-coxa.
The perfect functioning of the gamma circuits allows the green parallelogram formed by the vectors of extrafusal muscles (alpha stimulus) to be arranged in a mirror image to the parallelogram formed by the vectors of intrafusal muscles (gamma stimulus).

MF unit of latero-genu (la-ge)
Vectorial centre of coordination of the intrafusal muscles for the latero-genu MF unit (la-ge); it is located midway point between the knee and hip, over the iliotibial tract (CC).
If this fascia is fluid, then the primary and secondary afferents allow the alpha motor neurones to contract the motor units of latero-genu included in the short head of biceps femoris and the vastus lateralis muscles.

MF unit of latero-talus (la-ta)
Vectorial centre of coordination of the intrafusal muscles for the latero-talus MF unit (la-ta); it is located midway between the knee and ankle, over the lateral crural fascia (CC).
If this fascia is fluid, then the primary and secondary afferents allow the alpha motor neurones to contract the motor units of latero-talus.

MF unit of latero-pes (la-pe)
Vectorial centre of coordination of the intrafusal muscles for the latero-pes MF unit (la-pe); it is located over the muscle belly of the second and third dorsal interossei muscles.

Fig. 4.53. Normal functioning of the gamma circuit.
(From G. Chiarugi and L. Bucciante, Istituzioni di anatomia dell'uomo. Piccin Nuova Libraria, Padova 1983, modified)

ARTICULAR CONFLICTS IN THE LATEROPULSION UNITS, LOWER LIMB

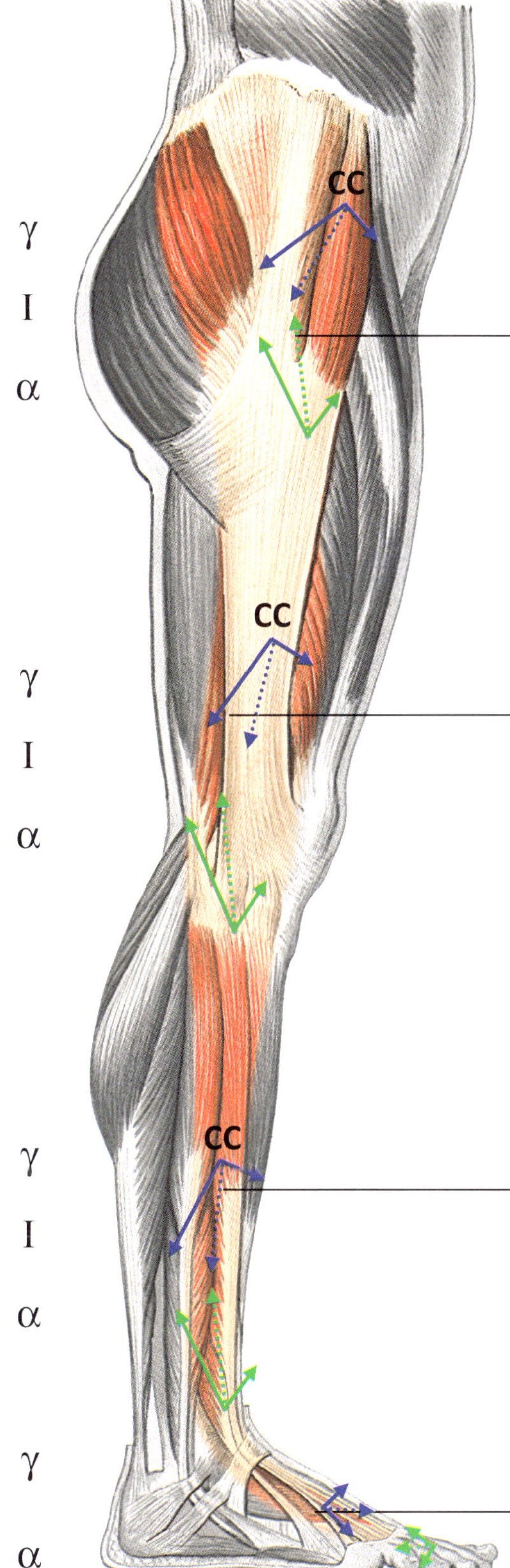

Pain during lateropulsion of coxa
If the fascia of the tensor fascia lata muscle is densified, then some intrafusal fibres are not able to contract and cannot activate all the extrafusal fibres of the la-cx MF unit. This dysfunction results in an abnormal stretching of the fascia with a cramping sensation during movements of abduction.
The densification of the fascia does not create a blockage of the gamma circuit but only its dysfunction. Both parallelograms are still in a mirror image but their resultant is no longer aligned with the joint axis.

Pain during lateropulsion of genu
If the iliotibial tract is densified, then some intrafusal fibres are not able to contract and cannot activate all the extrafusal fibres of the la-ge MF unit.
This dysfunction results in an abnormal stretching of the iliotibial tract with a burning sensation over the lateral region of the knee.

Pain during lateropulsion of talus
If the lateral intermuscular septum of the leg is densified, then some intrafusal fibres are not able to contract and cannot activate all the extrafusal fibres of the la-ta MF unit. This dysfunction results in an abnormal stretching of the joint sheath with pain and swelling over the lateral ankle.

Pain during lateropulsion of pes
If the vectorial centre of the traction of the extrafusal muscles of the latero-pes MF unit (la-pe) is densified, then a yield of the transverse arch of the foot is established with consequent pain underneath the II and III toes from nerve stress (Morton's neuroma).

Fig. 4.54. Dysfunction of the gamma circuit.
(From G. Chiarugi and L. Bucciante, Istituzioni di anatomia dell'uomo. Piccin Nuova Libraria, Padova 1983, modified)

LATEROPULSION SEQUENCE AND STRETCH REFLEX

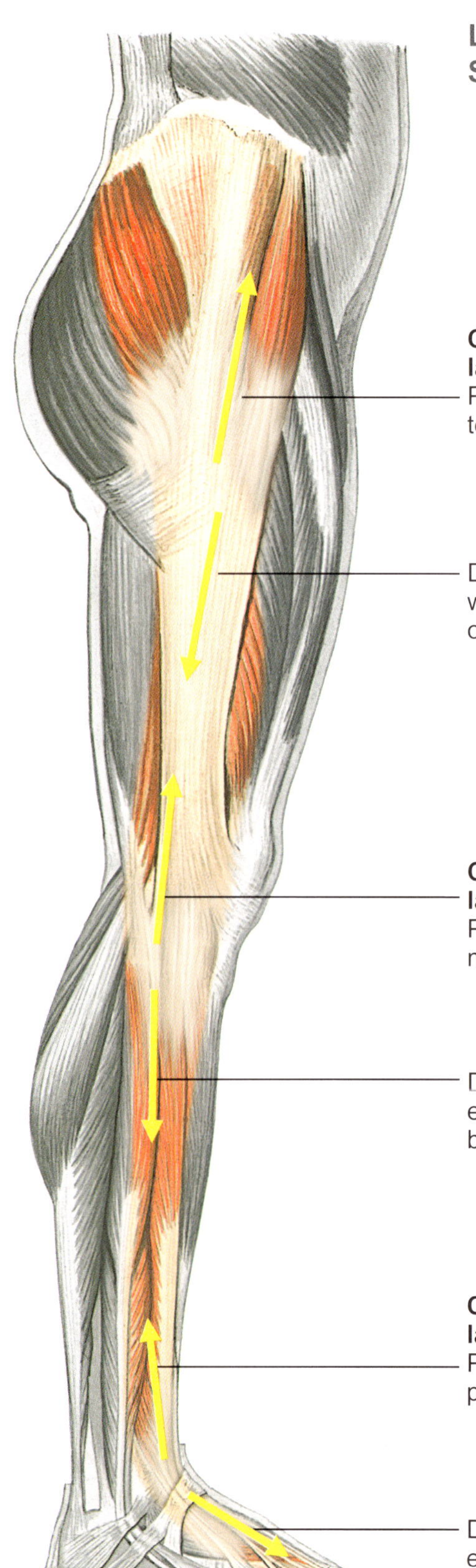

Coactivation of the MF unit of latero-coxa and latero-genu
Proximal traction of the iliotibial tract operated by the tensor fascia lata, gluteus medius and maximus muscles.

Distal traction of the iliotibial tract and lateral septum on which the short head of biceps femoris and vastus lateralis of the quadriceps muscles insert.

Coactivation of the MF unit of latero-genu and latero-talus
Proximal traction of the iliotibial tract by the gluteus maximus and tensor fascial lata muscles (Fig. 4.58).

Distal traction of the iliotibial tract expansions by the extensor digitorum longus and peroneus longus muscles, both are inserted on the septum dividing them (Fig. 4.60).

Coactivation of the MF unit of latero-talus and latero-pes
Proximal traction of the dorsal fascia of the foot by the peroneus tertius and extensor digitorum muscles (Fig. 4.59).

Distal traction of the dorsal fascia of the foot by the extensor digitorum brevis (superficial lamina) and dorsal interossei muscles (deep lamina).

Fig. 4.55. Synergy of the lateropulsion sequence in the lower limb.
(From G. Chiarugi and L. Bucciante, Istituzioni di anatomia dell'uomo. Piccin Nuova Libraria, Padova 1983, modified)

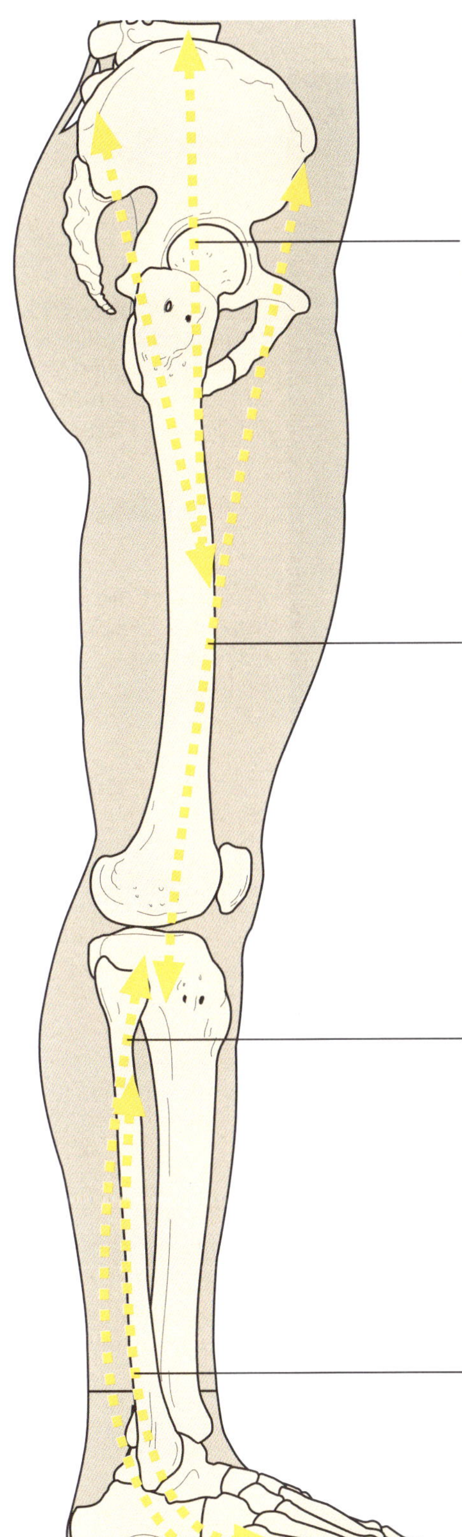

Fig. 4.56. Biarticular muscles for lateropulsion in the lower limb.

ACTIVATION OF THE GOLGI TENDON ORGANS

Connection between pelvis and coxa

The gluteal and tensor fascia lata muscles stabilise the pelvis and abduct the thigh.

"The iliotibial tract is formed proximally by the convergence of three components: anteriorly by the terminal tendon bundles of the tensor fascia lata muscle, posteriorly by the terminal tendon bundles of the gluteus maximus muscle, in between there are fibrous bundles derived from the fascia covering the gluteus medius muscle" (Chiarugi G. 1975).

Connection between coxa and genu

The muscle belly of the tensor fascia lata muscle is located at the level of the hip and its tendon (iliotibial tract) at the level of the knee. This is due to the fact that there are lateral movements at the hip, so the presence of muscle fibres are necessary, whilst in the knee only lateral stabilisation is occurring hence tendons and ligaments are sufficient.

Connection between genu and talus

The peroneus longus muscle also originates from expansions of the iliotibial tract.

"The fascia of the knee is reinforced by tendinous fibres of the tensor fascia lata muscle, together they form the iliotibial ligament or Maissiat band. These tendinous fibres are divided into two groups: the posterior fibres fixed to the fibular head and to the lateral condyle of the tibia, the anterior fibres fixed to the patella and to the medial aspect of the knee" (Testut L. 1987).

Connection between talus and pes

The extensor digitorum longus muscle acts upon both the ankle by deviating it laterally (talus lateropulsion) and the foot by bringing the toes superiorly and outwards.

The extensor digitorum longus muscle synchronises the action of the latero-talus MF unit (peroneus tertius muscle) with the action of the latero-pes MF unit (dorsal interossei muscles having connections with the distal tendons of extensor digitorum longus).

FASCIAE OF THE LATEROPULSION SEQUENCE IN THE LOWER LIMB

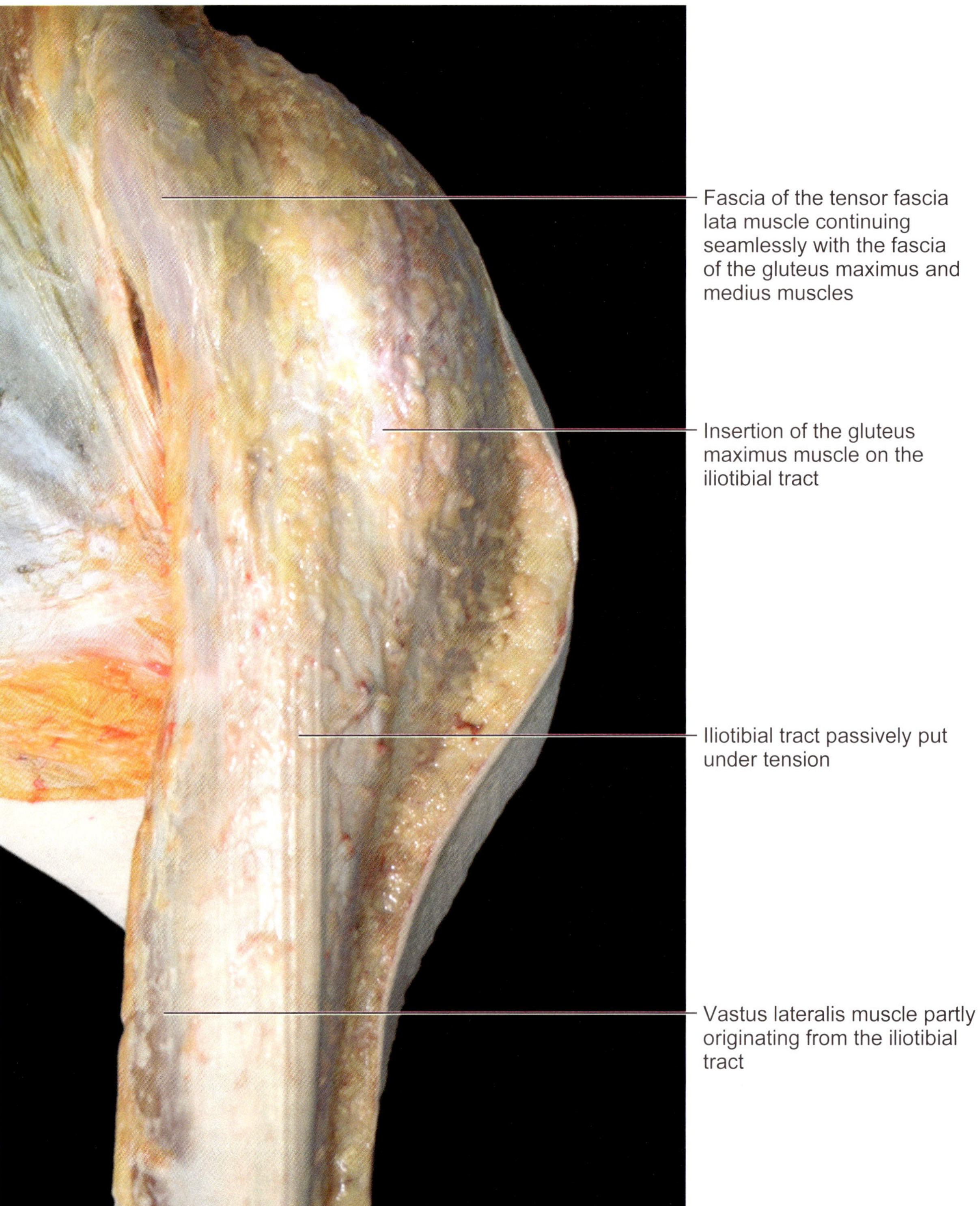

Fig. 4.57. Proximal retro-lateral fascia lata. When observed from the outside the fascia lata looks like a restraining sock but its internal wall is connected to the septa and to the epimysium and perimysium of muscles.

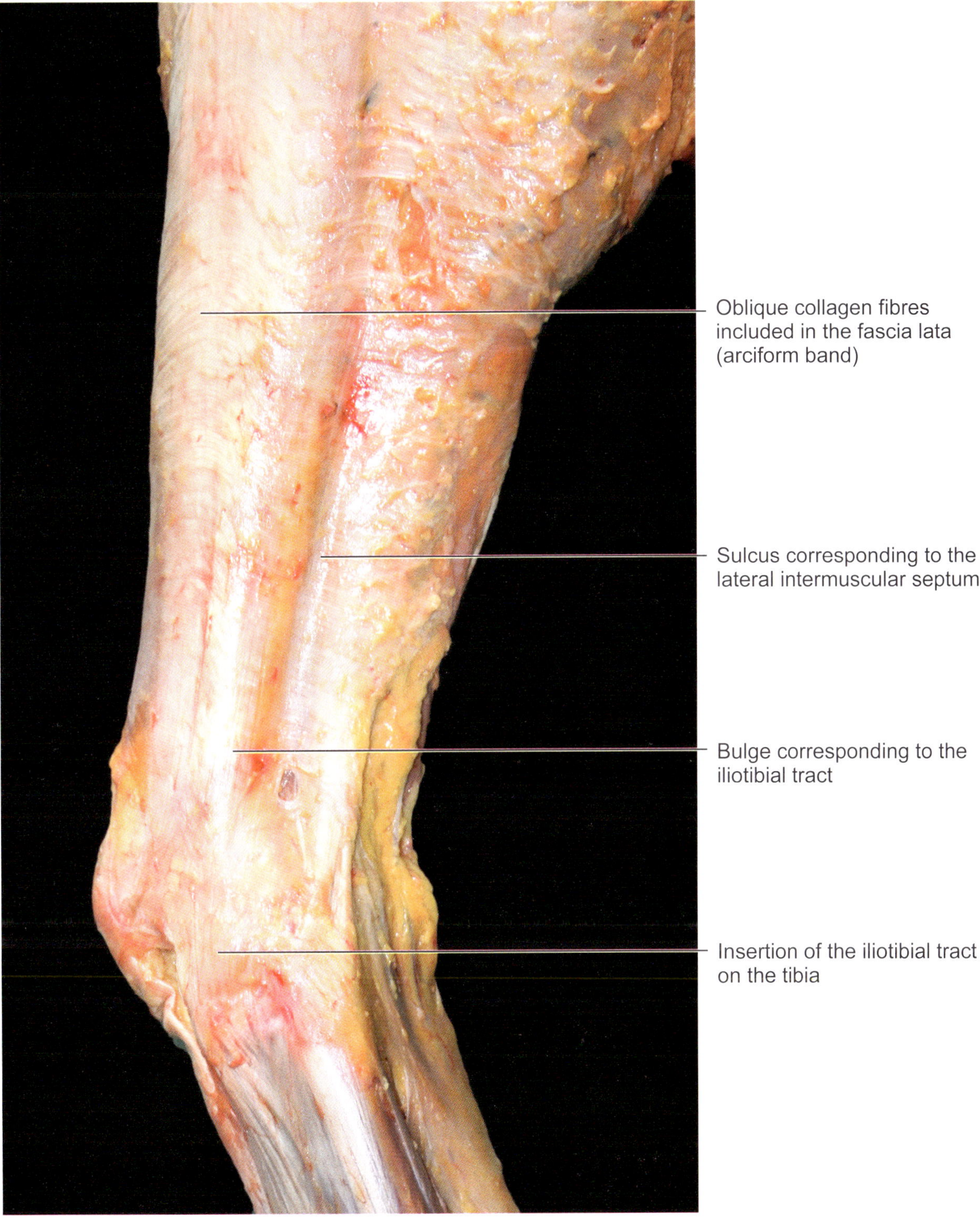

Fig. 4.58. Distal retro-lateral fascia lata. At the level of the knee, the fascia lata is thickened since it is connected to the periarticular structures: patellar retinacula, ligaments, external wall of the joint capsule, etc.

FASCIAE OF THE LATEROPULSION SEQUENCE IN THE LOWER LIMB

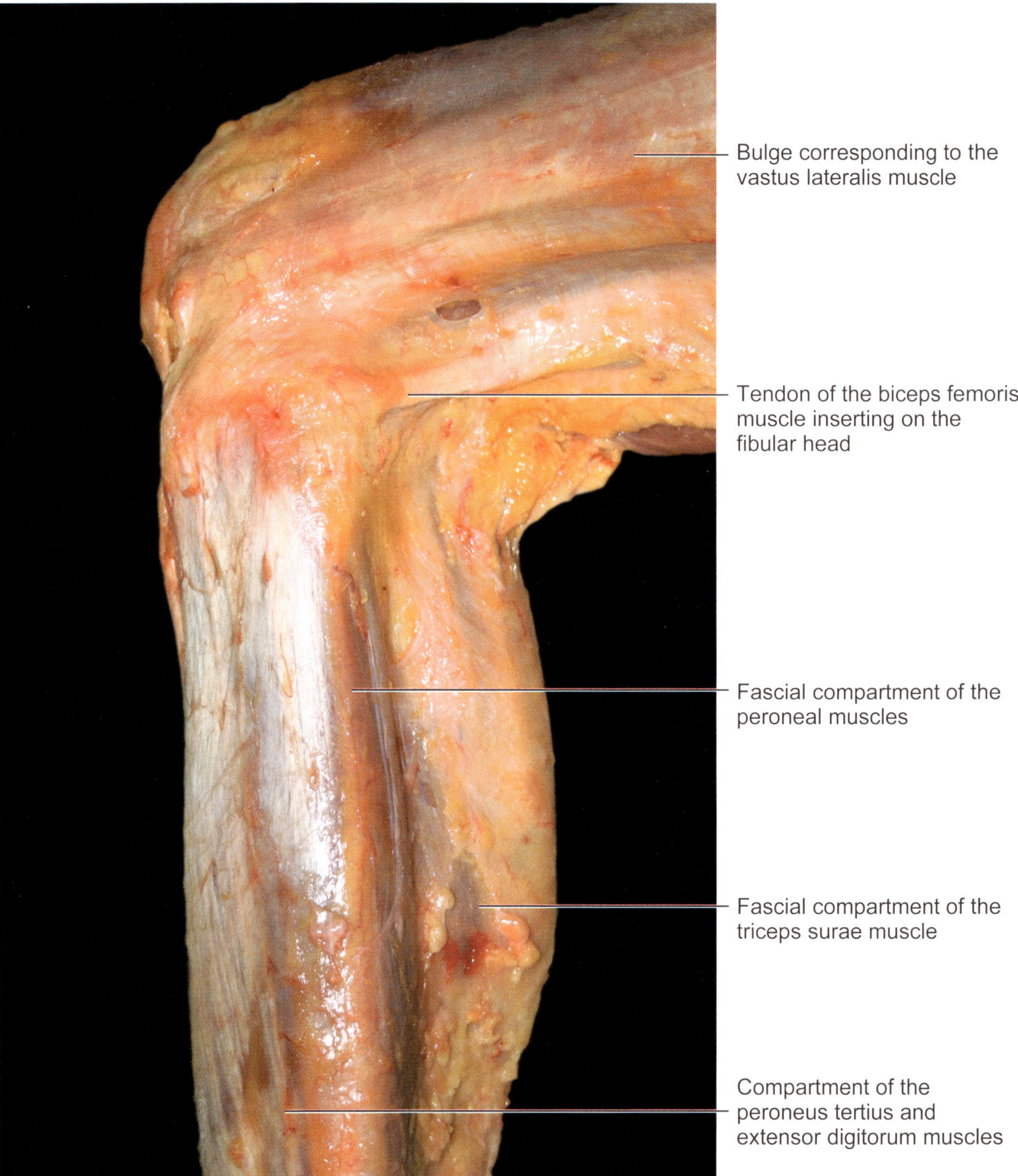

Fig. 4.59. Fascial compartments for the muscles of the leg. The deep fascia of the leg forms various muscular compartments or lodges, through the intermuscular septa, bones and interosseous membrane.

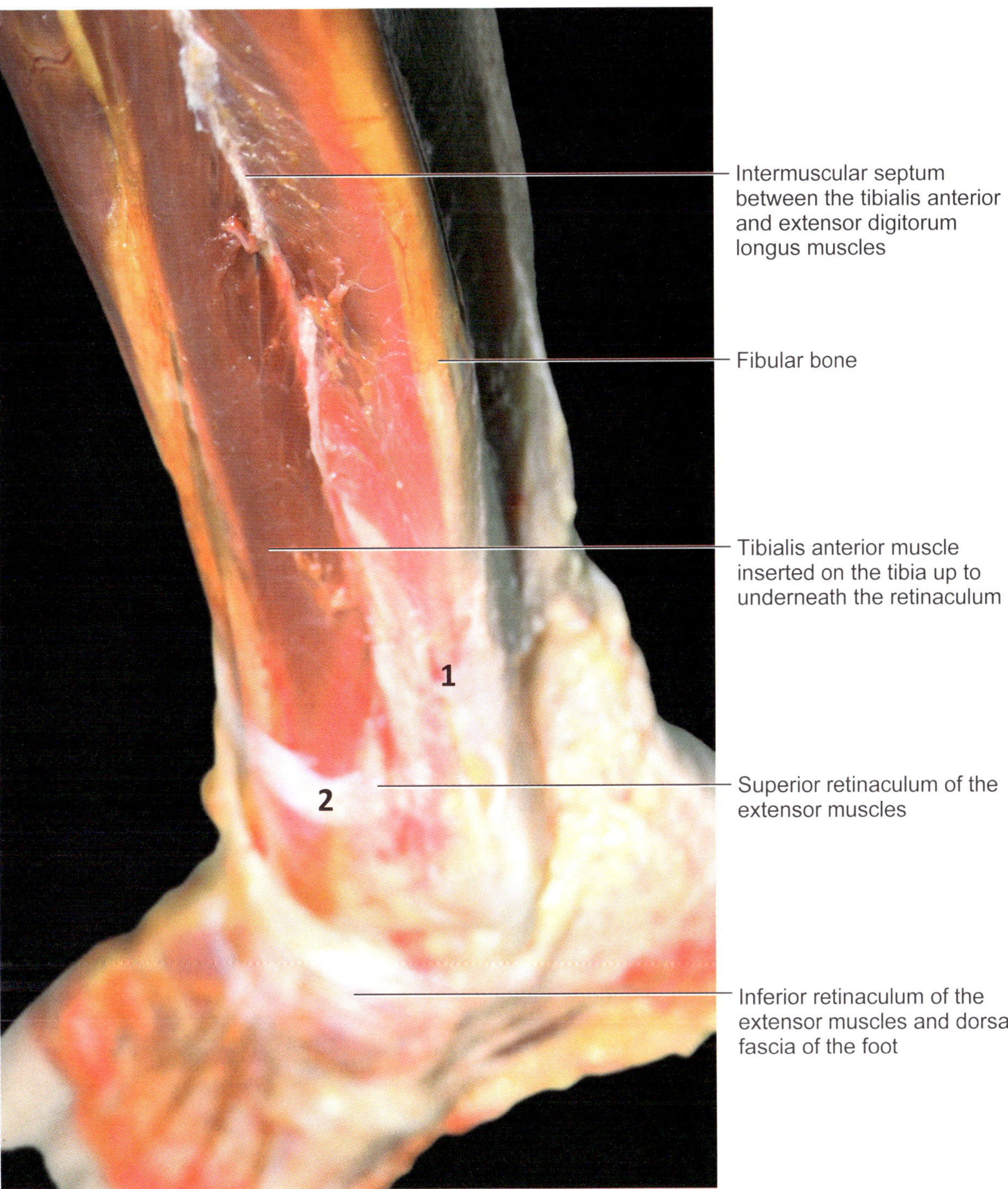

Fig. 4.60. Lateral intermuscular septum of the leg. The extensor digitorum longus muscle has insertions on the fibula nearly up to the malleolus (1) hence this insertion prevents the tendon from protruding during contraction and not the retinaculum (2).

POSTERIOR DEEP REGION OF THE LOWER LIMB, INTRAROTATION SEQUENCE

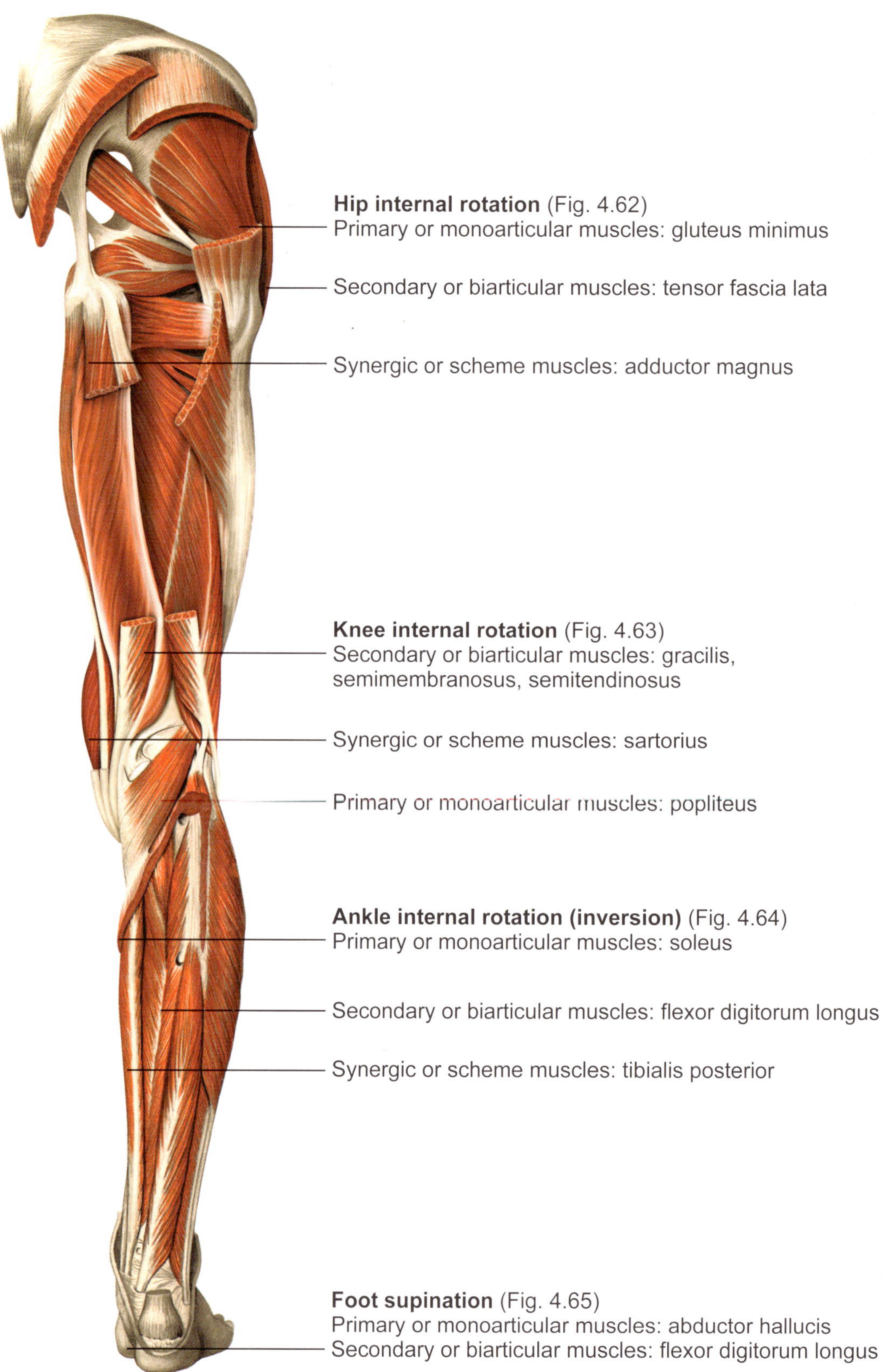

Fig. 4.61. Posterior deep region of the lower limb.
(From G. Chiarugi and L. Bucciante, Istituzioni di anatomia dell'uomo. Piccin Nuova Libraria, Padova 1983, modified)

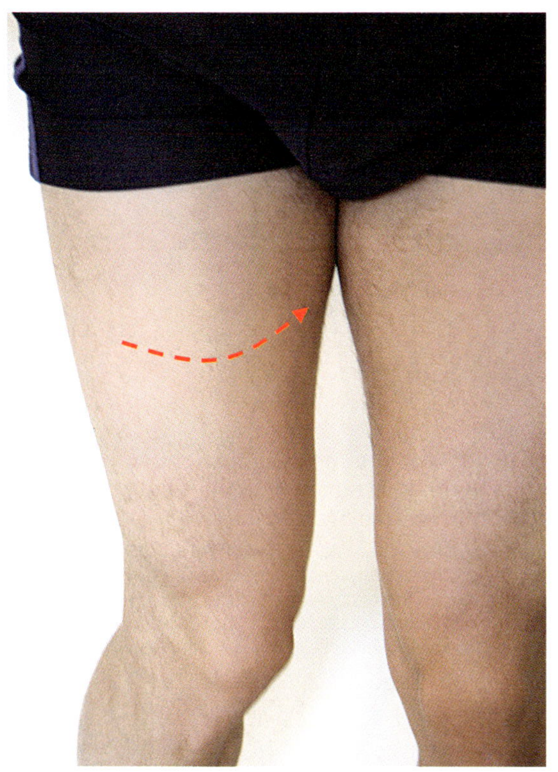

Fig. 4.62. Hip internal rotation coordinated by the myofascial unit of intra-coxa.

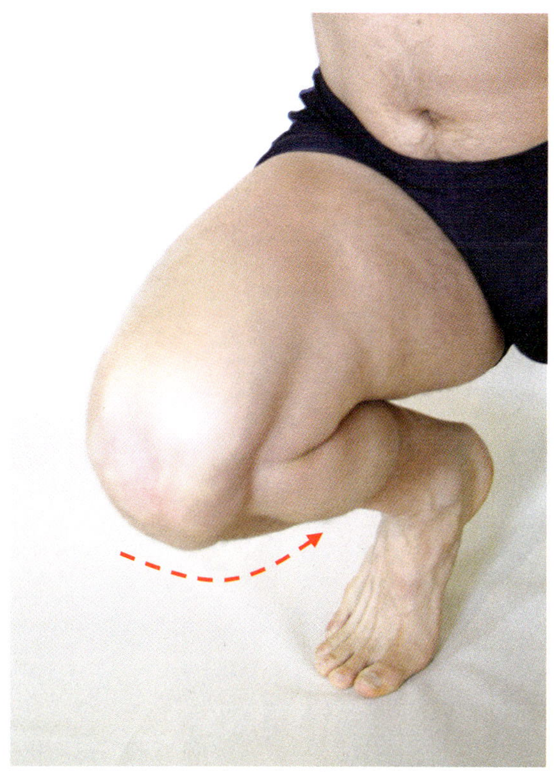

Fig. 4.63. Knee internal rotation managed by the myofascial unit of intra-genu.

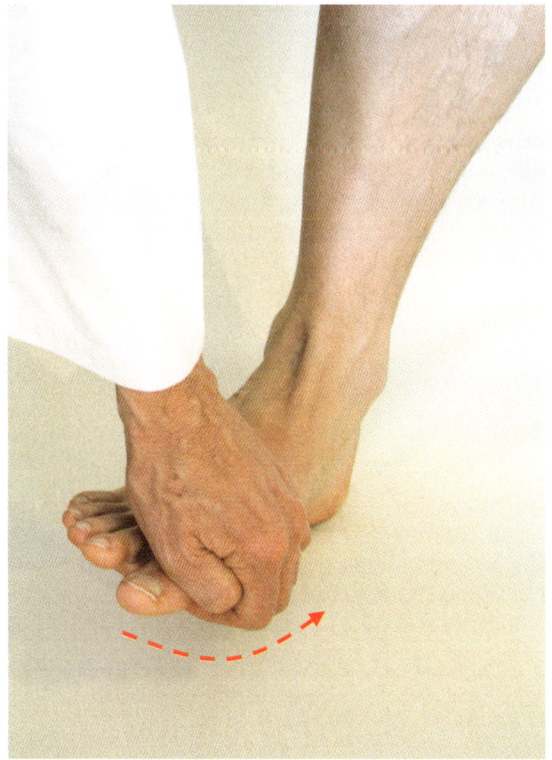

Fig. 4.64. Ankle internal rotation managed by the myofascial unit of intra-talus.

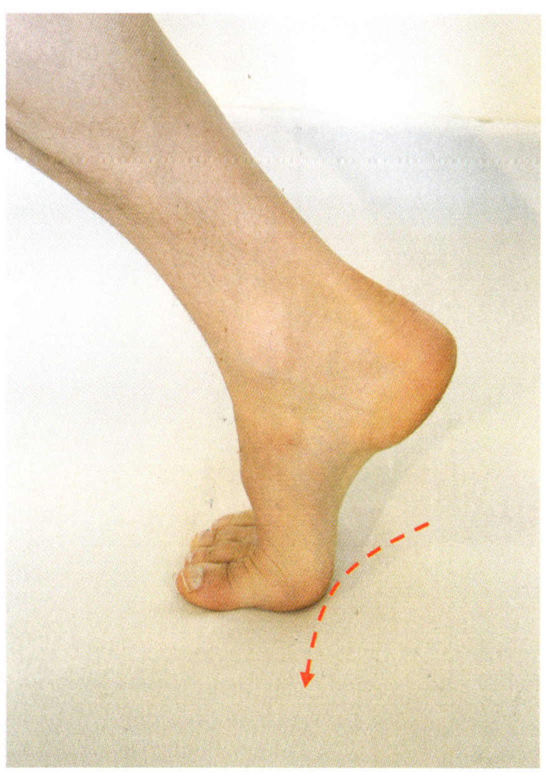

Fig. 4.65. Forefoot internal push managed by the myofascial unit of intra-pes.

COMPARTMENTS FOR THE MUSCLES OF INTRAROTATION, LOWER LIMB (Fig. 4.67)

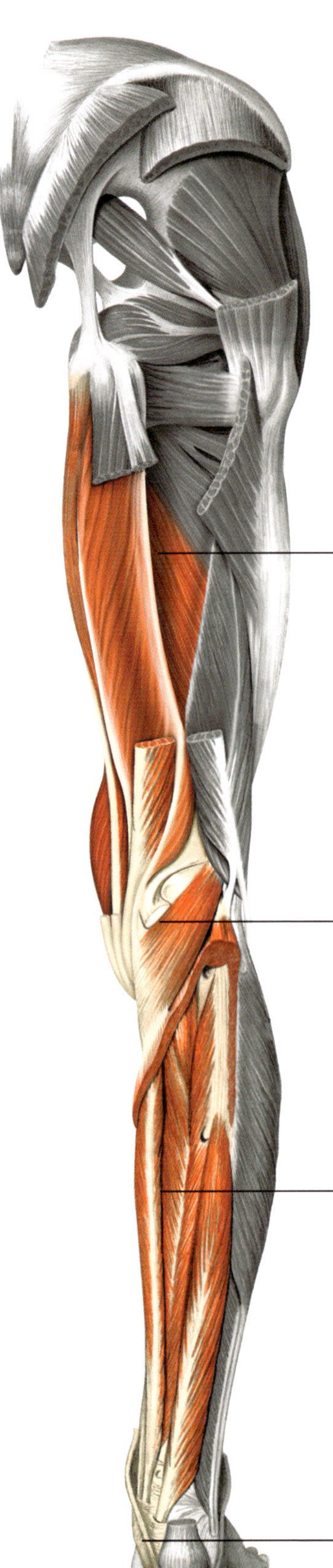

Fascial compartment for the intrarotation muscles of coxa
Adductor magnus is the internal muscle of the thigh carrying out internal rotation of the hip.

"A fibrous lamina detaches from the anterior wall of the adductor magnus muscle and is attached on the vastus medialis muscle thereby forming the adductor canal of Hunter. The distal tendon of the adductor magnus muscle stands together with the medial intermuscular septum. The adductor magnus muscle has remarkable similarities with the coracobrachialis muscle" (Chiarugi G. 1975).

Fascial structures for genu intrarotation
The popliteal fascia coordinates the intrarotation motor units of the knee distributed in many muscles.

"The internal rotation of the knee is only 10 degrees. The most energetic internal rotator is semimembranosus, with the smallest contributors being semitendinosus, gracilis, sartorius and popliteus muscles. Each gastrocnemius is able to produce a slight rotation ipsilaterally" (Chiarugi G. 1975).

Fascial compartments for talus intrarotation
The fascia of the leg sends septa forming four compartments: anterior, lateral, posterior superficial and posterior deep compartments. The latter compartment includes the muscles responsible for talus intrarotation.

Fascial compartment for the intrarotation muscles of pes
The abductor hallucis muscle takes origin from the laciniate ligament, or flexor retinaculum, through its contraction it contributes in bringing the forefoot inwards.

Fig. 4.66. Fasciae connected to intrarotation muscles.
(From G. Chiarugi and L. Bucciante, Istituzioni di anatomia dell'uomo. Piccin Nuova Libraria, Padova 1983, modified)

GLOBAL MOVEMENT IMPLEMENTED BY THE INTRAROTATION MF SEQUENCE

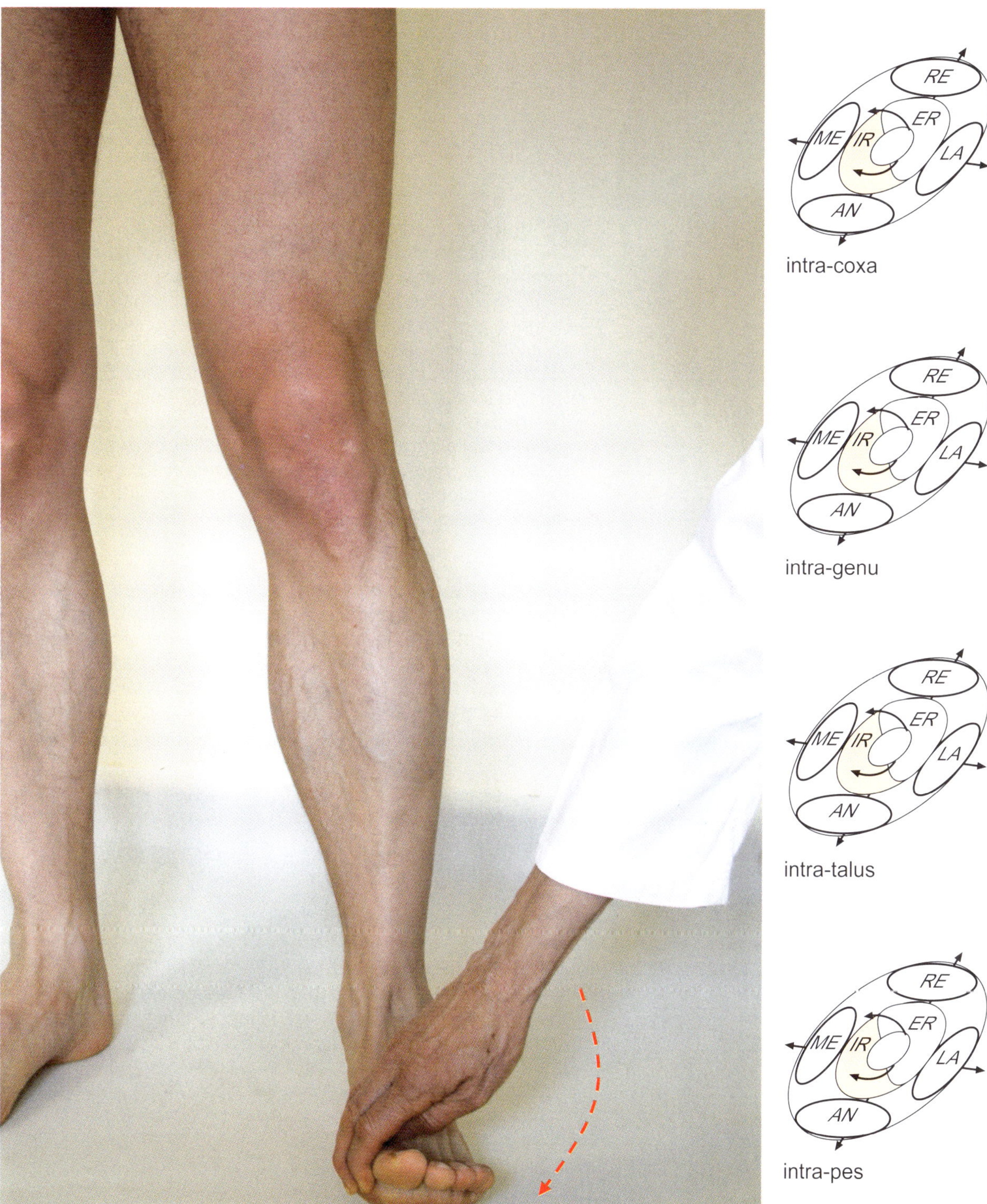

Fig. 4.67. Contraction of the intrarotation sequence rotates the entire lower limb internally.

Internal and external rotation of the lower limb are two movements that are mainly implemented involuntarily and are associated with other schemes or spiral movements. When these movements are dysfunctional then any small torsional movement of the limb creates a sharp pain.

PHYSIOLOGY OF THE INTRAROTATION MF UNITS, LOWER LIMB

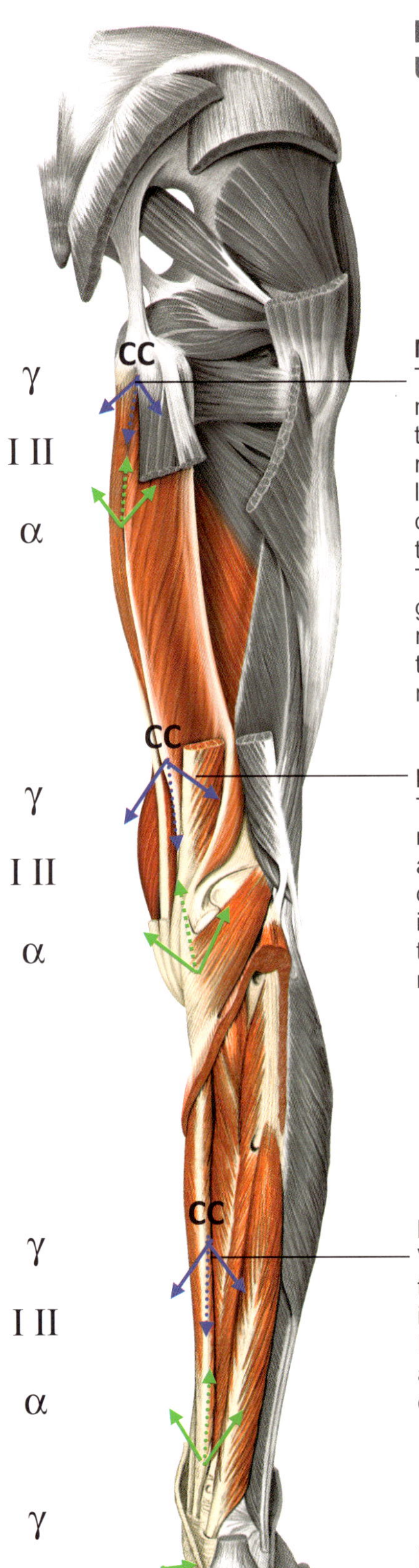

MF unit of intra-coxa (ir-cx)
The lateral internal rotator muscles of coxa (gluteus minimus and tensor fascia lata muscles) are connected to the medial internal rotator muscles of coxa (adductor magnus and pectineus muscles) through the inguinal ligament (Fig. 4.72) and the iliopectineal fascia. The centre of coordination is located at the lower margin of Scarpa's triangle for the motor units of the ir-cx MF unit.
The perfect functioning of the gamma circuits causes the green parallelogram formed by the vectors of the extrafusal muscles (alpha stimulus) to be arranged in a mirror image to the parallelogram formed by the vectors of the intrafusal muscles (gamma stimulus).

MF unit of intra-genu (ir-ge)
The motor units carrying out intrarotation of the knee are mainly located in the gracilis, sartorius, semimembranosus and semitendinosus muscles. These muscles are connected through the vasto-adductor membrane that is in turn located over the vastus medialis muscle. The CC of this MF unit is located over the fascia of the vastus medialis muscle.

MF unit of intra-talus (ir-ta)
Vectorial centre of coordination of the intrafusal muscles for the intra-talus MF unit (ir-ta); it is located midway of the leg, immediately behind the tibia (Fig. 4.74).
If the crural fascia (deep lamina) is fluid, then the primary and secondary afferents allow the alpha motor neurones to contract the intra-talus motor units.

MF unit of intra-pes (ir-pe)
Vectorial centre of coordination of the intrafusal muscles for the intra-pes MF unit (ir-pe); it is located over the muscle belly of the abductor hallucis muscle.

Fig. 4.68. Normal functioning of the gamma circuit.
(From G. Chiarugi and L. Bucciante, Istituzioni di anatomia dell'uomo. Piccin Nuova Libraria, Padova 1983, modified)

ARTICULAR CONFLICTS IN THE INTRAROTATION UNITS, LOWER LIMB

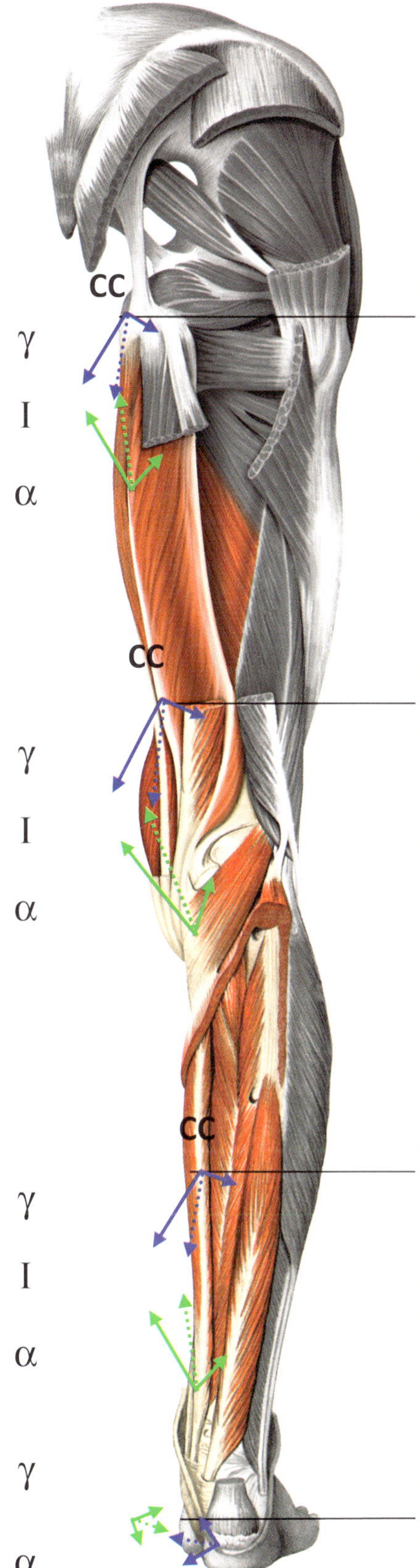

Fig. 4.69. Dysfunction of the gamma circuit.
(From G. Chiarugi and L. Bucciante, Istituzioni di anatomia dell'uomo. Piccin Nuova Libraria, Padova 1983, modified)

Pain in intrarotation of coxa
If the pectineal fascia is densified, then it does not adapt to the tractions of the intrafusal muscle fibres of the ir-cx MF unit; this does not allow the triggering of some afferents (II) and related alpha efferents. Consequently, only some extrafusal fibres will contract with repercussions on the joint capsule of the hip.
The densification of the fascia does not result in the blockage of the gamma circuit but only in its dysfunction. Both parallelograms are still in a mirror image but their resultant is no longer aligned with the joint axis.

Pain in intrarotation of genu
If the fascia lata lying over the vastus medialis muscle is densified, then it does not adapt to the tractions of the intrafusal muscle fibres of the ir-ge MF unit; this does not allow the triggering of some afferents (II) and related alpha efferents. Consequently, only some extrafusal fibres will contract with repercussions on the joint capsule of the knee.

Pain in intrarotation of talus
If the deep lamina of the crural fascia is densified then it does not adapt to the tractions of the intrafusal muscle fibres of the ir-ta MF unit; this does not allow the triggering of some afferents (II) and related alpha efferents. Consequently, only some extrafusal fibres will contract with repercussions on the joint capsule of the ankle.

Pain in intrarotation of pes
Vectorial centre and centre of perception of the MF unit intra-pes (ir-pe); normally both perceive internal rotation of the forefoot and in abnormal situations they perceive joint conflicts.

INTRAROTATION SEQUENCE AND STRETCH REFLEX

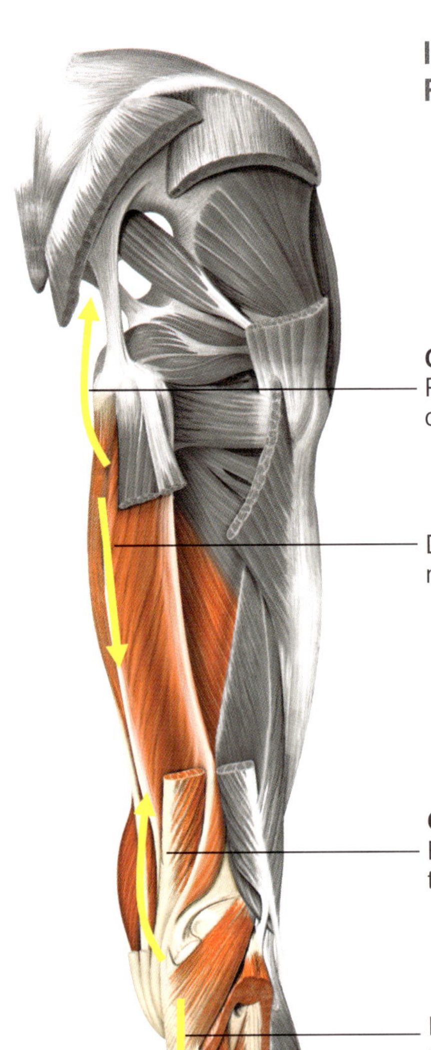

Fig. 4.70. Synergy of the intrarotation sequence in the lower limb.
(From G. Chiarugi and L. Bucciante, Istituzioni di anatomia dell'uomo. Piccin Nuova Libraria, Padova 1983, modified)

ACTIVATION OF THE GOLGI TENDON ORGANS

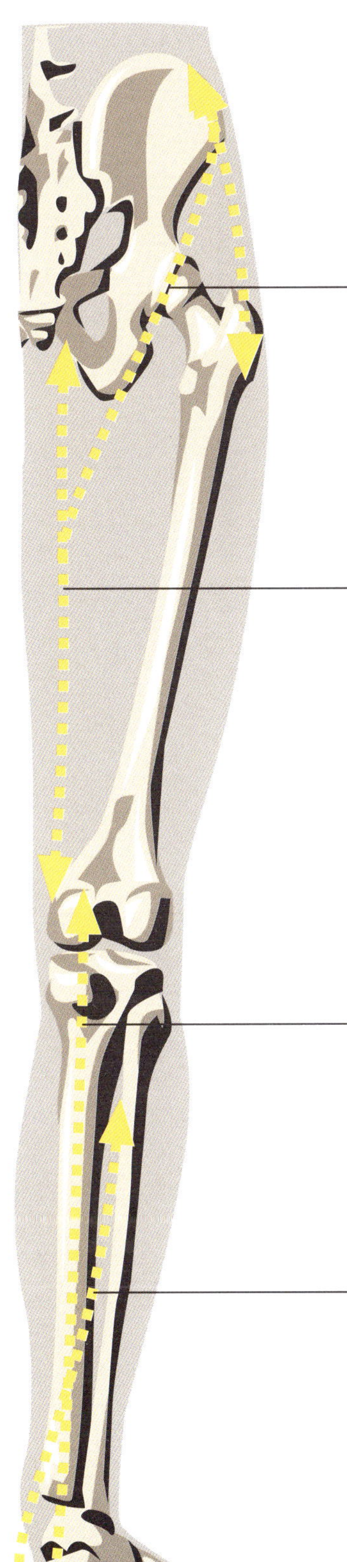

Fig. 4.71. Biarticular muscles for intrarotation in the lower limb.

Connection between pelvis and coxa
The anterior fibres of the gluteus minimus and tensor fascia lata muscles are connected through the inguinal ligament with the internal fasciae of the thigh surrounding the adductor magnus and sartorius muscles.

Connection between coxa and genu
The adductor magnus muscle internally rotates the hip and extends, through the medial collateral ligament, up to the pes anserinus where it is connected to the intrarotation forces of the knee.

Connection between genu and talus
The medial gastrocnemius muscle internally rotates genu and talus.

"The gastrocnemius muscles may receive additional bundles from the biceps, semitendinosus, semimembranosus and adductor magnus muscles. Some muscle fibres of the gastrocnemius originate from the joint capsule of the knee. The medial gastrocnemius partially participates in internal rotation of the knee and incidentally in internal torsion of the foot, hence it has a supinator action" (Chiarugi G. 1975).

Connection between talus and pes
The flexor hallucis longus muscle acts on the internal rotation of the ankle and foot.

"The flexor hallucis longus muscle originates from the fibula, from the fascia covering it and from the intermuscular posterior fibular septum separating it from the peroneal muscles. After travelling along the posterior wall of the talus, maintained in place by the deep layer of the laciniate ligament, it arrives in the sole of the foot and inserts on the base on the first and second phalanx. It is a flexor of the big toe, an extensor of the foot, as well as an adductor and supinator of the foot" (Chiarugi G. 1975).

FASCIAE OF THE INTRAROTATION SEQUENCE IN THE LOWER LIMB

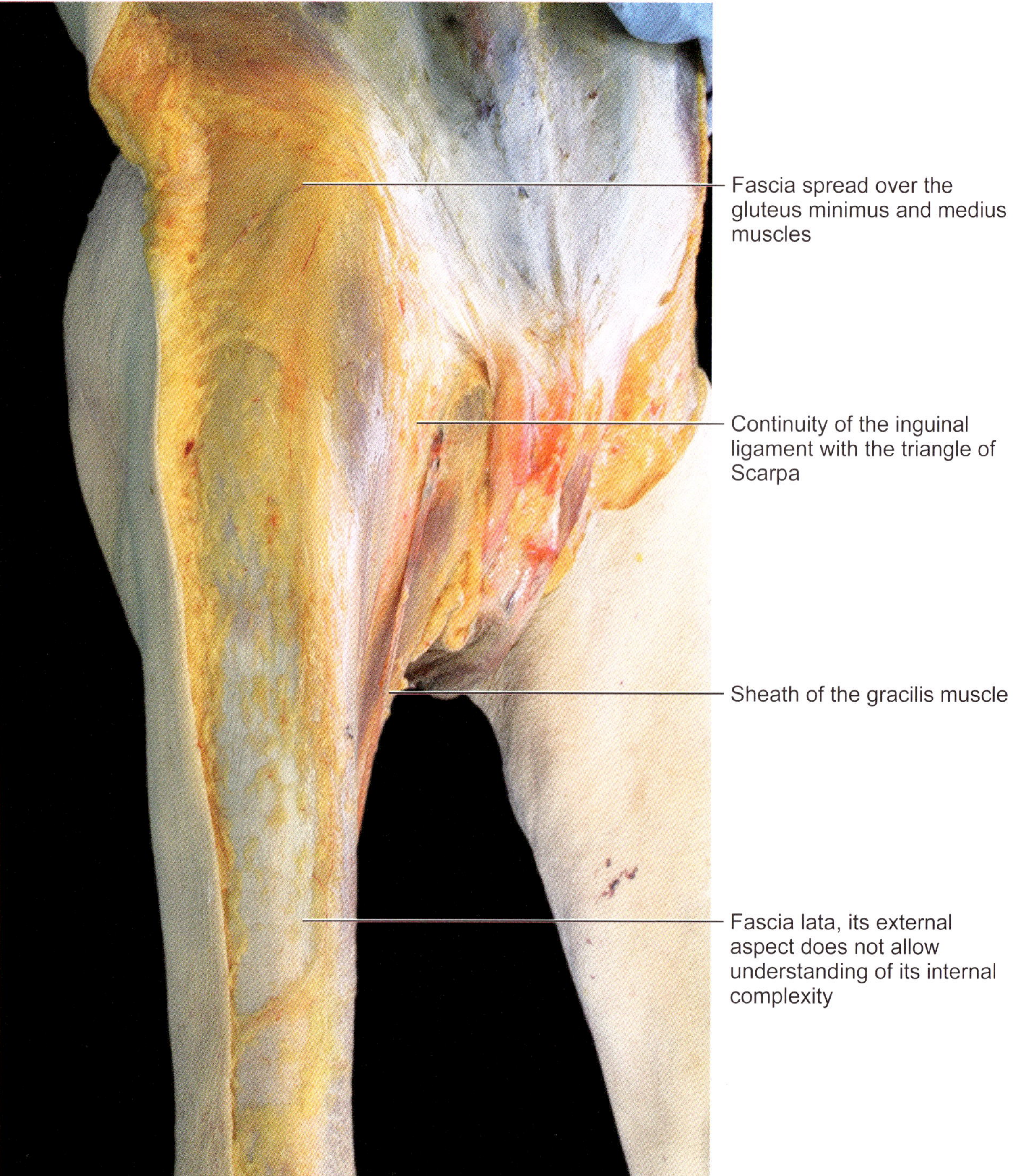

Fig. 4.72. Fascia lata in continuity with the gluteal and abdominal fasciae. The inguinal ligament connects the fascia of the gluteus minimus muscle with the fascia of the muscles included in the triangle of Scarpa.

FASCIAE OF THE INTRAROTATION SEQUENCE IN THE LOWER LIMB

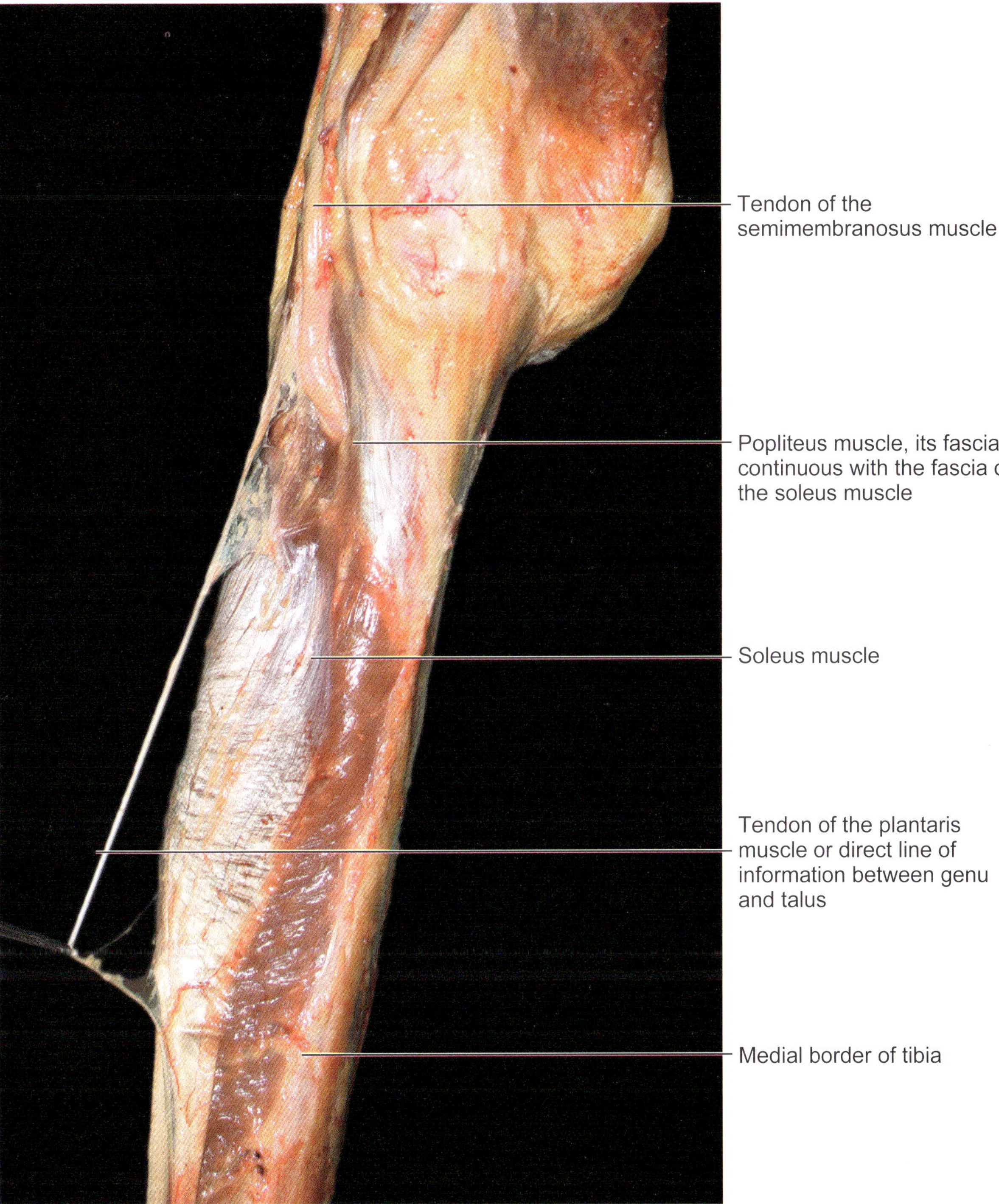

Fig. 4.73. Soleus muscle visible after removal of the gastrocnemii muscles. The removal of the muscles inserting on pes anserinus is helpful in highlighting the continuity between the tendon of semimembranosus with the fascia of the popliteus and soleus muscles.

FASCIAE OF THE INTRAROTATION SEQUENCE IN THE LOWER LIMB

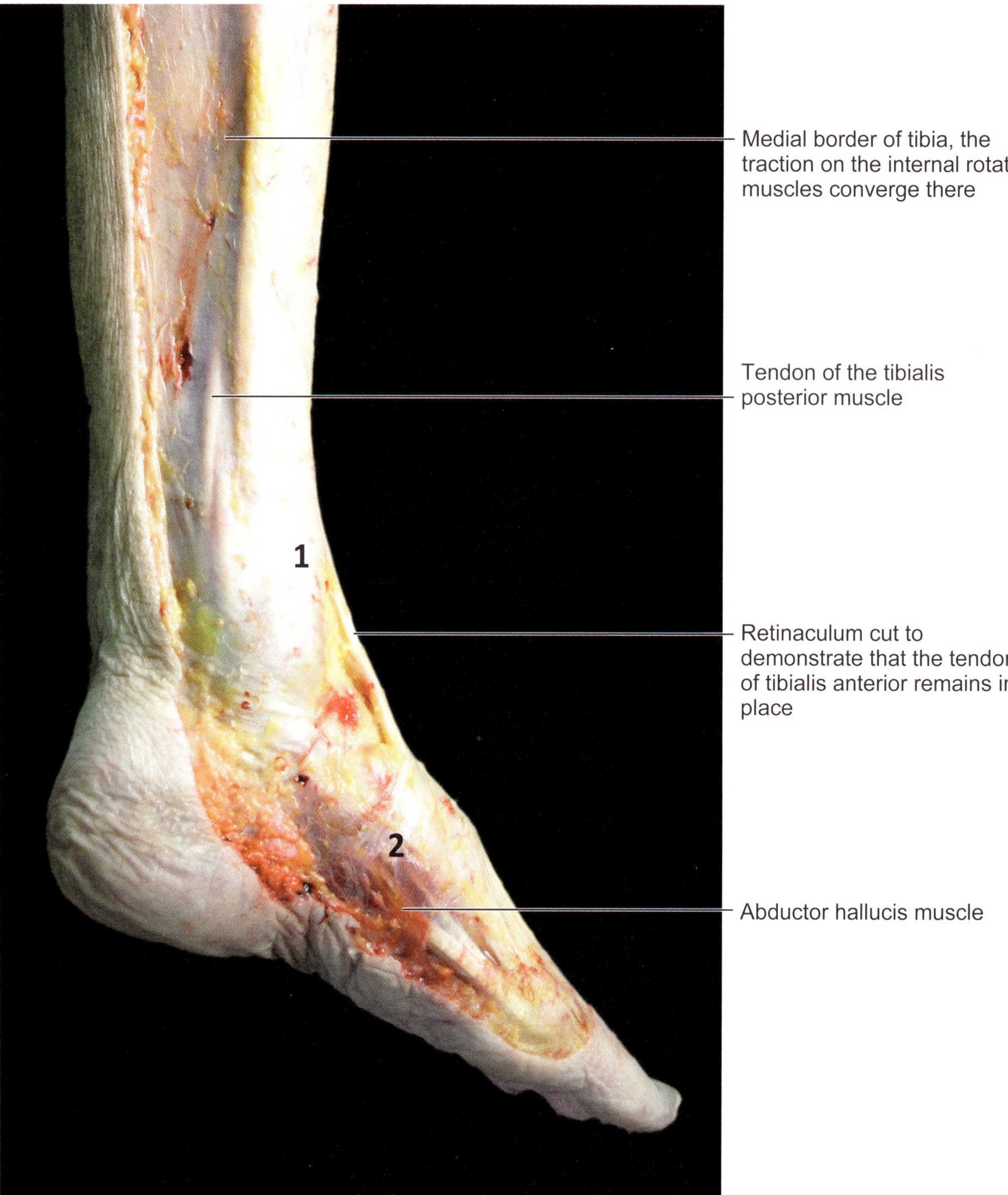

Fig. 4.74. Medial fascia of the leg and foot, superficial lamina. Even after cutting the extensor retinaculum (1), the tibialis anterior muscle remains in place by virtue of its origin and its insertion (2).

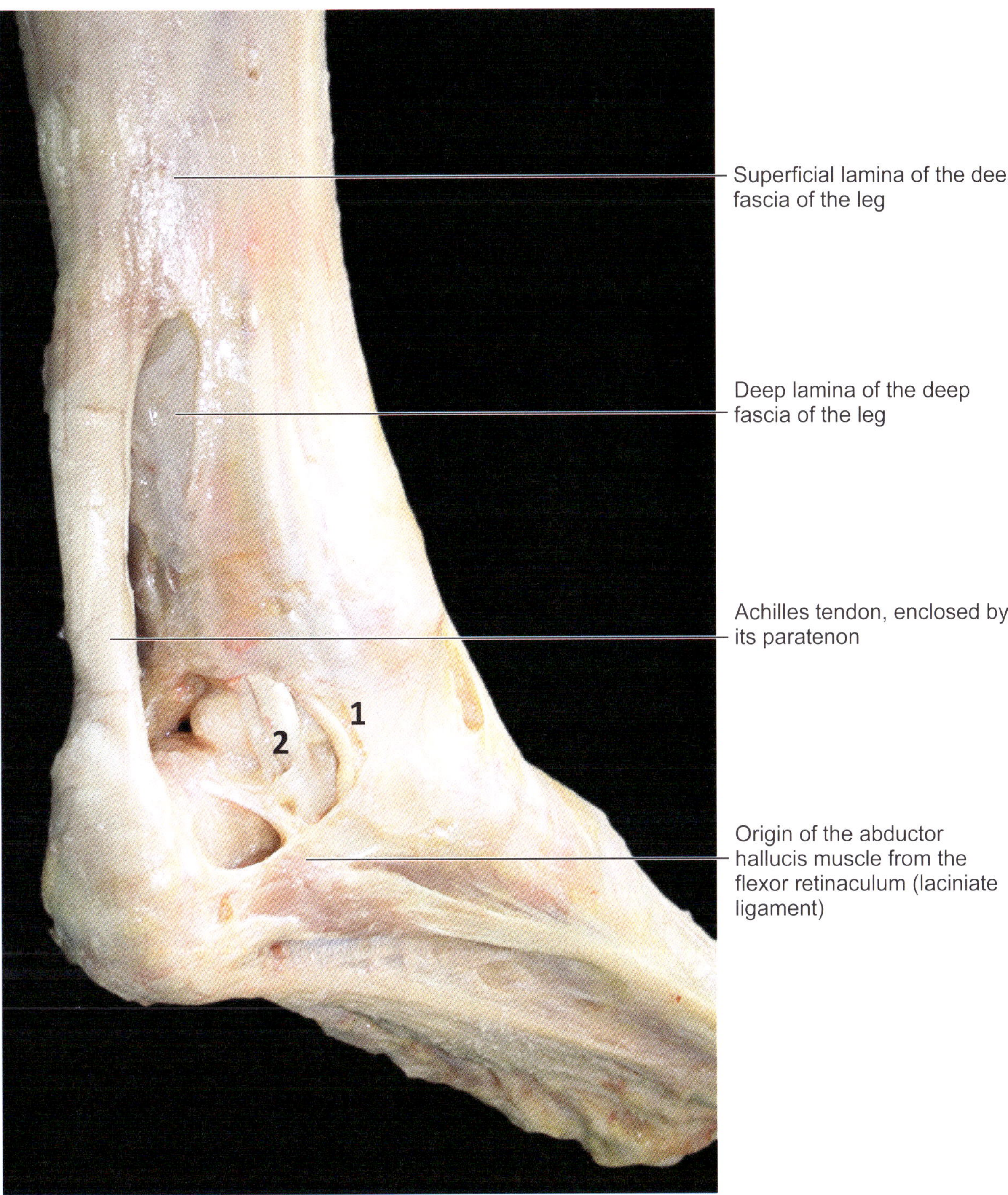

Fig. 4.75. Medial fascia of the leg and foot, deep lamina. The various laminae of the deep fascia (1) were cut, two tendons are visible behind the malleolus: that of flexor digitorum longus (2) and that of the tibialis posterior muscles.

POSTERIOR DEEP REGION OF THE LOWER LIMB, EXTRAROTATION SEQUENCE

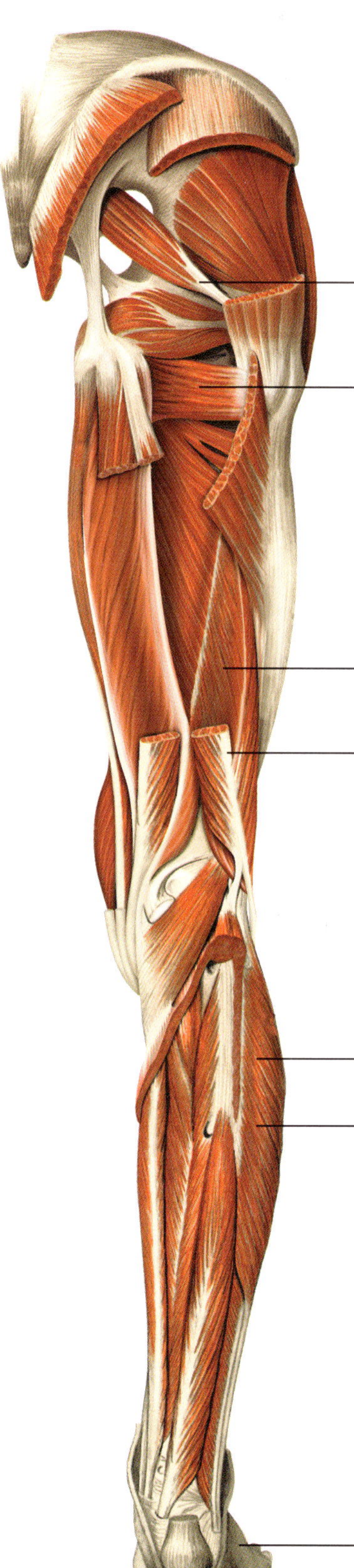

Hip external rotation (Fig. 4.77)
Primary or monoarticular muscles: piriformis, gluteus maximus
Secondary or biarticular muscles: iliopsoas, sartorius

Synergic or scheme muscles: quadratus femoris, obturator internus, adductor longus, brevis, magnus and minimus

Knee external rotation (Fig. 4.78)
Primary or monoarticular muscles: short head of biceps femoris

Secondary or biarticular muscles: long head of biceps femoris
Synergic or scheme muscles: lateral gastrocnemius

Ankle external rotation (pronation) (Fig. 4.79)
Primary or monoarticular muscles: peroneus brevis

Secondary or biarticular muscles: peroneus longus
Synergic or scheme muscles: peroneus tertius

Forefoot eversion (Fig. 4.80)
Secondary or biarticular muscles: extensor digitorum longus
Primary or monoarticular muscles: extensor digitorum brevis

Fig. 4.76. Posterior deep region of the lower limb.
(From G. Chiarugi and L. Bucciante, Istituzioni di anatomia dell'uomo. Piccin Nuova Libraria, Padova 1983, modified)

SEGMENTARY MOVEMENTS IMPLEMENTED BY THE MF UNITS OF EXTRAROTATION

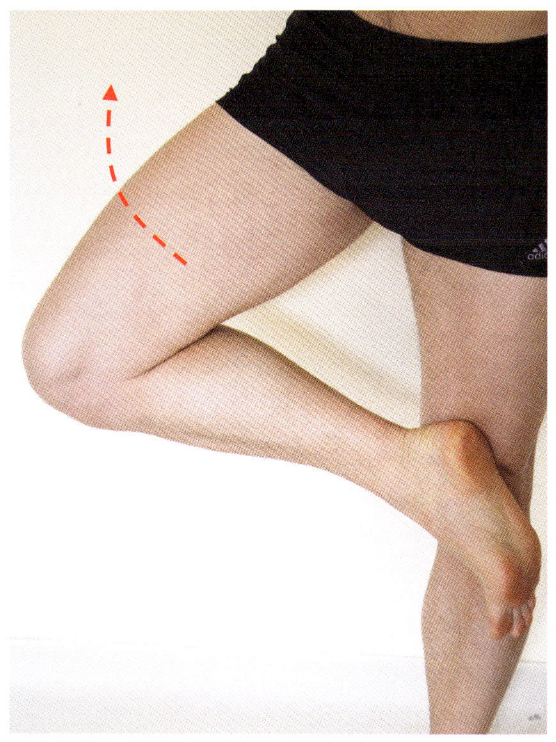

Fig. 4.77. Hip external rotation managed throughout its range by the myofascial unit of extra-coxa.

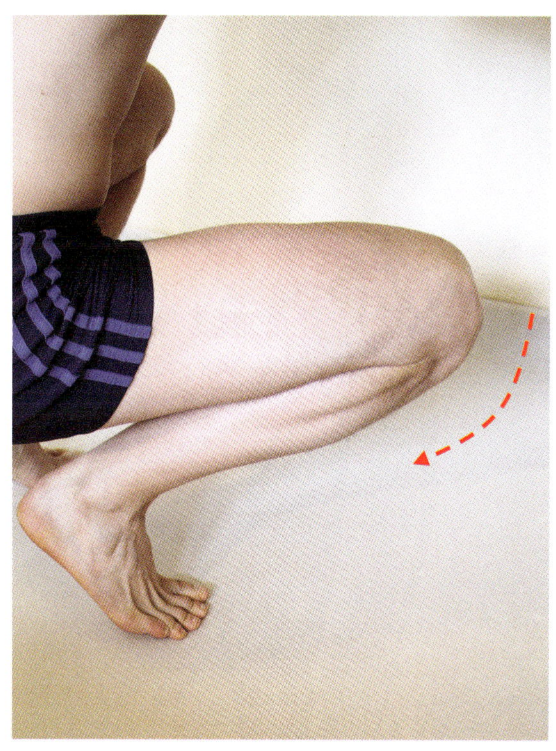

Fig. 4.78. Knee external rotation managed in the range of maximal flexion by the MF unit extra-genu.

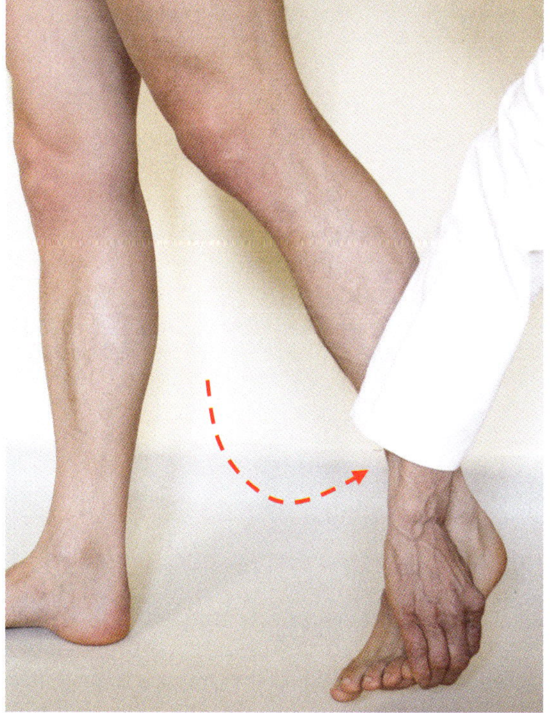

Fig. 4.79. Ankle external rotation coordinated by the myofascial unit of extra-talus.

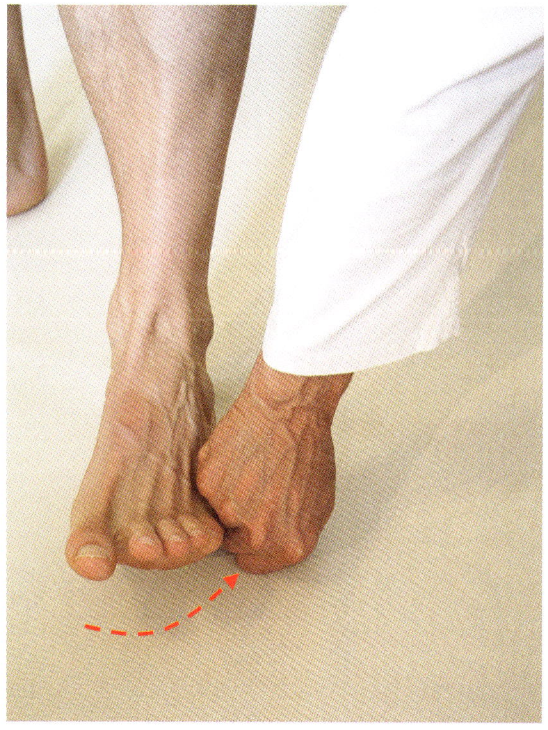

Fig. 4.80. Forefoot eversion managed by the myofascial unit of extra-pes.

The hand of the operator applies resistance to the movement which direction is indicated by the arrow.

COMPARTMENTS FOR THE MUSCLES OF EXTRAROTATION, LOWER LIMB (Fig. 4.82)

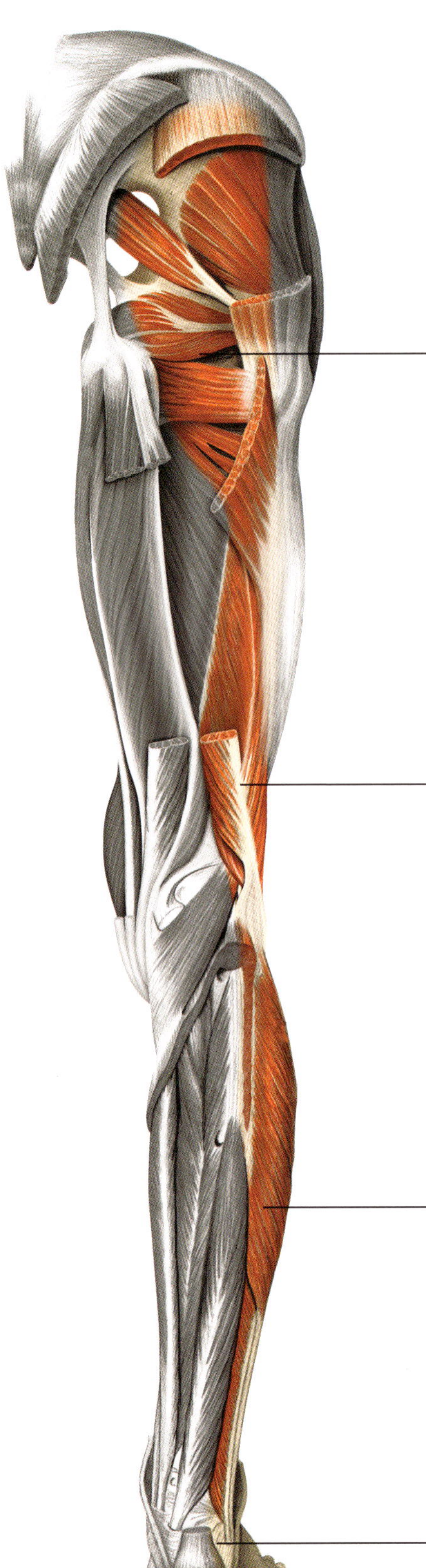

Fascial compartment for the extrarotation muscles of coxa

There are at least fifteen muscles contributing to the extrarotation of coxa. If the action of all these forces was not coordinated by the fascia uniting them, it would be like having many horses each acting on their own account.

"External rotation is produced by: gluteus maximus, quadratus femoris, obturator internus, gluteus medius and minimus with their dorsal fibres, iliopsoas, piriformis, sartorius, all the functional adductors except the pectineus muscle and the gracilis" (Platzer W. 1979).

Fascial structures for genu extrarotation

The fascia surrounding the biceps femoris muscle is connected to the fasciae of both soleus and peroneal muscles. Its tension determines a harmonic synchrony between these rotational forces.

Fascial compartments for talus extrarotation

Within the peroneal muscles there are motor units specific for the extrarotation of talus.

"Laterally the leg fascia sends one septum in front and one behind the peroneal muscles: the anterior and posterior fibular intermuscular septa. These septa are fixed on the fibula and help in the insertion of the peroneal muscles" (Chiarugi G. 1975).

Fascial compartment for the extrarotation muscles of pes

The extensor digitorum brevis muscle brings the foot outwards.

"The peroneus quartus is rarely present. It arises from the fibula, ... It may also send a small tendon to the fifth digit" (Platzer W. 2009).

Fig. 4.81. Fasciae connected to extrarotation muscles.
(From G. Chiarugi and L. Bucciante, Istituzioni di anatomia dell'uomo. Piccin Nuova Libraria, Padova 1983, modified)

GLOBAL MOVEMENT IMPLEMENTED BY THE EXTRAROTATION MF SEQUENCE

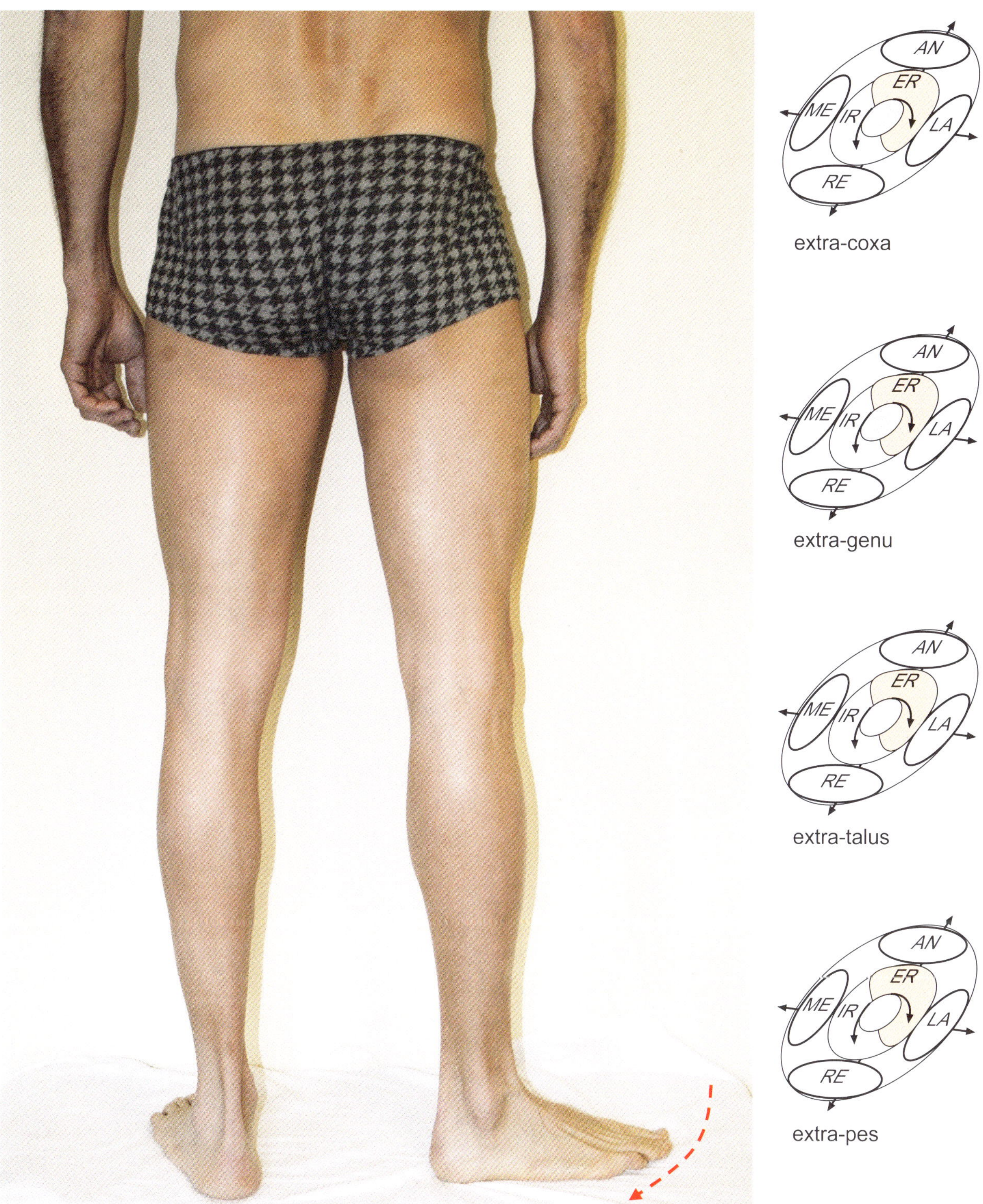

Fig. 4.82. Contraction of the extrarotation sequence rotates the entire lower limb externally.

In the limbs the intrarotation and extrarotation sequences do not form torque forces as in the trunk rather they act as antagonists to each other. When thinking of externally rotating the lower limb against a resistance as provided by the ground, the MF units of extra coxa, genu, talus and pes are activated. The stretching of the deep fascia connected to the extrarotation muscles sends specific afferents back to the brain for this direction.

PHYSIOLOGY OF THE EXTRAROTATION MF UNITS, LOWER LIMB

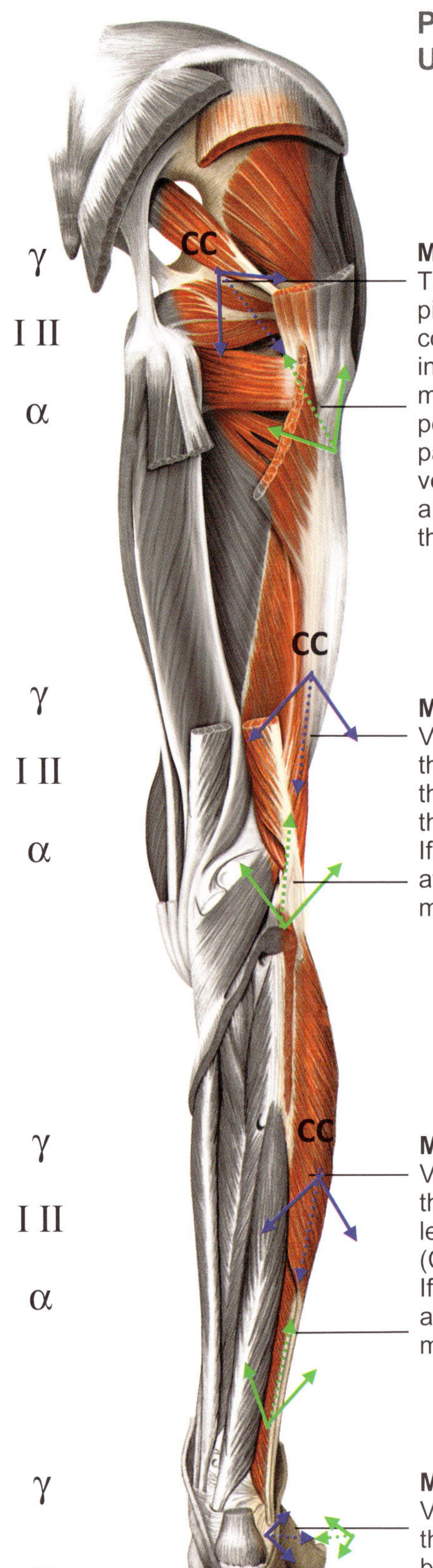

MF unit of extra-coxa (er-cx)
The external rotator muscles of coxa (gluteus medius, piriformis, etc) are connected together by the fascia covering them. The motor units of er-cx are distributed in those muscles, the centre of coordination of these motor units is located over the piriformis muscle. The perfect functioning of the gamma circuit causes the green parallelogram (convergence of the tendons) formed by the vectors of the extrafusal muscles (alpha stimulus) to be arranged in a mirror image to the parallelogram formed by the vectors of the intrafusal muscles (gamma stimulus).

MF unit of extra-genu (er-ge)
Vectorial centre of coordination of the intrafusal muscles for the extra-talus MF unit (er-ta); it is located midway down the thigh over the origin of the short head of biceps femoris on the lateral septum (Fig. 4.88).
If this fascia is fluid, then the primary and secondary afferents allow the alpha motor neurones to contract the motor units of extra-genu.

MF unit of extra-talus (er-ta)
Vectorial centre of coordination of the intrafusal muscles for the extra-talus MF unit (er-ta); it is located midway down the leg, over the fascial compartments of the peroneal muscles (CC).
If this fascia is fluid, then the primary and secondary afferents allow the alpha motor neurones to contract the motor units of extra-talus.

MF unit of extra-pes (er-pe)
Vectorial centre of coordination of the intrafusal muscles for the extra-pes MF unit (er-pe); it is located over the muscle belly of the extensor digitorum brevis muscle containing motor units for foot eversion.

Fig. 4.83. Normal functioning of the gamma circuit.
(From G. Chiarugi and L. Bucciante, Istituzioni di anatomia dell'uomo. Piccin Nuova Libraria, Padova 1983, modified)

ARTICULAR CONFLICTS IN THE EXTRAROTATION UNITS, LOWER LIMB

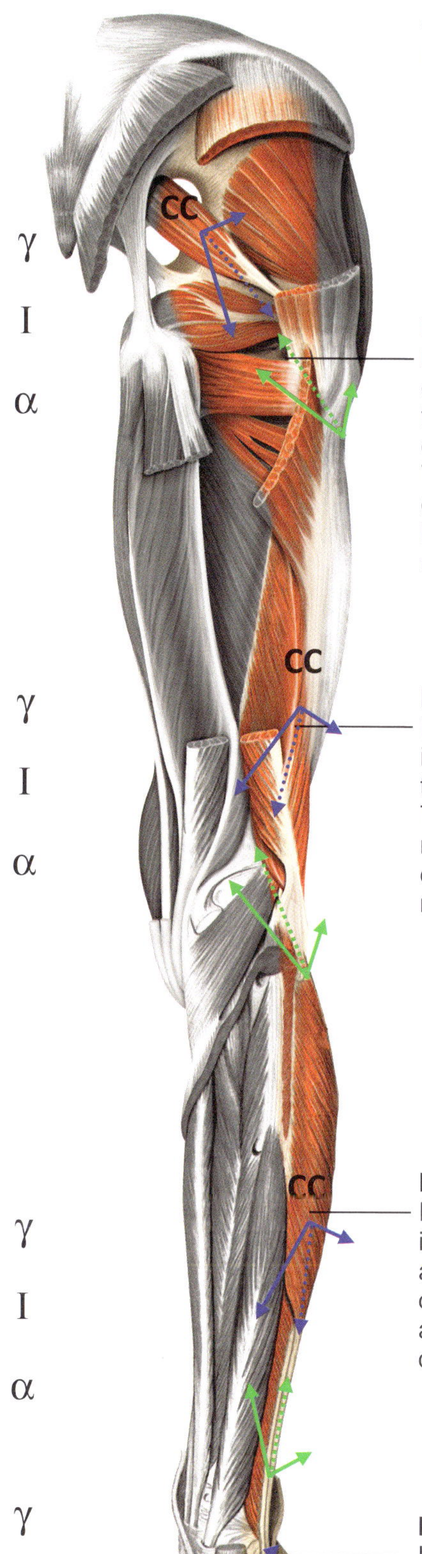

Pain in extrarotation of coxa
If the fascia of the piriformis muscle is densified, then it does not adapt to the tractions of the intrafusal muscle fibres of the er-cx MF unit; this does not allow the triggering of afferents (II) and related alpha efferents.
The consequent contraction of only some extrafusal fibres destabilises the coxofemoral joint.
Both parallelograms are still in a mirror image but their resultant is no longer aligned with the joint axis.

Pain in extrarotation of genu
If the latero-posterior fascia lata is densified, then some intrafusal muscle fibres are not able to contract and activate the related extrafusal fibres of the MF unit er-ge.
The excessive or deficient contraction of the biceps femoris muscle results in an articular conflict in the knee with consequent abnormal stretching of the capsule and hence receptors becoming nociceptors.

Pain in extrarotation of talus
If the retro-lateral crural fascia is densified, then some intrafusal muscle fibres are not able to contract and activate all the extrafusal fibres of the er-ta MF unit. If, for instance, only the muscle fibres of the peroneus longus are activated and not those of the peroneus brevis, then an incoordination occurs in the ankle.

Pain in extrarotation of pes
If the vectorial centre of the extrafusal muscle of the extra-pes MF unit (er-pe) is densified, then an excessive or deficient traction of the toe muscles is created with consequent deformation.

Fig. 4.84. Dysfunction of the gamma circuit.
(From G. Chiarugi and L. Bucciante, Istituzioni di anatomia dell'uomo. Piccin Nuova Libraria, Padova 1983, modified)

EXTRAROTATION SEQUENCE AND STRETCH REFLEX

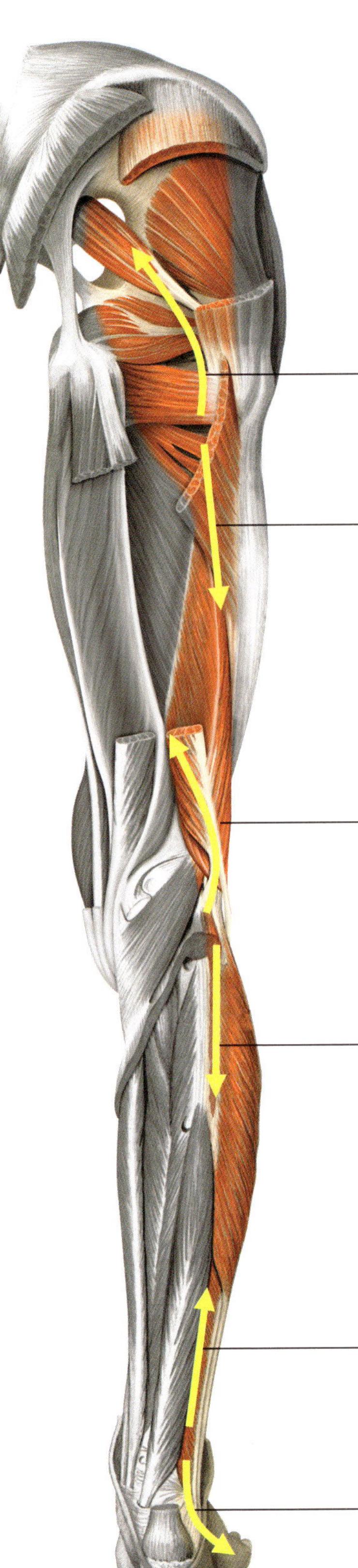

Coactivation of the MF unit of extra-coxa and extra-genu
Proximal traction of the lateral intermuscular septum operated by the gluteus maximus, piriformis and other external rotator muscles (Fig. 4.87).

Distal traction of the lateral septum operated by the insertion of the short head of the biceps femoris muscle.

Coactivation of the MF unit of extra-genu and extra-talus
Proximal traction of the lateral knee fascia by the biceps femoris muscle that also sends an expansion to the deep crural fascia.

"An expansion of the distal margin of the biceps femoris tendon continues in the fascia of the leg" (Chiarugi G. 1975).

Distal traction of the deep crural fascia by the peroneus longus and brevis muscles (Fig. 4.88).

Coactivation of the MF unit of extra-talus and extra-pes
Proximal traction of the dorsal fascia of the foot operated by the peroneus brevis muscle (Fig. 4.89).

Distal traction of the dorsal fascia of the foot and of the extensor retinaculum by the extensor digitorum brevis muscle (Fig. 4.90).

Fig. 4.85. Synergy of the extrarotation sequence in the lower limb.
(From G. Chiarugi and L. Bucciante, Istituzioni di anatomia dell'uomo. Piccin Nuova Libraria, Padova 1983, modified)

ACTIVATION OF THE GOLGI TENDON ORGANS

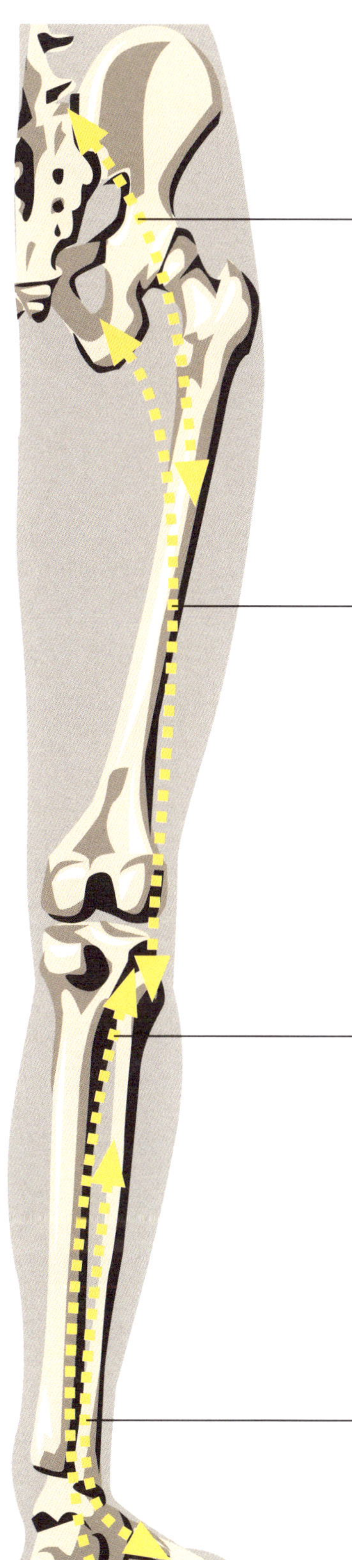

Fig. 4.86. Biarticular muscles for extrarotation in the lower limb.

Connection between pelvis and coxa
Extrarotation of coxa is implemented by the gluteus maximus and medius muscles, dorsal part. Both muscles are biarticular and their action on both joints is given by the fixed point upon which they exert a lever (pelvis or coxa).

Connection between coxa and genu
The piriformis muscle originates from the pelvic wall of the sacrum, the sciatic notch and the sacrotuberous ligament, where some fibres of the biceps femoris muscle take origin. This muscle inserts on the fibular head where it acts as an external knee rotator.

"The distal tendon of the biceps femoris muscle is fixed on the fibular head, it sends a big bundle in the anterior direction that includes the collateral fibular ligament and one of its expansion is continuous with the fascia of the leg" (Chiarugi G. 1975).

Connection between genu and talus
The peroneus longus muscle originates from the fibular head where the tendon of biceps femoris arrives. It also originates from the overlying fascia where the biceps femoris muscle attaches one of its tendinous expansion. The distal tendon of peroneus longus passes behind the lateral malleolus, it courses across the sole of the foot and fixes itself on the tuberosity of the first metatarsal bone. It gives the foot an outward torsional movement.

Connection between talus and pes
There are three fascial compartments within the peroneus brevis muscle containing three motor unit groups: the first is for extrarotation of the ankle and foot, the second is for extension of the ankle and foot, the third helps in lateral flexion of the ankle and foot.

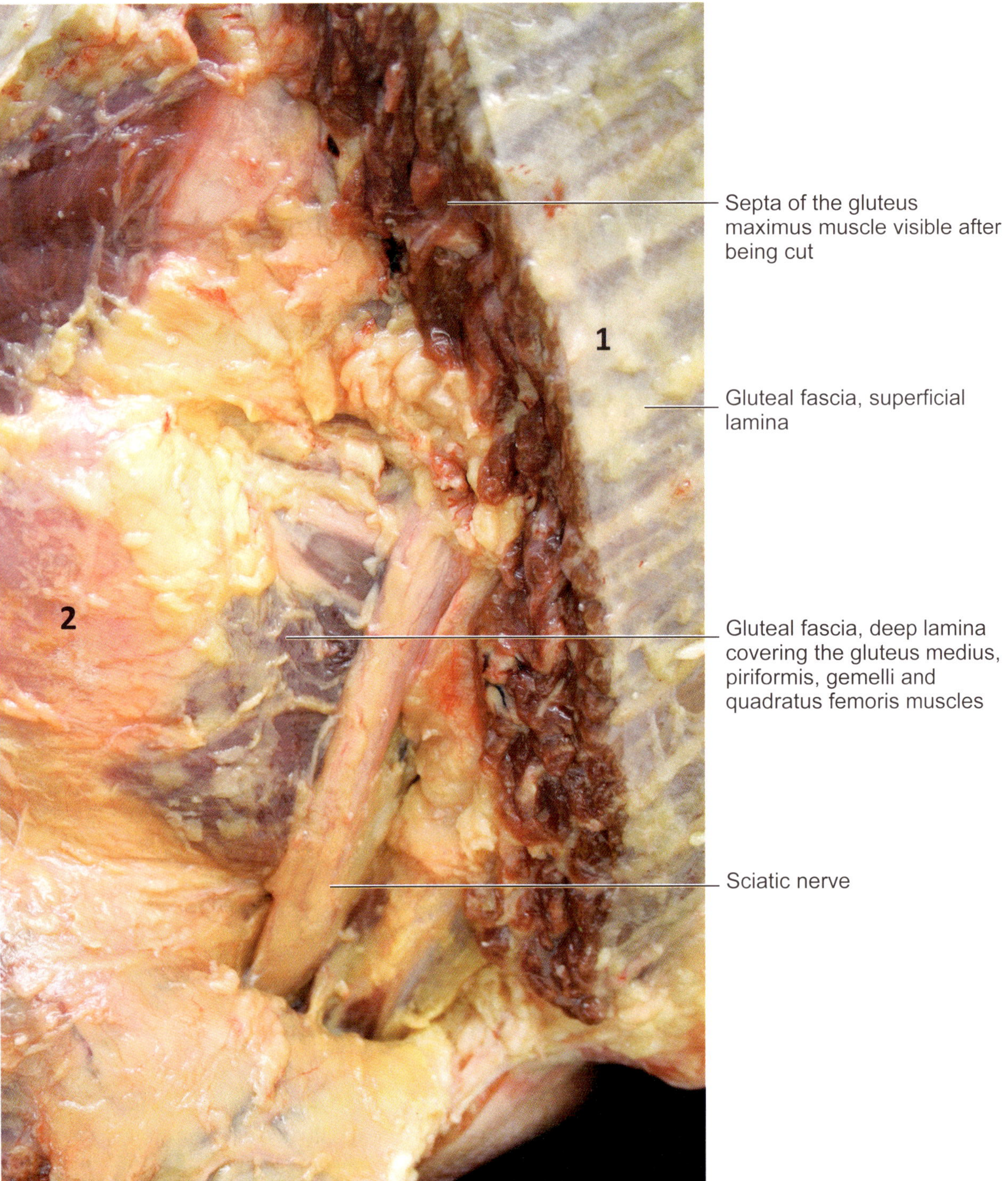

Fig. 4.87. Left gluteus maximus muscle. The gluteal fascia was cut (1) (superficial lamina), the tendon and loose connective tissue (2) were lifted laterally. Note the sciatic nerve and underneath it the gluteal fascia (deep lamina) covering the other external rotator muscles of the hip.

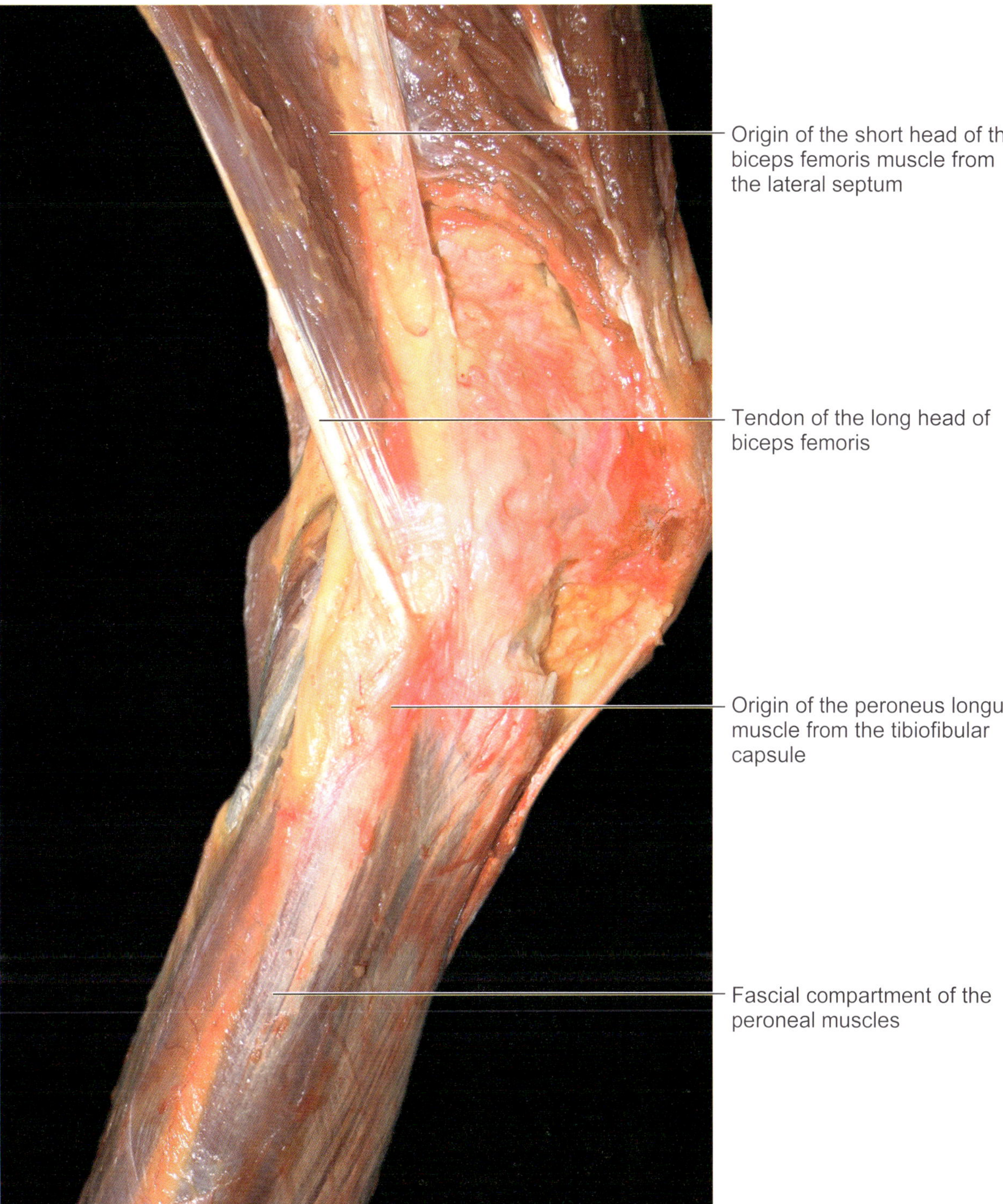

Fig. 4.88. Tendon of the biceps femoris muscle. When contrasting this picture with Figure 4.73, the mirror image of the disposition of the knee internal rotator with the external rotator muscles (biceps femoris muscle) is visible.

FASCIAE OF THE EXTRAROTATION SEQUENCE IN THE LOWER LIMB

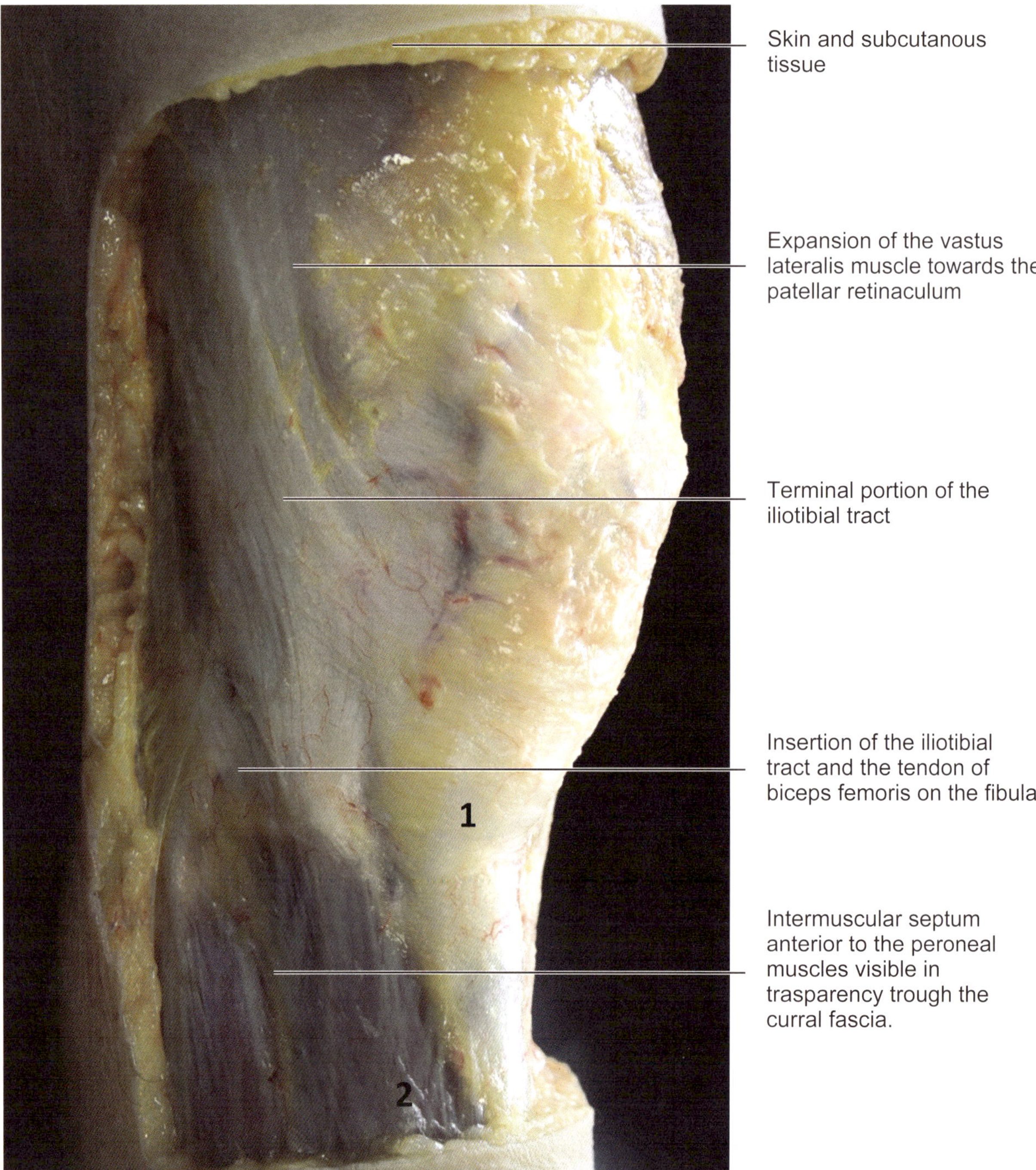

Fig. 4.89. Fascia of the lateral region of the knee. The tendon of the quadriceps (1) sends expansions to the anterior crural fascia where longitudinal collagen fibres (2) are formed. Laterally there are collagen fibres in continuity to the iliotibial tract. Posterior to the septum the collagen fibres are in continuity with the biceps femoris muscle.

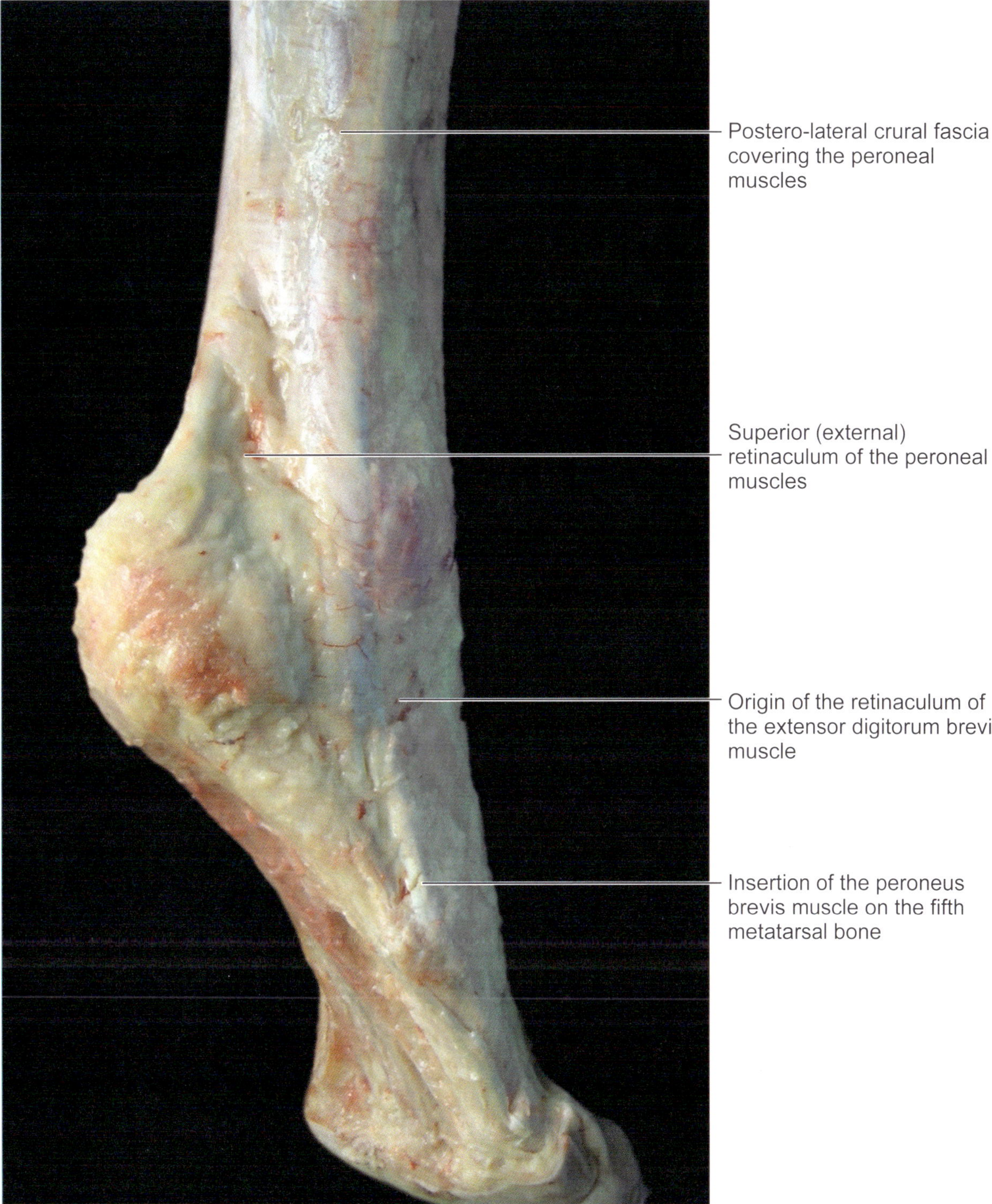

Fig. 4.90. Fascia of the retro-lateral region of the foot. "Both peroneal muscles since their respective tendons run behind the fibular malleolus, take advantage of this pulley, of the angle reflexion and achieve extension, abduction and pronation of the foot" (Chiarugi G. 1975).

CHAPTER 5

CENTRES OF FUSION AND DIAGONALS

MOTOR SCHEMES AND BIDIRECTIONAL MOVEMENTS

In this chapter the centres of fusion and motor schemes of the single segment along with global motor schemes of the entire limb (diagonals) are investigated.

If movement was only developed along the spatial planes, the centres of coordination (CCs) would be sufficient. Since movement is also developed along the intermediate degrees between one plane and the other, the centres of fusion (CFs) then become necessary. The CCs coordinate the vectors formed by the ipsidirectional motor units whilst the CFs coordinate the vectors formed by three myofascial units. The CCs are located on the epimysial fascia spread over the muscle belly whilst the CFs are located on the aponeurotic fascia spread over the tendons of muscles implementing, for instance, flexion, adduction and internal rotation (motor scheme of ante-medio-intra).

The fasciae overlying these tendons act like coachmen managing their intervention. Since a movement of scheme is implemented by several muscles, the fascia connected to them must fuse their actions together (centre of fusion or CF).

The vectors of the CCs belonging to the limbs have a proximal distal direction. The vectors of the CFs have a distal proximal direction since they must coordinate two MF units located in the proximal segment. The only exceptions are the CFs of the hand and foot since they must be able to perceive the tensions of the distal muscles and to transmit them to the proximal diagonal. In the trunk the vectors of the MF sequences and diagonals start from the head since it is the helm directing body movements.

The motor schemes along the intermediate degrees between two spatial planes can be implemented mainly in the shoulder and hip joints. For instance, the shoulder may be shifted from the antepulsion position to that of lateropulsion by passing through all the intermediate degrees since it is served by the pectoralis major and deltoid muscles. These muscles are structured like rheostats[1], namely with bundles of muscle fibres that are activated in succession. The same function is achieved by the three gluteal muscles for the movements of the hip.[2]

The movements along the intermediate range always take advantage of the movements of internal and external rotation.

The distal part of the diagonal perceives the intermediate movements of carpus-digiti and talus-pes.

The elbow and knee implement a static stabilisation of the corresponding intermediate diagonal.

The shoulder and hip move along all intermediate degrees required by the movement schemes of the extremity (Fig. 5.2).

Traditional medicine connects these movement schemes to cerebral motor patterns and to intraspinal reflex loops, but it does not refer to the peripheral myofascial organisation. Instead in all voluntary movements three organisations intervene: first the mind thinks about the movement that the hand or foot must realise; second the intraspinal reflex loops manage the alpha-gamma circuits; and third the myofascial stretching provides for the synchronisation of the various myofascial units based upon the transitions from one plane to the other and upon the changes in joint range.

Neural circuits are always activated in a similar manner (all or nothing) hence there must be an architecture in the periphery able to harmonise the stimuli from the central nervous system. The anatomical structure confirms the existence of this organisation. For instance, the biceps brachii muscle is divided into two parts since the long head participates in the motor scheme of ante-latero-humerus and ante-latero-cubitus whilst the short head participates in the motor scheme of ante-medio-humerus and ante-medio-cubitus. The same subdivision is found in the triceps brachii, triceps surae, quadriceps muscles, etc. Hence when the motor units distributed in all the regions of these muscles are activated then movement is managed by a CC. On the other hand, when the motor units belonging to only a region of these muscles are activated then movement is managed by CFs.

[1] All flat muscles, having a laminar shape and covering a large area of the body (i.e. muscles of the abdominal wall), are activated during natural movements but only several determined bundles of the muscular complex and those precise bundles inserted into the muscular chain implicated by the contraction are activated. (Benninghoff G. 1986)

[2] The muscle bundles of gluteus maximus, like the deltoid muscle, are easily individualised and separated by connective septa; they extend outwards and continue into the iliotibial tract of the fascia lata. (Chiarugi G. 1975)

CENTRES OF FUSION AND DIAGONALS OF THE UPPER LIMB

All muscles participate in multiple movements since they are the combination of multidirectional motor units. The deltoid is an example: its anterior portion is formed of motor units dedicated to antepulsion, the lateral portion is formed of motor units dedicated to lateropulsion, the posterior part is formed by motor units dedicated to retropulsion, its deeper fibres act upon rotation. This occurs because the deltoid is an ensemble of muscular fibres separated by intermuscular septa originating from the deltoid fascia. This fascia is connected to neuromuscular spindles and to Golgi tendon organs, and because of these connections, the fascia coordinates the various joint positions of the shoulder. For instance, when passing from antepulsion to lateropulsion a slight simultaneous rotation is also occurring. Only the CF ante-latero-humerus, located on the overlying fascia of the deltoid tendon, is able to manage the decrease in one MF unit and the increase in another MF unit during arm movements.

When descending along the limb other centres of fusion are found, they coordinate the intervention of two or three MF units when implementing motor schemes. A single muscle coincides with the CC of one MF unit, whilst the CF coincides with the convergence of two or three tendons (Fig. 5.1). For instance, over the epitrochlea the tendons of flexor carpi radialis (antepulsion vector), pronator teres (intrarotation vector) and flexor carpi ulnaris (mediopulsion vector) muscles are found. The centre of fusion of an-me-cu (ante-medio-cubitus) is located over this tendinous convergence whilst the centre of fusion an-me-ca (ante-medio-carpus) is found over the distal tendons of the same muscles. Unfortunately, the anatomical names of many muscles are misleading. For instance, the name of the flexor carpi radialis muscle implies an action only on the wrist, whereas it also acts upon elbow flexion, hence it participates to the motor schemes of both joints.

The two vectors or forces generated by two MF units converge into the centre of fusion, hence the CF corresponds to the resultant of two vectors. The diagonal connects the vectorial resultant of the centres of fusion placed in series: vectors of carpus, cubitus and humerus; the diagonal synthesises the intervention of each CF into a unique resultant.

At the level of digiti, the vectors have inverted their direction (proximal distal) since the motor needs of the hand and foot require the adjustment of the proximal muscles of the limbs. At the level of carpus, an interaction is created between the small muscles of the hand and the tendons of the powerful muscles of the forearm.

The recruitment of the proximal MF units[3] occurs during activities of the hand.

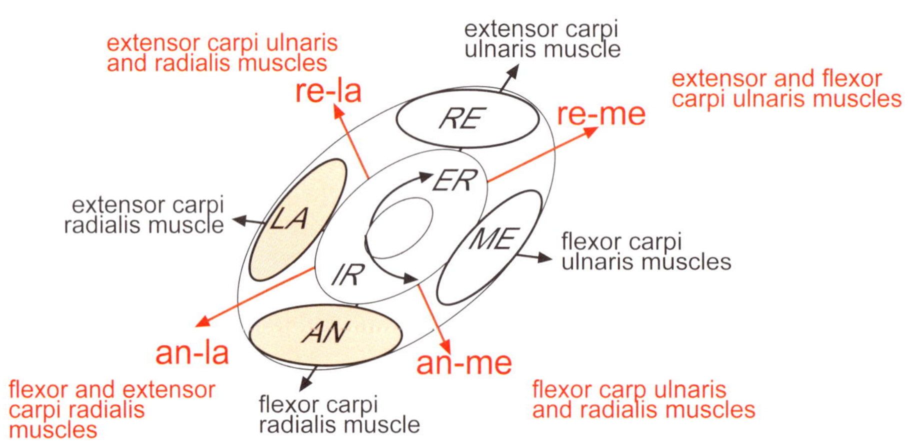

Fig. 5.1 Formation of the centres of fusion (CFs) from the association of two MF units or from two spatial directions. In this figure the forearm muscles were used as an example.

[3] "Resistance increases central excitation as a result from tension of the muscle, tendon and joint. With maximal resistance however, the contraction is not limited to a single muscle but is spread to other muscles through an irradiation process. Manual maximal resistance is fundamental to all facilitatory proprioceptive techniques." (Kabat H. 1954)

MOTOR SCHEMES OF THE UPPER LIMB IMPLEMENTED ACCORDING TO DIAGONAL PATTERNS

Fig. 5.2. Ante-latero diagonal or movement of the entire upper limb according to the an-la pattern.

Fig. 5.3. Ante-medio diagonal or movement of the entire upper limb according to the an-me pattern.

Fig. 5.4. Retro-latero diagonal or movement of the entire upper limb according to the re-la pattern.

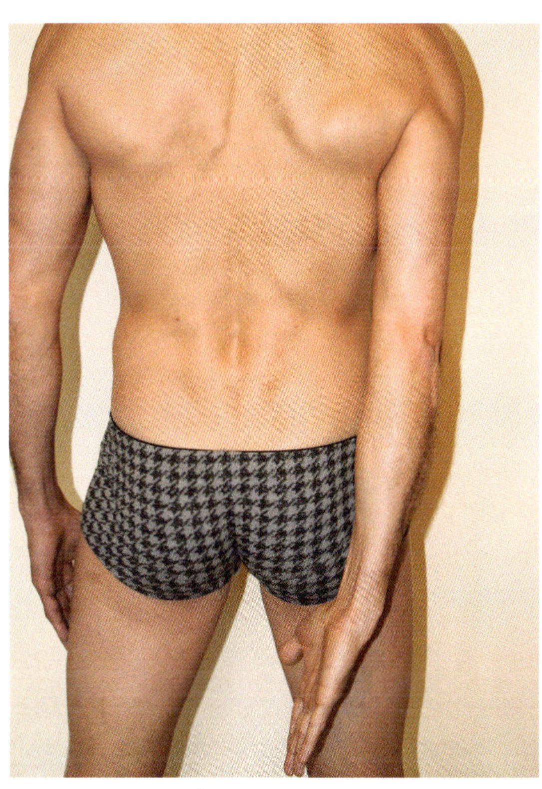

Fig. 5.5. Retro-medio diagonal or movement of the entire upper limb according to the re-me pattern.

ANTE-LATERO CENTRES OF FUSION, UPPER LIMB

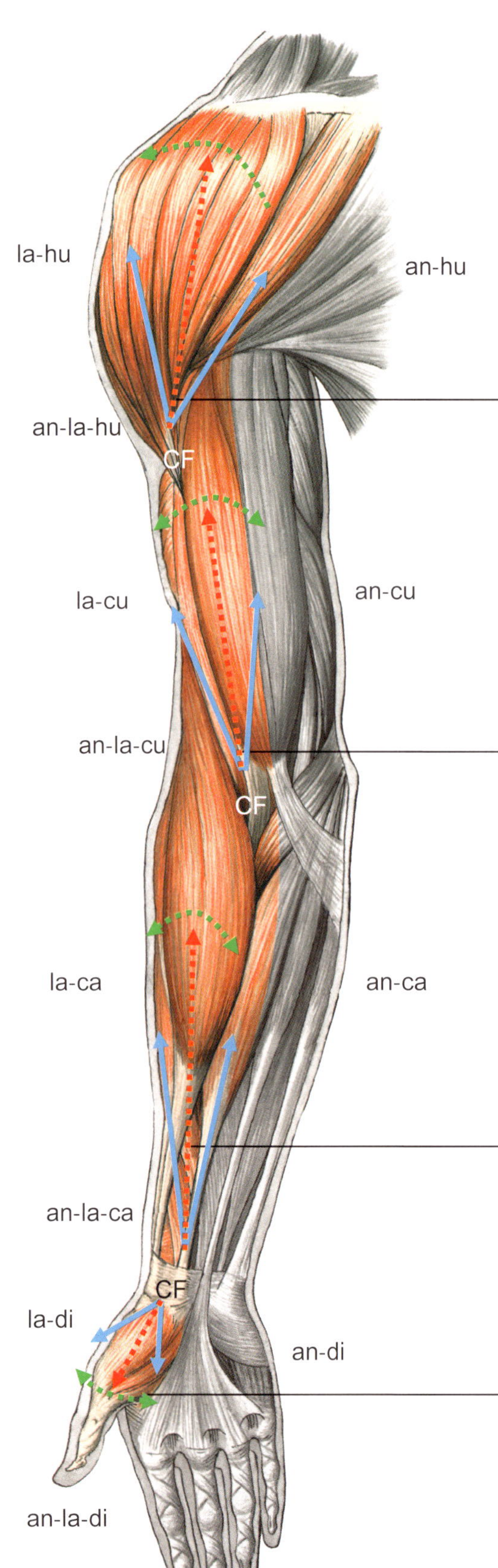

Motor scheme of ante-latero-humerus (an-la-hu)
The CF an-la-hu, located between the flexor and abductor tendinous fibres of the deltoid, interacts with the spindles and tendon organs of the MF units of an-hu and la-hu during movements of the humerus from one plane to the other.

Motor scheme of ante-latero-cubitus (an-la-cu)
The CF an-la-cu, located between the tendons of the biceps brachii, brachialis and brachioradialis muscles, interacts with the spindles and tendon organs of the MF units of an-cu and la-cu during movements of the elbow from one plane to the other.
The CC an-cu coordinates the motor units distributed in both muscle bellies of biceps brachii whilst the CF an-la-cu acts upon the motor units of the long head of the biceps brachii muscle, namely those included in its lateral portion (Fig. 5.6, 5.14).

Motor scheme of ante-latero-carpus (an-la-ca)
The CF an-la-ca, located between the tendinous fibres of the brachioradialis and flexor carpi radialis muscles, interacts with the spindles and tendon organs of the MF units of an-ca and la-ca during movements of the wrist from one plane to the other.

Motor scheme of ante-latero-digiti (an-la-di)
The CF an-la-di, located between the proximal tendinous fibres of the thenar eminence, interacts with the spindles and tendon organs of the MF units of an-di and la-di during movements of the thumb from one plane to the other.

Fig. 5.6. Centres of fusion of ante-latero, UL.
(From G. Chiarugi and L. Bucciante, Istituzioni di anatomia dell'uomo. Piccin Nuova Libraria, Padova 1983, modified)

ANTE-LATERO DIAGONAL, UPPER LIMB (Fig. 5.2)

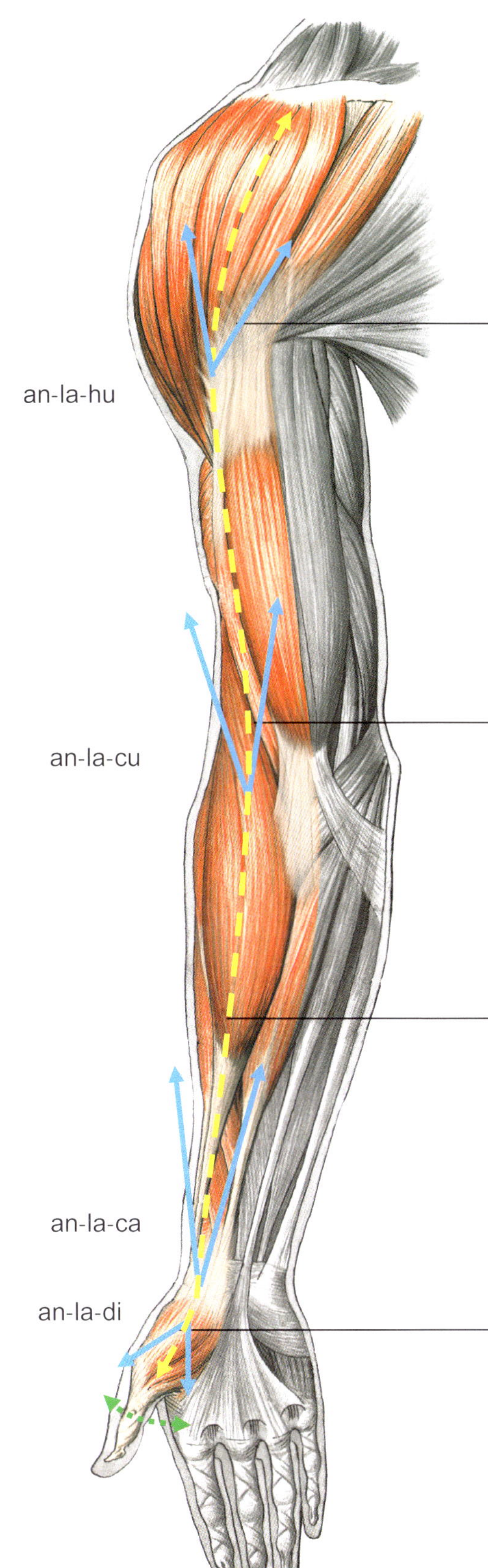

Fig. 5.7. Ante-latero diagonal, upper limb.
(From G. Chiarugi and L. Bucciante, Istituzioni di anatomia dell'uomo. Piccin Nuova Libraria, Padova 1983, modified)

Synergy of an-la-hu with the global scheme
The proximal part of the ante-latero diagonal synchronises the action of the CF an-la-hu with the motor pattern of thumb opposition. This longitudinal management of the CFs is similar to the management of the CCs by the myofascial sequences. In myofascial sequences the recruitment of the MF unit is more proximo-distal whilst in the diagonals the synergic recruitment of the CFs mainly occurs in a disto-proximal way.

Synergy of an-la-cu with the global scheme
The medial part of the ante-latero diagonal synchronises the CF an-la-cu with the motor pattern of thumb opposition and with the shift of the shoulder from ante to latero, hence its adaptation is proximo-distal and disto-proximal.

Synergy of an-la-ca with the global scheme
The distal part of the ante-latero diagonal synchronises the CF an-la-ca with the motor pattern of thumb opposition, hence there is a more prevalent proximo-distal adaptation.

Synergy required by the CF an-la-di
The movement of thumb opposition is implemented by the thenar eminence and flexor pollicis longus muscles. As the effort of these muscles progressively increases there is an adaptation or stretching of the retinaculum and hence, through the stretch reflex, the recruitment of the proximal CF occurs.

ANTE-MEDIO CENTRES OF FUSION, UPPER LIMB

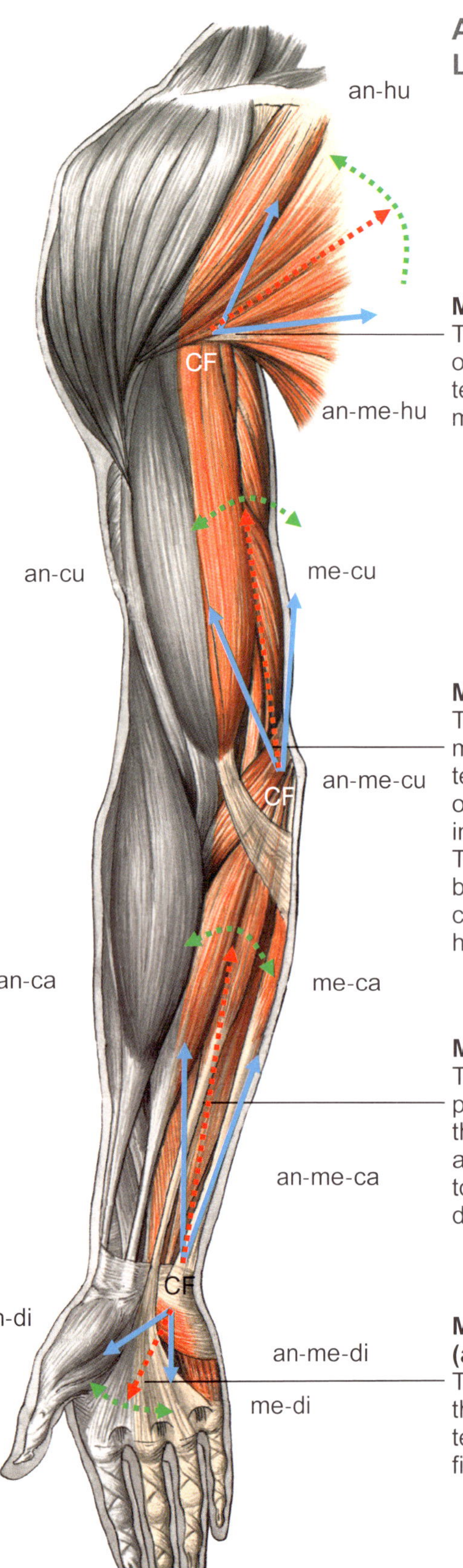

Motor scheme of ante-medio-humerus (an-me-hu)
The CF an-me-hu, located between the tendinous fibres of pectoralis major, interacts with the spindles and tendon organs of the MF units of an-hu and me-hu during movements of humerus from one plane to the other.

Motor scheme of ante-medio-cubitus (an-me-cu)
The CF an-me-cu, located between the tendons of the medial biceps brachii, flexor carpi ulnaris and pronator teres muscles, interacts with the spindles and tendon organs of the MF units of an-cu, ir-cu and me-cu during intermediate movements of the elbow (Fig. 5.15).
The CC an-cu coordinates the motor units distributed in both muscle bellies of biceps brachii whilst the CF an-me-cu coordinates the motor units located only in the short head of biceps brachii and other epitrochlear muscles.

Motor scheme of ante-medio-carpus (an-me-ca)
The CF an-me-ca, located between the tendons of palmaris longus and flexor carpi ulnaris, interacts with the spindles and tendon organs of the MF units of an-ca and me-ca during movements of the wrist from one plane to the other. The single CC interacts with the spindles during the degrees of flexion or adduction of the wrist.

Motor scheme of ante-medio-digiti, fifth digit (an-me-di)
The CF an-me-di, located between the tendinous fibres of the hypothenar eminence, interacts with the spindles and tendon organs of the MF units of an-di and me-di during fine movements of the fifth digit.

Fig. 5.8. Centres of fusion of ante-medio, UL.
(From G. Chiarugi and L. Bucciante, Istituzioni di anatomia dell'uomo. Piccin Nuova Libraria, Padova 1983, modified)

ANTE-MEDIO DIAGONAL, UPPER LIMB (Fig. 5.3)

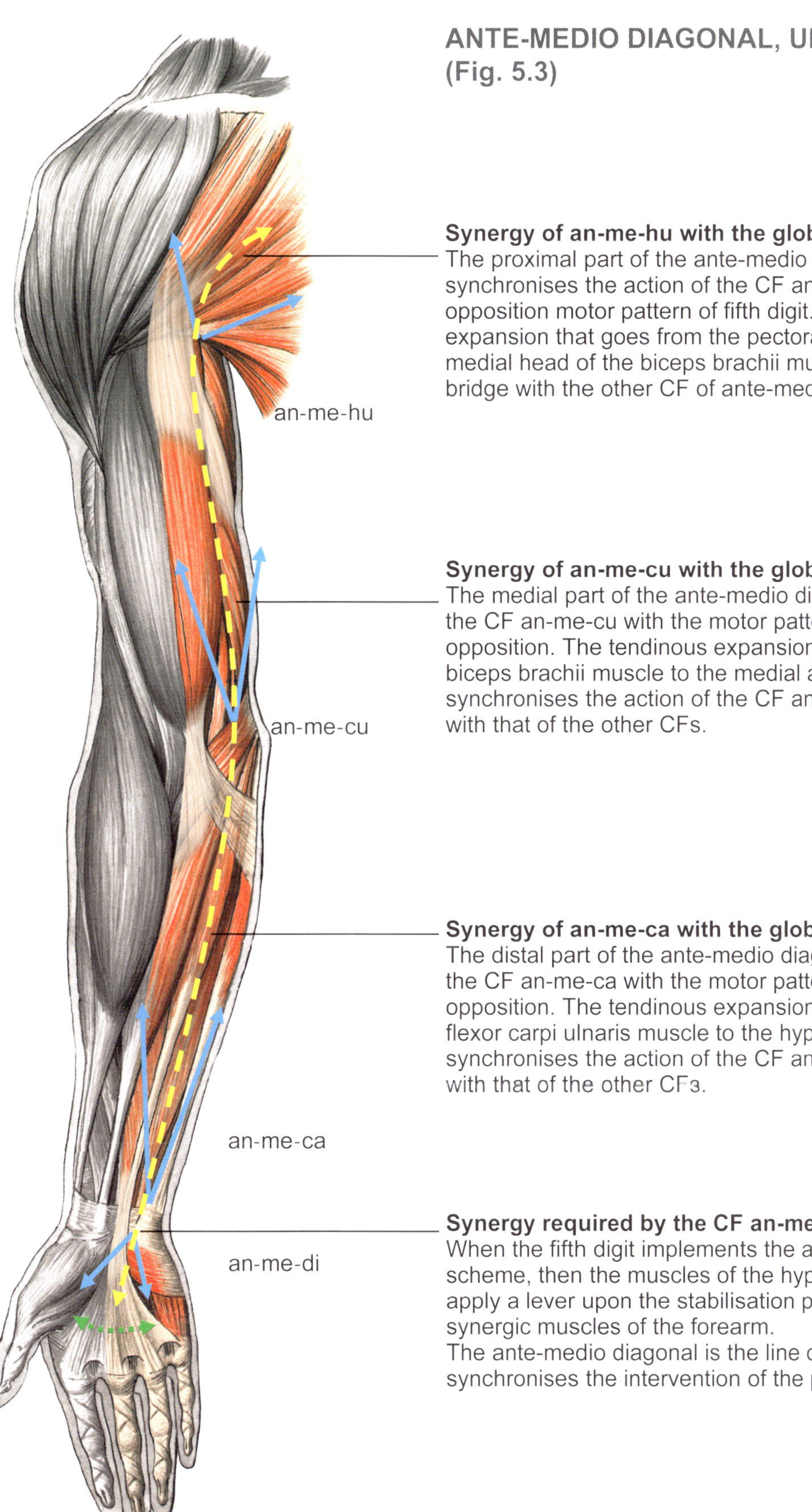

Fig. 5.9. Ante-medio diagonal, upper limb.
(From G. Chiarugi and L. Bucciante, Istituzioni di anatomia dell'uomo. Piccin Nuova Libraria, Padova 1983, modified)

Synergy of an-me-hu with the global scheme
The proximal part of the ante-medio diagonal synchronises the action of the CF an-me-hu with the opposition motor pattern of fifth digit. The tendinous expansion that goes from the pectoralis major to the medial head of the biceps brachii muscles creates a bridge with the other CF of ante-medio.

Synergy of an-me-cu with the global scheme
The medial part of the ante-medio diagonal synchronises the CF an-me-cu with the motor pattern of fifth digit opposition. The tendinous expansion that goes from the biceps brachii muscle to the medial antebrachial fascia synchronises the action of the CF ante-medio-cubitus with that of the other CFs.

Synergy of an-me-ca with the global scheme
The distal part of the ante-medio diagonal synchronises the CF an-me-ca with the motor pattern of fifth digit opposition. The tendinous expansion that goes from the flexor carpi ulnaris muscle to the hypothenar eminence synchronises the action of the CF ante-medio of carpus with that of the other CFs.

Synergy required by the CF an-me-di
When the fifth digit implements the ante-medio-digiti scheme, then the muscles of the hypothenar eminence apply a lever upon the stabilisation provided by the synergic muscles of the forearm.
The ante-medio diagonal is the line of force that synchronises the intervention of the proximal CFs.

RETRO-LATERO CENTRES OF FUSION, UPPER LIMB

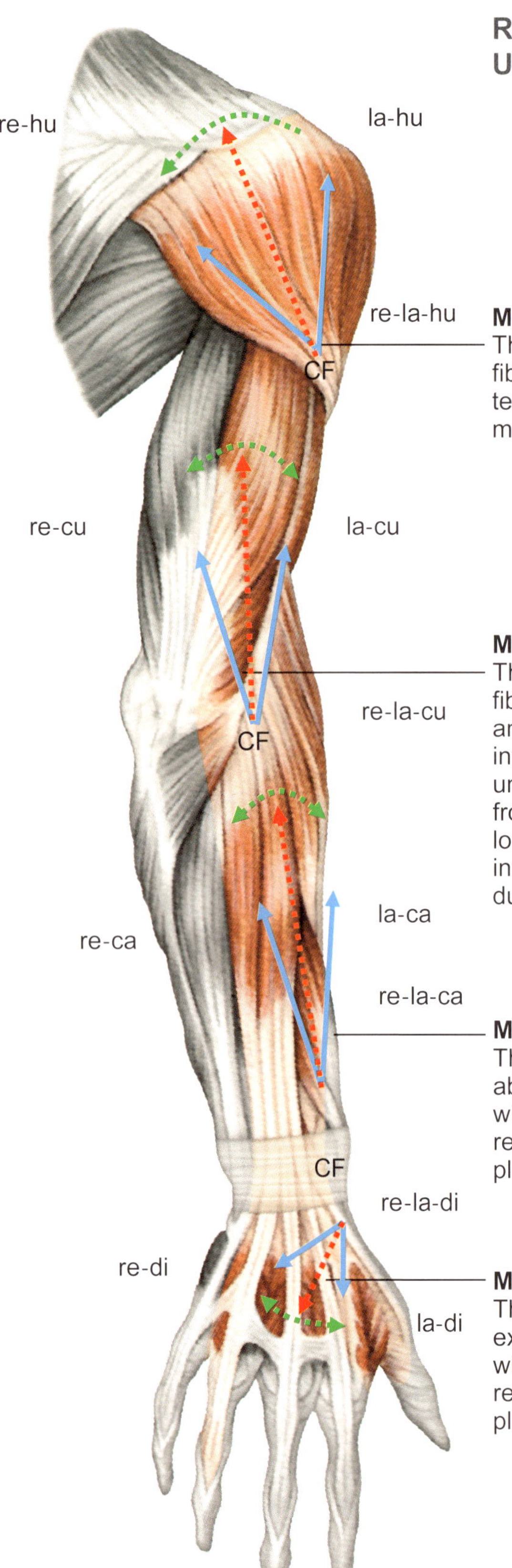

Motor scheme of retro-latero-humerus (re-la-hu)
The CF re-la-hu, located between the posterior tendinous fibres of the deltoid, interacts with the spindles and tendon organs of the MF units of re-hu and la-hu during movements of the humerus from one plane to the other.

Motor scheme of retro-latero-cubitus (re-la-cu)
The CF re-la-cu, located between the tendinous fibres connected to the lateral head of triceps brachii, anconeus, extensor carpi radialis and supinator muscles, interacts with the spindles and tendon organs of the MF units of re-cu and la-cu during movements of the elbow from one plane to the other (Fig. 5.16). The CC re-cu, located over the centre of the triceps brachii muscle, interacts with the spindles of the three heads of triceps during the various degrees of extension.

Motor scheme of retro-latero-carpus (re-la-ca)
The CF re-la-ca, located between the tendons of abductor and extensor pollicis longus muscles, interacts with the spindles and tendon organs of the MF units of re-ca and la-ca during movements of the wrist from one plane to the other.

Motor scheme of retro-latero-digiti (re-la-di)
The CF re-la-di is located between the tendons of extensor pollicis longus and brevis muscles. It interacts with the spindles and tendon organs of the MF units of re-di and la-di during movements of the thumb from one plane to the other.

Fig. 5.10. Centres of fusion of retro-latero, UL.

RETRO-LATERO DIAGONAL, UPPER LIMB (Fig. 5.4)

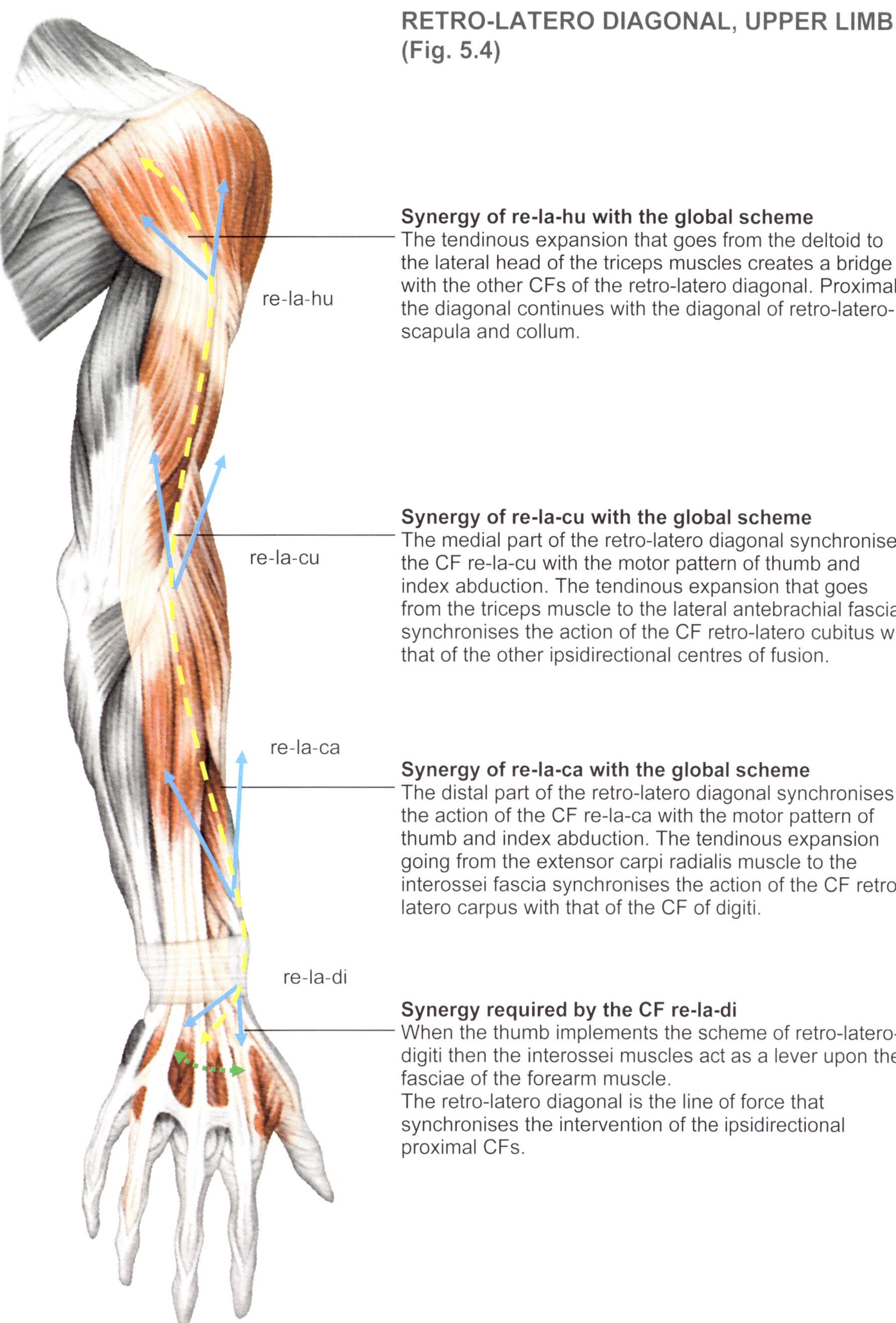

Synergy of re-la-hu with the global scheme
The tendinous expansion that goes from the deltoid to the lateral head of the triceps muscles creates a bridge with the other CFs of the retro-latero diagonal. Proximally the diagonal continues with the diagonal of retro-latero-scapula and collum.

Synergy of re-la-cu with the global scheme
The medial part of the retro-latero diagonal synchronises the CF re-la-cu with the motor pattern of thumb and index abduction. The tendinous expansion that goes from the triceps muscle to the lateral antebrachial fascia synchronises the action of the CF retro-latero cubitus with that of the other ipsidirectional centres of fusion.

Synergy of re-la-ca with the global scheme
The distal part of the retro-latero diagonal synchronises the action of the CF re-la-ca with the motor pattern of thumb and index abduction. The tendinous expansion going from the extensor carpi radialis muscle to the interossei fascia synchronises the action of the CF retro-latero carpus with that of the CF of digiti.

Synergy required by the CF re-la-di
When the thumb implements the scheme of retro-latero-digiti then the interossei muscles act as a lever upon the fasciae of the forearm muscle.
The retro-latero diagonal is the line of force that synchronises the intervention of the ipsidirectional proximal CFs.

Fig. 5.11. Retro-latero diagonal, upper limb.

RETRO-MEDIO CENTRES OF FUSION, UPPER LIMB

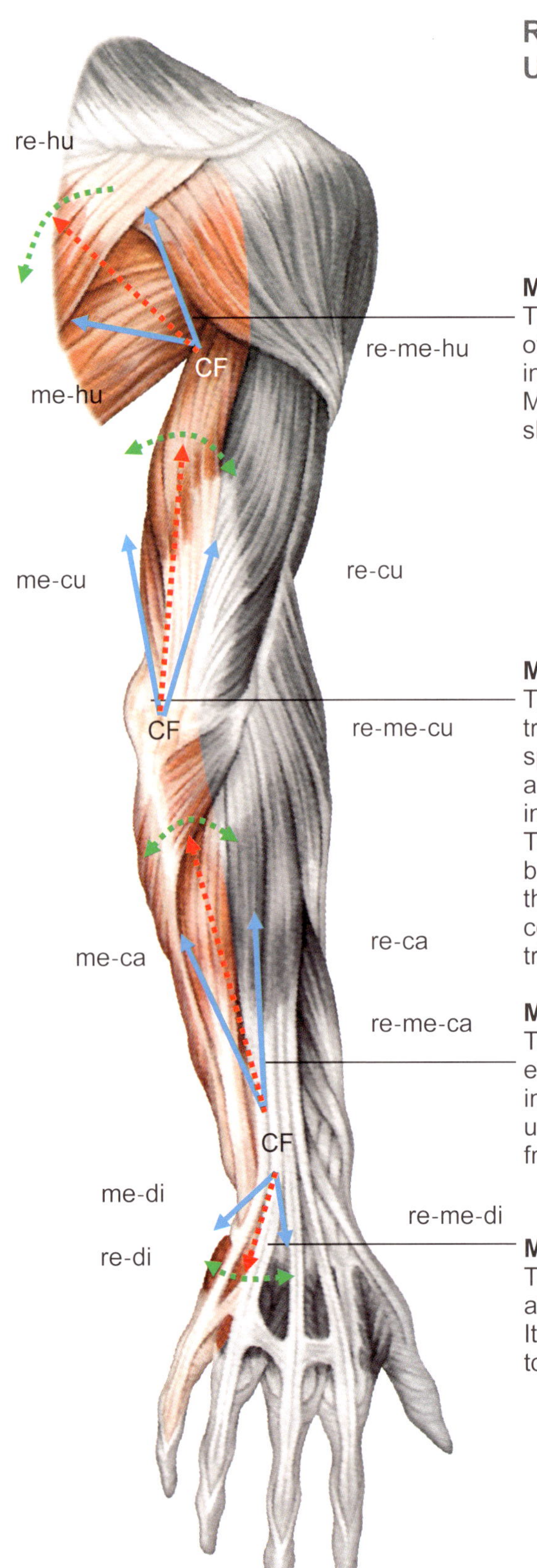

Fig. 5.12. Centres of fusion of retro-medio, UL.

Motor scheme of retro-medio-humerus (re-me-hu)
The CF re-me-hu, located between the tendinous fibres of the long head of triceps and latissimus dorsi muscles, interacts with the spindles and tendon organs of the MF units of re-hu and me-hu during movements of the shoulder from one plane to the other.

Motor scheme of retro-medio-cubitus (re-me-cu)
The CF re-me-cu, located between the tendon of the triceps muscle and the epitrochlea, interacts with the spindles and tendon organs of the MF units of re-cu and me-cu during movements of the elbow along an intermediate trajectory.
The CC re-cu is located over the muscle belly of triceps brachii and coordinates the motor units distributed over the medial and lateral heads whilst the CF re-me-cu only coordinates the motor units located in the medial head of triceps brachii (Fig. 5.17).

Motor scheme of retro-medio-carpus (re-me-ca)
The CF re-me-ca, located between the tendons of extensor carpi ulnaris and extensor digiti minimi muscles, interacts with the spindles and tendon organs of the MF units of re-ca and me-ca during movements of the wrist from one plane to the other.

Motor scheme of retro-medio-digiti (re-me-di)
The CF re-me-di is located over the insertion of the abductor digiti minimi muscle on the extensor retinaculum. It coordinates the transition of the last two digits from retro to medio.

RETRO-MEDIO DIAGONAL, UPPER LIMB (Fig. 5.5)

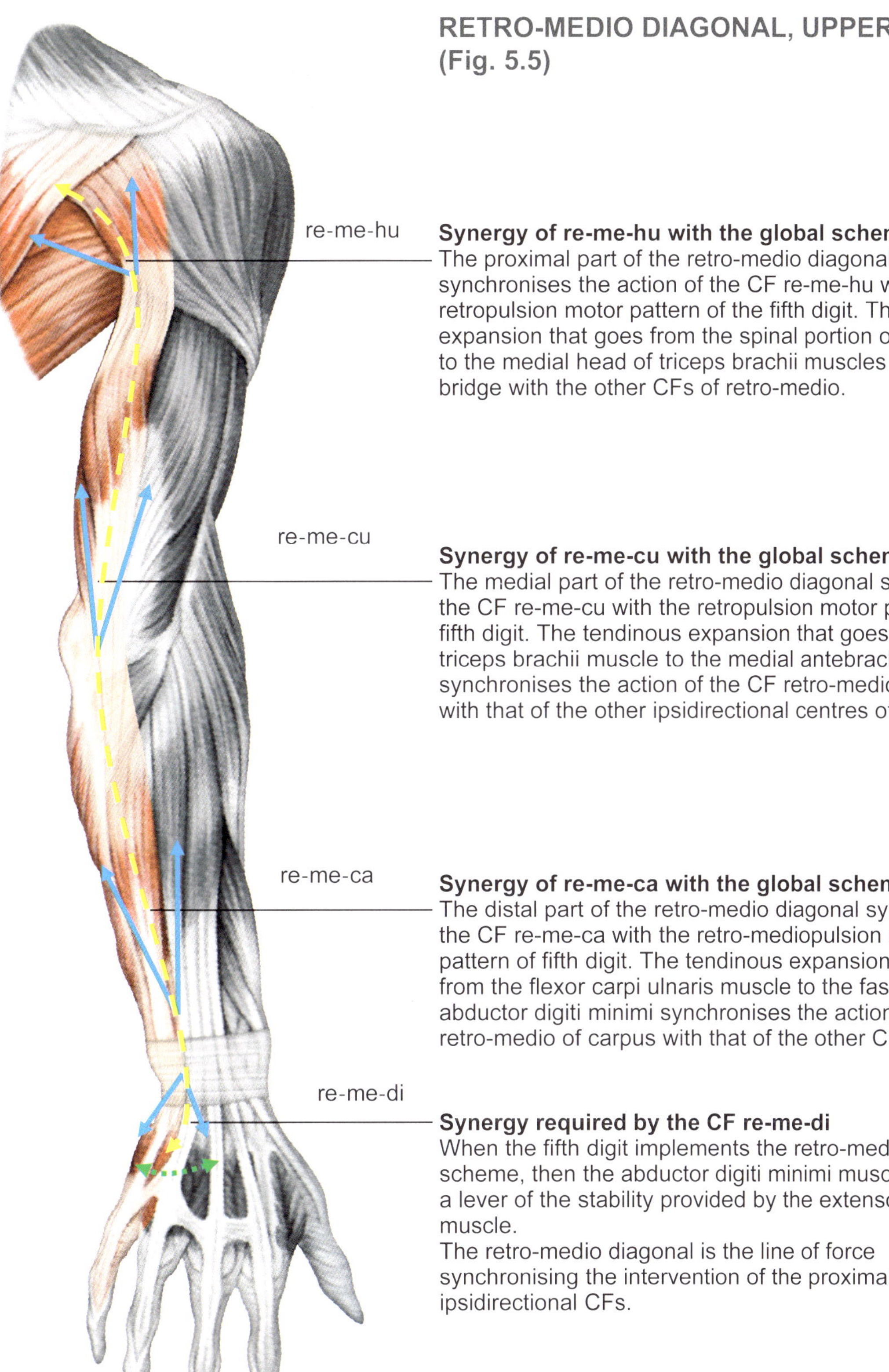

Fig. 5.13. Retro-medio diagonal, upper limb.

Synergy of re-me-hu with the global scheme
The proximal part of the retro-medio diagonal synchronises the action of the CF re-me-hu with the retropulsion motor pattern of the fifth digit. The tendinous expansion that goes from the spinal portion of deltoid to the medial head of triceps brachii muscles creates a bridge with the other CFs of retro-medio.

Synergy of re-me-cu with the global scheme
The medial part of the retro-medio diagonal synchronises the CF re-me-cu with the retropulsion motor pattern of fifth digit. The tendinous expansion that goes from the triceps brachii muscle to the medial antebrachial fascia synchronises the action of the CF retro-medio of cubitus with that of the other ipsidirectional centres of fusion.

Synergy of re-me-ca with the global scheme
The distal part of the retro-medio diagonal synchronises the CF re-me-ca with the retro-mediopulsion motor pattern of fifth digit. The tendinous expansion that goes from the flexor carpi ulnaris muscle to the fascia of abductor digiti minimi synchronises the action of the CF retro-medio of carpus with that of the other CFs.

Synergy required by the CF re-me-di
When the fifth digit implements the retro-medio-digiti scheme, then the abductor digiti minimi muscle applies a lever of the stability provided by the extensor ulnaris muscle.
The retro-medio diagonal is the line of force synchronising the intervention of the proximal ipsidirectional CFs.

LOCALISATION OF THE CF ANTE-LATERO-CUBITUS

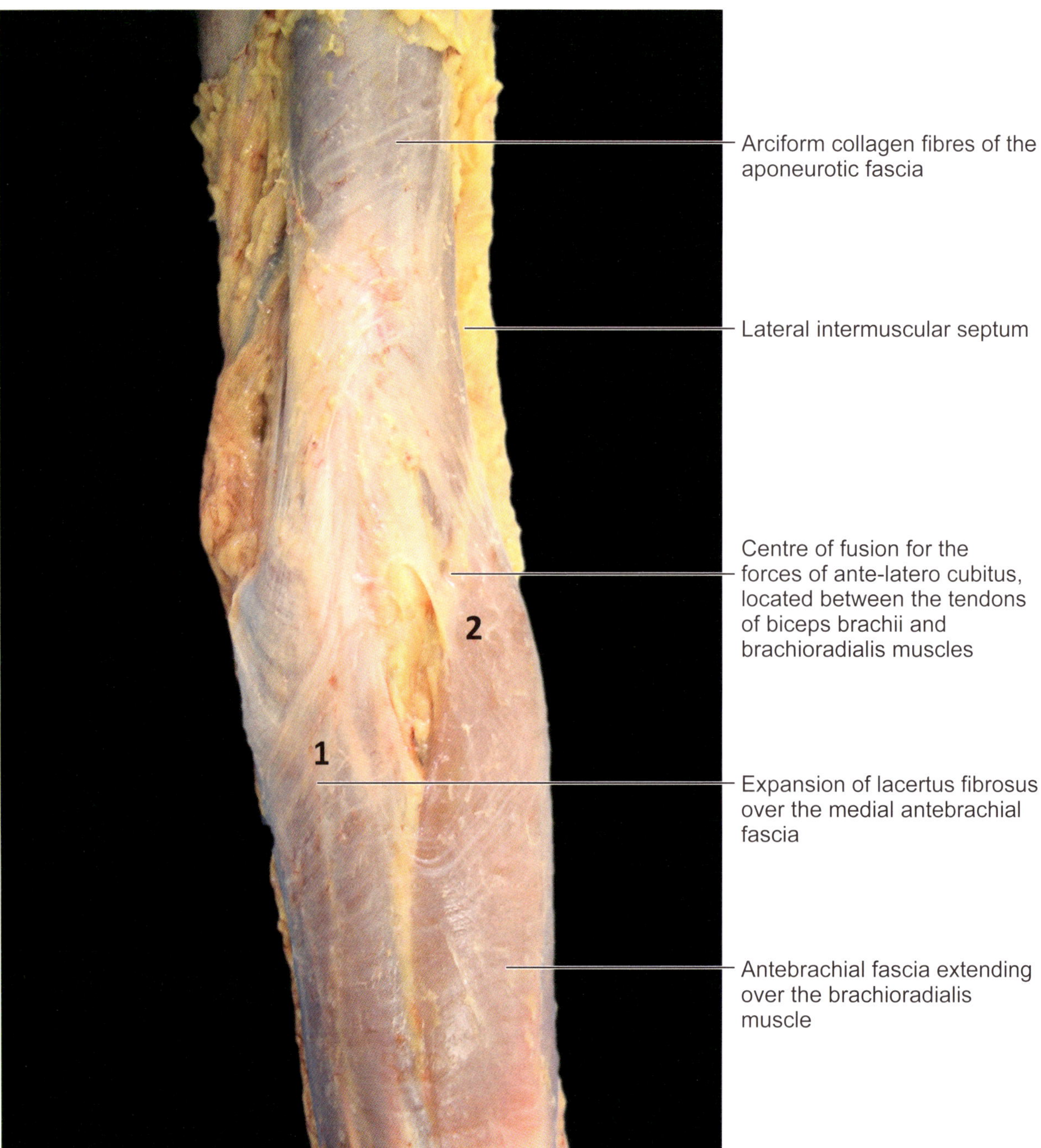

Fig. 5.14. Brachial and antebrachial fascia at the level of the elbow. The lacertus fibrosus tendon of the biceps brachii muscle is always represented with its medial portion going towards the ante-medio diagonal (1). A lateral fascial-tendinous portion (2) also exists coursing towards the diagonal of ante-latero-cubitus.

LOCALISATION OF THE CF ANTE-MEDIO-CUBITUS

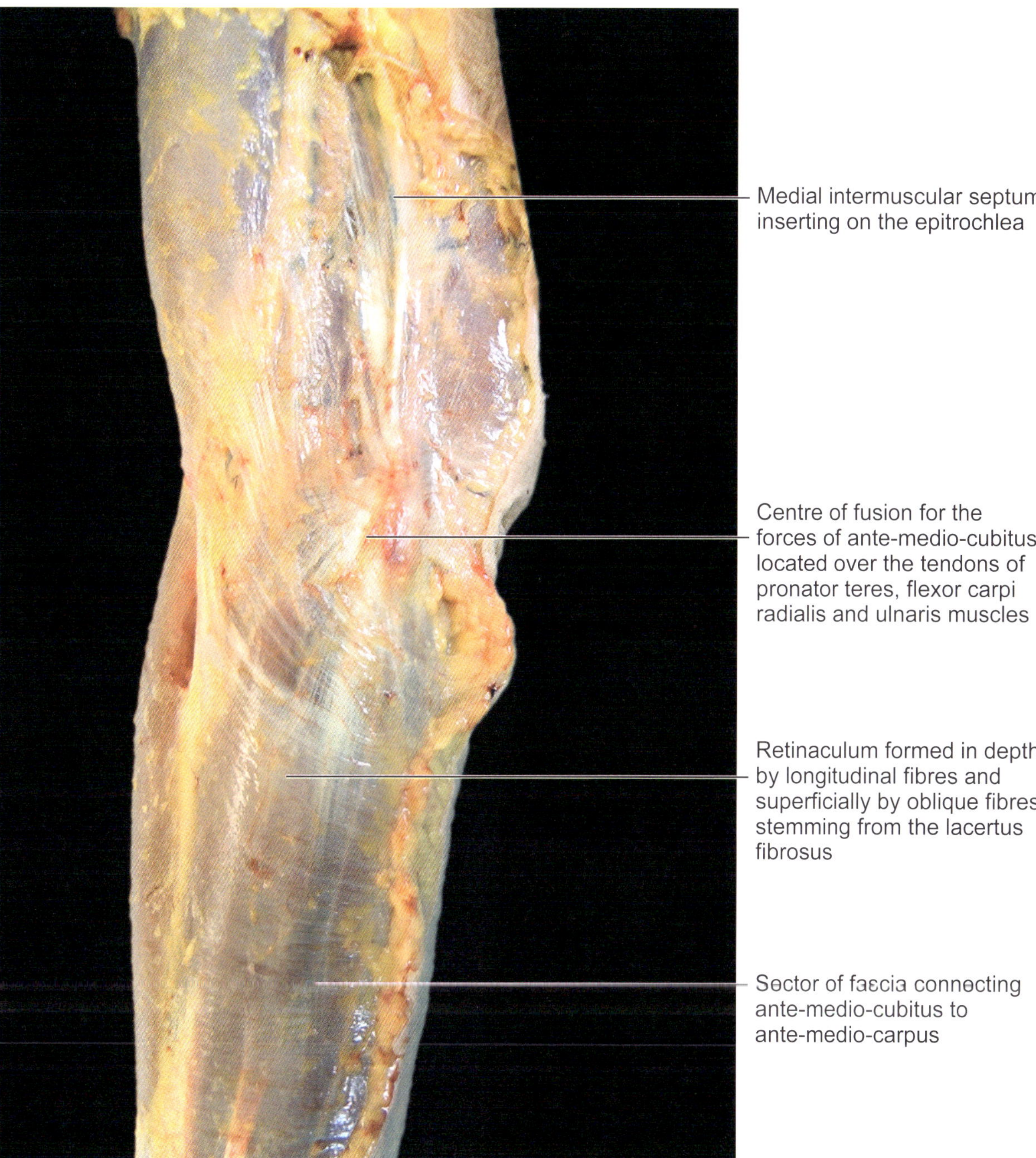

Fig. 5.15. Brachial and antebrachial fascia at the level of the epitrochlea. The lacertus fibrosus represents only a portion of the collagen fibres irradiating from the biceps brachii tendon towards the centre of fusion of ante-medio-cubitus.

LOCALISATION OF THE CF RETRO-LATERO-CUBITUS

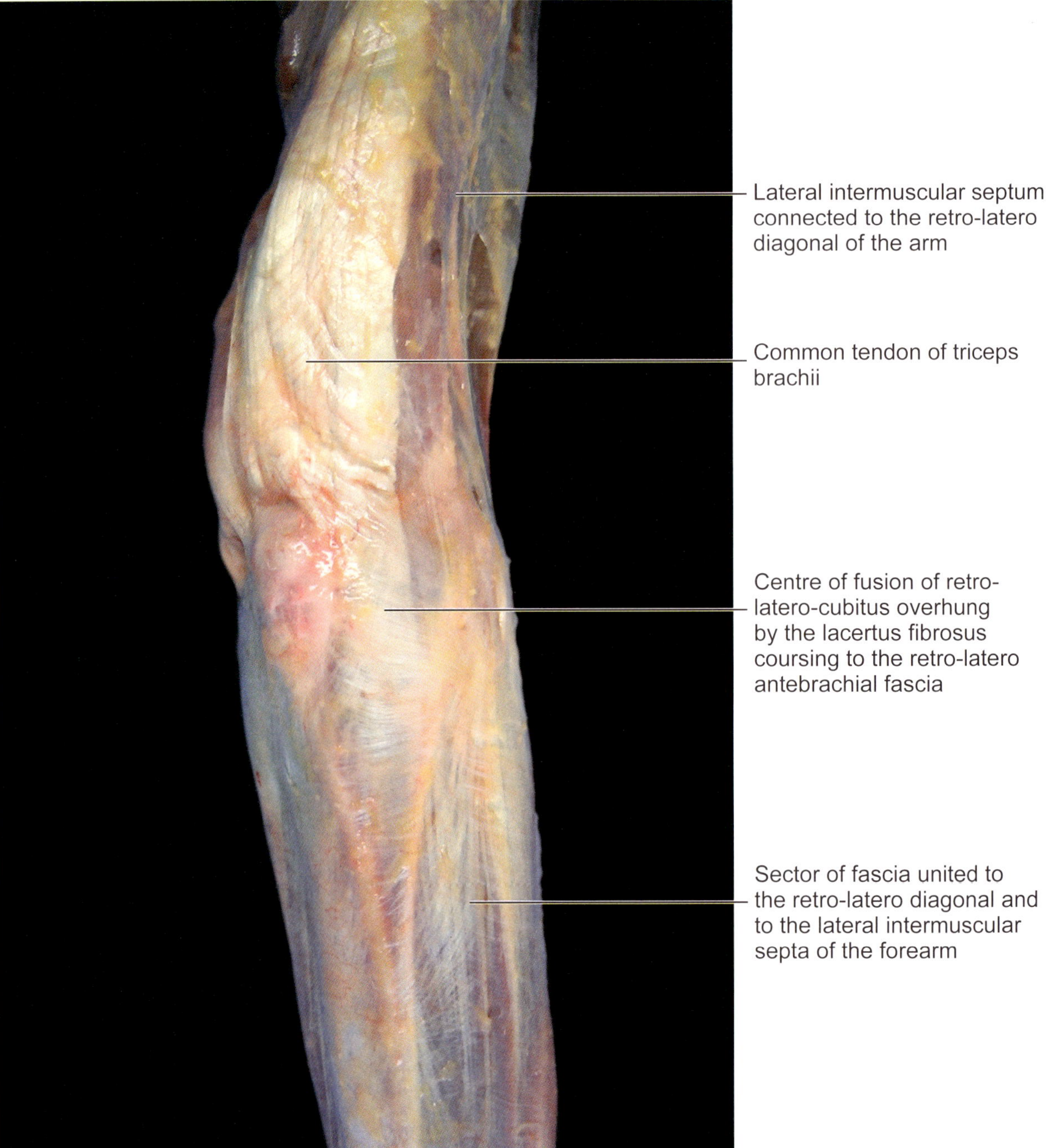

Fig. 5.16. Brachial and antebrachial fascia at the retro-latero level of the elbow. In the elbow the triceps brachii tendon is divided into three parts: the main portion inserts on the olecranon, a portion unites with the flexor carpi ulnaris muscle (retro-medio-cubitus) and the third portion unites with the centre of fusion of retro-latero-cubitus.

LOCALISATION OF THE CF RETRO-MEDIO-CUBITUS

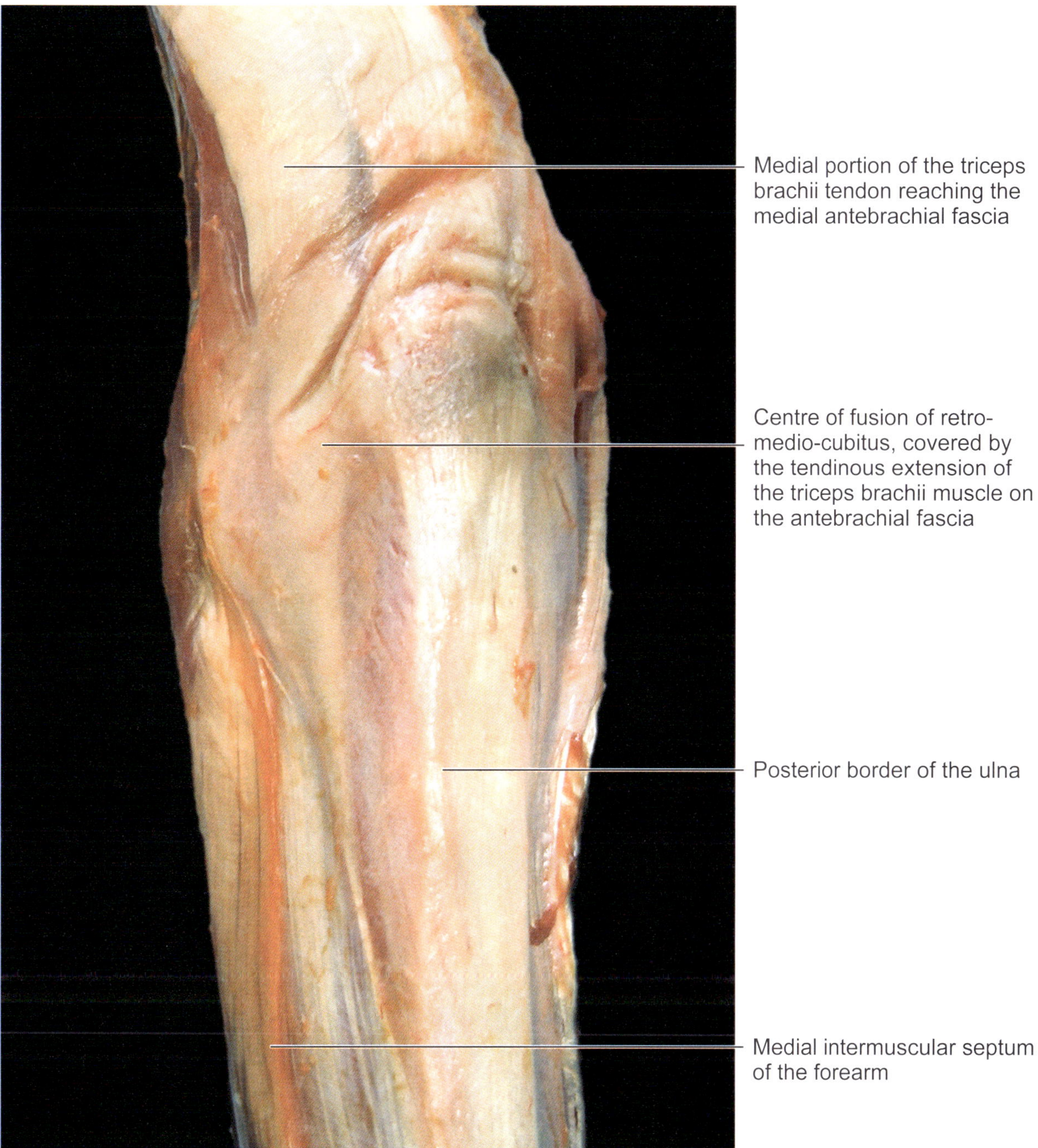

Fig. 5.17. Brachial and antebrachial fascia at the retro-medio level of the elbow. The centre of fusion of retro-medio-cubitus is located between the olecranon and the medial condyle. The forces of the flexor carpi ulnaris and medial head of triceps brachii muscles converge on this point.

CENTRES OF FUSION AND DIAGONALS OF THE TRUNK

Unlike in the limbs where there are four diagonals, in the trunk there are eight diagonals with four on each half of the body (Fig. 5.18). In the trunk, like in the limbs, during the movement from one plane to the other a slight rotation in intra or extra is also occurring.

The left ante-latero diagonal is the intermediate direction between the sequence of ante and the sequence of latero on the same side (Fig. 5.18, 5.19); whilst the retro-latero diagonal is the intermediate direction between the sequence of retropulsion and lateropulsion.

The ante-medio diagonals are located between the mediopulsion sequence and the antepulsion sequence (Fig. 5.20); whilst both retro-medio diagonals are located between the supraspinous ligaments (mediopulsion retro sequence) and both masses of the erector spinae muscles (retropulsion sequences) (Fig. 5.22).

The CCs of the trunk operate in pairs namely during trunk straightening both CCs of retro-lumbi on the right and left intervene together; whilst the CFs work individually during the return from trunk lateral flexion where only the ipsilateral retro-latero-lumbi CF intervenes.

In the limbs the intermuscular septa often have a course in parallel to that of the diagonals. These give insertions to muscles carrying out movements in two spatial planes.

From an anatomical point of view, there are lines of fusion in the trunk that are similar to septa corresponding to the course of the diagonals. Laterally to the erector sheaths there is fusion of the aponeuroses of the large muscles of the abdomen[4], forming the ante-latero diagonal. Close to the linea alba there is a second fusion of the aponeuroses of the muscles of the abdomen forming the ante-medio diagonal (Fig. 5.32).

In the posterior aspect of the trunk, laterally to the erector spinae muscles, there is fusion between both laminae of the thoracolumbar fascia forming the retro-latero diagonal and the retro-medio diagonal courses close to the supraspinous ligaments (Fig. 5.34).

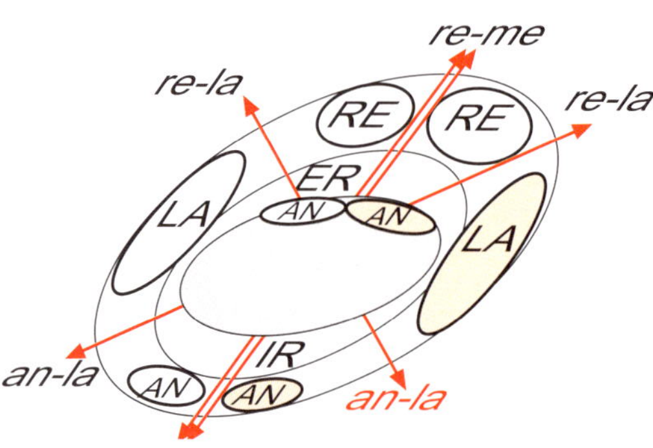

Fig. 5.18. Configuration of the centres of fusion (CFs) and the diagonals in the trunk.

In the trunk these lines of fusion from the aponeuroses synchronise the intervention of many muscles that singularly would act on a single plane.

Each diagonal is formed by the contribution of superficial and deep muscles of the trunk. For this reason, the anatomical drawings report both superficial muscles and the deep musculature including the rotational component implicated in all motor schemes.

[4] The aponeurosis of the internal oblique muscle when touching the lateral margin of the rectus abdominis muscle divides into two sheets. The anterior sheet passes in front of the muscle and fuses with the aponeurosis of the internal oblique muscle whilst the posterior sheet fuses in turn with the aponeurosis of the transversus muscle. In the inferior abdominal region, the above aponeuroses all course in front of the rectus muscle and the posterior compartment is closed by a thin fibrous sheet. The sheet is nothing but the posterior sheet of the fascia surrounding the transversus muscle also named fascia transversalis. (Testut L. 1987)

Fig. 5.19. Ante-latero diagonal; movement of the entire trunk according to the pattern of left an-la.

Fig. 5.20. Ante-medio diagonal; movement of the entire trunk according to the pattern of left an-me.

Fig. 5.21. Retro-latero diagonal; movement of the entire trunk according to the pattern of left re-la.

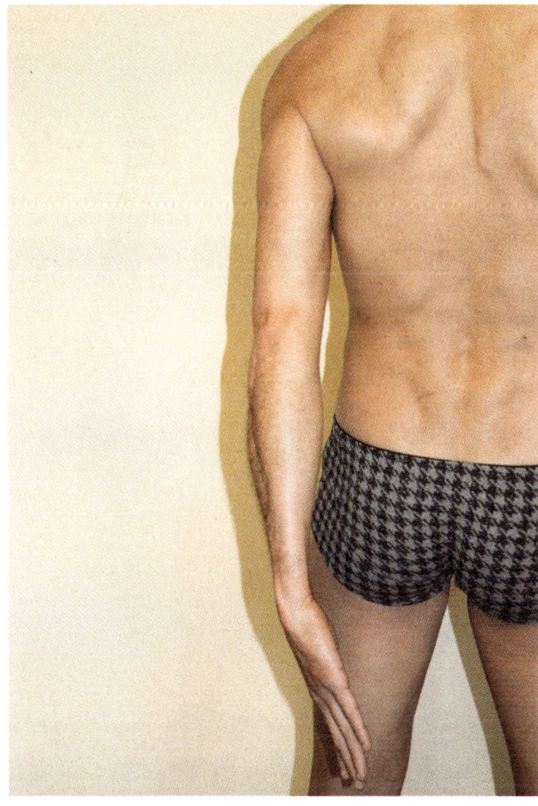

Fig. 5.22. Retro-medio diagonal; movement of the entire trunk according to the pattern of left re-me.

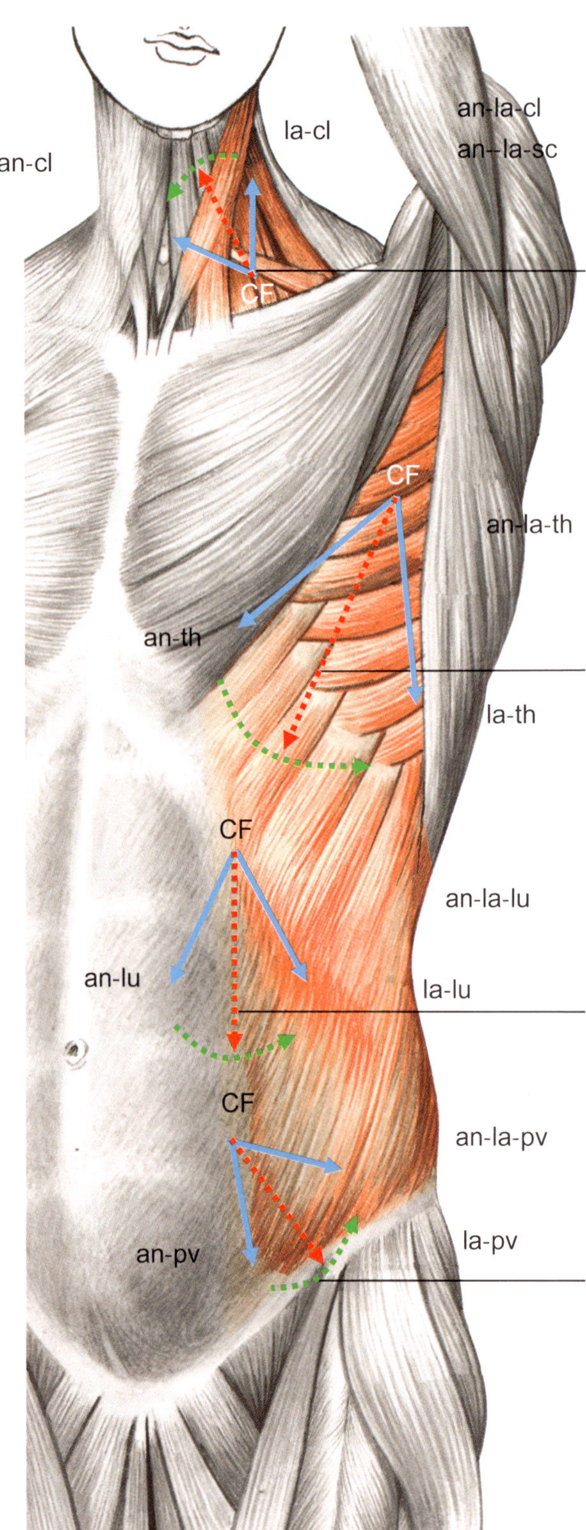

Fig. 5.23. Centres of fusion of ante-latero, TR.
(From G. Chiarugi and L. Bucciante, Istituzioni di anatomia dell'uomo. Piccin Nuova Libraria, Padova 1983, modified)

ANTE-LATERO CENTRES OF FUSION, TRUNK

Motor scheme of ante-latero-collum (an-la-cl, sc)
The CF an-la-cl is located over the angular ligament of the mandible. It cooperates with the CF an-la-sc that is located close to the rotator muscles (omohyoids).
These CFs interact with the spindles and tendon organs of the MF units of an-cl and la-cl during movements from one plane to the other.

Motor scheme of ante-latero-thorax (an-la-th)
The CF an-la-th is located over the fascia covering the muscle belly of serratus anterior. It interacts with the spindles and tendon organs of the MF units of an-th and la-th during movements from one plane to the other.

Motor scheme of ante-latero-lumbi (an-la-lu)
The CF an-la-lu is located along the line of fusion of the obliques and transversus adominis muscles laterally to rectus abdominis muscle. It interacts with the spindles and tendon organs of the MF units of an-lu (rectus sheath) and la-lu (fascia of the transversus muscle) during movements from one plane to the other.

Motor scheme of ante-latero-pelvis (an-la-pv)
The CF an-la-pv is located along the line of fusion of the abdominal muscles, from the umbilicus to the inguinal ligament. It interacts with the spindles and tendon organs of the MF units of an-pv and la-pv during movements from one plane to the other.

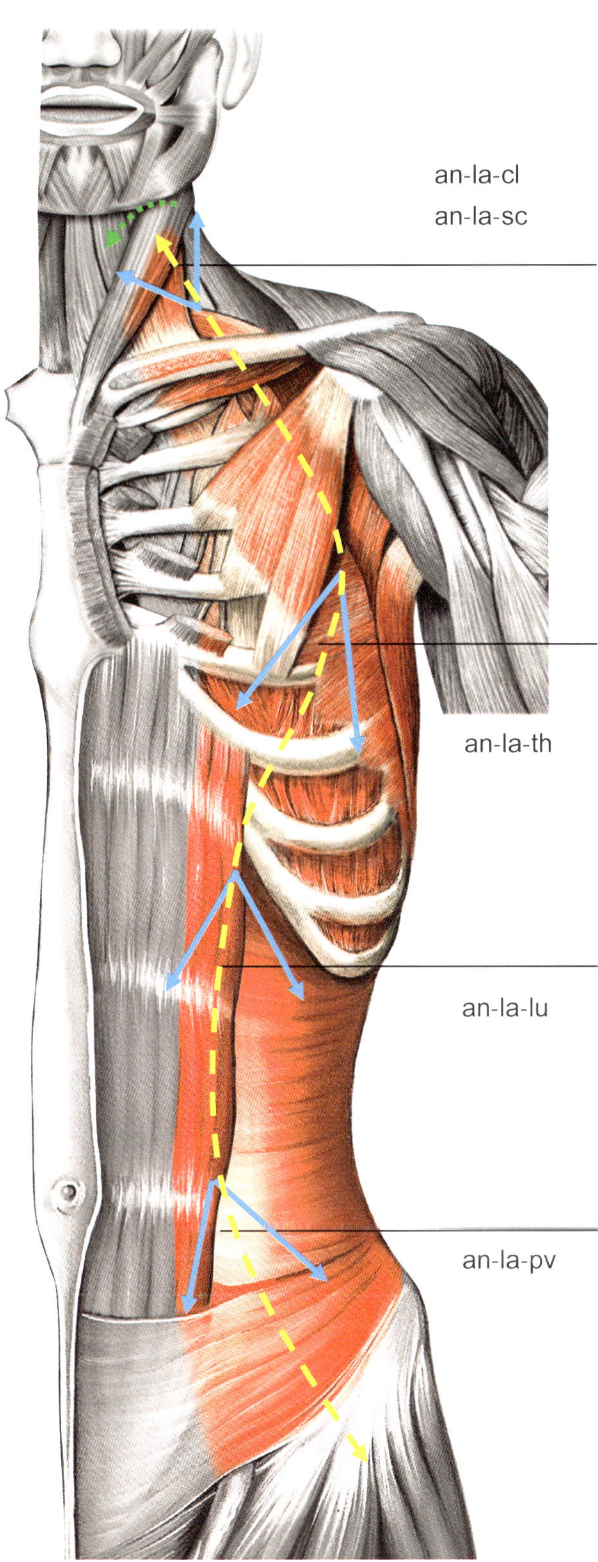

Fig. 5.24. Ante-latero diagonal, trunk.

ANTE-LATERO DIAGONAL, TRUNK (Fig. 5.19)

Synergy required from the CF an-la-cl and scapula
The diagonals of the limbs are at the service of the hands and feet whilst the diagonals of the trunk adapt to the necessities of the neck. The muscles implementing the ante-latero-collum scheme (sternocleidomastoid, scalenes, omohyoids, etc.) also act upon the scapula.

Synergy between an-la-th with the global scheme
The proximal part of the ante-latero diagonal synchronises the action of the scalene muscles (an-la-cl) with that of the intercostal and serratus anterior muscles (an-la-th) which are in direct continuity. Scapula is the element of pivot between the neck and the upper limb but also between the neck and the thorax.

Synergy between an-la-lu with the global scheme
The medial part of the ante-latero diagonal connects, through the external oblique fascia, the CF an-la-th to the rectus abdominis sheath above the umbilicus (an-la-lu) and to the rectus abdominis sheath below the umbilicus (an-la-pv).

Synergy between an-la-pv and the global scheme
The distal part of the ante-latero diagonal connects, through the fascia of the abdominal muscles, the pelvis to both the inguinal ligament and the ante-latero-coxa motor scheme (tensor fascia lata muscle).

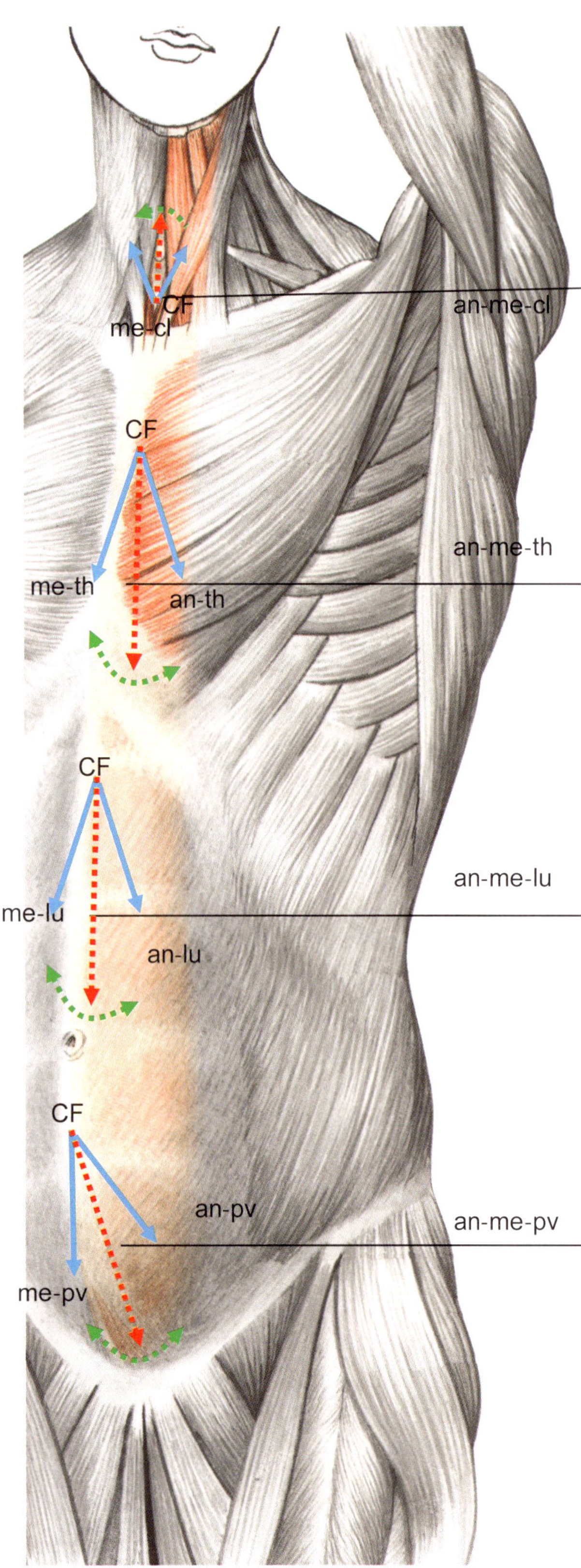

Fig. 5.25. Centres of fusion of ante-medio, TR.
(From G. Chiarugi and L. Bucciante, Istituzioni di anatomia dell'uomo. Piccin Nuova Libraria, Padova 1983, modified)

ANTE-MEDIO CENTRES OF FUSION, TRUNK

Motor scheme of ante-medio-collum (an-me-cl)
The CF an-me-cl is located against the sternal tendon of the sternocleidomastoid muscle. When moving the neck in ante-medio, the head is first moved away from the midline (medio) and forward (ante) to then finish in ante-latero. Hence the ante-medio motor scheme is the starting movement which is completed in ante-latero.

Motor scheme of ante-medio-thorax (an-me-th)
The CF an-me-th, located over the parasternal ligaments, coordinates the increase in forces of the an-th MF unit and the decrease of the me-th MF unit (longitudinal fibres of the rectus abdominis muscle working as a rheostat) (Fig. 5.31).
When bending the thorax forward and towards one side, the centre of gravity is moved outside the midline and it activates the ante-medio-thorax motor scheme.

Motor scheme of ante-medio-lumbi (an-me-lu)
The CF an-me-lu, located between the linea alba and the muscle belly of rectus abdominis, coordinates the increase in force of the an-lu MF unit on one side only, when starting from a standing posture (me-lu).

Motor scheme of ante-medio-pelvis (an-me-pv)
The CF an-me-pv, located laterally to the linea alba, coordinates the increase in force of the an-pv MF unit on one side only, it then relinquishes control to the ipsilateral an-la-pv (Fig. 5.32).
Mediopulsion in the trunk does not have its own motor units, but it corresponds only to the linea alba which is a collagen structure with a function of perception.

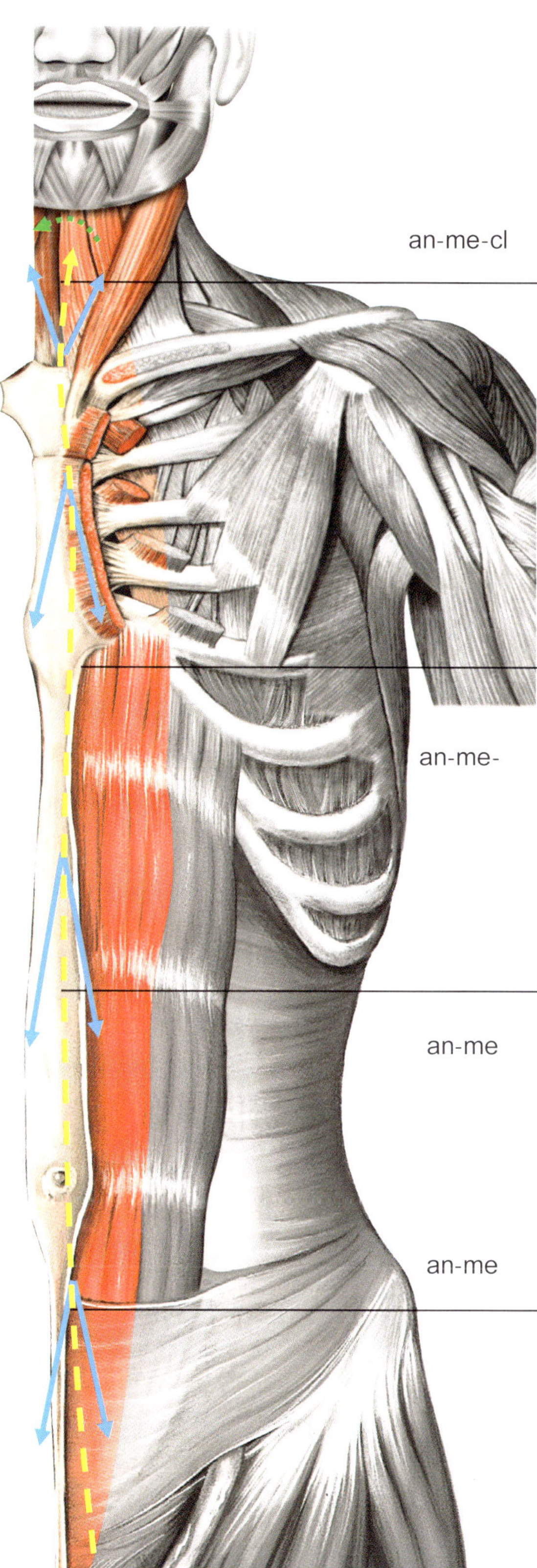

Fig. 5.26. Ante-medio diagonal, trunk.

ANTE-MEDIO DIAGONAL, TRUNK (Fig. 5.20)

Synergy required by CF an-me-cl and scapula
The muscles implementing the ante-medio-collum motor scheme (sternocleidomastoid, infrahyoids, etc.) insert their fascia on the sternum and clavicle where the fasciae for the CF ante-medio-scapula and an-me-th insert.
The lack of muscles in direct continuity between collum and thorax allows the neck to move independently from the trunk. The clavicle is the line of division between the fasciae of the neck and the clavi-coraco-axillary fascia (an-me-sc).

Synergy between an-me-th with the global scheme
The proximal part of the ante-medio diagonal corresponds to the suprasternal ligaments connecting the sternal tendon of sternocleidomastoid (an-me-cl) to the rectus abdominis sheath (an-me-lu). The fasciae of the pectoralis major and minor muscles also arrive on the sternum where the CF ante-medio-scapula is located.

Synergy between an-me-lu with the global scheme
The medial part of the ante-medio diagonal connects, through the rectus abdominis sheath, the CF an-me-th with the pelvis (an-me-pv) on one side only. The diagonal of ante-medio-lumbi extends from the xyphoid process to the umbilicus.

Synergy between an-me-pv and the global scheme
The distal part of the ante-medio diagonal, through the fascia of the abdominal muscles, connects the pelvis to the pubis and to the ante-medio-coxa motor scheme on one side only. Whereas the antepulsion sequence on one side always acts in pair with the one on the opposite side.

RETRO-LATERO CENTRES OF FUSION, TRUNK

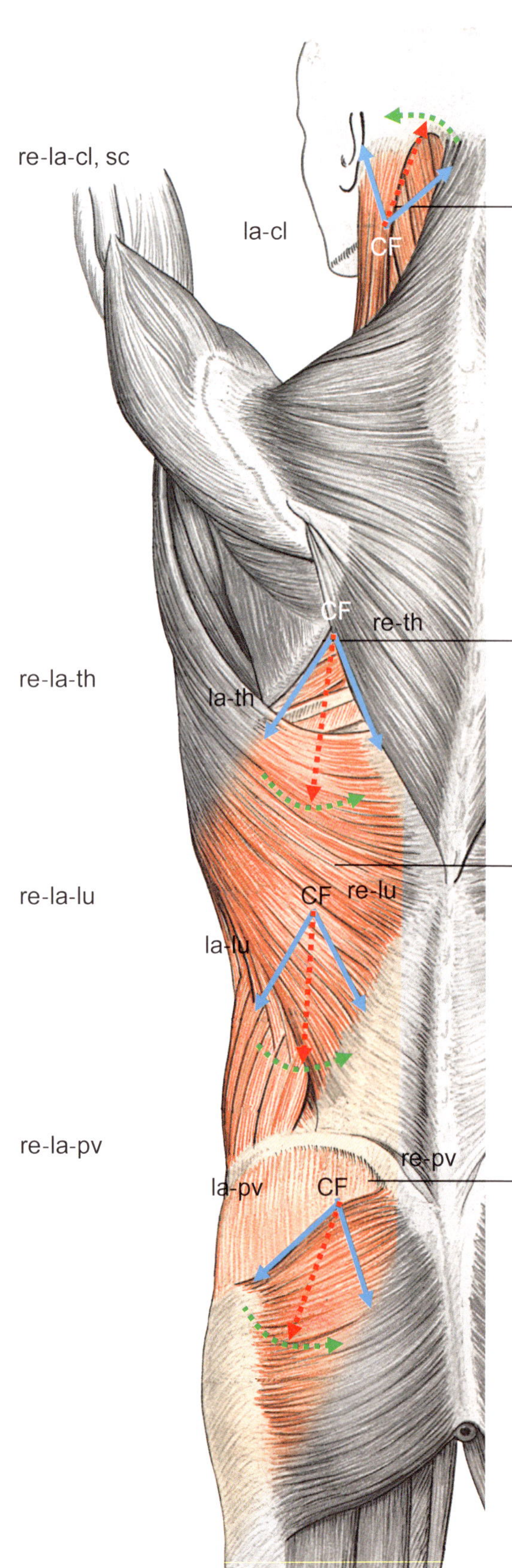

Fig. 5.27. Centres of fusion of retro-latero, TR.
(From G. Chiarugi and L. Bucciante, Istituzioni di anatomia dell'uomo. Piccin Nuova Libraria, Padova 1983, modified)

Motor scheme of retro-latero-collum (re-la-cl)
The CF re-la-cl, located over the splenius capitis muscle, coordinates the increase in force of the la-cl MF unit and the simultaneous decrease of the re-cl MF unit.
The image of the superficial muscles helps in better localising the point but the muscles mostly implicated in diagonals are the deep ones.

Motor scheme of retro-latero-thorax (re-la-th)
Initially, during the extension and lateral flexion of the thorax, the medial motor units of the paravertebral muscles prevail, towards the end the fibres located in the lateral portion of the same muscles prevail (Fig. 5.33).
The CF re-la-th, located on the iliocostalis thoracis muscle coordinates the increase in force of the la-th MF unit and the simultaneous decrease of the re-th unit.

Motor scheme of retro-latero-lumbi (re-la-lu)
Initially, during the extension and lateral flexion of lumbi, the medial motor units of the paravertebral muscles prevail and, towards the end, the fibres located in the lateral portion of the same muscles prevail.
The CF re-la-lu, located on the costal insertion of the quadratus lumborum muscle coordinates the increase in force of the la-lu MF unit and the decrease of the re-lu unit.

Motor scheme of retro-latero-pelvis (re-la-pv)
Initially, during the extension and lateral flexion of the pelvis, the motor units of the erector spinae muscles prevail and, towards the end, the fibres located in the lateral portion of the gluteal muscles prevail (Fig. 5.34).
The CF re-la-pv, located laterally to the posterior superior iliac spine coordinates the increase in force of the la-pv MF unit and the decrease of the re-pv unit.

RETRO-LATERO DIAGONAL, UPPER LIMB (Fig. 5.21)

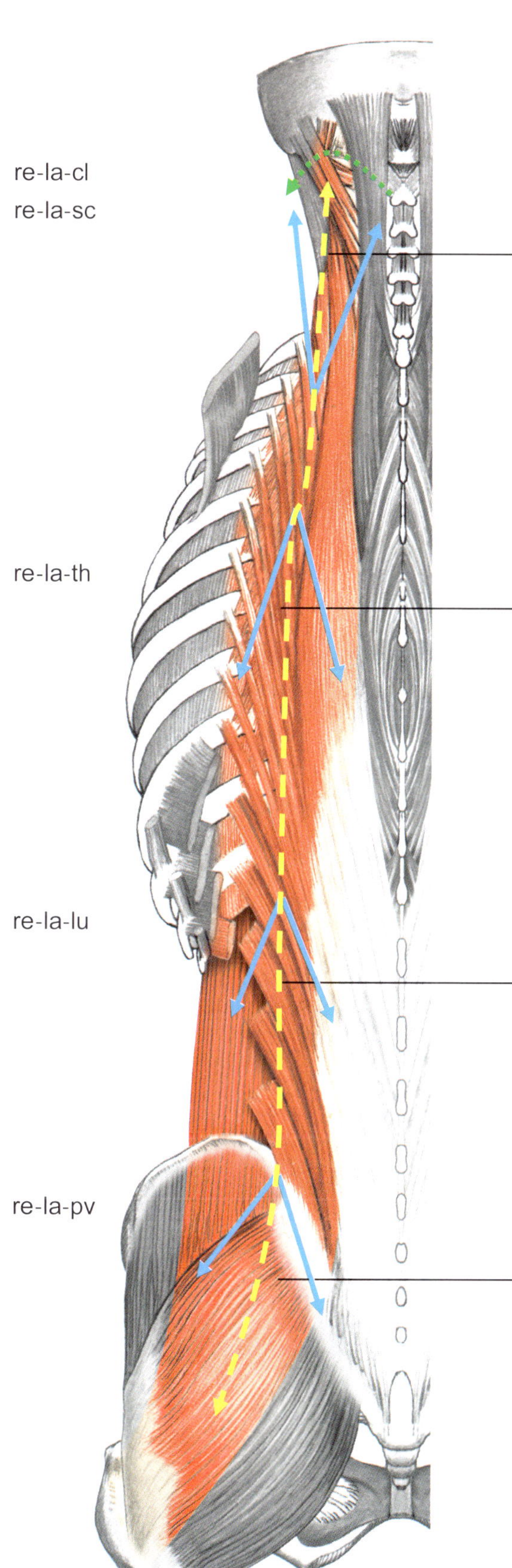

Fig. 5.28. Retro-latero diagonal, trunk.
(From G. Chiarugi and L. Bucciante, Istituzioni di anatomia dell'uomo. Piccin Nuova Libraria, Padova 1983, modified)

Synergy required by the CF re-la-cl and scapula
The splenius capitis and cervicis muscles create a movement of extension and lateral flexion in the neck.
These muscles work in connection with the levator scapula muscle participating in the execution of the re-la-sc motor scheme.
In the anterior region of the trunk, the neck has a certain motor independency whilst in its posterior region the muscular continuity is evident.

Synergy between re-la-th with the global scheme
The proximal part of the retro-latero diagonal corresponds to the splenii muscles connecting the neck to the thorax. Indeed, the splenii muscles are often fused together and descend up to the fifth thoracic vertebra (re-la-th).
The fascia of the iliocostalis muscle connects the CF re-la-th to the CF re-la-lu. At the thoracic level this diagonal corresponds to the septum separating the longissimus muscle from the iliocostalis muscle.

Synergy between re-la-lu with the global scheme
The medial part of the retro-latero diagonal, through the iliocostalis sheath connects the CF re-la-th with the low back and the pelvis (CF re-la-pv). The re-la diagonal intervenes on one side only whilst the retro sequence intervenes in pair with the contralateral one, the latero sequence works in pair with the anterior muscle (la-lu + an-la-lu).

Synergy between re-la-pv and the global scheme
The distal part of the retro-latero diagonal connects, through the fascia of the gluteus maximus muscle, the pelvis to the hamstring muscles (biceps femoris) and hence to the retro-latero-coxa motor scheme.

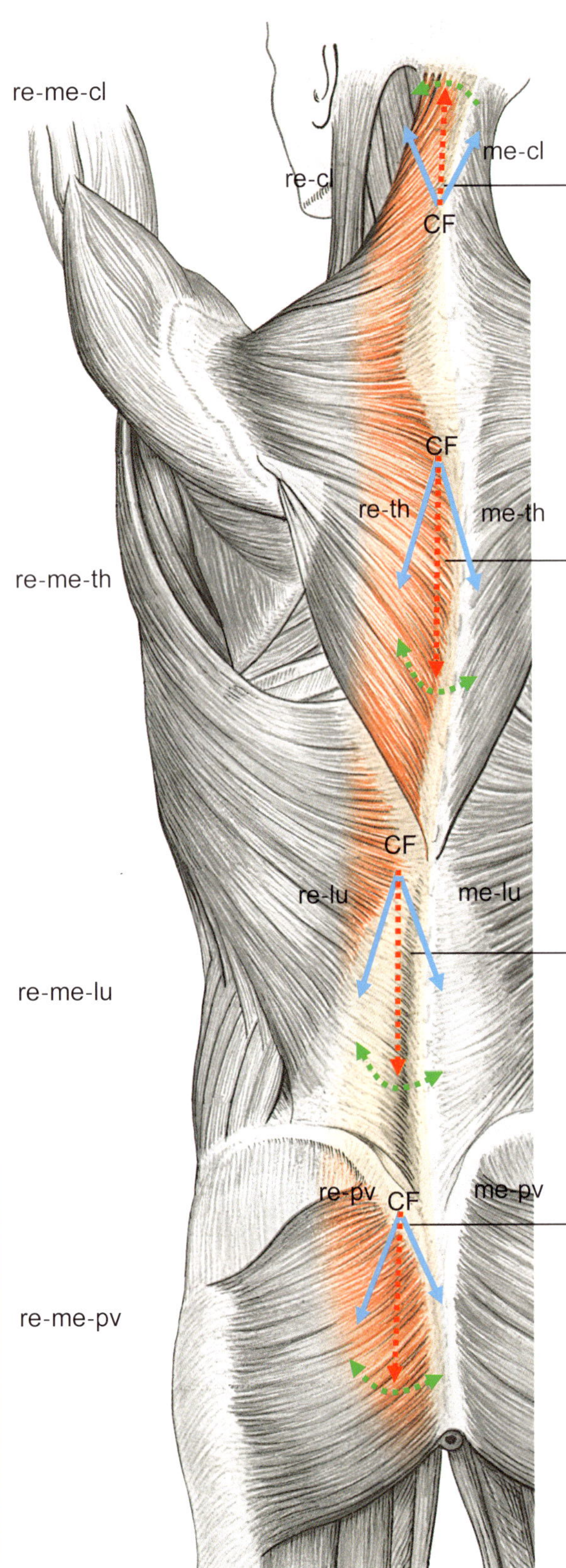

Fig. 5.29. Centres of fusion of retro-medio, TR.
(From G. Chiarugi and L. Bucciante, Istituzioni di anatomia dell'uomo. Piccin Nuova Libraria, Padova 1983, modified)

RETRO-MEDIO CENTRES OF FUSION, TRUNK

Motor scheme of retro-medio-collum (re-me-cl)
When moving the neck in retro-latero, movement is started by bringing the head away from the midline (medio) and backwards (retro) to then finish in retro-latero. Hence the retro-medio motor scheme is only the starting movement that is completed in retro-latero. The CF re-me-cl is located against the nuchal ligament.

Motor scheme of retro-medio-thorax (re-me-th)
When moving the thorax in retro-latero, movement is started by bringing the chest away from the midline (medio) and backwards (retro) to then finish in retro-latero. Hence the retro-medio motor scheme is only the starting movement that is completed in re-la-th. The CF re-me-th is located between the supraspinous ligament and the mass of the erector spinae muscles.

Motor scheme of retro-medio-lumbi (re-me-lu)
When moving the low back in retro-latero, movement is started by bringing the trunk away from the midline (medio) and backwards (retro) to then finish in retro-latero. Hence the retro-medio motor scheme is only the starting movement that is completed in re-la-lu. The CF re-me-lu is located between the supraspinous lumbar ligament and the mass of the erector spinae muscles.

Motor scheme of retro-medio-pelvis (re-me-pv)
When moving the pelvis in retro-latero, movement is started by bringing the chest away from the midline (medio) and backwards (retro) to then finish in retro-latero. Hence the retro-medio motor scheme is only the starting movement that is completed in re-la-pv. The CF re-me-lu is located between the supraspinous sacral ligament and the tendons the erector spinae.

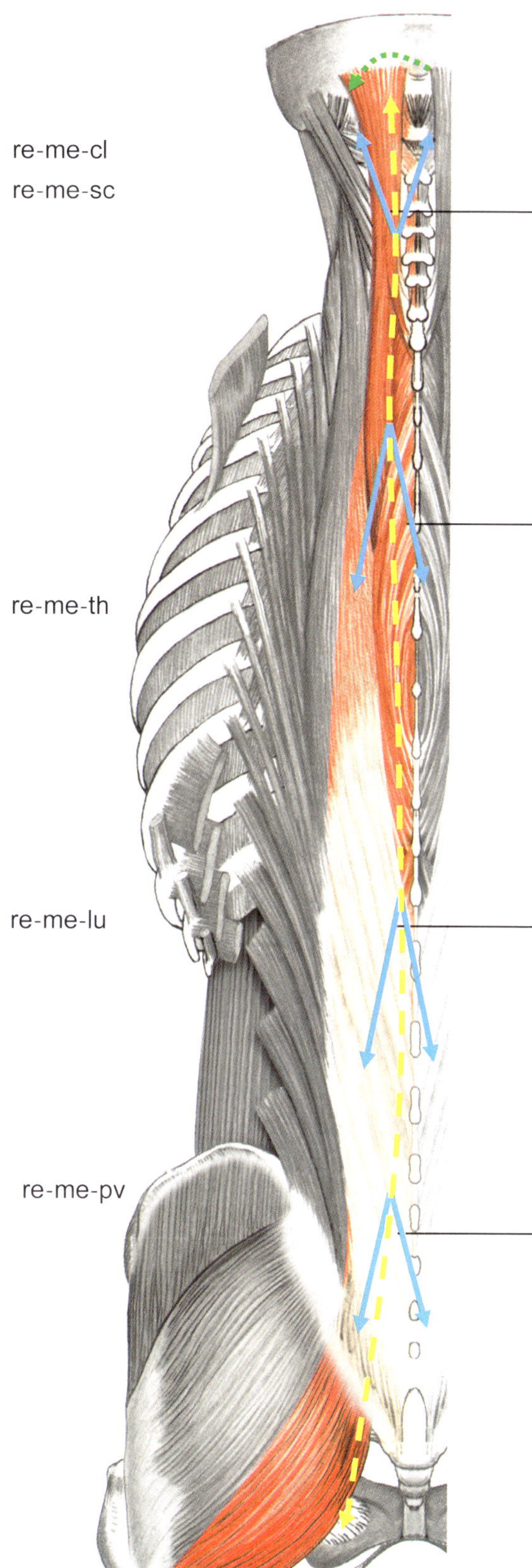

Fig. 5.30. Retro-medio diagonal, trunk.
(From G. Chiarugi and L. Bucciante, Istituzioni di anatomia dell'uomo. Piccin Nuova Libraria, Padova 1983, modified)

RETRO-MEDIO DIAGONAL, TRUNK (Fig. 5.22)

Synergy between the CF of re-me-cl and re-me-sc
The longissimus capitis and cervicis muscles on only one side in the neck imparts a movement of extension with a slight deviation from the midline. At the level of insertion on the last two cervical and first thoracic vertebrae, these muscles are connected to the rhomboid muscles carrying out the re-me-sc motor scheme.

Synergy between re-me-th with the global scheme
The proximal part of the retro-medio diagonal corresponds to the longissimus cervicis and thoracis muscles connecting the neck to the thorax (re-me-th). The fascia of the longissimus muscle extends up to the low back therefore coordinating the posterior musculature of the back to the motor requirements of the neck and head.

Synergy between re-me-lu with the global scheme
The medial part of the retro-medio diagonal connects, through the longissimus sheath, the CFs re-me-th with lumbi and pelvis (re-me-pv). The longissimus muscle (re-me) is separated from the iliocostalis muscle (re-la) by an intermuscular septum.

Synergy between re-me-pv and the global scheme
The thoracolumbar fascia covering the erector spinae muscles extends on the fascia of the gluteus maximus muscle. The distal part of the retro-medio diagonal, through the fascia of the gluteus maximus muscle, connects the pelvis to the hamstring muscles (semitendinosus) and hence to the retro-medio-coxa motor scheme.

CONTINUITY OF THE LINES OF FUSION IN THE ANTERIOR TRUNK

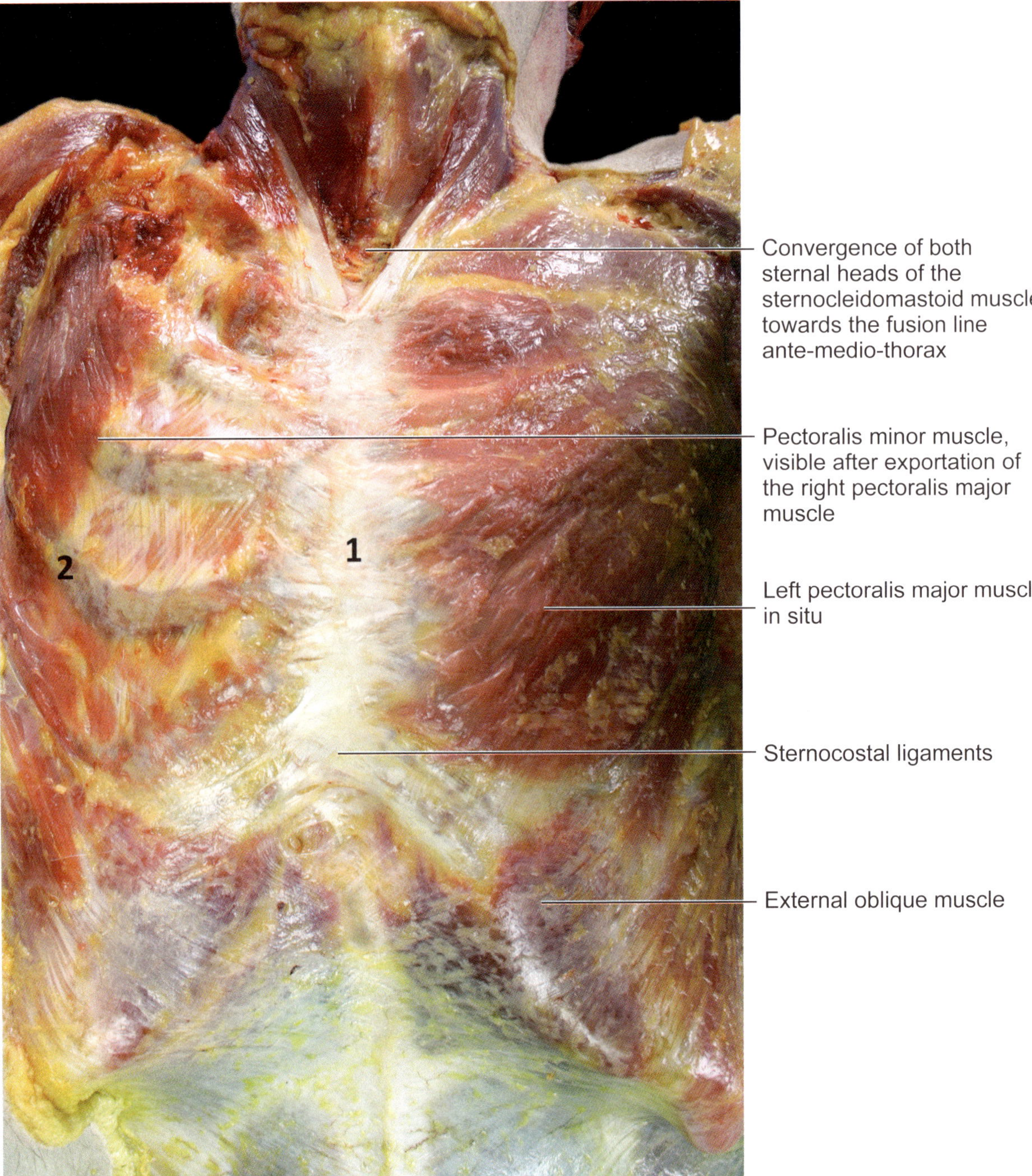

Fig. 5.31. Sternocostal ligaments. The fasciae of the right and left pectoralis major muscles (1) fuse over the sternum, where there is a convergence from the sternal tendons of the sternocleidomastoid muscles superiorly and from the linea alba inferiorly. Aligned with the pectoralis minor muscle the line of insertion of the serratus anterior muscle (2) is visible.

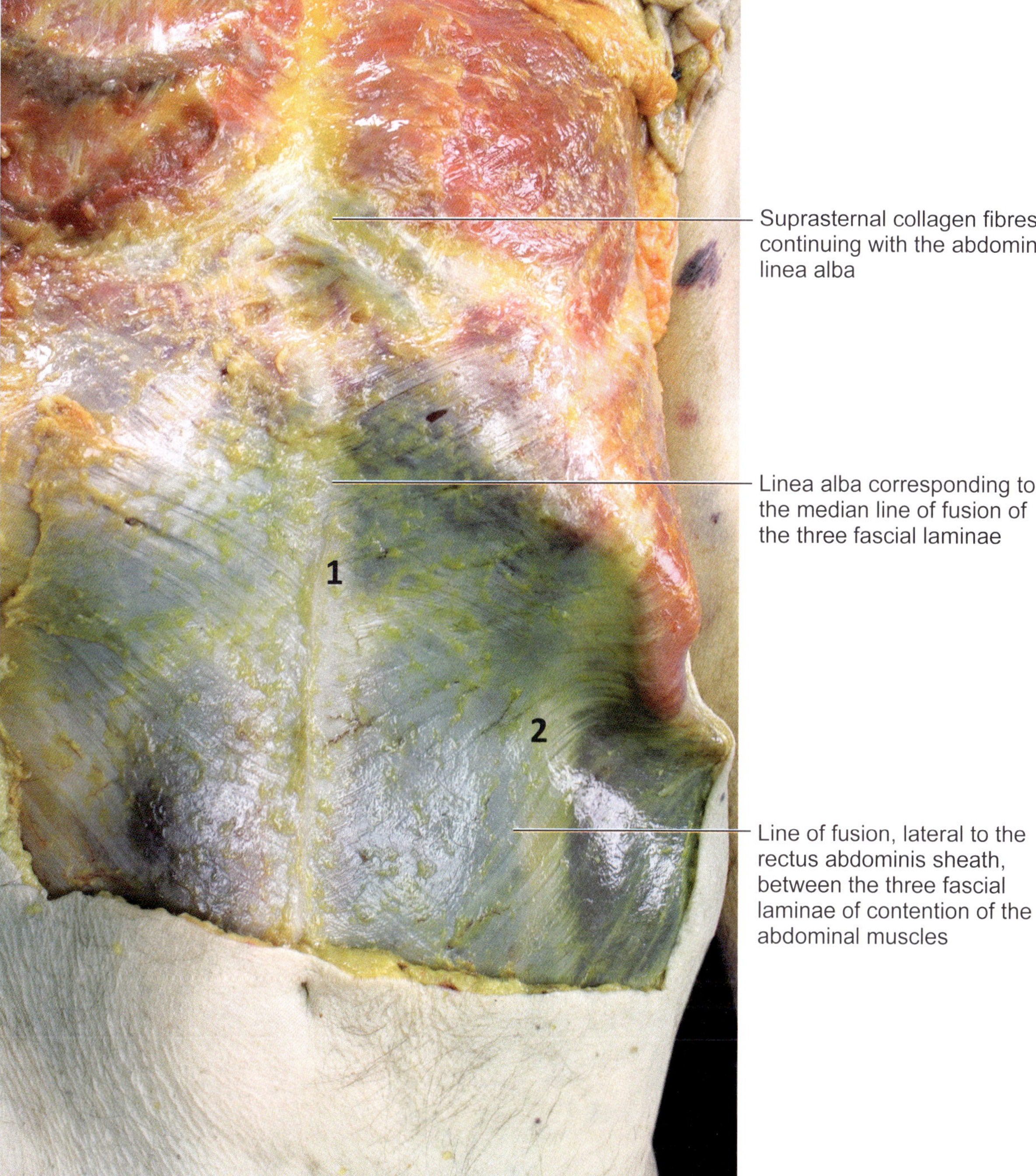

Fig. 5.32. Abdominal linea alba and lateral fusion line of the rectus abdominis sheath. The ante-medio-lumbi line of fusion is located lateral and to the left of the linea alba (1) within the rectus abdominis muscle. Whilst the ante-latero-lumbi line of fusion (2) is located lateral to the rectus abdominis sheath.

CONTINUITY OF THE LINES OF FUSION IN THE POSTERIOR TRUNK

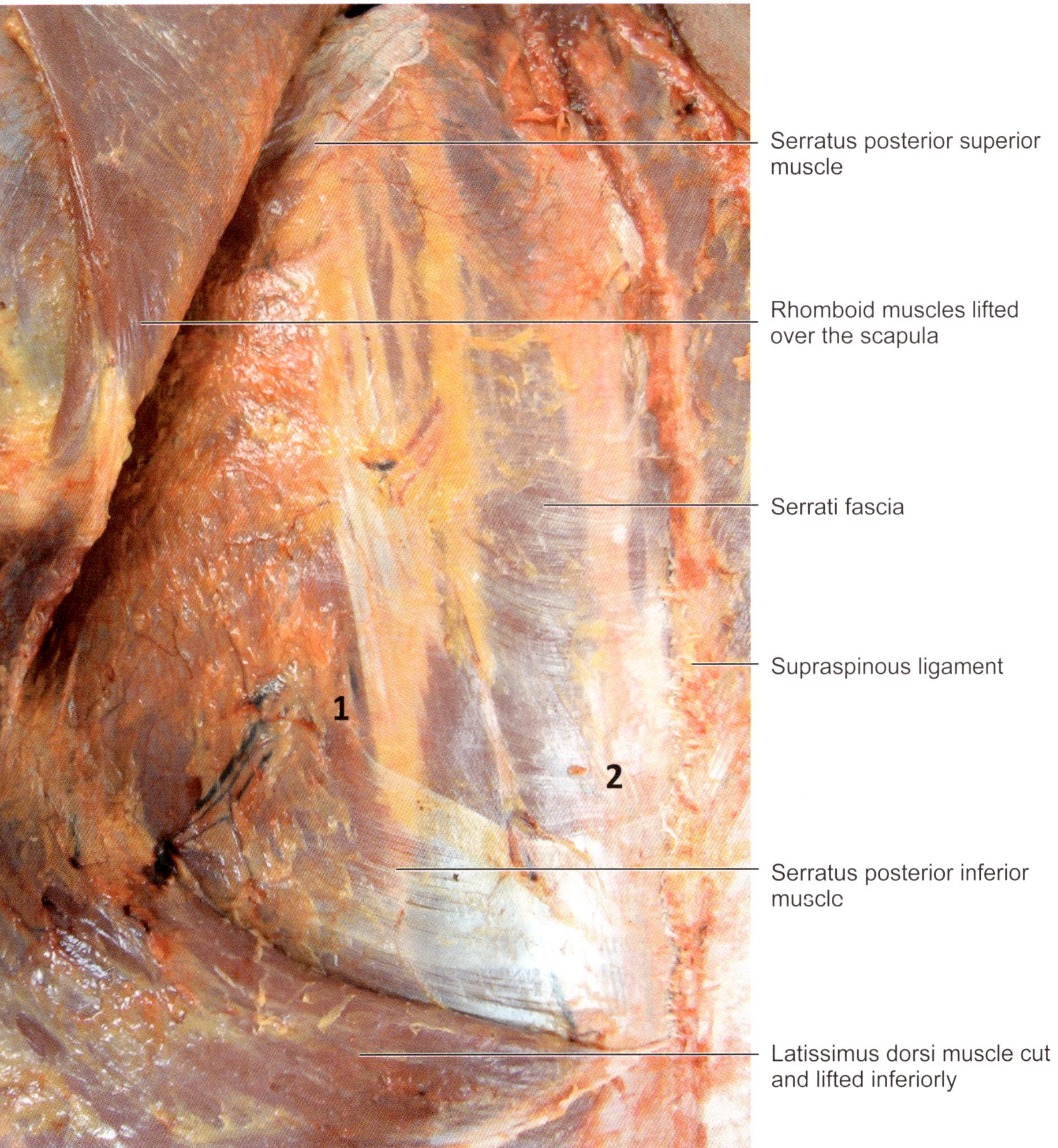

Fig. 5.33. Serrati fascia. Lateral to the iliocostalis muscle, the serrati fascia forms the line of fusion of retro-latero lumbi (1). Lateral to the supraspinous ligament the serrati fascia unites with the fascia of the latissimus dorsi muscle forming the retro-medio thorax and lumbi (2) line of fusion.

CONTINUITY OF THE LINES OF FUSION IN THE POSTERIOR TRUNK

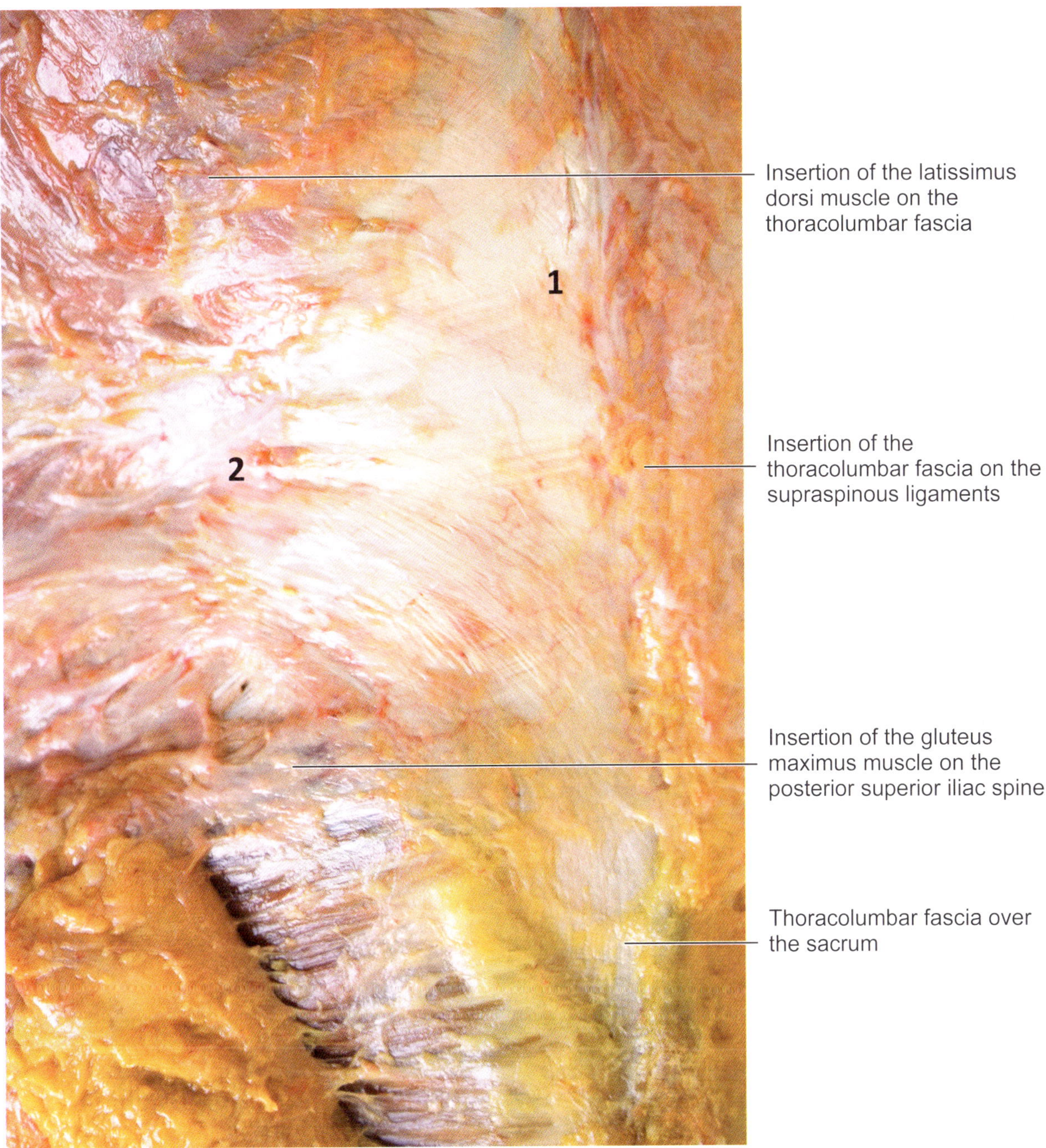

Fig. 5.34. Thoracolumbar fascia at the lumbar and sacral levels. The line of fusion of the medial fasciae (1) is located lateral to the spinous processes of the lumbar vertebrae. The union of the superficial lamina with the deep lamina of the thoracolumbar fascia forms the line of fusion retro-latero-lumbi (2).

CENTRES OF FUSION AND DIAGONALS OF THE LOWER LIMB

The myofascial architecture observed in the upper limb is repeated identically in the lower limb. In the thigh and leg, the ante sequence is interposed between the motor schemes of ante-medio and ante-latero. The retro sequence is interposed between the motor scheme of retro-medio and retro-latero (Fig. 5.35). Since the shoulder and hip may be moved from ante to retro by passing through the entire range of intermediated degrees, they have their own flat muscles (pectoralis major, deltoid, gluteus maximus) with muscle bundles set out as rheostats. The elbow and knee only have flexion-extension movements nonetheless they have ligaments and septa that guarantee the continuity of the ante-latero (Fig. 5.36), ante-medio (Fig. 5.37), retro-latero (Fig. 5.38) and retro-medio (Fig. 5.39) diagonals. The tensioning of the intermuscular septa determines the coordination and the afferents for each specific motor scheme.

The ankle and foot may be moved in rotation by the sequential activation of motor schemes in series, namely by the simultaneous contraction of two or more muscles that singularly would implement a unidirectional trajectory (Fig. 5.35). The figure shows how the recruitment of motor units of muscles is different in unidirectional movement where for instance the CC re-ta simultaneously recruits the motor units of the triceps surae muscle, compared to the CF re-ma-ta recruiting as a rheostat first the motor units of triceps surae and then those of the tibialis posterior muscle.

The techniques of Kabat "Proprioceptive Neuromuscular Facilitation" (Kabat H. 1954) may be defined as methods to evoke and speed up responses of neuromuscular mechanisms through the stimulation of proprioceptors. Proprioceptors are embedded in the muscular fascia hence this tissue should be the focus of attention for rehabilitators.

In peripheral lesions (plexus or cauda lesions) the threshold of excitation is very high, hence large stimuli are required to produce minor responses. Manipulation of the fascia helps in bombarding the posterior afferent ramus with afferent inputs so as to facilitate the passage of successive stimuli (temporal summation) and that of more simultaneous stimuli (spatial summation).

The schemes described by Kabat for neuromotor rehabilitation place muscle groups in a maximal state of stretch, permitting them to contract for the most efficient development of power. The movements follow well-defined schemes, in diagonal and spiral, implicating the muscles working in a global pattern. Diagonal movements are implemented with the limbs outstretched, whilst spiral movements are implemented by passing from extension to triple flexion and vice versa. The movement in the spirals takes advantage of the fibro-elastic structures for the winding and unwinding of pre-determined muscles.

In the lesions of the nervous system, motor coordination needs to be facilitated by starting from segmental movements (myofascial unit), followed by stimulation according to sequences (posture), diagonals (motor schemes) and finally by using spirals (fine motor movements).

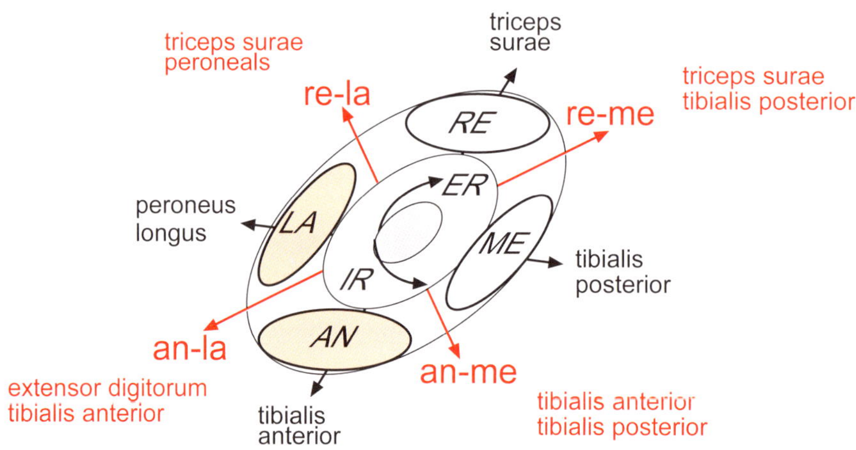

Fig. 5.35. Formation of motor schemes and of CFs as the resultant of two principal motor directions. In this figure only the leg muscles were taken into consideration.

MOTOR SCHEMES OF THE LOWER LIMB IMPLEMENTED ACCORDING TO DIAGONAL PATTERNS

Fig. 5.36. Ante-latero diagonal or movement of the entire lower limb according to the an-la pattern.

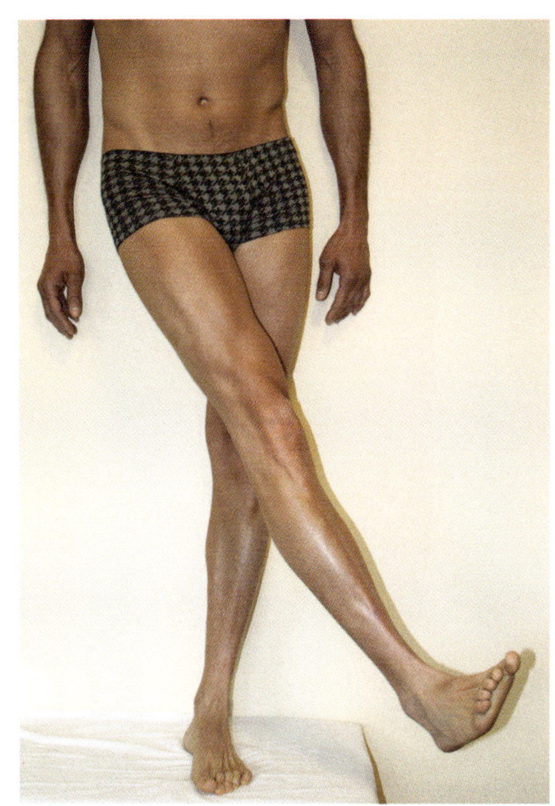

Fig. 5.37. Ante-medio diagonal or movement of the entire lower limb according to the an-me pattern.

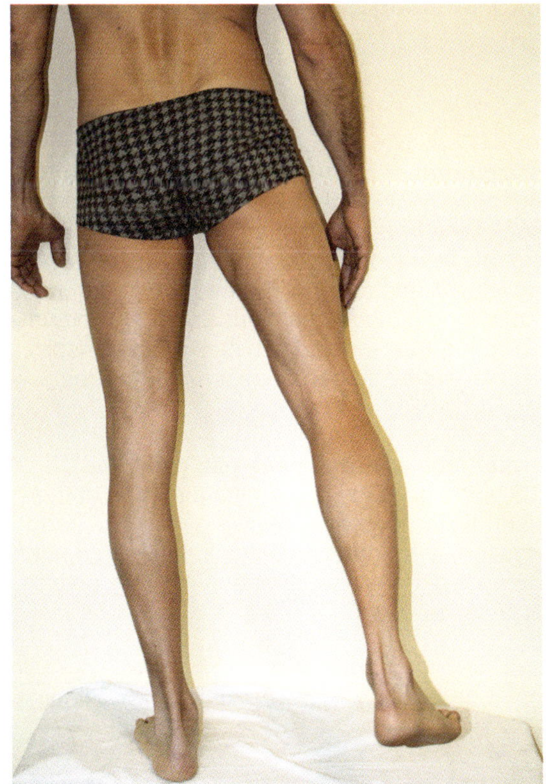

Fig. 5.38. Retro-latero diagonal or movement of the entire lower limb according to the re-la pattern.

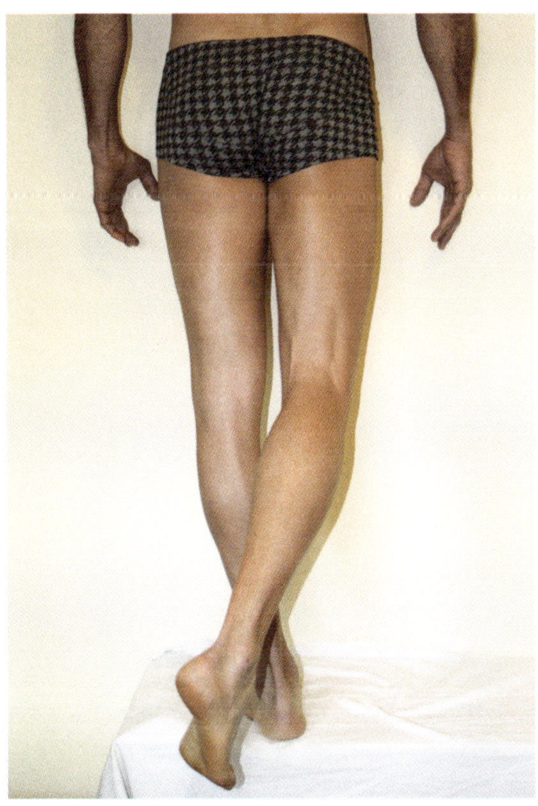

Fig. 5.39. Retro-medio diagonal or movement of the entire lower limb according to the re-me pattern.

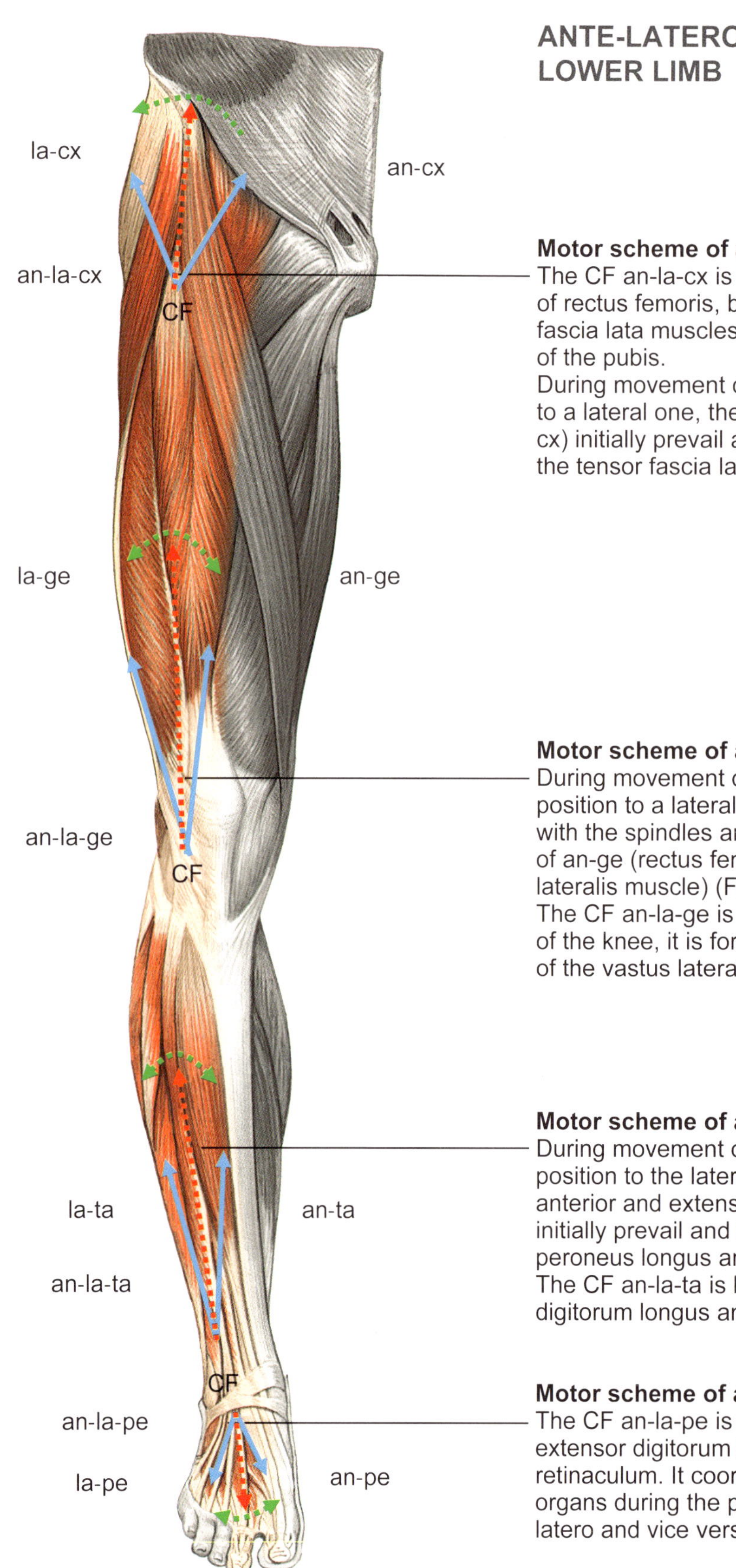

Fig. 5.40. Centres of fusion of ante-latero, LL.
(From G. Chiarugi and L. Bucciante, Istituzioni di anatomia dell'uomo. Piccin Nuova Libraria, Padova 1983, modified)

ANTE-LATERO CENTRES OF FUSION, LOWER LIMB

Motor scheme of ante-latero-coxa (an-la-cx)
The CF an-la-cx is located over the proximal tendon of rectus femoris, between the sartorius and tensor fascia lata muscles at the level of the inferior border of the pubis.
During movement of the hip from an anterior position to a lateral one, the fibres of the psoas muscle (an-cx) initially prevail and towards the end the fibres of the tensor fascia lata muscle (la-cx) prevail.

Motor scheme of ante-latero-genu (an-la-ge)
During movement of the knee from an anterior position to a lateral one, the CF an-la-ge interacts with the spindles and tendon organs of the MF units of an-ge (rectus femoris muscle) and la-ge (vastus lateralis muscle) (Fig. 5.48).
The CF an-la-ge is located on the lateral retinaculum of the knee, it is formed by the tendinous expansions of the vastus lateralis muscle.

Motor scheme of ante-latero-talus (an-la-ta)
During movement of the ankle from an anterior position to the lateral one, the fibres of the tibialis anterior and extensor digitorum muscles (an-ta) initially prevail and towards the end the fibres of the peroneus longus and tertius muscles (la-ta) prevail.
The CF an-la-ta is located between the extensor digitorum longus and peroneus tertius muscles.

Motor scheme of ante-latero-pes (an-la-pe)
The CF an-la-pe is located on the insertion of the extensor digitorum brevis muscle on the cruciform retinaculum. It coordinates the spindles and tendon organs during the passage of the foot from ante to latero and vice versa.

ANTE-LATERO DIAGONAL, LOWER LIMB (Fig. 5.36)

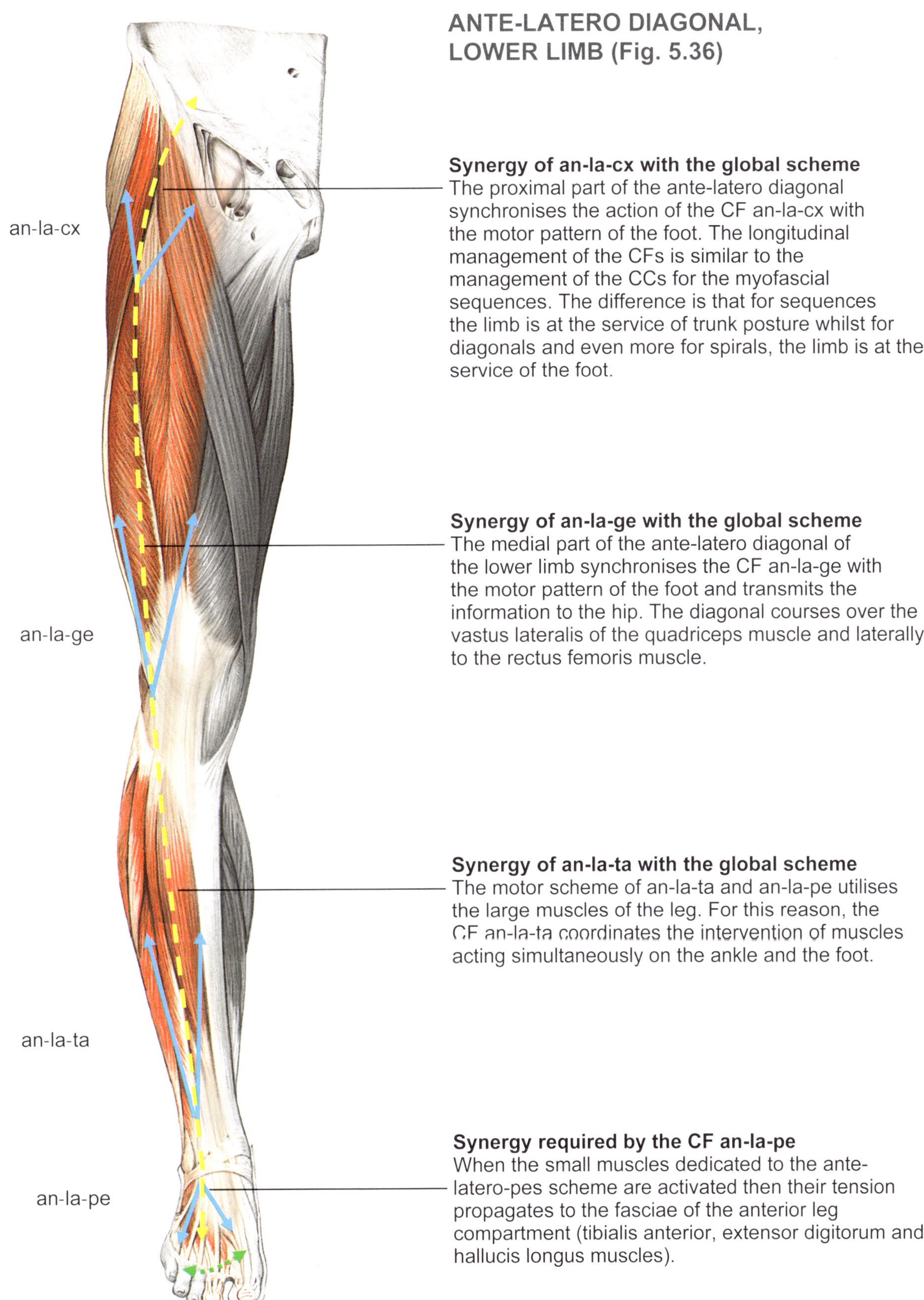

Synergy of an-la-cx with the global scheme
The proximal part of the ante-latero diagonal synchronises the action of the CF an-la-cx with the motor pattern of the foot. The longitudinal management of the CFs is similar to the management of the CCs for the myofascial sequences. The difference is that for sequences the limb is at the service of trunk posture whilst for diagonals and even more for spirals, the limb is at the service of the foot.

Synergy of an-la-ge with the global scheme
The medial part of the ante-latero diagonal of the lower limb synchronises the CF an-la-ge with the motor pattern of the foot and transmits the information to the hip. The diagonal courses over the vastus lateralis of the quadriceps muscle and laterally to the rectus femoris muscle.

Synergy of an-la-ta with the global scheme
The motor scheme of an-la-ta and an-la-pe utilises the large muscles of the leg. For this reason, the CF an-la-ta coordinates the intervention of muscles acting simultaneously on the ankle and the foot.

Synergy required by the CF an-la-pe
When the small muscles dedicated to the ante-latero-pes scheme are activated then their tension propagates to the fasciae of the anterior leg compartment (tibialis anterior, extensor digitorum and hallucis longus muscles).

Fig. 5.41. Ante-latero diagonal of the lower limb.
(From G. Chiarugi and L. Bucciante, Istituzioni di anatomia dell'uomo. Piccin Nuova Libraria, Padova 1983, modified)

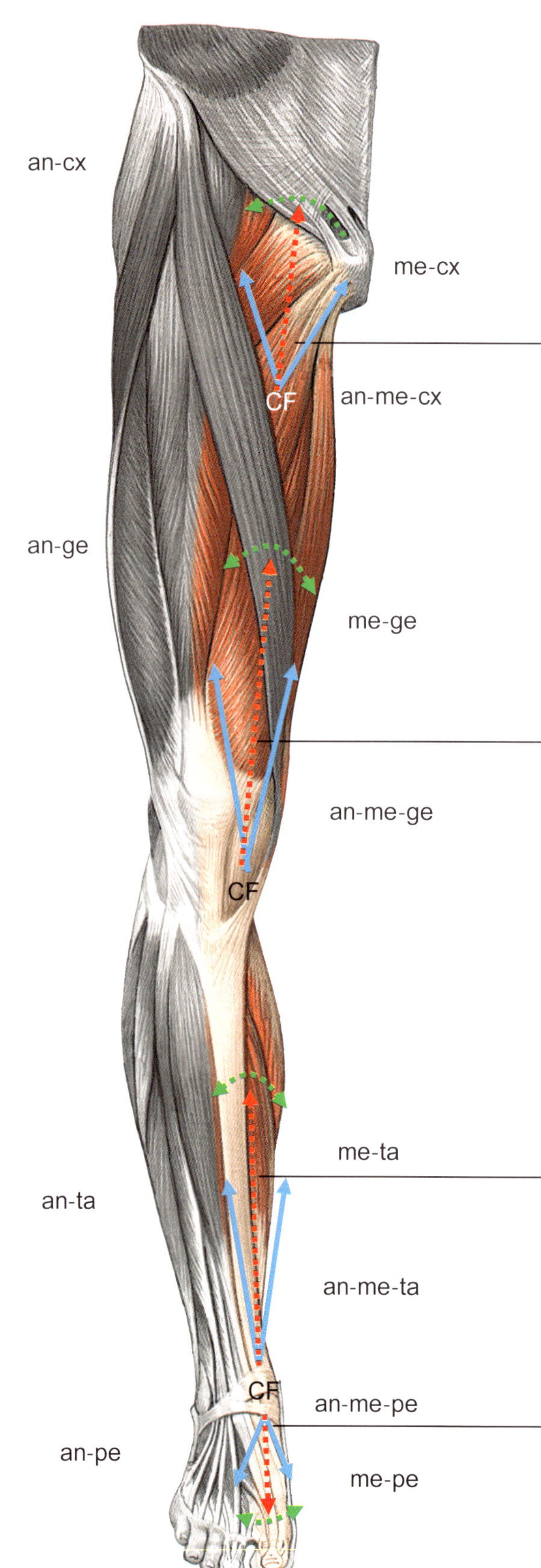

Fig. 5.42. Centres of fusion of ante-medio, LL.
(From G. Chiarugi and L. Bucciante, Istituzioni di anatomia dell'uomo. Piccin Nuova Libraria, Padova 1983, modified)

ANTE-MEDIO CENTRES OF FUSION, LOWER LIMB

Motor scheme of ante-medio-coxa (an-me-cx)
During movement of the hip from an anterior position (an-cx) to the medial one, the fibres of the psoas muscle initially prevail and towards the end the fibres included in the adductor muscles prevail.
The CF an-me-cx, located over the adductor tendon inserting on the pubis, coordinates the increase in force of the me-cx MF unit and the decrease of the an-cx unit.

Motor scheme of ante-medio-genu (an-me-ge)
During movement of the knee from an anterior position (an-ge) to the medial one (me-ge), the stabilising fibres of the quadriceps femoris muscle initially prevail and towards the end the fibres inserting into pes anserinus prevail (Fig. 5.49).
The CF an-me-ge, located between the vastus medialis muscle and pes anserinus, coordinates the increase in force of the MF unit me-ge and the simultaneous decrease of the an-ge unit. The CC of the an-ge MF unit coordinates the motor units distributed in the entire quadriceps muscle whilst the CF an-me-ge coordinates the motor units mostly located in the vastus medialis muscle.

Motor scheme of ante-medio-talus (an-me-ta)
During movement of the ankle from an anterior position to the medial one, the fibres of the tibialis anterior muscle initially prevail and towards the end the fibres of the soleus muscle prevail. The CF an-me-ta, located over the posterior border of the tibia in its distal third, coordinates the increase of the me-ta MF unit and the simultaneous decrease of the an-ta unit.

Motor scheme of ante-medio-pes (an-me-pe)
The CF an-me-pe is located over the retinaculum of the extensors and over the tibialis anterior tendon. It coordinates the passages of the foot from ante to medio and balances the force of the ankle with that of the foot.

ANTE-MEDIO DIAGONAL, LOWER LIMB (Fig. 5.37)

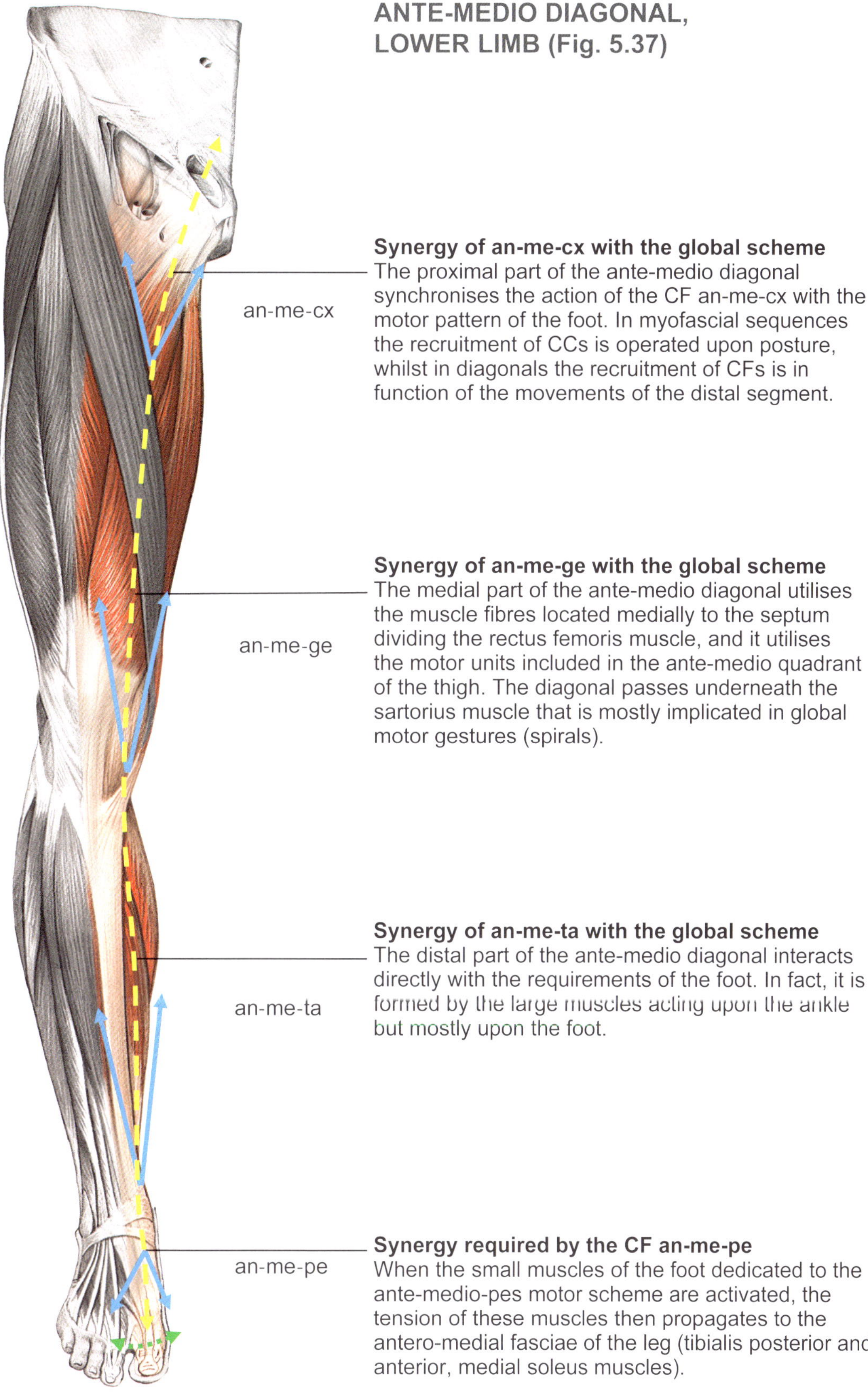

Synergy of an-me-cx with the global scheme
The proximal part of the ante-medio diagonal synchronises the action of the CF an-me-cx with the motor pattern of the foot. In myofascial sequences the recruitment of CCs is operated upon posture, whilst in diagonals the recruitment of CFs is in function of the movements of the distal segment.

Synergy of an-me-ge with the global scheme
The medial part of the ante-medio diagonal utilises the muscle fibres located medially to the septum dividing the rectus femoris muscle, and it utilises the motor units included in the ante-medio quadrant of the thigh. The diagonal passes underneath the sartorius muscle that is mostly implicated in global motor gestures (spirals).

Synergy of an-me-ta with the global scheme
The distal part of the ante-medio diagonal interacts directly with the requirements of the foot. In fact, it is formed by the large muscles acting upon the ankle but mostly upon the foot.

Synergy required by the CF an-me-pe
When the small muscles of the foot dedicated to the ante-medio-pes motor scheme are activated, the tension of these muscles then propagates to the antero-medial fasciae of the leg (tibialis posterior and anterior, medial soleus muscles).

Fig. 5.43. Ante-medio diagonal, lower limb.
(From G. Chiarugi and L. Bucciante, Istituzioni di anatomia dell'uomo. Piccin Nuova Libraria, Padova 1983, modified)

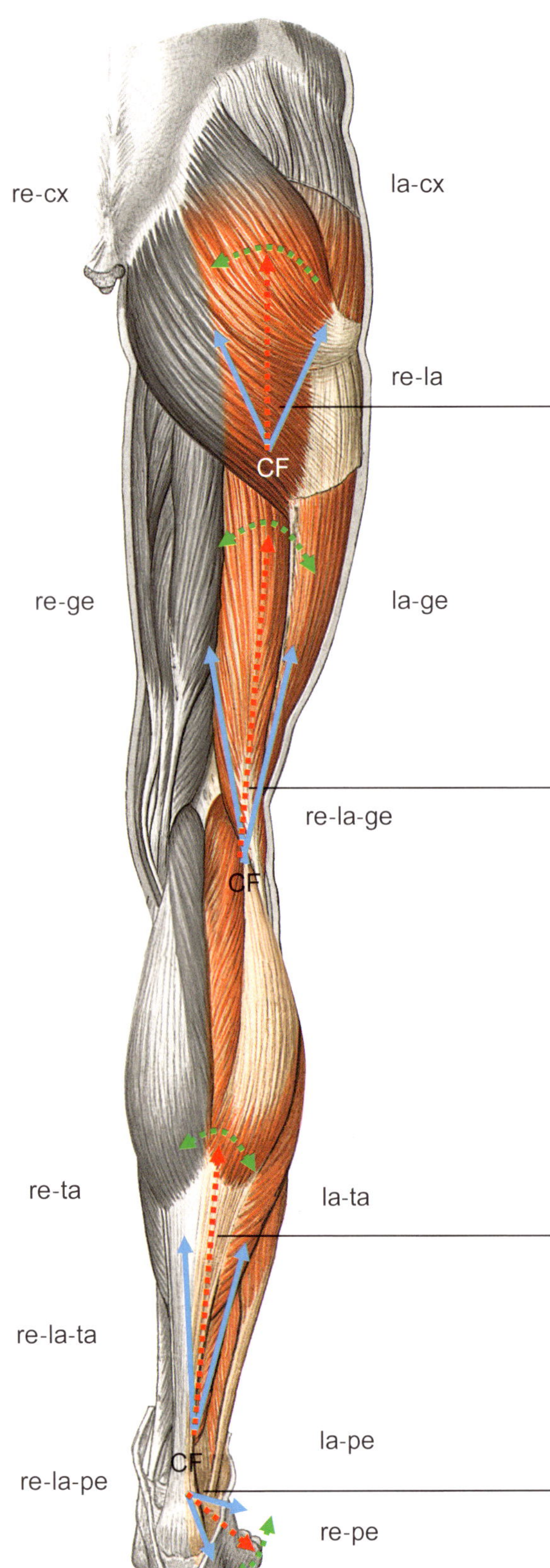

Fig. 5.44. Centres of fusion of retro-latero, LL.
(From G. Chiarugi and L. Bucciante, Istituzioni di anatomia dell'uomo. Piccin Nuova Libraria, Padova 1983, modified)

RETRO-LATERO CENTRES OF FUSION, LOWER LIMB

Motor scheme of retro-latero-coxa (re-la-cx)
During movement of the hip from the posterior position to the lateral one, the posterior fibres of the gluteus maximus muscle initially prevail and towards the end the lateral fibres of the same muscle and tensor fascia lata prevail.
The CF re-la-cx is located midway over the fibres of the gluteus maximus muscle, laterally to the ischial tuberosity.

Motor scheme of retro-latero-genu (re-la-ge)
The retro-lateral stabilisation of the knee is guaranteed by the CF re-la-ge coordinating the spindles and tendon organs of the MF units of re-ge and la-ge (Fig. 5.50).
The CC re-ge manages the motor units included in all hamstring muscles whilst the CF re-la-ge coordinates the motor units included only the biceps femoris muscle. The same occurs at the level of the ankle.

Motor scheme of retro-latero-talus (re-la-ta)
During movement of the ankle from the posterior position to the lateral one, the fibres of the triceps surae muscle initially prevail and towards the end the fibres of the peroneal muscles prevail. The CF re-la-ta is located laterally to the triceps surae tendon over the peroneus longus and brevis tendons. It coordinates the increase of force in the la-ta and er-ta MF units and the simultaneous decrease of the re-ta unit.

Motor scheme of retro-latero-pes (re-la-pe)
The CF re-la-pe is located on the superior and inferior retinacula of the peroneal muscles. It coordinates the interaction of the foot with the entire retro-latero diagonal.

RETRO-LATERO DIAGONAL, LOWER LIMB (Fig. 5.38)

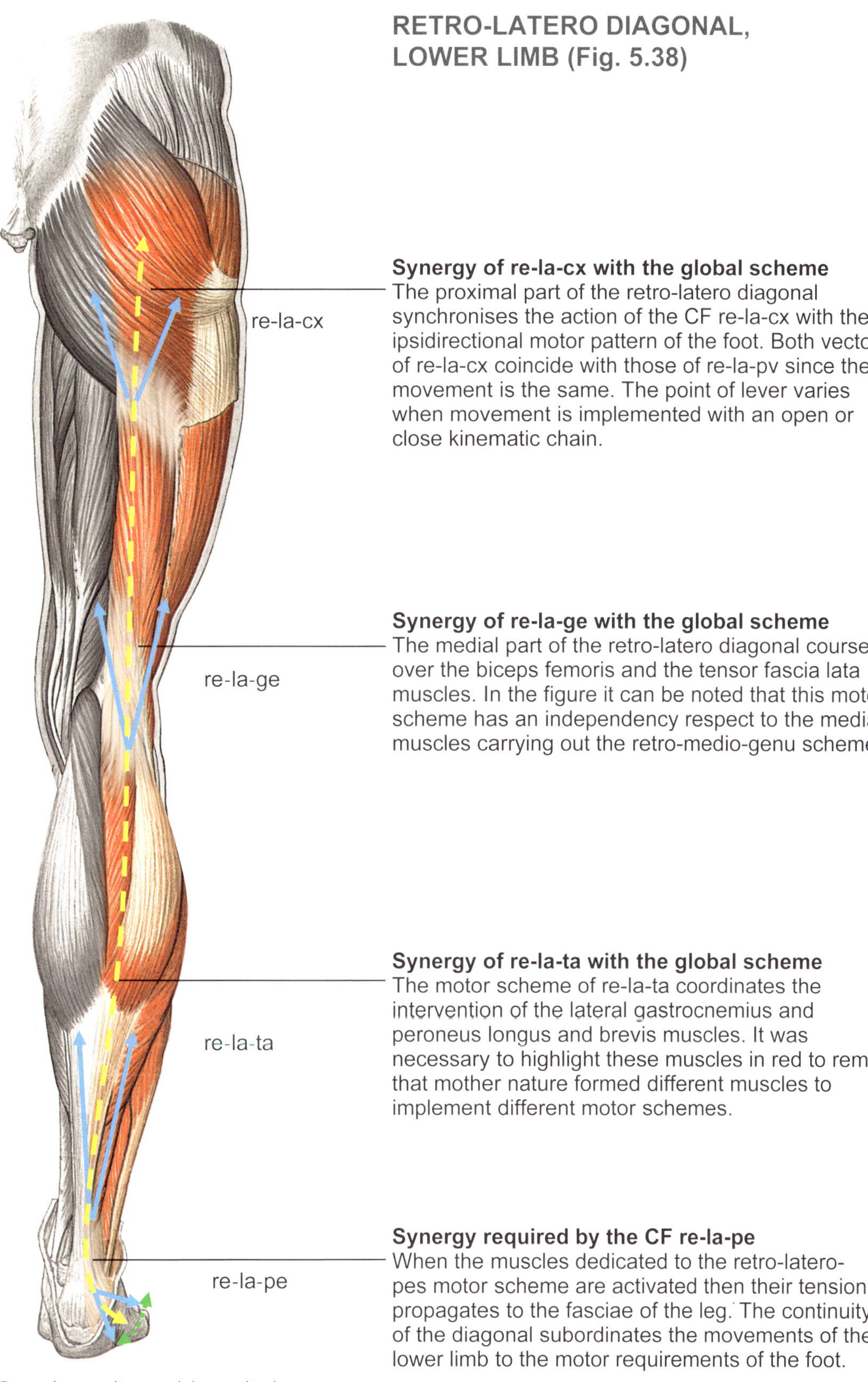

Synergy of re-la-cx with the global scheme
The proximal part of the retro-latero diagonal synchronises the action of the CF re-la-cx with the ipsidirectional motor pattern of the foot. Both vectors of re-la-cx coincide with those of re-la-pv since the movement is the same. The point of lever varies when movement is implemented with an open or close kinematic chain.

Synergy of re-la-ge with the global scheme
The medial part of the retro-latero diagonal courses over the biceps femoris and the tensor fascia lata muscles. In the figure it can be noted that this motor scheme has an independency respect to the medial muscles carrying out the retro-medio-genu scheme.

Synergy of re-la-ta with the global scheme
The motor scheme of re-la-ta coordinates the intervention of the lateral gastrocnemius and peroneus longus and brevis muscles. It was necessary to highlight these muscles in red to remark that mother nature formed different muscles to implement different motor schemes.

Synergy required by the CF re-la-pe
When the muscles dedicated to the retro-latero-pes motor scheme are activated then their tension propagates to the fasciae of the leg. The continuity of the diagonal subordinates the movements of the lower limb to the motor requirements of the foot.

Fig. 5.45. Retro-latero diagonal, lower limb.
(From G. Chiarugi and L. Bucciante, Istituzioni di anatomia dell'uomo. Piccin Nuova Libraria, Padova 1983, modified)

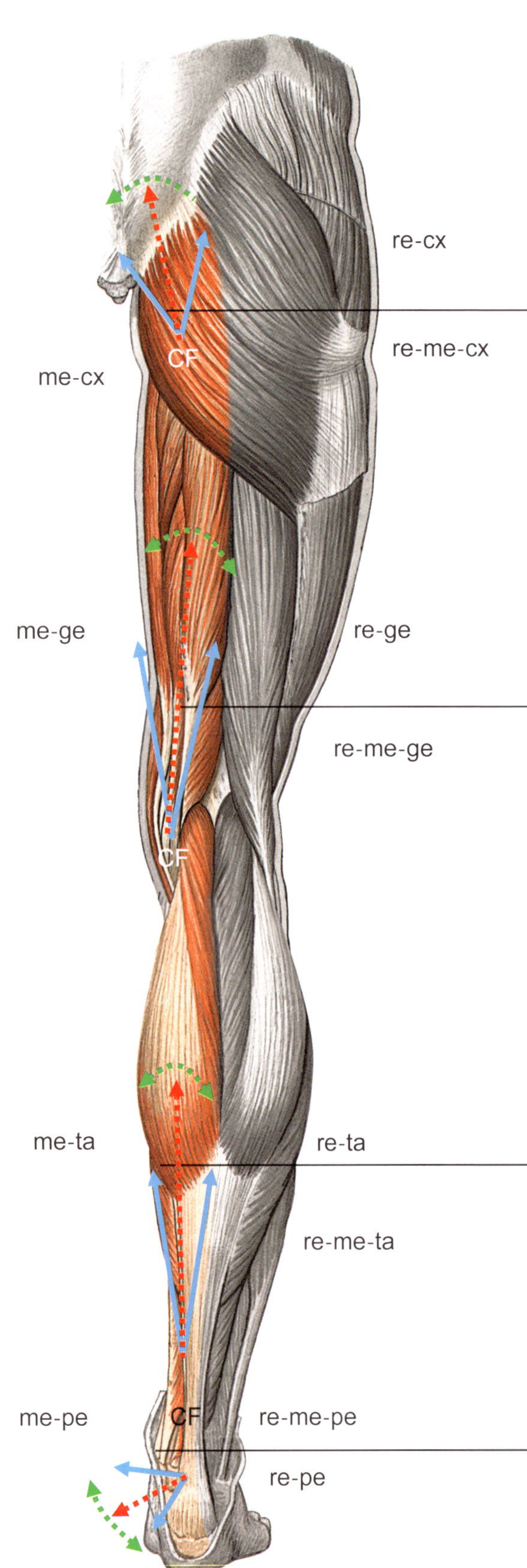

Fig. 5.46. Centres of fusion of retro-medio, LL.
(From G. Chiarugi and L. Bucciante, Istituzioni di anatomia dell'uomo. Piccin Nuova Libraria, Padova 1983, modified)

RETRO-MEDIO CENTRES OF FUSION, LOWER LIMB

Motor scheme of retro-medio-coxa (re-me-cx)
During movement of the hip from the posterior position to the medial one, the posterior fibres of the gluteus maximus muscle initially prevail and towards the end the fibres of the adductor magnus muscle prevail, midway through the range both forces are equal.
The CF re-me-cx is located over the gluteus maximus muscle laterally to the sacro-coccygeal joint.

Motor scheme of retro-medio-genu (re-me-ge)
The CF re-me-ge is located between the tendons of the semimembranous and medial gastrocnemius muscles since it must coordinate the force of both intervening muscles to implement this motor scheme (Fig. 5.51).
The CC re-ge coordinates the motor units distributed in all the hamstring muscles whilst the CF re-me-ge coordinates the motor units distributed in the semitendinosus and semimembranosus muscles.

Motor scheme of retro-medio-talus (re-me-ta)
During movement of the ankle from the posterior position to the medial one, the fibres of the medial gastrocnemius muscle initially prevail and towards the end the fibres of the flexor digitorum longus muscle prevail. The CC re-ta coordinates the motor units spread in the entire triceps surae muscle, whilst the CF re-me-ta coordinates the motor units spread only in the medial gastrocnemius and flexor digitorum longus muscles.

Motor scheme of retro-medio-pes (re-me-pe)
The CF re-me-pe is located over the flexor retinaculum in the deep fascia. It coordinates the adjustment of the proximal muscles to the requirements of foot movements.

RETRO-MEDIO DIAGONAL, LOWER LIMB (Fig. 5.39)

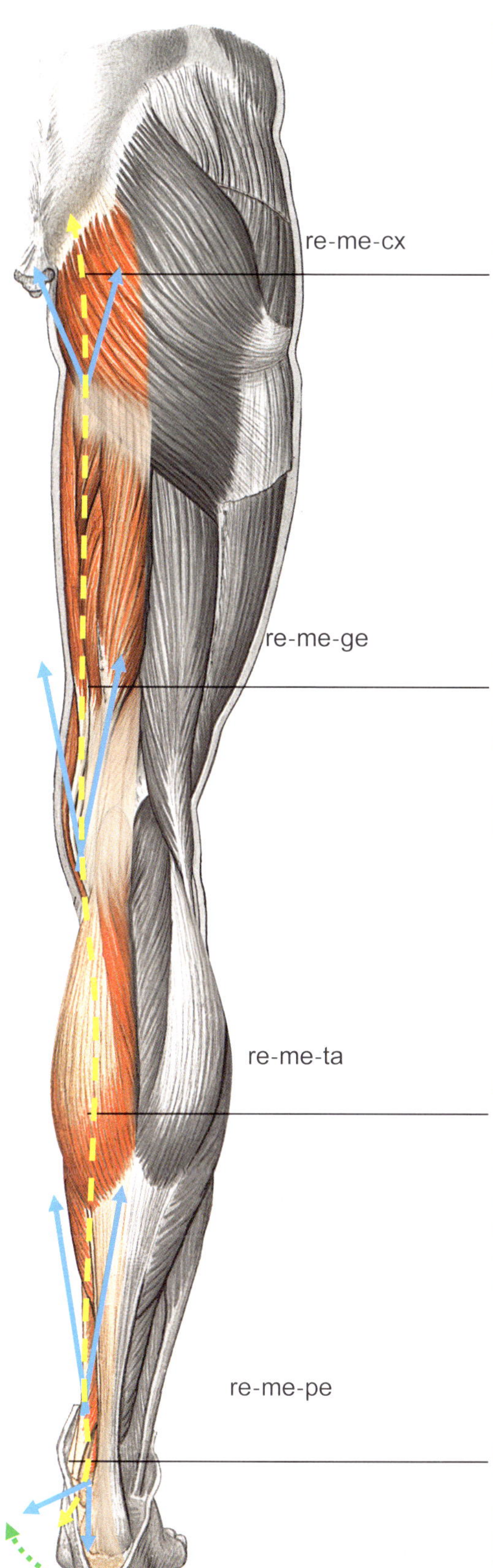

Fig. 5.47. Retro-medio diagonal, lower limb.
(From G. Chiarugi and L. Bucciante, Istituzioni di anatomia dell'uomo. Piccin Nuova Libraria, Padova 1983, modified)

Synergy of re-me-cx with the global scheme
When the entire limb implements the retro-medio scheme against resistance, then the CF re-me-cx must synchronise its force with that of the entire diagonal; the recruitment of the CFs is mostly disto-proximal.

Synergy of re-me-ge with the global scheme
In the medial part of the re-me diagonal, the continuity between the knee and ankle is confirmed by the connection of muscles. Indeed, fixing the knee in re-me is provided not only by the muscles of the thigh (semitendinosus, semimembranosus) but also by those of the ankle (gastrocnemius muscle).

Synergy of re-me-ta with the global scheme
The CF re-me-ta is located between the triceps surae tendon and that of the flexor digitorum muscle. In the distal part of the re-me diagonal, the continuity between ankle and foot is confirmed by the connection of muscles acting on the supination of both ankle and foot (tibialis posterior and flexor digitorum muscles).

Motor scheme of re-me-pe
When the muscles dedicated to the retro-medio-pes motor scheme are activated, then their tension propagates to the fasciae of the leg. The MF units of the foot have multiple muscles originating from the fascia and hence these determine a clear tensioning of the fascia in a disto-proximal direction.

LOCALISATION OF THE CF ANTE-LATERO-GENU

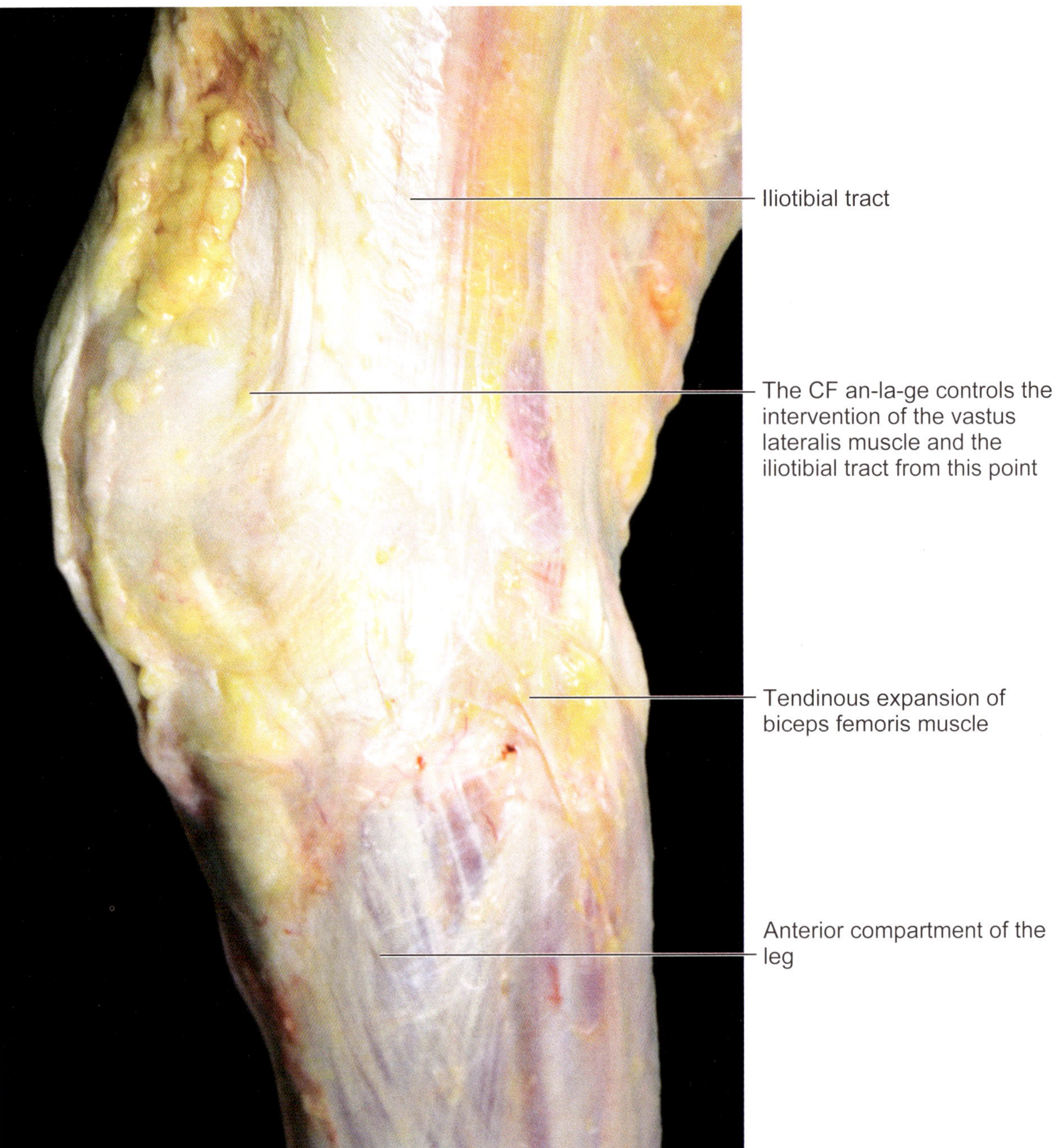

Fig. 5.48. Aponeurotic fascia of the antero-lateral region of the knee. Along the lateral collateral ligament of the knee there are collagen fibres forming a line of conjunction between the iliotibial tract and the anterior compartment of the leg.

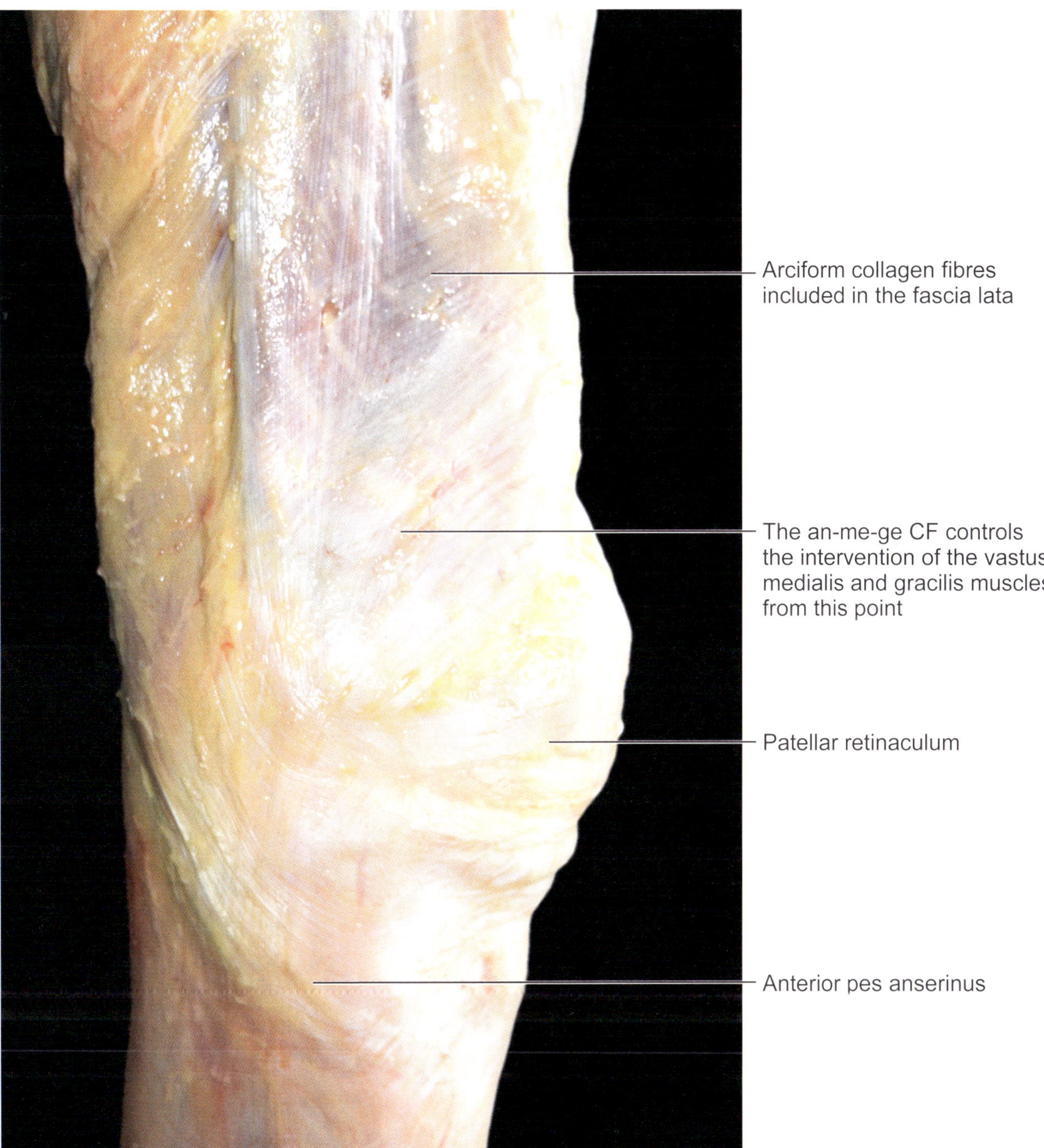

Fig. 5.49. Aponeurotic fascia of the antero-medial region of the knee. The anterior pes anserinus is a line of fusion since the tendons of the gracilis (medio), sartorius (ante) and the retinaculum of the vastus lateralis muscles converge in it.

LOCALISATION OF THE CF RETRO-LATERO-GENU

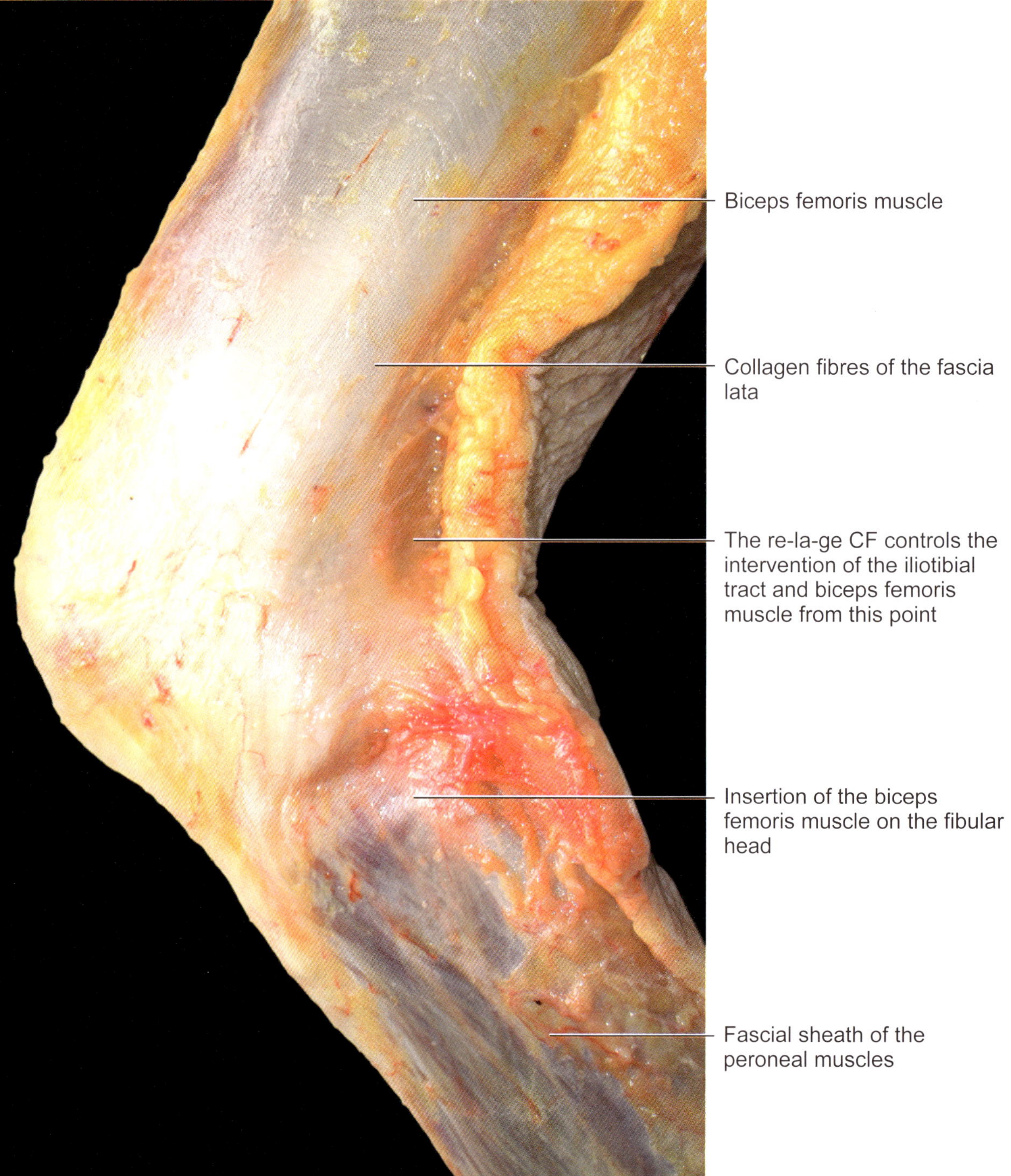

Fig. 5.50. Aponeurotic fascia of the retro-lateral region of the knee. The biceps femoris tendon through its three insertions forms a line of fusion since it acts in retropulsion, external rotation and lateral stabilisation of the knee.

LOCALISATION OF THE CF RETRO-MEDIO-GENU

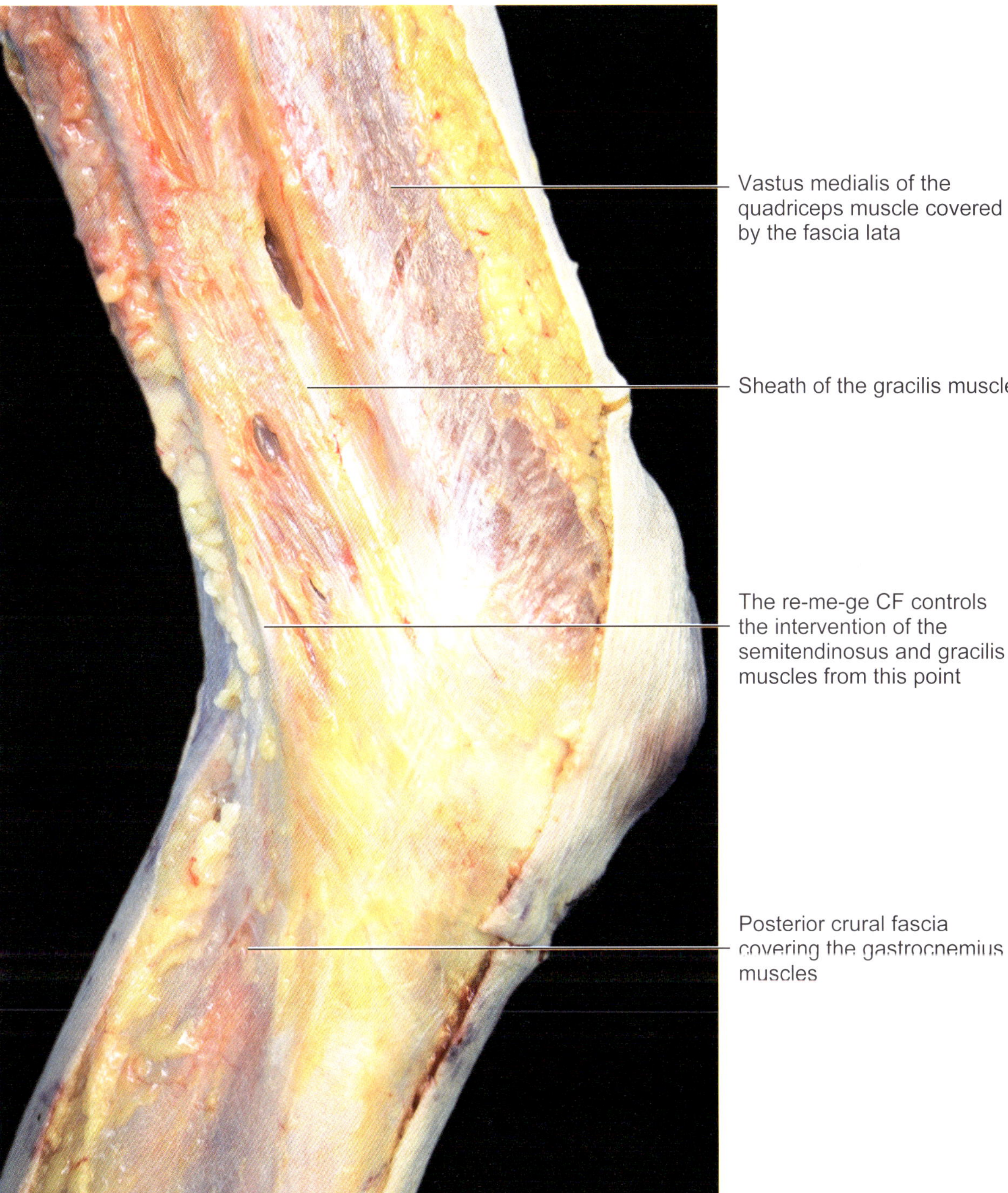

Fig. 5.51. Aponeurotic fascia of the retro-medial region of the knee. The posterior pes anserinus is a line of fusion or junction between retro-genu (semitendinosus muscle) and retro-talus (medial gastrocnemius muscle), between medio-genu (gracilis muscle) and medio-talus (soleus muscle).

CHAPTER 6

CENTRES OF FUSION AND SPIRALS

MOTOR GESTURES AND MULTIDIRECTION MOVEMENTS

Motor gestures include the typical activities of human kind like handling, jumping, throwing and grabbing. These activities represent the fundamental movements upon which all future motor learning in sporting and working activities are built. These activities are possible because the fasciae contain those structures which facilitate their organisation and peripheral motor memorisation.

In the newborn child the arrangement of the intrafascial collagen fibres is poorly organised. Then through repetition of motor gestures these collagen fibres are laid out in sequences, diagonals and spirals such that they function as motor memories. For instance, in order to remain standing a child initially widens the legs apart in order to increase the support base, then the child supports himself to an aid with his hands in order to move a leg forward, finally the lower limb is moved without triple flexion. The repetition of these motor gestures determines bipedal gait which is facilitated by the organisation of collagen fibres according to the stimuli they receive. Only when the spiral collagen fibres starting from the small muscles of the foot and the ankle retinacula are well structured can there be automatic gait, jumping and kicking with only one foot.

The same happens for hand motor gestures where the organisation and memorisation of collagen fibres occurs in a second time. For instance, writing is learned around six years old, and a pianist perfects hand gestures only after many repetitions of the pieces to play.

The periarticular retinacula of the wrist, ankle and head are included in the deep muscular fascia and are connected to the small muscles of the hands (Fig. 6.1), feet (Fig. 6.29) and head (Fig. 6.20). The stretching of the retinacula starts from these extremities[1] and propagates to the spiral mechanically, via mechanotransduction or via piezoelectrical effect, which determines the adjustment of the entire limb and trunk.

The motor gesture takes into consideration helicoidal movements of the distal segments (foot and hand) and spiral movements along the limbs and in the trunk. The helix is a spiral allowing movements in the three spatial planes[2].

The most frequent helicoidal movement is happening in the foot during gait: whilst the tibia internally rotates, the talus externally rotates and the calcaneus internally rotates. Trying to implement these movements voluntarily is not possible, this demonstrates that these are not organised by the brain but rather by a myofascial peripheral stretching. In order to implement a motor gesture the mind programmes the movement of the distal segments and these then recall, through their connections with the retinacula of the wrist and ankle, the adjustment of the proximal musculature. For instance, when tugging on a rope (Fig. 6.2) concentration is only given to the hands and without realising it the body implements a series of movements in the entire upper limb, trunk and lower limb.

Even footballers, when having to kick a ball, focus their attention on the foot and consequently the entire musculature of the lower limb and trunk adapts itself to this gesture.

The arrangement of certain muscles included in their own sheath derived from the aponeurotic fascia demonstrate how the spiral organisation functions. For instance the sartorius muscle, wrapped in its sheath derived from the fascia lata, participates in antepulsion and extrarotation of the thigh through its proximal tendon, whilst with its distal tendon implements retropulsion and intrarotation of the knee. Like the sartorius muscle, the sternocleidomastoid muscle intervenes to implement flexion, internal rotation and adduction of the neck through its sternal fibres, whilst carrying out extension, external rotation and lateral flexion of the neck through its fibres inserted on the mastoid process.

In many cases the CFs of the spirals are activated by intrafascial collagen fibres possibly through stretching or mechanotransduction. Certainly further studies are necessary to define how these collagen fibres interact with the neuromuscular spindles and with the Golgi tendon organs.

[1] "The voluntary extension of the lower limb when walking may be facilitated by the positive placing reflex, this is an extensor reflex induced by a pressure stimulus on the plantar surface of the foot: this stimulation allows the impulsion for gait". (Kabat H. 1954)

[2] Experience has demonstrated that the diagonal and spiral schemes of irradiation are often more effective. A spiral scheme is a voluntary motor scheme including a single movement, and simultaneously three components at the level of more joints: flexion or extension, abduction or adduction, internal or external rotation. (Kabat H. 1954)

CENTRES OF FUSION AND SPIRALS IN THE UPPER LIMB

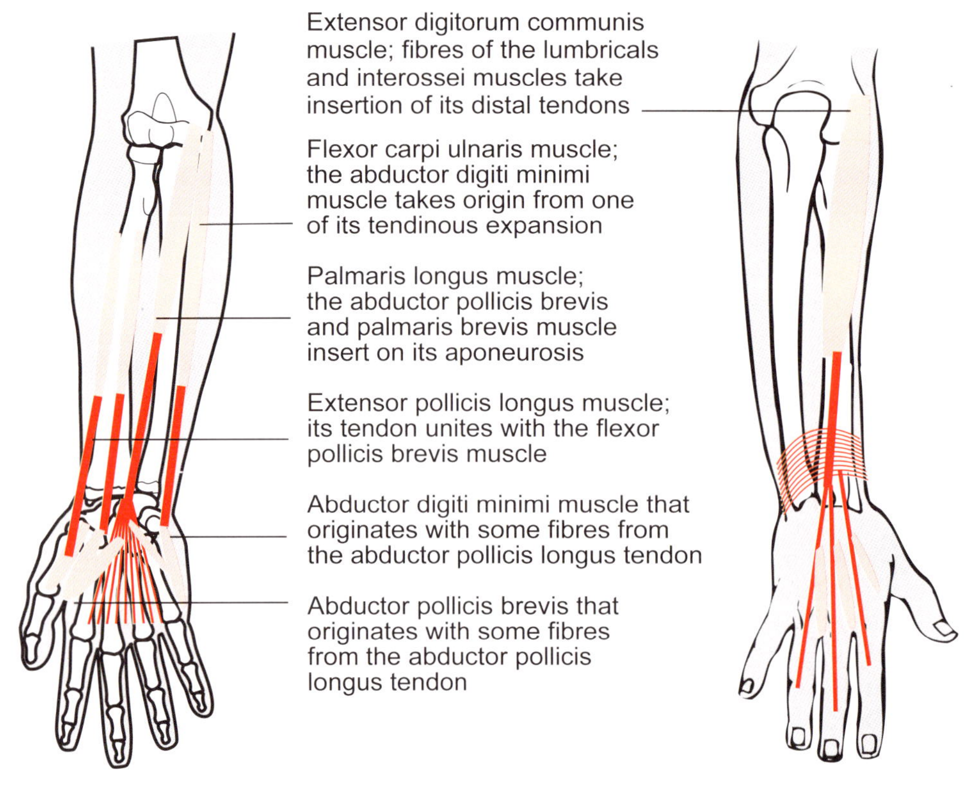

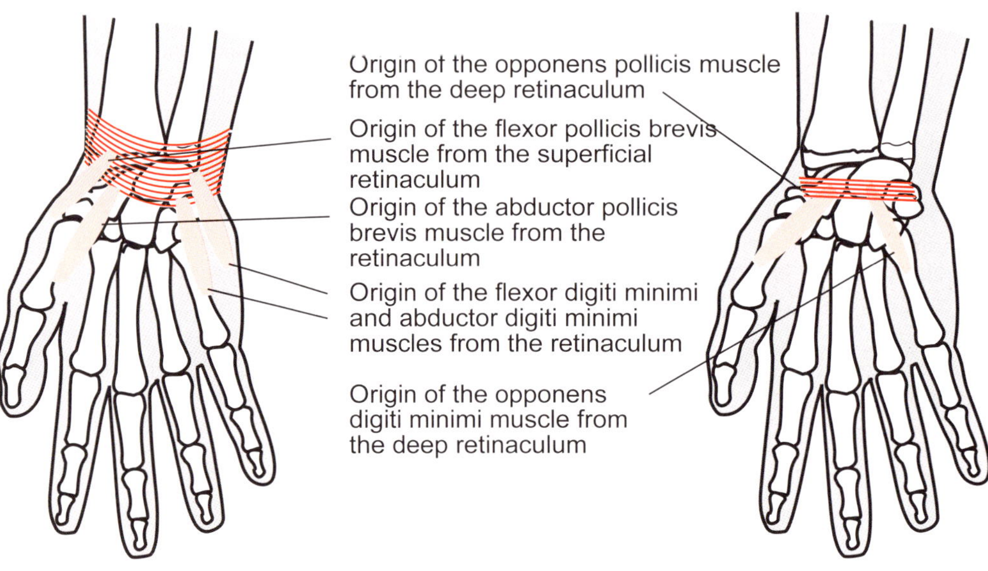

Fig. 6.1. Insertions of the hand muscles on the retinacula, ligaments and tendons. These determine a disto-proximal stretching with the activation of neuromuscular spindles included in the forearm muscles.

MOTOR GESTURE OF THE UPPER LIMB IMPLEMENTED BY THE AN-ME-DI SPIRAL

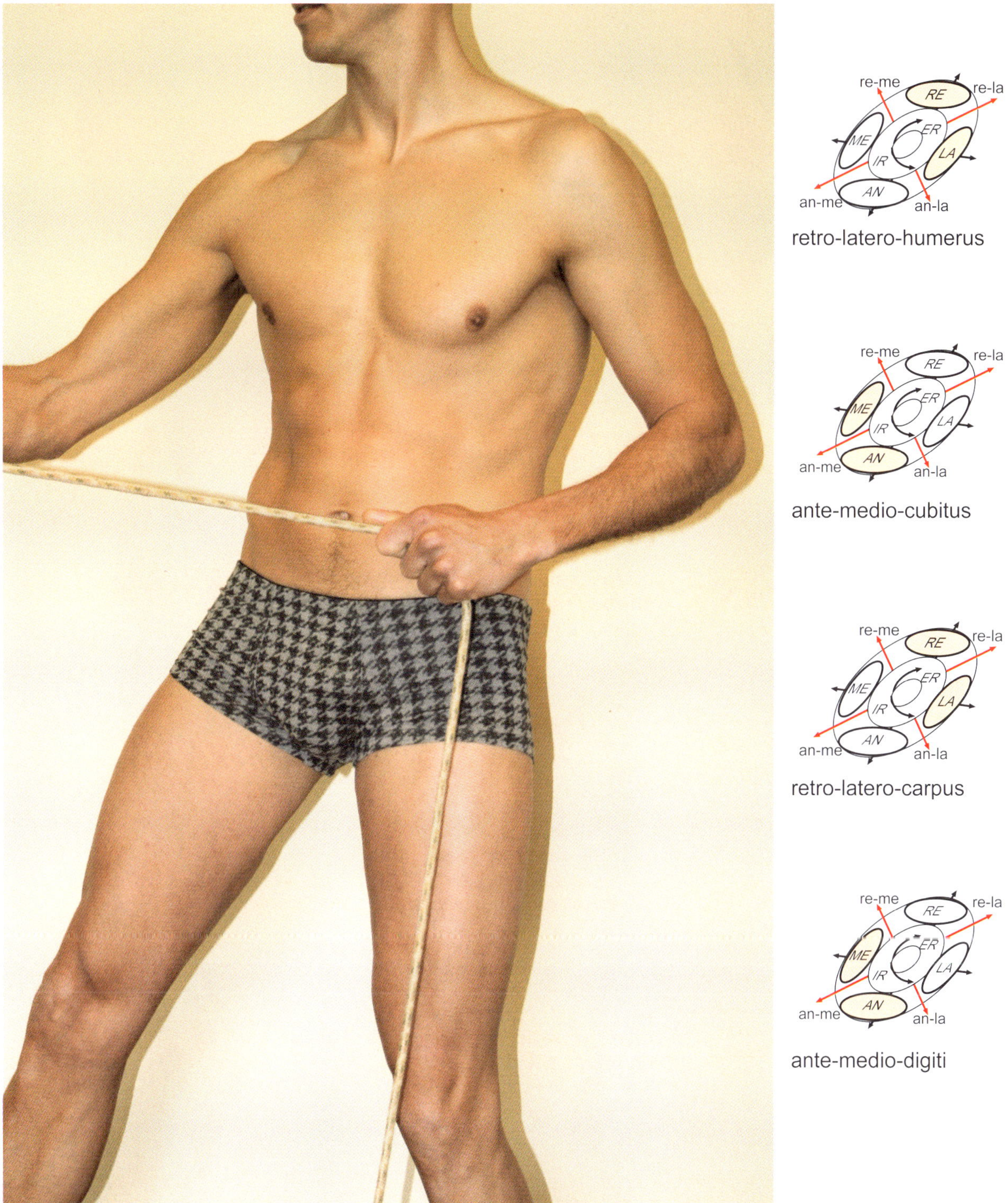

Fig. 6.2. Example of how the spirals are organised during the motor gesture of tugging on a rope.

The spiral coordinates the motor gestures requiring two adjacent joints to move in opposite directions. When tugging on a rope the fingers of the hand are disposed in ante-medio, the wrist goes in retro-latero, the elbow bends in ante-medio and the shoulder activates its force in retro-latero. Simultaneously the ante-latero-digiti, retro-medio-carpus, ante-latero-cubitus and retro-medio-humerus spiral is also activated. In other motor gestures the spirals of retro-medio-digiti and retro-latero-digiti are simultaneously activated.

AN-LA-DI SPIRAL

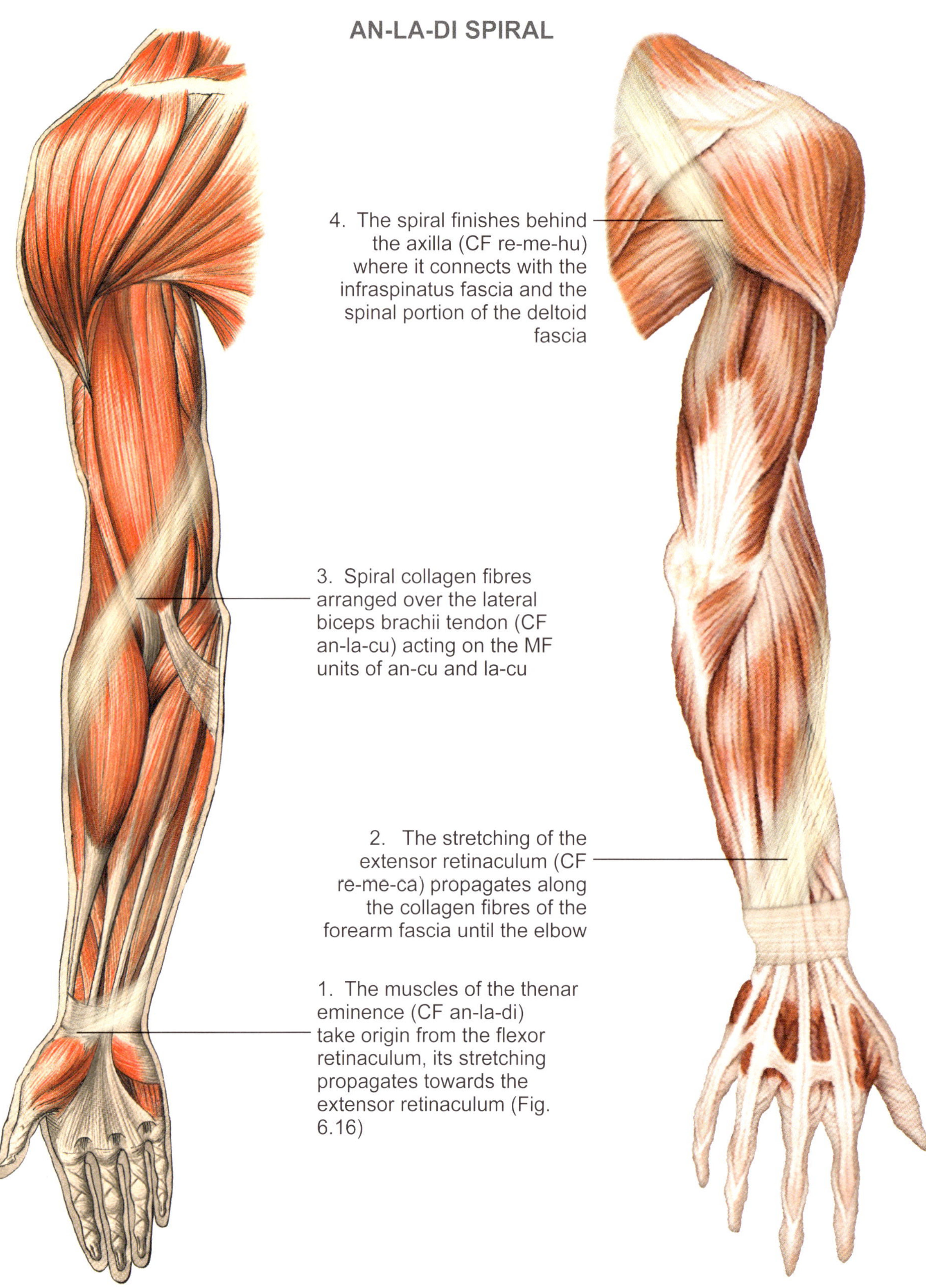

Fig. 6.3. Anterior course of the an-la-di spiral.
(From G. Chiarugi and L. Bucciante, Istituzioni di anatomia dell'uomo. Piccin Nuova Libraria, Padova 1983, modified)

Fig. 6.4. Posterior course of the an-la-di spiral.

NB. For a better understanding of the motor gesture it is advised to start reading from number 1 at the bottom of the page since the tensions of the hand muscles are responsible for the activation of the proximal muscles of the entire limb.

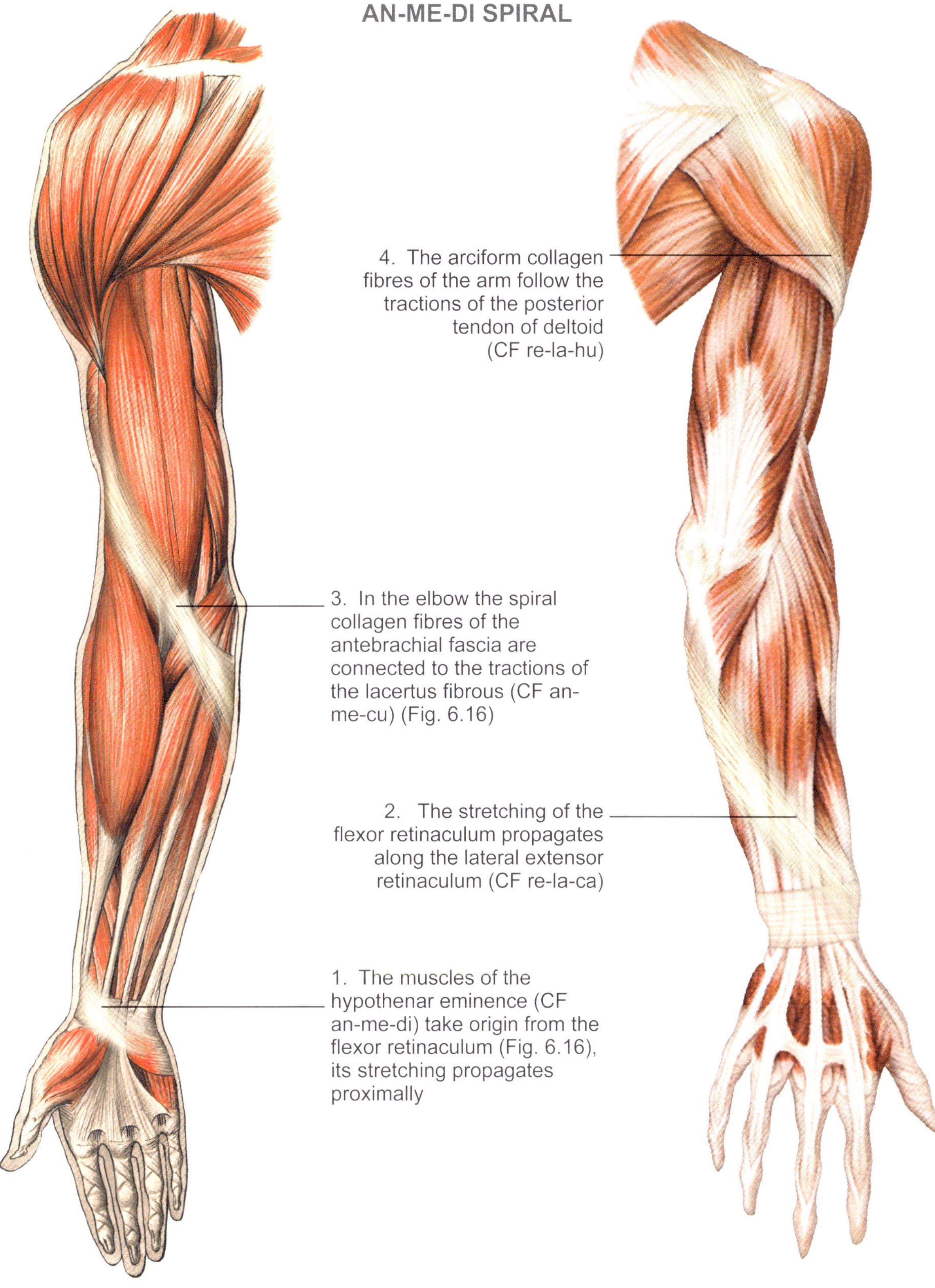

Fig. 6.5. Anterior course of the an-me-di spiral.
(From G. Chiarugi and L. Bucciante, Istituzioni di anatomia dell'uomo. Piccin Nuova Libraria, Padova 1983, modified)

Fig. 6.6. Posterior course of the an-me-di spiral.

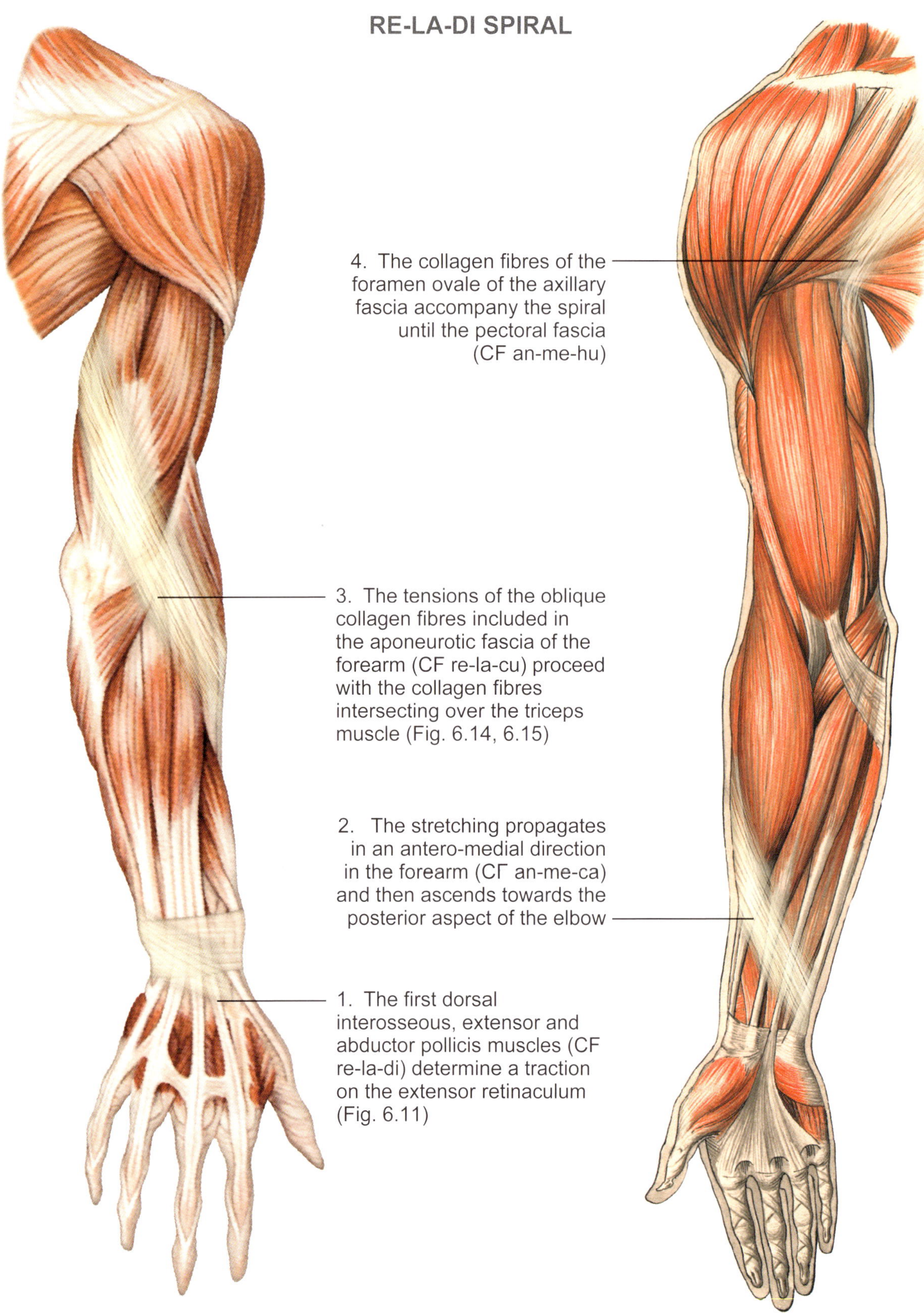

Fig. 6.7. Posterior course of the re-la-di spiral.

Fig. 6.8. Anterior course of the re-la-di spiral.
(From G. Chiarugi and L. Bucciante, Istituzioni di anatomia dell'uomo. Piccin Nuova Libraria, Padova 1983, modified)

RE-ME-DI SPIRAL

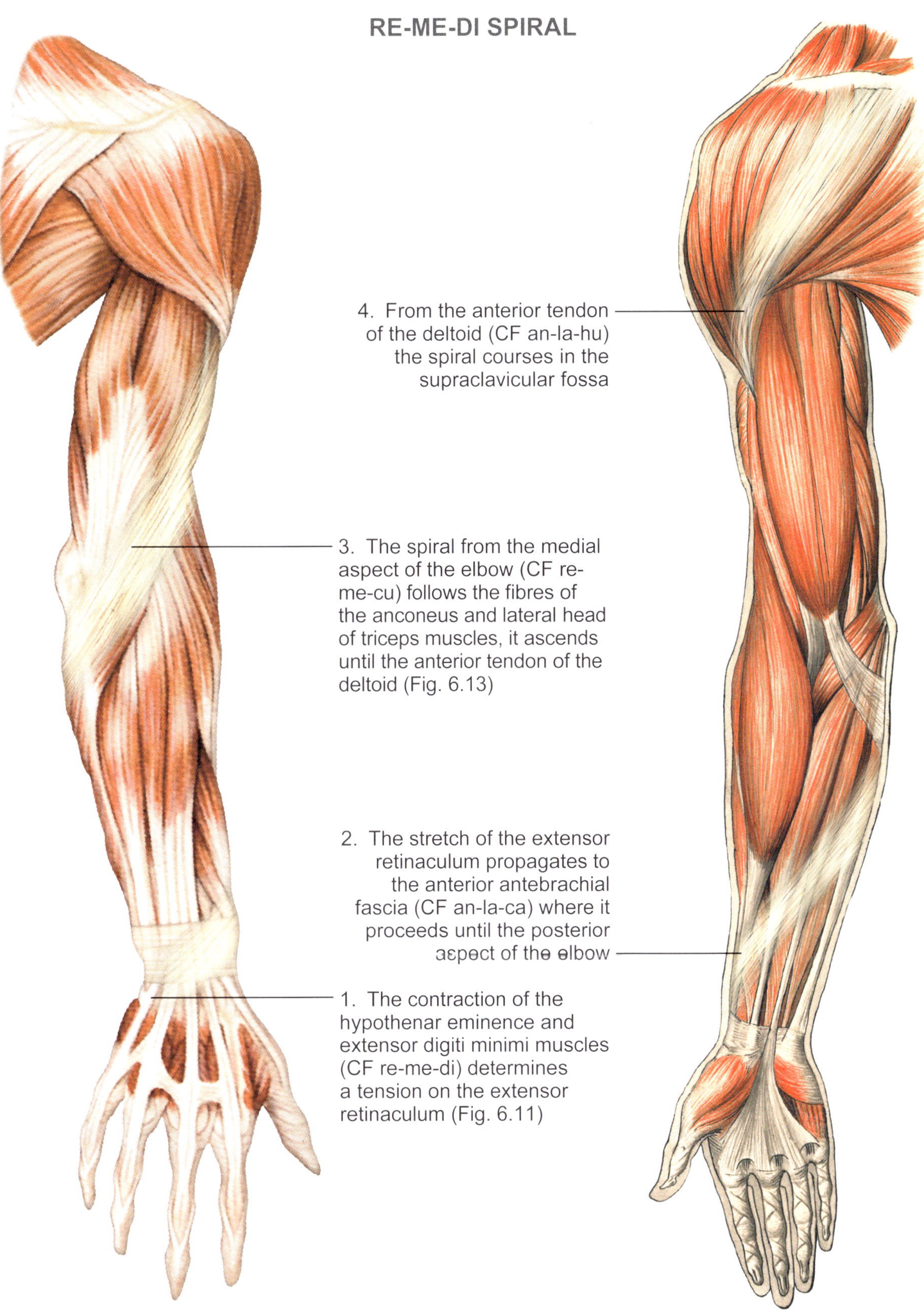

Fig. 6.9. Posterior course of the re-me-di spiral.

Fig. 6.10. Anterior course of the re-me-di spiral. *(From G. Chiarugi and L. Bucciante, Istituzioni di anatomia dell'uomo. Piccin Nuova Libraria, Padova 1983, modified)*

SPIRAL COLLAGEN FIBRES OF THE POSTERIOR HAND AND WRIST

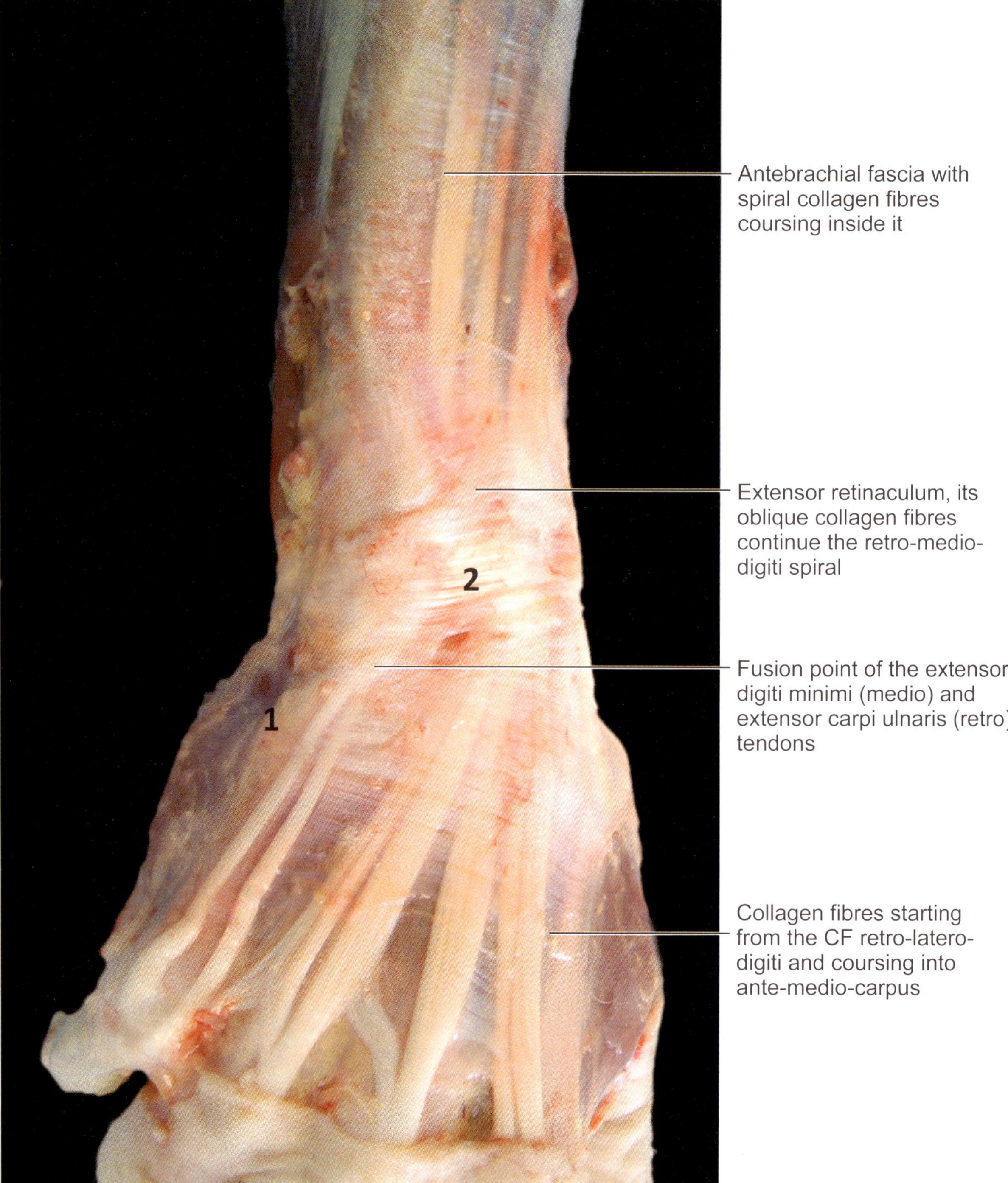

Fig. 6.11. Spiral collagen fibres of the dorsal fascia of the hand. Many collagen fibres originate from the hypothenar eminence (1) which then proceed in forming the extensor retinaculum (2). From the thumb-index commissure other collagen fibres start which are then connected to the flexor retinaculum.

SPIRAL COLLAGEN FIBRES OF THE ANTERIOR HAND AND WRIST

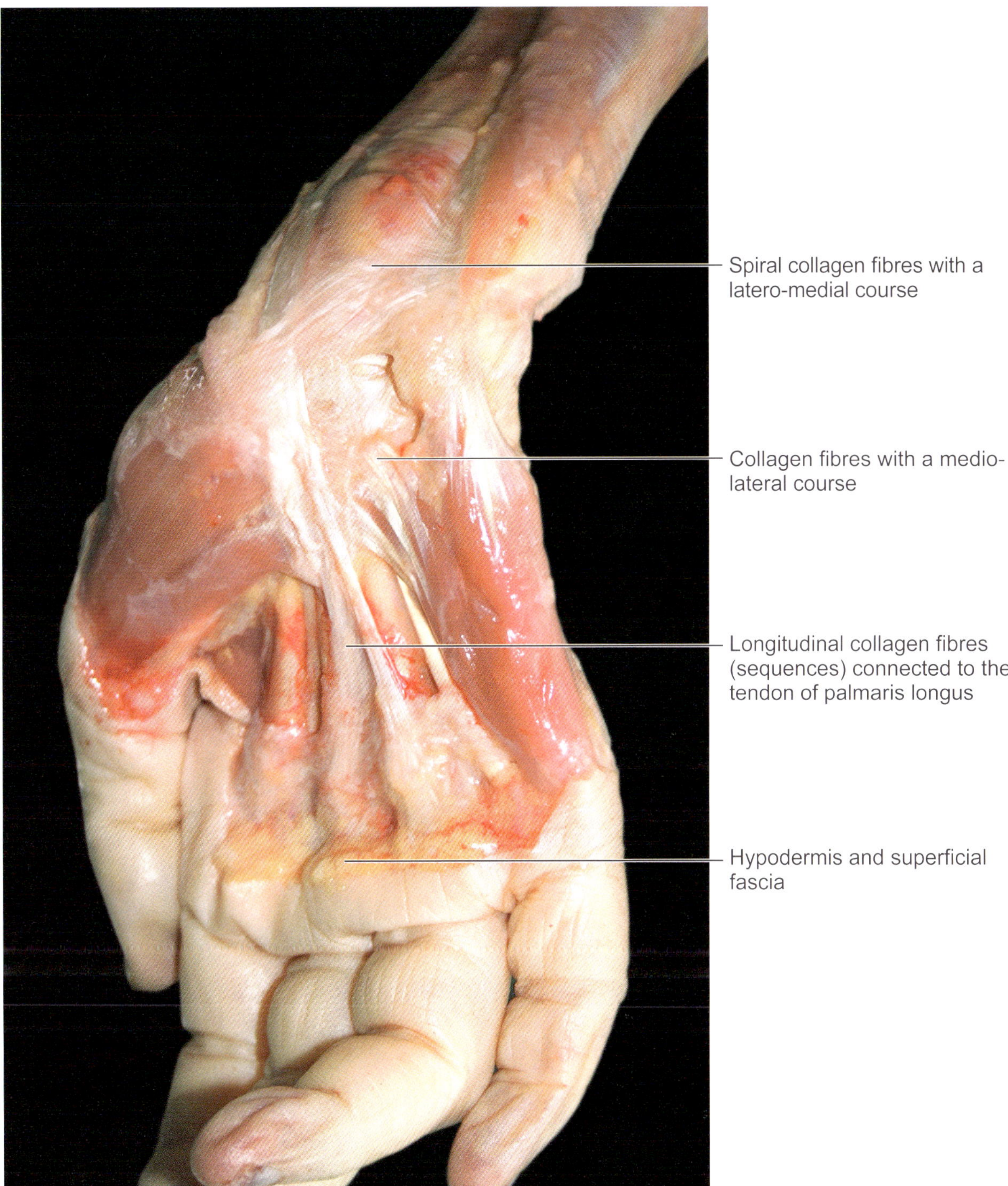

Fig. 6.12. Spiral collagen fibres of the palmar aspect of the hand. In the wrist the tractions of the thumb prevail in the superficial retinaculum and the tractions of the fifth digit prevail in the deep retinaculum.

In anatomical dissections the flexor and extensor retinacula were noted to have a different course to that represented in anatomical drawings. All artists have always represented them like fasciae of contention for tendons (Fig. 6.7, 6.8).

SPIRAL COLLAGEN FIBRES OF THE POSTERIOR ELBOW

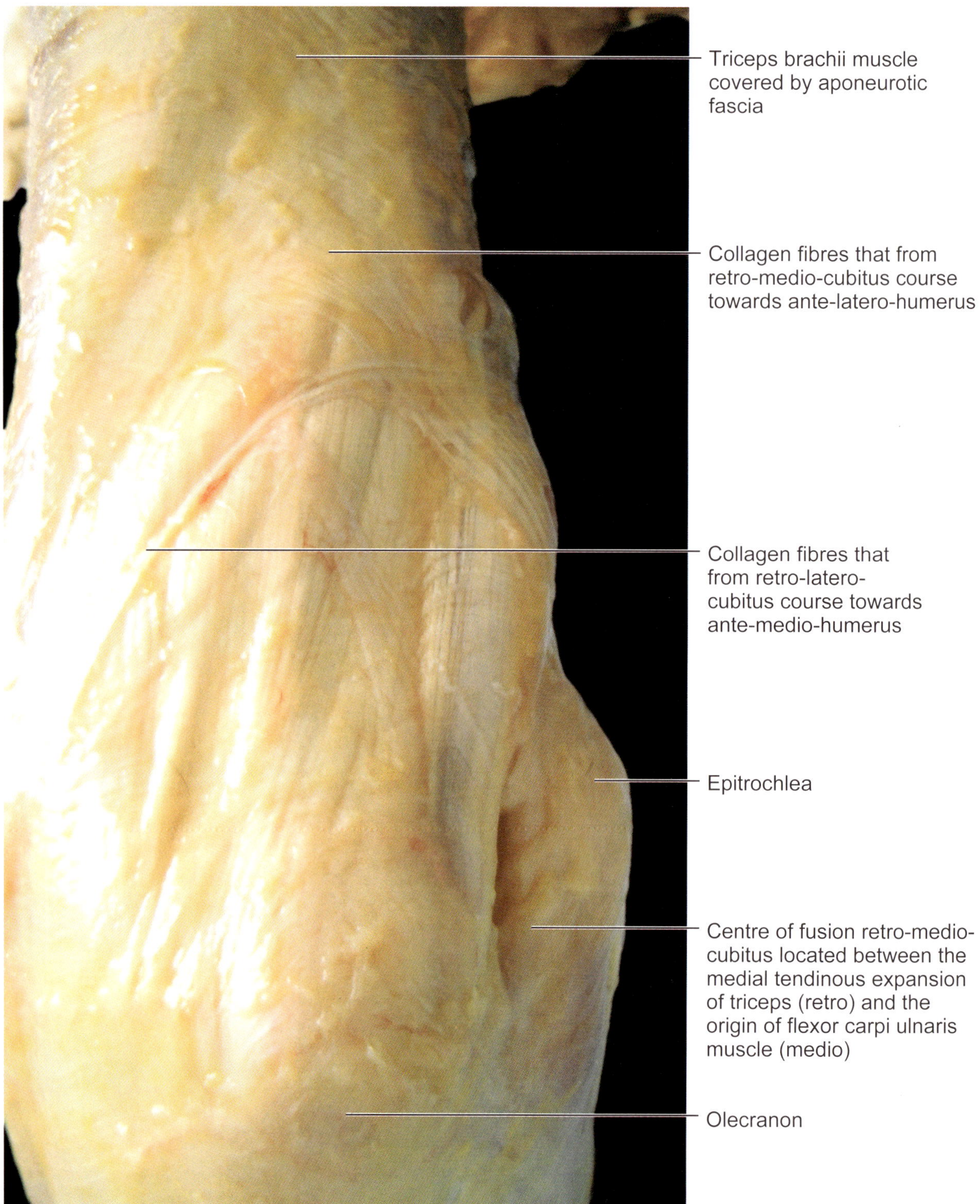

Fig. 6.13. Spiral collagen fibres of the posterior aspect of the arm. The collagen fibres course from the epicondyle towards the axilla and from the epitrochlea towards the deltoid region. This intersection of fibres forms a retinaculum which does not have a function of tendinous contention, but rather functions as a mesh for the transmission of motor forces from the elbow towards the shoulder.

SPIRAL COLLAGEN FIBRES OF THE POSTERIOR ELBOW

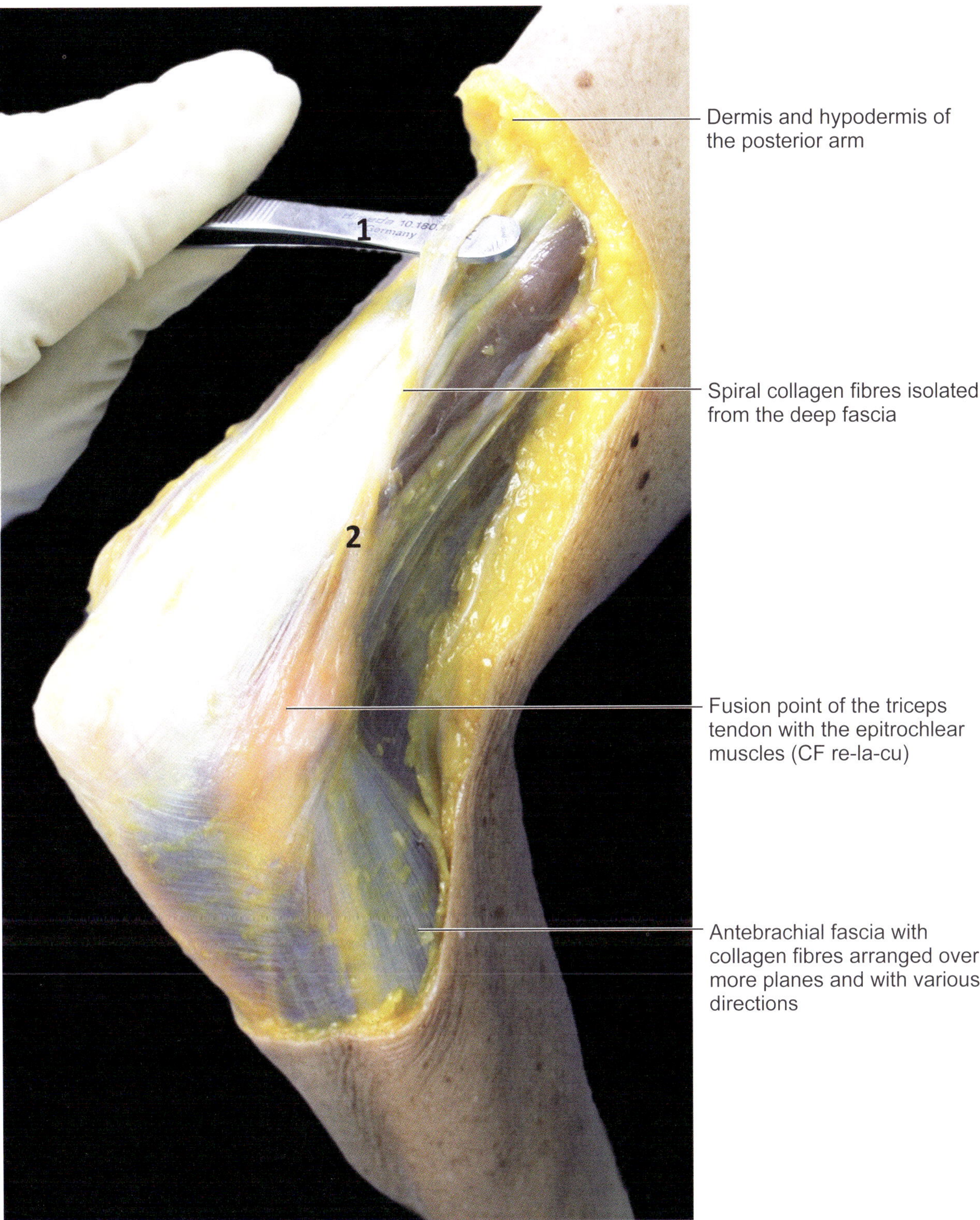

Fig. 6.14. Spiral collagen fibres isolated from the fascia. After isolating several collagen fibres and lifting them from the deep fascia (1), it can be observed that these form a bridge between the CF retro-latero-cubitus (2) and the CF ante-medio-humerus.

SPIRAL COLLAGEN FIBRES OF THE LATERAL ELBOW

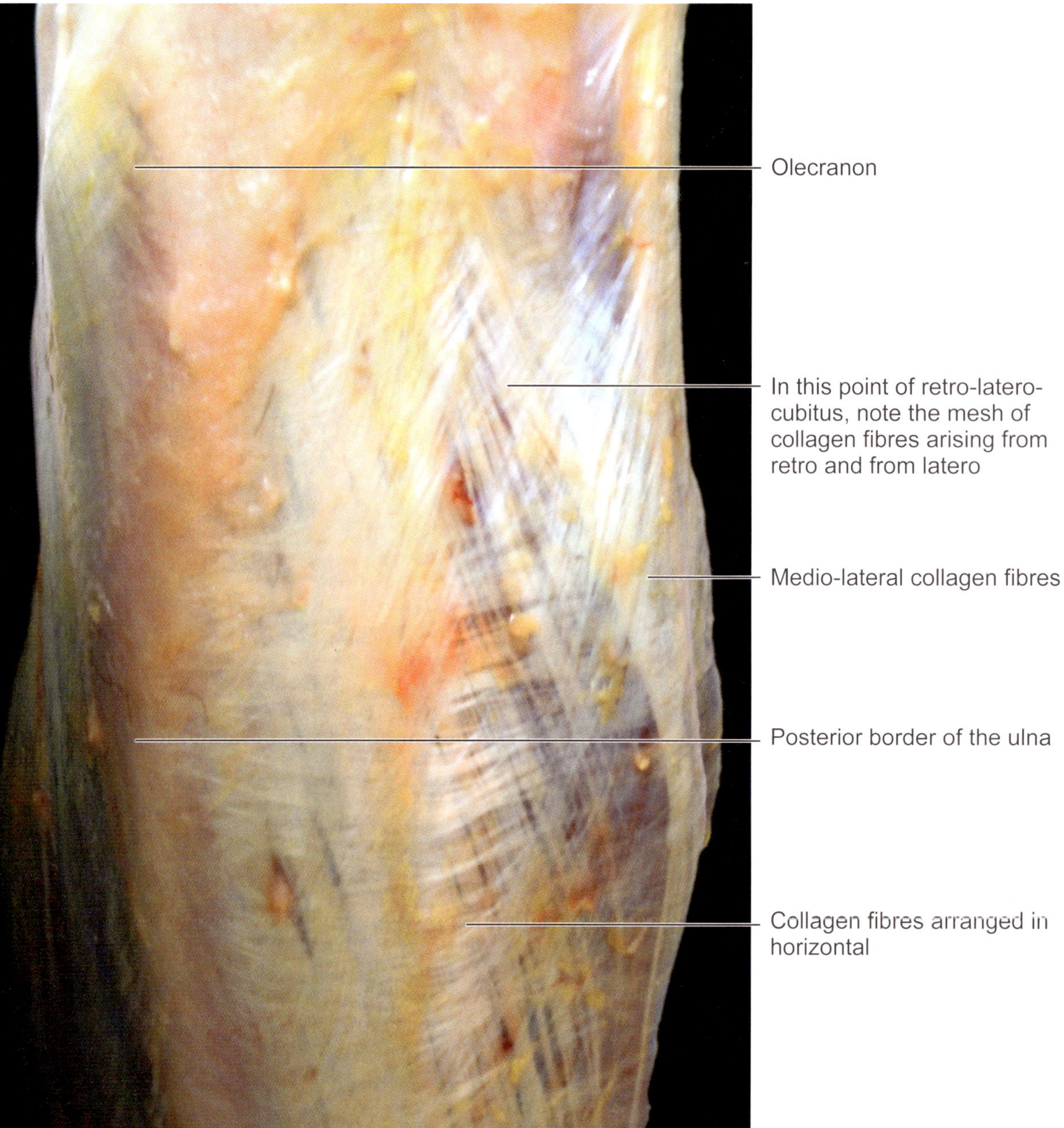

Fig. 6.15. Spiral collagen fibres of the postero-lateral fascia of the forearm. Each layer of collagen fibres is separated from the underlying one by loose connective tissue allowing its independent gliding. Thereby the oblique collagen fibres, connected to a spiral, may act independently with respect to the collagen fibres of another spiral.

SPIRAL COLLAGEN FIBRES OF THE MEDIAL ELBOW

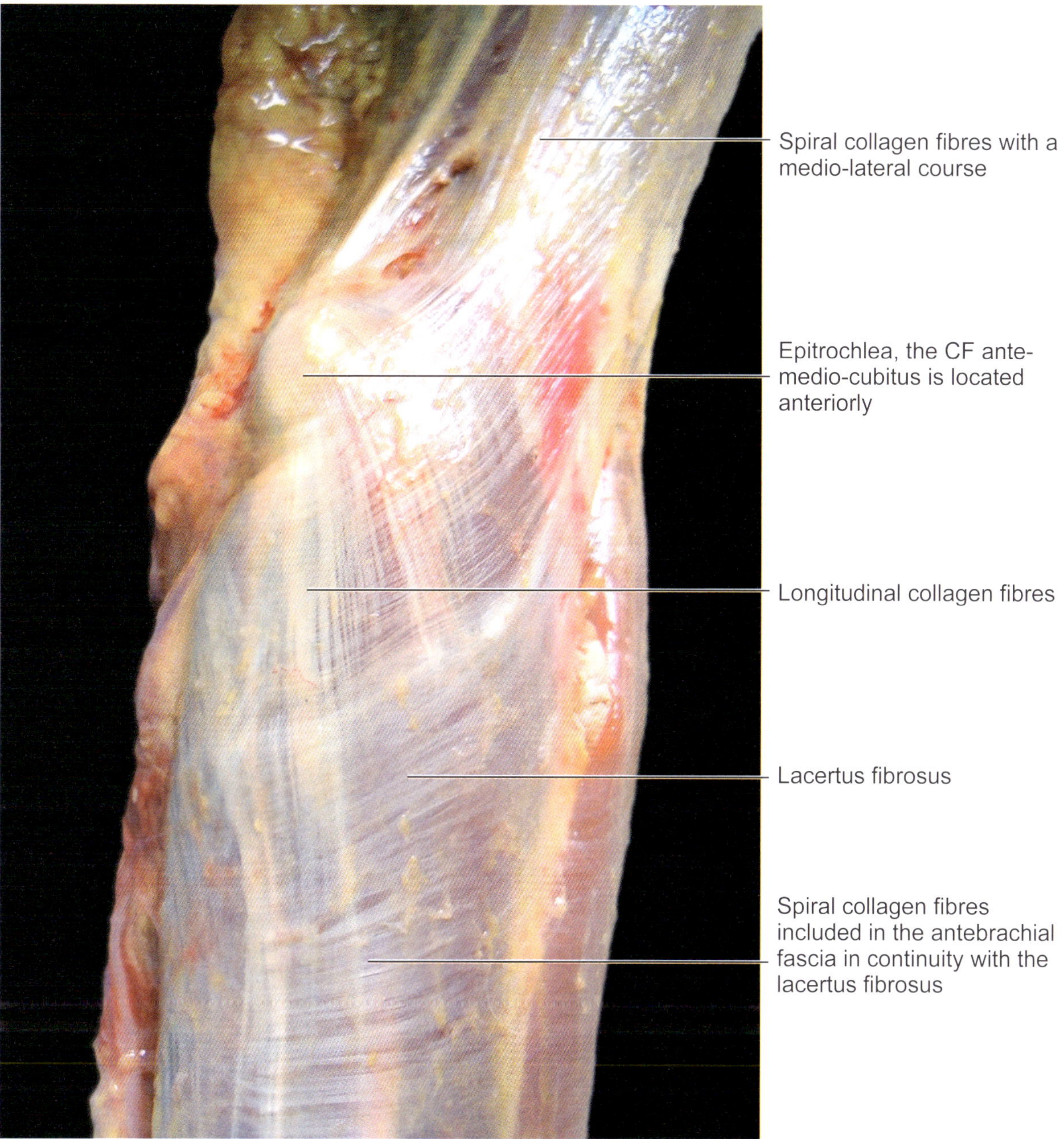

Fig. 6.16. Spiral collagen fibres of the anterior-medial fascia of the forearm. Each layer of collagen fibres corresponds to a specific tensional force. Note how the lacertus fibrosus is inserted in the spiral collagen fibres arising from ante-medio-digiti.

CENTRES OF FUSION AND SPIRALS OF THE HEAD AND TRUNK

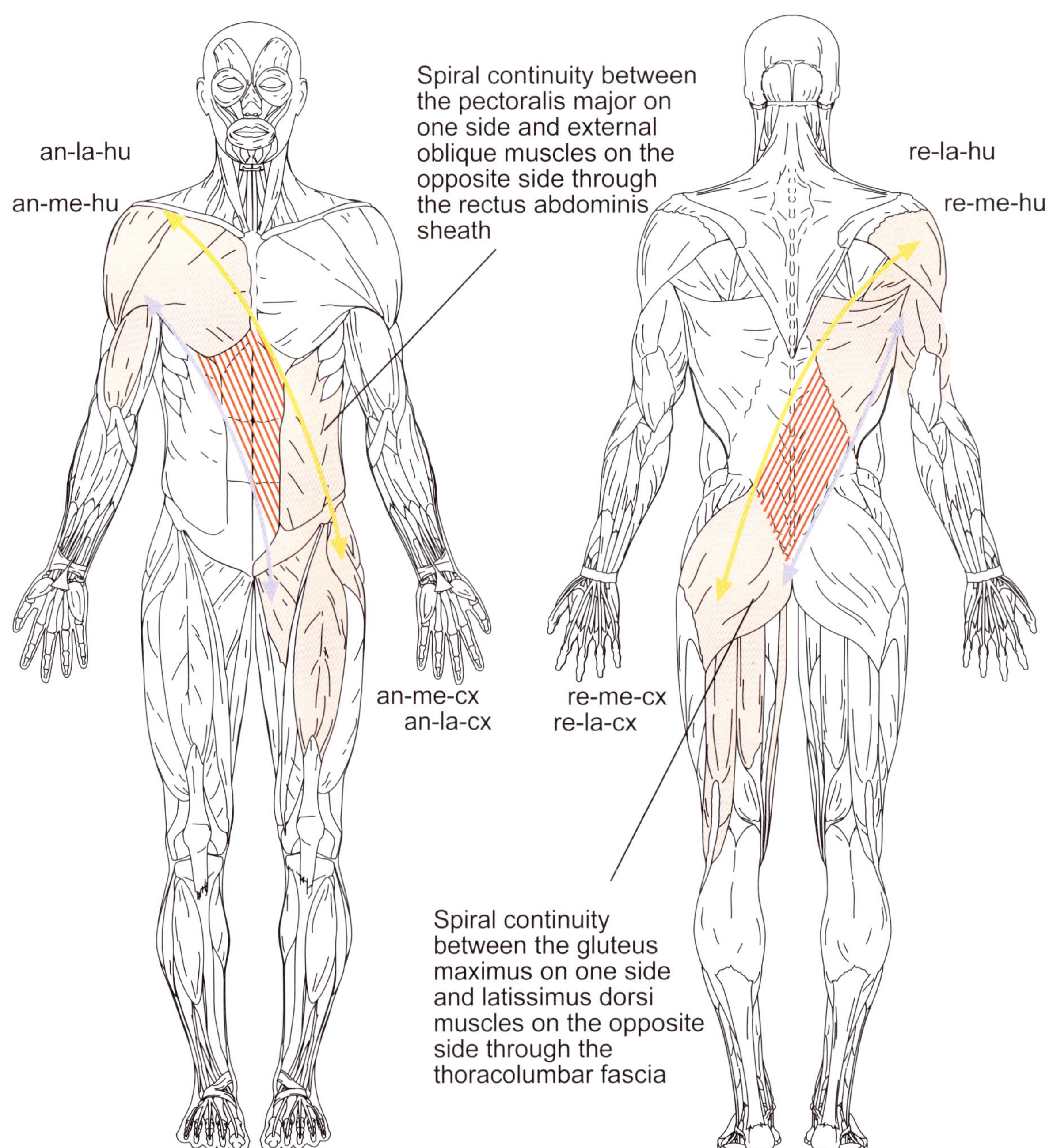

Fig. 6.17. Anterior and posterior short spirals of the trunk. During locomotion the short spirals of the trunk are activated, these are specific for managing the synchronisation of the lower limb on one side to the contralateral upper limb. When bringing the upper limb forward the MF units of ante, medio, and intra-coxa are initially activated and towards the end of gesture the units of ante-latero-extra coxa are activated. This gradual involvement of the lower limb fasciae is progressively transferred to the contralateral upper limb through the spiral.

The superficial muscles of the trunk wall (appendicular muscles) serve as the coordinating element for the crossed gait pattern between the four limbs. These muscles are also present in quadruped mammals. During gait both short spirals connecting the scapular girdle to the pelvic girdle prevail.

MOTOR GESTURE OF THE TRUNK MANAGED BY THE AN-ME AND AN-LA SPIRALS

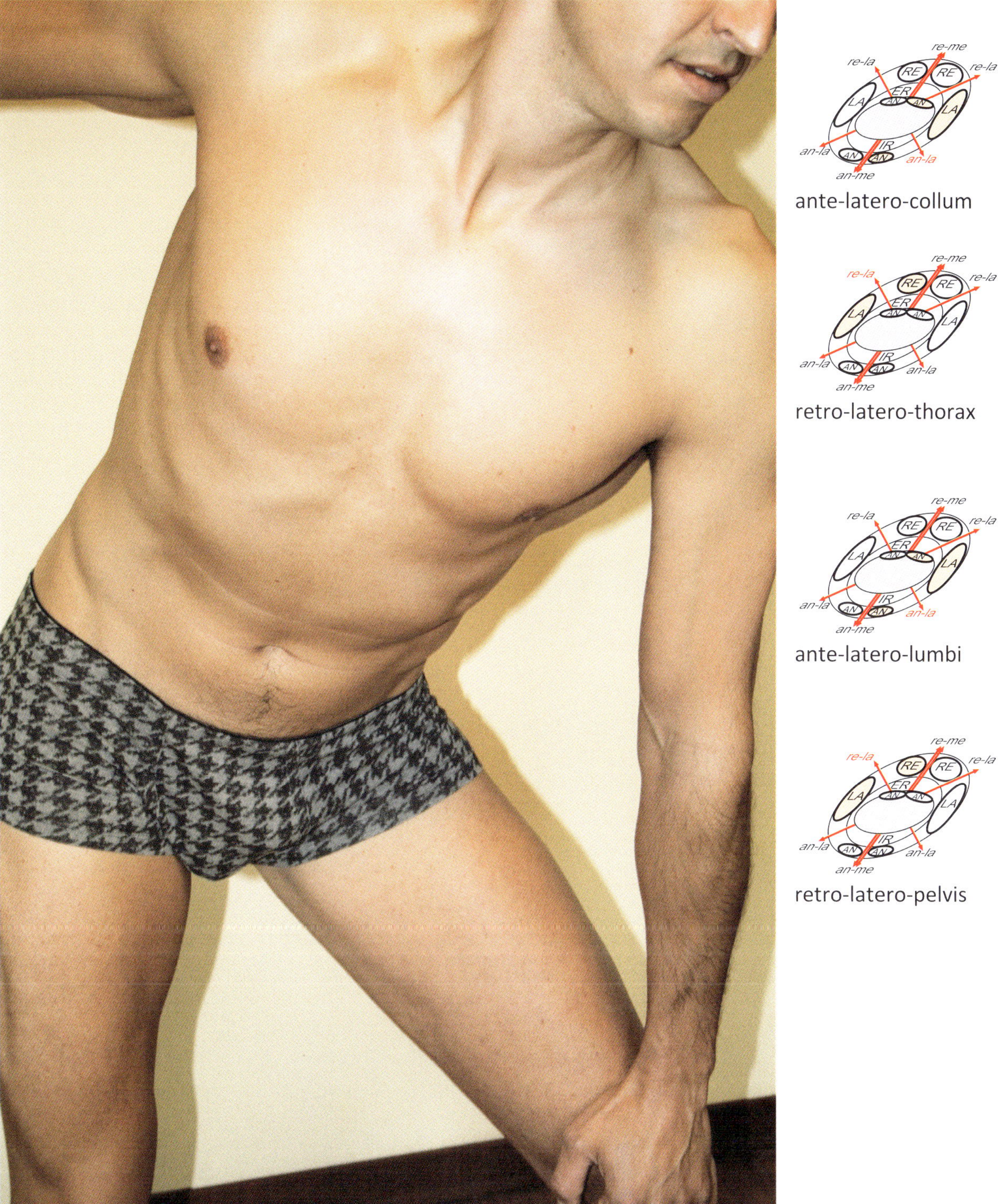

Fig. 6.18. Motor gesture of discus throw. During global motor gestures the long spirals of the trunk are activated, these are specific for organising the spirals of the trunk with the spirals of the neck. For instance, when throwing a discus, the neck goes in ante-latero towards the left, whilst the upper limb and right thorax go in retro-latero. Simultaneously the left low back rotates in ante-latero and the right pelvis is positioned in retro-latero. Moreover, the long spirals continue in a different manner with the spirals of the limbs.

During global motor gestures one spiral shortens and the antagonist spiral lengthens or becomes stretched. The stretching of the spiral collagen fibres allows the storage of energy which is freed in series as in a rheostat when the muscles connected to it contract.

SPIRALS INCLUDED IN THE SUPERFICIAL FASCIA OF THE NECK AND HEAD

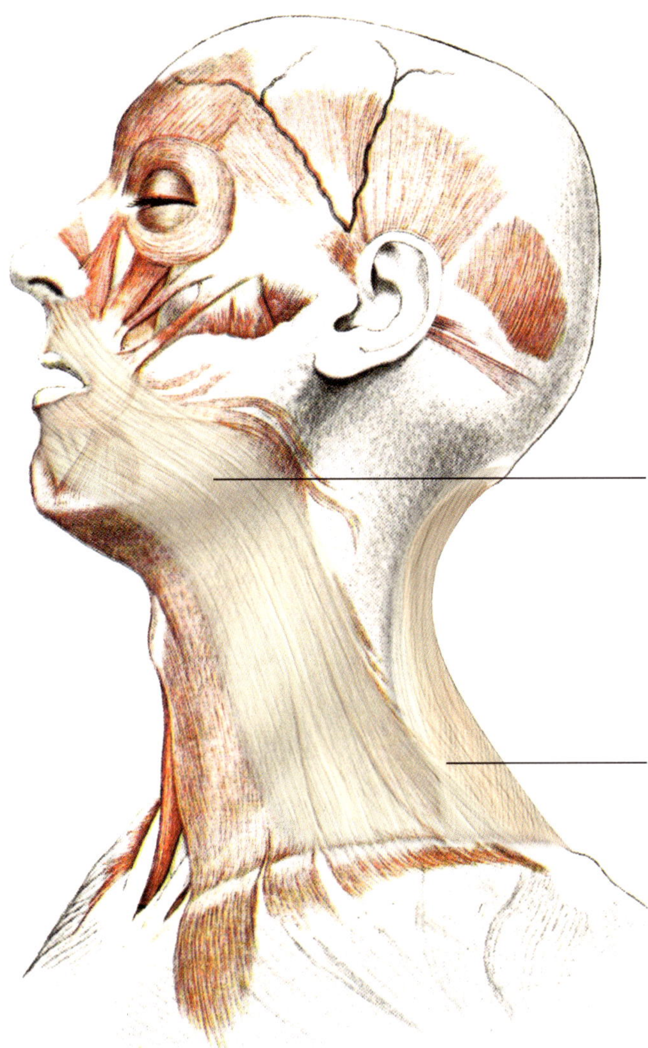

The platysma muscle is included in the superficial fascia (Fig. 6.23); its proximal fibres are continued in the face with the orbicularis oris muscle (CFs an-me-cp, an-la-cp). At the level of the clavicle the platysma muscle continues with the fascia containing the CFs an-la-sc and an-me-sc.

The trapezius muscle originates from the occipital bone (CFs re-me-cp, re-la-cp) through the short aponeurotic fibres (superior aponeurosis). It descends and inserts on the superior external aspect of the scapula (CFs re-la-sc and re-me-sc); this continuity unites the CFs along a diagonal and not according to a spiral. Only the sternocleidomastoid implements a real spiral action.

Fig. 6.19. Superficial spirals managing facial mimicry.
(From G. Chiarugi and L. Bucciante, Istituzioni di anatomia dell'uomo. Piccin Nuova Libraria, Padova 1983, modified)

In the neck there are muscles arranged in spirals included in both the superficial fascia and in the laminae of the deep fascia (trapezius, sternocleidomastoid, hyoid muscles).
The platysma muscle is included in the superficial fascia and is defined as a mimic or cutaneous muscle since it participates in skin movements of the neck and face.
The platysma muscle has origin and insertion on many muscles of the face which are in continuity with the contralateral ones (spiral). The small cutaneous muscles participate in the movements of mastication, phonation and respiration. These movements have a directional component (sequences and diagonals) and have a spiral organisation (complex motor gestures). The "cutaneous mimic" muscles are under voluntary control, hence they necessitate fascial coordination and perception like all the other muscles included in the deep fascia. In the figure (Fig. 6.19) the spiral formed by the left platysma is highlighted. The zygomaticus and mentalis muscles are found at a deeper plane compared to the superficial fascia of the face, they combine with the right platysma.

SPIRAL INCLUDED IN THE DEEP FASCIA OF THE HEAD AND NECK

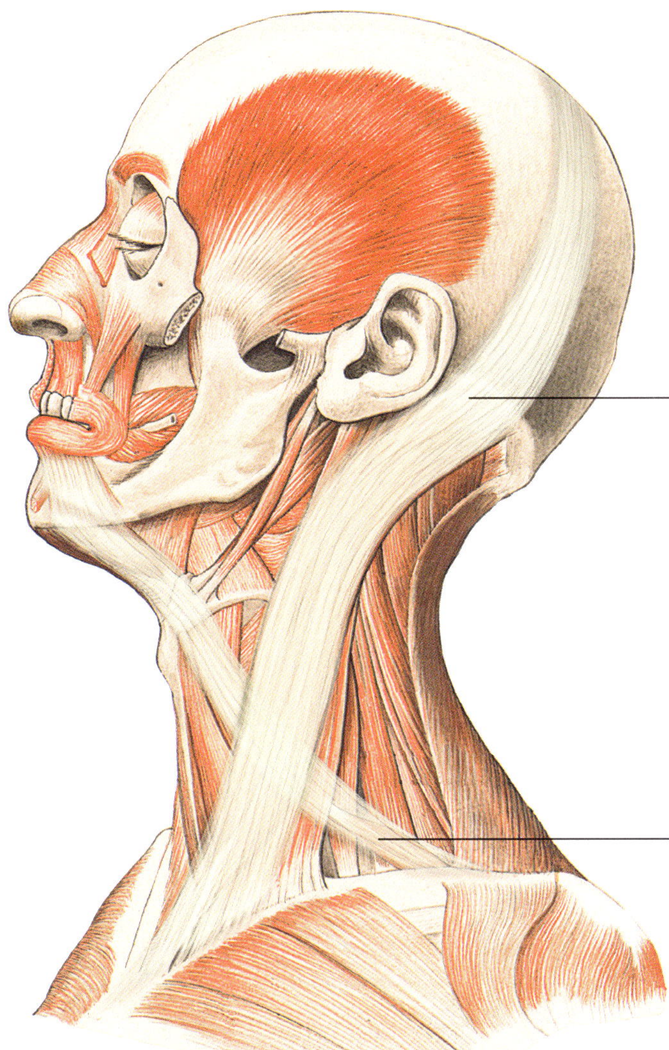

The sternocleidomastoid muscle (SCM) originates from the mastoid process (CF re-la-cp), where the epicranial fascia lying underneath the galea capitis also inserts. The SCM muscle inserts with its anterior head to the sternum where the CF an-me-cl is located. Hence this spiral, like in the sartorius muscle, has placed side by side muscular fibres and spiral collagen fibres.

The fascia of the depressor labii inferioris muscle (CF an-me-cp) is continuous with the anterior belly of the digastric muscle. The intermediate tendon of this muscle is fixed on the hyoid bone where the omohyoid muscle, originating from the scapula (CF re-la-sc), is inserted.

Fig. 6.20. Deep spiral managing movements of the neck.
(From G. Chiarugi and L. Bucciante, Istituzioni di anatomia dell'uomo. Piccin Nuova Libraria, Padova 1983, modified)

The spiral, unlike the sequences of intra and extrarotation, does not perform its intervention on one half of the body, rather it passes from one side of the body to the other. For instance, in the posterior aspect of the cranium some tendinous fibres of the sternocleidomastoid muscle on one side continue with the collagen fibres of the contralateral cranial fascia. This continuity explains why in some patients the compression of the right cervical fascia irradiates to the left eye.
The omohyoid, mylohyoid and anterior part of the digastric muscles are located in the intermediate cervical lamina. These muscles have a spiral arrangement opposite to that of the sternocleidomastoid muscle.
The continuity of the stylohyoid with the sternohyoid muscle on the opposite side is located in a still deeper fascial plane to the intermediate cervical fascia. The motor complexity of the cervical segment is made possible by this mesh of muscular fibres included in the three fascial laminae that become intertwined and form a large retinaculum.

SHORT SPIRALS OF THE ANTERIOR TRUNK: AN-ME AND AN-LA

The sheath of the rectus abdominis muscle forms a large spiral within which the ante-medio and ante-latero spirals are activated sequentially.

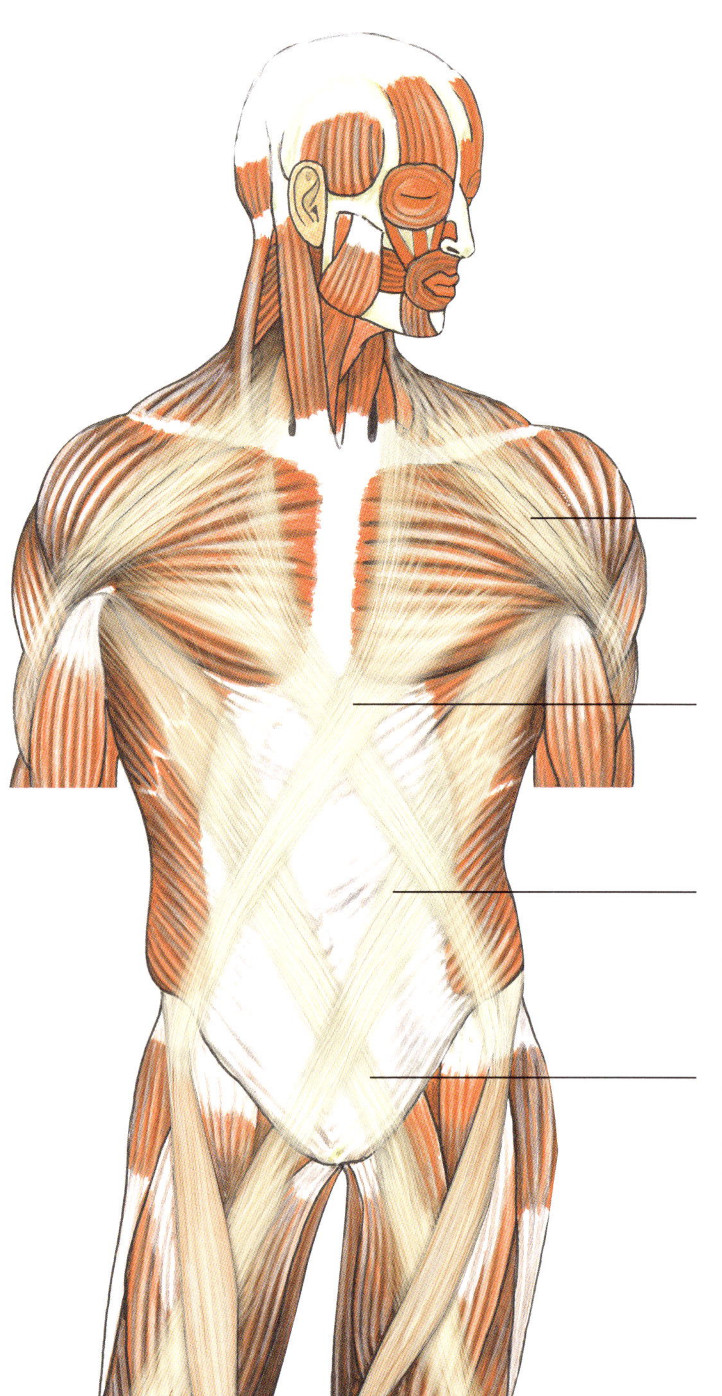

Fig. 6.21a. Course of the ante-medio and ante-latero spirals of the trunk.

During locomotion, when the lower limb is brought forward, the traction of ante-medio-coxa is initially activated; it propagates towards the CF ante-medio-humerus. During the last phase of gait the an-la-cx spiral is activated which is connected to the CF an-la-hu.

SHORT SPIRALS OF THE POSTERIOR TRUNK: RE-ME AND RE-LA

The thoracolumbar fascia forms a large spiral within which the spiral of retro-medio and retro-latero are activated sequentially.

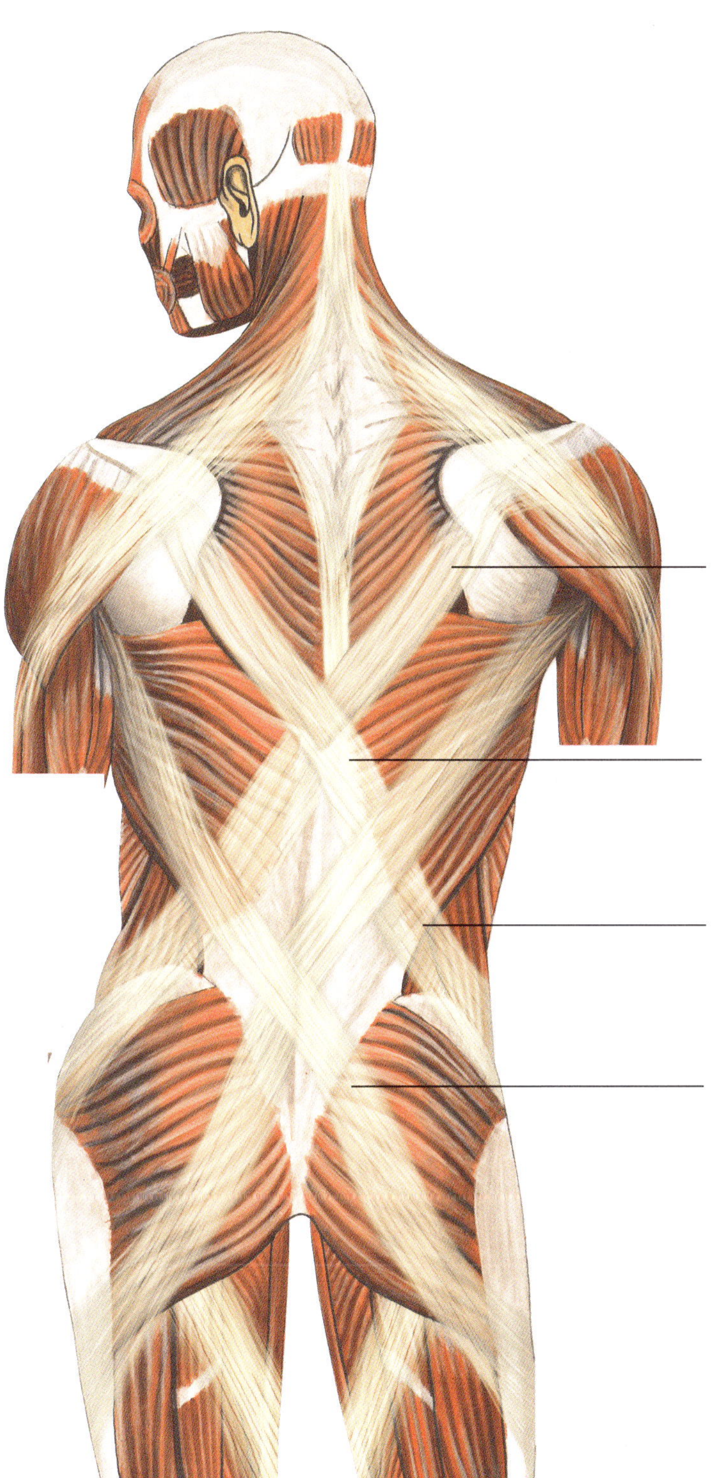

The inferior border of the trapezius is in contact with the CF re-la-th; the superior part of this muscle contains the CF re-la-sc and continues seamlessly with the deltoid fascia where the CF re-la-hu is located.

The trapezius muscle is included in the superficial lamina of the deep fascia, with its ascending fibres it fuses with the latissimus dorsi muscle in the CF re-me-th.

Lateral to the erector spinae muscles the superficial sheet of the thoracolumbar fascia fuses with the deep sheet forming the CF retro-latero-lumbi (Fig. 6.27).

Point of fusion of the gluteus maximus fascia with that of the erector spinae muscles and with the thoracolumbar fascia. The CF retro-medio-coxa on the right connects to the CF retro-medio-pelvis on the left in a mirror image to what happens in the anterior trunk wall (Fig. 6.28).

Fig. 6.21b. Course of the retro-medio and retro-latero spirals of the trunk.

During locomotion, when the lower limb is pushed backwards the traction of the retro-medio-coxa spiral is initially activated; it connects with the CF retro-medio-humerus. Towards the end of the push the re-la-cx spiral is activated, it is connected to the CF re-la-hu.

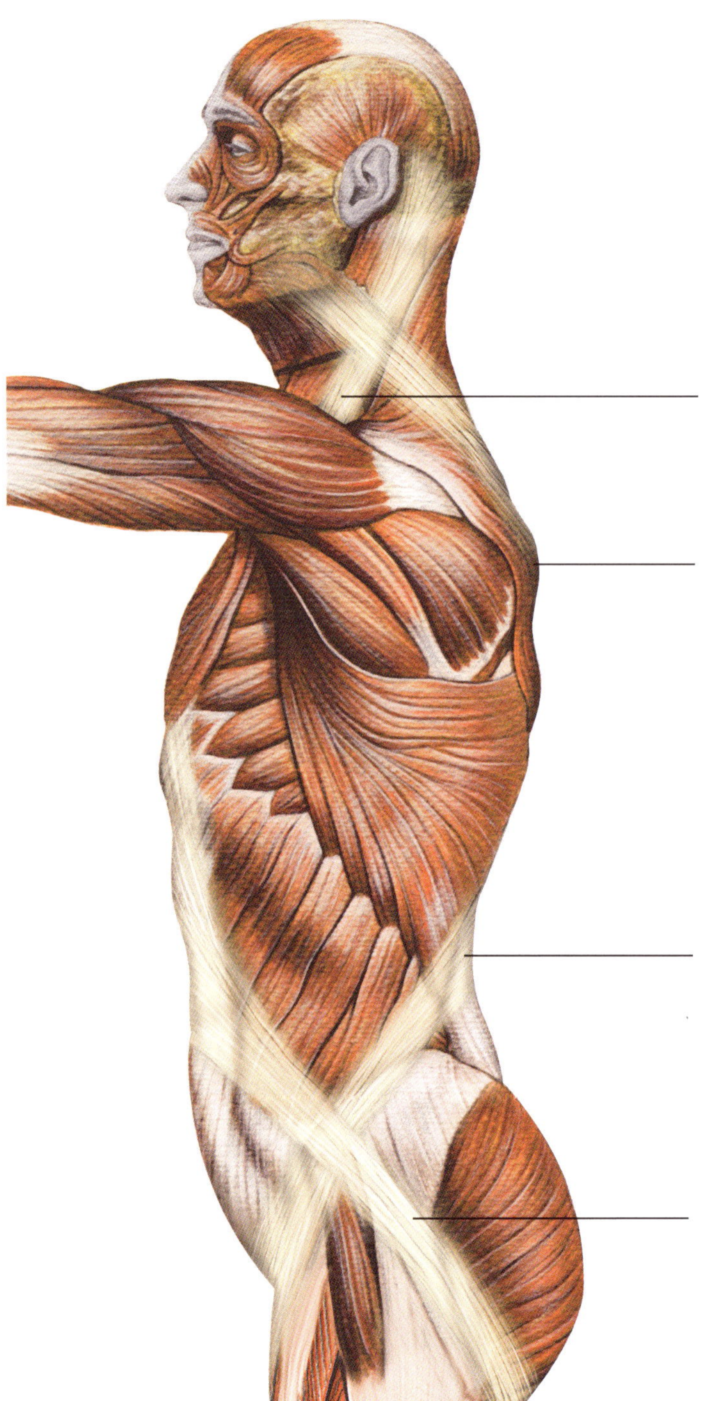

LONG SPIRALS STARTING FROM THE LEFT COXA: AN-LA AND RE-LA

Differences between intra and extrarotation sequences and spirals: sequences have a course along the same flank whilst spirals transit from the front to the back and from one side to the other.

The collagen fibres of the left clavicoracoaxillary fascia (CF an-la-th) continue with the fascia of the right sternocleidomastoid muscle (CFs an-me-cl, re-la-cp 3).

The fibres of the left posterior superior serratus muscle continue with the fibres of the splenius cervicis (CF re-me-cl) and right stylohyoid muscles (CF an-la-cp 3). Both spirals are also connected with the spirals of the upper limb.

During global motor gestures the myofascial tensions from the internal aspect of the thigh (CF an-me-cx) are transferred along the inguinal ligament towards the external part (CF an-la-cx). This ligament provides insertion to the external oblique muscle which fascia transmits the anterior tensions towards the low-back (CF re-la-lu).

During global motor gestures the deep gluteal fascia unites the tractions of the hamstring muscles (CFs re-me-cx and re-la-cx) and channels them towards the fascia of the gluteus medius muscle. This fascia is connected to the oblique muscles (CF an-la-lu).

Fig. 6.22a. Course of the ante-latero and retro-latero spirals of the left coxa ascending towards the low back and finishing in the head and neck.

During global motor gestures the CF an-me-cx, through the inguinal ligament, is connected to an-la-cx. This traction, through the fascia of the external oblique muscle, activates the CF re-la-lu. From there the spiral proceeds with the fascia of the latissimus dorsi muscle on the opposite side of the body (Fig. 6.22a), it then joins the clavicoracoaxillary fascia and the contralateral anterior cervical fascia.

LONG SPIRAL COURSE OVER THE RIGHT SIDE OF THE TRUNK

The global gestures of the spirals are managed by the large and superficial muscles of the trunk with the exceptions of the scapular and posterior cervical regions where the spirals proceed with intermediate muscles.

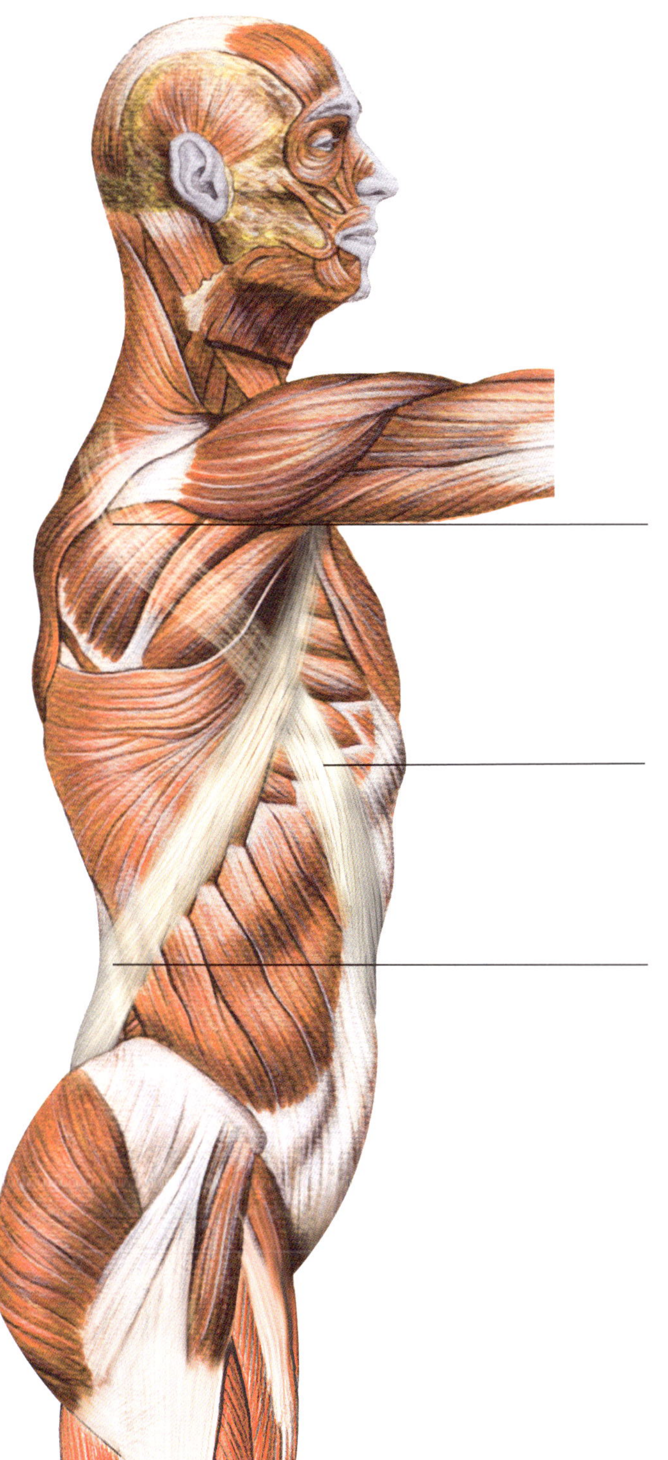

In the intermediate plane the fascia of the rhomboid muscles (CF re-me-sc) which is in continuity with the fascia of the serratus anterior muscle (CF an-la-th) is joined with the fascia of the serratus posterior superior muscle at the level of their common vertebral insertions.

The fascia of the right external oblique muscle continues caudally with the fascia of the opposite oblique muscles (CF an-la-lu) and cranially with the fascia of the serratus anterior (CF an-la-th) and rhomboid muscles. These muscles connect the long spirals to the gestures of the upper limb.

The fascia of the right latissimus dorsi muscle (CF re-la-lu) continues caudally with the opposite thoracolumbar fascia (CF re-la-lu) and cranially it continues with the axillary fascia and with the clavicoracoaxillary fascia.

Fig. 6.22b. Course of the retro-latero and ante-latero spirals of the trunk originating from the left low back.

During global motor gestures the CF re-la-cx directs the traction of the CF re-me-cx through the deep gluteal fascia. This traction goes in the direction of the iliac crest (Fig. 6.22b) stretching the fascia of the internal oblique muscle (CF an-la-lu). From there the spiral proceeds with the fascia of the serratus anterior muscle of the opposite side of the body. The spiral then continues with the intermediate lamina of the thoracic fascia and posterior cervical fascia.

SPIRAL COLLAGEN FIBRES OF THE ANTERIOR HEAD AND NECK

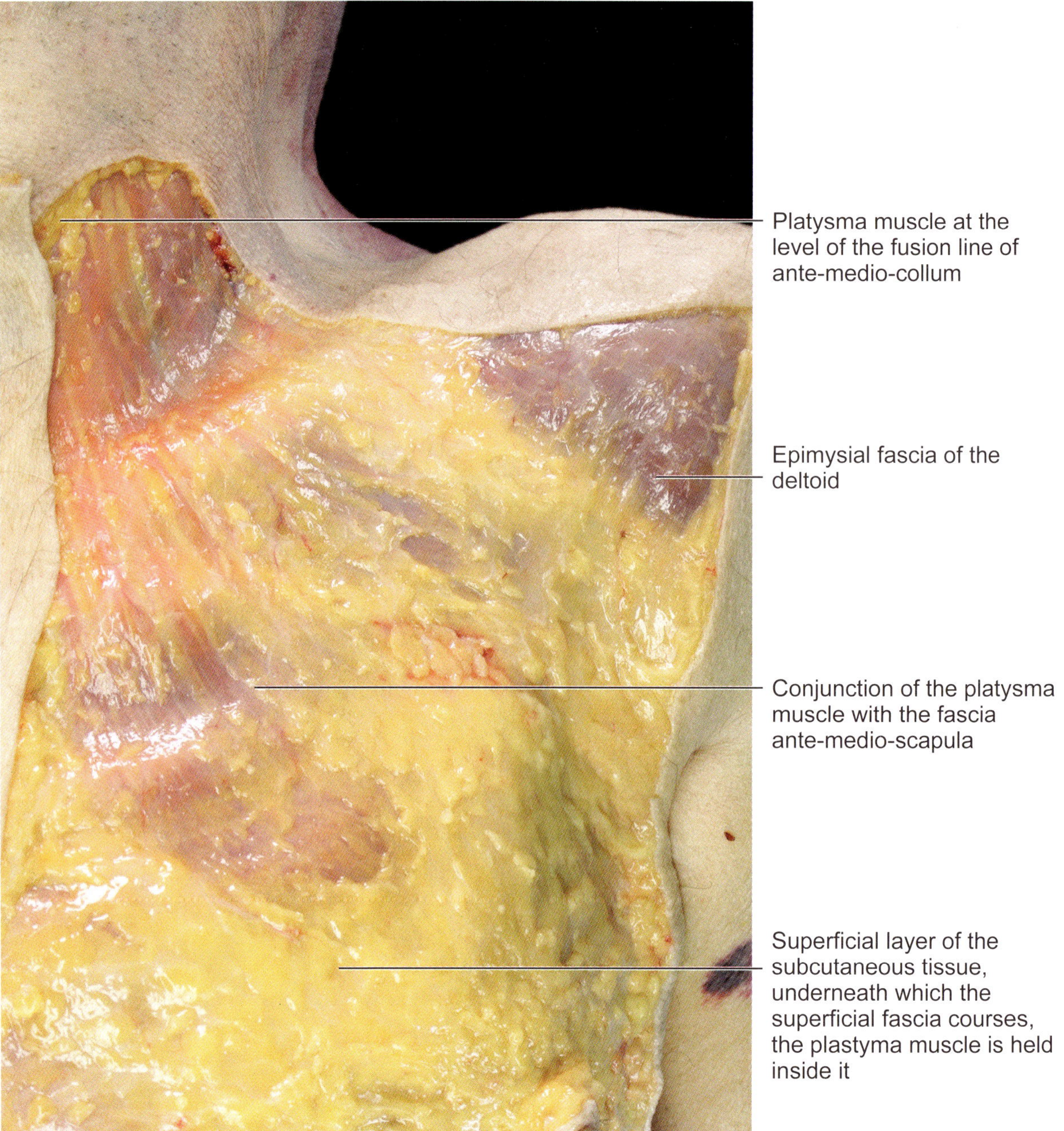

Fig. 6.23. Platysma muscle included in the superficial fascia of the neck and thorax. The platysma muscle forms a spiral that only partially connects complex movements on the neck to the spiral movements of the trunk.

SPIRAL COLLAGEN FIBRES OF THE ANTERIOR TRUNK

Fig. 6.24. Spiral collagen fibres of the rectus abdominis sheath. Retinacula were given this name since their criss-crossing fibres appear as a mesh (or retinaculum in latin).

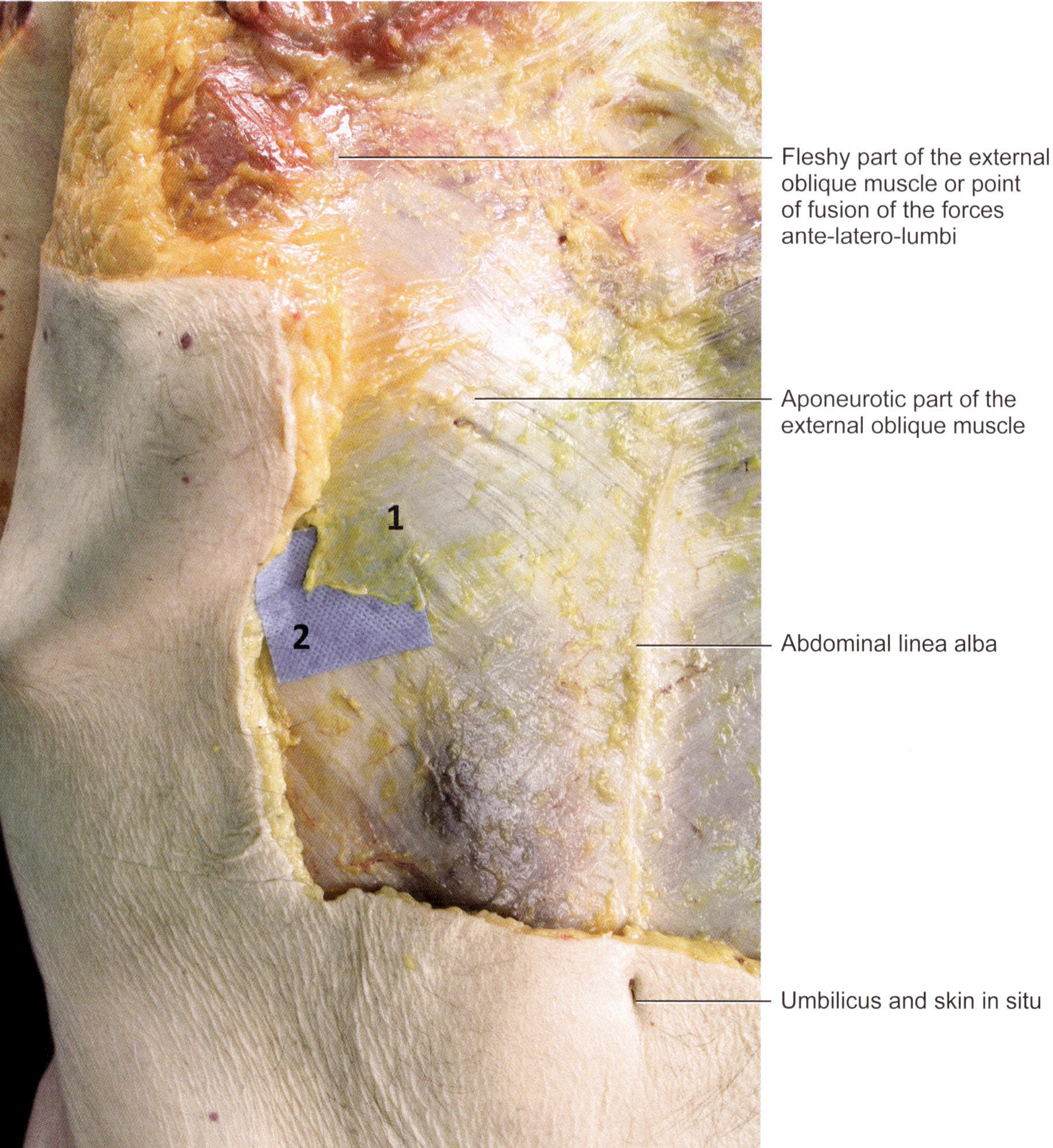

Fig. 6.25. Deep abdominal fascia. A small fascial strip of the external oblique muscle was isolated (1), the operator inserted a piece of paper underneath it (2) to highlight the separation between the elastic fascia and the aponeurotic one. The perceptive fascia of the external oblique muscle is formed by a higher number of elastic fibres whilst the aponeurotic fascia is formed by many collagen fibres.

SPIRAL COLLAGEN FIBRES OF THE ANTERIOR TRUNK

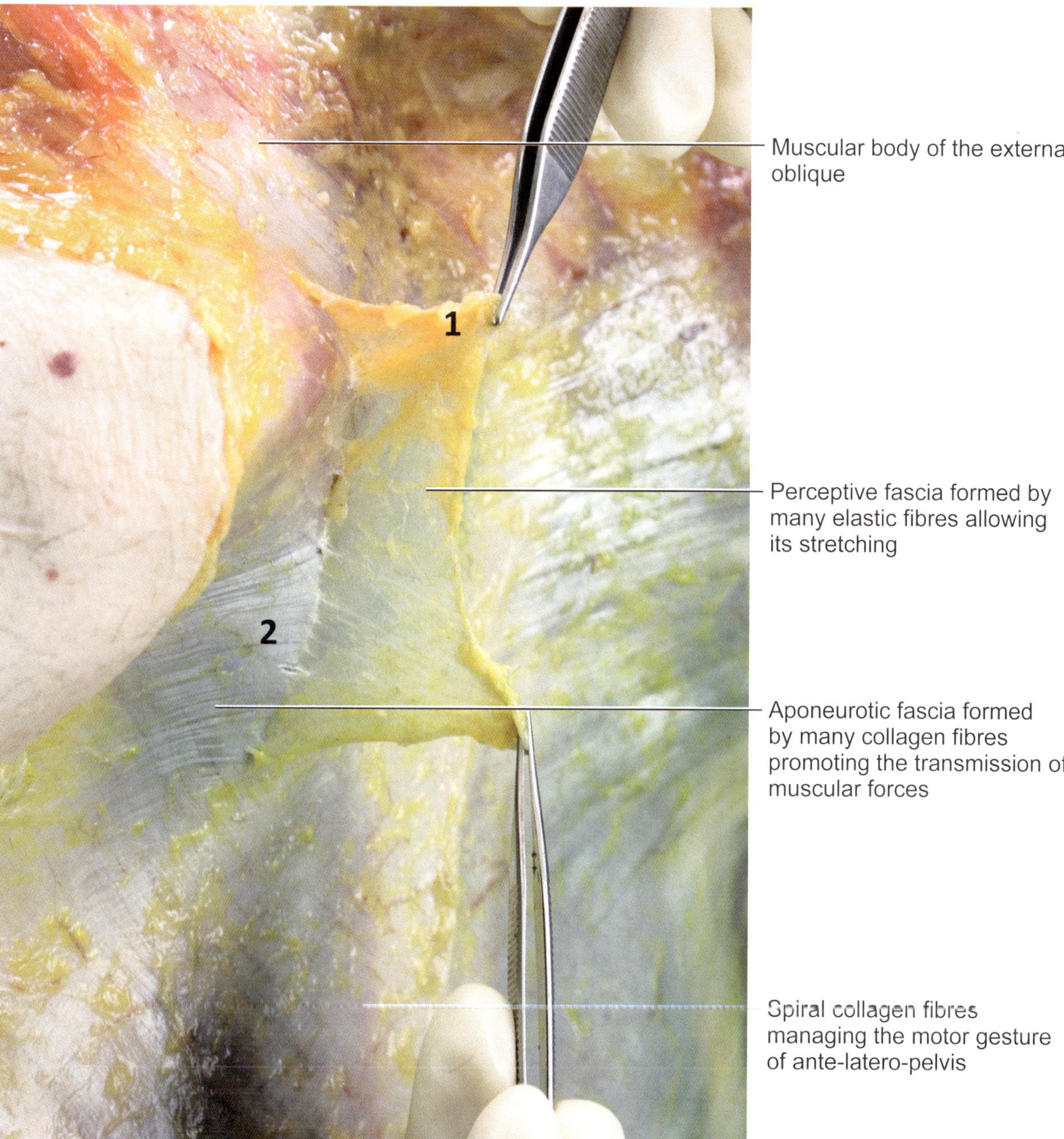

Fig. 6.26. Abdominal fascia, elastic lamina. With the forceps (1) the operator lifts a strip of perceptive fascia to highlight the underlying aponeurotic fascia of the external oblique muscle. The perceptive fascia, being elastic allows the stretching of proprioceptors that are sensitive to stretching. The aponeurotic fascia, being little elastic, favours the transmission of muscular forces.

The aponeurotic fascia performs the function of a flat tendon. The boundaries between both structures are very blurry since fusiform or flat tendons contain collagen fibres suitable for both transmission of muscular forces and for the Golgi tendon organs. Since these organs contribute to motor coordination, a property of the fasciae, then a part of the tendons and aponeuroses may also be considered fasciae.

SPIRAL COLLAGEN FIBRES OF THE POSTERIOR TRUNK

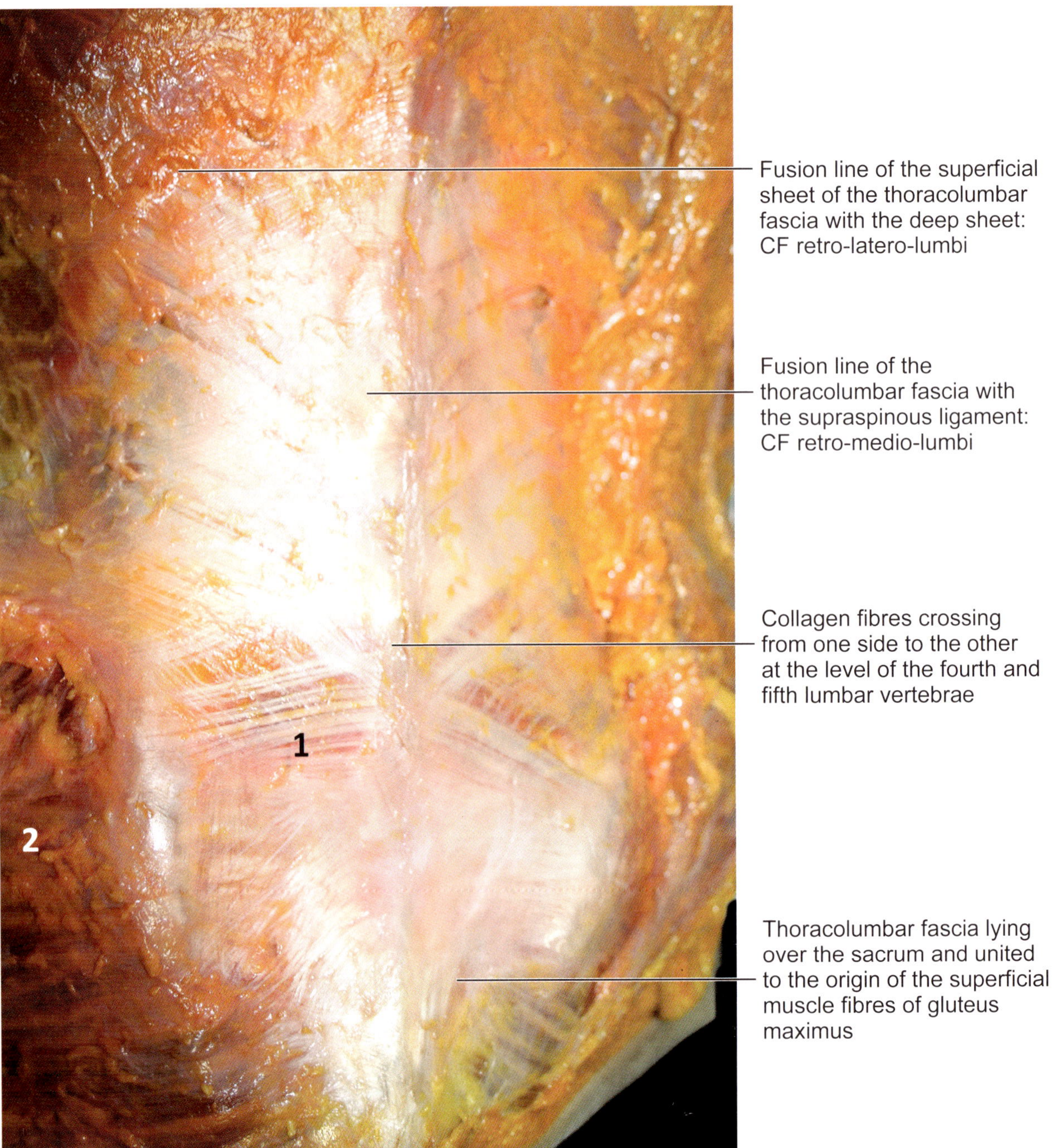

Fig. 6.27. Spiral collagen fibres of the thoracolumbar fascia. This picture highlights how the centre of fusion retro-medio-pelvis (1) works in synergy with the CF retro-latero-pelvis (2). These are located along the same collagen fibres forming the short spiral of the trunk.

SPIRAL COLLAGEN FIBRES OF THE POSTERIOR TRUNK

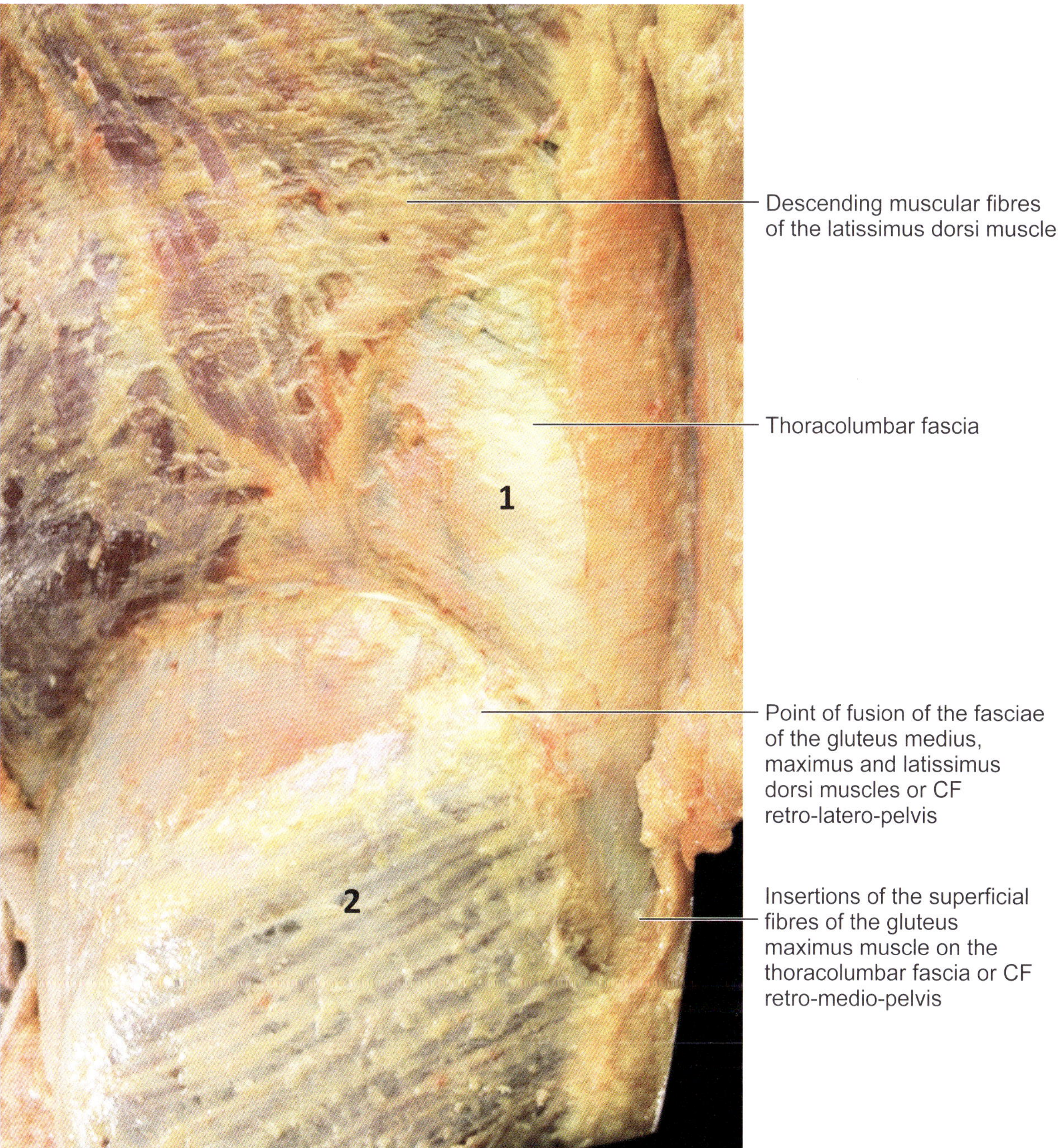

Fig. 6.28. Spiral collagen fibres corresponding to the septa of the left gluteus maximus muscle. The fibres of the latissimus dorsi muscle have a descending course (1), whilst the fibres of the gluteus maximus muscle have an ascending direction (2). The spiral direction may be understood when taking into consideration the gluteus muscle opposite to the latissimus dorsi muscle.

CENTRES OF FUSION AND SPIRALS OF THE LOWER LIMB

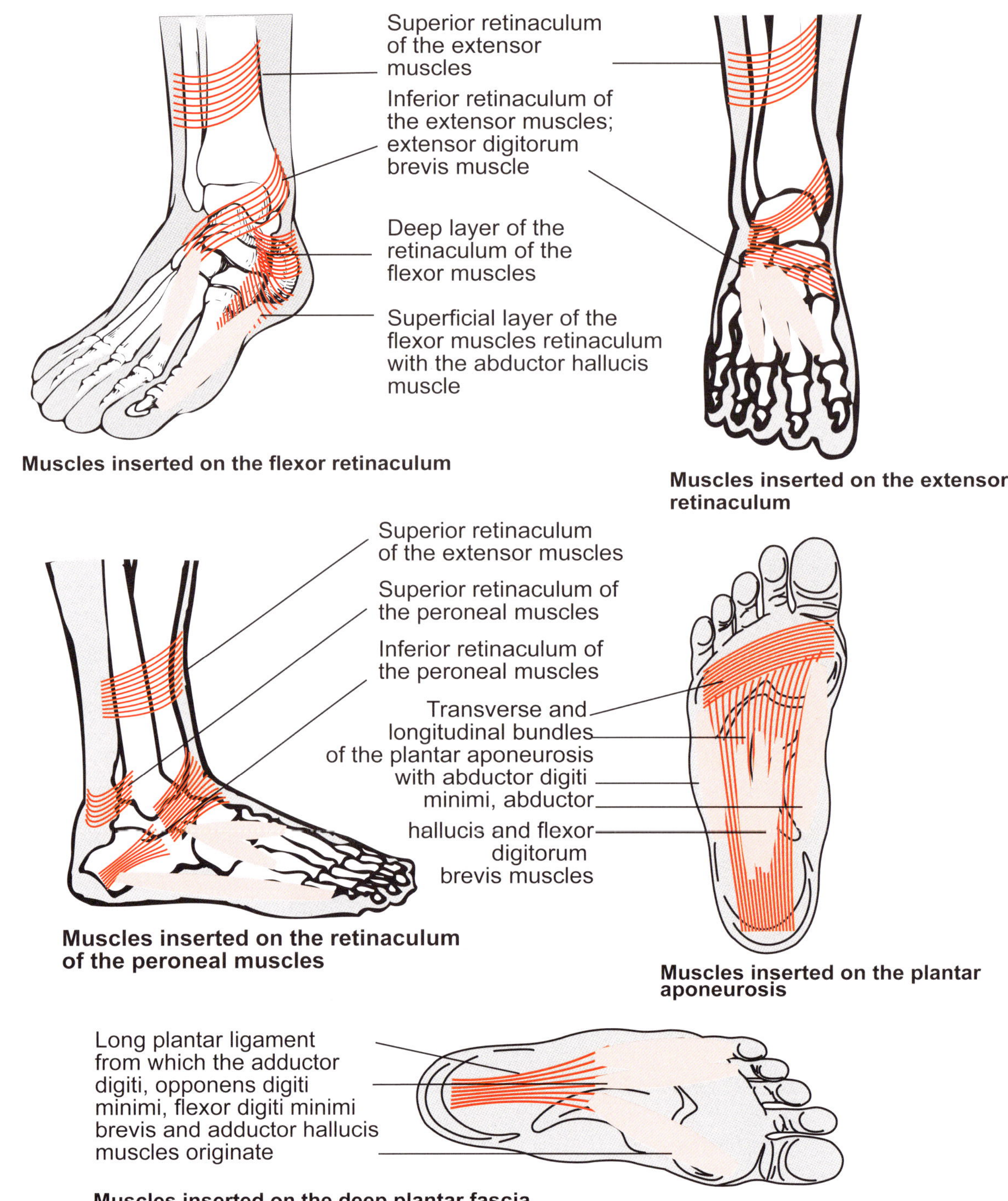

Fig. 6.29. Origin of the foot muscles from the retinacula and tendons of the leg muscles. If the muscles of the foot only had the function of moving joints, then they would originate and insert only on bones; their fascial origins leads to the hypothesis that their function is to start the motor gesture organisation in spiral.

MOTOR GESTURE OF THE LOWER LIMB MANAGED BY THE AN-ME-PE SPIRAL

Fig. 6.30. Example of how the spirals of the lower limb are organised when high jumping.

The insertions of the foot muscles on the ankle retinacula determine a stretching that propagates proximally along the spiral collagen fibres. For instance, when jumping the foot is positioned in ante-medio, the ankle is pulled in retro-latero, the knee muscles contract in ante-medio and those of the thigh in retro-latero. This spiral contracts in association with that of ante-latero-pes, but for clarity one spiral is described at a time.

AN-LA-PE SPIRAL

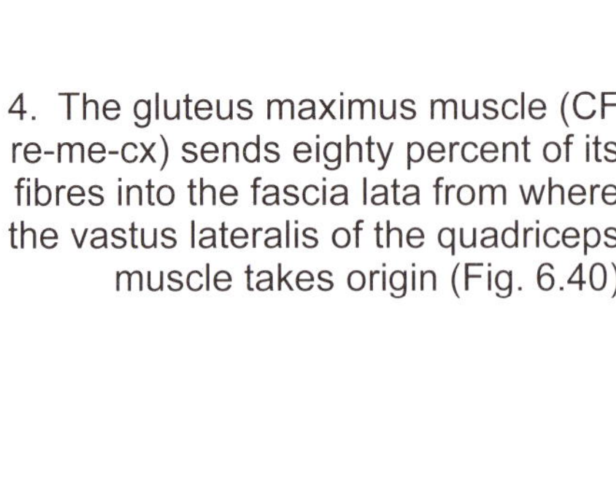
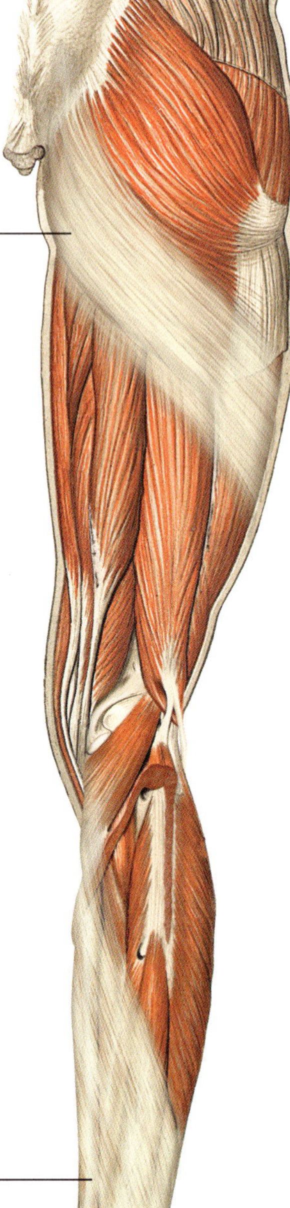

Fig. 6.31. Anterior course of the an-la-pe spiral.
(From G. Chiarugi and L. Bucciante, Istituzioni di anatomia dell'uomo. Piccin Nuova Libraria, Padova 1983, modified)

Fig. 6.32. Posterior course of the an-la-pe spiral.
(From G. Chiarugi and L. Bucciante, Istituzioni di anatomia dell'uomo. Piccin Nuova Libraria, Padova 1983, modified)

NB. For a better understanding of the motor gesture it is advised to start reading from the number 1 at the bottom of the page since the tensions of the foot muscles are responsible for the activation of the proximal muscles of the entire limb.

AN-ME-PE SPIRAL

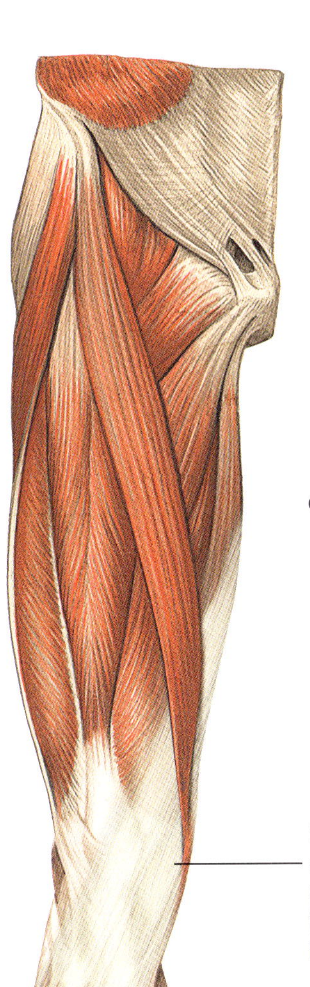

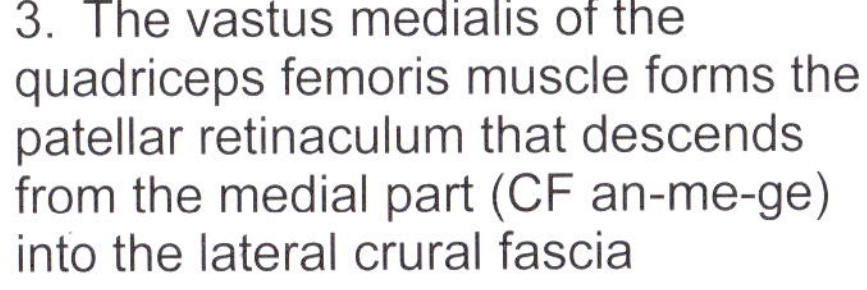

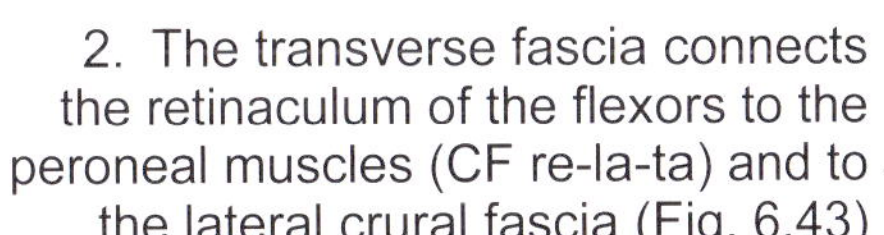

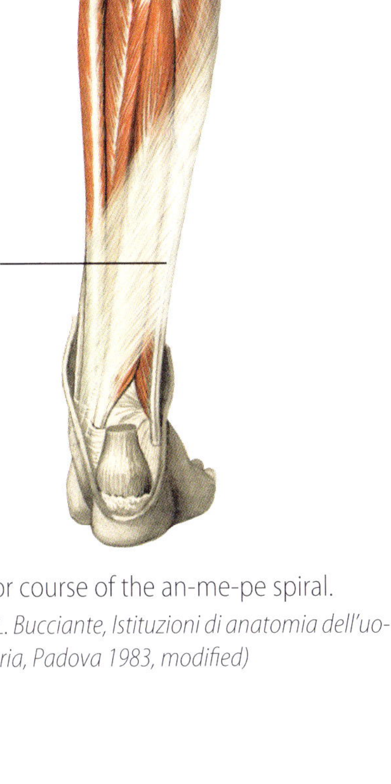

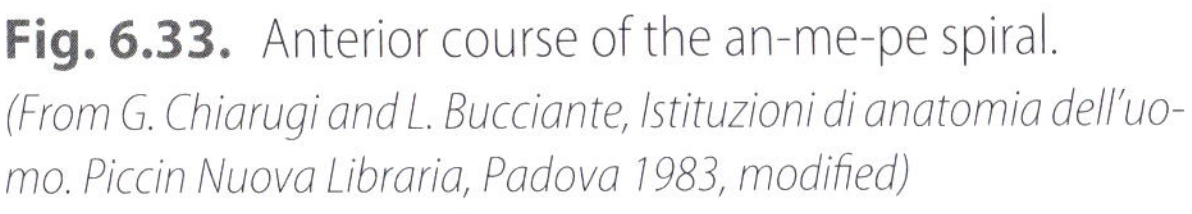

Fig. 6.33. Anterior course of the an-me-pe spiral.
(From G. Chiarugi and L. Bucciante, Istituzioni di anatomia dell'uomo. Piccin Nuova Libraria, Padova 1983, modified)

Fig. 6.34. Posterior course of the an-me-pe spiral.
(From G. Chiarugi and L. Bucciante, Istituzioni di anatomia dell'uomo. Piccin Nuova Libraria, Padova 1983, modified)

RE-ME-PE SPIRAL

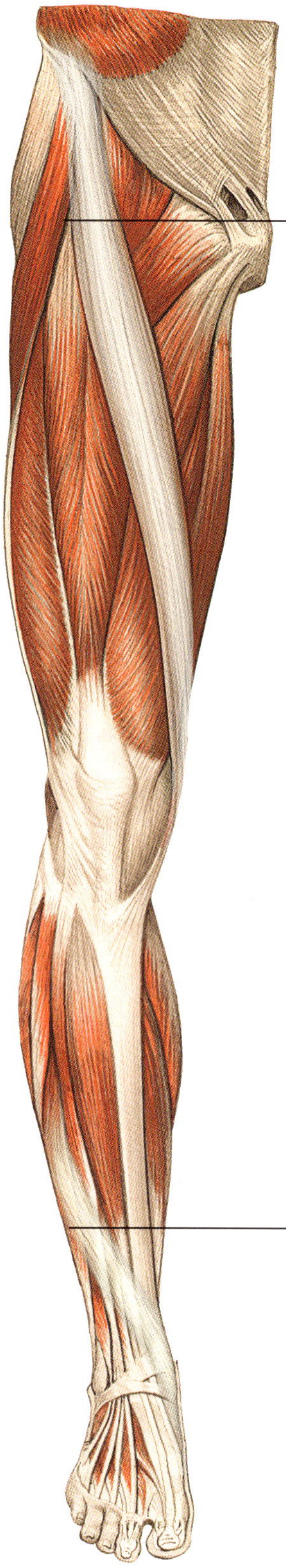

Fig. 6.35. Anterior course of the re-me-pe spiral.
(From G. Chiarugi and L. Bucciante, Istituzioni di anatomia dell'uomo. Piccin Nuova Libraria, Padova 1983, modified)

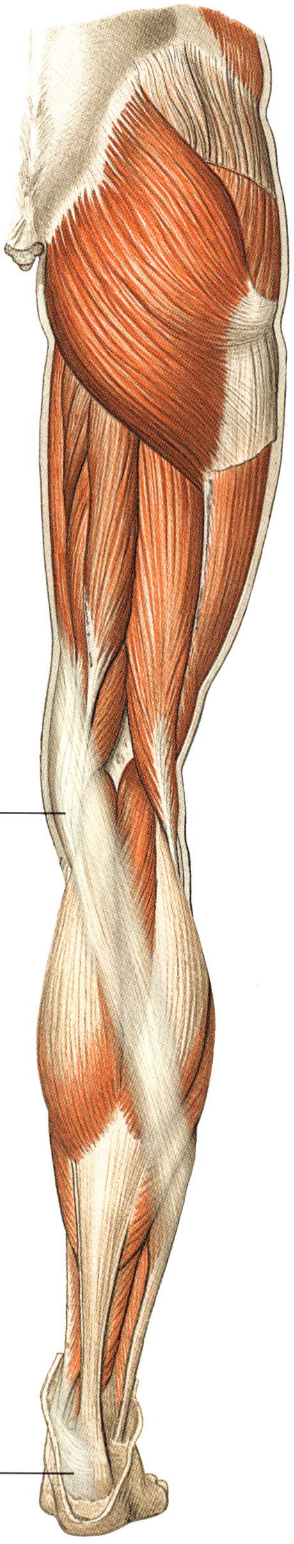

Fig. 6.36. Posterior course of the re-me-pe spiral.
(From G. Chiarugi and L. Bucciante, Istituzioni di anatomia dell'uomo. Piccin Nuova Libraria, Padova 1983, modified)

RE-LA-PE SPIRAL

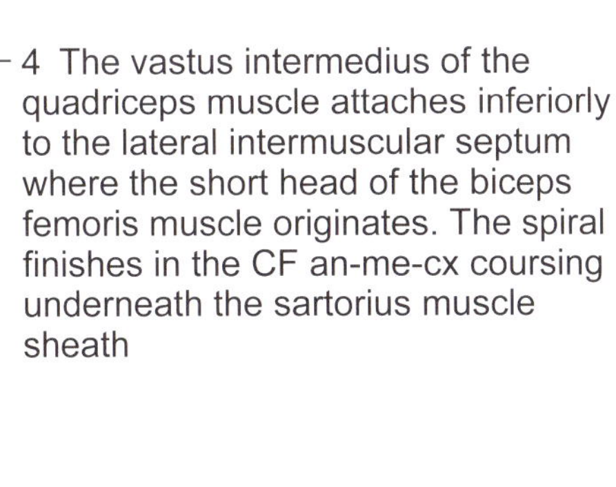

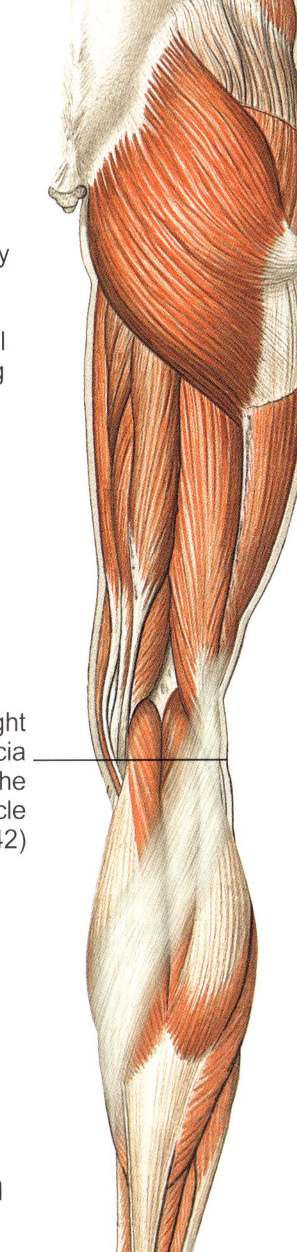

Fig. 6.37. Anterior course of the re-la-pe spiral.
(From G. Chiarugi and L. Bucciante, Istituzioni di anatomia dell'uomo. Piccin Nuova Libraria, Padova 1983, modified)

Fig. 6.38. Posterior course of the re-la-pe spiral.
(From G. Chiarugi and L. Bucciante, Istituzioni di anatomia dell'uomo. Piccin Nuova Libraria, Padova 1983, modified)

SPIRAL COLLAGEN FIBRES OF THE LOWER LIMB

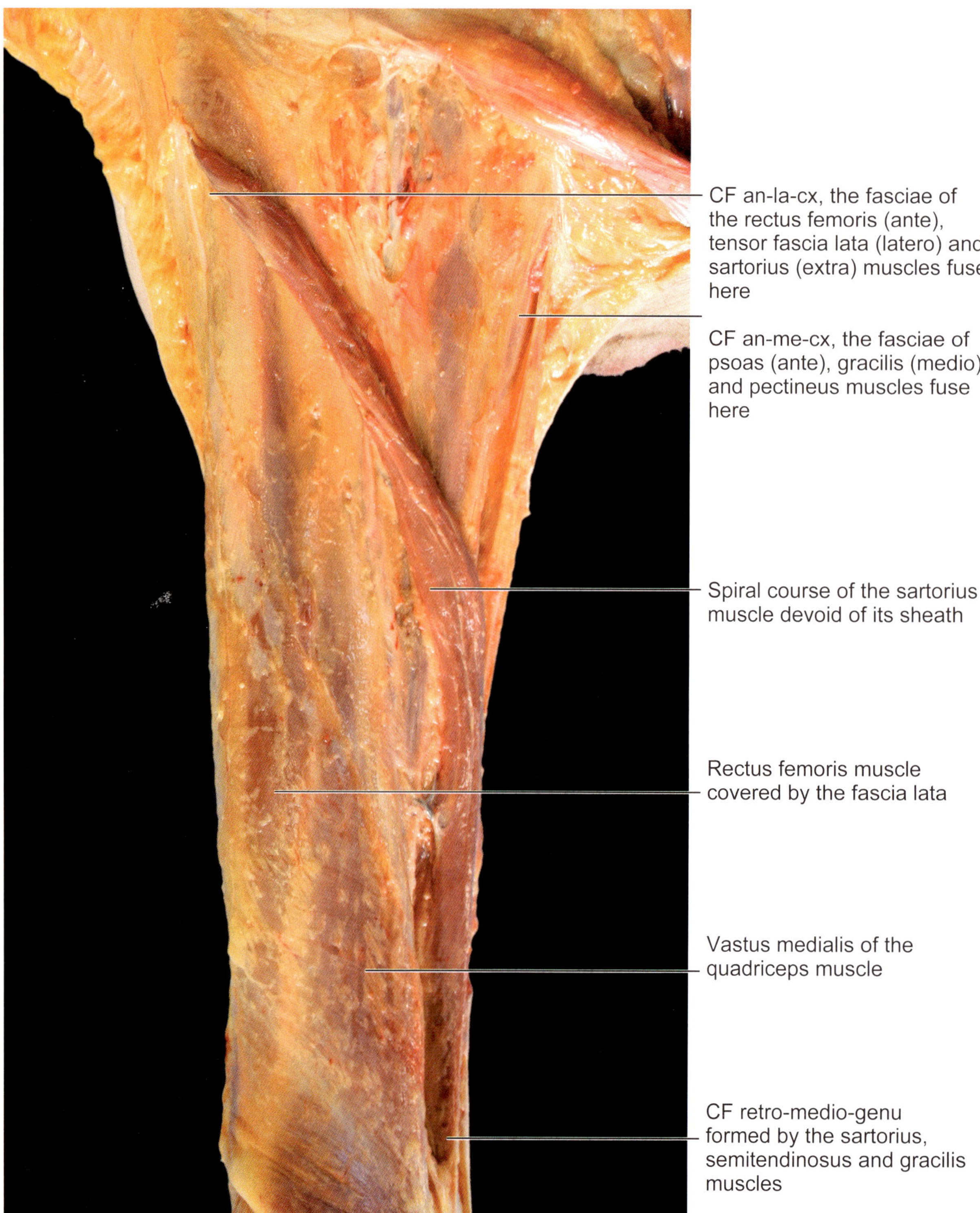

Fig. 6.39. Spiral course of the sartorius muscle. The dissection has isolated and removed the sheath of the sartorius muscle to highlight its independence from the fascia lata. The sartorius muscle implements the ante-latero-coxa scheme whilst at the level of the knee it implements the retro-medio-genu scheme, hence it executes the typical function of a spiral.

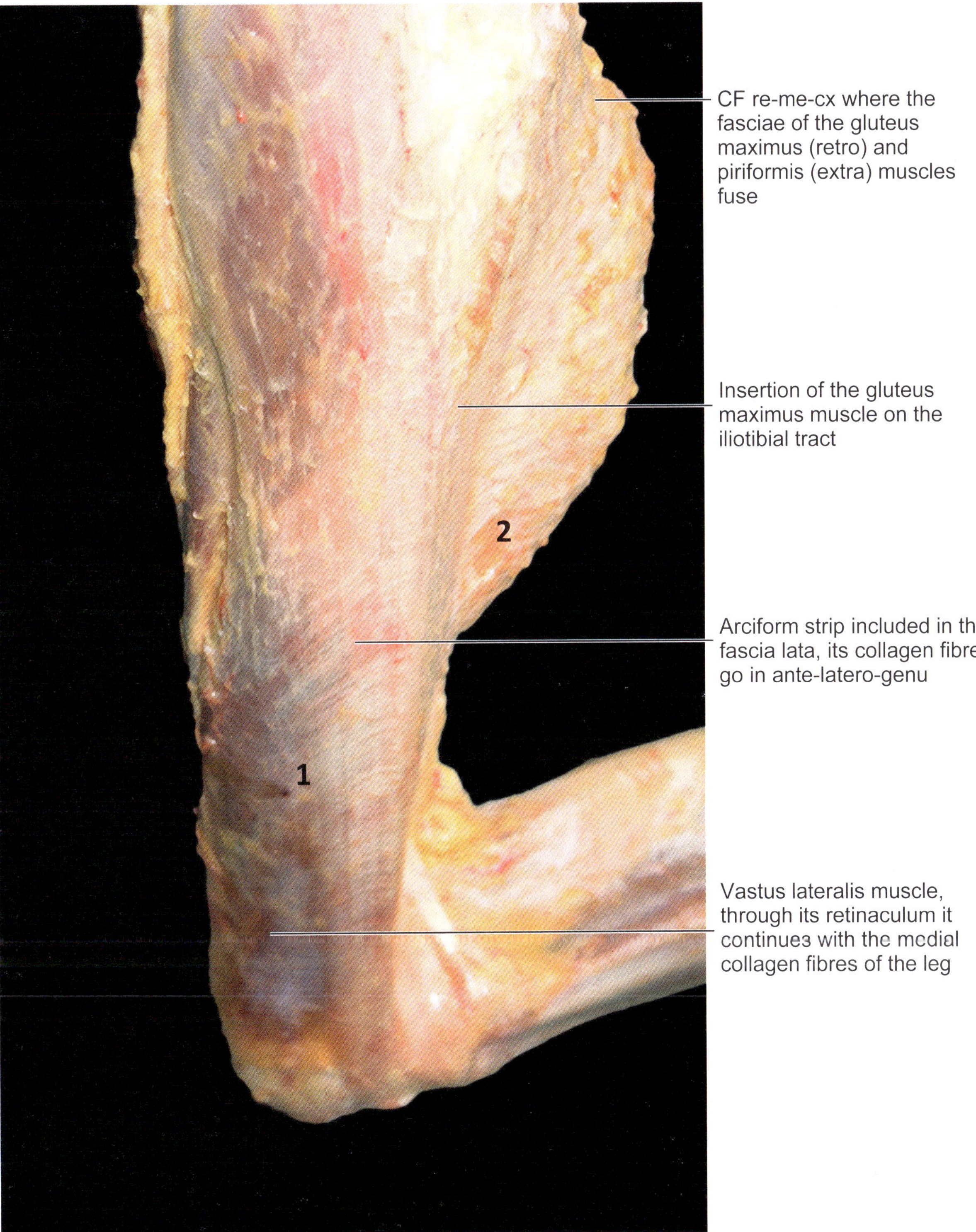

Fig. 6.40. Spiral collagen fibres of the lateral thigh. This photograph shows how the gluteus maximus muscle inserts with around 80% of its tendinous fibres on the iliotibial tract and fascia lata. The arciform collagen fibres included in the fascia lata are arranged in spiral (1) accordingly to the tractions of the gluteus maximus muscle (2).

SPIRAL COLLAGEN FIBRES OF THE LOWER LIMB

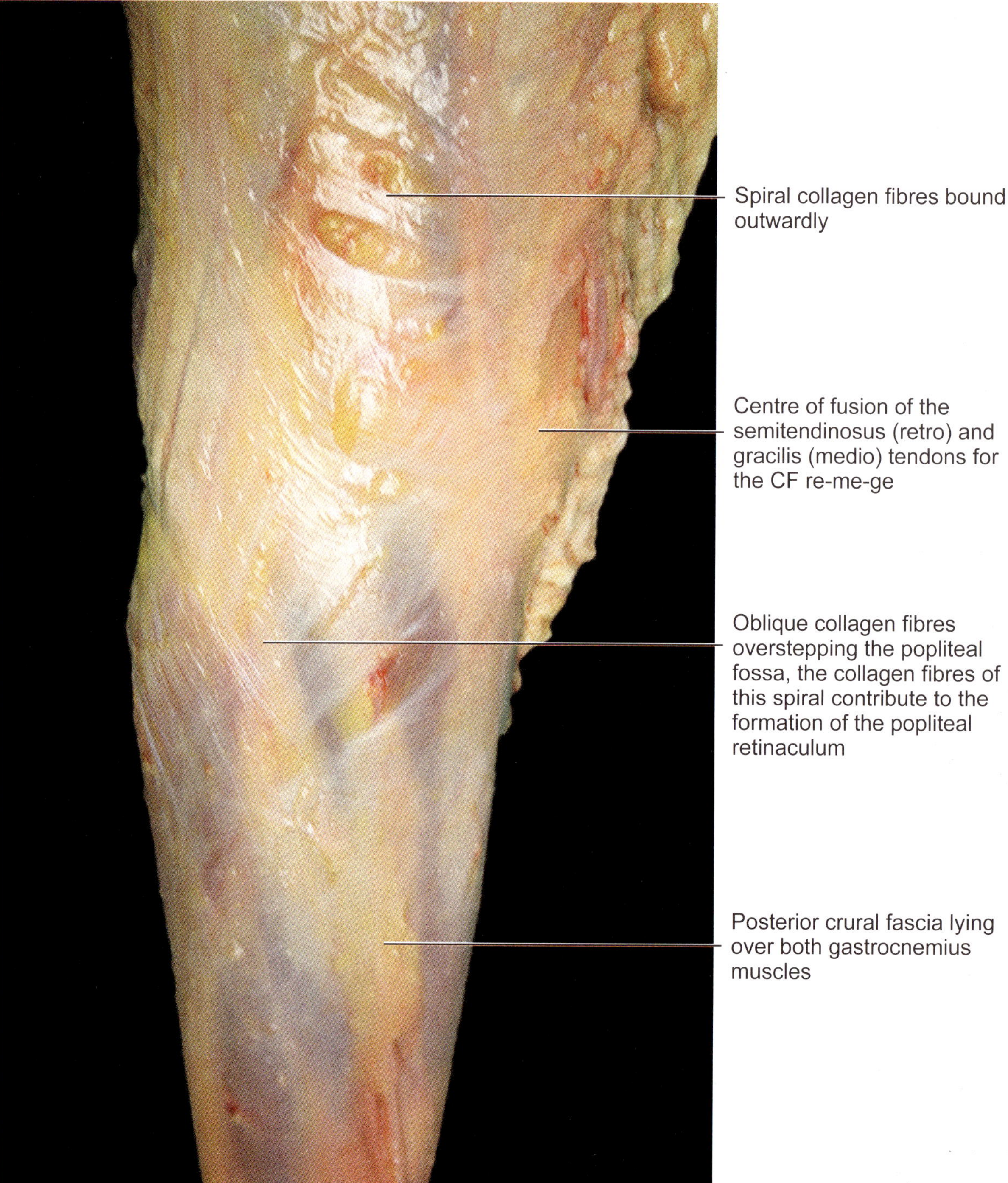

Fig. 6.41. Spiral collagen fibres of the posterior retinaculum of the knee. No anatomical textbook presents the posterior retinaculum of the knee but the arrangement of the collagen fibres clearly demonstrates the presence of a mesh of collagen fibres intersecting with each other.

SPIRAL COLLAGEN FIBRES OF THE LOWER LIMB

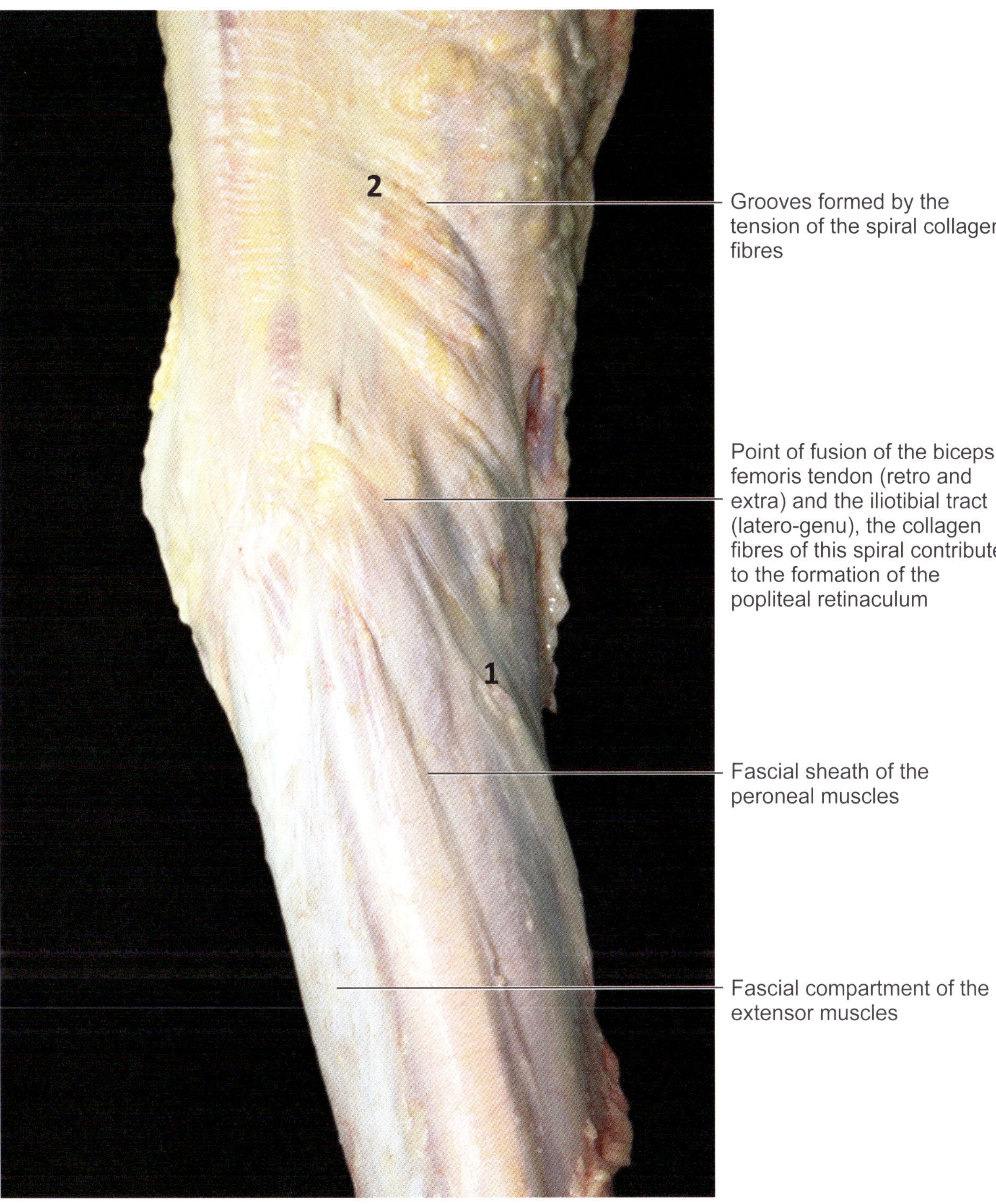

Fig. 6.42. Spiral collagen fibres of the retro-lateral fascia of the knee. The arrangement of the spiral collagen fibres has the ability to transmit tensions, indeed when internally rotating the leg passively (1), it can be observed that the collagen fibres form grooves in a spiral disposition (2) from above the knee.

SPIRAL COLLAGEN FIBRES OF THE LOWER LIMB

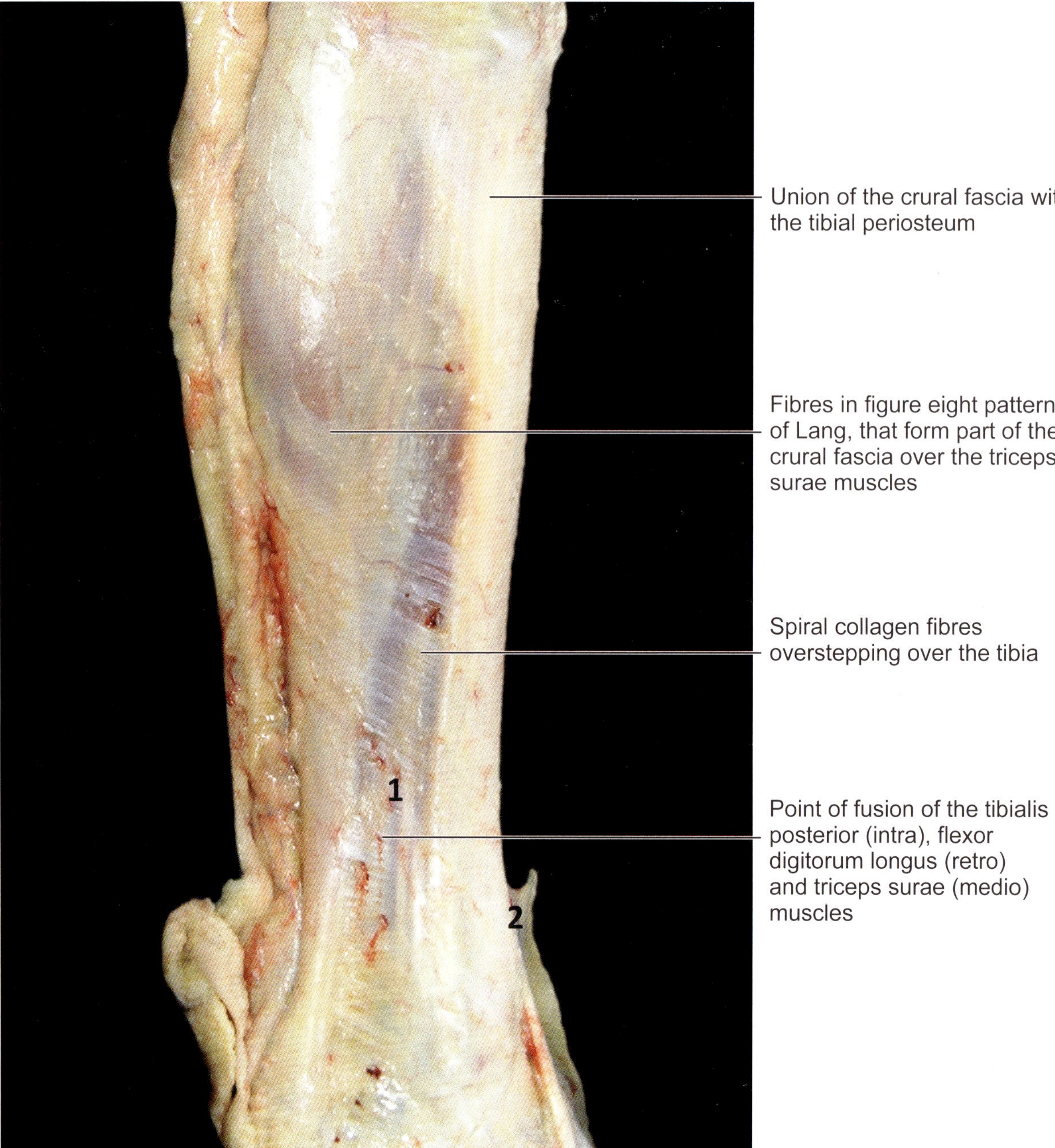

Fig. 6.43. Spiral collagen fibres of the medial crural fascia. In the proximal third of the leg, the crural fascia unites with the periosteum of the tibia, whilst in the distal third the oblique collagen fibres (1) course over the periosteum and form a continuity with the superior extensor retinaculum (2).

SPIRAL COLLAGEN FIBRES OF THE LOWER LIMB

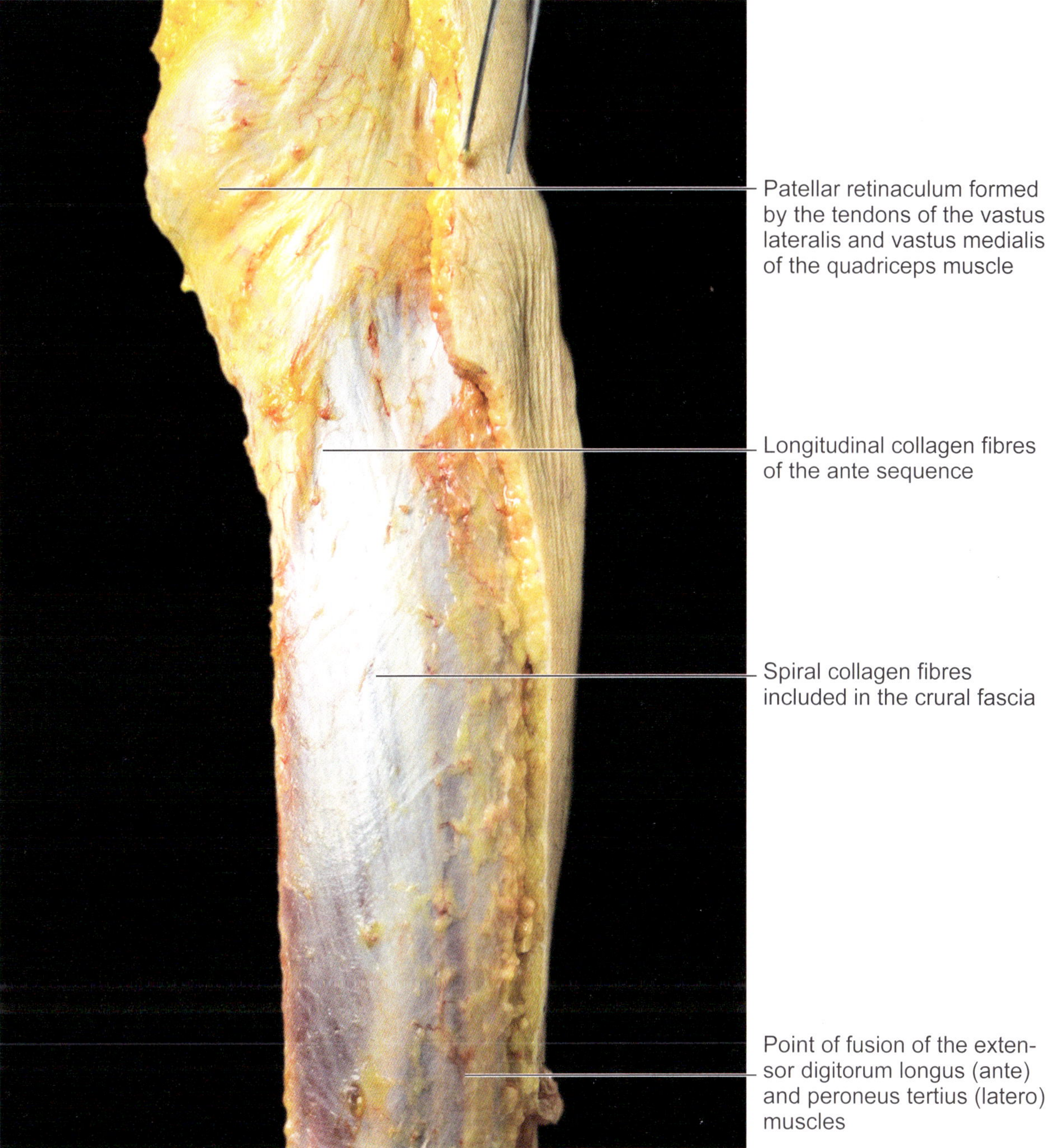

Fig. 6.44. Spiral collagen fibres of the lateral crural fascia. A point of fusion is never a precise point as the vectorial centre of coordination; indeed the CF is often located along the line of convergence of more tendons and hence of more forces intervening in series during multidirectional movements.

SPIRAL COLLAGEN FIBRES OF THE LOWER LIMB

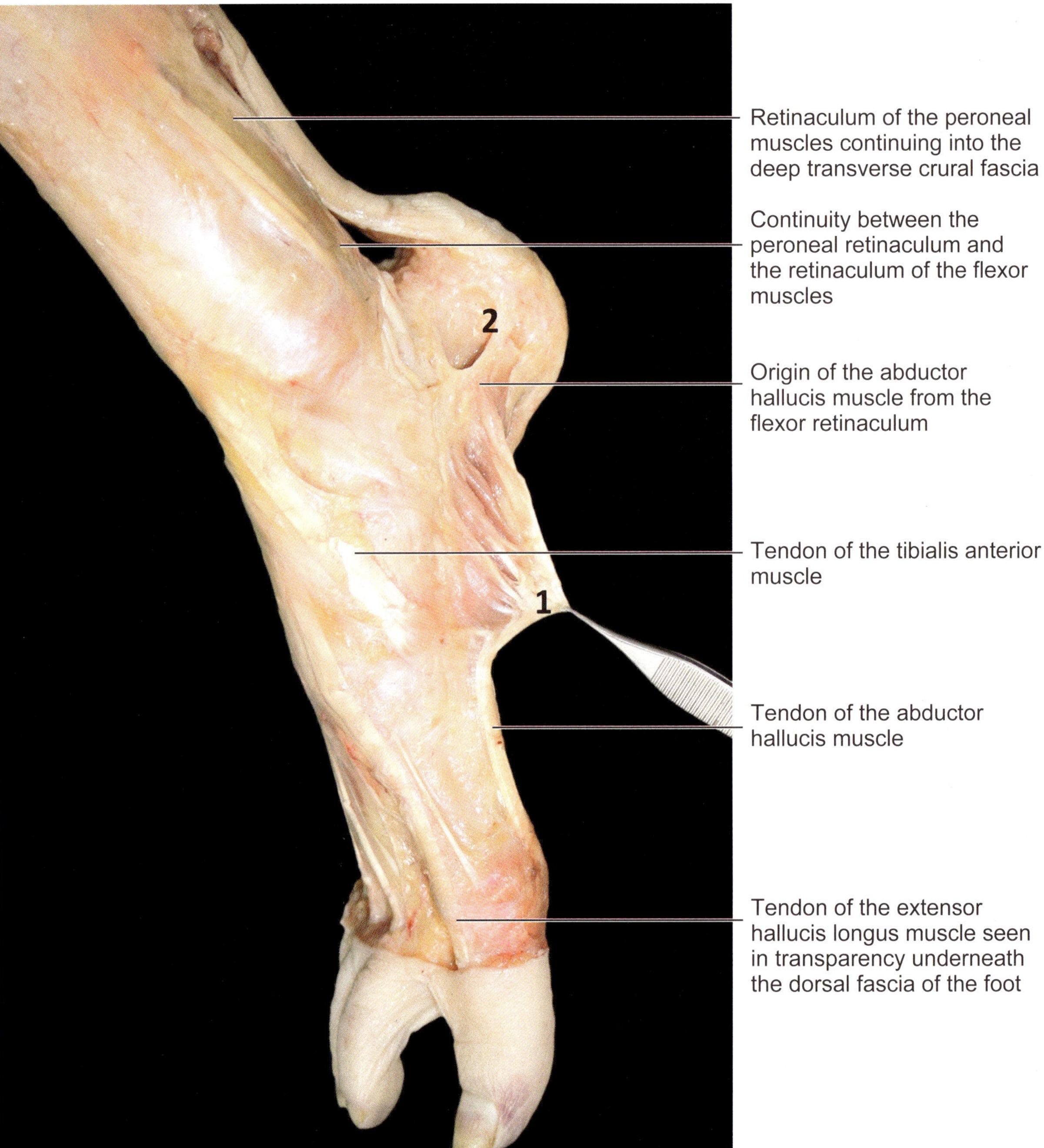

Fig. 6.45. Fascia of the medial region of the foot. After cutting and lifting the medial plantar aponeurosis medially (2), the insertion of the abductor hallucis muscle on the fascia itself is visible. This muscle also originates from the superficial and deep sheet of the flexor retinaculum (2) or laciniate ligament.

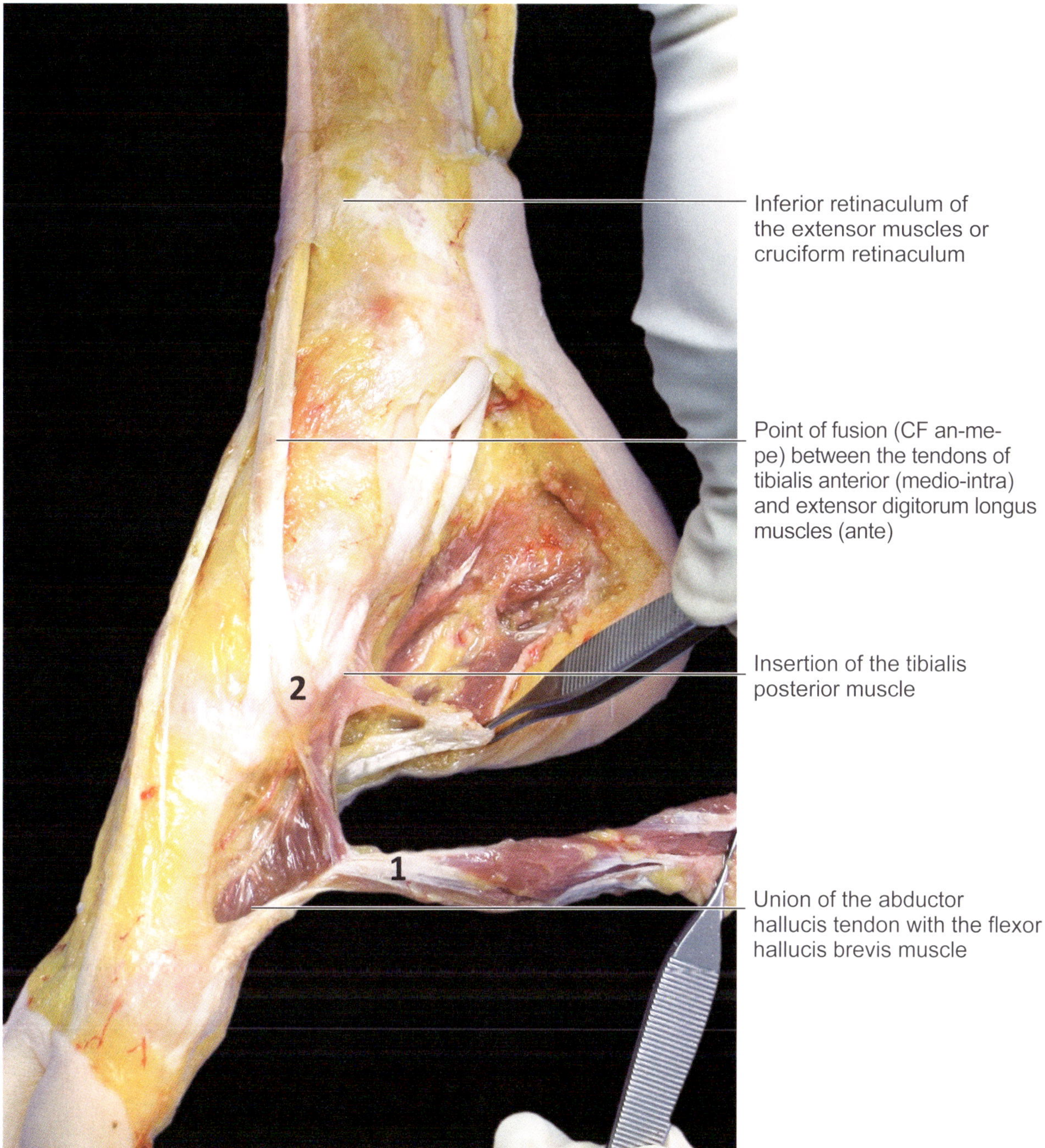

Fig. 6.46. Fascial insertions of the abductor hallucis muscle. The abductor hallucis muscle was cut and lifted medially, the union of its tendon (1) is visible with the flexor hallucis brevis muscle. The flexor hallucis brevis muscle in turn takes origin from the tendons of tibialis anterior and tibialis posterior muscles (2).

CONCLUSIONS

Physiologists and Anatomists sustain that the brain[1] programmes movements according to spatial planes, motor schemes and global gestures, nevertheless textbooks continue to convey movements as implemented by single muscles.

Physiologists and Anatomists admit that around 40% of muscular fibres are inserted in the surrounding fasciae (Huijing P.A. 2003), nevertheless in atlases muscles keep on being cleaned up of the fasciae.

Physiologists and Anatomists recognise that the neuromuscular spindles and Golgi tendon organs are essential for the coordination of muscles (Gray H. 1993), nevertheless in books these nervous endings keep on being inserted with proprioceptors.

This atlas of anatomy and physiology presents the locomotor system not by examining the single muscle, nerve or bone but rather by putting muscular tissue, fascial tissue and nervous tissue together (myofascial unit).

This atlas connects in series the ipsidirectional myofascial units of an entire limb and of the entire trunk (myofascial sequences).

This atlas does not want to change anatomy but wants to bring back to the locomotor apparatus the fasciae with their collagen fibres arranged longitudinally, in diagonals and in spirals.

This atlas subdivides movement in its three fundamental manifestations:

- **unidirectional movements.** These are movements implemented in the three spatial planes; these movements are achieved by the six myofascial units of each body segment. The fascia overlying muscle bellies is connected to the perimysium where the neuromuscular spindles of the ipsidirectional motor units (CC) are inserted. The ipsidirectional MF units are reunited longitudinally by the myofascial sequences in order to manage the posture of the entire body;
- **bidirectional movements.** These are the movements implemented in intermediate ranges between two spatial planes; these movements correspond to the motor scheme of each single segment. When all the segments of a limb are displaced along an intermediate trajectory between two MF sequences, then the myofascial diagonals intervene. The fascia lying over the tendons (CF) arising from two myofascial units manages the passage from one plane to the next;
- **multidirectional movements.** These are motor gestures that move body segments in opposite directions, such as walking, throwing or running. The retinacula of the ankle and wrist perceive the small movements of the hand and foot and transfer them to the muscles of the limbs. The endofascial collagen fibres arranged in spiral in the limbs and trunk synchronise the motor gestures of the various segments in the entire body.

Further research is necessary to demonstrate this new approach to the locomotor system although examining anatomical dissections in the light of these proposals already provides a good support. If each body structure has its significance, then one should wonder what functions do all the fasciae and collagen fibres forming a large part of the human body have.

The explanations presented in this atlas do not claim to be exhaustive, but it is hoped that these will spark curiosity in those who have the means to better scientifically document what intuition alone cannot achieve.

[1] The threshold stimulation of a single point of the motor cortex gives rise to a muscular response in many muscles according to a specific scheme of irradiation rather than to the contraction of a single muscle. (Gellhor E. 1949)

REFERENCE

Atti IV Fascia Research Congress, Washington, September 2015.

Baldissera F. Fisiologia e biofisica medica. Poletto, Milano, 1996.

Benninghoff G. Trattato di anatomia umana. Piccin, Padova, 1986.

Burkholder TJ. Mechanotransduction in skeletal muscle. Front Biosci 2007, Jan;1(12):174-91.

Carroll AM, Biewener AA. Mono-versus biarticular muscle function in relation to speed and gait changes: in vivo analysis of the goat triceps brachii. J Exp Biol 2009, Oct;212(Pt 20):3349-60.

Chaitow L. Fascial dysfunction, manual therapy approaches. Handspring, Edinburgh, 2014.

Chalmers G. Re-examination of the possible role of Golgi tendon organ and muscle spindle reflexes in proprioceptive neuromuscular facilitation muscle stretching. Sports Biomech 2004, Jan;3(1):159-83.

Chanaud CM, Pratt CA, Loeb GE. Functionally complex muscles of the cat hindlimb. II. Mechanical and architectural heterogenity within the biceps femoris. Clin Neurophysiol 2013, Jan;124(1):114-9.

Chiarugi G, Bucciante L. Istituzioni di anatomia dell'uomo. Vallardi-Piccin, Padova, 1975.

Cronin NJ, af Klint R, Grey MJ, Sinkjaer T. Ultrasonography as a tool to study afferent feedback from the muscle-tendon complex during human walking. J Electromyogr Kinesiol 2011, Apr;21(2):197-207.

Crossman AR, Neary D. Neuroanatomy, Elsevier S. Philadelphia, 2002.

Denning D, Paukshto MV, Habelitz S, Rodriguez BJ. Piezoelectric properties of aligned collagen membranes. Biomed Mater Res B Appl Biomater 2014, Feb;102(2):284-92.

Diong J, Bilston LE, Gandevia SC, Lichtwark GA. The Journal of Physiology 2015, Jan;593(2):441-55.

Downes L, Ashby P, Bugaresti J. Reflex effects from Golgi tendon organ (Ib) afferents are unchanged after spinal cord lesions in humans. Neurology 1995, Sep;45(9):1720-4.

Drunen P, Maaswinkel E, van der Helm FC, van Dieën JH, Happee R. Identifying intrinsic and reflexive contributions to low-back stabilization. J Biomech 2013 May, 31;46(8):1440-6.

English AW, Wolf SL, Segal RL, Compartmentalization of muscles and their motor nuclei: the partitioning hypothesis. Phys Ther. 1993; 73:857-867.

Findley T, Chaudhry H, Dhar S. Transmission of muscle force to fascia during exercise. J Bodyw Mov Ther 2015, Jan;19(1):119-23.

Forsythe M, Zellner D, Cogan E, Parker S. Attractiveness difference magnitude affected by context, range, and categorization. Perception 2014;43(1):59-69.

Fumagalli Z et al. Anatomia macroscopica dell'uomo. Piccin-Vallardi, 1974.

Gellhor E. Proproception and the motor cortex. Brain, 1949.

Georgopoulos AP, et al. Neuronal population coding of movement direction. Science 1986, Sep 26;233(4771):1416-9.

Gosling JA, Harris PF. Anatomie humaine. Atlas couleur. deBoeck, 2003.

Gottschal JS, Nichols TR. Head pitch affects muscle activity in the decerebrate cat hindlimb during walking Exp Brain Res 2007, Sep;182(1):131-5.

Gray H. Anatomia, Zanichelli, Bologna 1993.

Gregory JE, Brockett CL, Morgan DL, Whitehead NP, Proske U. Effect of eccentric muscle contractions on Golgi tendon organ responses to passive and active tension in the cat. J Physiol 2002, Jan 1;538(Pt 1):209-18.

Hammer W. Functional soft-tissue examination and treatment by manual methods. J Barlett, Massachussetts, 2007.

Hauk O, Johnsrude I, Pulvermuller F. Somatotopic representation of action words in human motor and premotor cortex. Neuron 2004, Jan 22;41:301-7.

Heine H. Anatomical structure of acupoints. J Tradit Chin Med 1988, Sep;8(3):207-12.

Herbert RD, Héroux ME. Changes in the length and three-dimensional orientation of muscle fascicles and aponeuroses with passive length changes in human gastrocnemius muscles. J Physiol 2015, Jan 15;593(2):441-55.

Huijing PA, Maas H, Baan GC. Compartmental fasciotomy and isolating a muscle from neighboring muscles interfere with myofascial force transmission within the rat anterior crural compartment. J Morphol 2003, Jun, 256(3):306-21.

Huijing PA, Smeulders MJC, Kreulenn M. Spastic muscle properties are affected by length changes of adjacent structures. Muscle Nerve 2005, Aug, 32(2):208-15.

Kabat H, Knott M. Proprioceptive facilitation therapy for paralysis. Physiotherapy 1954, Jun, 40(6):171-6.

Kandel ER et al. Principi di neuroscienze. Casa Editrice Ambrosiana, Milano 1994.

Kistemaker DA et al. Control of position and movement is simplified by combined muscle spindle and Golgi tendon organ feedbak. J Neurophysiology 2013, 109;1126-39.

Kistemaker DA et al. Equilibrium point control cannot be refuted by experimental reconstruction of equilibrium point trajectories. J Neurophysiology 2007, Sept, 98;1075-82.

Langevin HM. Connective tissues: a body wide signaling network? Medical Hypothesis 2005;66:1074-7.

Loram ID, Lakie M, Di Giulio I, Maganaris CN. The consequences of short-range stiffness and fluctuating muscle activity for proprioception of postural joint rotations: the relevance to human standing. Journal of Neurophysiology 2009, Jul 1, 102;1:460-74.

Macefield VG, Walton DK. Susceptibility to motion sickness is not increased following spinal cord injury. J Vestib Res 2015, Jan 1;25(1):35-9.

Mazzocchi G, Nussdorfer G. Anatomia funzionale del sistema nervoso. Ed. Libreria Cortina, Padova 1996.

Moccia D, Nackashi AA, Schilling R, Ward PJ. Fascial bundles of the infraspinatus fascia: anatomy, function, and clinical considerations. J Anat 2015, Sep 25. doi: 10.1111.

More HL, et al. Sensorimotor responsiveness and resolution in the giraffe. Journal of Exper Biology, 2013, Feb, 216;1003-11.

Mugge W, David A et al. A rigorous model of reflex function indicates that position and force feedback are flexibly tuned to position and force tasks, Experimental Brain Research 2009;10:1007-9.

Myers TW. Meridiani miofasciali. Tecniche Nuove, Milano 2006.

Pirola V. Il movimento umano, Cinesiologia. Edi-Ermes, Milano 1998.

Platzer W. Color atlas of human anatomy: locomotor system, 6th ed. Thieme, 2009.

Pozzi F, Snyder-Mackler L, Zeni J Jr. Relationship between biomechanical asymmetries during a step up and over task and stair climbing after total knee arthroplasty. Clin Biomech (Bristol, Avon) 2015, Jan;30(1):78-85.

Prochazka A et al. Positive force feedback control of muscles. J Neurophysiology 1997;77(6):3226-36.

Proske U. The role of muscle proprioceptors in human limb position sense: a hypothesis. J Anat 2015, May 14, doi: 10.1111.

Proske U, Gregory JE. Signalling properties of muscle spindles and tendon organs. Adv Exp Med Biol 2002;508:5-12.

Purslow PP. Strain induced reorientation of an intramuscular connective tissue network: implications for passive muscle elasticity. J Biomech 1989;22(1):21-31.

Rosatelli LA et al. Three-dimensional study of the musculotendinous architecture of lumbar multifidus and its functional implications. Clin Anat 2008;21:539-546.

Rowe RW. Morphology of perimysial and endomysial connective tissue in skeletal muscle. Tissue Cell 1981;13(4):681-90.

Sakamoto Y. Histological features of endomysium, perimysium and epimysium in rat lateral pterygoid muscle. J Morphol 1996;2277(1):113-9.

Schilder A, Hoheisel U, et al. Sensory findings after stimulation of the thoracolumbar fascia with hypertonic saline suggest its contribution to low back pain. Pain 2014, Feb;155(2):222-31.

Schleip R, Findley TW, Chaitow L, Huijing P. Fascia: the tensional network of the human body. Churchill Livingstone, 2012.

Simons DG, Travell J. Myofascial trigger points, a possible explanation. Pain 1981, Feb;10(1):106-13.

Stahl VA, Nichols TR. Short-term effect of crural fasciotomy on kinematic variability and propulsion during level locomotion. J Motor Behavior 46(5):339-49.

Standring S. Gray's Anatomy, 40th ed. Churchill Livingstone, London 2008.

Stecco A, Busoni F, Stecco C, Mattioli-Belmonte M, Soldani P, Condino S, Ermolao A, Zaccaria M, Gesi M. Comparative ultrasonographic evaluation of the Achilles paratenon in symptomatic and asymptomatic subjects: an imaging study. Surg Radiol Anat. 2015 Apr; 37(3):281-5.

Stecco A, Gilliar W, Hill R, Fullerton B, Stecco C. The anatomical and functional relation between gluteus maximus and fascia lata. J Bodyw Mov Ther 2013, Oct;17(4):512-7.

Stecco A, Meneghini A, Stern R, Stecco C, Imamura M. Ultrasonography in myofascial neck pain: randomized clinical trial for diagnosis and follow-up. Surg Radiol Anat 2014, Apr;36(3):243-53.

Stecco C. Functional atlas of the human fascial system. Elsevier, 2015.

Stecco C, Corradin M, Macchi V, Morra A, Porzionato A, Biz C, De Caro R. Plantar fascia anatomy and its relationship with Achilles tendon and paratenon. J Anat. 2013 Dec;223(6):665-76.

Stecco C, Pavan PG, Porzionato A, Macchi V, Lancerotto L, Carniel EL, Natali AN, De Caro R. Mechanics of crural fascia: from anatomy to costitutive modelling. Surg Radiol Anat 2009, Aug;31(7):523-9.

Stecco C, Porzionato A, Lancerotto L, Stecco A, Macchi V, Day JA, De Caro R. Histological study of the deep fasciae of the limbs. J Bodyw Mov Ther 2008;12:225-30.

Takeoka A, Vollenweider I, Courtine G, Arber S. Muscle spindle feedback directs locomotor recovery and circuit reorganization after spinal cord injury. Cell 2014, Dec 18;159(7):1626-39.

Testut L, Jacob O. Trattato di anatomia topografica. UTET, Firenze 1987.

Travell JG, Simons DG. Dolore muscolare, diagnosi e terapia. Ghedini editore, Milano, 1996.

Treccani Enciclopedia, www.treccani.it.

Watanabe K, Kouzaki M, Ando R, Akima H, Moritani T. Non-uniform recruitment along human rectus femoris muscle during transcutaneous electrical nerve stimulation. Eur J Appl Physiol 2015, Jun 10.

Weisman MH et al. Surface electromyographic recordings after passive and active motion along the posterior myofascial kinematic chain in healthy male subjects. J Bodywork Movement Ther 2014;18:452-61.

West CR, Bowden AE. Using tendon inherent electric properties to consistently track induced mechanical strain. Ann Biomed Eng. 2012 Jul;40 (7): 1568-74.

INDEX

A

C

D

O

P

R

S

T

U

INDEX

Finished printing
in the month of September 2016
by Arti Grafiche Casagrande di Colognola ai Colli (VR)
for Piccin Nuova Libraria S.p.A., Padova, Italy